THE HOLY GRAIL

THE HOLY GRAIL

India's Quest for Universal Elementary Education

R.V. VAIDYANATHA AYYAR

OXFORD UNIVERSITY PRESS

OXFORD
UNIVERSITY PRESS

Oxford University Press is a department of the University of Oxford. It furthers the University's objective of excellence in research, scholarship, and education by publishing worldwide. Oxford is a registered trademark of Oxford University Press in the UK and in certain other countries.

Published in India by
Oxford University Press
YMCA Library Building, 1 Jai Singh Road, New Delhi 110 001, India

First Edition published in 2016

ISBN-13: 978-0-19-946347-3
ISBN-10: 0-19-946347-6

Typeset in Berling LT Std 9.5/13
by The Graphics Solution, New Delhi 110 092
Printed in India by Replika Press Pvt. Ltd

CONTENTS

PREFACE

> We are so often caught up in our destination
> that we forget to appreciate the journey

India is striving to be a country where every child receives basic education—or, to use jargon, striving to universalize elementary education. This endeavour began in 1817 when Maharani Gouri Parvati Bayi of Travancore issued a Royal Rescript, 73 years before the Imperial Rescript of Japan's Emperor Meiji, declaring that 'the State should defray the entire cost of education of its people in order that there might be no backwardness in the spread of enlightenment among them, that by diffusing education, they might become better subjects and public servants and the reputation of the State might be advanced thereby'. In pursuance of the rescript, vernacular schools were established in every village with at least two teachers, and a strict system of inspection was instituted. The policy of the Maharani was carried forward during the reign of Maharaja Sri Moolam Thirunal Rama Varma; Dewan V.P. Madhava Rao (1904–6) made primary education free in the state. Other native states and British provinces began the journey towards the goal of universal education decades later, a fact which explains the head start Kerala had. Almost two centuries after the Royal Rescript, we have reached a new phase of the journey. Beginning from the late 1990s, a spectacular progress was made to universalize elementary education. The number of out-of-school children in the age group 6–14 is reported to be near about 60 odd lakhs in September 2014 as compared to 2.5 crores in 2002. The net enrolment ratio in the primary stage (classes I–V) is 99.8 per cent; shorn of jargon, almost every child in the age group 6–11 is in school. However, it is premature to 'declare victory and go home' for several reasons. The net enrolment ratio at the upper primary level (classes VI–VIII) is still around 70 per cent only. Those who are still out of school are hard-core marginalized groups, and it is a moot point whether in the near future the school system can reach out to them and retain them till they complete elementary schooling. The dropout rates are still substantial. However, it would be fair to say that the foremost challenge now is improvement of quality and learning achievement. Data of the unofficial and much popular Annual Status of Education Reports (ASER) as well as the data available with the government indicate that there is a great crisis of poor learning in government schools. The Right to Elementary Education, which the Constitution guarantees, now would be nugatory or illusory if it is limited to attending a school with all the facilities and teachers mandated by the 'Right of Children to Free and Compulsory Education Act (RTE Act), 2009'; learning should come to be the pivot of the efforts to implement the RTE Act, 2009, and to universalize elementary education. Getting all children, irrespective of background, is only the first step in a long march towards making elementary education inclusive; making all children feel at home in the school and complete elementary education and achieving equity in learning outcomes involves a long and more arduous journey.

As we enter a more strenuous phase of the journey, it would be expedient to take stock of the journey so far and of the new challenges. That is what I propose to do in this book as a participant observer. During 1988–97, I was intensely associated with many of the policy and programme initiatives at the state, national, and international levels. Among others, I was associated with the revision in 1992 of the National Policy on Education (NPE), 1986, and its Programme of Education, and the development of District Primary Education Programme (DPEP), which, along with its progeny, the Sarva Shiksha Abhiyan (SSA), was responsible for bringing the nation to the current stage in the long march towards universal elementary education. I was also the pointsman for managing the interface between the Union Department of Education and external agencies including the Department for International Development (DFID), Swedish International Development Agency (SIDA), European Commission,

United Nations Development Programme (UNDP), United Nations Educational, Scientific and Cultural Organization (UNESCO), United Nations Children's Emergency Fund (UNICEF), and the World Bank. I was privileged to have occasional opportunities even after retirement from the government to get fleeting but meaningful glimpses of the developments at the national and international levels. In writing this narrative I tried to be as objective and self-critical as a human being could be and chose to write in third person singular, employing the pseudonym 'K' after the protagonist of Kafka's *The Castle*. As part of my attempt to be objective, I deliberately eschewed the *prashasti* (panegyric) style of writing about great people that is customary in our country and chose to follow Oliver Cromwell's injunction to his painter: 'to paint my picture truly like me, and not flatter me at all; but remark all these roughnesses, pimples, warts and everything as you see me'. My objective was not to run down any one or settle scores but offer an unbiased assessment of men and matters to the extent humanly possible. However, I am conscious of the fact that being human and only all too human I did not succeed in totally eschewing my personal preferences and prejudices, and what follows is not so much history as *his-story*. Yet I think this narrative has merit by virtue of the fact that when dust settles down and a historian could write of this period as an *outsider* and not as one lived through by him, he needs sources. Personal narratives have a special value in a country like ours in which, in spite of legal provisions, public records do not reach archives as they ought to—a fact of which I have experiential knowledge from my stint as Secretary, Culture, Government of India, whose remit includes supervision of the National Archives of India (NAI). Suffice it to say, this *his-story* would serve as a source for future historians of Indian education.

All in all, the years after NPE, 1986, constitute a watershed in the history of India's quest for universal literacy and universalizing elementary education. Yet, while there have been articles—maybe even a book or two—on some aspects of the quest since 1986 of universal elementary education, there is no comprehensive narrative that covers *all* major developments and places them against the backdrop of national and global political, economic, and educational developments. Even as accounts of individual developments, most articles have two limitations. First, almost all miss out the politics and process of policy and programme development, of engagement between the centre and states in a federal polity, as well as of engagement between a country and funding agencies. A good example is external funding for elementary education. Even good studies miss out the complexity of DPEP, a programme which was implemented in many states and financed by multiple funding agencies, and which tenaciously adhered to a policy of self-reliant strategy of planning, implementation, and capacity development. They miss out the challenge of getting everyone on board a newly assembled Noah's Ark with novel features such as an arm's length relationship between the funding agencies and the states—the funding agencies behaving like mere financing agencies with no role in planning and implementation and states being compelled to focus on outputs and outcomes instead of being obsessed with spending the grants provided by the central government. There were so many to be got on board: the main funding agencies (namely the World Bank, the European Community, and the Overseas Development Administration [United Kingdom]), agencies such as UNICEF and UNESCO which were keen to have a piece of action, states (seven to begin with and progressively increasing to eighteen), and the central government ministers and organizations concerned such as Finance Commission, Planning Commission, National Council of Educational Research and Training (NCERT), and National Institute of Educational Planning and Administration (NIEPA). There were battles and tests of wills in which the Ministry of Human Resource Development (MHRD) had to prevail in conflicts. Suffice it to say, by treating the dynamics of the engagement as a black box, the published studies failed to explore the most important feature of the engagement. The second limitation of the extant studies is that most are vitiated by the fact that they are either a panegyric (as with Total Literacy Campaigns [TLCs]) or unremittingly censorious viewing some of the developments, such as DPEP through a narrow prism of an ideology which considers institutions such as the World Bank to be unmitigated evil, and further any departure from the idea that education should be public funded and managed and provided as a basic service to be a heresy.

This book is part personal reminiscences and part history. Without the illumination provided by the past one cannot grasp the present, what has changed, and what continues. Study of the past helps us to understand 'how we got here' which is as interesting as understanding how different the present is from the past. The study of history dispels the facile belief of many decision-makers that 'the world was new, all problems fresh', and controls the tendency 'to offer quick fixes for complex problems'.[1] Quite a few of the contemporaneous educational challenges were also addressed in the past by great minds and statesmen, and their thoughts and actions are of great value in understanding the nature of contemporaneous challenges. The lessons of history help identify promising avenues and blind alleys, and cure one of solipsism and hubris. If I have tried to look at the 'present' from the perspective of the 'past', I also attempted the converse of it, namely look at the 'past' from the perspective of the 'present'. Unusual for a book on education, I attempt to bring in multiple perspectives to illuminate the events and developments. This is a book about many things. The book throws light on educational developments at the state, national, and international levels. It also is about changing trends in development co-operation and the functioning of bilateral, regional, and multilateral organizations such as DFID, UK, the European Union, and the World Bank. A history describing events as they occurred and the impact of those events is only one aspect of history; far more interesting is *why* history: It provides explanations of the forces driving events and attempts to understand the meaning of events. It therefore embeds the narrative in theoretical concepts related to decision-making, negotiation theory, and international relations. All in all, it provides information few, even experts, are aware of. Every piece of information has been thoroughly documented.

By happenstance, the narrative in this book has acquired unexpected salience because of the recent developments captured by the expression 'cooperative, competitive federalism'. Consequent to the acceptance of the recommendations of the Fourteenth Finance Commission and devolution to the states of a higher proportion of its tax revenues, the Narendra Modi government had decided to prune the list of Centrally Sponsored Schemes (CSS), and to alter the financing pattern of those schemes which were retained and reduce its budgetary outlay on those schemes. Among the schemes which were retained are the SSA, the Rashtriya Madhyamik Shiksha Mission (RSMA), and the Rashtriya Uchchatar Shiksha Mission (RUSA). By and large, the decision to devolve a higher

[1] Richard E. Neustadt and Ernest R. May, *Thinking in Time: The Uses of History in Decision-making*, New York: The Free Press, 1986, p. xi.

share of the central government's tax revenues and prune the list of CSS had been widely welcomed; however, concerns had been expressed that the additional resources which would be passed on to the state governments might not be used by those governments to boost their social sector spending in the aggregate, and further that the additional resources would not be sufficient to offset the reduction in the outlay of the central government on schemes such as SSA. An equally important but less noted point is that in the new federalism which is sought to be ushered, the greater scope for the states to display policy and programme initiatives does not imply a less proactive role of the central government. This book makes two significant points. First, DPEP and its progeny, SSA, had established that in a centrally sponsored scheme it is eminently possible to marry a national frame and strategy with tremendous flexibility and scope for states to innovate. This counter-intuitive point is missed out in official reports as well as the discourse on Centrally Sponsored Schemes. Second, the central government cannot divorce itself from its paramount responsibility of steering the nation towards achievement of overarching national goals, and to that end it would have to define the objectives, lay down a broad national strategy, and use policy levers to prod the states to compete and innovate within the national frame. The government's 'Make in India' campaign is a good example of this approach; what is good in the economic arena is equally good with education and health. This book highlights that without the central government steering the nation towards universal elementary education and discerningly using the fiscal lever, the counter-productive brick-and-mortar approach to education would not have been abandoned and universal participation in elementary education would not have been brought within sight. Improving quality and learning achievement in all areas and at all stages of education, universalizing secondary education, development of skills and competencies of all types, expanding access to higher education, rejuvenating the moribund state universities, and establishing world-class universities are transcendent national challenges which could be grappled with only by replicating the role of the central government in DPEP and SSA. With quest for universal elementary education at its final stage of improving quality and learning outcomes, RSMA moving towards the take-off stage and RUSA just moving out of the drawing board, the need for the central government's strategic, advisory, and fiscal roles is definitely more and not less.

I would like to thank Vrinda Sarup, Maninder Kaur Dwivedi, and Mahammed Ariz Ahammed of MHRD for their forbearance towards a former colleague with his unending demands for information.

This book would not have been possible without the encouragement and patience of my wife, Seetha Vaidyanathan. It is the second part of what was to be a trilogy but now looks like a quartet. For years I have been and continue to be engrossed in writing; such engrossment is burdensome for a spouse at a stage of life when loneliness is an ineluctable existential condition.

ABBREVIATIONS

ADB	Asian Development Bank
AICTE	All India Council of Technical Education
AIU	Association of Indian Universities
ANER	adjusted net enrolment ratio
AP	Andhra Pradesh
APEID	Regional Programme of Educational Innovations for Development of Asia and the Pacific
APPEAL	Asia-Pacific Programme on Education for All
APPEP	Andhra Pradesh Primary Education Project
bn.	billion
BEP	Bihar Education Project
BGVS	Bharat Gyan Vigyan Samiti
BRAC	Bangladesh Rural Advancement Committee
BRC	Block Resource Centre
BSPP	*Bihar Shiksha Pariyojna Parishad* (BEP Governing Council)
CABE	Central Advisory Board of Education
CARE	Cooperative for Assistance and Relief Everywhere
CCEA	Cabinet Committee on Economic Affairs
CCPA	Cabinet Committee on Political Affairs
CEDAW	Convention on the Elimination of Discrimination against Women
CIDA	Canadian International Development Agency
CMP	Common Minimum Programme

CPRHE	Centre for Policy Research in Higher Education
CRC	Convention on the Rights of the Child
CRC	Cluster Resource Centre
CSS	Centrally Sponsored Scheme
DEA	Department of Economic Affairs, Ministry of Finance
DFID	Department for International Development, United Kingdom
DG	Director General
DIET	District Institute of Education and Training
DISE	District Information System for Education
DOE	Department of Education, MHRD
DPE	Domestic Political Environment
DPEP	District Primary Education Programme
DRDA	District Rural Development Agency
ECCE	Early Childhood Care and Education
EdCIL	Education Consultants India Limited
EEC	European Economic Community
EFA	Education for All
EFA FTI	Education for All Fast-track Initiative
EFA-9	EFA Summit of Nine High-Population Countries (New Delhi, December 1993)
EFC	Expenditure Finance Committee
EGS	Education Guarantee Scheme of Madhya Pradesh
ESCAP	Economic and Social Commission for Asia and the Pacific
EWLPs	Experimental World Literacy Projects
FAO	Food and Agriculture Organization
FCI	Food Corporation of India
FDR	Franklin Delano Roosevelt
FTFLP	Farmers Training and Functional Literacy Project
GDP	gross domestic product
GER	gross enrolment ratio
GOBI	growth of the child, breastfeeding, oral rehydration, and immunization
GOI	Government of India
GTZ	Deutsche Gesellschaft für Technische Zusammenarbeit

HDI	human development index
IAS	Indian Administrative Service
IBRD	International Bank for Reconstruction and Development
ICDS	integrated child development services
ICICI	Industrial Credit and Investment Corporation of India
ICR	implementation and completion report
ICSSR	Indian Council of Social Science Research
IDA	International Development Agency
IDBI	Industrial Development Bank of India
IDRC	International Development Research Centre
IEG	World Bank's Independent Evaluation Group
IGNOU	Indira Gandhi National Open University
IIEP	UNESCO's International Institute of Educational Planning, Paris
IIM	Indian Institute of Management
IIT	Indian Institute of Technology
ILO	International Labour Organization
IMF	International Monetary Fund
ISCE	Indian School Certificate Examinations
JNU	Jawaharlal Nehru University
JRM	Joint Review Mission
KSG	Kennedy School of Government, Harvard University
KSSP	Kerala Sastra Sahitya Praishad
LDC	least developed country
LPG	liberalization, privatization, and globalization
LSA	Lok Sampark Abhiyan
MOA	Memorandum of Association
LSK	Lok Shiksha Kendra (Adult Education Centre)
MDGs	Millennium Development Goals
MHRD	Ministry of Human Resource Development
mn.	million
MINEDAP-VI	Sixth Meeting of the Ministers of Education of the Asia-Pacific Region
MLLs	minimum levels of learning
MNC	multinational corporation
MORD	Ministry of Rural Development

MP	Madhya Pradesh
MS	Mahila Samakhya
NAEP	National Adult Education Programme
NAS	National Assessment Survey
NCERT	National Council of Educational Research and Training
NCF	National Curricular Framework
NCG	National Core Group
NCLP	National Child Labour Policy, 1985
NCTE	National Council of Teacher Education
NCW	National Commission for Women
NDA	National Democratic Alliance
NEEM	National Elementary Education Mission
NER	net enrolment ratio
NGO	non-governmental organization
NIEPA	National Institute of Educational Planning and Administration
NIT	National Institute of Technology
NORAD	Norwegian Agency for Development Cooperation
NRF	National Renewal Fund
NRG	National Resource Group, MS
NSS	National Sample Survey
NSSO	National Sample Survey Organisation
NTR	N.T. Rama Rao
NUEPA	National University of Educational Planning and Administration
ODA	Overseas Development Administration, United Kingdom
ODA	Official Development Assistance
OECD	Organization for European Cooperation and Development
PAB	Project Approval Board
PBA	programme-based approach
PDS	Public Distribution System
PIL	public interest litigation
PISA	Programme for International Student Assessment
P-MOST	Programmes of Mass Orientation of School Teachers
POA	Programme of Action

PPP	private–public Partnership
PROPEL	Promoting Primary and Elementary Education Project
PV	P.V. Narasimha Rao
REC	Regional Engineering College
RMSA	Rashtriya Madhyamik Shiksha Abhiyan
ROEAP	Regional Office for Education in Asia and Pacific
Rs	Rupees
RTE Act	Right of Children to Free and Compulsory Education Act
RUSA	Rashtriya Uchchatar Shikhsha Mission
SAL	structural adjustment loan
SAP	Structural Adjustment Programme
SBM	Saakshar Bharat Mission
SCs	Scheduled Castes
SCERT	State Council of Educational Research and Training
SHGs	self-help groups
SEMIS	Secondary Education Management Information System
SIDA	Swedish International Development Agency
SOP	South Orissa Project
SSA	Sarva Shiksha Abhiyan
SSN	social safety net
STs	Scheduled Tribes
SWAp	sector-wide approaches
TAPs	Technical Assistance and Administrative Procedures
TET	Teacher's Eligibility Test
TLC	Total Literacy Campaign
TSG	DPEP Technical Support Group
U-DISE	Unified District Information for System for Education
UDHR	Universal Declaration of Human Rights
UEE	Universal Elementary Education
ULIE	University of London, Institute of Education
UNDP	United Nations Development Programme
UNESCO	United Nations Educational, Scientific, and Cultural Organization
UNFPA	United Nations Population Fund

UNICEF	United Nations Children's Fund
UP	Uttar Pradesh
UPA	United Progressive Alliance
UPE	Universal Primary Education
USAID	United States Agency for International Development
VECs	Village Education Committees
WCEFA	World Conference on Education for All (Jomtien Conference)
WDS	Women's Development Programme
WFP	World Food Programme
WHO	World Health Organization

I

THE TINSEL TOWN

One fine morning, in May 1988, before the break of daylight, Joseph K woke up to receive a telephone call from the chief minister. In his theatrical style the chief minister, N.T. Rama Rao, or NTR as he was popularly referred to, told him, 'K *garu*, I want you to be my Education Secretary. Come over immediately.' Thus began K's engagement with educational policy, planning, and management; over the next 28 months he operated at the state level, and for seven years thereafter at the national and international levels. Even after retirement, he continued to dabble in educational planning and management once in a while. All in all, K spent about a quarter of his career in the area of education.

Looking back, his experience as State Education Secretary was invaluable in that he acquired a good understanding of the education system as a whole as well as of its parts, of the organizational dynamics and culture of different categories of educational institutions and of teacher unions, as well as of the interplays of different kinds: interplay between the government and heads of department, between central and state governments, and between government and universities. With about a quarter of the state government's budget, about 2.5 lakh teachers, 70,000 educational institutions, over a crore of students, the maximum number of heads of department[1] (19), and 11 autonomous

[1] In states, ministries are called departments and the secretary is the administrative head of a department; each department has executive arms called directorates or commissionerates. The head of a directorate is called a head of the department.

organizations (ten universities and the State Council of Higher Education) attached to any department, the education department was the largest department of the state government. No other department had such diverse institutions and subjects in its remit: schools, technician institutions, colleges, universities, employment exchanges, museums, archives, archaeology, libraries, sports organizations, and youth services. While the minister is *de jure* responsible for proper functioning of the department and its constituents, the secretary is *de facto* responsible to ensure that the department and its constituents are in fine fettle, joined up both horizontally and vertically, and perform to the satisfaction of the chief minister, minister of the department, the government, and the citizenry at large. Managing a vast organization and coping with the unending problems of personnel, patronage, logistics, and coordination is very challenging. Looking back, K was administering a mammoth licence-permit-inspectorate Raj which was collapsing under its own weight. The government felt duty bound to protect the interests of parents, students, teachers, and staff, and there was pressure on the government from parents to regulate fees even of private schools which were highly sought after, and from teachers' unions to regulate their salaries and service conditions even in institutions which received no grant-in-aid from the government. Consequently, the government regulated every conceivable aspect of the functioning of every educational institution, dotting every 't' and crossing every 'i', private or public, and whether it funded an institution or not. However, enforcement was erratic, vexatious, and ineffective; the more enterprising educational entrepreneurs could get around the rules with impunity. When confronted with the evidence of institutions violating the rules, and demands for action against errant institutions, the government tended to tighten the rules further, leading to a vicious cycle of over-regulation and weak enforcement, thereby spawning many adverse consequences. The administrative machinery was so overwhelmed by the burden of enforcement that it could not give adequate attention to the more important issue of academic supervision. With the expansion of educational institutions, and the proliferation of regulations, rigorous academic inspections by officials of the education department became a rarity. Inspections of colleges by universities and of universities by University Grants Commission (UGC) committees were equally perfunctory. The burden of enforcement of regulations was increased manifold by a culture in which no one would take a 'no' for answer, and the administrative system was willing to relent and revise an earlier order if only the supplicant had enough perseverance and the skill to work on key functionaries in the government. Given the culture of lobbying the government, K would be continually besieged all day long by an uninterrupted stream of visitors, even in respect of matters where a vice chancellor or K's subordinate had the power to take a decision. Rare would be a day when K did not have long meetings with teachers' trade union leaders. The departmental functionaries, all along the line of control from K himself to the grassroots functionary, were bogged down with the management of institutions and teachers. The officers of the department had to contend with multiple unions aggressively competing in a game of one-upmanship, vigorously espousing not only collective demands but also individual claims of thousands of teachers and lecturers, each such claim being based on a subtle historical and critical analysis of rules and regulations going back to East India Company days. Few departments were as much involved in litigation as the education department; handling thousands of cases in the High Court and Supreme Court was challenging enough. Compounding the challenge was the frequent use of contempt proceedings to browbeat the department and its functionaries. Rare was a week in which K did not have to appear before the High Court as a contemnor. As State Education Secretary, K often used to crack the joke that he had little time for education; this self-deprecating remark alluded to the fact that managing a vast administrative system was so demanding that he did not have adequate time to properly address the challenge of educational reform, or, in other words, the routine was crowding out what was important.

It was an exciting time to be a State Education Secretary. It was a fascinating experience to work closely with Chief Ministers N.T. Rama Rao and M. Channa Reddy, both of whom took enormous interest in education. A living legend of Telugu cinema, Rama Rao was an artist in politics, while Channa Reddy was an artist in the use of power. More importantly, the NPE of 1986 was just two years old, and there was great excitement in the air. It reconstructed the nation's vision for educational development and outlined the strategies for realizing that vision; the Programme of Action (POA) detailed the strategies. Dealing with elementary education offered K the exhilarating experience of leading a daunting mission of ensuring that every child in the state received elementary education. A bold vision, clear goals, strategies which seemed well thought out, and hefty infusion of resources from the central government to support the implementation of these strategies, all these seemed to be in place, and to coalesce to form an overarching purpose. The new programmes initiated after NPE, 1986 overturned the work style of functionaries of a hitherto insulated and self-engrossed department; functionaries who were steeped in an organizational culture of supervision and control were now called upon to be managers and 'deliver' programmes as well as outcomes such as ensuring that every child in their jurisdiction was enrolled in schools and once enrolled did not drop out. The new programmes required the functionaries of the education department in the districts to shed their insularity, to establish new working relationships with other departments. It was not an easy task to wean the education functionaries in the field away from inspectorate culture, and get them to embrace a development and managerial role and acquire an outcome orientation. His experiential learning as State Education Secretary was a perfect foil for his work later in Delhi in the Department of Education. The experiential knowledge he acquired in the state was about the education system *as is*, while that in Delhi was about what education *ought to be*; correspondingly, the skills he acquired in the state were for managing the education system and those in Delhi for transforming the education system. In military parlance, he honed his tactical skills in Hyderabad as a prelude to acquiring strategic skills in Delhi.

State of the School System

When K was a boy, the annual inspection of his school was a big event that sent a shudder down the spine of the management and teachers, since the payment of grants to the institution was conditional on satisfactory performance of the students in the tests administered by the inspecting officers. Should the inspectors be unsatisfied, they could curtail or even stop grants, thereby impairing the jobs of teachers. Teachers made extra effort to coach the students so that they impressed the inspecting officers with their scholastic abilities and demeanour. The saying that there is nothing new under the sun is validated to a considerable extent by the history of modern education in India. Private provision and public funding, and performance-linked matching grants were principles that were practised for a century before the modish New Public Management in the 1980s, elevated them into cardinal principles for organizing the delivery of basic services such as education. Even after Independence, state governments continued to largely follow the policy put in place by the Indian Education Commission of 1882. That policy differentiated between primary education and other stages of schooling. While it was the duty of the state to provide elementary education, at other stages of education private effort was to be encouraged through a system of grant-in-aid. The payment of the grant-in-aid was on a matching basis in that the government did not fully provide the recurring expenditure needed to pay the salaries of teachers and staff. Further, grant-in-aid was linked with performance. In keeping with the spirit of the times when economics was literary and not an inferior branch of mathematics, performance was assessed through impressions and perceptions rather than quantitative performance indicators. After Independence, state governments were more willing than during the British Raj to set up schools of their own; however, the grant-in-aid policy continued to be relied upon to expand upper primary and secondary education. The result was that the higher the stage of a school, the higher was the proportion of private aided schools. Thus, even in 1986–7 (when NPE came into effect) private aided schools accounted for 66.77 per cent of higher secondary schools, 52.65 per cent of secondary schools, 23 per cent of upper primary schools, and 7.60 per cent of primary schools. Further, the proportion of private schools was much higher in urban areas compared with rural areas. Thus, private institutions played an important role in providing access to upper primary and secondary education, a fact missed out in contemporaneous policy discourse. To complete the story, the British did establish some schools and colleges to serve as models for Indians to emulate. Government institutions were expected to set standards, generate healthy competition, and enhance the quality of non-government educational institutions.[2] Yet even by 1953, the Secondary Education Commission had observed that many of the government schools could not be models because of poor infrastructure.[3] With the expansion of

[2] Clive Whitehead, *Colonial Educators: The British Indian and Colonial Educational Services, 1858–1983*, London: I.B. Tauris, 2003, p. 5.

[3] Ministry of Education and Social Welfare, *Report of the Secondary Education Commission (October, 1952–June, 1953)*, 1972, p. 180.

the educational institutions and the proliferation of regulations, rigorous inspections became a rarity by the mid-1970s. An important aspect of inspections by the officers of the State Education Departments was academic supervision, which, among others, would comprise assessing how well teachers are transacting the curricula and offering guidance for more effective teaching. The collapse of academic supervision impaired the quality of education in government and government-aided schools even as education was being transformed from elite to democratic (mass) education, and extra efforts were needed to ensure effective learning for the bulk of students who were either first-generation learners or those whose home environment did not support the learning process or both. Also, it put an end to performance-linked grant-in-aid system that had been in vogue for about a century.

Another practice that conforms to the saying that there is nothing new under the sun was the collection of fees. In the contemporaneous discourse on private schools, champions of private schools contend that payment of fees strengthens the chain of accountability to parents. Teachers in private schools are directly accountable to managers who can fire them for non-performance; in turn, the managers are directly accountable to parents who are more demanding by virtue of having to shell out fees and will withdraw their children if they feel that teaching is inadequate. In contrast, the accountability chain is much weaker in government schools as teachers hold permanent jobs with salaries and promotion unrelated to their performance. As early as 1854, the famous Wood's Despatch, which laid the foundation for education during the British Raj, laid down the principle that some fees, however small, should be collected as people do not value anything free, and the payment of a fee promotes seriousness of purpose on the part of the student and his parents.[4] So strongly entrenched was the view articulated by the Wood's Despatch that even in 1964 when the landmark Kothari Commission began its work, fees were being charged in primary schools even though the Constitution obligated the state to endeavour to provide free and compulsory education to all children by 1960. During 1949–55, student fees were Rs 3.50 a month for classes VI, VII, and VIII, and Rs 6.50 a month for classes IX, X,

[4] Ministry of Education, *Education and National Development: Report of the Education Commission, 1964–66*, 1966, Volume I, pp. 199–200.

and XI. The report of the Kothari Commission triggered the move towards the abolition of school fees in government and government-aided private schools.[5] The Kothari Commission also recommended extension of the principle of 'equal work, equal pay' to teachers working under different managements, and revision of the grant-in-aid so as to fully cover the teachers' salary.[6] Teachers' trade unionism ensured a quick adoption of the principle by state governments. The grant paid to private aided schools ceased to be matching as governments began to fully reimburse teacher and staff salaries. Being so, it made no sense for the government to finance aided institutions when the recurring expenditure that the government had to reimburse for private unaided schools was no different from what it had to bear if it ran the school itself. It was as though the government funded private individuals and bodies to exercise power over admissions and teacher appointments. Andhra Pradesh (AP) became the first state in the country to bring the curtain down on the century-old grant-in-aid system when it declared through legislation that grant-in-aid would not be provided to new private colleges established after September 1985, and to private schools established after March 1985. Many other states followed suit so that with passage of time, the relative importance of government-aided institutions declined enormously; as access to elementary and secondary education was sought to be expanded through programmes such as DPEP, SSA, and RMSA, state governments sought to establish institutions of their own, or of local bodies rather enlist private effort. Thus, from 1973–4 to 2011–12, the proportion of government-aided schools declined from 5 per cent to 3 per cent at the primary stage, 17.8 per cent to 9.5 per cent at the upper primary stage, and 57 per cent to 25.8 per cent at the higher secondary stage.[7] In a country of continental size like India, there are bound to be interstate variations, but what is significant is that trends are more or less similar in almost all states. From a historical perspective, the decline of private aided schools marks the end of an era of modern education in India.

[5] *Report of the Education Commission, 1964–66*, Volume I, pp. 202–4.

[6] *Report of the Education Commission, 1964–66*, Volume I, p. 87.

[7] Ministry of Human Resource Development, *Statistics of School Education (As on 30th September 2011)*, 2014.

As State Education Secretary, K was intrigued by the fact that in Hyderabad city fewer students were getting enrolled in government institutions, as a result of which many institutions had far too many teachers than what their student strength warranted; even renowned institutions from the Nizam's era such as the Mahaboobia College with its landmark building were no exception. On inquiry, K came to know that an increasing number of parents preferred private English medium schools to government Telugu medium ones. K was not a stranger to the lure of English medium; though he himself studied in the Telugu medium, like everyone in the social class, he sent his daughter to an English medium school. Strange but true, it was during the British Raj that the common school system with the local language as medium of instruction was predominant, and Independence gave an enormous impetus to English medium schooling. Following the Education Despatch of 1854, vernacular languages were introduced as the media of instruction in secondary schools, and preparation of text-books in vernacular languages got a fillip. At the time of Independence, almost everyone who studied in schools studied in the main language of the place in which he lived. English medium schools were a rarity in mofussil towns, and the few which existed were located in large towns and hill stations, and catered mostly to Anglo-Indians and children of expatriates and of the affluent who were not rich enough to send their children to schools in England the way Maharajas and highly successful professionals such as Motilal Nehru did. English medium schools in India were mostly run by Christian missionary organizations and they prepared their students for the secondary examinations conducted by the University of Cambridge. In 1956, the Council for the Indian School Certificate Examinations (CISCE) was established to replace the overseas Cambridge School Certificate Examination by an all-India examination. The Council was a private body, and the schools affiliated it to it were predominantly schools run by Christian missionary organizations. In 1962, another all-India board offering education in English medium emerged when the central government constituted the Central Board of Secondary Education (CBSE) in its present form so that schools with a common medium of instruction could be set up all over the country to cater to the educational needs of those students whose parents were employed in the central government and had frequently transferable jobs that took them to different parts of the country. In contrast to schools which were affiliated to CISCE, CBSE schools were predominantly either central government schools or government schools in union territories such as Delhi, or private non-denominational schools. As the demand for English medium shot up, the number of private schools affiliated to CBSE began to rise in many parts of the country, and the students were seldom children of central government employees. CBSE was only too willing to extend affiliation without bothering to check whether its liberal policy of granting affiliation was not causing the proliferation of English medium schools and thereby defeating the policy postulate that school education should be imparted in the mother tongue of the child. As almost everyone of consequence began to send his or her children to English medium schools, those schools mushroomed all over the country, and CBSE emerged as the predominant all-India board. Also, small towns such as Ongole where K's daughter had her first schooling began to have 'convent' schools. Almost every senior educational administrator and academic that K was to know in his career sent their children to English medium schools; among the few exceptions was Venka Reddy. The irony of educationists serving in government and governmental institutions unwilling to send their children to government schools was captured by the aphorism of J.P. Naik that educationists were *planning for the best education of other people's children.*[8] As one looks around, one finds that even most social activists who ferociously condemn dualism in education and strongly advocate equality in education are no different. In his stint in education in Hyderabad as well as Delhi, K came to recognize how prized admissions to many of these English medium schools are, and how extraordinary was the clout that principals and managements of these schools had because of their power to grant or refuse admissions, and how much they were courted by the Lords of the Administrative Universe such as private secretaries to ministers. No wonder, two successive principals of Delhi Public School, R.K. Puram, were awarded the national honour of Padma Shri. As he probed further the reasons for the decline in enrolment in government schools in Hyderabad city, K found that the parents who preferred to 'vote' for private unaided schools 'with their feet' were drivers, peons, and

[8] Ministry of Education and Social Welfare, *The National Education Policy, 1947–1978*, July 1979, p. 41.

other parents of lower middle classes, and the names of the schools they preferred invariably began with the word 'Saint' and ended with the word 'Convent'. The middle name did not matter; it could be anything, say Amar, Akbar, or Antony. While these schools did impart education in the English medium, they were a world apart from the English medium schools to which the better-off sent their children, in terms of the facilities they had, the fees they charged, which were relatively low, and the ease of admission. However, to be honest, even in his wildest dreams K did not anticipate the spectacular growth and diversification of private unaided schools which began to take place about a decade later.

APPEP: Getting to Know an Externally Funded Project

K's experiential understanding of elementary education would have been incomplete without his association with the Andhra Pradesh Primary Education Project (APPEP), which was funded by the British Overseas Development Administration (ODA), the predecessor of DFID (Department for International Development). APPEP started as a pilot project in July 1984. Typical of the projects funded by external funding agencies before the World Conference on Education for All, held in Jomtien, Thailand, March 1990 (popularly known as Jomtien Conference), the scope of APPEP did not cover the whole gamut of elementary education but was limited to some, namely school building construction and improvement of the quality of education. Known as Phase I, the pilot project had an outlay of 1 million pounds; it covered 11 of the 23 districts. A total of 84 school buildings were constructed (out of over 50,000 elementary schools in the state) with innovative designs and generous norms of space, storage facilities, and ventilation. In-service training was imparted to 795 primary teachers (out of over 100,000 elementary school teachers in the state) working in 320 elementary schools (out of about 50,000 elementary schools in the state). Universal enrolment and retention were not vowed objectives of APPEP; however, ODA functionaries claimed that there was substantial increase in enrolment and retention in project schools because of better classroom environment and practices. When K joined the State Education Department, the pilot project was about to be completed in a year, and the central government was engaged in negotiations with ODA for further funding of APPEP. The negotiations culminated in the launch of Phase II, with an outlay of 32 million pounds spread over five years (1989–94). This phase envisaged construction of 3,400 classrooms and 1,104 teacher training centres, as well as training of all the elementary education teachers and their supervisors in the state. Historically, Phase II of APPEP was the first elementary education project in India with substantial external funding. The key pedagogic innovation of APPEP was activity-based child-centred learning, the key institutional innovation setting up a Teacher Centre at mandal headquarters, mandal being a sub-district administrative unit covering about ten villages, and the key process innovation systematic planning of in-service training. At the heart of the pedagogic innovation that APPEP sought to pioneer were six principles which aimed at transforming the student from a passive recipient of instruction into an active player in the learning process.[9] The first principle called upon the teacher to generate activities which would guide the pupils' learning instead of merely lecturing all the time. The second principle sought to promote learning by doing, discovering, and experimenting. The third principle commended use of group work to promote learning. It was expected that the application of these three principles would together transform the 'quiet classroom dominated by the teacher's voice into 'a lively place filled with the buzz of children's talk and discussion'. The fourth principle was extremely valuable. It explicitly recognized that children develop differently as individuals, and that their development in subject areas would also vary considerably. This principle exhorted teachers to provide for individual differences in the teaching–learning process. The fifth principle encouraged teachers to draw upon the local environment (for example, local fauna and flora, local landscape, local institutions, and so on) amidst which the pupils live in order to stimulate their interest in learning. The principle also recommended the use of locally available low-cost material for activities such as waste paper to cut, tamarind seeds to count, and so on. The sixth principle suggested transforming a dull classroom with bare

[9] Y. Ravi and Seshagiri Rao, 'APPEP', in Angela Little, Wim Hoppers, and Roy Gardner, eds, *Beyond Jomtien: Implementing Primary Education for All*, London: Macmillan, 1994, p. 35. The article written by two project officials is a good account of the project; also see Digumarthi Bhaskar Rao, *Success of a Primary Education Project*, New Delhi: APH Publishing Corporation, 2007.

walls into an inviting and exciting place decorated with the display of children's work. The display of good work was expected to counter the belief that tests were the only means of expressing the value of education provided. In-service training of teachers, teacher trainers, as well as supervisory staff focussed on getting the trainees to internalize the six principles, and equipping them to apply those principles in actual classroom practice. NPE, 1986, was announced during the third year of the pilot project, and by happy coincidence the child-centred and activity-based learning that the policy prescribed was being piloted in APPEP's in-service training. In pursuance of the policy, a country-wide Programme for Mass Orientation of Teachers (P-MOST) was organized. In AP, the six APPEP principles were incorporated in P-MOST.

A visit to Britain, courtesy of the British Council, provided K a splendid opportunity to understand what the British experts wanted to accomplish in APPEP. It was an educational tour which took him to many schools and teacher centres in London and Sussex, the University of London, Institute of Education (ULIE), which was providing the technical support to ODA, the Open University, Milton Keynes, Cambridge University, and the BBC studios producing educational TV programmes. From a professional point of view, K was particularly privileged to be in England when an intense debate raged over the National Curriculum that was in the offing. In retrospect, K was witness to an era that was to end soon, an era in which schools and teachers could decide what to teach and how to teach without any external direction. Schools laid down their own curriculum, and teachers decided what projects and activities students should undertake without being hemmed by fixed textbooks. In every educational institution K visited, and in every conversation he had with educators, the ongoing educational reforms constituted a staple topic of conversation, and he could not miss the palpable anxiety about the reforms. Although he did not realize then the full import of the reforms, the anxiety of educators he met arose from the challenge the reforms posed to the role perception of educators, and to their cardinal beliefs about what the objective of education should be, and how it should be imparted. The welfare state was built on the assumption that the state functionaries such as civil servants and teachers who delivered public services were knights who were competent, and predominantly public spirited and altruistic; they could correctly gauge the public needs and provide them competently.

Conversely, those who received the benefits of public services such as students and patients were considered to be incapable of knowing what was good for them, and taking independent action to procure what they ought to have.[10] Therefore, the society was deemed better off if education of children was left to teachers, health to doctors, and so on. From the late 1970s, the ideological foundations of the welfare state began to be assailed from the Left as well as the Right. The Left continued to believe that the state alone could further common good; however, it was sceptical of the willingness of rulers and state functionaries to further common good, and advocated social mobilization, empowerment of the people, particularly the disadvantaged groups, and vigilante activism that would name and shame the errant state functionaries, prod them to give up aberrant behaviour, and further the public interest as they ought to. Human rights and entitlements came to be a morally resonant language to articulate the objectives and strategies that the Left preferred. Those at the other ideological extreme had a greater faith in the efficacy of markets and a tendency to be concerned with government failure much as the earlier generation was with market failure. The Thatcherite assault on the welfare state was predicated on the belief that all human beings including state functionaries were self-interested, and it would be a grave error to construct government institutions and formulate public policies in the belief that the state functionaries were altruistic knights, and citizens incapable of discernment and autonomous action. The Thatcherite critique of education proceeded from the premise that far too much money was spent on achieving far too little, and that increases in public spending on education had not led to higher standards for the reasons that there was no external compulsion on schools and teachers to perform better, and far too many schools lacked firm direction and clear priorities and were 'adrift in a sea of fashionable opinions about what children should not, rather than should be, taught' because the education establishment was a secret garden of cosy sensuality that valued vague notions of personality development above measurable attainment.[11] If educational

[10] Julian Le Grand, *Motivation, Agency and Public Policy: Of Knights and Knaves, Pawns and Queens*, Oxford: Oxford University Press, 2003.

[11] Eric Evans, *Thatcher and Thatcherism*, 2nd Edition, London: Routledge, 2004, pp. 71–2.

attainment in Britain was not to fall behind that in other industrialized countries, a decentralized school-based curriculum without any compulsion to achieve minimum levels of learning should give way to a school system with National Curriculum for major subjects and National Achievement Tests at ages 7, 11, 14, and 16; the results of Achievement Tests would provide reliable information about pupil, teacher and school performance, and could guide parents' choice of schools. The public service reforms initiated by Thatcher were carried forward by the successor governments of Tony Blair and Gordon Brown so much so that the title of Simon Jenkins's book, *Thatcher & Sons: A Revolution in Three Acts*[12] captures faithfully the historic truth that the New Labour governments of Blair and Brown were a continuation of the conservative governments of Thatcher and Sir John Major. It would be facile to dismiss the British educational reforms as an offshoot of neo-liberal prejudice against the state and its functionaries. Thatcher only brought passion and conviction to a debate not of her instigation. It was the Labour Prime Minister James Callaghan, 'who could truly be said to have emerged from the bowels of the Labour movement', who called for a Great Debate on education.[13] In his famous Ruskin College speech, he asked the fundamental questions—why so many students were leaving schools with inadequate levels of literacy and numeracy, whether the curriculum met the needs of most students, and why students who completed higher education preferred to stay in academic life or find their way into the civil services rather than join the industry. Education was too important to be left to educationists; parents, learned and professional bodies, representatives of higher education and both sides of the industry, and the government, all had an important part to play in formulating and expressing the purpose of education and the standards that the country needed. The education establishments had no answer except for saying, 'Trust us to do the best and invest more in education.'

In retrospect, what was happening in British education during K's visit was part of a global trend that over the next three decades

[12] Simon Jenkins, *Thatcher & Sons: A Revolution in Three Acts*, London: Penguin, 2006.

[13] *Toward a National Debate*, speech by Prime Minister James Callaghan, at Ruskin College, Oxford, on 18 October 1976.

impacted on many areas of governance including education. Virginia Woolf famously declared that 'on or about 1910 … all human relations have shifted—those between masters and servants, husbands and wives, parents and children',[14] and that the change in human relations gave birth to modernity in literature, social relations, and religion. However, it was not a change that happened all at once or one that happened uniformly all over the world; it was only after passage of time imparted a perspective did the small shifts of everyday practice and possibility jell together to reveal fully the significance of the immanent shift. What Virginia Woolf wrote about shifts in human relations applies to other shifts such as the way people think about the state and what it ought to do and ought not to do. The 1980s witnessed a major shift in the perceptions about the state and markets, leading to mainstream economists placing great faith in the efficacy of markets, and emphasizing government failure as much as market failure. In addition, policy praxis began to be increasingly influenced by mainstream economic thinking, as a result of which New Public Management, an offshoot of Institutional Economics and the Public Choice theory, came into vogue. While there are various shades of New Public Management, the core belief that is common holds that the government should confine itself to core activities for which it has a comparative advantage, and that features of competitive markets should be introduced in public systems. The measures advocated by votaries of the New Public Management include providing greater choice for the 'consumer' of public services, inculcating in public sector functionaries a 'customer' orientation, laying down and monitoring precise quantitative performance targets, and linking remuneration and career advancement to the fulfilment of performance targets. The area of education was not insulated from the intellectual winds of change that swept other areas of governance; consequently, enhancing the efficiency of the school system, measuring and monitoring learner attainment, and promoting parental choice through grant of vouchers gained currency among policymakers.

To get back to his British visit, seeing is believing. After seeing what was happening in British education, K was particular that ODA did

[14] Virginia Woolf, 'Mr Bennett and Mrs Brown', in *Virginia Woolf: Selected Essays*, Oxford World Classics, Oxford: Oxford University Press, 2008, pp. 32–54, at p. 38.

not 'transfer' obsolete 'education technology' to APPEP, and that the pedagogic practices sought to be disseminated were not out of step with the emerging international practices. Soon after K returned from London, at his behest, ODA organized a colloquium in Hyderabad to discuss the on-going reforms in India and Britain. Among others, Roy Gardener of ULIE and Paul Scoop, a former Inspector of Schools, attended the colloquium. Gardener was candid enough to say that no one knew as yet how the National Curriculum would work out, and whether teachers would begin teaching for tests or would continue the present approach which laid stress on processes and personality development in the expectation that if the means were taken care of the end (learning achievement) would take care of by itself. It would be necessary for the British teachers to adapt to the pedagogic processes so that the objectives of the National Curriculum were achieved and all students reached the learner achievement levels expected. At the end of the colloquium, it was decided that in-service teacher training should clearly convey the message that the pedagogic practices that APPEP wished to disseminate should not be viewed in isolation, but should be treated as instruments for achieving the objectives of the AP state curriculum, and for transacting the textbook lessons.

As State Education Secretary, and later as Joint Secretary in the central education department, K supervised the implementation of Phase II of APPEP all through; he could therefore closely observe the impact of APPEP's educational interventions on classroom practice, and educational outcomes. The key institutional innovation of setting up a Teacher Centre at mandal headquarters and the key process innovation of systematic planning of in-service training was successful and well sustained. In contrast, the six principles that APPEP pioneered did not take root. A major thrust of NPE, 1986, was enhancing teacher competence and motivation, in pursuance of which a new Centrally Sponsored Scheme of Strengthening Teacher Education was launched to support the states to revamp pre-service training and to organize for the first time periodic in-service training of elementary education teachers. Hitherto the training infrastructure was limited to an institution at the state headquarters, the State Council of Education Research and Training (SCERT) in some states, and the State Institute of Education in others. The scheme on teacher education financed the states to deepen the training infrastructure by setting up a District

Institute of Education and Training (DIET) in every district. This was a welcome step; however, given the large number of teachers in most districts, a single institution in a district was not sufficient to systematically organize in-service training for all the teachers. The Mandal Teacher Centre pioneered by APPEP filled a critical gap in the training infrastructure. The APPEP innovation was mainstreamed and adapted throughout India, first through DPEP and later the Sarva Shiksha Abhiyan (SSA) so much so that teacher training resource centres at sub-district levels—blocks and clusters of about ten villages—have come to be an important feature of the Indian educational landscape. With training, 'hard' is 'soft', and 'soft' is 'hard'. The construction of brick and mortar buildings is the easiest part of training. Far more difficult are the 'soft' aspects: recruitment of suitable faculty, defining training objectives, choice of appropriate training methodologies, development of training modules and material, training the trainers for transacting the training modules, systematically planning and organizing the training programmes, evaluation of the training, and refining the training programmes by using the feedback from evaluations. And no less important is bringing about a change in the attitude of the participants and their superiors towards in-training, since the traditional attitude towards training was one of flippancy. The first large-scale in-service training programme for teachers in the country was the Special Orientation Programme for Primary School Teachers (SOPT) launched in the wake of NPE, 1986. As State Education Secretary, K heard hilarious accounts of SOPT from Ramana Reddy, a functionary of the National Council of Educational Research and Training (NCERT) who was the very antithesis of an 'organization man', an opposite of a man who not only works for an organization but 'belongs' to it.[15] A rationalist who was brutally honest and who took great delight in calling a spade a spade, Ramana Reddy poured ridicule on the SOPT training camps that NCERT organized in association with SCERT, and regaled K with stories of participants and the trainers turning into tourists and decamping from training to pleasant spots nearby. Needless to say, it is as important to generate a demand for training as to 'supply' training; K had seen for himself the wonders which would be accomplished when teachers come to realize the value

[15] William H. Whyte, *The Organization Man*, New York: Simon and Schuster, 1956.

of improving their competence. A case in point is the Subject Teacher Forums which secondary teachers established in Karnataka on their own initiative after in-service training. The members of these forums formed a virtual community and used open source operating systems to interactively develop and disseminate teaching aides for putting across abstract scientific concepts and mathematical theorems to students. Whatever it is, for the first time in the country, APPEP organized well-planned, systematic, large-scale in-service training of teachers. K can still visualize the tall, gaunt Scoop stooping over a table and spending hours drawing up the training calendar. The problem of participant absenteeism was solved by organizing training for all the teachers in a mandal as a group and closing all the government schools in the mandal during the training period, thereby leaving no room for participants to abstain. Luckily for the state, the establishment of DIETs synchronized with the implementation of the training under Phase II of APPEP; consequently, DIETs became functional earlier in AP than in other states. For the first time in the country, APPEP introduced the cascade system of training on a large scale: the DIET staff were trained first, the DIET staff in turn trained master trainers (mandal education officers, mandal resource persons, and select teachers), and the master trainers in turn trained the teachers. The in-service training was reinforced by periodic meetings of teachers at Mandal Teacher Centres for exchanging notes on good pedagogic practices.

Kaki pilla kaki ki muddu (a crow's offspring is cute to the crow) is a Telugu proverb of universal validity. Rare is a programme whose organizers do not declare it to be a success while it is being implemented. It is not unusual for the funding agencies and managers of programmes to turn evaluation into an occasion for securing fulsome praise by appointing 'friendly' experts for conducting the evaluation. Many ODA functionaries and British experts saw evidence of the six principles taking root in classroom practice. Thus, after field visits, Kenneth King, an expert on the politics of aid, claimed that 'the Herbertian Steps for lesson planning', steps that were central to traditional teaching in schools, 'are at last being dethroned'. Systematic lesson planning was no doubt abandoned by most teachers but nothing replaced it so that the quality of instruction did not improve as it should. K himself was greatly impressed by what he saw in the project schools: colourful display and the din and buzz of activity offered a stark contrast to the normal ambience of a classroom. He was no less impressed by the contribution that activity-based learning could make to informed understanding of concepts. He saw students learning the concept of an 'angle' through cutting paper and forming shapes. Although he spent long years studying mathematics and science, K was surprised to discover that his understanding of an 'angle' was inadequate. An angle was formed only by the intersection of two straight lines and not of any two lines; if two curved lines intersect what was formed was a corner and not an angle. Appearances are deceptive. From his 'surprise' visits to schools without any intimation, he discovered that the traditional classroom practices continued to rule roost, and that what he witnessed during visits which were previously announced were 'Potemkin villages', special shows of activity-based learning staged for visiting British and Indian dignitaries. At that time, K was inclined to scoff at the pretensions of ODA functionaries who claimed success where there was none. However, as years rolled by, K acquired a better and more mature understanding of human behaviour and of the dynamics of organizational change, and he came to be more appreciative of the efforts that were made by ODA functionaries against heavy odds. Human motivation is complex: street-level bureaucracy (functionaries such as the teacher in the school, *anganwadi* workers in the child care centre, and auxiliary health workers), which actually implements policies and programmes at the grassroots, fails to implement new instructions for many reasons. There would be many who are slaves of habit and are not inclined to adapt their working styles to the demands of the new instructions. There would be many others who do not hesitate to subvert a policy or programme for private gain or because they are just cussed or are inclined voluntarily or involuntarily to please the local power brokers. However, even those who are scrupulous may find it difficult to implement the new instructions because of inadequate resources or working conditions. Conducting the classroom transaction in accordance with the six principles of APPEP requires smaller classes with a more favourable teacher–pupil ratio and a lighter curricular load. Many teachers felt that with the size of the classes they had to handle they could not cover the entire syllabus using the activity-based approach. Many had not internalized activity-based instruction method sufficiently enough to be able to apply that method to topics that were not covered in the training programmes they attended. Furthermore, many schools in rural areas did not have a teacher for each class, and consequently a teacher had to teach multiple classes simultaneously; activity-based learning was more difficult to organize with such 'multigrade' teaching.[16] Also, parents were not happy with the activity-based learning that was propagated under the APPEP project; for them, cutting and pasting, building clay models, singing, and dancing that were central to activity-based learning were play and not the education they wanted their wards to have. Replacing the traditional rote learning by a more creative way of learning continues to remain a major challenge.

Dealing with an Agency: The First Lessons

APPEP was the first project funded by an external funding that K supervised, and that experience offered valuable lessons in the intricacies of managing such projects as well as managing the 'development partners' as funding agencies are called these days. Managing smooth flow of funds from the funding agency to the project implementation units, utilizing aid, and completing project activities in accordance with the schedules agreed with the funding agency are major challenges. The release of funds for project activities was irregular even though the State Finance Department received ODA assistance as an advance from ODA through the central government. This problem was not unique to APPEP but characteristic of all activities implemented by state departments and financed by the central government with either its own resources or resources mobilized from agencies. Money being fungible, state finance departments tended to release funds with a view to ensure that ways and means of the state government are balanced, rather than making available on time resources for the project activities. K was witness to many occasions when his colleagues in the Finance Department tried to regulate expenditure in the face of acute ways and position by closely monitoring the bills presented to the treasury and deciding which bills the treasury officials should clear and which ones they should hold in abeyance, so much so that one was not sure whether one would receive payment from the treasury of an amount due and sanctioned by the government. Anil Bordia, K's boss, came up with a solution to this systemic problem by way of setting up a legal

[16] Ravi and Rao, 'APPEP', p. 29.

entity registered under the Society Registration Act for the management of externally funded projects. Funds would directly flow from the central government to that legal entity short-circuiting the state finance department. The solution was first tried out in Shiksha Karmi, and scaled up in the Bihar Education Project (BEP) and later extended to all other elementary education projects funded by external agencies, and much later to RMSA, a programme started in 2009 to universalize secondary education. However, midway through the implementation of APPEP, it was not possible to alter the organizational arrangements for managing APPEP, and smooth flow of funds remained a problem throughout the implementation of APPEP.

David Theobald, Education Adviser in the British High Commission, supervised APPEP. He was an astute *India hand* with excellent knowledge of the Indian Government and the bureaucracy, a good judge of men, adept in handling officials, and capable of using the right tactic for the moment; he kept close tabs on the central and State Education Departments, and was *au courant* with all the developments. No wonder his supervision of APPEP earned him an honour from the Queen, an Officer of the Most Excellent Order of the British Empire. Theobald's supervision was greatly facilitated by the fact that ODA had an office in Hyderabad which functioned like the residency of the Raj period in Native States; in effect, the native ruler reigned while the resident ruled. ODA's hands-on management was also facilitated by the vestiges of the colonial mindset still prevalent in India, so virulently described by R Vaidyanathan:

> It is time we stopped getting awed by the West ... [a low level functionary]—generally called a side-kick in Bollywood films—... gets immediate *darshan* [audience] with our Prime Minister. ... [We tend] to practice *shashtanga namaskaram* (complete prostration) when we meet 'experts' from multilateral institutions or from the US or Europe. ... Any white man or woman is assumed by definition to be 'experts'.[17]

The ODA Office in Hyderabad worked in close association with the state government's project office, which functioned more as an enclave of ODA than a state government office. K lost his temper on many

[17] R. Vaidyanathan, 'Developing Healthy Contempt is a Must', *Daily News and Analysis*, July 1, 2008, http://www.dnaindia.com/report.asp?newsid=1174759.

occasions when he found the officials of the project office acted as subordinates of ODA than as officials of the state government. Every interaction between a secretary and a manager of the funding agency is a negotiation, even if it does not have the customary trappings of a formal negotiation. 'Knowing the other', information about what the other party to negotiations really thinks about the negotiation and wants from the negotiation, gives formidable power in negotiations; Theobald brought to bear on his interaction with K the insider knowledge that K's deputies in the project office provided him. What irritated K further was the fact that the officials of the project office used Theobald to intercede with K on their behalf in personal as well as official matters. Such behaviour reminded K time and again that the British conquered India with Indian soldiers, and with the treacherous support of avaricious aspirants for power such as Mir Jaffar. K often rudely gave vent to his indignation at the attitude of the officers of the project office. Once he hissed at a lady officer in the project office, saying, 'Get a British passport', much like the 'Iron Lady', Margaret Thatcher, telling her dissenting Europhile ministers in a cabinet meeting that if they disagreed with her, they should get on a boat to Calais, put on a beret, and pay 80 per cent of their earnings to the French government.[18] On another occasion, he was ruder, shrieking at an officer, 'Carry their shoes', a veiled and distorted reference to the episode in *Ramayana* in which Bharatha meets Rama at Chitrakoot, fails in his efforts to persuade Rama to return from exile and rule the kingdom, returns carrying Rama's shoes on his head, places the shoes on the throne, and rules the kingdom as a proxy of Rama. Theobald was suave and pleasant; most British consultants were gentlemanly without a trace of condescension. However, once in a while, K came across Blimps, British version of the *Ugly American*. One day, a Wheeler turned up in the company of Theobald. Wheeler was a consultant appointed in the British High Commission to supervise construction of school buildings in APPEP. He brusquely demanded that all tender documents should be submitted to him for prior scrutiny, and declared pompously that he would visit every classroom and teacher centre under construction and issue directions. K was equally brusque, and peremptorily told him that

[18] Julian Barnes, 'Daddy's Girl', *New York Review of Books*, 23 February 2012.

he would not succeed even if he equipped himself with a company of the British army and a squadron of the Royal Air Force. The agreement with ODA did not provide for prior scrutiny of tenders by ODA, and single-handedly he could not visit thousands of classrooms scheduled for construction which were scattered all over a sprawling state such as AP, which was larger than the United Kingdom itself. Theobald hastily intervened to say that adequate arrangements could be worked out to the satisfaction of the state government.

British experts associated with APPEP were first-rate professionals, well-meaning and meticulous in their attention to detail. Their contribution to APPEP, operationalization of the DIETs in AP, and the designing and operationalization of subdistrict cluster-level resource centres were very laudable. However, locals and local institutions were not associated in any significant way, not to speak of national resource institutions such as NCERT. No doubt APPEP had a component for capacity building: study tour of Britain by officials such as K and training of a few teachers at ULIE. Those who visited Britain benefited from exposure to a foreign country and foreign institutions; however, by and large, as a system, the State Education Department was not benefited from such visits. A measure of capacity building is the extent to which officials of the recipient government, local institutions, and local experts are associated with the planning, detailing, monitoring, and evaluation of the project. Judged by this standard, APPEP built little capacity. In the Union Education Department, K came to be the department's pointsman for interaction with multilateral and bilateral agencies, and K's association with APPEP came to be a defining experience which conditioned his attitude to the external agencies. K carried with him to Delhi his concern that capacity development should not be impaired by continuous 'mothering' by a local agency office and by hordes of expatriate consultants and officials descending on states and districts at short or no notice. That concern underlay the new institutional arrangements he developed for DPEP whereby agency functionaries or their consultants would not be associated with planning or implementation; they could visit states and interact with programme functionaries in the field only for the purpose of appraisal and later only once in six months as part of the six-monthly joint review missions and nothing else. In short, supervising APPEP was a rich educative experience, offering lessons on what should be done and what should not be done while engaging external funding agencies, and that experience stood in good stead for dealing with a wide variety of multilateral and bilateral agencies.

Bordia was the Union Education Secretary when K was State Education Secretary. He was a compulsive traveller and a fine headhunter; spotting and recruiting acolytes was an important activity he undertook during his restless tours. In 1989, he descended upon K in Hyderabad and reviewed the implementation of centrally sponsored programmes in AP. K hosted a lunch for him at Lakeview, the state guesthouse. After lunch, they were on their way to the Secretariat to resume the review. All of a sudden, Bordia asked the driver to halt at Panchagutta. Followed by K, he rushed to a *paan* shop, and as the *paan* (betel leaf [*Piper betle*] with areca nut , slaked lime paste, and other ingredients) was being rolled, he asked K, '*Yar* [Hi, buddy], there is a post of Joint Secretary falling vacant soon in my department. Would you like to join?' K was a trifle surprised at the offer, but never one to let go a bird in hand, he answered in the affirmative. Bordia was not sure that it was a categorical acceptance. He asked K, '*Yar*, you have been in an economic ministry. Would you really join the education department?' K replied, 'Sir, I would be happy to join as it saves me the bother of lobbying for a job'. Thus began K's exodus from the state government to which he did not return to serve.

II

THE GREAT MASTER

After reaching Delhi in August 1990, K spent the first few days looking up friends and colleagues. Gayatri looked puzzled when K mentioned to her that he would be joining Bordia's department; she was a colleague from his State cadre, a Delhi girl from a family of senior civil servants who were *au courant* with the ways of Delhi. Daffney Rabello, a colleague in Bordia's department who was also from K's State cadre, greeted him as he entered her room with the words, 'Welcome to the madhouse.' Maybe she was jealous, thought K, as he mulled over her unusual greeting. Everyone was surprised when K was allocated not a substantive charge but a variety of odd subjects—administration, policy, planning, coordination, country's relations with UNESCO, external academic relations, and an assortment of small programmes funded by external agencies such as the Mahila Samakhya (MS), a women's empowerment programme, Shiksha Karmi, a programme for providing education in remote villages of Rajasthan through para-teachers, and the Bihar Education Project (BEP), which was still very much in the air. All these were portents of what was in store for K. He was in for many shocks and surprises. Very soon K found that his new workplace was a fine setting for a prolonged fit of despair. Bordia the boss was not Bordia the head-hunter; lest K should have any doubt, Bordia made that explicit in the very first meeting. A couple of days after K joined the department, Bordia pulled him up for the bad state of restrooms. Although as head of the administration division, K was technically in charge of the upkeep of restrooms, K could not help wonder whether he had come all the way from Hyderabad to spruce up the restrooms. Being an avid reader who liked to relate himself to what he read, K recalled the plight of the land surveyor K of Kafka's *The Castle*. The land surveyor arrived in the Count's village thinking that the Count expected him, only to find that the Count and his Castle were remote and inaccessible. Thereafter he spent all his life trying to ascertain in vain whether at all he was needed in the first place. K felt his plight was worse; for one moment he was the royal guest at the Castle and the very next cast into the heavy snow in the village below. One moment, Bordia exuded bonhomie, jovially bantered and bluffed, but in a trice turned into an imperious and inconsiderate master. As one of his non-governmental organization (NGO) friends, who went on to win along with her husband the Magsaysay Award, said to his great delight, Bordia had a remarkable ability to turn men into mice. As Bordia's moods swung, K was metamorphosed back and forth, from being yar to Dr K; he could be never sure which Bordia he would face at any given moment, the yar or utterly inconsiderate boss, and whether he himself was a human being or a giant bug. One was not sure whether the swing in moods was a personality trait or a management technique. K believed it was the latter, and recalled that it was said of Prime Minister Thatcher that she was Machiavellian, that she believed that it was far better for the boss to be feared than loved, and that the fear she evoked operated at two levels: face-to-face intimidation and ruthlessness. As the officer in the department responsible for administration, K once brought to his notice the request of an officer to be designated as Education Adviser. Bordia was in no mood to oblige, and demanded to know why that officer wanted such a designation. K replied, 'To be kept in good humour, have good morale and motivation.' Bordia curtly said it was not his job to keep people in good humour, and that if anyone wanted to be in good humour, he should read poetry. K wanted to tell him that great poetry was about tragedy and emotional scars, but dared not, and the words stopped in his mouth. Unlike Thatcher, the lady who was 'not for turning', Bordia often reversed orders and acted as if he had not issued a different order earlier, as a result of which K and his colleagues drew Bordia's ire for following up his earlier instructions. Bordia had the utmost consideration for the welfare and personal problems of his acolytes like K, and yet his work style and the demands he placed on them were such that they could have no personal life. A compulsive workaholic, he would hold long meetings on Sunday late evenings and, as the meeting broke, would command K to have a document ready by 8 a.m. the very next day. K would slog all night to get the document ready only to find that Bordia would just set it aside and begin working on the document himself. The slightest error was enough to provoke Bordia's mighty wrath. And further, Bordia would elicit views of his deputies only to scorn those that were not to his liking. Once in a meeting with funding agencies, Bordia quipped that he was the Pope; in another, he quipped that 'they (his deputies) would say what I would like them to say'. His witticisms always had a grain of truth. He brooked no difference of opinion, much like the Grand Inquisitor of Seville in Dostoyevsky's *Brothers Karamazov*, who commanded Christ himself to be silent and threatened to burn him at the stake for coming in his way. K recalls an incident in which the financial adviser of the department showed Bordia a copy of the existing instructions on issue of grants to NGOs, and said that so long as those instructions existed they had to be complied with. Thereupon, Bordia ceremoniously tore the copy to pieces, much like the District Collector in the Raj period who observed on a Government of India Act which he received in the mail that 'this Act would not apply in my district'. In his interactions with Bordia, K was often reminded of imperious viceroys such as Marquis Wellesley, Dalhousie, and Curzon. Maybe, thought K, the inability of Bordia, like that of Wellesley, to see anyone else's point of view as well as his tremendous certainty of respect due to him gave Bordia the cutting edge to get things done.[1]

The 21 months of tutelage with Bordia were a fiery ordeal for K; it was living in 'a reign of danger full of nightmares which might easily turn into reality'. However, it was an ordeal that K, in retrospect, would not give up for his dear life. The challenge of coping with Bordia and his exacting demands was a great learning experience. K learnt about human nature, and to live with the ineluctable fact that Man is a bundle of contradictions. His career was richer for that ordeal; he watched a great master at work. Learning by observation and reflection on what was observed helped K acquire administrative skills, particularly of articulation, negotiation, and, more importantly, grand design and execution.

[1] Philip Woodruff, *Men Who Ruled India*, Volume I, London: Jonathan Cape Ltd., 1971, p. 202.

The tutelage was at a stage in K's career when he could set his eyes on being a General (Secretary to Government of India [GOI]) soon; there was no better way of learning to be a General than being a close aide to a temperamental and slave-driving Patton-like General whose brilliance dazzled and nearly blinded everyone around. Bordia was an extremely capable and exceptional administrator. He was one of the all-time Greats. If he is not reckoned as an L.P. Singh or an L.K. Jha, it is because in the administrative pecking order education is rather lowly. While everyone says education is important, the education department ranks low in status and prestige, as a young lady Indian Administrative Service (IAS) officer once quipped. The peer evaluation of education is no different in Whitehall, as the memoirs and the biographies of Thatcher would bring out. Thatcher headed just one department—education—before she moved on to lead the Tory party and later the nation. In appointing her, Heath thought that education was about her ceiling. A Cinderella department, it was not considered a department for an outstanding minister to make a mark. By its very nature, education is an isolated department with relatively little impact on other departments, which meant the Education Minister sits on very few cabinet committees or, correspondingly, the permanent secretary on very few official committees. It does not provide the visibility and the sense of movement that gives momentum to official and political careers. Nevertheless, Bordia was not only, to use *officialese*, an outstanding civil servant, but also exceptional. As a master, he was very exacting much like the Rishis and gurus, with oceans of knowledge and wisdom, and rather temperamental with awesome powers to curse and bless. *Gurukulavasa*, residential study with gurus, would have been a nerve-wracking experience but for the belief that knowledge is transmitted only through revelation and that revelation is only through the medium of gurus.

Bordia was a quintessential *un homme de government*. As a maestro in administration, Bordia had superb mastery over the essential tools of his trade. Bordia was a fine wordsmith, very precise in his expression, and as he often said, he was very sticky with drafting. He himself would prepare for his deputies the communications they should send. To begin with, Bordia's corrections of his drafts irritated K a great deal and hurt his *amour proper*. However, over time, he began to appreciate the corrections and the purpose underlying them. Bordia was a past master in the use of *constructive ambiguity*, deliberate use of ambiguous language on a sensitive issue in order to advance the objective in mind. In a negotiation, for example, constructive ambiguity might be employed not only to disguise an inability to resolve a question on which the parties remain far apart but also to do so in a manner that enables each to claim that some concession on it has actually been obtained. K learnt from Bordia the invaluable art of deliberately introducing constructive ambiguity or greater precision as the context and implication warranted. People in high position have to be, to use the metaphor of Machiavelli, a fox as well as a lion. K learnt from K.V. Ramanathan, his previous boss in the central government, the need to stand firm, and courageously and frontally repulse attacks by opponents like a lion. However, that learning was not enough, as it was necessary to learn to recognize traps like a fox, and the art of outflanking and outmanoeuvring the opponents. From Bordia he learned enough to spot the guiles of others, and be on the alert. Bordia's practice of what is called in management jargon as *backward mapping* was superb. He carefully assessed in every situation who mattered and who did not, and relentlessly sought to win over all those who could be won over and neutralize those who could not be. He was an artist in the use of power; he always meticulously assessed the power configuration of the moment and appropriately adapted his persona. He was a consummate actor. With ministers and those to whom he thought deference was due, he was humility personified, and he could teach Sir Humphrey of *Yes Minister* fame a trick or two. Even as humility personified, he could resist the wishes of the minister by every possible means through his consummate command of all the arts of thwarting and checkmating bosses. If he wanted to comply, he could move with the speed of not light but of thought, cutting through the jungle of red tape like wild fire. He was the classic example of a person who *could* if he *would*. He was quick to seize the tactical implications of any development. He could march with a parade of elephants through an opening as minute as the head of a needle. He was a virtuoso in manipulating men and systems, relentlessly pursuing the accomplishment of what he set his heart on with a ferocious tenacity, never quailing before obstacles, and never hesitating to stoop to conquer, if bluff and bluster or his irresistible charm did not work. He assiduously cultivated media deftly using it as an arena for the continuation of his battles by other means. He was engaged in a cold war with his minister Arjun Singh; once in a while his journalist friends would write stories criticizing Arjun Singh for being indifferent to education and spending his time in politicking instead of attending to his ministry. He was a battle-hardened veteran of bureaucratic jungle warfare, and in every development he discovered opportunities to advance his objectives. Nothing with him was spontaneous, including his breathing. He often joked about his convoluted mind. He left nothing to chance; instead he meticulously planned every move. He orchestrated every event and every meeting, clearly laying down the role and script for his deputies, specifying who would do and say what, and planning ahead the stratagems to thwart those who may oppose. He was a virtuoso in the game of co-opting; consequently, professionals whose job was evaluation of his programmes were generally less demanding than what professional integrity required. Bordia was a capable negotiator, an invaluable skill in governance; however, at times, his bluff and bluster was counterproductive. Nonetheless, K could not have asked for more: study of negotiation theory at Harvard, one of the world's very best institutions, and internship with a great master.

As ever, Bordia charmed his visitors with the visions he conjured, the breadth of his knowledge about contemporary international developments in education, and the passion with which he spoke about India's effort in universalizing elementary education and literacy. Bordia was a great communicator and a great performer too. His delivery, modulation of voice, and body language all would do a thespian proud. As mentioned earlier, he always sought to overawe his foreign visitors with his bold and difficult demands. It seemed to K that in these encounters Bordia was entering into high level of psychological warfare, not so much a war of attrition as of blitzkrieg. Just an example would suffice: the visitors were from the Swedish International Development Agency (SIDA), which had been financing Shiksha Karmi (education worker), an innovative project in Rajasthan. Bordia was now keen that SIDA should fund a more comprehensive basic education project in the same state, basic education as defined by the Jomtien Declaration comprising an assortment of primary education for children, non-formal education (NFE) for children who do not complete schooling, and adult and non-formal vocational education for youth. Basic education so defined did not include formal vocational education and was different from the Gandhian concept of basic education wherein primary education was sought to be imparted through the medium of work. Bordia personally served tea to his visitors and joked about the polluted water and milk in India, thereby trying to strike a rapport with the foreign visitors scared of catching the dreaded Delhi belly. As the conversation turned to the business at hand, Bordia tried to get the visitors commit themselves on the scale of funding and a probable date by when the project could start. What they would all say was that while SIDA was keen to fund the project preparation the approval cycle had to be gone through. When charm failed, Bordia turned to bluff and bluster. With or without SIDA support, the project would start in three months, that is to say January 1991, lest the astrologically favourable constellation of stars should go away. To jump the story ahead, the project with an exotic name, Lok Jumbish (People's Movement), started about two years later, as a pilot with a modest outlay, that too only after the due process of the project cycle was gone through and after a bitter fracas over the appraisal report of a three-member team of Swedish consultants.

Obsessional bureaucratic animals like Trevelyan and Curzon are abnormal people and do not make easy company. Bordia was no different; like the heroes in Greek tragedies, he had tragic flaws in his character. His hubris, fretfulness, and vindictiveness undid much of what he so deftly planned. Like an artist, he was temperamental; he never hesitated to make foes; in fact, he made more foes than necessary. Consequently, he had as many, if not more, detractors than admirers. Except for four or five favourites of his, the rest of his office corps was disgruntled, and quite a few of them looked to Arjun Singh and his factotums for succour; quite a few were emotional wrecks. Decades later K came to read about Sir Robert Morant, a reforming British civil servant who left a deep impression on the English education system; Morant appeared to be a previous *avatar* of Bordia. Morant was 'the supreme civil servant', and remained, even after his death, 'a figure of acrid controversy'. Morant was a man of the highest intellect, 'had a passion for making the instruments of public service more effective, and was consumed and destroyed by it.... There was no intermittence in his volcanic energy. He knew no rest and enjoyed no leisure'. A colleague, perhaps less well-disposed, described him as suffering from 'chronic diarrhoea of the pen'.[2] Beatrice Webb of the Fabian Society fame was a fellow

[2] John W. Wheeler Bennett, *John Anderson: Viscount Waverley*, New York: St. Martin's Press Inc., 1962, p. 311.

member of the Haldane Committee on the machinery-of-government inquiry (1918); she once described Morant as 'the one man of genius in the Civil Service ... a strange mortal not altogether sane'.[3] It is said that he was one of the greatest autocrats who ever dwelt in the Civil Service, and that 'he was not unprincipled but he was unscrupulous'. He fell out with many colleagues and unleashed a vendetta against everyone he fell out with.

Internship with Bordia was not just about the methods of managing men and matters. It was also about understanding the historical and social context of education, about imbibing the essence of education. As State Education Secretary, K was engrossed in managing a vast machine and in coping with the unending problems of personnel and patronage, as well as living under not one Damocles Sword but hundreds of them, by way of contempt petitions. He did not have adequate time to adequately address the challenge of educational reform. It was only after K joined Bordia that he began to know what education was about. To Bordia, education was not just a job; it was a calling. In his classic essay on Tolstoy's view of history, *The Hedgehog and the Fox*,[4] Isaiah Berlin contrasts the fox which knows many things with the hedgehog which knows one big thing, and goes on to proclaim that Tolstoy was a fox who spent his life wishing he were a hedgehog. Bordia was very much like Tolstoy except that unlike Tolstoy he could also fulfil his wish of being a hedgehog. Although he was an ace IAS officer capable of many things, he chose education as the passion of his life. Bordia was inspired by his father, a school teacher, and wanted to follow in his footsteps. He had his schooling at the innovative Vidya Bhawan School, Udaipur, where grades were not the be-all-and-end-all of education, and students were encouraged to be creative and broad-minded. Half his career was devoted to education, and rather unusual for an IAS officer, he chose to have adult education as his specialization during his foreign training. His tryst with adult education began in 1965 when as a young Additional Director of Primary and Secondary Education, Rajasthan he came into close contact with

[3] Peter Hennessy, *Never Again: Britain 1945–51*, London: Jonathan Cape Ltd., 1993, p. 53.

[4] Isaiah Berlin, *The Hedgehog and the Fox: An Essay on Tolstoy's View of History*, London: Widenfeld & Nicolson, 1953.

the internationally well-known adult educators Roby Kidd and James Draper who were then consulting at the University of Rajasthan. Kidd had been the President of the UNESCO Second World Conference on Adult Education (Montreal, 1960), and later created the International Council for Adult Education in 1972 to promote literacy in Third World countries with President Julius Nyerere of Tanzania as honorary president, and Malcolm Adiseshiah, then with UNESCO, as working president. It was at the Ontario Institute for Studies in Education where Kidd was Chairman of the Department of Adult Education that Bordia had his foreign training. In his first stint in the Union Education Ministry, in the late 1970s, Bordia was associated with the launch of the National Adult Education Program. At the end of his first stint, he went on for a stint to the UNESCO's International Institute of Educational Planning (IIEP), Paris, which helped him build up international contacts and be *au courant* with international education.

Bordia had a strong sense of history, and talking to him when he was in an expansive mood was education by itself. It was from chats with Bordia that K got to know for the first time about officials of yesteryears such as J.P. Naik and Raja Roy Singh who did stellar work in the field of education. Raja Roy Singh was Joint Education Adviser in the Ministry of Education, the first Director of NCERT, and went on to be the Chief of UNESCO's Regional Office for Education in Asia and the Pacific, Bangkok. It was Bordia who encouraged K to study the history of Indian education, thereby helping K to acquire a better perspective of the educational challenges that the nation was grappling with. Bordia strongly believed and acted on the belief that he was a legatee of a grand Indian tradition of education with luminous stars such as Ishwar Chandra Vidaysagar, Gopal Krishna Gokhale, Zakir Hussain, D.S. Kothari, and J.P. Naik. Through his tutelage under Bordia, K also came to feel he was part of a *guru shishya parampara* (teacher–disciple lineage); K was proud of his *parampara* and strove to live up to that parampara. However, he was not a blind believer in tradition, and acted to live up to the maxim of Aristotle that *amicus Plato, sed magis amicas veritas* (Plato is dear but dearer is truth). It has been said, rightly so, that whoever reads history with application would perceive the same scenes repeated with different actors and different settings. As mentioned earlier, K noticed many of the contemporary educational challenges addressed in the past by great minds and statesmen, and their thoughts and actions to be of great value in getting to know the nature of contemporaneous challenges, for the past far from being dead is often not even past. The lessons of history help in identifying promising avenues and blind alleys, and cure one of solipsism and hubris. Also, the further back one looks, the farther forward one can see and envision alternative futures. From his study of the history of education, K lost his patience with name-calling and labelling and with the customary attribution of all the ills of Indian education to Macaulay, and to erosion of values. Richard E. Neustadt and Ernest R. May addressed their classical work on the uses of history for decision-making to the very many in Washington who thought that the world was new, all problems fresh, and were prone to offer quick fixes for complex problems.[5] Delhi was no different, and once Universal Elementary Education (UEE) and Education For All (EFA) became fashionable, there were magic bullets and quick fixes galore. There was a UNICEF Resident Representative, for example, who thought UEE could be achieved in one shot the way polio was eradicated through immunization, and what came in the way was lack of political will. He was absolutely certain that the advocacy of UNICEF and the NGOs it had been funding would drum up the requisite political will, and make UEE a reality in a couple of years. From his study of the history of education, K learnt that the challenges of access, participation, quality, and equity were not amenable to quick fixes, that best can often the enemy of the good, and that practical programmes that carry forward educational reform process were needed rather than rhetorical pleas for uprooting the existing systems. Achieving UEE was like running a marathon and not a sprint, and quick fixes distract attentions, instil false hopes, and would sooner than later lead to dejection and cynicism. The test of an idea for reforming education does not lie in its loftiness, or the eminence of the figure who espouses it, but whether it can be acted upon by ordinary human beings, and whether it is acceptable to 'stakeholders'. Statesmanship in any field including educational reform consists in recognizing that administration is the art of the possible and yet striving to extend the limits of what is possible. The challenge of education demands not *ad hominem*, knee-jerk reactions, but a well-considered response, which

[5] Richard E. Neustadt and Ernest R. May, *Thinking in Time: The Uses of History in Decision-making*, New York: The Free Press, 1986, p. xi.

positions the challenge in its proper perspective, draws lessons from history, and builds upon the efforts of the past and visions of the future. To paraphrase Newton, what was needed was to stand up on the shoulders of giants to see further and go further. K was deeply conscious of the lack of institutional memory in government ministries arising from poor, if not non-existent, documentation, particularly of the process underlying the trajectories of policies and programmes. A Third Law of Thermodynamics of sorts operates in government ministries. Just as natural systems tend towards more and more disorder, information and knowledge tend to get dissipated, and soon acquire the status of dark matter. In the absence of efforts to prevent the natural tendency to dissipate institutional amnesia becomes common. Consequently, every initiative comes to be a voyage of adventure, a voyage without the guidance of the compass of institutional memory. To mix the metaphor, proven blind alleys emerge as promising avenues. Shorn of historical connectivity and the benefit of learning experience, initiatives get stultified. There is often much motion without movement.

What Would Naik Saheb Say?

As Education Secretary, Bordia chose to stay put in a smaller room than secretaries do, the room that J.P. Naik occupied as Education Adviser. Naik's photograph was embedded in a wall of that room—an altar of sorts. Naik saheb was an eternal presence with K and his deputies in Bordia's fiefdom. Hardly a day passed without him being mentioned. It seemed to K that with every issue Bordia encountered, he wondered what Naik saheb would think about that issue, and that, therefore, the key to understand Bordia's worldview on education and what he strove to achieve as Secretary of the Department of Education (DOE) lay in understanding the life and work of Naik, and the ideas which influenced him.

In his eventful life, Naik was a man who played many roles: freedom fighter, social activist, Education Adviser to GOI and as such a pillar of the educational establishment, a prolific writer on education, a historian of modern Indian education whose seminal work constituted the first systematic exploration of the subject from a nationalistic perspective,[6]

[6] J.P. Naik and Syed Nurullah, *A Student's History of Education in India (1800–1973)*, 6th edition, Delhi: Macmillan, 1974.

a leading light on the international educational circuit and educational planner, and a distinguished and a political and educational radical. The fountainhead of Naik's eminence as an educational thinker was his historical perspective; he carried 'in his head not only the facts and their history but also the whys and wherefores of each educational event which he is able to build into a systematic and integrated theory'.[7] In addition, he also compiled select educational records through archival research; such compilations are invaluable for historical research.

Naik began his career as a political activist who plunged into the Civil Disobedience Movement, courted imprisonment, dedicated his life for Mahatma Gandhi's rural reconstruction movement, and engaged himself in teaching in a primary school, running a rural dispensary and promoting *Khadi*. Later, he was an activist who turned into a pillar of educational establishment. As an Education Adviser in the Union Education Department, he came to be Mr Education, and as Member-Secretary he was a major architect of the report of the epochal Kothari Commission (1964–5). In this phase, he sought to work *within* the system and strove to bring out the educational transformation he cherished from positions of vantage. He was also an institution builder playing an important role in the setting up of NCERT, the Asian Institute of Educational Planning which evolved into NIEPA and later into a deemed university, and the Indian Council of Social Science Research (ICSSR). He also emerged as a major figure in the international education circuit, and a major achievement of his was the development of the Karachi Plan, a plan for providing UEE that was adopted by the Asian Member-States of UNESCO at Karachi in 1959. During this phase, Naik entertained the hope that education was the one and only instrument that could bring about a large-scale social transformation in the country, and that it could obviate the need for a violent revolution; this hope was sharply articulated in the report of the Kothari Commission which called for 'a revolution in education which will set in motion the much desired social, economic, and cultural revolution'.[8] This view of education was rooted in the tradition–modernity paradigm which

[7] Malcolm Adiseshiah, *Foreword* to J.P. Naik, *The Education Commission and After*, 2nd edition, New Delhi: A.B.H. Publishing Corporation, 1997, p. viii.

[8] Ministry of Education, *Education and National Development: Report of the Education Commission, 1964–66*, Volume I, 1966, p. 9.

dominated the international thinking on development and education.[9] The modernization ideals included the belief that governance should be guided by rational considerations; in turn, a rational approach to governance necessitated a replacement of traditional values and attitudes such as fatalism and adopting attitudes such as diligence, punctuality, preparedness for change, and alertness to opportunities as they arise in a changing world. In short, what was needed was a 'wholesale metamorphosis of habits, a wrenching reorientation of values concerning time, status, money and work … unweaving and weaving of the fabric of daily existence'.[10] The quest of development as well as planning for development followed from the application of a rational approach to the economic and social arena. Rise of productivity, levels of living, and reduction of economic disparities came to be commonly shared goals of development. What distinguished the Western tradition–modernity paradigm from the communist doctrine was the belief that the cultural change by way of new values and attitudes could be readily acquired through education, and that cultural change would suffice for socio-economic transformation of the newly independent countries; change in the social and economic structure through a violent revolution was not needed. In this phase of Mr Education, Naik also believed that comparative educational thinking and best practices in other countries could be adopted in India in spite of the diversity in socio-political context, a belief explicitly stated in the resolution of GOI setting up the Kothari Commission.

> While the planning of education for India must necessarily emanate from Indian experience and conditions, Government of India are of the opinion that *it would be advantageous to draw upon the experience and thinking of educationists and scientists from other parts of the world in the common enterprise of seeking for the right type of education which is the quest of all mankind, specially at this time when the world is becoming closely knit together in so many ways*. It has, therefore, been decided to associate with the Commission, either as members or as consultants, some eminent scientists and educationists from other countries. (emphasis added)

[9] Gunnar Myrdal, *Asian Drama: An Inquiry into the Poverty of Nations*, Three Volumes, Volume I, New York: Pantheon, pp. 54–69.

[10] Robert Heilbroner, *The Great Ascent*, New York: Harper and Row, Inc., 1963, p. 66, cited in Ministry of Education, *Education and National Development: Report of the Education Commission*, Volume I, p. 8.

Exceptions apart, men grow conservative with age; the youthful rages give way to mellow, politically correct utterances, and the bulldog turns into a bigwig, and stays a bigwig.[11] Naik was an exception. In the 1970s, Naik moved away from the belief of his Mr Education phase that education could be used to bring about a large-scale social transformation in the country. He ceased to be an *education wallah* and laid emphasis on political action. Commenting on the view, which is widely prevalent even now, that education is better left to academics and that education would be better off if politicians keep their hands off it, he wrote:

> When the Education Commission was appointed, Mr. M.C. Chagla boasted that it consisted only of academics and that he had not appointed a single politician on it. But this isolation makes educationists blind too many aspects of the educational reality ... [many issues] cannot be solved except jointly by politicians and educationists . .. educationists desire full political support without any political interference [which is their concept of autonomy].... A situation of this type does immense harm.[12]

In this phase, Naik began to stress the importance of political mobilization for the creation of the new egalitarian social and economic order, and importance of education, particularly adult education, in creation of the awareness necessary among the poor, thereby enabling them to struggle for the new egalitarian social order. He was disenchanted by Western (more accurately liberal democratic) models of development and education, and regretted that India turned its back on the Mahatma, uncritically accepted as a model for the highly industrialized, consumer-oriented societies of the West, and thoughtlessly adopted Western educational systems. He called for a Swadeshi movement that would create a distinctive society which would combine science and technology with our hoary spiritual and moral values.[13]

[11] Roy Porter, 'A Seven-Bob Surgeon: "Pope" Huxley and the New Priesthood of Science', *Times Literary Supplement*, 18 November 1994. Porter narrates how Thomas Henry Huxley, the iconoclastic scientist, accused Robert Owen, the noted social reformer of Victorian Era, of being a 'great conservative'. Owen retorted 'And so will you be after forty.' Owen proved to be right.

[12] J.P. Naik, *The Education Commission and After*, pp. 238–9.

[13] Naik and Nurullah, *A Student's History of Education in India (1800–1973)*, p. 487.

While the Mahatma was a perennial source of inspiration, he felt that Marx was also relevant, and that 'what is needed is a dialogue between Gandhism and Marxism which will enable us to discover the most effective programmes of educational and social reconstruction suited to the unique civilization that is India'.[14] He was also influenced by the radical ideas from diverse sources such as Ivan Illich and Paulo Freire from Latin America, and Cultural Revolution of China. If K's memory serves him right, a quotation of Mao Zedong used to adorn the wall of the room which Bordia used to occupy. Suffice to say, radical ideas from anywhere or anyone was grist to Naik's mill, and he seemed confident that all such ideas irrespective of their differences in conceptual foundations, preferred course of action, and prognoses could be harmoniously synthesized and harnessed to advance the creation of a new social order and educational reconstruction.

One cannot miss the strong influence of Freire and Illich on the later Naik and Bordia's views on UEE and adult education. Freire as well as Illich were products of the hothouse environment of Latin America which produced exotic theories in diverse fields such as liberation theology in Christianity, *dependencia* (the theory that in the existing international economic order, underdeveloped countries were doomed to be hewers and drawers of water unless they disengaged from the capitalist economies and embarked on a path of self-reliant development and structural transformation of the economy), and structuralism (a milder version of *dependencia*) in economics. Freire held that the ignorance of the poor was a result of their economic, social, and political oppression; the educational system was an instrument to keep the poor oppressed. The process of learning should compel them to reflect on their environment and existential condition, and instil a determination to break the shackles of oppression, or to use the jargon lead to *conscientization*. Learning to read and write must be a means of self-liberation, a twentieth-century enunciation of the ancient Sanskrit saying *sā vidyā yā vimuktaye* (that learning is true learning which liberates the learner). Freire explored the avenues open for individuals to realize their potential for freedom and creativity while living in the midst of politically, economically, and culturally oppressive structures. Illich was no less

[14] J.P. Naik, *Equity, Quality and Quantity: The Elusive Triangle in Indian Education*, New Delhi: Allied Publishers, 1975, p. 115.

damning of the education system. The school, in his view, was no more than a despicable system which dehumanized societies, and suppressed and alienated individuals. It was absurd to think that universal education was feasible through schooling. The school's position in society and the play of forces to which it was subjected made it incapable of being the instrument of true education in the service of mankind or endowing the students with *conviviality*, that is to say, capacity for independent creative relationships with other people and the environment. Rather than go to school, young people can form their characters and learn to earn by living within the community and performing practical tasks. The ideas of Freire and Illich were extremely influential; their works, particularly Freire's *Pedagogy of the Oppressed* (1970) and Illich's *Deschooling Society* (1971), came to acquire a canonical status; ideologically, they are poles apart from the *functionalist* view espoused by economists. The functionalist view, of which the human capital theory is a highly refined version, values education for imparting skills and knowledge which enhance the productivity and income-generating capabilities of individuals and, by extension, the economic development and international competiveness of the country's economy. It also values education for grooming children and youth as enlightened citizens of the country who would discharge their duty to their country and to fellow citizens. It also values education for enabling the poor to avail the benefits of the developmental and welfare programmes introduced by the government. All in all, functional education is designed for the economic man (*homo economicus*) and a citizen of a liberal democracy. In contrast, the views of Freire and Illich are the education version of liberation theology; the whole purpose of education is political in the sense in that its objective is to organize the poor to seize their destiny in their own hands, assert their rights and entitlements, and ideally overthrow the oppressive State, its rulers, and lackeys. This view of education influenced the writings of Naik in his later phase, and the design by Bordia of his favourite programmes such as MS, and TLCs.

Mainstream educators considered that the ideas of Freire and Illich were not of much help in elaborating alternative educational systems, although they admirably exposed 'the human damage' of the existing educational system, challenged people and organizations who claimed to be 'aligned with the poor to think very deeply about what they were offering as solutions', and laid 'the groundwork for the conception of school more attentive to the needs of its environment , to the realities of its pupils' lives, and to the efficient acquisition of socially relevant knowledge'. Illich's writings were considered to be 'founded essentially on intuitions, without any appreciable reference to the results of socio-educational or learning research. His criticism evolves in a theoretical vacuum, which may explain the limited acceptance his educational theories and proposals find today'.[15] His condemnation of the school was considered too Utopian to be to be put into practice, with the result that even those who endorsed his views had to concede that some form of schooling was necessary for learning. Mainstream educators were inclined to tone down the message of liberation and empowerment that emanated from the oeuvre of Freire and Illich, and treat it as a stronger version of the creed emphasized time and again since the 1950s that active participation of the people was necessary in any programme designed for their benefit. They also held that 'the question of whether radical educational work can take place within state institutions or state-funded projects has still to be tackled more thoroughly'.[16]

With the end of the Emergency and the emergence of the Janata Government in 1977, Naik felt that he was witness to what was then perceived as the second dawn of Independence; here was a rare second chance to usher in transformative changes in polity that could and should have been effected in 1947. The millennial hopes that the downfall of Indira Gandhi aroused were dashed soon, thereby reinforcing Naik's scepticism. With the return to power of Indira Gandhi in 1980, Naik ceased to be a part of the educational establishment, and he retired to the Institute of Education, Pune, which he established in 1941, and he died soon thereafter in 1981. In his radical phase, Naik was clear that an inegalitarian society would not create an egalitarian educational system and *vice versa*. He believed that by itself education would no doubt bring out social changes but such changes would be of a limited extent and would take a very long time too. However, he seemed to be uncertain about what ought to

[15] Marcelo Gajarado, 'Ivan Illich', in *Thinkers in Education*, Volume 2, Paris: UNESCO Publishing, 1995, pp. 711–20, at p. 719.

[16] Heinz-Peter Gerhardt, 'Paulo Freire', in *Thinkers in Education*, Volume 2, Paris: UNESCO Publishing, 1995, pp. 439–58, at p. 452.

be done. In some writings in his last phase, he was a romantic optimist believing that a simultaneous advance in both educational and social reordering was necessary, and, more importantly, possible.[17] In some other writings, however, he was a hard realist who discounted the possibility of simultaneously advance in both educational and social reordering. 'In regard to major social change', he wrote, 'education has only a minor role to play … it can only prepare for, complete, or consolidate a social change decided elsewhere whether by bullet or ballot'.[18]

In his historical evaluation of Mahatma Gandhi, the eminent historian R.C. Majumdar highlights the Indian tradition of indulging in *prasasthi* (eulogy) of great leaders, of 'reverence' for such leaders 'standing in the way of ascertaining the truth',[19] and of the aversion to objectively evaluate the achievements of the Great. The Mahatma had set out clearly that his life was his message; as the apt title of his autobiography put it crisply, his life was a continual experiment to discover truth. That being so, to deify him and to treat every view of his as Gospel truth that has to be implicitly accepted as truth is to be un-Gandhian. A.R Kamat's critique of Naik is exceptional, and resembles Majumdar's attempt to objectively evaluate Mahatma Gandhi's historic role. In spite of his close association with Naik, Kamat observed that except for minor issues, for all his efforts Naik failed in his 'grand objective [of fundamental reconstruction of Indian education]', and that this magnificent failure stemmed from the 'inherent weaknesses in his conceptual edifice', and 'the very socio-structural forces of the Indian situation'. Kamat further observed that 'like the post-independence slogans about "socialism" and "socialist pattern", his [Naik's] [radical] writings have induced many Indian educationists, politicians and educational planners and administrators to use "radical phraseology

[17] Naik and Nurullah, *A Student's History of Education in India (1800–1973)*, pp. 482–3, 487; J.P. Naik, *Policy and Performance in Indian Education 1947–74*, Dr. K.G. Saiydain Lectures, 1974, New Delhi: Allied Publishers, 1975, pp. 18–19.

[18] J.P. Naik, *Equality, Quality and Quantity: The Elusive Triangle in Indian Education*, New Delhi: Allied Publishers, 1975, pp. 110–11.

[19] R.C. Majumdar, *Three Phases of India's Struggle for Freedom*, Bombay: Bharatiya Vidya Bhavan, 1961.

in education'".[20] Naik himself bemoaned the fact that 'in short, while we have talked of "revolutionary charges", we have practiced only a "moderate reformism", thus providing one more illustration of the divorce between theory and practice which characterises our lives'.[21] During his tutelage under Bordia, K had plenty of opportunities to come across that radical phraseology and attempted to put in practice the ideas conveyed by that phraseology. He was also witness to the possibilities as well as the limitations of mass mobilization to further adult literacy and UEE. He could also discover through observation and reflection an answer to the quintessential question arising from Freire's theories whether radical educational work can take place within state institutions or state-funded projects.

Dvaita or Advaita?

In Hindu philosophy, there are three main schools of thought: Advaita (monism) which holds that the universal and human souls are one and the same, Dvaita (dualism) which holds that the universal and human souls are different, and the *Vishishtadvaita* (qualified monism) whose position is in-between the other two schools. Tyagaraja's[22] famous *krithi* '*dvaitamu sukhama advatiamu sukhama*'—which is better, Advaita or Dvaita—poses a perennial question which engaged the attention of Indian philosophers and saints. Likewise the question whether UEE could be achieved only through one system (school) or whether that achievement requires two systems (school and NFE) evoked a ferocious controversy after NPE, 1986, postulated that school system alone cannot lead to UEE, and a large NFE education programme was launched in the wake of NPE, 1986. Or to borrow the metaphor of Mao Zedong, UEE could be reached only by walking on the two legs of primary school and NFE. The Advaita (monism) school held that UEE could

[20] A.R. Kamat, 'Naik', in 'The Pilgrim's Progress', *Bulletin of the Indian Institute of Education*, Pune, J.P. Naik Special issue, III(1982), pp.104–18; 'J.P. Naik', in *Thinkers in Education*, Volume 3, Paris: UNESCO Publishing, 1995.

[21] J.P. Naik, *Educational Planning in India*, New Delhi: Allied Publishers, 1965, pp. 19–20.

[22] Tyagraja is one of the foremost composers of Carnatic Classical Music whose *krithis* (musical compositions) are famous and continue to be widely performed in concerts.

be achieved only through an improved school system, and that NFE was inferior education designed to 'get away with the failure of ensuring universal elementary schooling', was 'less accountable than formal system', and worse made 'the system further segregative'.[23] Adherents of this school were unwilling to accept the argument of the dvaitins that without NFE lakhs of working children would be deprived of educational opportunities; they posed the counter-question as to why child labour should be permitted at all. One of the key issues in the engagement with external funding agencies was whether the projects funded by the agencies should cover NFE. The controversy raged till NFE was outlawed by the RTE Act 2009. As international trends in ideas cast a long shadow on the national debate over systems, it is worthwhile to narrate the course of international thinking.

From the perspective which time can only provide, the decade from mid-1960s to 1970s can be characterized as the *Age of Alternatives*: developing countries demanded in the UN system the replacement of the extant unequal global economic system by a New International Economic Order, the extant economic growth models received a mighty challenge from an alternative theory which demanded a direct attack on absolute poverty in developing countries, and the relevance of Western capital-intensive technologies for developing countries was challenged by advocates of appropriate/intermediate technologies. Education was not exempt from the spirit of the times. Apart from the radical ideas of Freire and Illich, a paradigmatic shift on the thinking on education began in mid-1960s, at about the time the Kothari Commission was going about with its work. This shift was aligned with the shift in the mainstream economic thinking and development praxis; it did not question, as Freire and Illich did, the bona fides of the state or of the existing international economic order. Among those in the vanguard of the paradigm shift in education were Roy Prosser, a British adult educator with great experience in developing countries, and Philip Coombs who was the Founding Director, UNESCO's IIEP, Paris. Since the early 1950s, education ministers, educational administrators, and planners believed as an article of faith that linear expansion of existing educational systems would lead to swift educational development,

[23] Poromesh Acharya, 'Universal Elementary Education: Receding Goal', *Economic and Political Weekly*, XXIX, no. 1–2, 1–8 January 1994: p. 27.

and to the attainment of all the great objectives of education such as democratization of education, and creating the manpower required for the modernization and development of economy. This rosy optimism began to fade by mid-1960s, and a 'new framework of problems took shape', and doubts began to be expressed about the capability of school systems to meet the demand for education, the ability of countries to provide the school systems with the massive resources required, and the desirability to continue the development of education along the lines hitherto followed. Philip Coomb's classic *The World Educational Crisis* (1967) spread the belief that the world education was in fact in the grip of a systemic crisis.[24] In spite of the valiant efforts made by many developing countries 'to carry their people over the hump of mass illiteracy, to level gross educational inequalities, and to widen access to education at successively higher levels of instruction' the results were disappointing in many countries. Coombs highlighted the fact that the impressive increase in enrolment and enrolment ratios recorded in developing countries masked a dark side. The increase did not reveal the 'vast social waste and the human tragedy in the high rate of drop-outs and failures'; nor did the increase say anything about the nature, quality, and usefulness of the education received. There being nothing new under the sun, the observation of Coombs was nothing new; 40 years earlier, just as the Great Depression sharply squeezed revenues of provincial governments, the Hartog Committee made an identical observation about the adverse consequences of the considerable expansion of elementary education that took place after the introduction of diarchy in provinces, and Indian ministers taking charge of education. What was at work whether in the India of the 1920s or the developed countries in the 1950s and 1960s was a process similar to that underlying the Kuznets's curve. As an economy begins to develop and per-capita income begins to rise, inequality may initially rise, reaching a maximum at an intermediate level, and then decline as income levels characteristic of mature developed economy are reached. This is because early in *development* investment opportunities for those who have money multiply, while wages are held down by an influx of cheap rural labour to the cities; in contrast, in mature economies, labour is

[24] Philip H. Coombs, *The World Educational Crisis: A Systems Analysis*, New York: Oxford, 1967.

relatively scarce and wages are higher. Similarly, in the initial phases of the expansion of the school system, there are relatively more first-generation learners, and there are more inexperienced teachers freshly recruited from the labour market; consequently, there is more wastage and stagnation, and even deterioration in quality as compared to the position when education was limited to elites. The Hartog Committee earned the hostility of nationalist Indians by recommending that provincial governments should abandon the policy of 'hasty' expansion and opt for a policy of consolidation. Where Coombs differed from the Hartog Committee was that even in the face of wastage, stagnation, and deterioration in quality, and deterioration in the economic conditions of many developing conditions, he wanted expansion of access to education to continue and came up with cost-effective alternatives. The shift on the thinking on education also highlighted the fact that even in developed countries, there was disconnect between education and employment as well as between education and the development needs of societies. In a society or economy that was in constant flux, and in the face of seemingly limitless explosion of knowledge, the old concept of education seemed to be obsolete and too narrow. The old concept held that education took place only in an institution such as the school or college, that such education could meet, once and for all, the essential learning needs that an individual might require in his lifetime, and that such education took place during the student phase of an individual before he joined the workforce. The old concept gave way to new concepts which held that if one's knowledge and skills were not to be obsolescent one needs to constantly upgrade one's stock of knowledge and skills throughout life, and that life-long learning or continuous education could take place even outside the school by self-study or in settings outside the formal education system.

Naik was active in the international education circuit, and always kept abreast of the latest international thinking on education; that apart Coombs was one of the consultants engaged by the Kothari Commission. No wonder the winds of change in educational thinking wafted through the Kothari Commission's report. The paradigm shift in the thinking on education received an official imprimatur from *Learning to Be* (1972), the landmark report of UNESCO's Faure Commission. The report expounded an enlarged concept of education; learning wherever it took place, even if it were outside the formal system, however it took place, and at whatever age it took place was proclaimed to be education. Education was a lifelong process, spanning all the years from infancy to life's end. Even while offering many suggestions for strengthening the formal education system, it suggested that in a world of rapidly growing and changing learning needs, and also by the unacceptable gross inequities, it was essential to give attention also to strengthening other modes of education.

The paradigm shift in the thinking on education also gave a big impetus to the growth of NFE. The term 'NFE' was first used in Jane King's *Planning Non-formal Education in Tanzania* (1967),[25] which was influenced, and carried a foreword, by Coombs. Coomb's classic *The World Educational Crisis* (1967) had a whole chapter 'Non-formal Education: To Catch Up, Keep Up, and Get Ahead'. NFE was a new term used to describe activities that were not entirely new. Within about five years of the submission of the Kothari Commission report, a 'non-formal fashion' gripped educators and development agencies. NFE was literally an idea whose time had come in that it made its debut precisely at a time when the new-fangled 'poverty economics' created demand for training on a large scale and in a variety of fields, a demand which schools and other formal educational institutions could not cater to. The non-formal fashion also gave a fillip to use of communication media such as radio and films to deliver educational messages as well as instruction; in literature, communications and media came to be sometimes described as the third channel of education, the first being schooling, and the second NFE. It would take as many shapes as the legendary Proteus of Greek mythology; it was capable of as many interpretations as the cryptic Delphic utterance or *Da* of the Upanishadic Brahman. For the crusaders against poverty it was just the vehicle they were looking for to equip the poor who might have missed schooling with minimum learning needs such as functional literacy and numeracy, knowledge and skills for productive activities, family planning and health, child care, nutrition, sanitation, and knowledge required for civic participation. To alternate education thinkers who were concerned about what formal schooling did to rural children—deracinating them even when

[25] Jane King, 'Planning Non-formal Education in Tanzania', in *Educational Development in Africa: Volume III: Integration and Administration*, Paris: International Institute of Educational Planning, 1967.

towns offered few of them gainful livelihood—it offered the prospect of amending the curriculum to match the exigencies of future rural life, and to economists and hard-pressed educational administrators unable to cope with the burgeoning numbers of school-age population it was a low-cost alternative to schooling. To educational planners it was an exciting and daunting challenge—how to integrate it in a planning frame the extraordinary variety of programmes that go under the rubric of NFE which is 'any organized activity outside the formal education system'—imparting of 3Rs outside the school, pre service and in-service skill training, agricultural training in areas such as literacy, family planning, and health. It was all things to all people and, with the exception of International Development Research Centre (IDRC), all agencies plumbed for the fashion, and United States Agency for International Development (USAID) was in the forefront along with UNICEF and the World Bank.

Simplistically, there were two strands of NFE: the first is an alternative or a complement to the elementary schooling which imparts education similar to that of elementary schools to children who failed to enrol in schools or having enrolled did not complete the full cycle of elementary education; the second, non-formal training which imparts skills to a variety of clientele such as farmers, wanna be entrepreneurs, professionals, para professionals, and so on. Ministries of Education in India and other developing countries were mainly concerned with the first strand, and with non-formal training to a limited extent in post-literacy programmes. In contrast to the first strand, the second stand spanned the domain of several ministries such as agriculture, health, industries, and so on. K's experiential knowledge is limited to the first strand, and that being so whatever he has to say about NFE is limited to that strand. Two publications of Coombs, *New Paths to Learning for Rural Education and Youth* (1973) co-authored with Roy Prosser and Manzoor Ahmed and commissioned by UNICEF, and *Attacking Rural Poverty: How Nonformal Education can Help* (1974) co-authored with Manzoor Ahmed and commissioned by the World Bank, put in place for the first time a conceptual framework for educational activities outside the school system, helped create a favourable climate for NFE, and were quite influential in shaping the operational policies of agencies such as UNICEF and the World Bank. To begin with however, the response of UNESCO was decidedly frosty.[26] Many educators felt that Coombs and his collaborators went too far in criticizing the schools, and willy-nilly conveyed the impression that NFE was an alternative to schooling, and was a panacea. By late-1970s, schooling and NFE moved closer, and many educators were willing to acknowledge that NFE could be a useful complement to the school system. The new conventional wisdom laid down that even while pressing with the expansion of the school system, and making schools less rigid and more attractive, non-formal programmes should be put in place to compensate for the inadequacies of the school system. The deterioration in the global economic environment that followed the first oil crisis of 1973 made NFE an attractive complement to formal schooling in countries with a large population of out-of-school children. However, there was widespread concern about the learning outcomes in NFE, and many strongly felt that NFE was a 'poor cousin to mainstream education', and that promoting NFE distracted governments from the main challenge of reforming the school system. Supporters of NFE argued that the actual choice faced by many out-of-school children was either NFE or no education at all; the critics were prone to respond by contending that NFE was no better than having no education. Followers of Illich initially welcomed NFE for its sharp critique of schooling; however, as NFE and schooling came closer, and the objective of NFE began to be defined as compensating for the lack or inadequacies of schooling, they grew sharply critical. For them, the education outside the school they propagated was an alternative to the mis-education that took place in the school; mis-education does not cease to be mis-education just because it took place outside the formal educational structures. In general, the Left had been sharply critical of NFE for offering to the poor inferior education and aggravating inequalities in the society. To jump the story, the non-formal fashion faded out by early 1980s, and in their operations agencies such as the World Bank equated primary education with primary schooling. After a great deal of haggling, UNDP, UNESCO, UNICEF, and the World Bank, the co-sponsors of the Jomtien Conference, agreed to expound an expanded vision of

[26] Maggie Black, *The Children and the Nations: The Story of UNCEF*, New York: UNICEF, 1986, p. 322.

Education for All in the Jomtien Declaration. Even while setting down that the main delivery system for basic education was the school system, the Declaration recognized that the basic learning needs of children, youth, and adults were diverse, and that, therefore, these needs should be provided by a variety of delivery systems such as primary schooling, NFE, and adult education. However, in their follow-up of the Jomtien Declaration, the co-sponsors and bilateral agencies were not inclined to support all the delivery systems equally, and in his engagement with the external agencies, this was an issue which Bordia strongly took up with agencies, particularly the World Bank.

Within a few years of the submission of the Kothari Commission report, Naik began to espouse NFE for out-of-school children with his customary vigour and enthusiasm. As Bordia once put it, Naik wanted to formalize the NFE system and non-formalize the school system. The non-formal system should enable the learners to learn at their own pace at their own time and yet its levels of learning should be comparable to the formal system, and the learners should be able to join the formal system if they choose to. Likewise, the formal system should be more flexible to allow for individual differences among students. The formal school system provided for a single-point entry, that is to say children could generally enrol only in class I. It is sequential in that a child is expected to complete one class every year before rising to the next class after passing the annual examination. Further, the formal school system imparted full-time education. Naik strongly held that elementary education could not be universalized through the formal school system as it stood. It was necessary to non-formalize it by replacing the single-point entry by multi-point entry, and by doing away with the sequential character. Thus, the reformed school should allow older children of 9, 11, or 14 years to join the schools in separate classes specially organized for their needs. Further, it should also allow older children join the prescribed courses at any time and could complete them in a much shorter period. The non-formalized school system should be complemented by a large programme of NFE which should be organized so as to suit the convenience of working children. While Bordia was a fervent advocate of a large NFE and battled fiercely with critics of NFE, it came out from his stance on the recommendation of the Ramamurti Committee that he did not believe that non-formalizing the school was a feasible proposition. Naik also felt that it was necessary to do away with the exclusive reliance on full-time teachers; it was necessary to opt for part-time teachers and to enlist volunteers who would act as instructors.[27] Naik's view was widely adopted in the organization of NFE and other alternatives to schooling such as the Shiksha Karmi. Even in formal schooling, from the 1980s states began to appoint teachers on contract and offering remuneration less than that for regular teachers.

As Education Minister, Nurul Hasan strove to popularize the idea of NFE; however, he was not successful in launching NFE during the Fifth Five-Year Plan (1974–9). It was the short-lived Janata government (1977–9) which began to extend specific grants for NFE in nine educationally backward states. During the revision of NPE, 1986, NFE turned out to be the most controversial provision of NPE, 1986.

Bordia's Education Mission

Bordia's educational mission was driven by a few articles of faith which he shared with Naik. The first was that UEE and elimination of illiteracy are at the heart of educational transformation, and the second that without social mobilization, the education system by itself, however much reformed, cannot meet the transcendent challenge of UEE and universal literacy. The objective of social mobilization was to *conscientize* (in the Freirean sense of shaping a new consciousness among the oppressed so that they strive to change their destiny and thereby alter the social reality) the poor and enlist the local community and a large army of dedicated volunteers to participate in the struggle for educational transformation. The third article of faith was the belief that given the Indian socio-economic reality, UEE can be achieved only through two systems—formal and non-formal—with provision for moving from one system to another, or to use the imagery of Mao by walking on the two legs of formal school system and NFE. For Bordia, the litmus test of commitment to UEE was support to a large non-formal programme. It was this test he administered to the World Bank to test the sincerity of the Bank's claim that it was deeply committed to the expanded vision of basic education that the Jomtien Declaration (adopted by the Jomtien Conference) put forth, and that it was prepared 'to be as flexible and

[27] J.P. Naik, *Elementary Education in India: A Promise to Keep*, Delhi: Allied Publishers, 1975, pp. 46–52.

accommodating as Government of India may consider necessary'. The fourth article of faith was that the central government has to lead the educational transformation by laying down the broad national goals and strategies, and, no less importantly, financially assisting the state governments and NGOs for implementing programmes designed to usher the educational transformation. Given his participation in the freedom struggle and the Mahatma's rural reconstruction programme, Naik was passionately attached to reduction of the over-importance attached to English, the development of Hindi as the link language for the country, the use of regional languages as the media of instruction at all stages, work with the hands, and social or national service being an integral part of all education with a view to creating a work-based culture and to minimizing the large traditional gap between the intelligentsia and the people. In contrast, Bordia was more inclined to take note of the historical experience, and was less passionate in the matter of work experience and language. Although he was effusive in expressing his love of Hindi, and made fun of the Tambrahms who, he claimed, were running the department—Additional Secretary S. Gopalan, L. Narayan, Financial Adviser, and K—for their poor knowledge of Hindi, as a realist he was keen to let sleeping dogs lie—better to stay away from that highly inflammable subject of language lest his plans for education were to be incinerated.

Bordia's second stint in the Education Department (August 1985 to May 1992) coincided with a defining moment of education in post-independent India. In the first two years of Rajiv Gandhi's reign (1984–6), his government seemed to be a Camelot. The body politic displayed signs of exuberant youth. It was as if the country would make it to the twenty-first century before the advent of the third millennium. There was a flurry of policy initiatives and breakthroughs. Among these initiatives was the formulation of NPE, 1986. In August 1985, Bordia moved in as Additional Secretary, and assisted Anand Sarup in the formulation of the NPE; when he succeeded Sarup in March 1987, it fell upon Bordia to carry forward the implementation of NPE, 1986. Bordia's tenure as Education Secretary was a defining moment in another sense. India's efforts to provide a new impetus and direction to UEE and universal literacy in the light of NPE, 1986, were coeval with the build-up of the EFA movement internationally. With his customary gusto and élan, Bordia plunged into the EFA movement. As happened when he was around, he began to lead the movement from the front; he played an important role in the landmark Jomtien Conference (March 1990) and the follow-up of its Declaration nationally and internationally. He came to be a major presence in UNESCO and EFA forums, and with his charm, wooed major educationists from all over the world, particularly those who shared his worldview.

Privilege to Be an Intern

K joined Bordia five months after the Jomtien Conference just as Bordia began as to gear himself for following up the Jomtien Declaration with flagship EFA projects. As Education Secretary, Bordia had four ruling passions: protecting NPE, 1986, from attempts by the National Front Government which succeeded the Rajiv Gandhi Government to drastically modify it, MS, TLCs, and the design of EFA projects. K was closely associated with Bordia's pursuit of all his passions except for TLCs; even with TLCs, he had a ringside opportunity to its planning and monitoring. Looking back, K was fortunate to join Bordia at an historic moment and have an historic opportunity to shape the country's quest for UEE. Contrary to his own and everyone's expectations, K's charge came to be extremely important and offered great opportunities for learning and career development. His charge was such that he came to be associated with every major issue and programme in the field of education; K is ever grateful to Bordia for assigning a charge that appeared insignificant but was a real and not elusive El Dorado in the making. K came to be the workhorse, and his room the engine room of the department. MS offered a rare insight into the women's movement, and the discourse of human rights. Unusual for an officer not serving in ministries such as external affairs or commerce or economic affairs, K acquired enormous experience in dealing with a variety of multilateral and bilateral organizations, and good knowledge of international organizations, donor politics and behaviour, development cooperation, and negotiation praxis. All in all, K's tutelage under Bordia was the best preparation for K to seize the historic opportunity to develop DPEP which set the country firmly on the fast track to UEE.

III

THE LONG JOURNEY
Early Days

The Nationalist Saga

One can list a long litany of policy pronouncements starting from the Educational (Wood's) Despatch of 1854, which highlights the responsibility of the government to 'the great mass of people, who are utterly incapable of obtaining any education worthy of the name, by their own unaided efforts'. The lopsided and inadequate development of education during the British Raj proves the point that what matters with a policy is not what it says but how it is implemented, and implementation in turn depends on the appropriateness of the policy levers chosen, human and financial resources provided for implementation, and the determination of the government not to swerve from the policy objectives and priorities in the face of pulls from and pressures by interest groups. At the time of Independence, India inherited a system of education which was not only quantitatively small in relation to the size of its population, but also characterized by disparities of many kinds as well as structural imbalances. At the commencement of the First Five-Year Plan (1951–6), educational facilities were provided for only 40 per cent of the children of the age group 6–11, for 10 per cent of those in the age group 11–17, and for 0.9 per cent of those in the age group 17–23. Only 18 per cent of the population over five years of age was literate; only 37.8 per cent of children were enrolled in a primary school, and only 16 per cent of children moved from the primary stage to the upper primary stage. In relation to the school-going population, the population attending colleges and universities was higher than that in England or Germany, so much so as aptly described by the Sarjent Committee, the superstructure of the education system developed before the main building was erected on a broad and sound foundation.[1]

By the late nineteenth century, nationalist opinion began veering round the view that the illiteracy of the masses can be eliminated rapidly *only* through the introduction of a system of free and compulsory primary education. And as in many other areas, the practice in Britain influenced nationalist thinking. There were three elements of free and compulsory education in the British legislations: specifying the age group of children who were to be provided free education, establishing enough number of schools for the education of those children, and legally compelling parents to send their children to school. Many Indian witnesses represented to the Indian Education Commission, 1882, that as in Britain, elementary education should be made free and compulsory. However, in its report the Commission took no notice of the representations, and did not go beyond general propositions. Elementary education of the masses should be the main part of educational system to which strenuous effort of the State needed to be directed in a still larger measure than before; education should be imparted through vernacular languages, and control of elementary education should be transferred to newly set up district and municipal boards. However, it was a recommendation which was not categorical enough for the nationalists; in fact, till the Right of Children to Free and Compulsory Education Act, 2009 was enacted, a seemingly never-ending battle raged between the proponents of free and compulsory education and the governments of the day over the question whether provision of free and compulsory education should be linked with availability of resources or not. There were two notable exceptions. As early as in 1817 Maharani Gouri Parvati Bayi of Travancore issued a rescript declaring that 'the State should defray the entire cost of education of its people in order that there might be no backwardness in the spread of enlightenment among them, that by diffusing education, they

[1] Ministry of Education, *Post-War Educational Development in India (January 1944)*, 1964, p. 18.

might become better subjects and public servants and the reputation of the State might be advanced thereby'. In pursuance of the Rescript, vernacular schools were established in every village with at least two teachers, and a strict system of inspection was instituted. The policy of the Maharani was carried forward during the reign of Maharaja Sri Moolam Thirunal Rama Varma; Dewan V.P. Madhava Rao (1904–6) made primary education free in the state and, in pursuance of the policy of universal education, introduced measures such as a double shift in schools and a higher pupil–teacher ratio, measures that were advocated over three decades later by R.V. Parulekar to make free and compulsory education affordable. Even in the 1990s, double shift in schools was advocated by many and practised in quite a few areas. No wonder at the time of Independence, the literacy rates in Travancore and the adjoining native State of Cochin, which adopted the policy of its neighbour, were the highest in the country and compared favourably with some of the Western countries. However, the policy and practice of these Native States at the southernmost tip of India did not catch the attention of those advocating free and compulsory education. It was the introduction of free and compulsory education in Baroda state which attracted the attention of the nationalists; in 1884, Maharaja Sayojirao Gaekwad introduced free and compulsory education in Amreli Taluq, and 15 years later, extended it to the whole of his state. His initiative was seen by nationalists as establishing that free and compulsory education was a feasible proposition. It is to the credit of Gopal Krishna Gokhale that he made free and compulsory primary education a national issue by raising the issue repeatedly in the Imperial Legislative Council, the highest legislative forum of the country, and introducing an elementary education bill in 1910. Gokhale was unsuccessful in his attempt to get the Council even to refer the Bill to a Select Committee; however, he was eminently successful in deeply planting the idea of free and compulsory education in the psyche of nationalists, and in inducing even the Raj to pay more attention to primary education by creating a DOE in GOI, and committing itself in the *Government Resolution on Education Policy*, February 1913 to 'the widest possible expansion of primary education on a voluntary basis', and to that end 'double in the not-so-distant future' the number of public primary schools, and the enrolment in them.

Mahatma's Experiment with Education

It is significant that till about the mid-1960s, Gandhian basic education was the dominant model for achieving UEE. Even though basic education itself was abandoned, one of the key ideas of basic education, namely that education should be linked with work so as to eliminate a false sense of values and an aversion to manual work, continues to hold sway. Being so, it is worthwhile to recount in some detail the basic education moment in Indian education. Following the GOI Act, 1919, and introduction of the scheme of diarchy, school education was entrusted to Indian ministers in the provinces. Even though these ministers did not belong to the Congress party, many of them evinced greater interest in primary education than the British officials did. During 1919–30, Compulsory Education Acts similar to Gokhale's Bill were enacted in most provinces of British India. Official reports such as the *Quinquennial Report of the Progress of Education in India, 1927–32*, and the *Report of the Hartog Committee* (1929) note that education came to be regarded as an indispensable agency for nation-building, legislative councils in the provinces gave considerable attention to education and poured large sums of money into education, a burst of enthusiasm swept children into schools with unparalleled rapidity, even communities which had hitherto neglected education, such as 'Muhammadan', 'Depressed Classes', and 'tribal aborigines', pressed forward with eagerness to obliterate past deficiencies in education, and a larger proportion of people than before began to demand education as a right.[2] Expansion of elementary education was to go hand in hand with adult literacy programmes so that the country was set on a path that would eliminate illiteracy. For the first time in the country they opened night schools to impart literacy to adults. Although the adult literacy programmes were very modest in scope and coverage, they created public awareness of the importance of adult literacy and sprouted ideas such as compelling employers to make their employees literate and enlisting students, local bodies, co-operatives, and other semi-official and non-official organizations in adult literacy work. While these

[2] J.P. Naik and Syed Nurullah, *A Student's History of Education in India (1800–1973)*, 6th edition, Delhi: Macmillan, 1974, pp. 324–5.

developments were heartening, the provincial governments soon hit the wall of financial constraint and extension of free and compulsory education to new areas slowed down. The provinces had to rely on their own revenues as devolution of educational grants from the central government to the provinces ceased after the GOI Act, 1919, came into effect. Furthermore, from 1930, the Great Depression began to severely impact on government revenues all over the world. Against the backdrop of Compulsory Education Acts coming into force, and the provincial education ministers being committed to the implementation of those Acts, the perennial question of how to lower the cost of providing schooling and how to make free and compulsory education affordable, and how to reduce 'wastage and stagnation', or to use modern nomenclature reducing dropouts and repetition of classes, cropped up with greater severity. The most noteworthy attempt to reduce unit costs of formal schooling was made by R.V. Parulekar who followed Gokhale's lead in coming up with models of schooling whose prime objective would be banishing illiteracy. Parulekar suggested concentrating all funds and energy on the liquidation of mass illiteracy, limiting the duration of primary education to four years, and simplifying its curriculum so as to cover mainly the three Rs, enhancing the age of entry to seven so as to reduce stagnation, raising the teacher–pupil ratio, introducing part-time education for older children, and introducing double shift in schools. His ideas had some impact in the Bombay Province; primary education in Maharashtra covered only classes I–IV till RTE Act, 2009, mandated that it should be five years.

Once the GOI Act, 1919, gave way to the GOI Act, 1935, and popular Congress party ministries assumed office in the provinces in 1937, the perennial questions assumed greater salience, all the more so as Mahatma Gandhi described illiteracy as the sin and national shame of India, and starting of night schools and village libraries were an important component of his rural reconstruction programme. The financial constraint turned out to be more pressing as the Congress party was irrevocably committed not only to free and compulsory education but also to prohibition. As Mahatma Gandhi put it, the problem of education was unfortunately mixed up with the disappearance of 'drink revenue'. Huge sums of money were needed to spread elementary education, and even as more resources were needed, the Congress governments were committed to introduce prohibition and forgo substantial excise revenue, all the more so at a time when the recovery from the Great Depression was not yet complete and provincial budgets were under severe stress. Congress governments were on the horns of a dilemma: which commitment should they give up, UEE or to prohibition? They could not have both. Like a *deux ex machine* in a play, the ideas of the Mahatma on primary education that go by the name of the Wardha Scheme of Basic Education appeared on the scene which held out the promise of knocking out two great barriers at one stroke: the fiscal barrier which impeded the expansion of free elementary education, and the class barrier that separated the toiling, illiterate masses from the small group of people who thought that manual work was degrading, and yet receive the benefits of education and dominated the society.

There is no philosopher or statesman who had not seriously thought about education; of the hundred eminent thinkers on education covered by a seminal UNESCO publication, very few are professional educators.[3] A thinker's visualization of an ideal society and polity invariably shapes his thinking on education; the educational model suggested is conceived as a key instrument to usher in and sustain the ideal society and polity. No wonder that Mahatma Gandhi wrote extensively about education and experimented with his ideas in Tolstoy farm, South Africa, and elsewhere. No one rejected colonial education as sharply and as completely as Gandhi, nor did anyone else up forward an alternative as radical as the one he proposed.[4] He was critical of the education that the British introduced for being too literary, for alienating the student from his society, for inculcating a false sense of values and an aversion to manual work, and for the tremendous wastage of time and labour involving in learning a foreign language. In his famous Chatham House speech, which was delivered in 1931 when he visited Britain to participate in the Second Round Table Conference, he claimed that a strong indigenous system existed in Indian villages before British rule, the British uprooted the 'beautiful tree' of Indian education, and the cost of formal schooling was too high to ensure

[3] Zaghloul Morsy, ed., *Thinkers on Education*, Four Volumes, Paris: UNESCO Publishing, 1994.

[4] Krishna Kumar, 'Mohandas Karamchand Gandhi' , in Morsy, ed., *Thinkers in Education*, Volume 2, pp. 507–17, at p. 507.

universal education.[5] The Mahatma's conceptualization of education went far beyond change in the content of education and medium of instruction. His views are best expressed in his own words:

> Our education has got to be revolutionised. The brain must be educated through the hand. If I were a poet, I could write poetry on the possibilities of the five fingers. Why should you think that the mind is everything and the hands and feet nothing? Those who do not train their hands, who go through the ordinary rut of education, lack 'music' in their life. All their faculties are not trained. Mere book knowledge does not interest the child so as to hold his attention fully. The brain gets weary of mere words, and the child's mind begins to wander.[6]

These ideas are in synch with voguish principles of activity-based learning and full development of personality espoused by pedagogues as ideal for educating young children. The Mahatma went beyond such pedagogic ideas in that the activity in which he wanted the pupils to be engaged was designed to teach a craft; teaching of that craft was also expected to simultaneously develop his intellect and impart the education one receives through conventional schooling. Basic education, as envisaged by the Mahatma, was a single activity of education *through* craft, and did not comprise two activities of imparting education as well as training for a craft. He illustrated his idea with reference to spinning:

> Look at *takli* [spindle] itself, for instance. The lesson of this *takli* will be the first lesson of our students through which they would be able to learn a substantial part of the history of cotton, Lancashire and the British empire.... How does this *takli* work? What is its utility? And what are the strengths that lie within it? Thus the child learns all this in the midst of play. Through this he also acquires some knowledge of mathematics. When he is asked to count the number of cotton threads on *takli* and he is asked to report how many did he spin, it becomes possible to acquaint him step by step with good deal of mathematical knowledge through this process. And the beauty is that none of this

[5] M.K. Gandhi, *Future of India*, An Address given at Chatham House on 20 October 1931, London: Royal Institute of International Affairs.

[6] Mahatma Gandhi, 'Discussion with Teacher Trainees', *Harijan*, 18 February 1939, in *The Collected Works of Mahatma Gandhi*, Volume 68, pp. 372–3.

> becomes even a slight burden on his mind. The learner does not even become aware that he is learning. While playing around and singing, he keeps on turning his *takli* and from this itself he learns a great deal.[7] (emphasis added)

By making work the axis of the teaching–learning process, the Mahatma's basic education and its more expanded version Nai Talim (New Education), which he expounded after his release from prison in 1945, altered the very meaning and process of education. The educational institution was turned into a place of work; curriculum was built around the teaching of craft, and whatever literary skills and values that were to be imparted were expected to be imparted through the medium of learning and practicing craft. Like the village community he visualized, the schools and colleges he visualized were self-reliant institutions financed by the productive work of the students and the faculty. In specific terms, the Mahatma suggested that primary education should be extended at least to seven years, and at the end of it a student should, except for knowledge of English, acquire the competencies a student would acquire at the matriculation standard, as well as the skills needed to pursue a vocation. The Mahatma himself claimed that self-sufficiency was the acid test of his proposals. Vocations such as spinning and weaving, embroidery, tailoring, paper-making, book-binding, carpentry, and so on could easily be learnt and handled without much capital investment, and as the sale of products of craft could recover the recurring costs, the educational institution would be self-sufficient. It is significant that in terms of learning outcomes, the Mahatma's basic education goes far beyond the Gokhale–Parulekar model of providing free and compulsory education of four years focussing on three Rs; it sought to prepare the students to be conscientious citizens, productive members of the society, and above all, fine human beings. That was the reason why the duration of basic schooling was longer than the four years of schooling suggested by Gokhale and Parulekar.

The Mahatma's ideas about basic education were discussed at the First Conference on National Education held at Wardha on 22–23

[7] Excerpted from the address by Mahatma Gandhi at the Wardha Education Conference, 22 October 1937, Translated from Hindi, *Hindustani Talimi Sangh*, 1957, pp. v–vii. Cited in NCERT, *National Focus Paper on Work in Education*, 2007, at p. 4.

October 1937; the Conference was attended by several educationists and the education ministers of the seven provinces ruled by the Congress Party. The Conference decided that free and compulsory education should be provided for seven years throughout the nation, and that the medium of instruction should be the mother tongue. It endorsed basic education in the expectation that it would gradually cover the remuneration of teachers. It appointed a committee under the chairmanship of Dr Zakir Hussain to prepare a detailed syllabus for basic education. The report of the Zakir Hussain Committee (December 1937) elaborated the principles and objectives of basic education in terms of pedagogic doctrines and educational psychology, worked out elaborate syllabi for a number of crafts, and outlined various aspects of implementing basic education such as the training of teachers, academic supervision, examinations, and administration. It took a great deal of effort to play down the claim that basic education would be self-financing, and emphasized that basic education should be welcomed because it was educationally sound, and was an important measure of national reconstruction. That basic education would cover the *major* portion of its running expenses was an incidental benefit. In fact, it warned against the dangers of over-emphasizing the financial aspects of basic education. Teachers might devote most of their attention and energy to extracting the maximum amount of labour from children, while neglecting the intellectual, social, and moral implications and possibilities of craft teaching. To jump the story, the Sarjent Report in 1943, while endorsing basic education, explicitly stated that it was 'unable to endorse the view that education at any stage and particularly at the lowest stages can or should be expected to pay for itself. The most which can be expected is that the sales of the products produced should cover the cost of the additional materials and equipment required for practical work'.

The Haripura Congress (February 1938) endorsed the Zakir Hussian Report and resolved to build up a national system of education which would, among others, aim at providing education 'through the medium of some productive trade or handicraft and, to the extent possible, all other activities be built around this central craft, the latter being chosen in accordance with the conditions in which the child is placed'. Thereafter, the provinces ruled by the Congress party began to introduce basic education with gusto; however, before the implementation could pick up momentum, the Congress governments resigned from office in September 1939 over the unilateral proclamation by the Viceroy of a state of war emergency without consulting the central or provincial legislatures. It is significant that even while the Congress governments were in power, there was a considerable body of nationalist opinion which was sceptical of basic education. Basic education was an embodiment of the Mahatma's perception of an ideal society as one consisting of small, self-reliant communities. Few, not even devout followers such as Nehru, subscribed to his perception of an ideal society. The Wardha Scheme coincided with the setting up by the Congress Party of the National Planning Committee (NPC) with the avowed objective of creating a controlled planned economy and rapid expansion of large-scale industries. NPC's sub-committee on general and technical education was reluctant to recommend a shift from the existing system, more so when there was an increase in the efficiency of the primary schools under the Congress ministries. It was of the view that 'it would, therefore be wrong to displace the movement by one in favour of basic education'. The subcommittee saw serious flaws in the Wardha Scheme. Too much stress on vocation at such a young age was 'spiritually harmful and teaching of general subjects through a single narrow-down medium makes the knowledge of the subject superficial and defective'. It could not accept the idea that the output of the children's work at school would financially sustain the school; it even went to the extent of claiming that to a certain work children's work at school 'will mean the existence of child labour in schools'. In conclusion, the subcommittee recommended that the 'introduction of basic education should be a process of grafting on to the elementary education'.[8] After Independence, however, GOI took the stand that basic education had gone beyond the stage of experimentation and should be adopted as the national pattern.

After Independence, only Uttar Pradesh (UP) heroically converted all existing elementary schools into basic schools without investing the complementary resources required for the conversion. Other states were cautious in recognizing that expansion of basic education schools

[8] National Planning Committee, *General Education and Technical Education and Development Research*, Reports on the Sub-Committees Series, Vora: Bombay, 1948, pp. 140, 142, cited in Krishna Kumar, at pp. 512–13.

was linked with the provision of trained teachers, space, equipment, and materials, and attempted to graft basic schools on the existing school system. The graft wilted away all over the country for many reasons, including the unwillingness of poor parents to settle for what they perceived to be a second-best education. Some states experimented with basic education even at the secondary stage; rural institutes such as the Gandhigram Rural Institute were set up by devout Gandhians. Basic education faced the perennial dilemma of radical schemes: they could succeed only if everyone in the society including better-off sections adopted it, and yet there was no way a democratic society could compel the elite to adopt schemes which were inferior in their view, and the poor not to try to emulate the better-off. Opposition was particularly vociferous in Madras Province. Teaching through craft was far from making schools self-supporting and was more costly than normal teaching in formal schools because of the need to procure equipment and materials. With his remarkable ingenuity, Chief Minister C. Rajagopalachari sought to overcome resource constraint by letting students learn craft from their parents at home in out-of-school hours. This triggered a shrill criticism in that province with a long-standing anti-Brahmin movement that the chief minister was trying to perpetuate Brahminical hegemony by forcing lower-caste children to stick to the occupations of the castes in which they were born. The scheme was dubbed as *Kula Kalvi Thittam* (Hereditary Caste Education Policy) designed to perpetuate the caste system—to ensure that 'a cobbler's son would only be a cobbler, a washer man's son a washer man, a potter's son a potter and so on'. Basic schools came to be a convenient stick for the opponents of Rajagopalchari within the Congress Party to mount a challenge to his leadership; eventually the scheme of basic schools was withdrawn.

Blossoms in the Dust, an insightful travelogue much popular in the early days of K's administrative career, vividly brings out that many poor all over the country saw education as a ladder that helps them up in the social hierarchy, and were reluctant to opt for alternatives which the better-off in the society did not patronize. The author, Kusum Nair, was a sociologist who toured almost the whole country in 1958, and distilled from her 36 bulky volumes of copious field notes a string of short-story-like chapters vividly portraying strikingly dramatic change that was transforming rural India, and the attitudes and motivations of the poor that restricted their ability to take benefit of the developmental programmes. In the collieries of Dhanabad, Bihar, Kusum Nair came across miners for generations sending their children to school for the first time; they ridiculed the suggestion of Kusum Nair that after study they should join the mining profession.

> 'What an idea', they said. 'It is like the saying we have: '*padho pharsee becho tel*'—that man should study Persian (and become a scholar) and then sell oil. How can that be?'
>
> Even near Sewagram Ashram, where the Mahatma spent the later part of his life, the villagers spoke of basic education with contempt.
>
> 'We do not send our children to the *ashram* school … because those who pass out of *nai talim* cannot get jobs. So our boys go to Wardha town; they walk four miles to study in a conventional school.… We don't want to remain tillers forever. We also want to become lawyers and doctors. *Nai talim* is no good for it'.[9]

The reluctance of the poor to opt for alternate education that has perhaps more relevance for their lifestyle but prevented them from emulating their better-offs, and thwarted their aspiration to move up, is universal. Like the Mahatma, Jomo Kenyatta of Kenya and Julius Nyerere of Tanzania thought that traditional rural societies had systems of education more suited to their environment than anything that colonial administrators and missionaries wanted to put in its place. After independence, Kenya opened village polytechnics, and Upper Volta a network of rural education centres designed to impart 'basic education', the knowledge and skills to make a modest, but better living in villages. Tanzania was more ambitious in its plans of reconstruction of its entire primary education system. Nyerere's education policy that went by the name Education for Self-Reliance wanted schools to promote cooperative rather than individual success, and to teach pupils how to transform within, rather than despise, the socio-economic mores of village life. The school was a laboratory where new techniques and entrepreneurial activities benefitting the entire community should be pioneered. Every community school established farming plots, and each class spent some of its school day farming, building chicken coops, and tending goats. The profits from these activities were expected to

[9] Kusum Nair, *Blossoms in the Dust: The Human Factor in Indian Development*, New York: Praeger, 1961, pp. 162–3, 186–7.

help offset the costs of the school. In addition, the improved techniques tried out in these schools were expected to be passed on to the villagers. The community schools were also expected to provide day-care for infants and organize adult literacy classes. All in all, these schools were expected to be embedded in the local community. Like the coal miners of Dhanbad and the villagers of Sewagram, the African parents who wanted their children to be educated were keen to send their children to conventional schools, and did not want them to spend their time hoeing groundnuts and minding chickens which they could have done more usefully if they had stayed at home.[10] Suffice it to say, educational innovations which cover only schools attended by the poor are doomed to fail. All in all, Mahatma's basic education started as a promising avenue but turned out to be a blind alley. However, the idea that productive work should have a central place in school curriculum has an enduring charm, and is a hardy perennial in educational discourse[11] and policies.

Hope Trumps Reality

Two issues relating to elementary education figured in the making of the Constitution: first, who should bear the responsibility for the development of elementary education, the Union or states, or both, and second whether free and compulsory elementary education should be a justiciable Fundamental Right or a non-justiciable Directive Principle which the Constitution proclaimed to be fundamental in the governance of the country. Education was one of the subjects which witnessed a keen contest between 'centralizers' and 'provincial politicians' during the making of the Constitution. With a few modifications, the Constitution-makers decided to maintain the distribution of responsibilities between the Union and the states prevailing since the coming into force of the GOI Act, 1935. Consequently, elementary and adult education continued to be state subjects. The demand that free and compulsory education should be a fundamental right had been a long-standing one. In 1925, at the behest of Annie Besant a group of

[10] Maggie Black, *The Children and the Nations: The Story of UNICEF*, New York: UNICEF, 1986, pp. 316–19, 322–3.

[11] NCERT, *National Focus Paper on Work in Education*, 2007.

Indians drafted a Commonwealth of India Bill, and George Lansbury, Labour Member of the Parliament, introduced that Bill in the House of Commons in 1925; the Bill provided for a right to free elementary education which was to be enforceable as soon as arrangements for educational facilities could be made. The Fundamental Rights of the Nehru Report of the Congress Party (1928) not only included a right to free elementary education but also a special provision for the elementary education of minorities.[12] Given the historical background it is no wonder that there were demands in the Constituent Assembly for making free and compulsory primary education a fundamental right. However, the demand was not conceded, a prime reason being that during the freedom struggle no distinction was made between negative civil rights and positive social, economic, and cultural rights, and now that the former 'agitators' were officeholders, the question of feasibility came to the fore. The salience of a fundamental right lay in its justiciability, and going by the way judiciary functioned those days, it was difficult to conceptualize how Directive Principles like a right to education could be made justiciable. What M. Anantasayanam Ayyangar had to say about the amendment to make Article 45 (Article 26 in the draft stage) a fundamental right makes interesting reading in these days of pervasive judicial activism.

> In Article 26 it is said that the State should within a period of ten years introduce free compulsory education.... Let us assume that the State does not do so, then can any court of law enforce it? Against whom? In case a decree is granted by a court of law, who will carry it out? If the Government does not carry it out, can the High Court or the Supreme Court enforce it? Is it open to the Supreme Court to change such a government? With its authority, can it by an officer of the Court, an Amin or a Sheriff imprison all the Ministers, and bring into existence a new set of Ministers? In the nature of things, these are only directives and cannot be justiciable rights at all ...
>
> These are [Directive] principles which the Government must keep in mind, whatever Government may be in power, and they must be carried out. We have incorporated them in the Constitution itself because we attach importance to them. But to classify them as Fundamental Rights as in Part III would be to take away the difference between the

[12] Granville Austin, *The Indian Constitution: The Cornerstone of a Nation*, Oxford: Clarendon Press, 1966, pp. 39, 54–5, 82.

> one set and the other, and making all the rights justiciable, which, in the nature of things, is impossible. *There is no use being carried away by sentiments. We must be practical.* (emphasis added)[13]

While Constitution-makers were not carried away by sentiment in making compulsory primary education a fundamental right, they were 'romantic rather than clear-eyed, more well-intentioned than practical' in respect of some directive principles; the fixation of a time limit of 10 years for providing free and compulsory elementary education is a good example. Except for Article 45, no other Directive Principle sets a time limit for the State to comply with the obligation arising from the Principle. How the time limit of ten years for Article 45 came about is an interesting tale by itself. The Sarjent Committee recommended that a system of universal, compulsory, and free education for all children should be introduced as early as possible. It was emphatic that education from 6 to 14 years should be treated as an organic whole, and would lose value if not so treated. In view of the practical difficulties, the report concluded that it would take under the most auspicious auspices 30–40 years before a system of universal, compulsory, and free education for all boys and girls between the age of 6 and 14 years could be brought into operation.[14] The report estimated that about 18 lakh trained teachers would be required for providing UEE. In contrast to this requirement, the annual output of teacher training institutions was no more than 20,000 per year. As it was, about 40.6 per cent of the school teachers (about 5,18,000) were untrained. In retrospect, the time frame envisaged by Sarjent Committee was realistic; as would be elaborated below, about two decades after the Sarjent Committee, in 1966 the Kothari Commission envisaged universalization of elementary education by 1985–6. Even as late as 2009, the RTE Act provided for the central government relaxing the minimum qualifications required for appointment as a teacher if a state does not have teachers possessing minimum qualifications in sufficient numbers. However, the Sarjent Committee came for severe criticism

[13] *Constituent Assembly* Debates on 19 November 1948, *Constituent Assembly of India*, Volume VII, http://indiankanoon.org/doc/682692 (last accessed on 22 May 2015).

[14] Ministry of Education, *Post-War Educational Development in India*, pp. 17–18, 86–7.

for projecting a far too long time frame for universalizing elementary education. In 1948, the Central Advisory Board on Education (CABE) revisited the prognosis of the Sarjent Report when it appointed a Committee of Experts under the chairmanship of B.G. Kher, Premier of Bombay Province, to suggest the ways and means of reducing the period for achieving UEE. By 1948, Native States were not yet amalgamated in the Indian Union, and therefore the Kher Committee's remit was limited to the provinces which, before Independence, constituted British India. In its interim report, the Kher Committee opined that universal compulsory basic education could be introduced within a period of 16 years through two five-year and one six-year plans. By 1960, all children in the age group 6–10 were to be covered by free and compulsory education, and by 1966, UEE was to be achieved by providing free and compulsory education to all children in the age group 6–14. The Kher Committee estimated that the expenditure on elementary education would have to expand from Rs 9.38 crore in 1949–50 to Rs 288.97 crore by 1964–5, and recommended that the central government should provide the provinces 30 per cent of the expenditure required. At the CABE meeting in January 1949, Maulana Azad, the Education Minister, announced that his Ministry accepted the Report of the Kher Committee, and tried to provide the provinces the funds required; however, in view of the acute financial crisis, his Ministry was compelled to postpone consideration of the scheme 'for the time being'. One factor which weighed with Azad was that the contribution of the central government would be effective only if provinces could contribute their share, and the financial position of the country was such that it was doubtful that provinces could find the necessary resource.[15] Surprisingly, the Kher Committee turned optimistic and suggested in its final report that UEE be achieved by 1960. After some discussion whether free and compulsory education should be a justifiable right or not, the Constitutional Assembly decided to incorporate it as a Directive Principle of the Constitution (Article 45) in line with the recommendation of the Kher Committee. The manner in which the target of 1960 was set for achieving UEE is a commentary on the manner in which time and again good intentions triumphed

[15] Proceedings of the Fifteenth Meeting—January, 1949, in *Central Advisory Board on Education (1935–60): Silver Jubilee Souvenir*, 207–9.

over reality, and unrealistic targets continued to be set so much so that targets lost meaning.

Article 46 casts a special obligation on the State to promote the educational and economic interests of scheduled castes, scheduled tribes, and other weaker sections of society. The Constitution also guaranteed special protection to the interests of linguistic and religious minorities. Article 29(1) provides that 'any section of the citizens residing in the territory of India or any part thereof having a distinct language, script or culture of its own shall have the right to conserve the same'. Article 29(2) prohibits denying of admission of any citizen to government- or private-aided educational institution on the grounds only of religion, race, caste, language, or any of them. Article 30 (1) vests in all minorities, whether based on religion or language, the right to *establish and administer* educational institutions *of their choice*. The scope of this right had been adjudicated in High Courts and Supreme Court for several decades separately as well as part of the adjudication of the power of central and state governments to regulate private unaided institutions.[16] Article 30(2) prohibits the State from discriminating against any educational institution in the matter or providing grant-in-aid on the ground that it is under the management of a minority. The Constitution (Seventh Amendment) Act, 1956, introduced Article 350A which obligated every state and every local authority to provide adequate facilities for instruction in the mother tongue at the primary stage of education to children belonging to linguistic minority groups. Article 350A authorizes the president to issue such directions to any state as he considers necessary or proper for securing the provision of such facilities.

Kothari Commission and NPE, 1968

The Kothari Commission explored in detail the reasons for UEE being elusive and came up with meaningful recommendations. It made it clear that the programme of providing good general education of seven years' duration to every child would require (*a*) the provision of a school within easy distance from the home of every child, (*b*) the enrolment

[16] *P.A. Inamdar and Others v. State of Maharashtra and Others*, 2005 (6) SCC 537.

of every child of the prescribed age in class I 'through propaganda, persuasion, and even penal action, if necessary', and (*c*) the retention of every child in school till he reaches 14 years of age. It made it clear that universal provision, universal enrolment, and universal retention should go hand in hand with simultaneous improvement in the quality of education because universe enrolment and retention depend largely on the attracting and holding power of the schools. Even while outlining what the thrust in elementary education should be, the Kothari Commission was pragmatic in setting the targets for fulfilling the constitutional obligation, and offered an elaborate justification for the targets it proposed. Five years of *good and effective* education (classes I–V) should be provided all over the country by 1975–6 (ten years from the submission of the report), and seven years of such education by another ten years hence in 1985–6. Stagnation and wastage should be halved by 1976 and almost eliminated by 1986. The report contended that while the targets proposed 'may appear modest', 'a close examination would show that they were really formidable and the nation would have to strive its utmost to realise them'. Thus, the enrolment had to more than double from 500 lakhs in 1965–6 to 1250 lakhs in 1985–6, and reduction of wastage and stagnation, and improvement of quality were more onerous challenges than increasing enrolment. The report suggested that each state, and even each district, should prepare a perspective plan for fulfilling the Constitutional obligation as early as possible, and that each state and district should be assisted to go ahead at the best pace it can, and that the 'progress in no area shall be allowed to be held up for want of essential facilities or financial allocations'. Here is the germ of idea which underlay DPEP in 1994 and its progeny SSA in 2001.The Kothari Commission explicitly recognized the educational needs of a teeming army of children and youth who did not and would not in the near future complete the schooling necessary for permanent literacy and acquiring to use contemporary jargon, livelihood skills, its prescience lies in introducing the concept of multiple-entry education outside the portals of educational institutions through part-time courses and self-study. The Kothari Commission incorporated the state-of-the-art thinking by postulating that there were three channels of education: the first channel of formal education, the second channel of part-time education, and the third channel of self-education. Reliance on full-time education in a school or college as the sole channel of instruction was inadequate in a modernizing and changing society. Education should be recognized as a lifelong process. Being so, it was necessary to complement the channel of formal full-time education in an institution by the second channel of part-time study in an institution, and the third channel of self-study. The two alternative channels of part-time and self-study should be developed on a large scale at every stage and in every area of education, and should be given the same status as full-time education. Children in the age group 11–14 who were not attending schools and did not complete the primary stage should be required to attend literacy classes at least for a year. Children who have completed primary stage, and who desire to study further but could not attend schools, should be imparted part-time education; such education should be elastic and determined according to the needs and aptitudes of the children receiving it. The proposals of the Commission drew heavy criticism from the Committee of Members of Parliament (MPs) mainly on the ground that the period envisaged for achieving UEE was far too long. NPE, 1968, which announced the decisions of the government on the Commissions' report did not commit itself to a firm target date for UEE , and merely said that 'strenuous efforts should be made for the early fulfilment of the Directive Principle under Article 45 of the Constitution seeking to provide for free and compulsory education for all children under the age of 14', and that 'suitable programmes should be developed to reduce the prevailing wastage and stagnation in schools and to ensure that every child who is enrolled in school successfully completes the prescribed course'. The Kothari Commission's recommendation for state- and district-level planning for fulfilling the constitutional obligation was not acted upon till 1994 when DPEP was launched.

NPE, 1968, post-Independence India's first NPE embodies the decisions of the government on the Commission's report. It was a bland document full of generalities and exhortations basically because 'the time is out of joint' and the nation was in the grip of acute political and economic crises. Even while declaring that the government was convinced that a radical reconstruction on the broad lines recommended by the Education Commission was necessary, the 1968 Education Policy failed to act on almost all the major recommendations of the Kothari Commission. Thus NPE, 1968, failed to specify a time frame as recommended by the Kothari Commission for the realization of Universal Primary Education (UPE) and UEE but also the recommendations suggesting compulsory literacy classes for children in the age group 11–14 who did not complete primary education, and provision of flexible part-time courses for children who had completed primary stage, and who desired to study further but could not attend schools. The government considered inexpedient to appear that it was diluting the Constitutional obligation to provide free and compulsory education under Article 45 by suggesting alternatives to schooling. NPE, 1968, made no mention about any programmes for out-of-school children. It was in higher education that part-time education received a big boost, mainly because cash-strapped state universities discovered that correspondence courses were a cash cow which they could profitably harness; though perhaps well-intentioned, this move aggravated the poor quality of higher education. A major issue that Bordia had to encounter as Education Secretary was the proliferation of substandard B.Ed. programmes offered through correspondence courses; students of these programmes had no classroom experience worth the name in spite of such experience being vital for the practice of teaching. Over a course of time, the ascendancy of the idea that education is a lifelong process and can take place in many settings led to the growth of open universities. The growth of new technologies for dissemination gave and continues to give a great impetus to open learning outside educational campuses. Starry-eyed techno-optimists see in the contemporaneous growth of massive open online courses (MOOCs) the beginning of a trend which would lead to the universities being no more than one of the sites for management of MOOCs.

Constitutional Amendment, 1976

Till the 42nd amendment to the Constitution in 1976, education was essentially a state subject except for certain items specified in the Union List such as determination of standards in institutions of higher education and research, and establishment and maintenance of central universities as well as specified institutions for scientific or technical education and research. The objective of incorporating education in the Concurrent List in 1976 was to facilitate evolution of all-India policies in the field of education. Viewed in a proper perspective, the

1976 Constitutional Amendment did not shrink the role of the states in educational development and regulation; it only expanded the role of the Union beyond the domain the original Constitution conferred on it. After the Amendment in 1976, the Union no doubt has the power to legislate on any area or aspect of education, and its legislation would prevail over any prior state legislation unless an existing state legislation had secured President's assent. After that amendment, technically, the Union could have enacted the whole of NPE, 1986, as a central Act but such a move would have been imprudent and ran contrary to convention. In terms of the number of educational institutions established, the proportion of students enrolled in state government institutions, and the budgetary resources allocated to education (over 90 per cent of total expenditure of Centre and states in 1992), the states *as a whole* dwarf the centre. States are constitutional entities in their own right. While the centre could legislate for a small segment of education and enforce that legislation there is no way it could legislate for education as a whole and enforce it, all the more so as it does not have the organizational machinery to enforce such a sweeping legislation. Even if such a central machinery were to be established it would have to be gargantuan. The statement of Sir Girija Shankar Bajpai, a celebrated Indian member of the Indian Civil Service (ICS) who as Member of the Viceroy's Executive Council in charge of education, played a lead role in the revival of CABE in 1935, that 'None of us would, even if we could, centralise educational initiative or control', embodies administrative wisdom.[17]After the Constitution was amended in 1976, only two Central acts were legislated in exercise of the powers vested by the entry in the Concurrent List; they were the National Commission for Minorities Educational Act, 2004, and the Right of Children to Free and Compulsory Elementary Education Act, 2009.

Suffice it to say, the NPE, 1986, definition of concurrency as a partnership is absolutely correct. The central and state governments are locked up in a state of mutually interdependent relationship. Disagreements are intrinsic to any partnership; in a federal polity, disagreements arise between the centre and states as well as among the states themselves about what ought to be done and how one ought to

[17] Government of India, Ministry of Education, *Central Advisory Board on Education (1935–60): Silver Jubilee Souvenir,* 1960, p. 14.

go about even if there is agreement on what ought to be done; this is all the more so in case of concurrent subjects over which the central and state governments have overlapping jurisdictions. Consequently, tensions and even conflicts are inevitable. Given the inevitable disagreements and tensions intrinsic to a federal polity, mechanisms are needed to deliberate and discuss issues and iron out disagreements. Historically, CABE, which was established in 1921, has been playing that role; chaired by the Union Minister it has all the state education ministers as well as select experts as members.

Central funding has been the policy lever that the central government has been employing for inducing the states to continue implementing national policies. The objective of CSS is to induce states to implement national policies through provision of *tied grants*. Where there is no such financial lever and where some of the state governments are ruled by parties of a different ideological disposition, the central government has been unable to secure nation-wide implementation of all the provisions of its national framework policies. A CSS creates an implicit contractual relationship between the centre and the states. The centre offers grants in exchange for the state implementing the scheme in accordance with the scheme parameters and guidelines.

IV

COURSE CORRECTION
NPE, 1986

The formulation of NPE, 1986, is an illustration of the proposition that policymaking is more packaging, combination, and re-combination of 'old', pre-existing elements rather than conjuring new ideas out of thin air. Any policy on elementary education needs to address a set of questions: what is the target date for achieving UEE? And, how should one go about? The second question in turn gives rise to a few other questions: why is it that in spite of spectacular expansion of access UEE proved elusive? How can it be ensured that *all* children in the age-group 6–14 years are enrolled in schools, complete eight years of elementary education, and equally importantly, learn whatever the syllabus and curriculum expect them to? How can the reach, grasp, and effectiveness of the schools be improved to the level necessary to achieve UEE? Even with all the improvements possible, in the given socio-economic situation can one rely solely on schools to achieve UEE?

When NPE, 1986, was being formulated, UEE was nowhere is in sight in spite of spectacular expansion in access and enrolment. Over the period 1950–1 to 1986, the number of elementary schools nearly tripled, from 2.23 lakhs to 6.68 lakhs; by 1986, 94.5 per cent of the rural population had a primary school within a walking distance of 1 km. During the same period, the number of teachers in these schools increased fourfold from 6.2 lakhs to 26.2 lakhs. Enrolment in the primary stage (classes I–V) increased more than fourfold from 192 lakhs to 899 lakhs, and in upper primary (classes VI–VIII) stage ninefold from 31 lakhs to 288 lakhs. The Gross Enrolment Ratio (including children over as well as below 14 years of age) rose from 42.6 to 95.9. Yet about 188 lakh children, about 20 per cent of the 6–11 age population, were outside the school.[1] Dropout rates were high; out of every 100 children enrolled in class I only about 40 survived to class V and 25 to class VIII. Regional and gender disparities, and dropout rates, though showing considerable improvement since 1950–1, remained unconscionably high. While UEE was still far away, the remarkable expansion of the elementary education system since Independence contradicts the voguish view of the 1990s that UEE was not achieved because it was neglected by central and state governments and did not receive adequate investment. Among the explanations put forth for the neglect were the cultural explanation put forth by Amartya Sen[2] and the class explanation put forth among others by Naik,[3]Ashok Mitra,[4] and Myron Weiner.[5] Amartya Sen attributed the high literacy rates in Buddhist countries such as Burma and Sri Lanka as compared to India, and the Indian bias in favour of higher education and against elementary education to the fact that in contrast to the relatively egalitarian and populist traditions of Buddhism, both Hinduism and Islam have considerable inclination towards religious elitism, with reliance, respectively, on Brahmin priests and *mullahs*. The class explanation has it that oligarchical groups who are in power sustain their power by limiting access to primary education and thereby prevent the spread of political and social awareness among masses. However, the neglect hypothesis is right only to the extent that the state failed to take the necessary measures to ensure that the 'capacity' of the expanded school system was fully utilized and that *all* the children, irrespective of class, caste, creed, or sex, attended the schools set up and stayed long enough to complete primary education. A defining characteristic of higher education ever

[1] Estimated from the data in POA, 1986, at p.. 13.

[2] Amartya Sen, 'How Is India Doing?', *New York Review of Books*, 29, no. 20 (16 December 1982). http://www.nybooks.com/articles/archives/1982/dec/16/how-is-india-doing/ (last accessed on 22 May 2015).

[3] J.P. Naik, *Policy and Performance in Indian Education 1947–74*, Dr K.G. Saiydain Lectures, 1974, New Delhi: Allied, 1975, pp. 11,16.

[4] Ashok Mitra, 'How Is India Doing? An Exchange', *New York Review of Books*, 30, no. 3, (3 March 1983). http://www.nybooks.com/articles/archives/1983/mar/03/how-is-india-doing-an-exchange/ (last accessed on 22 May 2015).

[5] Myron Weiner, *The Child and the State in India*, Princeton, NJ: Princeton University Press, 1991, pp. 5–6.

since English education was introduced in the country has been that in contrast to the deficient demand in elementary education, particularly among girls and in rural areas, the demand for education that held out job opportunities was in excess of supply. That being so, unlike higher and technical education, special measures are needed, to use the jargon of economists, to pump-prime demand for primary education. The poor, particularly rural poor, did not avail provision of basic services, such as, education, for a number of reasons including lack of adequate information about the services, social taboos such as the education of girls, and a culture of apathy and low level of aspirations arising from centuries of poverty, ignorance, and fatalistic religions and tradition. Therefore, providing schools was not sufficient; it was also necessary to alter the traditional attitudes and mores either through public action and mobilizing the local communities for persuading the households to avail the benefit of primary education or by compelling school attendance. Unlike the communist countries which relied on political mobilization, the political parties in power in India relied exclusively on the bureaucracy to deliver social goals. While school teachers and officials of the State Education Departments organized enrolment drives, they were not oriented towards engaging the parents and local community so as to ensure that the children enrolled continued to attend the school and completed primary education.

The question the policymakers faced in 1986 was whether they should take note of the grim reality and go in for realistic targets or to skirt around the issue as NPE, 1968, had done when it declared that the strenuous efforts would be made for the early fulfilment of the obligation cast under Article 45. NPE, 1986, did not opt for the soft option chosen by its predecessor; it followed the recommendation of the Kothari Commission and set specific targets: while the attempt to set targets was commendable, the targets set were unrealistic. There was no way that just in four years—by 1990—primary education would be provided to all children, and in another five years—by 1995—elementary education would be provided to all children. The same worry which haunted the Constitution-makers as well as the committee of MPs and the government when the Kothari Commission was being processed haunted the makers of NPE, 1986; a realistic target would be construed as lack of commitment to achieve UEE. In extenuation of the unrealistic targets one can only say that one has to be a politician before one is a statesman, and that being so top policymakers shy away from seeing issues in black and white terms and choose to recognize various shades of grey and live with ambivalence. The choice the NPE, 1986, policymakers faced is either to be brutally honest and make the target a matter of controversy detracting from the objective of moving ahead or to waffle; they chose pragmatism over forthrightness. While the policymakers waffled over the target they were extremely perceptive in their conceptualization of UEE; UEE was conceptualized to be universal enrolment and universal retention of all children up to the age of 14 years and substantial improvement in the quality of education.

In four significant respects, NPE, 1986 and its POA departed from the national strategy hitherto followed for achieving UEE which excessively relied 'on opening of new schools, appointment of teachers, and launching of enrolment drives': (*a*) ensuring that every elementary school had minimum infrastructure and facilities, (*b*) improving teacher quality by revamping pre-service education, and putting in place a system of in-service training, (*c*) explicitly recognizing the need to put in place a large NFE system to supplement formal schooling, and (*d*) replacing ineffectual enrolment drives by microplanning and social mobilization.

For the first time, NPE, 1986, specifically postulated that a child-centred and activity-based process of learning should be adopted at the primary stage. It proposed to undertake two sets of measures to improve the quality of education and introduce a child-centred and activity-based process of learning. For the first time ever, minimum criteria were laid down for a primary school—every elementary school was to have at least two teachers, two all-weather classrooms, and a set of minimum essential teaching–learning aids and play material, and elementary teacher education training was proposed to be reorganized. The inclusion of teaching–learning aids in the minimal criteria was based on the premise that in the absence of such aids teachers exclusively depended on textbooks for teaching and were concerned only with completing the textbooks before the academic year closed and not with how interesting their teaching was or whether children learned at all. It was expected that the use of the teaching–learning aids would place the individual child at the centre of classroom process, make teaching more learner oriented, and lead to a radical departure from the institutionalized form of teaching and learning. All existing schools were to be upgraded so as to fulfil the minimum criteria, and no schools were in future to be sanctioned unless they fulfilled the minimal criteria; in other words, there could be a backward region but not a backward school. There were to be two strands of the reorganization proposed in elementary teacher education training: (*a*) creation of institutional infrastructure to leaven pre-service teacher training, as well as organize systematic in-service training for teachers, NFE, and adult education instructors, and (*b*) put in place a strong regulatory system to enforce standards and quality of elementary teacher education. A new institution called DIET was to be set up in every district, and the SCERT, apex organizations responsible for providing resource support for all stages and aspects of school education in states were to be strengthened. The National Council of Teacher Education (NCTE), which was an advisory body in existence from 1973, was to be vested with statutory powers to lay down and enforce standards and norms for institutions of teacher education, and to accredit and disaccredit institutions of teacher education.

NPE, 1986, also gave its imprimatur to the *Dvaita* doctrine (Chapter II). The POA elaborated the principles for developing an extensive system of NFE that would cater to the educational needs of children outside school. The essential characteristics of the NFE system envisaged were organizational flexibility so that learners could learn at their own pace, relevance of curriculum, and diversity in learning activities so as to relate them to learners' needs. Modern technological gadgets such as solar packs for provision of power in NFE centres and audio-visual aids were to be used to improve the learning environment of NFE centres. Efforts would be made to evolve different models of NFE programmes, and agencies implementing the NFE programme were to be encouraged to adapt the model most suitable for the learner groups they were catering to.

Apart from outlining the development of a large NFE system, the strategies which NPE, 1986, and the POA outlined included microplanning and social mobilization. In doing so, they drew upon the Report of the Kothari Commission, and the ideas articulated by Naik in his radical phase. The Kothari Commission recommended that the enrolment of every child of the prescribed age in class I should be ensured 'through propaganda, persuasion, and even penal action, if necessary', and, to that end, involve the local community in the management of education. Penal action was deemed impractical;

Bordia, who was opposed to a compulsory legislation, used to quote Naik's quip that in many educationally backward states with huge out-of-school child population, punitive education would result in more parents being in jails than children in schools. In the writings of his radical phase, Naik was critical of exclusive dependence on the bureaucracy and had strongly suggested massive mobilization of teachers, and social and political workers to bring about big reforms in education. Building on these ideas, NPE,1986, spoke of 'constant microplanning and verification to ensure the enrolment, retention, and successful completion of courses do not fail at any stage'. The POA went one step ahead by extending the concept of microplanning to all children of the age group 6–14, and weaving into that concept social mobilization strategies. It explicitly declared that enrolment by itself is of little importance if children do not continue education beyond even one year, many of them not seeing the school for more than a few days, and that emphasis would, therefore, shift from enrolment to retention and completion by all children of at least five years of education. Enrolment drives would be replaced by systematic house-to-house survey in which the teachers, in cooperation with the village community, would educate the parents about the essentiality of their children receiving education, and interact continually with them so as to ensure regular attendance of the children. The POA envisaged that planning for UEE would be decentralized, and teachers and local community involved in the planning process. The Village Panchayat and the Village Education Committee were envisaged the principal instruments through which the community would be enlisted for the cause of UEE. Suffice it to say, the emphasis NPE, 1986, laid on micro-planning and social mobilization addressed the 'neglect' of elementary education outlined above.

From the perspective which time provides, it comes out that all the elements of the strategy which NPE, 1986, and its POA envisaged did not fall in place with the result that, instead of concerted steps being taken to hasten the march to UEE, disjointed efforts were made to improve school facilities and set up NEF centres and DIETs. The grand ideas essayed about microplanning and social mobilization remained on paper. In the absence of financial assistance and technical support by DOE, the states lacked the financial wherewithal, incentive, and expertise to undertake microplanning. Talk about social mobilization was not followed by action; it was a good example of the use of radical phraseology in education which Kamat bemoaned was a legacy of Naik. A silver lining was the fact that NIEPA began to study the modalities of participatory microplanning for UEE. Till 1994, when DPEP was launched, planning for UEE remained a concept occasionally tried in isolated pockets.

NPE Programmes: OB and DIETs

School improvement was sought to be effected through a CSS with the evocative name of Operation Blackboard (OB); at the same time, two other CSSs were launched, one for the establishment of DIETs, and the other for organizing NFE centres. In terms of numbers, the achievement of OB was quite impressive. A distinctive feature of OB was the stipulation that at least one of the two teachers in every school should be women, and that, in the recruitment of teachers, preference should be given to women; in other words, there should be no single-teacher school anywhere in the country. By 1999–2000, as many as 1.74 lakh teachers (of whom about half were women) were recruited and 136,000 classrooms were constructed. In the mid-1990s, this scheme was expanded to cover upper primary schools and also provide a third teacher to primary schools with enrolment more than 100. When one moves from outputs to outcomes, the achievements are less promising. The quality of teachers recruited varied widely. For want of adequate number of trained teachers, quite a few states were constrained to appoint teachers without pre-service teacher training, and the programmes put in place to prepare the teachers so recruited for undertaking effective teaching were usually inadequate. Strange but true, during the first few years of the scheme there was a fall in the total number of elementary teachers in the country as many states recruited only teachers sanctioned by OB programme without filling the vacancies which arose every year because of retirement; that is to say, they utilized the funds released by the central government to substitute the expenditure they would have incurred in normal course. The construction of classrooms fell short of the norm as it was the responsibility of the state governments to finance the construction either from their own resources or by tapping the funds released by the Ministry of Rural Development for asset creation. NIEPA's National Evaluation revealed that by 1999–2000 there were still schools without any buildings in nine states including Bihar, Haryana, Tamil Nadu, and UP; every state except for Delhi and Sikkim had schools with a single all-weather classroom.[6] Suffice it to say, the OB norm of every school having at least two all-weather classrooms was not fulfilled. The fiscal capacity of most states was far too stressed to undertake the construction programme on the scale necessary, and the funds released by the Ministry of Rural Development were meagre in relation to the competing demands such as road building, minor irrigation, and school building construction. Procurement of teaching–learning aids and play material was the weakest element of implementation. As State Education Secretary, K found that the direction of DOE suffered from both type of errors, the error of doing what ought not to be done as well as of not doing things what ought to be done. NCERT went overboard with the specifications it stipulated for teaching–learning aids and play material. A case in point was the ludicrous and pedantic specifications fixed about the size and bounce of the ball to be procured. With the wisdom of hindsight, DOE's release of funds distorted the market for teaching–learning aids and play material. Never before were funds of such magnitude available for procurement of teaching–learning and play material with the result that demand outstripped supply, and overnight hucksters appeared to make quick buck or to mix metaphor make hay while the sun shone. Flimsy books were touted as supplementary reading material, and ragtag grotesque sketches as maps. Ideally DOE ought to have closely scrutinized the material procured and calibrated the release of funds with the availability of material in the market. Calibrated release might be fiscally prudent but organizationally imprudent as utilization of funds is an important factor in the fixation of the budgetary allocations for the programme in the next year. If a department prudently spends less it stands to lose. DOE made some efforts to get the National Book Trust and Children's Book Trust to produce supplementary reading material; however, these efforts were inadequate. A fatal flaw of the supply-augmenting strategy of DOE was the exclusive reliance upon government organizations and shying away from the more enterprising

[6] National Institute of Educational Planning and Administration, *Implementation of Operation Blackboard Scheme in Primary Schools in India*, National Evaluation of Operation Blackboard, Document 1, 2006.

private publishers. As a response to the recurring complaint by states about the lack of flexibility in supply of the teaching–learning material, some changes were made in the procurement whereby broad categories were defined within which the state governments could decide the items to be procured. Even though the state governments were expected to provide teaching–learning materials to larger schools which were not covered by OB, they did not. Even in schools provided with the material teachers were reluctant to use the material lest they should be held accountable for damages. Even though the state governments were required to replace the teaching–material consumed or damaged, few did. A study by Caroline Dyer[7] and an evaluation by NIEPA brought out that the transformation expected from OB did not materialize. The National University of Educational Planning and Administration (NUEPA) evaluation brought out that the OB objective of doing away with single-teacher schools was fulfilled only in Delhi; for the country as a whole, 15 per cent of schools were single-teacher schools; schools without two all-weather classrooms continued to exist in 26 out of the 28 states and union territories, and that utilization of available teaching–learning material was negligible. Suffice it to say, OB mainly served the purpose of offering a lesson in what not do in the matter of providing grants to schools for teaching–learning and play material, namely that it makes no sense for DOE to steer the utilization of grants given for school improvement. The system of providing freewheeling grants to schools and letting the schools decide what they wanted to procure was first tried out in APPEP, and became the national norm first in DPEP and later in SSA and RMSA.

In terms of numbers, the attempt to establish DIETs was highly successful. Over a course of time, a DIET was established in every district even though the number of districts increased from about 450 in 1985 to about 670 now because of the reorganization of districts. However, as with OB the outcomes are far less impressive. Institution building is not just building a campus; staffing DIETs with competent and committed faculty still remains a challenge more than a quarter century of

[7] Caroline Dyer, 'The Improvement of Primary School Quality in India: Successes and Failures of Operation Blackboard', Edinburgh Papers in South Asian Studies Number 4, 1996, Centre for South Asia Studies, University of Edinburgh.

the launch of the scheme to set up DIETs. In terms of their training capacity, DIETs by themselves were inadequate to organize periodic in-service training of all elementary teachers; it was only after Block and Cluster Resource Centres began to be set up on a large scale first by DPEP and later by SSA that the requisite capacity could be created. The intake of DIETs for pre-service training was too inadequate to meet the demand for trained teachers which got a boost first from OB, and later from DPEP and SSA. Hence, there was no choice but to depend on private Teacher Training Institutes and Colleges of Teacher Education offering B.Ed. degrees to meet the demand. It was only in 1993 that enabling legislation was passed by the Parliament to vest NCTE with statutory powers, and NCTE came into existence only in 1995, nearly a decade after NPE, 1986. Till then, the only lever DOE had to persuade the state governments to prevent the proliferation substandard institutions was to hold out the threat that grants for establishment of DIETs would be withheld. It was not an effective policy lever as withholding grants would run contrary to the other objective of creating DIETs. Even after NCTE came into existence, it was no more successful than the All India Council of Technical Education (AICTE) in curbing the proliferation of substandard institutions. While the teacher education scheme helped SCERTs to improve their facilities, rejuvenation of SCERTs did not take place and they continued to be dysfunctional.

NPE Programmes: NFE

Even in respect of NFE the numbers were quite impressive. Although the focus of the NFE scheme was the educationally backward states of AP, Arunachal Pradesh, Assam, Bihar, Jammu & Kashmir, Madhya Pradesh (MP), Orissa, Rajasthan, UP, and West Bengal, the scheme covered urban slums, hilly, tribal and desert areas, and areas with concentration of working children in the other states as well. DOE fully financed the expenditure incurred by the educationally backward states for managing NFE centres for girls and half the expenditure of NEF centres catering to boys. DOE fully financed the expenditure incurred by NGOs for operating NFE centres; it also supported the development of innovative models by fully financing the expenditure incurred on innovative and experimental models. The number of NFE centres increased from 126,000 in 1986 to 255,000 by March 1994 and the enrolment from 3.65 million to 6.4 million. During this period, the number of girls' centres increased from 20,500 to 96,766. Over 425 voluntary agencies were participating in this programme. Alongside, around 50 experimental and innovative projects and 22 district resource units were in operation for in-depth work. It is significant to note that unlike the TLCs or MS, the NFE scheme adopted a functionalist approach imparting 3Rs and livelihood skills rather than seeking to 'empower' the participants in NFE centres. However, to be honest, the outcomes were disappointing.

There were quite a few acclaimed NFE programmes such as PROPEL (Promoting Primary and Elementary Education Project) spearheaded by Chitra Naik, which was chosen by UNESCO as a 'showcase project' to promote elementary education for rural children, particularly girls, in developing countries. The most acclaimed of NFE programmes was Shiksha Karmi (literally, education worker), which innovatively addressed only the question of access in remote villages. A chronic problem in such villages is that schools do not function most of the time because of teacher absenteeism. Almost all teachers in such villages are from outside the community and do not like to live in such inaccessible areas. Launched in 1987, Shiksha Karmi sought to improve the enrolment of boys and girls in remote, socio-economically backward districts of Rajasthan where the existing elementary schools were dysfunctional, and further to build a level of learning equivalent to class V. The basic idea underlying Shiksha Karmi is that best is often the enemy of the good, and that people in remote rural villages are better off if basic education and health services are provided by local persons with minimal qualifications and training than by more qualified professionals from outside the village who would not stay in the village and are likely to be irregular in providing their services; the same idea underlies Mao Zedong's barefoot doctors. Shiksha Karmi traces its lineage to an experiment in the three villages of Tilonia, Buharu, and Phaloda, Rajasthan, during 1975–8 by the Social Work and Research Centre (SWRC), Tilonia.[8] SWRC is also known as Barefoot College and was set up by the famous activist Bunker Roy, under the influence of Mao Zedong. The idea underlying Shiksha Karmi, however, is

[8] S.N. Methi and Sharada Jain, *The Shiksha Karmi Project in Rajasthan, India (SKP)*, in Angela Little et al., pp. 146–62.

not new. In his famous Chatham House speech, in which he spoke of the 'beautiful tree' of Indian education being uprooted by the British, Mahatma Gandhi asserted that it was impossible 'to fulfil a program of compulsory primary education of ... masses inside of a century with the schools introduced by the British', and urged revival of 'the old village schoolmaster' and dotting every village with traditional village schools which were part of the local community (Chapter III).[9] Further the idea underlying Shiksha Karmi was also tried elsewhere earlier, for example, as early as 1944, Baron Christoph von Fürer-Haimendorf, whose work among tribals in the Nizam's dominions is legendary and akin to the work of Verrier Elwin's work among tribals of North-East India, tried imparting basic education through local youth in the tribal villages of Adilabad in AP. The novelty of Shiksha Karmis therefore lies not in the originality of the basic ideas but in its scale and duration as well as its institutional and process innovations. The existing dysfunctional school was rejuvenated by replacing the regular teachers by Shiksha Karmi who were from the village and lived there, by making the curriculum flexible and relevant, and learning related to learner's environment and made joyful through games, songs, and excursions. In addition to schools, the project also operated night schools, Aangan Pathshalas (courtyard schools) for school-age girls, and Prahar Pathshalas (non-formal classes) for imparting NFE for adolescent girls. In order to improve the enrolment of girls who have to attend to siblings at home, Mahila Sahayogis (women escorts) were appointed to escort girls from home to school and back, and take care of girls' siblings during school hours. The minimum education qualification for a Shiksha Karmi was class VIII for men and class V for women. In the selection of Shiksha Karmis, the preference of the villagers was taken into account, and greater preference was given to willingness and ability to function as a social worker rather than education qualifications alone. The appointment was on contract; after eight years of satisfactory service, Shiksha Karmis were put in the regular grade. To overcome lack of educational qualifications, Shiksha Karmis were given intensive induction training as well as periodic refresher course. The training gave emphasis on working with the community for ensuring universal access and retention. An NGO, Sandhan, assisted the project in developing curriculum, training,

[9] M.K. Gandhi, *Future of India*.

motivation, planning, and evaluation. The Institute of Development Studies, Jaipur, assisted the project by organizing participatory evaluation. A major institutional innovation was the management of the project by a parastatal organization embedded in the department and yet functioning autonomously and associating actors outside government in the governance structures. The design of the parstaatal organization implicitly followed the celebrated thesis of the famous business historian, Alfred Chandler Jr., that organizational structures should follow the compelling strategy.[10] Strategy is the determination of long-term goals and objectives, courses of action, and allocation of resources, while structure is the way the organization is put together to administer the strategy, with all the hierarchies and lines of authority that the strategy implies. An innovative strategy for the universalization of elementary education requires complementary innovation in administration structures and procedures; this necessarily involves a certain amount of debureaucratization of structures. The management of the Shiksha Karmi project was vested in an autonomous Rajasthan Shiksha Karmi Board with representatives from government and the NGOs. The Executive Council of the Board is headed by the State Education Secretary, and the Governing Council by the State Education Minister. The Executive Council manages the programme and takes decisions on issues pertaining to finance, management, and support to NGOs, while the Governing Council annually reviews the progress and issues policy guidelines. This innovative structure was modified and adapted in all externally funded projects that were started subsequently, except for the Janashala programme.

SIDA funded Phases I (1987–94) and II (1992–8) of Shiksha Karmi. DFID stepped in after SIDA terminated assistance following the Pokhran nuclear test in May 1998. Phase III (1999–2004) was originally envisaged to last for five years but was extended by two more years. During Phase I, an expenditure of Rs 21.2 crore was incurred, of which SIDA provided 90 per cent and the rest was born by the Rajasthan government. During Phase II, an expenditure of Rs 72.21 crore was incurred; however, at 50 per cent the share of the Rajasthan government was higher than in Phase I. In 1988–9, the Shiksha Karmis

[10] Alfred Dupont Chandler, Jr., *Strategy And Structure: Chapters in the History of the American Industrial Enterprise*, Cambridge, MA: MIT Press, 1962.

project operated 2,600 schools, 48,229 Prahar Pathashalas, and 98 Aangan Pathshalas in 146 out of a total 237 blocks in the state. 2.16 lakh children were enrolled in these institutions, of whom 40 per cent were girls. Although retention rates at 50 per cent between class I and class V were still low, they were higher than the 30 per cent in 1989 .While overall enrolment rates did increase markedly, the gender gap did not close significantly. Thus, while the enrolment of boys had increased from 50 to 88 per cent, that of girls had increased only from 21 per cent to 65 per cent.[11] During Phase III (1999–2004), an expenditure of Rs 70.13 crore was incurred, of which DFID contributed 50 per cent; in the extended period of Phase III, an expenditure of Rs 72.21 crore was incurred; however, the share of the DFID was higher at 75 per cent. When the project ended, it operated 3,477 schools, 1,885 Prehar Pathshalas, and 97 Aangan Pathshalas in 3,650 villages in 150 blocks of 31 districts in Rajasthan. The enrolment in these institutions was 2.74 lakh children; in all 8,655 Shiksha Karmis were employed. It was claimed that learning achievement was as good as in regular schools. The basic idea underlying Shiksha Karmi is very appealing, and it received wide recognition and inspired quite a few states to go in for similar alternate schools in habitations that have no schools. The most celebrated of such state programmes is the MP Education Guarantee Scheme (EGS) started in the year 1997 (Chapter 20). However, the word 'Shiksha Karmi' got debased as it was used in many states for teachers appointed on a contract with no fixity of tenure and a remuneration which was often less than a third of a regular teacher's.

Exceptions prove the rule. As K sat through the discussions on NFE, meetings of the Grant-in-Aid Committee, which sanctioned proposals for establishing NFE centres by NGOs, and review meetings of implementation, K could not help feel that NFE was a good example of the Indian mindset at work. A 1990 study estimated that by 1995, nearly 30 million children, a third of child population in the age group 6–11, had to be served by non-formal programmes.[12] Yet,

[11] Government of India, Planning Commission, 'Partnerships in Education: Shiksha Karmi and Lok Jumbish, Rajasthan', in *Successful Government Innovations and Best Practices: Experience from Indian States*, New Delhi: Academic Foundation, 2003, pp. 90–101.

[12] National Institute of Educational Planning and Administration, *Education for All by 2000: An Indian Perspective*, New Delhi, March 1990.

even when NFE was at its peak, the reported enrolment did not exceed 6.5 million; centres run by NGOs accounted for only about a tenth of the reported enrolment. The reason for inadequate coverage is not far to seek for more attention was paid to dilate upon the attributes of good NFE and its essentiality than to think through the organizational challenges and come up with concrete and coherent solutions. As a concept, the strength and attractiveness of NFE lay in its flexibility and client specificity. Children out of school varied diversely in their socio-economic situation, educational attainment, and learning needs. It was possible in principle for NFE to introduce in diversity in the timings, curriculum, and pace of learning so as to match the diversity of the clientele; however, that entailed planning responsibility being totally decentralized and placed as close to the learners as possible',[13] and treating each NFE class being a specific setting. On a small scale, it is possible to approximate the organization and instruction of NFE to the ideal. K knew of many such examples within government. Thus, Kumud Bansal, Secretary Education, Maharashtra, organized NFE for children of parents who migrated to sugar cane districts in Maharashtra during the sugarcane harvesting seasons; an enterprising Director of the AP DPEP Society organized NFE for children of labourers from Orissa who worked in brick kilns around Hyderabad. He got Oriya primers all the way from his counterpart in Orissa. While small could be 'beautiful', the large was beset with problems as the rub lay in scaling up. The problems of scaling up were never thought through adequately. It is difficult for any large organization, even if it were an NGO and, not to speak of the governmental entities, to provide the enormous flexibility required to manage myriads of specific non-formal settings, and to imbue instructors and supervisors with the commitment and empathy required to teach out-of-school children most of whom are hardened by the harshness of life. Not every NGO or government entity could secure the strong institutional support and dedicated leadership of the Shiksha Karmi project. NFE centres were similar to adult education centres. Even while it was abandoning adult literacy centres on the ground that such centres were dysfunctional, DOE was encouraging state governments to establish NFE centres, glossing over the

[13] David Evans, *The Planning of Non-formal Education*, Paris: International Institute of Educational Planning, 1981, p. 86.

question how such centres could be made to succeed when their adult education counterparts did not.

NGOs were considered as a great white hope by the CSS of NFE; however, it was not easy to identify enough number of NGOs which were committed to working with the poor and disadvantaged, and were efficient and immune to the lure of making money without delivering results. What was needed was an effective, institutionalized arrangement for identifying and accrediting NGOs; such an arrangement did not exist. Ideally, self-regulation would have been ideal but attempts by some activists to introduce self-regulation fell through because of the aversion of many NGOs to accept the idea that external screening and scrutiny of their activities were desirable. Many central government departments extended financial assistance to NGOs for programmes administered by then; yet the standard procedure put in place to screen the NGOs was inadequate. It did not prevent hucksters who saw the governmental financial support as a business opportunity for accessing central government funding; yet at the same time, many genuine NGOs were frustrated with the elaborate process as well as the caprice of the inspecting officials. What was in place was a system of trial and error; however, the media, audit, and parliamentary committees were unforgiving when instances of error came to public notice. This, in turn, set in a vicious cycle of making the process more stringent, aggravating the hassles of genuine NGOs, and exacerbating adverse selection of NGOs. Having no mechanism of their own, central government departments relied on their state counterparts to verify the competence and bona fides of NGOs applying for assistance, and to monitor the implementation of the programme by the NGOs assisted by them. However, it was not unusual for the central government departments to directly fund NGOs without the intermediation of the state government departments on the ground that the latter did not recommend the cases of some NGOs because of either the cussedness of the officials concerned or political considerations. This often resulted in substitution of subjectivity by one level of government by another. Bordia brought to bear on the identification of NGOs his extraordinary passion for headhunting; however, there was only that much an individual could do. Further, headhunting by Bordia was inevitably subjective, and his eagerness to promote NGOs of his choice, if need be in relaxation of the eligibility criteria, sometime led to unpleasant situations for officials of the

Internal Financial Division who had the responsibility to ensure that the criteria were fulfilled in each and every case, as well as for officials of the state government. NGOs that were chosen directly by Bordia did not bother about state government officials, and this attitude vitiated the relationship between such NGOs and state government officials who were duty bound to monitor the performance of those NGOs. And, it was not unusual for Bordia to change his opinion about an NGO of whom initially he thought highly of. Further the guidelines provided that for being eligible to receive grant an NGO should have been in existence for three years; however, the guidelines also provided that this eligibility criterion cold be relaxed in case of deserving NGOs. The scope for relaxation acted as a thin edge of the wedge for a minister's office to exert pressure on officers dealing with the grants to approve cases in which they were interested. All in all, the process for selection of NGOs was dysfunctional, and to say the least, direct funding of NGOs by the central government departments in a vast country like ours was queer. All in all, the true believers in NFE were over-optimistic in their expectations about the scale at which NFE could be operated.

The pedagogic objectives that the true believers expected from NFE were no less over-optimistic. The curriculum was expected to be custom-built for the learning needs of the learners; the learners were to be permitted to learn at their own pace and at timings suitable for them; the quality of NFE was expected to be comparable to formal schooling, and the learners were to be permitted to laterally enter the school system should they chose to do so. Fulfilling all these objectives simultaneously was the pedagogic equivalent of squaring the circle. The closer the curriculum of NFE was to that of the school, the easier was the lateral entry to the school system; there was a cost though. The learner had to put in longer hours each day, which he might not be able to; or, alternately, he would have to have extraordinary motivation for staying put in each class for a long period, longer than he would have to spend in the school. Compared to school teachers, non-formal instructors were less qualified and less paid, and except in exceptional cases of extraordinarily high motivation of instructors and learners, it was difficult for the quality of NFE to be on par with that of schooling. All in all, as with great problems of life, there are only awkward adjustments and no neat solutions to the challenge of imparting education to out-of-school children. That being so, pragmatic educators went by the principle of the best being the enemy of the good, and limited the pedagogic objectives. Thus, Gokhale and Parulekar were prepared to settle for a curriculum that was limited to three Rs, holding that banishing mass illiteracy was the first priority, and quality could wait. Or to give another example, the M.V. Foundation organized NFE as a bridge programme of limited scope, namely to acclimatize out-of-school children to the school ambiance and facilitate their joining schools. The rhetoric of NFE ruled out anything but the best.

All in all, the basic premise underlying Dvaita was unexceptionable, for to eschew any alternative to schooling on ideological considerations in the face of millions of out-of-school children was to flaunt a dogmatism that would do pride to the Grand Inquisitor of Seville in Dostoyevsky's *Brothers Karamazov* or a die-hard Stalinist culture commissar. However, the dvaitins were not faultless as they shirked away from the million-dollar question as to how NFE could be provided on a scale required for millions of out-of-school children, and how lateral movement from non-formal stream to formal education system could in actuality be ensured on a large scale. To be honest, when he was under the tutelage of Bordia, K did not recognize the challenges intrinsic to NFE with the clarity he has now, for that clarity is the product of experiential knowledge he had accumulated coupled with decades of reflection. However, even then, K instinctively realized the limitations of NFE. His position was in between that of the Dvaitins and Advaitins; he was a *Vishistadvaitin* (qualified monism) who strongly believed that UEE could be achieved mainly through a school system with an enhanced reach, grasp, and quality and yet was catholic to encourage promising NFE initiatives. Realization, like freedom, could be a burden. The ordeal of coping with Bordia's work style and swings in his moods was exacerbated by Bordia's angst arising from ideological and temperamental differences with Bordia. K could not believe that with his powerful intellect and rich administrative experience, Bordia was not aware of the limitations of NFE, and yet all along he went about as if an NFE programme large enough to encompass all out-of-school children could be put in place, and all the pedagogic objectives could be realized.

To jump the story, Carol Bellamy succeeded Jim Grant as Executive Director, and under her helmsmanship UNICEF began to actively espouse the UN Convention on the Rights of the Child (CRC) and adopted a rights approach to its operations. Thereafter, child rights acquired ascendancy in the vocabulary of discourse of NGOs, and the Advaita School gained ascendancy. The UNICEF Resident Representative who wanted UEE to be tackled like immunization labelled NFE as educational apartheid. From the mid-1990s, there was increasing demand for declaring free and compulsory elementary education to be a fundamental right, and to abolish child labour in its entirety so that government was obligated to provide enough schools and parents were obligated to send their children to school. The RTE Act, 2009, that was enacted after the Constitution was amended in 2002 and UEE made a fundamental right, relies exclusively on schooling. Suffice to say, Advaita had triumphed, and the theological dispute between the Dvaita and Advaita schools is now consigned to the limbo of history. When the RTE Act came into force as many as 37.5 lakh children were enrolled in alternative schooling funded by SSA. SSA was required to mainstream all such children in regular schools.

Official life presents comic interludes. Once Bordia demitted office and S.V. Giri succeeded him, the department was suffused with a refreshing breeze of freedom, and the officials felt free to express their views without inhibition. G.R. Khairnar, an overzealous official of Bombay Municipal Corporation, was very much in the news for taking on no less than Sharad Pawar, Chief Minister of Maharashtra, and was much lionized by the media for acts which an inquiry committee headed by a High Court judge held to be over-stepping of authority and making wilful misstatements. The department had a Khairnar on hand when the undersecretary dealing with NFE declared that it was a total failure in an article he published in the *Times of India* titled 'Removing the Stigma of Child Labour'. The Press Information Officer of the department whose job was to project the department and its activities in favourable light was grievously upset, and requested Giri to take action against the undersecretary for publishing an article without obtaining the prior permission of the government as required under the Conduct Rules. In turn, the matter was remitted to K as head of the administration division. K held that the undersecretary no doubt made sweeping observations, was indiscrete, and violated the Conduct Rules; however, punishment was not expedient. He gave vent to widely prevalent views, and punishing him would make him a martyr, place the department in an unfavourable light, and give enormous publicity to the article and his pronouncement that NFE was a failure. It was better to emulate the example of senior officers during the Raj, as well as K's early days in service, and be indulgent to the folly of youth. When a young officer committed an indiscretion, the senior would call for him, give him a dressing down, and close the case recording that the officer was spoken to. That was what K did with that undersecretary.

V

*SĀ VIDYĀ YĀ VIMUKTAYE**

Bliss it was in that dawn to be alive
But to be young was very heaven

William Wordsworth, *The Prelude*

Of all the programmes K was associated with, the one for which K has the fondest memories is Mahila Samakhya (MS), which means women speaking with the same voice. The programme was just over a year old when K joined DOE and there was great excitement all around. As he got acquainted with the programme, the imagery which cropped in K's mind was that of a mountain stream descending from snowy hills with crystal-clear bubbling water and a torrential pace which seemingly attempted to wash out the rock boulders which stood in its way. An ideologue himself, what impressed K most was the ideological conviction and the Promethean spirit of the inner circle of the programme. The expectations were so high that even the sky did not seem a limit. The programme was expected to grow into a major, if not the main, vehicle for women's empowerment in the country. The programme was purportedly in a pilot phase, and was being implemented in 10 districts spread over Gujarat, Karnataka, and UP. Looking back, the expression 'pilot phase' was a misnomer in that unlike an utterly novel programme there was absolute clarity about the manner in which the programme should move ahead. Figuratively, the programme did not look like a toddler stumbling and trying to walk; it was a youthful

* Knowledge is that which liberates.

sprinter bracing to win the race. This was because MS was attempting to scale up the Women's Development Programme (WDS) which was started five years earlier in six districts of Rajasthan when Bordia was the Development Commissioner. To mix metaphors, the learning curve was skimmed down a great deal, and the path that was to be traversed was already marked even if not paved with cement and concrete. About a year and half later, in January 1992, MS was started in Bihar as part of BEP; as would be elaborated later, it was distinct from MS elsewhere in that it was not ethereal and more focussed on the education of girls. MS in BEP was adopted as a model by DPEP and the MS interventions of BEP tried out in the DPEP states. By the time K's association with MS ended in 1996, the programme was extended to AP; it was being implemented in 2,252 villages spread over 16 districts in four states (three of AP, four each of Gujarat and UP, and five in Karnataka). In terms of outlay, it was a pretty small programme with an annual outlay of the order of Rs 4 crore, infinitesimally small in comparison with the outlay of any other programme of DOE or of State Education Departments. Yet it had a unique élan. In addition to the regular MS programme implemented with Dutch assistance, in 1996, BEP-style MS was being implemented in 2,252 villages spread over seven districts of BEP, six of the UP Basic Education Project, and three each of the districts of Assam and MP covered by DPEP.

MS was truly an exceptional programme in many respects, and sought to demonstrate the transformative power of education, education in the loftiest sense of liberating the learner from ignorance and bondage. Even in societies where over decades successive waves of feminist movement had enhanced the status of women, subtle discrimination exists in various forms. A good example is the *glass ceiling* which perpetuates disparity in salaries, and acts as a formidable barrier to women rising to the top positions in corporate world, politics, and government. In a society like ours where even after six decades of working a democratic Constitution the society continues to be a jumble of castes and communities and the principle that every citizen is entitled to equal consideration as an individual without regard to gender is not even accepted as a notion by large numbers, the discrimination is more open; the *khap panchayat* is one of the many manifestations of a patriarchal social order. Suffice it to say that few women in the world are exempt from the need to struggle against the destiny which biology and social values attempt to impose on women.

Traditionally, one can discern three strands of efforts to eliminate the discrimination against women: legal, economic, and psychological. Figuratively the legal effort seeks to replace the old *Manusmriti* which declared *na stree swatantramarhati* (no woman is entitled to freedom) by a new *smriti* (code of laws) which declares that a woman is equal to a man in all respects, and outlaws social practices which reduce women to the status of chattels. The new smriti also includes laws which positively discriminate in favour of women such as reservation for women in educational institutions, employment, and panchayat raj bodies. The legal approach also includes developing international covenants such as the Convention on the Elimination of Discrimination against Women (CEDAW), 1979, ensuring that all national laws are amended so as to be in conformity with CEDAW, and further ensuring that the amended laws are earnestly enforced. The economic approach seeks to enhance opportunities for women in education, employment, and income generation in the belief that the enhancement of economic status of women would lead to enhancement of their social status. The economic approach could be dubbed a Marxian approach if one attaches far too importance to the proposition that people with economic power control society; as women acquire economic power, they begin to share with men control of the society, and unequal gender relations would cease to exist. Most development and welfare programmes adopt the economic approach, be they the employment generation and asset creation programmes of yesteryears, or the current programmes built around the formation of women's self-help groups (SHGs). By happenstance, the genesis of the SHG affinity movement was coeval with WDS; while WDS started in 1984, the first SHGs were formed in 1985.[1] Going by contemporary accounts, SHGs are being used in many parts of the country to sensitize and motivate women to struggle against iniquities and malgovernance. If true, economic opportunity could as well be the entry point for the process of socially and politically empowering women. The economic approach commends

[1] Aloysius P. Fernandez, 'History and Spread of the Self-Help Affinity Group Movement in India', Occasional Papers, Knowledge for Development Effectiveness, Rome: International Fund for Agricultural Development, 2006.

encouraging participation of girls and women in education with a view to enhance their opportunities for employment and to take advantage of various women-oriented programmes of governments.

In contrast to the legal and economic approaches, the psychological approach seeks to eliminate gender discrimination by erasing widely prevalent stereotyped, negative images of women. Paraphrasing the famous credo of the UNESCO charter, the MS implicitly proceeds from the belief that it is in the minds of men and women that the defences of a just gender order should be built. Traditionally, educationists had sought to mould human mind and alter values and attitudes through changes in curricula, textbooks, gender sensitization of teachers and educational administrators, and transaction of curricula; likewise, governments attempted to gender sensitize its functionaries. Such an approach can be compared to the theory of economic development which was regnant till 1970s, and posited that the benefits of economic growth would automatically trickle down to the poor. The trickle-down theory got discredited when, during the 1960s, many developing countries registered record economic growths and yet the benefits of economic growth did not trickle down to the poor as much as expected, and employment did not grow as expected; consequently, the new conventional wisdom commended a frontal attack on poverty. Likewise, the attitudinal change expected from curricular reform and sensitization programmes may fall short of expectations, and therefore a frontal attack on gender inequity has to be waged through a new pedagogy which goes beyond conventional views on education. Bondage begins in the minds of women who are prepared to acquiesce in the discriminatory social values and attitudes; consequently, a frontal attitude on gender inequities succeeds best when the discriminatory social values and attitudes entrapped in the psyche of women are shattered. MS added a gender dimension to Freirean pedagogy. The basic idea of MS is that it is necessary to shape a new consciousness among the women so that they strive to change their destiny and thereby alter the social reality; conscientization is best done in collectives (*sanghas*) and these collectives could lead the struggle for gender equality by serving as forums in which women could reflect critically on their predicament, analyse their position in relation to their wider society, shed the negative image that is etched on their psyche, and develop the self-confidence to challenge the unequal gender order. Central to MS was the creation of sanghas in each of the villages covered by the programme. All in all, MS sought to recondition the psyche of women, and it can be loosely compared with the psychoanalytic approach of Freud. MS is exceptional in that unlike all other government programmes it did not offer any services or pecuniary benefits or incentives; it offered only freedom from bondage. It gave full freedom to conscientized women's groups to choose the activity they wish to pursue. Over the quarter of a century that MS had been in existence, the sanghas chose a wide variety of issues including seeking literacy and numeracy skills for themselves, education of their children, vocational skills such as repairing handpumps, health issues, livelihood issues, participation in local governance, and ensuring effective delivery and functioning of government services and structures. What was also remarkable about MS was that it was led by modernist, educated, emancipated feminists, and yet rather than work with the relatively easier target group of urban educated women, they chose to conscientize poor illiterate women. They were not in a hurry to show success.

Only an exceptional, unconventional civil servant like Bordia could have conceptualized an exceptional programme like WDP and its progeny MS, and furthermore organized it as a unique partnership between the central government, select state governments, and feminists. The section in NPE, 1986, dealing with 'Education for Women's Equality' is quite eloquent:

> 4.2 Education will be used as an agent of basic change in the status of woman. In order to neutralise the accumulated distortions of the past, there will be a well-conceived edge in favour of women. The National Education System will play a positive, interventionist role in the empowerment of women. It will foster the development of new values through redesigned curricula, textbooks, the training and orientation of teachers, decision-makers and administrators, and the active involvement of educational institutions. This will be an act of faith and social engineering. Women's studies will be promoted as a part of various courses and educational institutions encouraged to take up active programmes to further women's development.
>
> 4.3 The removal of women's illiteracy and obstacles inhibiting their access to, and retention in, elementary education will receive overriding priority, through provision of special support services, setting of time targets, and effective monitoring. Major emphasis will be laid on

> women's participation in vocational, technical and professional education at different levels. The policy of non-discrimination will be pursued vigorously to eliminate sex stereo-typing in vocational and professional courses and to promote women's participation in non-traditional occupations, as well as in existing and emergent technologies.

Its eloquence notwithstanding, implementation of NPE, 1986, did not call for developing a programme anchored in Freirean pedagogy; it would have been adequate if the traditional approach of encouraging the participation of girls in education, restructuring the curriculum, and sensitization of teachers and educational administrators was implemented with verve. But for Bordia, MS would have never come into existence. Once he succeeded Anand Sarup as Education Secretary in March 1987, he went full steam ahead in conceptualizing and grounding the ethereal programme that MS was building upon the experiences of the WDS.[2] Common to WDS and MS are three defining features. First is the provisional nature of the project document; the logical corollary of this proposition is that a project continually evolves , and except for the broad financial parameters and structures for policy direction and implementation everything else is in a state of flux. Consequently, there is infinite scope for innovation, trial, and testing as well as for adapting the programme to suit the requirements of every particular group, area, or problem. The second is the firm refusal to set any quantitative targets in the belief that they exert pressure on functionaries to exaggerate performance and, at the same time, run counter to the overarching objective of the programme by constricting the time and space required for conscientization. Bordia often used to quip that UP registered a phenomenal increase in enrolment after the Twenty Point Programme of Indira Gandhi was expanded to include enrolment of children in elementary schools; the third defining feature was the assignment of a predominant role to NGOs in the conceptualization, implementation, monitoring, and evaluation of the programme. Figuratively, the government was to be like the crow which offers its nest to the cuckoo (NGOs) to lay its eggs. These defining features were articles of faith for Bordia which he sought to extend even to basic

[2] Maitreyi Das, 'The Women's Development Program in Rajasthan: A Case Study in Group Formation for Women's Development', Working Papers, Women in Development, World Bank, WPS 913, 1992.

education projects. However, TLCs were exempted from the articles of faith. They were driven by a target orientation: the districts covered by TLCs were required to acquire 90 per cent literacy in the age group 15–35 to become eligible to be declared fully literate.

In its initial years, education was not central to MS except in the sense of conscientizing women. MS questioned the perception that literacy had to be the entry point and corner stone of adult education, and contended that education was not to be confused with literacy. It turned the argument of literacy campaigners upside down by arguing that empowerment was a critical precondition for the participation of women and girls in the formal or NFE. The question which should come up first adult education in the broadest sense or literacy was one of the contentious issues during the review of NPE, 1986, by the Ramamurti Committee. The Committee precisely echoed the MS philosophy when it drew a distinction between adult education and literacy, and recommended that literacy should come in only as and when it came to be perceived as a felt need by the learners. Against this backdrop, the Committee decried the undue emphasis on literacy in the TLCs and other activities of the National Literacy Mission (NLM), all the mores so as the Ernakulum model of TLC was deemed it inappropriate for districts with high levels of illiteracy. The Committee's stance upset Bordia a great deal, and DOE, under his direction, found fault with the Ramamurti Committee for putting forth propositions that did not conform to 'well established postulates regarding adult education', and ignoring the symbiotic relation between adult education and literacy, as well as of the fact that 'literacy provides minimal entry point to education and through this, access to the world of information, communication, modernisation, and innovation'. Truth to be told, consistency was not a virtue prized by Bordia; as with lawyers, his propositions and arguments were contingent upon the context. To put it more charitably, the challenge of educational and societal reconstruction required multiple approaches which might be based on divergent propositions. If in TLCs literacy was the entry point for adult education and conscientization, it was the other way round in MS.

Project Formulation started in March 1988; Vimala Ramachandran and Srilatha Batliwala developed the programme based on discussions with diverse groups across the country. Vimala Ramachandran went on to be the first National Project Director and Srilatha Batliwala the first State Programme Director in Karnataka. With Dutch funding, the programme was started in April 1989. The organizational structures at the national, state, district, and village levels were so designed so as to provide ample room for enlisting activists and entrusting the implementation of the programme. At the apex was a National Resource Group (NRG) to provide policy advice and guide the implementation; it predominantly comprised gender and development experts and activists. Officials in charge of the programme in DOE like Bordia and K (after he joined DOE) were also members. Except for the ministerial supporting staff, the programme staff including the National and State Project Directors programme staff were gender or development experts or activists drawn from outside the government. At the state level, the management structure of MS differed significantly from that of WDP in that the management was entrusted to a hybrid structure which was legally distinct and 'joined-up' with the state government, and not to a state government department. In each of the states chosen for implementation, the programme was managed by a society registered under the State's Societies Registration Act; the General Council was headed by the Chief Minister or the Education Minister, and the Executive Committee by the State Education Secretary. Like NRG, gender and development experts and activists were associated with the governing bodies of the state society; so were DOE representatives so that they could guide the implementation of the programme and yet at the same time keep track of implementation. This society model of implementation was later adopted by basic education projects such as BEP, UP Basic Education Project, Lok Jumbish, DPEP, and SSA.

A National Project Office was located in DOE with the overall responsibility of implementing the programme and interacting with the funding agency. As a matter of deliberate design, Bordia chose to set up an office within DOE instead of setting up a society at the national level so that the programme is insulated from interference by the minister. From the days of Nurul Hasan, if not earlier, many ministers in charge of Ministry of Education and later MHRD, irrespective of the party to which they belonged, had been packing the organizations attached to their ministry with their favourites. For instance, appointing ruling party loyalists to the National Commission for Women (NCW) was the rule rather than exception both during the time of

Arjun Singh as well as his ideological antipode and successor Murli Manohar Joshi. Whatever be the motive, the propriety in a democratic polity of a civil servant managing a programme to the exclusion of his minister is questionable. That apart, there is a basic contradiction in expecting the state societies to be apolitical while shying away from the formation of a national-level society on the ground that it would be politicized. The only explanation which K could surmise is that Bordia thought that the alternative of implementation by the State Education Department would be worse, and that he was confident that the state governments could be managed making use of the awe in which most provincials held GOI, and if need be, hold out the threat that the Dutch would withdraw funding to the state if it did not play by the rules set by DOE. K's own impression is that by and large ministers and chief ministers did not bother about the programme, mainly because in terms of funding as well as scale MS was so minuscule as to come to their notice. And further, in those days they would not take liberties with a programme funded by the central government and external funding agencies. Problems arose when the education secretaries were not provincials and not awed by the mystique of the Bharat Sarkar. The programme sailed smoothly in Karnataka because the first Director, Srilatha Batliwala, was suave, and socially and politically well connected. When she decided to pave the way for a successor, K had to work on his friend Teresa Bhattacharya to get an outsider who could provide leadership to the programme appointed. Even the masterly Bordia could not dissuade the Gujarat government from appointing a provincial civil service officer as state director. Problems arose in UP when the second project director had to be appointed and the state education secretary quoted chapter and verse of the society regulations to contend that DOE had no say in the appointment of the director. Mercifully the state government was dismissed and President's rule imposed before the argument was concluded. Subsequent events show that managing the state governments was a perennial challenge for the National Programme Director and DOE.[3] On the whole, it should be said that entrustment of the implementation to the state societies did not amount to be an unmanageable problem mainly because the

[3] C. Gouridasan Nair, '"Mahila Samakhya" Caught in a Spat', *The Hindu*, 1 July 2002.

programme was too small for a state secretary to bother, all the more so as any action considered to be adverse by women's groups would have elicited voluble criticism, and most senior officers did not wish to be perceived as politically incorrect male chauvinists.

MS built its mobilization and training strategies based on the WDP Programme. The Mahila Sangha was the nodal point of MS, and all activities were planned and organized around the Sangha. The Mahila Sangha was expected to provide the space where 'women can meet, be together, and begin the process of reflecting, asking questions, speaking fearlessly, thinking, analysing and above all feeling confident to articulate their needs through this collective action'.[4] They were also expected, where possible, to try and seek solutions to their problems such as fuel, fodder, drinking water, etc., by initiating action and interacting with the block and district administration. In WDP, a woman volunteer was chosen from the local community and intensely trained to mobilize women and initiate the process of reflection and conscientization; called *sathin* (literally, comrade or friend) she operated in about ten villages, and was the core link in the programme. Every community development block had a *pracheta* (literally animator or initiator) who supervised ten sathins. It was noticed in WDP that to be effective a sathin needed to co-opt another functionary like, say, the Anganwadi worker. MS took note of this fact and opted to replace the sathin by a team of two women each of whom is called *sakhi* (friend). The term pracheta was replaced by the term *sahayogini* (facilitator). At the district level, the programme was managed by the District Implementation Unit which consisted of a District Program Coordinator, a resource person, and support staff.

Interacting with the key persons associated with MS such as Sharada Jain, Srilatha Batliwala, and Abha Bhayya was a rewarding experience, and offered a fascinating glimpse of an alternate world of which K had little knowledge. Visits to the field was equally rewarding and soul-filling; tears would roll down K's cheeks when he met poor hapless women—literally the wretched of the earth—exuding confidence and Promethean defiance. However, such moments were ephemeral, and the scepticism of intellect would assert itself, and he would be seized

[4] Ministry of Human Resource Development, Department of Education, *We Can Change Our World: The Mahila Samakhya Experience*, 1997, p. 7.

by gnawing doubts. No doubt, there were telling examples of the MS strategy making a difference to the lives of women and of some sanghas leading the struggle against iniquities and malgovernance. However, K was not sure whether a few examples, however telling, were adequate to pass a judgement on a programme. Could one judge a programme solely on fleeting impressions without any hard information on how many women were conscientized, how deep and sustained was the conscientization, and what the sanghas did after the conscientization process was concluded? He was not sure. He could not help ask: empowerment for what and what it did it accomplish in concrete terms? An account of the WDS, the prototype of MS, which he read a few years after he left MS brought out that his feeling was not unique. That account noted that in the absence of the quantitative monitoring of the work done by prachetas, sathins, and the sanghas what was available were 'interesting illustrations of the kind of work which prachetas and sathins have done, the kind of processes they have set in motion—episodes which illustrate the manner in which bondage of women can be loosened and they can face in unison suppression within family, the neglect by the developmental agencies, and the oppression of the police and the criminal elements'. The question of what was to be done with the sanghas once they formed remained an open question even eight years after WDS was launched. There appeared to be a deliberate focus away from economic activities 'in part by the ideology and agenda of the individuals and NGOs (notably Institute of Development Studies, Jaipur, which provided the resource support for the programme) who have formed the top management of the program'. The question, training for what, needed to be asked as training sessions were such an intense, personal experience for the trainers as well as the trainees that it became difficult to view the outside world realistically, and sathins and prachetas internalized the idiom of women's solidarity and a new feminist self-image so completely that they sometimes lost the idiom with which to communicate with the village women.[5]

K was happy that under the leadership of Sister Sujita, MS in BEP began to focus straight away on the education of girls. *Jag-jagi* (awakening of the world), the education component of MS-BEP, was very vibrant, and undertook activities such as striving for enrolment and

[5] Maitreyi Das, 'The Women's Development Program in Rajasthan', pp. 51, 71.

retention of children of deprived groups in schools through activities such as *school tayyari karyakram* (preparing children for school), encouraging women to participate in village education committees, organizing *kishori jag-jag* (education of adolescent girls), and promoting Mahila Shiksha Kendras which helped girls who dropped from schools to prepare for the matriculation examination.[6] Apart from influencing the MS component of the UP Basic Education Project and DPEP, MS-BEP influenced MS itself; in due course, girls' education emerged as a key intervention in MS itself after a debate within NRG whether a focus on girls' education would lead to a dilution of focus on women's education and empowerment. What clinched the debate was the feedback from the field which indicated that once women were conscientized, they invariably got concerned about the futures of their girl children, and voiced strong demands for alternative learning streams that enabled adolescent girls to get an opportunity to learn. The adoption of a focus on girls' education led to the mobilization and organization of *balika/kishori* (girls and adolescents) sanghas.[7]

Come to think of it, MS is the only programme initiated in the wake of NPE, 1986, which continues to exist a quarter of century later. MS was extended to AP in 1996 and Kerala in 1998. In April 2002, the Ninth Five-Year Plan ended and so did Dutch assistance which financed MS from the beginning. MS was being implemented in over 9,000 villages in 53 districts spread over 10 states, and reportedly two lakh women were mobilized. During the Tenth Five-Year Plan, the programme was continued with the funds which spilled over from the previous plan, and in 2007, DFID stepped in as a donor, and the programme witnessed a rapid expansion. In March 2013, MS reportedly covered 11 states, 122 districts, and 39,566 villages and had mobilized about 12.7 lakh women.[8] True to the Hegelian dictum that quantity

[6] Sister Sujita, 'Case Study of Bihar Mahila Samakhya', in Carolyn Medel-Ationuevo, *Women Reading the World: Policies and Practices of Literacy in Asia*, Hamburg: UNESCO Institute for Education, 1996, pp. 59–64.

[7] Jandhyala Kameswari, 'Empowering Education: The Mahila Samakhya Experience', Background Article for the EFA Global Monitoring report 2003/4, Paris: UNESCO, p. 12.

[8] Government of India, Ministry of Human Resource Development, Department of School Education and Literacy, *Fourth Joint Review Mission of Mahila Samakhya (12 to 21 March 2013)*, p. 19.

becomes quality, MS, since 2002, is qualitatively different from that from 1989 to 2002. There is greater insistence by the government as well as DFID to expand rapidly, and to ensure that MS has a demonstrable impact. This had resulted in stipulations such as baseline surveys, coverage of minimum number of villages in every district covered by the programme so that the programme acquires a critical mass, monitoring through a results framework, and a qualitatively different modality of evaluation.[9] That apart, issues directly relevant to lives of women were brought to the forefront; MS no longer solely relies on the sangha model wherein all the members of the sangha play an active role in selecting issues to be taken by a sangha. Instead each sangha has a committee of *karyakarinis*—women who work on specific issues such as health, law, environment, employment, literacy, and political action. The remuneration which would have gone to the sakhi is paid to the sangha to be used for its activities.[10] All these changes do not fit easily with the philosophy of MS as originally conceived. Over the quarter of a century that the programme was in existence, secretaries, joint secretaries, and national project directors had come and gone in DOE; so did state education secretaries and state project directors. However, rather miraculously quite a few gender experts and activists who were associated with the programme in the initial years continued to be associated with the programme so much so they try to act as conscience keepers of the programme. All in all, Bordia's pessimistic prognosis that 'it [MS] will be destroyed' was proved wrong. Bordia based this prognosis on the fact that:

> The inherent problem [arises] because programs like this are working in a very simmering or overt manner against a system that is totally rallied against [them]. And here is a person who stands between those forces and empowering processes, if you remove that person, a dismantling [of the program] can happen.... If there is an assault on the program is led by the Government, then there is little chance of its continuance. Particularly on gender issues, it is a very serious matter.[11]

[9] Jandhyala Kameswari, 'Ruminations on Evaluation in the Mahila Samakhya Programme', *Indian Journal of Gender Studies*, 19, no. 2 (2012), pp. 211–31.

[10] Aradhana Sharma, *Logic of Empowerment in Neoliberal India*, Minneapolis: University of Minnesota Press, 2008, p. xxviii.

[11] Aradhana Sharma, *Logic of Empowerment in Neoliberal India*, p. 50.

The rationale Bordia adduced is impeccable except perhaps the proposition that a single functionary, presumably an official like himself, can defy the hostile forces of the governmental system and society, and that continuation of radical programmes such as MS require successive good-hearted supermen. If in spite of the impeccable rationale adduced by Bordia, why did MS set a record by continuing to exist for about a quarter of a century? Is it because it became less abstract and more 'result oriented'? These are million-dollar questions whose exploration would illuminate the strengths and weaknesses of the strategy adopted by MS.

MS demonstrated that radical education work could take place within a programme funded by a state whose ruling class, to say the least, is not committed to a total uprooting of the prevalent hierarchical society. MS also demonstrated that strategy could make a difference to the lives of many women. However, at the same time it is abundantly clear that the expectation that MS would emerge as a major vehicle for the empowerment of women was not fulfilled. In K's view, the expectation was not fulfilled not because the programme was located within the state or because the state and its functionaries later turned hostile to the programme but because of the limitations and internal contradictions of the strategy adopted by the programme. As a matter of deliberate strategy, MS opted for making haste slowly—rather too slowly—lest the sanctity of the process of conscientization should be compromised. However, an unintended consequence of the strategy was that MS turned out to be too minuscule to make a difference; the survival of the programme so long could be traced to the fact that it was too small to 'upset the apple cart'. By April 2002—more than a decade after the launch of the programme—when financing by the Dutch, who were more empathetic to the MS philosophy, came to an end reportedly two lakh women were mobilized spread over 9,000 villages in 53 districts spread over 10 states—figuratively a drop in the ocean of rural poor women. Even that would not have mattered if all the women conscientized took the discriminatory social order head-on, thereby radicalizing more and more women, or to draw an imagery triggering a chain reaction. This did not happen because of another element of the MS strategy: the sanghas were given total freedom to choose the issues they wished to address. No attempt was made even to systematically collect evidence on the issues individual sanghas were addressing. To draw an analogy, MS did not wish to the play the vanguard role that the Communist Party played in the Soviet Union to lead the proletariat in the right direction. Consequently, nothing prevented the sanghas from addressing bread and butter issues (such as health, public distribution, and livelihood) instead of challenging head-on the discriminatory social order. Such issues could have been addressed even without MS, for to K's knowledge there is no comparative study of the way in which MS sanghas and SHGs addressed bread and butter issues, and there is no evidence that the sangha women addressed such issues better than those organized in SHGs. In fairness to the 'founding fathers' of the programme, ideas were mooted to hive off the programme as an independent entity outside the government; however, they were given up. The idea of well-organized sanghas exiting from the government fold and coming together as federations at the level of the Community Development Block was also mooted, and some federations were indeed organized. Yet as the Fourth Joint Review Mission (2013) noted, the 'thorny questions' of what autonomy of federations means and the implications of such federations for the programme are yet to be critically addressed.

When MS was conceptualized, there was a turf war between the Department of Women and Child Development (WCD) and DOE, both constituents of MHRD, where the programme should be located. DOE won because of the forceful personality of Bordia and the keen desire of gender activists that MS should be located in DOE so as to send a strong message that gender issues should not be the concern of a single department of the central or state government but of the governments as a whole, and further that if located in WCD it would be more difficult to depart from the tradition of women being considered to be passive recipients of welfare generously offered by the government instead of being treated as autonomous individuals capable of intelligent choices and independent action. The expectations from locating MS in DOE might have been fulfilled if MS grew to scale, and had emerged as a major programme competing with other programmes for women. As MS was located in DOE and State Education Departments and not in the nodal departments in central and state governments with the responsibility for the empowerment and economic betterment of girls and women, the MS methodology was not mainstreamed, an example of the law of unintended consequences. The lesson that K would like to draw from the MS experience is that while a focus on processes is important it cannot be the be all and end all of programmes; it is necessary to be have targets though not driven by them. Not to have any targets because of the apprehension that a programme that has targets would be driven by them would be like throwing out the baby with the bath water. Bordia himself recognized this point with TLCs. Output and outcome orientation cannot be altogether *verboten*.

VI

AKSHARA KERALAM TO *AKSHARA BHARATHAM**

Total Literacy Campaigns loomed large during K's tutelage under Bordia. They figured conspicuously in most meetings that K attended, constituted a 'hot button' topic during the review of NPE, 1986, and came up again and again in Bordia's intimate conversations with his acolytes which, illuminated his inner thoughts. Once the campaign approach to achieve 'total literacy' was demonstrated successfully first in Kottayam city and then in Ernakulum district, the dissemination of the TLC model was extremely fast. By mid-1991, TLCs, to use contemporary neologism, had gone viral. In May 1991, Frederico Mayor, Director General (DG), UNESCO, made a pilgrimage to Wardha, home to Mahatma Gandhi in his later years, to declare Wardha district fully literate. Kerala Sastra Sahitya Praishad (KSSP), which collaborated with the state government in making Ernakulum district wholly literate, was awarded the UNESCO King Sejong Literacy Prize for the year 1990, and the West Bengal government the UNESCO Noma Literacy Prize for the year 1991. In his address to the Education Commission of the UNESCO General Conference in October 1991, Bordia could proudly announce that 12 districts spread over the states of Kerala, Pondicherry, and West Bengal had become totally literate, that about 60 lakh people were made functionally literate in these 12 districts, that a campaign to make Kerala *Akshara Keralam* (a Kerala which

* From Totally Literate Kerala to Totally Literate India.

is totally literate) was under way and that 'the literacy wave which started from the southern and eastern provinces was now beginning to extend to practically all the States of the country'. In 1992, Puduvai Arivoli Iyakkam (Movement for Light of Knowledge), Pondicherry, won the UNESCO King Sejong Literacy Prize. By January 1992, TLCs were in progress in 65 districts, and over 10 lakh volunteers and 4 crore learners were reportedly participating in the TLCs. A movement of this scale reminded many of the freedom struggle; many literacy enthusiasts claimed that a second freedom struggle was under way, that very soon India would become *Akshara Bharatham* (an India that is totally literate) and that very soon the masses would seize their destiny with both hands, and push the country on to a fast track to a just and equal society and polity. No other programme launched in the wake of NPE, 1986, and its POA attracted so much of media attention, largely due to the imaginative use of media by Bordia and later by Sudeep Banerjee.

Why and What Adult Education?

The distinction between literacy and education is too well known to require elaboration. 'Literacy is not enough' is a creed that dominates the praxis of adult education whatever the modality of organizing adult education, be it the campaign mode or teaching in adult education centres. It has been axiomatic that literacy work should be conflated with adult education designed to perform specific functions; however, adult education programmes vary in the manner in which they define functionality. Functionality in turn is designed by the organizers of the adult education programme to further social, political and economic objectives they desire. Historically, the first and foremost objective of adult education campaigns had been legitimation and consolidation of the regime, and uprooting the *otherness* of the citizens. However, this objective is perceived differently by Marxist and single-party governments on the one hand and democratic governments on the other. In Marxist countries, be it the Soviet Union, China, Cuba, or Mengistu's Ethiopia, loyalty to the leader, the regime, the party, and antipathy to the class enemies were the most important elements of functionality. Literacy campaigns were often intertwined with campaigns against class enemies and enemies of the state such as *kulaks* and capitalists.

Women, given their low literacy rate, were regarded as having the highest potential for becoming the 'modernizers' of Soviet society. To further extend their reach to the peasant community, the Bolshevik's built reading rooms in villages across the country. Serving as a propaganda centre rather than library, a literate peasant would act as the room's *Red Reader* and lead discussions on texts sent by the party directive with members of the local community. Attendance was most often mandatory, as the reading rooms proved to be one of the party's most successful propaganda tools.[1] Although the Bolshevik leadership which succeeded Lenin believed that literacy was a political tool, they also viewed literacy as an important step towards modernization of society and economy. Thus, some of the agitational pamphlets published during the campaign exhorted women to learn and read in order to ensure the health of their children. The literate worker, Bolsheviks believed, would be more productive and so increase the economic well-being of the society.[2] On the whole, in countries with Marxist and single-party governments political functionality had been the primary objective of mass literacy campaigns and other objectives secondary.

Like Marxist and single-party governments, newly formed democratic countries also sought to uproot the *otherness* of the citizens. During the 1950s and 1960s, among newly formed nations, nation building was voguish. Nation building had three components. The first is crafting a distinct national identity and instilling in their citizens a strong sense of collective destiny and purpose; the underlying challenge is captured by the saying that 'Italy has been made; now we must make Italians'. The second component is civic education which educates the populace of their rights and duties as citizens. The third component is what could be called development education enabling the populace to participate more effectively in the economic and social progress of their community, to avail the benefits of development and to acquire the values and attitudes needed for modernization of the society and economy. Modernization requires a replacement of traditional

[1] Peter Kenez, *The Birth of the Propaganda State: Soviet Methods of Mass Mobilization, 1917–1929*. New York: Cambridge University Press, 1985, pp. 137–8.

[2] Charles E. Clark, *Uprooting Otherness: The Literacy Campaign in NEP-era Russia*, Cranbury, NJ: Associated University Presses, 2001, p. 9.

values and attitudes such as fatalism and adopting attitudes such as diligence, punctuality, preparedness for change, and alertness to opportunities as they arise in a changing world. Adult education programmes which went by the name of fundamental or social education catered to these needs of nation-building. As nations ceased to be nascent, economic functionality gained ascendancy; the predominant objective of adult education programmes came to be acquainting the illiterate farmers and workers with the ability to apply modern technologies. A defining characteristic of a democracy is the space provided for dissent; it was but natural that individuals and groups questioned the nature of the regime in which they lived or, alternately, the way the regime failed to function as it *ought to*. These dissenters saw the function of adult education to shape a new consciousness among the poor and oppressed so that they strive to change their destiny and thereby alter the social reality. Under the influence of Paulo Freire this conceptualization of adult educators gained ascendancy among adult educators in the 1970s. With the ascendancy of the language of rights from mid-1980s, the objective of adult education was to enable the poor to assert their rights and receive their entitlements. Suffice to say, one can notice changing fashions in the conceptualization of the functionality of adult education; the reigning fashion at a given moment, or to use jargon paradigm, usually shapes the objectives and design of adult education in individual countries. Social education was the dominant fashion till late 1950s, economically functional literacy in the 1960s, conscientization-driven adult education in the 1970s and early 1980s, and right- and entitlement-driven adult education from mid-1980s. While adult educators may have grand objectives in mind, adult learners can spare only a limited amount of time for adult education because of the exacting demand which work places on working men and women, and domestic chores on all women. That being so, the practical question that arises is how much emphasis should be laid on literacy, and how much on other aspects of adult education. This is not a hypothetical question even though it is often evaded in the rhetoric of adult education programmes. In practice, however, only some aspects of the literacy so defined get attended to and subjected to evaluation.

Mass literacy campaigns are a class apart from the 'night schools' designed to impart 3 'R's to adult illiterates mainly because of their scope in terms of functionality and intensity of coverage. Historically, mass literacy campaigns were preceded by politically landmark events. India also is not an exception to the historical trend if one could think in time and recall the mass literacy campaigns that were started by the Congress Party governments in provinces in 1938. The formation of these governments constituted a major political transformation in that provincial governments were, for the first time, vested with full autonomy under the GOI Act, 1935, and Congress Party, which was so far engaged in political struggle with the Raj, assumed office for the first time at the provincial level. The political nature of these campaigns was made explicit by Dr Syed Mahmud, Education Minister, Bihar, who chaired a pace-setting CABE Committee on Adult Literacy (1938–9); in his address to that Committee, he quoted Lenin's saying that 'The liquidation of illiteracy is not a political problem; it is a condition without which it is impossible to speak of politics. An illiterate man is outside of politics, and before he can be brought in he must be taught the alphabet. Without this there can be no politics- only rumours, gossip, tales and superstitions'.[3] The course of these campaigns was documented[4] by Frank C. Laubach, an American literacy pioneer who developed the famous technique of 'Each One Teach One' in the Philippines; this slogan and technique was much in vogue in India when K was State Education Secretary. Laubach was in India from 1935 to 1939, addressing a number of adult education conferences and developing innovative literacy primers based on images and keywords in many Indian languages. In his promotion of adult education, Laubach received the support of the Mahatma, Tagore, Rajagopalachari, and Nehru. The duration of these campaigns varied from 4 to 6 months, and the learners belonged to the age group 10–50 years. These campaigns elicited the participation of students, teachers, and many sections of the society. The literacy campaign in Bihar was considered to be the most successful in terms of coverage as well as establishment of libraries which helped the neo-literates to continue their education. The most effective of these campaigns was that conducted in the Princely State of Aundh whose exceptional ruler was singled out for praise by the

[3] J.P. Naik and Syed Nurullah, *A Student's History of Education in India (1800–1973)*, Delhi: Macmillan, p. 390.

[4] F.C. Laubach, *India Shall Be Literate*, 1940. Nagpur: National Church Council; reprinted in 2015 by Andesite Press.

Mahatma for being the only ruler who devolved power on his subjects. During the campaign which started on 21 January 1938, the Raja and his Rani went from village to village singing *kirtans* (paeans) on literacy. The Raja did what visionary educationists such as Naik dreamt of by closing all schools during the campaign so that students and teachers can participate in the campaign. In the first two months of the campaign, the literacy rate of that tiny state increased by about 50 per cent when about 12,000 people learned how to read and write. Literacy campaigns in the provinces ruled by Congress Party lost their momentum after the Congress governments tendered their resignations following the Viceroy's unilateral declaration that India was at war with Germany without consulting the provincial governments or the Central Legislature. However, surprisingly, the colonial government continued to provide financial support to literacy movements mainly to divert the attention of the students and the educated from the freedom struggle; the Indian leaders viewed them as a means of keeping in touch with the masses and motivating them to participate in the freedom struggle. However, during the period 1938 to 1942, it was estimated that 2.77 crore adults attended literacy classes, of whom about 1.38 crore were reported to have become literate.[5]

Rather surprisingly, though the Congress provincial governments, which came into office after the 1946 elections, organized mass literacy campaigns before transfer of power; the campaign mode faded away after Independence. The euphoria generated by Independence was a great opportunity to launch mass literacy campaigns; however, with the exception of Maharashtra government's *Gram Sikshan Mohim* (Village Education Movement), the mass campaign approach to eradication of illiteracy was given up till 1989. One could only surmise the reasons for giving up a programme which the Congress provincial governments had earlier set great store by. In the aftermath of Independence and the Partition, there were more pressing problems than mass illiteracy. The central government was too engrossed in coping with challenges such as communal violence, rehabilitation of refugees, integration of the 500 odd native states with the Indian Union, and invasion of

[5] S.Y. Shah, 'Adult Education', in J.S. Rajput, ed., *Encyclopaedia of Indian Education*, Volume I, Delhi: National Council of Educational Research and Training, 2004, pp. 21–41, at pp. 26–7.

Kashmir by Pakistan to turn its attention to adult illiteracy. No less importantly, the new Indian government did not need legitimation and consolidations of power through mass literacy campaigns as in, say, the Soviet Union or Cuba. Once the government had the time and space to address development issues, it relied on Community Development for rural uplift; it constituted in Nehru's words 'the dynamo for the successful implementation of the Five Year Plans' (*Asian Drama*, Volume II, p. 870). As Community Development encompassed everything needed for rural uplift and was envisaged as a people's programme, it was perhaps felt that no separate mass campaign for literacy was necessary. Social education was one of the extension activities undertaken in community development blocks; it was expected to spread literacy among grown-ups and inculcate a lively sense of rights and duties of citizenship as well as the attitudes required for participating in 'community uplift through community action'. Initially, Community Development evoked considerable enthusiasm; however, it did not take long for the mass enthusiasm to fade and 'the hopeful vision of massive uplift throughout the rural population' to be clouded. It had to come to rely on grants from the government and efforts of government servants rather than of village volunteers (*Asian Drama*, Volume II, pp. 1342–3). Furthermore, in practice, Community Development gave scant attention to social education and no serious concentrated effort was made to put an end to illiteracy in villages (Government of India, *Evaluation Report on Working of Community Projects and N.E.S Blocs*, Volume I, 1957, p. 35, cited in *Asian Drama*, Volume III, p. 1689).

In the mid-1960s, social education gave way to *functional literacy* in which functionality came to be defined in terms of enhancing the productivity of the economic activities of the learners. In this phase which lasted about a decade, adult education programmes sought to integrate imparting reading and writing skills with dissemination of occupation-specific skills and knowledge which would help the learners to be economically more productive. Thus, the Farmers Training and Functional Literacy Project (FTFLP), which was in operation in for about a decade from 1968, aimed at improving the efficiency of farmers in the context of the Green Revolution. Like social education, the FTFLP followed the global fashions of the day; in fact, it was financed partly by UNESCO and UNDP, and was part of the Experimental World Literacy Projects (EWLPs) implemented in 11 countries under the aegis of UNESCO with a view to rigorously evaluate the linkage between literacy and development. Functional literacy got a body blow in the mid-1970s with the change in the intellectual climate and the findings of the 1976 evaluation of EWLP. That evaluation did not find clear evidence for the effectiveness of functional literacy in enhancing the productivity of learners or improvement in the consumption of goods. A 1976 evaluation of FTFLP was no different.

Even before the evaluation of EWLP was published, the intellectual climate that dominated international relations had changed dramatically. In the early 1970s, the rhetoric of New International Economic Order cast a long shadow on the deliberations of the UN system. UNESCO, under the leadership of Amadou-Mahtar M'Bow who succeeded Maheu in 1974, positioned itself in the vanguard of the movement to restructure the international order, and embarked on an extraordinarily broad-ranged refection on major world problems and promotion of concepts such as endogenous development and a New World Information and Communication Order. Literacy and schooling themselves were not insulated from the gales of radicalism that swept the UN system and the thinking on international relations. The mid-1970s were the high tide of Freirean pedagogy, and the Declaration of Persepolis (1975) was a Freirean manifesto for adult education and a clarion call to arms against oppressive structures whether social, political, or economic. The Declaration was adopted by an International Symposium on Literacy, organized by the Iranian government and the International Coordination Secretariat for Literacy. The Symposium was not an official conference, and one wonders whether the Declaration would have been adopted had it been one, for few Member States would have been at ease with a 'subversive' manifesto. The Declaration rejected the previous notions of functionality which linked adult literacy programmes with citizenship or individual or group economic betterment. The tone and tenor of the deliberations were set up by a working document entitled *Functionality of Literacy* presented by Malcolm Adiseshiah who had by then left UNESCO and was on his way to become an *éminence grise* of Indian education. That document redefined functionality to be:

> A wider package of literacy and education which promotes the need of the poor person to organise himself/herself and his/her fellow sufferers and fight against the existing power centres, the irrelevant

decision-making processes, the growing poverty he/she is living in and for equitable and just social and political order.[6]

The new perception of the functionality of literacy was embraced by Roby Kidd, a distinguished adult educator and long-time associate of Bordia (Chapter II). In a state-of-the-art review he prepared for the International Development Research Center (IDRC), Kidd reaffirmed the definition of functionality set out by the Persepolis; functional literacy meant more than the ability to function economically and 'should not be tied to such things as growing cotton'. Literacy was 'functional when it arouses in the individual a critical awareness of social reality, enabling him or her to understand, master, and transform the reality'.

Five days after the promulgation of the Emergency in June 1975, Indira Gandhi announced a Twenty-Point Economic Programme, whose implementation, D.K. Barooah, the Congress President, claimed, 'would open up immense possibilities of changing the face of rural India, for liberating the rural poor from the age-old chain of exploitation and poverty'.[7] Eliminating adult literacy in the age group 15–35 by 1990 was one of the points in that programme; however, this was sought to be achieved by making more effective the programmes initiated already rather than by launching a mass literacy campaign that would conscientize the masses. The government took no notice of the Persepolis Declaration. The Janata government which came to office after the Emergency set a high priority on adult education. In April 1977, about a month after it came to office, the Parliament adopted a policy resolution which spelt out the government's resolve 'to wage a clearly conceived, well-planned and relentless struggle against illiteracy to enable the masses to play an active role in social and cultural changes'. Figuratively, heads rolled after the Janata government was formed in that several personalities who wielded enormous power in the previous regime were displaced. However, Naik was an exception, and in the new government, he came to be a stronger pillar of education establishment than he was earlier. By then Naik was in his radical phase under the deep influence of Ivan Illich, Paulo Freire, and

[6] Malcolm S. Adiseshiah, 'Literacy's Functionality and the Fight for Social Justice', *Convergences*, 8, no. 24 (1977), p. 23.

[7] Cited in Francine R. Frankel, *India's Political Economy, 1947–1977: The Gradual Revolution*, Princeton: Princeton University Press, 1978, p. 553.

the Chinese Cultural Revolution, and the radicalism was reflected in the Policy Statement on Adult Education and the conceptualization of the National Adult Education Programme (NAEP). The objective of NAEP was nothing short of imparting 'literacy, functionality, and awareness' to approximately 10 crore persons in the age group 15–35 over a five-year period. NAEP mainly relied on adult education centres to impart literacy, each of which catered to about 25–30 adult illiterates. The Janata government began with a bang and ended with a whimper; NAEP started by it fared no better. The Janata government lost office just about eight months after the launch of NAEP. After Janata government collapsed, NAEP was continued with a few modifications. However, as many evaluation reports brought out, only imparting literacy received attention; other elements of NAEP such as functionality and awareness received little attention. According to some estimates, some 130,000 literacy centres were active under NAEP, where some 36.4 lakh adults were enrolled. At least 10 per cent of those enrolled learned to read and write; 30,000 functionaries—instructors, supervisors, and writers of books and primers—were trained. Some 3,000 literacy and post-literacy texts and materials were published.[8]

Developments after 1984

Come to think of it, neither NPE, 1986, nor its POA visualized TLCs which came to be the main mode for imparting adult education after 1988. NPE rhetorically declared that

> The whole Nation must pledge itself to the eradication of illiteracy, particularly in the 15–35 age group. The Central and State Governments, political parties and their mass organisations, the mass media and educational institutions must commit themselves to mass literacy programmes of diverse nature. It will also have to involve on a large scale teachers, students, youth, voluntary agencies, employers, etc.

[8] H.S. Bhola, 'A Policy Analysis of Adult Literacy Education in India: Across the Two National Policy Reviews of 1968 and 1986', *Perspectives in Education*, 4, 1988, p. 218; Vimala Ramachandran, 'Adult Education: A Tale of Empowerment Denied', *Economic and Political Weekly*, XXXIV, no. 15 (1999), pp. 870–80.

However, when it came to specifics, the NPE repeated the variety of modalities which were in vogue for a long time, such as establishment of centres in rural areas for continuing education; workers' education through the employers, trade unions, and agencies of the government; post-secondary education institutions; wider promotion of books, libraries, and reading rooms; use of radio, TV, and films, as mass and group learning media; creation of learners' groups and organizations; programmes of distance learning; organizing assistance in self-learning; and organizing need- and interest-based vocational training programmes. Taking note of the idea of technology mission which was floating within the government, the POA mentioned that eradication of illiteracy would be launched as a technological and societal mission on the presupposition that 'we are the threshold of momentous scientific, technological and pedagogic changes, which may, besides augmenting the range of communication system, make the process of acquiring literacy quicker and easier'.

Soon enough, the NLM was launched in 1988, one of the six missions set up by Rajiv Gandhi and led by the messianic Sam Pitroda. K also had an occasion to attend in Delhi a meeting of the newly constituted NLM. That meeting was a surrealistic bazaar of technical gadgets: plastic blackboards that could be rolled, solar lamps, a TV-cum-VCP with a politically evocative label Indira Priyadarshini (the maiden name of Indira Gandhi), and so on. According to the chief of the public sector unit which manufactured Priyadarshini, what all had to be done to achieve literacy *nirvana* was to provide each village with a Priyadarshini and a few audio-visual lessons. The sight of alphabets being animated on a TV monitor was impressive. However, grappling as he was with the logistics of implementing NTR's 10,000 TV-VCP programme, K was sceptical of the sales pitch. K recalled the saying that armchair generals dabble in grand strategy while real generals wrestle with logistics. As he gained experience in educational administration and as he interacted with educational experts from all over the world, K learnt that at the school stage the claims for educational technology including computer-assisted learning were often exaggerated. Whatever, K came away with a poor impression of the missionaries who fervently believed that technology was the magic bullet that could cure *all* of India's problems, and that the best way to fire that bullet was the mission mode. As months rolled, NLM retreated from its blind alley of technological fixation for which full credit should be given to Bordia. As set out earlier, in India, no one had better technical credentials than him in the field of adult education, for he picked up the praxis of adult education from luminaries such as Naik, Kidd, and Draper, studied at the Ontario Institute for Studies in Education, and acquired valuable experiential knowledge as Director of the National Adult Education Programme (NAEP), 1978 (Chapter II). During one of his many head-hunting expeditions for locating good performers whom he could draft as his deputies as well as promising initiatives, he spotted the Ernakulum experiment and immediately recognized its potential as a new model that would help adult education escape from the 'centre-based' approach of NAEP as well as techno-fixation of NLM. In Ernakulum, an activist District Collector K.R. Rajan who was a member of KSSP for two decades and had been Vice President of KSSP forged a partnership with KSSP to make the whole district fully literate in a year. The Ernakulum model provided him an opportunity to take the literacy movement beyond what Naik and he tried to do in 1980, and launch TLCs.

What distinguishes a mass literacy campaign from a literacy programme with night schools as the vehicle is a sense of urgency, passionate fervour, and crusading spirit. Campaigns to eradicate illiteracy are replete with military metaphors such as campaigns, battles, and crusades. M.P. Paraemwaran, President of KSSP and a leading light of Bharat Gyan Vigyan Samiti (BGVS), summarized the key aspects of the Ernakulum campaign to be: (*a*) *massive approach*—entire district taken up in one go; (*b*) *saturation environment building—no member of society*, literate or illiterate, *could escape* from the impact of this environment building campaign; (*c*) meticulous spatial and temporal planning *as in war* for the deployment of human and material resources, and for organizing mobilization and learning; (*d*) integration of people's enthusiasm with administrative machinery; and (*e*) delinking the implementation machinery from governmental bureaucracy to increase dynamism and flexibility, and at the same time ensuring accountability through stringent monitoring by the public.[9]

[9] S. Sivadas, *How Ernakulum Became the First Literate District of India*, Notes, Comments. No. 195, UNESCO-UNICEF-WFP Cooperative Programme, June 1991, pp. 9–10.

Bordia strongly believed that success begets success, and that it was essential to dispel the widely held perception that, like chasing a mirage, it would be futile to attempt to achieve universal literacy in the country in a few years. To that end, he believed that it was imperative to create a series of success stories and widely broadcast the successes. He used to tell K often that *antyodaya*—targeting the most deprived—though appealing, is unlikely to create and sustain the momentum necessary for pushing forward a difficult programme. However, being gloriously inconsistent, he did not hesitate to apply the antyodaya principle whenever it was expedient as with the choice of Bihar for the first flagship EFA project, and the choice of UP for the first World Bank-financed basic education project in the country. He recognized in a trice that there could not have been a more promising locale for creating a literacy success story through government–NGO partnership than Kerala with its high literacy rate, a rich tradition of social and political mobilization, and organizations such as KSSP eager to spread their base and activities. Literally he latched on to the Ernakulum experiment and, like John the Baptist, worked overtime to spread word that the Kingdom of Heaven (fully literate India) was around, and that a Messiah (the Ernakulum model) who would lead the country to full literacy was born. Bordia literally seized the opportunity of the formation of the V.P. Singh government which was dependent on the support of the Leftist parties for survival to forge a special partnership with BGVS, an organization with so many activists of leftist persuasion that many considered it to be a front organization of the Left. Generalizing, a few strands of thought were interwoven in the conceptualization of the TLCs. The first was the creed that while literacy was the entry point for adult education, it could not be the be-all-and-end-all of TLCs. The second was that, to succeed, TLCs should be inspired by a bold, nay a daring vision; the objective should be nothing less than eliminating the scourge of illiteracy from the country within a stipulated time frame. Even for a semblance of success such a bold vision necessitates total mobilization of the nation as in war, the unstated exemplars being literacy campaigns in countries such as the Soviet Union. The third was that, to succeed, TLCs should, like military campaigns, be meticulously planned and deftly executed with minute attention to logistics and coordination. The fourth was that, as in military campaigns, the psychological front held the key to sustain the momentum of TLCs and expand their coverage. A country might win all the battles and yet lose the war if its citizens lose heart and come to believe that the war could not be won or that the war their country has been waging is unjust. The American defeat in Vietnam is a classic example. The victory on the battlefield is easier if one could convince the enemy comes to believe defeat is inevitable. The TLCs were no different. It was imperative to drum up enlistment in the campaign, to boost morale of the participants, and to unnerve the sceptics; to that end, propaganda by way of creative success stories and spreading disinformation about the sceptics was essential. There is no better way to grasp these strands than trace their historical evolution. The fifth was that TLCs were expected to be organized, to use a contemporaneous jargon, in a private–public partnership (PPP) mode. It was, however, a PPP with a difference in that the partners of the government were not business entities, but NGOs and social activists whose cooperation with the government, even at the best of circumstances, is antagonistic. The partnership operated at two levels: in the districts and at the national level. Central to the Ernakulum model is a registered district-level literacy society with the District Collector as Chairman, and representatives of the NGOs, social activists, and Panchayat Raj bodies as members; the society was expected to steer the planning and implementation of the TLC. The model aimed at harnessing the positional power of district collectors, and the prowess of NGOs and activists in social mobilization. At the national level, the PPP technically operated through a contract between DOE, MHRD, and BGVS whereby BGVS was entrusted with the task of organizing socio-cultural mobilization across the length and breadth of the country to promote TLCs. It was not exactly an arm's length contract in that BGVS itself was formed with the encouragement of DOE, extension of its network in states and districts was financed by DOE, and the General Council of BGVS had representatives of DOE and many of the leading lights of the BGVS members of the NLM Executive Council. It is axiomatic that any partnership is beset with tensions, a fact underlying the saying, 'God take care of my friends, I would take care of my enemies myself'. It is not easy to manage a partnership with an organization of activists uncomfortable with, if not antipathetic to, most policies and all procedures of the government. The way in which Bordia managed the tensions intrinsic to such a partnership, and ensured that he had his way all the time, was just masterly. All in all, the strategy sought to operationalize the principle of 'unity of opposites' much advocated by Mao Zedong and forge an alliance between the 'opposites' of the state and the 'Civil Society'. An important element of the strategy was innovative use of folk culture and modern communications, and enlisting celebrities such as U. Ananthamurthy and Girish Karnad.

There had been many and perhaps more successful mass literacy campaigns before the TLCs, but every one of them was initiated during periods of political upheaval, revolutionary transformation, and civil strife; thus, the mass literacy campaign was launched in the Soviet Union after the Bolshevik Revolution, that in North Vietnam after the Communists came to power, those in China, Vietnam, Somalia, Ethiopia, Mozambique, and Nicaragua after a civil war in which a Marxist or radical group captured power, those in Brazil and Burma after a military coup , and that in Julius Nyerere's Tanzania after the highly respected leader turned radical. The TLCs stood out in that they were not preceded by a political discontinuity; in fact, they owed their rapid spread to the remarkable entrepreneurship of a civil servant, namely Bordia. And further, they were the first major campaign organized in a democratic federal polity with governments of different political hues holding power at the centre and in the states. Another distinctive feature was the PPP described above.

As part of the build-up for the TLCs, Bordia got the prime minister himself to travel down on 4 February 1990 to Ernakulum to declare the district as the first fully literate district in the country. The states ruled by the Left Front such as Kerala and West Bengal were purposively chosen to replicate the Ernakulum model so that cadres required for mobilization needed for a mass campaign were available in plenty; so was Fatehpur, the constituency of the Prime Minister even though it had none of the conditions necessary for the success of a TLC. And then he practised agitprop with a finesse which would make a political commissar proud. He creatively used media to create euphoria about the TLCs and relentlessly debunk and thwart sceptics and critics. By early 1991, the euphoria generated by success stories was transformed through media and communications into a tidal wave of we-can-do confidence, which engulfed large parts of the country. Herd instinct is particularly strong among civil servants, all the more so if an activity is seen as likely to bring laurels. Soon district collectors all over the country were vying with each other to make their districts totally literate. In a couple of years, TLCs appeared to be ubiquitous, even in many districts of BIMARU states,[10] which in terms of educational indicators were as far from the Kerala districts as chalk from cheese. TLCs spread with the irresistible momentum of a Juggernaut: 17 districts in 1990, 40 in 1991, and 65 districts in January 1992. District after district declared itself totally literate. Millions of people were reported to have become literate, and several more million volunteers were reported to be involved in TLCs. The inexorable march of TLCs continued even after the retirement of Bordia in 1992; in fact, the expansion in BIMARU states picked up momentum in 1993; and by 1994, TLCs were being conducted in 258 districts. Lest it should lose credibility, in 1994 the NLM itself divested the district collector of the authority to declare his district to be totally literate. Only after satisfying itself through an evaluation would NLM certify a district to have achieved total literacy. A little later, even the very idea of a totally literate district was given up, and NLM was willing to fund a TLC to be undertaken in a part of a district.

The Real World

Within a few minutes of K joining his new post in Shastri Bhavan, Bordia whisked K away in his car to a meeting of the Executive Committee of the NLM; participation in that meeting turned out to be K's rite of passage in Bordia's fiefdom. The meeting of the Executive Committee had the ambience of a revival meeting in which the faithful chant with gay abandon hymns to the glory of God. The faithful rejoiced over the glad tidings about the TLCs that were pouring in from Kerala and West Bengal, and were keen to spread the word to new territories. Bordia introduced K to the audience with élan, extolling K for coming away to the meeting instead of reporting to duty, thereby displaying his commitment to adult education; hearing him say that convinced K that

[10] BIMARU are the Hindi-speaking states of Bihar, MP, Rajasthan, and UP, educationally the most backward states of India. Bihar has since been bifurcated into Bihar and Jharkhand, and MP into MP and Chhattisgarh.

banter and fibs were the staple of his new boss. After a brilliant overview of the developments by Bordia, the Executive Committee took up for consideration proposals from districts for funding TLCs; these included Chittoor, one of the three proposals which K sponsored from AP. To his utter surprise, K found that the Executive Committee took up an additional proposal from his state, of which he had absolutely no clue, namely Cuddapah; his surprise turned into amazement when he found that Parimala, the District Collector, Cuddapah, himself had turned up to present his proposal to make his district fully literate. After his presentation, Bordia praised Parimala and his presentation to the sky; like a medieval knight bowing to his lady love, Bordia bowed to Parimala and said, 'I salute you for coming out with a programme of this nature. It is an excellent presentation by an excellent man. You have answers for all the questions.' In contrast to Parimala, the presentation by Nagarjuna, District Collector, Chittoor, was ill received. Nagarjuna was one of the most earnest IAS officers K had known, and he was utterly devoted to education like his cousin Shanta Sinha who did stellar work to get out-of-school children admitted to schools and later rose to be the Chairman of the National Child Rights Commission. However, Bordia found nothing right with Nagarjuna's presentation. Parimala's proposal was approved as it was with applause, and Nagarjuna's returned for refinement. The central government funded only three fourth the outlay of a TLC; the rest was required to be provided by the state government or mobilized from private sources. Having jumped the gun, Parimala was now worried that the state government might not fund the TLC; nothing to worry, Bordia assured him and said he and K would sort out the matter with the state government. For a straight bat Tambrahm officer procedure was God, and violating procedure cardinal sin. K was therefore shocked beyond words by the arbitrary decision-making which favoured the proposal of a favourite and rejected a sound proposal of an extremely competent and socially committed officer, and by the insouciance with which a proposal which cast a liability on a state government was approved without that government having any idea whatsoever of that proposal. Over time, K found that the approval of Parimala's proposal was not an isolated case but a pattern. Short-circuiting the state governments and dealing directly with districts and even villages—or to use the colourful slogan attributed by press to Mamata Banerjee, 'from PM [Prime Minister] to DM

[District Magistrate] with no CM [Chief Minister]'[11]—was a practice introduced by Rajiv Gandhi government, and Bordia did not hesitate to follow that practice when it suited him. The results were not always beneficial. Thus, after a couple of years after Parimala's proposal was approved, the NLM was compelled to recover all the funds released to Cuddapah as the grant NLM provided was used not for literacy but for environment building that popularized *Parimala Prabhandha*—a heroic ballad that extolled the virtues and legendary successes of the Great Collector. Quite a few state governments objected to their being blindsided by the NLM; thus, at the meeting of CABE in May 1992, C. Aranganayagam, Tamil Nadu Education Minister, lodged his protest against the central government going about with the selection of an NGO as State Resource Centre and of the Chief Co-ordinator of the TLC in Kanyakumari district without consulting the state government. When the MP government issued a circular prohibiting the district collectors from directly approaching the NLM, a journalist-friend of Bordia published a story criticizing the state government for politicizing the TLCs.

The TLCs were largely driven by district collectors except perhaps in Kerala and West Bengal and a few odd districts elsewhere. Although BGVS and its affiliates were expanding their organizational base, their reach and grasp were not commensurate with the demands of a programme that spread over a hundred and odd districts spread over several states. That was perhaps the reason why the approval of a TLC was largely dependent on Bordia's assessment of the commitment of the district collector and the extraordinary efforts made by Bordia and the DG, NLM, to ensure that such committed district collectors and commissioners were not transferred out, and that those who were suspect in their eyes were shifted. There is no better way to implement in the districts a programme that relies on government functionaries than anchoring it in the district collector; however, such anchoring comes with some costs. The 'We are the Government syndrome' is not

[11] *Indian Express*, 31 July 2009. Mamata Banerjee, according to the report, was insistent that central government funds to provide relief to the victims of the Alia cyclone that hit the Sunderbans, West Bengal, should flow directly to district boards controlled by her, and that she was upset when the funds were released by Pranab Mukherjee to the West Bengal government.

extinct in the IAS with the result that implementation bears strongly the impress of the collector's personality. Such an impress could be very beneficial if the collector were public spirited and enterprising; however, it also carries the danger of the programme objectives and processes going awry if the collector perceives the programme as an opportunity to shoot into prominence, make a splash, and then move on. More importantly, the change of district collector marks a discontinuity in a programme as that change is figuratively like the change of government. It is said of the American government that a new administration 'tends to believe that history began on its Inauguration Day, and its predecessor was totally wrong about everything and that all its acts must therefore be cancelled'.[12] During the Mohammaden era of Indian history, the word *khilaf* changed its connotation from 'in succession' to 'opposition', reflecting the relationship that generally prevailed between the preceding and the successive ruler.[13] The relationship between a predecessor and his successor is not usually different in the case of district collectors. Exceptions apart, every district collector wants to begin afresh, and seeks to create a new edifice by pulling down the edifice put up by his predecessor. Bordia was very much aware that it would be a rare thing if a successor in government would protect a radical programme initiated by his predecessor, and went out of the way to ensure that his Chosen Few were at the helm in the districts with a tenacity that Robert Bruce would admire. Thus, he went on badgering Mukund Prasad, Laloo Prasad Yadav's Secretary, and Arun Pathak, the Chief Secretary, to cancel the transfer of the Commissioner, Muzaffarpur Division, who was his acolyte, and who he felt was doing outstanding work in BEP and literacy. The chief secretary was not amused as the transfer was effected so that that the official could attend to emergent relief work in north Bihar. Bordia sought to take advantage of the awe with which state government functionaries hold foreigners and foreign agencies, particularly if they finance projects in the state, to creatively spin and convey the story that the UNICEF headquarters, New York, was gravely concerned about the impact of the transfer on

[12] Alexander Haig, *Caveat: Realism, Reagan and Foreign Policy*, New York: Macmillan, 1984, p. 105.

[13] Nari Rustomji, *Enchanted Frontiers: Sikkim, Bhutan, and India's North-eastern Borderlands*, New Delhi: Oxford University Press, 1971, p. 136.

the implementation of BEP which it financed. His ploy failed; reportedly, Laloo Prasad Yadav observed that if UNICEF was so concerned about the transfer of an official, it could as well run Bihar. TLCs were only one of the many tasks attended to by the district collector and commissioner, and no state government would like commitment to TLCs being the sole criterion for the appointment or shift of a collector or a commissioner. That being so, the tendency to short-circuit the state governments was counterproductive as the state government which was side-lined saw no reason to concede the request of Bordia or the DG, NLM to retain their favourite.

In his many intimate moments, Bordia would quip that it was necessary to repeat the simple message of success so that it is reinforced and comes to be accepted as a truth. The way Bordia addressed the psychological aspects of the TLCs was again masterly. There was scepticism all around, whether total literacy was feasible at all, whether the campaigns could be taken up on a massive scale, and whether the learning outcomes would be satisfactory. Bordia employed three tactics to win the psychological battles: first, vesting the TLCs with an aura of success so as to take advantage of the human traits to be associated with something good and noble as well as to be on the winning side; second, securing the endorsement of celebrities, particularly of well-known critics of the establishment so as to vest the aura of success with a ring of authenticity; and third, an attack strategy of labelling those who were sceptical as cynical, and those officials and governments who, he felt, were not adequately cooperative as either vested interests or trying to politicize education. All in all, the tactics were those of classic *agitprop*. His co-option of a media celebrity renowned for her *exposés* of government failure is classic. One day he worked all his charm on her over dinner, and in an accusatory tone, he asked her, 'Are you for female literacy?' compelling her to confess that she was indeed for female literacy. Having trapped the quarry, he gave an offer: 'Why don't you visit places where the literacy campaigns were doing well and report on them rather reporting all the time only negative features of public life.' When the TV episodes produced by her were telecast, many viewers were persuaded to accept that something remarkable must be happening when a government-baiter like her was so appreciative of literacy campaigns. Thanks to the excellent media management by Bordia, reports about NLM and TLCs were predominantly appreciative, although here and there were discordant notes of criticism. Apart from reports of inflated achievement, there were reports of district collectors using their power to coerce the illiterate to join the TLCs. Thus, it was reported that in the Durg district the measures taken to promote TLC were reminiscent of the family planning drive during the Emergency. One such measure was the stipulation requiring any illiterate who wished to procure rations from a fair price shop to produce a certificate from an Akshar Sainki (literacy soldier) that he was a participant of the literacy classes.[14]

While some of the districts chosen for praise no doubt performed very well, quite a few chosen for tactical considerations did not. It appeared that the flavour of the season changed continuously, and when a new flavour made its debut, the earlier ones just faded away. When V.P. Singh was the Prime Minister, UP came in for praise; in a Conference of State Education Secretaries, the secretary came in for praise for plastering all the walls of the vast state of UP with NLM slogans, and for the campaign in Fatehpur, the Prime Minister's constituency. A little later, it was Pondicherry which was singled out for praise, then Bijapur and Dakshina Kannada districts in Karnataka, then Durg district in MP, and once PV was the Prime Minister, Nizamabad and Nellore districts of AP. The Municipal Commissioner, Hyderabad, came in for praise for setting up an *Akshara Jyothi*, a literacy flame similar to the eternal flame at the Tomb of the Unknown Soldier at the India Gate, in the heart of Hyderabad near the Ambedkar statue. After a couple of weeks, the flame vanished without leaving a trace and without any impact on the literacy in Hyderabad. When Laloo Prasad Yadav had to be courted for support to BEP, Madhepura was showered with praise. There were reports of millions of the newly literate rushing forward to send their children to schools. That was not all. It seemed that the transformative power that educationists claimed for education was at work on a continental scale. There were heart-warming stories of the wretched of the earth being empowered, of casting away age-old crippling fatalism, and of taking control of their lives with fierce determination. There was no doubt an element of truth in many stories for it is but human nature, particularly in a surcharged atmosphere, to secure social approval by behaving in the manner expected by peers

[14] 'Literacy by Compulsion in Durg', *Hindustan Times*, 20 April 1992.

and superiors; however, what upset K was the element of exaggeration, tendency to ignore other forces at work and to convey the impression that the behavioural and attitudinal change noticed was permanent. Thus, the DG, NLM, went to town with the story of the Muslim learners of Srirangapatna, Karnataka, learning Kannada; to K who spent much of his time as a child in the shop of Mushkinda, a Muslim owner of a paan shop (a stall that sells betel leaves, nuts, cigarettes, etc.) near his father's hotel, the story appeared bizarre. Like almost all Muslims in South India, Mushkinda mingled with his Hindu neighbours and spoke Telugu, the language of the region in which he lived. Those days, Muslims of southern states were no different from Mushkinda. Another story was that of the neo-literate women of Nellore in AP. Much was made of the anti-liquor movement in AP which was reportedly inspired by *Seethamma Katha*, a lesson in their adult education primer wherein a woman teaches her drunkard husband a lesson. There was a protest indeed by the women of Dubugunta, Nellore district, against the relaxation of prohibition, and many of the protestors were neo-literates; however, that protest was not the *only* trigger that launched the state-wide prohibition movement, nor was it solely responsible for its spread in the state. Soon after he assumed office as the chief minister, N.T. Rama Rao introduced a new liquor policy as well as populist measures such as supply of rice at two rupees a kilogram, which together crippled the fiscal capacity of the state government to undertake developmental programmes. After N.T. Rama Rao lost office in 1989, his government's liquor policy was relaxed by the successor government making liquor more easily available. Even before January 1990, when the TLC began in Nellore district, there were rumblings of protest in the state against the new liquor policy; the dissidents within the Congress party as well as the opposition parties saw prohibition as an issue to embarrass Janardhana Reddy, the chief minister. It was opportune for them to highlight the protest of women in Dubugunta, a village in the district from which the chief minister hailed. The prohibition movement picked up momentum when a few freedom fighters such as Vavilala Gopalakrishniah joined the movement, and *Enadu*, the Telugu daily with the largest circulation among Telugu newspapers, supported the campaign with missionary zeal through its columns and the brilliant front-page cartoons of Sridhar. In 1995, after NTR regained power, prohibition was reintroduced, but a few years later, the government of his own party progressively did away with prohibition as the state government could not afford to lose substantial excise revenue, and as criminal gangs engaged in illicit manufacture and sale of liquor had sprung up all over the state. The campaign to reintroduce prohibition faded away.

As 1990 rolled, it was increasingly becoming clear that the Ernakulum model had limitations, and could not be replicated in the low-literacy districts of BIMARU states and elsewhere. The Ernakulum model made sense only if the number of literates in a district vastly exceeded the illiterates so that sufficient volunteers could be mobilized to instruct all the illiterates in a swift campaign of, say, a year or so. It is not given to man to live far too long in the rarefied air of romantic idealism and to be engaged indefinitely without remission in a war-like campaign. Thus, the attainment of Independence required no less than three major campaigns—the non-cooperation movement, the Salt Satyagraha, and Quit India—and, on the top of it, a World War which totally debilitated England's economic and military prowess. Thousands of volunteers could not be expected to altruistically impart literacy for years and years. Lest anyone should miss that point, the Ramamurti Committee pointed out the limitations of the Ernakulum model and suggested that a variety of approaches should be tried, evaluated, and that successful models should be encouraged. In the CABE Committee on Policy, Ram Dayal Munda questioned the appropriateness of treating the Ernakulum model as being applicable all over the country. In a light-hearted manner, Bordia brushed off all such reservations about the universal validity of the Ernakulum model as due to inadequate understanding or cynicism. The Ernakulum model was touted as a panacea for eliminating illiteracy wherever it existed in India, and success stories touted, a task easier because of the fact that TLCs created touching spectacles of mobilization which made good copy for journalists, and provided good images for television even though, by themselves, they were all froth and no substance. K was puzzled by the contrasting attitudes adopted by Bordia to UEE and adult education. Bordia explicitly recognized that UEE could not be achieved in the near future by relying on the school system alone, and that therefore schooling needed to be supplemented by an extensive system of non-formal education that would cater to the educational needs of children outside school; yet when it came to adult education, he was inclined to hold that the one size of TLC would fit all districts irrespective of wide variations among districts in literacy levels as well as the tradition and potential for social mobilization. Of course, in Bordia's fiefdom, even the slightest whiff of dissent was a sure recipe for courting calamity, and K was not one who had the moral courage to court calamity; he confided his agony and angst to himself and his journal. However, if at all anyone was capable of infusing realism in the dissemination of the Ernakulum model it was Bordia, and he failed to infuse realism, may be because he thought that it was rather premature. To put a generous interpretation on Bordia's efforts, one can say that perhaps he felt that overzealous effort was worthy in itself, that success, however short-lived and limited, would provide good exemplars and give heart to those outside the government to put pressure on the government to move in the right direction. However, once TLC acquired a halo of success, it was difficult for his successors to appear politically incorrect and sound a note of caution, all the more so as the environment building of TLC lends itself easily to expansion and consolidation of political base of shrewd political leaders. It is therefore no wonder that with Arjun Singh continuing to be the Minister, the inexorable expansion of TLCs to the Hindi heartland picked up momentum.

The cynic he was, K could not suspend disbelief and swallow feel-good stories which were too good to be wholly true. To him what seemed to be at work were human imagination, inclination to conjure faith-sustaining myths, and the disinclination of well-intentioned persons to discredit something that was good *per se* and seemed to be doing well. Whenever he heard stories about the miraculous transformation that TLCs brought about, with his feverish imagination and tendency to recall historical analogies, K could not but recall Homeric legends, the story of Rosie the welder in wartime America, the Horst Wessel song of Nazi Germany, and the Stakhnovite miracles of Stalin's Russia. While K was all admiration for what was happening and what Bordia did to make that happen, by early 1992 he was disturbed by the systematic attempt to exaggerate achievements and impact of TLCs, and the attempt to brush away any criticism. Those days, at no point was the NLM in a position to give district-wise details of the millions of volunteers and learners reported to have been enlisted by the TLCs even though there were requests for such information from the Planning

Commission. It was obvious that illiteracy was being addressed with a vigour never before displayed in the country, but everything was not hunky dory. K agonized a great deal over the consistent exaggeration of the achievement of TLCs and wondered whether it was necessary and whether it was proper to distort the truth to achieve something good in public life. He was haunted by questions such as do end justify means, and is public morality different from private morality. In order to succeed programmes need what is now called social marketing; in any marketing advertising plays a key role. And furthermore, 'manufacturing reality' or resorting to what Shakespeare called 'lies like truth' is central to advertising. That being so, is not exaggeration for a good cause excusable? What about truth in advertising? K could not come to any definitive conclusion. He admired Bordia for being not afflicted with the pessimism of the intellect, despite being endowed with a towering intellect. Bordia never let his worries and doubts come in the way of plunging into action, and briskly move ahead. Bordia was pretty aware of the potentiality as well as limitations of TLCs, for in his *Table Talk* he would again and again burst into his trademark horse laughter, describe how he had vested TLC with an aura of success, and in his candid moments, worry that the far too rapid expansion of coverage would end in *band baj jayegi* (bubble would burst).

What Did TLCs Achieve?

There is no doubt that no other educational programme in the history of Indian education spread so fast and mobilized so many adult learners and volunteers as TLCs. Beginning in 1988–9, the TLCs expanded in quick succession to seventeen districts in 1990, 40 in 1991, 65 in January 1992, 258 in 1994, 561 in December 2000, and 587 out of 600 districts by March 2003; 95 per cent of India's villages and people were covered by the adult literacy programmes by March 2003.[15] Nearly 400 of these districts have, after completing TLC, moved on to post-literacy and subsequently to continuing education stage. The NLM's monitoring data indicated that from 1988 till March 2005, approximately 12 crore persons were made literate under various schemes.

[15] Government of India, Ministry of Human Resource Development, *Education for All: National Plan of Action INDIA* (New Delhi), 2003.

Census data indicate that during the period 1981–91 the population in the NLM's target group of 15–35 years increased by 3.3 crores, and yet the number of illiterates in that age group decreased by 80 lakhs; this fact was touted as proof of the success of the TLCs.[16] However, the marked reduction in illiterate population cannot be wholly attributed to TLCs as there was expansion of enrolment and completion of primary education during the 1990s.

While much of the criticism levelled against TLCs could be dismissed as being uniformed or carping or motivated, it was difficult to similarly brush away a sharp critique by Sumanta Banerjee, an activist of impeccable radical credentials, published in June 1993 soon after DOE decided to set up a committee of experts to evaluate the TLCs.[17] He was appreciative of the beneficial outcomes in districts where TLCs were successful; there was a general rise in the enrolment in primary schools and greater acceptance of immunization. However, he was critical of the disturbing trends in several districts not only in BIMARU states but also in AP, Karnataka, Maharashtra, and Tamil Nadu. Although the campaign had run for well over a year, the performance level still remained below 20 per cent of the target. At the end of their TLCs, very few districts had gone in for a summative evaluation by any external agency as envisaged by the NLM. Many had approached the NLM with claims of having achieved total literacy on the basis of some 'internal evaluation' and sought approval and financial assistance for launching the post-literacy campaign, even though illiterates far outnumbered neo-literates. External evaluation in some districts such as Narsinghpur in MP and Shimoga in Karnataka had shown that claims of total literacy were inflated. Even in some districts such as Burdwan where external evaluation had confirmed that 60 per cent to 80 per cent of the illiterates had reached the NLM norms of literacy about a year ago, there were disquieting signs of a relapse among a large number of neo-literates.

Turning from 'fictional literacy', as he put it, to 'functional literacy', Banerjee dwelt upon the perennial question of how much of social

[16] A. Mathew, 'Literacy: Real Options for Policy and Practice in India', Background Paper prepared for the *Education for All Global Monitoring Report 2006*, 'Literacy for Life', p. 15.

[17] Sumanta Banerjee, 'Revisiting the National Literacy Mission', *Economic and Political Weekly*, XXVIII, 25 (1993), pp. 1274–8.

transformation and attitudinal change could literacy and education promote. Is it 'functional literacy' that motivates the people to become 'aware of the causes of their deprivation' and to move towards 'the amelioration of their condition through organization'? Or, is it the other way round? During the environment-building phase of TLC, the organizers tend to cast education as 'a weapon in everything from the war on poverty to the fight against communalism!', and convey simplistic messages suggesting that once the poor get literate, they would get their minimum wages, medicines and health care, better jobs, and so on. While acquiring literacy augments the capacity to struggle for one's rights, illiteracy could not be equated with ignorance and considered 'an impassable barrier against participation in political struggles and socioeconomic movements by the illiterate'. Banerjee turned the claim of literacy enthusiasts on the head by asserting that literacy movements took root mainly in areas where struggles and socio-economic movements 'created a social base for a felt need for literacy', and paved the way for popular acceptance of literacy classes. Banerjee's assertion complements international experience of mass literacy campaigns; campaigns were reportedly successful mostly in countries ruled by parties with a leftist persuasion and a political ideology aiming at a radical transformation of the polity and society. Banerjee cited as specific examples the anti-arrack movement in AP, the mobilization of women quarry workers in Pondicherry to run their own quarries, and the high political consciousness and critical awareness generated by organized movements in Kerala and West Bengal. In effect, the 'effect' of TLCs rapturously hailed by literacy enthusiasts is not the effect but actually the 'cause' of successful TLCs. Banerjee went on to make a point not dissimilar to the one made by the John Bowers of the UNESCO Secretariat in the 1950s, and the Ramamurti Committee by asserting that literacy should come in as and when it becomes a felt need. In inaccessible tribal districts of Orissa, immediate problems of survival, such as starvation, lack of drinking water, and dearth of medicines and health care need to be tackled first before literacy campaign is started so that ' the potential learners can find themselves in the necessary physical and mental shape to attend the literacy classes'. A similar point was later made by Denzil Saldanha, a sociologist who studied minutely the BGVS and evaluated the TLCs. A 'contributory factor to the relative failure of literacy campaigns in low literacy districts with low social development indicators' was that 'in these districts, socio-economic survival was the legitimately felt priority and literacy would be accepted only if seen to be contributing to and accompanied by interventions that enhance the quality of that survival'.[18]

Banerjee's observations on the literacy levels achieved in some districts were confirmed by the expert group appointed by DOE to evaluate the TLCs. The group observed that progress reports from each TLC district were normally based on information gathered through the routine channels within the district and such reports were not always equally dependable for all districts. 'Quite a few of the reports', the group commented, 'give a picture far removed from the reality'. The NLM analysed 41 external evaluation reports (EERs) prepared by independent agencies and came to the conclusion that the achievement was 58 per cent of the achievement reported in the progress reports received from the TLC districts. Referring to these EERs, the expert group expressed serious reservations as a large number of them were deficient in terms of coverage, sample design, size of sample, and, above all, the estimation procedures adopted to arrive at district-level estimates.[19] The expert group suggested a more scientific evaluation system. The background study prepared for UNESCO's EFA-Global Monitoring Report (1996) by Mathew noted that even the external evaluations 'undertaken after the expert group's report, and adopted by NLM, could [not] be said to be above the needle of suspicion', that 'NLM's figures about numbers made literate are not based on the EERs, but on the internal progress reported by the districts', and that 'the public credibility dimension at least in regard to the number claimed to have been made literate never seemed to influence or affect NLM claims'.[20] Even in regard to the Kerala TLCs a bit of scepticism seems to be justified. On 18 April 1991, Kerala was declared a fully literate state by virtue of having achieving a rate of 93.58 per cent, higher than the norm of 90 per cent literacy rate for a district to be declared fully

[18] Denzil Saldanha, *Civil Society Processes and the State: The Bharat Gyan Vigyan Samiti and the Literacy Campaigns*, Jaipur: Rawat Publications, 2010, p. 31.

[19] Government of India, Ministry of Human Resource Development, Department of Education, *Evaluation of Literacy Campaign in India: Report of Expert Group*, 1994.

[20] Mathew, 'Literacy: Real Options for Policy and Practice in India', p. 15.

literate. However, according to the 1991 census, the literacy rate was only 89.81 per cent on 1 March 1991; even according to the 2001 census, the literacy rate was only 90.86 per cent. More interestingly, the literacy rate of women in Kerala was only 87.86 per cent in 2001, which, if true, is less than the threshold limit of 90 per cent for declaring an area to be totally literate. Whatever the actual figures, the difference between the literacy figures reported after the TLCs were concluded and those reported by the censuses, and the very small rise between the 1991 and 2001 censuses raise the question of what happened to all those who became literate in the TLCs. This question has been the subject of a number of studies.[21] According to a study of the neo-literates in Ernakulum itself, by 1999 only 40 per cent of the neo-literates could still read and write to an acceptable level. While regression to illiteracy was not total, the 'world of letters' had not become part of many neo-literates.[22]

In 1995, by when its relations with NLM had cooled off, the BGVS General Council expressed concern about the indiscriminate expansion of TLCs to districts without even 'minimal ground-level preparation' resulting in 'an alarmingly growing number of districts with stagnant TLCs', increasing bureaucratization of TLCs leading to subversion of the 'basic spirit of the "people's movement" character of the campaigns', increasing instances of *zilla saksharata samitis* (district literacy councils) becoming a vehicle for patronage and corruption, and 'increasingly falsified reporting of achievements as well as undue pressures to make declarations of total literacy'. The BGVS General Council urged the NLM to reconsider the approach to mass literacy campaigns.[23] To be honest, these concerns were nothing new; they were immanent in the strategy adopted in 1990 to adopt the Ernakulum model as the only vehicle for eliminating illiteracy all over the country, and to build up

[21] Pamela Clayton, *Literacy in Kerala: Report of Research Undertaken November 2005–October 2006*, University of Glasgow, Scotland, November 2006. http://www.scribd.com/doc/17375060/Literacy-in-Kerala.

[22] P.K. Michael Tharakan, 'Ernakulum Re-Visited: A Study of Literacy in the First Totally Literate District in India', in M. Karlekar, ed., *Reading the World: Understanding the Literacy Campaigns in India*, Bombay: Asia South Pacific Bureau of Adult Education, 2000, pp. 33–79 cited in Pamela Clayton, *Literacy in Kerala*.

[23] Denzil Saldhana, *Civil Society Processes and the State*, pp. 47–8.

that model as a panacea. And furthermore, BGVS was very much associated with this strategy.

All this is not to deny the ineluctable fact that in the history of India TLCs comprise the most significant attempt to make a direct attack on illiteracy; instead, it is to make the point an uncritical adulation is undesirable. In his historical evaluation of Mahatma Gandhi, the eminent historian R.C. Majumdar highlights the Indian tradition of indulging in *prasasthi* (eulogy) of great leaders, of 'reverence' for such leaders 'standing in the way of ascertaining the truth',[24] and of the aversion to objectively evaluate the achievements of the Great. That tradition extends to assessment of programmes widely considered to be lofty because of their pro-poor orientation; that tradition, however, neither furthers the programme objectives nor eventually benefits the poor. Suffice it to say, mass literacy campaigns constitute a valuable approach to eradication of illiteracy but they are not without limitations; their efficiency is likely to be low unless they extend over a long duration and the mobilization total, conditions that are unlikely to be fulfilled is in a democracy. No less important is the need to make strong efforts to keep the neo-literates literate; an important factor in the relative success of the Soviet effort was the compulsion to participate in literacy campaigns and attend the local library, a compulsion difficult to enforce in a democracy. Like the campaigns in the freedom struggle, the TLCs of the1990s have to be followed by repeated efforts at suitable intervals to make a dent on adult illiteracy; that, however, necessitates an 'objective' and not a 'committed' assessment of what happened and what did not.

How Much of Radical Educational Work Is to Be Done in a Government Programme?

It is now opportune to turn to the seminal question whether Freirean conscientization and radical educational work can take place within state institutions or state-funded projects. In other words, how far can radical phraseology be translated into practice in a country whose government wishes to effect social change through the modalities

[24] R.C. Majumdar, *Three Phases of India's Struggle for Freedom*, Bombay: Bharatiya Vidya Bhavan, 1961.

of a parliamentary democracy and not through extra-parliamentary struggles and direct action. A hallmark of the mobilization organized by BGVS was the innovative use of culture to encourage the poor to make them aware of their environment and existential condition, and instil a determination in them to break the shackles of oppression by becoming literate. Even about a quarter century later, K still has vivid memory of the stirring performances put up at the function organized to commemorate the International Literacy Day, 1991. One of the performances was enactment of a few scenes from a Hindi adaptation of Bertolt Brecht's play *The Mother*; those scenes exhorted the poor and hungry to become literate in order to understand the causes of their poverty and bring about a radical transformation of the society. In one scene, the worker-learners in dull, drab overalls are puzzled when the 'bourgeois' teacher teaches them how to spell the word *bulbul* (nightingale); a hothead screams at the teacher and asks him to stop teaching gibberish. The wise Mother who is with the workers asks the hothead to be patient and smartly advises the teacher to spell the word *mazdoor* (worker). With great reluctance, the teacher does as the Mother suggested; the workers are thrilled. Coached by the Mother, the teacher teaches his students the spelling of words such as *vargha sangharsh* (class conflict), *shoshan* (oppression), and other standard words of Marxist discourse. The scene ends with the whole group bursting into the singing of the literacy song that Safdar Hashmi, celebrated playwright and member of the Communist Party of India Marxist (CPM), composed for the NLM

> *Padhna likhna sikho, o mehnat karne walon*
> *Padhan likhna sikho, o bhook se marne walon*
> (Learn to read and write, Oh, all those who are labouring
> Learnt to read and write, Oh, all those who are dying of hunger)

The melody of that song still haunts K. In one of the memorable scenes of Brecht's *Mother,* the Mother rejects God in favour of a new faith in revolutionary violence. The Hindi adaptation which was enacted had a scene making fun of the priest who was performing a *havan*.

As he watched the play, K fell into a reverie. He was transposed to his student days when he was infatuated with the leftist creed and worldview, and imbibed with great relish the heady, intoxicating poetry of

Sri Sri. In the dream world, he again ran into the blind beggar who was singing the song *sengodi ki jai jai* (Hail the Red Flag) on the train from Kerala to Madras about a quarter of a century earlier, and he was once again moved to tears. He recalled his reading in one go Maxim Gorky's *The Mother* and being mesmerized by its evangelical spell. The reverie did not last long, and his mind wandered to recent events in Europe. The Berlin Wall had fallen, and the Communist states in Eastern and Central Europe fell like dominoes. The Soviet Union itself was tottering. In 1953, when the uprising in East Berlin was put down with the support of the Soviet army, Brecht initially came out in support of the East German government, but a little later, the social critic in him was provoked to pour ridicule on the East German government in his poem *Die Lösung* (The Solution)

After the uprising of the 17th of June
The Secretary of the Writers Union
Had leaflets distributed in the *Stalinallee*
Stating that the people
Had forfeited the confidence of the government
And could win it back only
By redoubled efforts. *Would it not be easier*
In that case for *the government*
To dissolve the people
And elect another? (emphasis added)

As it turned out, it was not the government which dissolved the people but the people who dissolved the government, and by the simple expedient of 'voting with their feet', a voting that reminded K of Lenin's characterization of Russian soldiers deserting the army on large numbers as voting for peace with their feet. K could not miss the irony of enacting scenes from the most overtly agitational and unequivocally communist of Brecht's play when nothing seemed to be left of the Left. He was reminded of the quip that it was only in India that one could still meet people who speak Victorian English; it appeared that true believers were left only in India. In Brecht's play, one of the momentous scenes was the moment in October 1917 when on the eve of the Czar's overthrow Mother becomes free to carry and raise her own Red Flag. K could not miss the historical fact that after the Revolution in Russia and Communist takeover in Eastern and Central Europe, 'oppression' did not cease but acquired a different character and meaning.

Could life imitate art? This question provides an answer to the question whether Freirean conscientization and radical educational work can take place within state institutions or state-funded projects. Even as art, Hashmi's literacy song ran into trouble with Doordarshan; NLM could persuade Doordarshan to telecast free and repeatedly a one-minute spot on literacy that included a condensed version of the song with the line *padhan likhna sikho, o bhook se marne walon*. Soon enough, the line aroused objection on the ground that the state channel could not run a spot again and again which spoke of people dying of hunger when the government claimed that it abolished starvation deaths.[25] As a compromise between the two wings of the government, one advocating literacy and another eulogizing the achievements of the government, the phrase *o bhook se marne walon* was replaced by *padhna likhna sikho*. The 'hunger line' was to arouse a controversy in the post-literacy campaign in Pondicherry, a Union Territory which won laurels for its TLCs. A primer had a song that asked: 'Freedom for the country, but why poverty for us?' The chief minister took umbrage at the song, summarily transferred the key officials of the literacy programme, and sacked the NGO which was implementing the post-literacy campaign.

As he watched Brecht's play, K wondered whether environment building linked with leftist ideology would not enmesh NLM with controversies. The traditionalist he was, K was worried about the propriety of using the government funds for propagating an ideology that was not accepted by any government in the country except perhaps the Leftist governments of Kerala and West Bengal, and which was not in synch with NPE, 1986. K did not have to wait for long. Even as the International Literacy Day was being celebrated, the country was in the grip of general elections to the Parliament and state assemblies in a few states such as Kerala. The Left Democratic Front lost power in those elections, and two or three weeks later, K. Karunakaran, the incoming chief minister, dubbed the literacy movement 'a politically motivated Marxist hoax', and declared that his government had little interest in continuing a campaign inspired and led by the 'leftist' KSSP and CPI(M)-affiliated teachers' unions. Bordia's media brigade sprang

[25] Avik Ghosh, *Communication Technology and Human Developments: Recent Experiences in the Social Sector*, New Delhi: Sage, 2006, pp. 101–2.

into action criticizing Karunakaran for politicizing the literacy campaign. If the Kerala government politicized literacy, wrote a columnist, it would be detrimental to the whole country and to the nascent movements in other districts of the country; so far the literacy effort was perceived to be a 'national integration effort'; everyone was coming together, and it was a great unifying factor. Therefore, injecting politics into literacy would be equivalent to poisoning it. Another opined that 'while it is true that those with left ideology (not necessarily workers of the Communist Party [Marxist]) dominated the movement and formed the core of the grassroots workers of the literacy movement, the movement had drawn all sections of the society and all political hues into its fold'. Anything was grist to the mill, even the customary transfer of a chief secretary following the change in the ruling party or coalition. The movement, the columnist thundered, received a 'blow in solar plexus' with the shift by the new government of the Chief Secretary Padma Ramachandran who worked with dedication for the literacy movement, and the appointment of S. Padmakumar as Padma's successor. She expressed fear that the new government would pack the district literacy councils with politically motivated workers replacing committed workers with a stake in literacy. Arjun Singh, the incoming Minister of MHRD, stepped in to get Karunakaran on board and persuade him to continue the post-literacy movement, never mind if he chose to restructure the councils in whatever manner he chose. After all that was what he himself did with nominations to committees and organizations, and for that matter what every government in the country irrespective of political affiliation did. Soon thereafter, in the CABE Committee on Policy, E.T. Mohammad Basheer, the new Education Minister of Kerala, criticized the previous government for politicizing the literacy movement, and yet hailed the achievement of the Kerala state and people in achieving total literacy. Freirean conscientization ran into trouble in other states as well. In AP, the state government, for example, withdrew *Seethamma Katha* from the primers used in the state in the wake of the prohibition movement that was embarrassing the government. At the CABE meeting in May 1992, Aranganayagam criticized the Chief Coordinator of the Kanyakumari TLC selected by the central government of attempting political proselytization through volunteers who were ex-card holders; he also blamed the State Resource Centre, again chosen by the central government without consulting the state government, of printing literature which was not in synch with NPE, 1986. There were similar complaints from Gujarat, which then had a Congress government. In UP and Gujarat, BGVS volunteers and literacy workers belonging to Gandhian organizations were engaged in battle of words.

For all the radical slogans and agitprop, TLCs were largely collector-driven. Even in the districts of Kerala and West Bengal where the TLCs might have been successful in the Freirean sense, little attention was given to imparting skills that would help the learners improve their economics status during the campaign or post-literacy phase. Consequently, in effect TLCs confined themselves to imparting 3 'R's. Some literacy enthusiasts had faulted the district collectors for eschewing sensitive issues and conscientization in the TLCs. Of course, most of the district collectors were motivated by a concern for career advancement and, exceptions apart, were averse to infuse in TLC activities which might not be to the liking of the state government and its key functionaries. Some, however, felt that it did not behove of them to play the role of a political and social activist if they were to promote conscientization on their own without direction from a democratically elected government. K's own position is elegantly articulated by André Beteille, the eminent sociologist, in an article he specially wrote for retreat of some IAS officers. An official can no more be a social activist than a patron for:

> The social activist can take independent initiative in political action; the civil servant can do so only within limits set by others. *The civil servant's relation to the public is defined by the obligations of his office; it is fundamentally different from that of the social activist who is besides, free to choose an appropriate public, or segment of the public to act upon.* The Indian Administrative Service is not a voluntary association whose members are free to determine their own terms and conditions of work.[26]

Suffice to say, the scope for officials or NGOs or activists to foster Freirean consceintization was limited in TLCs, a state-sponsored programme.

[26] André Beteille, 'Experience of Governance: A Sociological Overview', in R.K. Dar, ed., *Governance and the IAS*, New Delhi: Tata McGraw-Hill company, 1999, pp.198–230, at pp. 201–2.

The partnership between DOE and BGVS that Bordia forged continued even after he retired for the reason that Arjun Singh built his political career around a fiery commitment to secularism, leftist economic ideology, and social justice, and the ideological commitment he professed served him well in his battles with political rivals. However, increasingly his political agenda rather than that of BGVS guided the activities of NLM and the extraordinarily fast expansion of TLCs in the Hindi heartland; that explains the 1995 resolution of BGVS expressing disenchantment with the way TLCs were functioning. Among some activists of BGVS, there is a feeling that the special relation that DOE forged with BGVS was due to Bordia, and once he and his band of committed deputies exited from DOE, the special relationship ceased. Such a feeling is only partly true; had the political context been different, Bordia himself would not have forged the relationship or sustained it. To ignore objective conditions such as political context and to bank on the cooperation of individual officers for moving forward social agenda is to say the least un-Marxian.

Law of Unintended Consequences

'Pace-setting' programmes such as TLCs or DPEP or SSA lead to positive outcomes in the nature of spin-offs which are not anticipated when the programme is designed. TLCs might not have ushered in 'total' literacy or Freirean conscientization, but without any doubt whatsoever they did hasten the march to universal literacy. They moulded the opinion of men who matter. Once the goal of total literacy was achieved, or thought to have been achieved, in a district, the district collectors and activists began to look for new ventures. UEE came to be the legitimate candidate for the new venture. It did not take much for them to recognize that their achievement would be ephemeral, a nine-day wonder, if an inadequate schooling system spawned year after year a new brood of illiterates. The questions that sprung up involuntarily among the activists were: Why cannot the district be the arena for a systematic campaign for UEE? Why cannot the administrator–activist partnership be brought to bear on the hitherto elusive UEE? As district after district reported success with TLCs, the questions that involuntarily crossed the minds of Bordia and K were: Why cannot the district be the arena for a systematic planning for UEE? Why cannot the methodology of planning used by TLCs be extended to UEE? These cogitations awakened interest in the idea of district planning of UEE, an idea that was, figuratively speaking, hibernating since it was articulated by as early as 1941 by the eminent economist D.R. Gadgil[27] and later by the Kothari Commission (1968)[28] and J.P. Naik in 1969.[29] The district-based approach to UEE was operationalized on a large scale by DPEP whose progeny SSA is. Thus, a major contribution of TLCs was to impart a sense of urgency to the pursuit of UEE and pave way for DPEP and SSA.

Saakshar Bharat Mission (SBM)

Saakshar Bharat (literate India), the 'new variant' of the NLM, was launched by Prime Minister Manmohan Singh on 8 September 2009, and a new CSS was introduced. Initially the scheme was to last during the Eleventh Five-Year Plan (2007–12) but it was extended to the Twelfth Five-Year Plan. The mission's focus is on women and adolescents, and it looks at gender in conjunction with caste, ethnicity, religion, and disability. It seeks to provide functional literacy to 70 million people, of whom 60 million would be women so that the national adult literacy rate reaches 80 per cent by the end of 2017, the terminal year of the Twelfth Five-Year Plan. While not eschewing the campaign approach of TLCs, SBM fell back on the centre-based approach. *Lok Shiksha Kendras* (LSK, Adult Education Centres) were

[27] Deputy Chairman of the Planning Commission (September 1967 to March 1971). Among his pioneering contributions to Indian planning was the planning exercise he attempted in the 1930s to reform primary education in Wardha district. He and V.M. Dandekar were also commissioned by the Director of Public Instruction, Bombay Presidency, to study primary education in the Satara district of Maharashtra. D.R. Gadgil and V.M. Dandekar, *Primary Education in Satara District: Reports of Two Investigations*, Pune: Gokhale Institute of Economics and Politics, 1955; Nilakantha Rath, 'D.R. Gadgil on Planning at the District Level', *Economic and Political Weekly*, 37, 23 (2002), pp. 2219–22.

[28] Ministry of Education, *Education and National Development: Report of the Education Commission, 1964–66*, 1966, Volume II, pp. 267–8.

[29] J.P. Naik, *Educational Planning in a District*, New Delhi: Asian Institute for Educational Planning and Administration, 1969.

envisaged as the operational arm of SBM and were responsible for the organization and delivery of classes. Adult education centres were established in gram panchayats (local self-government at the village level) on the basis of one per a population of 5,000. Each centre was manned by two paid *preraks* (coordinators), of which at least one is a woman. The centre offered various services: registration, a venue for teaching, a library, and reading rooms. It was also used as a centre for promoting and practicing sports, adventure, and cultural activities. A voluntary literacy educator who is a local resident acts as a mobilizer, trainer, and teacher and is responsible for imparting literacy on average to 8–10 learners. Two features sharply distinguished SBM from TLCs: literacy efforts are anchored in Panchayat Raj institutions, and SBM seeks to focus on vocational education and skill development. And further, only two categories of districts were eligible for coverage under an SMB: district whose adult female literacy rate was 50 per cent or below according to the 2001 census, and Left Wing extremism affected districts irrespective of their literacy rate. By 2013–14, SBM covered 383 of the 410 eligible districts. A major task of SBM was to rejuvenate the NLM structures which became moribund due to the hiatus in literacy programmes during the Tenth Five-Year Plan (Twelfth Five-Year Plan (2012–17), Social Sector, Volume II, 2013, p. 88). During the three-year period, 2009–12, reportedly 14.4 million adult learners were assessed and certified for their proficiencies in reading, writing, and numeracy.[30] UNESCO awarded NLM the King Sejong Literacy Prize for the year 2013. While outlining the salient features of SBM UNESCO's EFA Global Monitoring Report 2015 observed that 'as with other such campaigns, its cost-effectiveness and capacity to promote sustainable reading skills on a large scale have not been evaluated independently'.[31]

[30] Jagmohan Singh Raju, 'Saakshar Bharat Mission', 2013, UNESCO Effective Literacy Website, http://www.unesco.org/uil/litbase/?menu=9&programme=132.

[31] United Nations Educational, Scientific and Cultural Organisation, *Education for All 2000-15: Achievement and Challenges*, EFA Global Monitoring Report, 2015, Paris: UNESCO Publishing, p. 147.

VII

INDIA AND JOMTIEN

By a magnificent coincidence, India's efforts to provide a new impetus and direction to UEE and universal literacy in the light of NPE, 1986, were co-eval with the build-up of the Education for All (EFA) movement internationally. The climacteric event of that movement was the World Conference on Education for All, held in Jomtien, Thailand, March 1990, (popularly known as Jomtien Conference). The Jomtien Conference was the largest international gathering on education with about 1,500 participants; almost all the countries, almost all donors, and international and regional NGOs engaged in the field of education were in full force. The list of sponsors, co-sponsors, and associate sponsors was pretty long. While UNDP, UNESCO, UNICEF, and the World Bank were the sponsors, UNFPA, ADB, Inter-American Development Bank, USAID, Islamic Educational, Scientific and Cultural Organization, Japan, Denmark, Finland, Norway, and Sweden were co-sponsors, and WHO, ESCAP, Canadian International Development Agency (CIDA), International Development Research Centre (IDRC), Italy, Switzerland, and Bernard van Leer Foundation were associate sponsors. Never before had the entire 'development assistance industry' and all the countries came together on a single platform to give a clarion 'call to action': to ensure singly and jointly that the basic learning needs of all are met, and while doing so, give priority to the education of girls and women, and to removing educational disparities. The concept of basic education visualized by the Declaration of the Jomtien Conference brought together for the first time primary schooling,[1] NFE, and adult education which were hitherto treated as different segments of education. Equally importantly, a paradigm shift in the economic thinking about education ushered a new intellectual climate which imparted a sense of urgency to universalization of primary education by countries which were yet to do so. It is this new climate which ensured that Jomtien Conference was not yet another conference like the series of regional conferences on the development of education organized by the UNESCO between 1960 and 1966, one each for African, Asian, Latin American, and Arab regions. These conferences set ambitious targets: African, Asian, and Arab countries were to attain universal and free primary education by 1980 and Latin American countries by 1970 itself. Of particular relevance to India is the Karachi Plan adopted in 1960 by 15 Asian countries.[2] These conferences aroused great hopes that 'endless resources unleashed by disarmament' would be available to educational development, and 'the dream of universal free education of at least 7 years' was real and realizable.[3] However, the hopes of endless resources turned out to be a pipe dream, and given the extant economic thinking on education, few external funding agencies were willing to fund primary education; the programmes financed by UNESCO were, to use jargon, *upstream* activities such as studies and workshops, and few *downstream* programme activities. At best only innovations, studies, and workshops were supported, and not direct efforts to promote education. In contrast, the new intellectual environment ensured that after the Jomtien Conference most development agencies extended priority to basic education in their operations and displayed a willingness 'to put money where mouth is'. According to a background study for the World Education Forum, Dakar (2010)—the sequel of the Jomtien

[1] In international parlance what is termed in India as elementary education is now termed primary education; hence, in this chapter primary education and elementary education are used interchangeably, and so are universal primary education (UPE) and universal elementary education (UEE).

[2] Fernando Valderrama, *A History of UNESCO*, Paris: UNESCO Publishing 1995, p. 129.

[3] Anand W.P. Guruge, 'Growing up with UNESCO in ROEAP' in 'UNESCO in Asia and the Pacific: 40 Years on', *Bulletin of the UNESCO Office for Education in Asia and the Pacific*, Number 27, November 1986, Section Two, p. 20.

Conference a decade later[4]—during the 1990s bilateral agencies' commitments to basic education (as a percentage of commitments to all education) had increased from a very low level to an average of 28 per cent; in absolute terms, the total value of bilateral funding earmarked for basic education increased to around $500 million. Among multilaterals, aid commitments to basic education increased from $550 million to an annual average of $1.5 billion in the second half of the decade. The World Bank doubled its lending for education from $918.7 million to an average of $1.9 billion a year. It also increased the percentage of its lending devoted to basic education from 27 per cent to 44 per cent of the lending to education, and increased the lending for girls' education to an average of $860 million per year. The priority that basic education came to acquire in operations of agencies comes out more sharply when set against the gloomy backdrop of declining aid. ODA levels in current price terms were 10 per cent lower by 2000 than those in 1992 because of a number of reasons such as global economic downturn, the raison d'etre for 'political aid' ceasing to exist with the end of the Cold War, large fiscal deficits in developed countries which are major providers of ODA, a number of academic studies which concluded that 'aid did not work', and the increasing demands for humanitarian assistance because of the expanding numbers of people affected by natural calamities and local conflicts. It should be mentioned, however, that notwithstanding the expanded vision of basic education that the Jomtien Declaration expounded almost the whole of ODA went to primary schooling; Jomtien did not make any difference to the tendency of most agencies to stay away from adult education. The fact that the Jomtien Conference did make a difference in terms of outcomes is brought out by the *Final Report* of the Dakar Conference.[5] While the indicative targets of the Jomtien Declaration and Framework were not met in their entirety, there was 'ample evidence that a large number of countries have taken serious steps to implement the Jomtien agenda, many of which have been successful'. Symptomatic of the impact of the Jomtien Conference was the fact that 'some 10 million more children

[4] World Education Forum, Education for All Assessment, *Funding Agency Contributions to Education for All*, Thematic Studies, Dakar, Senegal, 26–28 April 2000.

[5] World Education Forum, Dakar, *Final Report*, Paris: UNESCO, 2000.

have been going to school every year, which is nearly double the average increase in the preceding decade'. The report made special mention of the fact that 'China and India have made impressive progress towards achieving universal primary education, especially with regard to girls'.

Power of Ideas Makes the Jomtien Conference Exceptional

A *what* history, describing events as they occurred and the impact of those events, is only one aspect of history; far more interesting is *why* history. Why it was that so many agencies came together for the first time at Jomtien to espouse basic education? And furthermore, after Jomtien why did the agencies step forward to fund primary education on an unprecedented scale? These questions can be answered only by drawing upon the history of the ideas about what constitutes development and how best development can be fostered. While the views of educationists about what education ought to be, and how education systems should be organized, do influence top-level policymakers in national governments and agencies, their views alone do not matter. What distinguishes public policy from polices made by other organizations such as business and not-for-profit organizations is the distinctiveness of government as an organization, the vast scope of public policy and its far-reaching impact, multiplicity of considerations and decision criteria, multiplicity of 'actors', and the permeability of the decision-making process to 'outside' influence. Every public policy question needs to be looked at from multiple perspectives, and there can be no policy unless the multiple perspectives are reconciled. Education is no exception. The priority to be given to, say, public expenditure on education is not a matter for educationists alone. Thus, educationists consider that providing educational opportunities to all children and adults who miss out schooling is a moral imperative which transcends mundane considerations such as availability of resources. It is common to come across the viewpoint that there would be no dearth of resources for education and other social services if only wasteful expenditures such as military expenditure were reduced. Thus, in her Frank McDougall lecture delivered in Rome in 1981, Indira Gandhi bemoaned the arms race and observed that the expenditure on building a new intercontinental ballistic missile was equal to the cost of establishing 3 lakh primary schools. The website for the EFA Global Monitoring Report claims that '6 days of military spending by aid donors would close the US$16 billion Education for All external financing gaps'. However, any government of the day cannot afford to look at public expenditure on education only from the perspective of educationists without regard to other competing demands. It would be wonderful to have a world free of arms build-up and vices, and where everyone is altruistic. Unfortunately, policy has to be formulated for the world *as is* and not the world as it *ought to be*. In the real world, simple choices do not exist as in a scholarly paper or a rhetorical speech; it is not a question of guns versus butter but of guns as well as butter. It is juvenile to consider that all defence expenditure is a waste disregarding the fact that without securing itself a nation can neither develop in any manner nor take up welfare programmes of any kind. In the real world in which power is the currency of international relations, unilateral disarmament is a recipe for disaster. In the face of inadequate resources and competing demands, prioritization is inevitable, and the question is not of absolute priorities but one of relative priorities, not whether education is valuable or not but how much of budgetary support could be provided to education in the face of competing demands. While there is scope to improve the efficiency of public spending, the scope for shift of budgetary resources from one area to another is far less than advocates of spending in a given area would like. That is one of the main reasons why successive Indian governments could not fulfil the promise of allocating 6 per cent of GDP to education.

All policy questions need to be looked at from different perspectives: the perspective of the subject matter under consideration as well as legal, economic, and managerial perspectives. The legal perspective is important as any policy has to conform to a binding legal obligation, domestic or international. From mid-1990s, the demand for a legislation to provide free and compulsory elementary education gained momentum as the proponents believed rightly that if a legal liability is created the government cannot plead lack of resources as a ground for justifying its inability to provide free and compulsory elementary education to every child. On the international plane, in the run up to Jomtien the legal perspective was not important. The Universal Declaration of Human Rights (UDHR), 1948, the Declaration of the Rights of Child (1959), and the International Covenant on Economic,

Social, and Cultural Rights (1966; entry into force 3 January 1976) had declared that free and compulsory elementary education was a human right. However, in actuality it was only after the Convention on the Rights of the Child (CRC) entered into force in 1990, and UNICEF wholeheartedly embraced a rights-based approach did the idea of primary education as a human right acquire a strong champion. Till the Cold War ended in 1989, for strategic reasons Western democracies were prone to stress civil and political rights while Soviet Bloc countries tended to hold that civil and political rights were of no consequence in the absence of economic and social rights. Bertolt Brecht's characterization of freedom of speech as a lapidary bourgeoisie luxury typifies the Communist approach to rights. 1979 was the International Year of the Child, and a major objective of the celebration was to provide a framework for advocacy on behalf of children. Poland took the opportunity to submit to the UN Commission on Human Rights a proposal to transform the Declaration of the Rights of Child (1959) into a binding international instrument. CRC was such an instrument, and it took ten long years for the CRC to be adopted by the UN General Assembly as Poland's move was taken to be a Cold War ploy and, even within the UN system, there was little support. James Grant, Executive Director, UNICEF, initially had reservations about child rights because he felt that rights advocates were too preoccupied with child protection to the detriment of child development and survival, or to put it in a colourful language, too much obsessed with individual abuse—'one child being flogged'—and too little interested in the crimes of omission which condemned millions of children to poverty and disease. Grant strongly believed that the success of the mass immunization programme he was steering very much depended on mobilizing political will and the co-operation of the national governments. His was a Keynesian view which placed governments at the heart of all efforts to promote child development survival. Adopting a rights-based approach would entail a profound shift in UNICEF's attitude towards governments. Instead of applauding governments for saving lives, with a rights-based approach, UNICEF would be accusing governments for failing to meet their legal obligations and letting children die. However, for reasons not yet known in the public domain, from 1986 onwards UNICEF began to play an active role in the drafting of the CRC, and ensuring that the child protection focus of the original text of CRC was expanded to cover all aspects of children's needs. Even while doing so, UNICEF ensured that the landmark World Summit on Children (September 1990) held 6 months after the Jomtien Conference was kept separate and distinct. UNICEF fully embraced CRC only after Carol Bellamy succeeded Grant in May 1995, and unequivocally declared that CRC was UNICEF's mandate. It was thereafter UNICEF enthusiastically began to finance NGOs for rights-based advocacy, and 'naming and shaming' governments for acts of omission and commission in the enforcement of child rights, and in 1998, UNICEF adopted a rights-based programming of its activities. K was associated with UNICEF in two spells from 1990 to 1996, and again from 2001 to 2013. The UNICEF in the second spell was qualitatively a distinct organization from the one he knew in the 1990s.

In the absence of a binding legal obligation to provide every child basic education, the economic perspective was predominant as every policy choice has financial implications and resources being scarce and demands many a choice has to be made among competing demands. While governments do make choices based on non-economic considerations, they cannot wholly eschew financial, if not economic, considerations. In deciding the choice among competing demands, the staple concepts and tools of economist's trade such as allocative efficiency, cost-effectiveness, the relation between inputs and outputs, and the contribution the choice can make to the productivity, growth, and competiveness of the economy come to the fore. The managerial perspective assumes importance because of the ineluctable fact that a policy is as good as its implementation.

With the legal perspective being not relevant, the educationist's perspective received a mighty challenge from the perspective of economists. The policies and programmes of multilateral organizations are shaped by the world view of its dominant professional group. Thus, the educational policies and programmes UNESCO espouses are shaped by educationists who are its dominant professional group, and that being so, its policies and programmes might not be wholly in synch with those advocated by development economists; however, there are limits to the 'independent line' of UNESCO for the compulsion to raise resources over and above the financial contributions of the Member States—or to use jargon, extra-budgetary resources—compel UNESCO not to stray far too away from the extant conventional wisdom of the development economics profession. In contrast to UNESCO, the World Bank is first and foremost a bank, and its policies and practices can be best understood and should be assessed on that basis only. Only for its soft credit arm, the International Development Association (IDA), does the World Bank receive contributions from developed countries; the bulk of its funding has to be raised from the market. Consequently, financial and economic considerations largely dictate its operational policies. In the World Bank, economists constitute the most influential professional group, and the conventional economic wisdom conditions the policy of the Bank; this 'monopoly of single professional interests' is resented by other professional groups such as educators. The intense professional rivalry between educators and economists within the Bank was too palpable to be missed by K when he was attending the meetings of the World Bank External Advisory Panel appointed by President Wolfensohn of which K was a member; that rivalry was to impact on Bank's policies and policy advice.

Ever since the end of the Second World War when the process of decolonization began and economic development came to be a preoccupation of underdeveloped countries, development economics underwent far-reaching changes again and again. In parallel to the trajectory of the reigning ideas of economic development, the placement of education in the development process had also undergone a vast change from education being a provider of the critical manpower to being an objective by itself and central to the very idea of what development is about; relative priorities to be given to different areas of education also underwent far-reaching changes. Particularly in regard to primary education, one could discern four phases;[6] in the first phase from 1946 to late 1960s, most economists viewed primary education to be a non-economic factor which did not directly contribute to economic development. In keeping with the regnant development planning models, most countries assigned a higher priority to investment in technical and higher education than other stages of education as education was valued for its supply of the critical skills and knowledge necessary for planned development. Aid was available mostly for investment in industry and physical infrastructure; the little aid that went for education was earmarked for engineering, vocational, and agricultural education, and for

[6] Any periodization is bound to be arbitrary; the periods indicated are ballpark figures.

deputation of technical experts. In the second phase (mid-1960s to end of 1970s), the view that a minimum basic education should be provided to all as soon as available resources permit gained ascendancy among economists. The third phase spanning roughly a 15-year period from 1980 to 1995 was the high noon of the view that countries which are yet to universalize primary education should accord primacy to primary education in the matter of investment and development. The corollary of this view was that in such countries it would be iniquitous and inefficient to divert the available resources for education from primary education to higher education. With the rise of the new information technologies and the consequential eagerness of countries to become knowledge societies and economies, the primacy of primary education gave way to the belief that national education systems need to develop in a balanced manner, and that higher education is as much an investment priority as primary education.

Primary Education Becomes 'Cool'

During the 1980s, the idea that providing primary education to every child is a development imperative which should be given an overriding priority in countries which were yet to universalize primary education acquired the status of conventional wisdom. And furthermore, the new conventional wisdom required governments to protect public expenditure on primary education even during harsh times of fiscal austerity. The paradigm shift in the economists' and agencies' perception of inter se priorities in education occurred due to a confluence of three streams of thought originating from three different, and to a certain extent antagonistic, sources. The first source comprises mainstream neo-classic economists, the second economists who were sharply critical of neo-classical economics, and the third those who wanted child labour to be eradicated.

Turning to neo-classical economists, once manpower planning fell from favour, the question as to how investment priorities in education should be determined came to the fore, and cost–benefit analysis by way of rate of return studies came to be seen as providing a plausible answer to the question. Rates of return on education began to be calculated in the 1960s, but it was only in late 1970s that these calculations under the research leadership of George Psacharopoulos entered the centre stage of policy debate. Rates of return studies conducted by Psacharopoulos and his team showed that in almost all developing countries rates of return to investment on education exceeded the long-run opportunity cost of capital, making education investment an excellent investment; in countries which were yet to achieve UPE, the rates of return for primary education, were higher than those of other stages of education. The conclusions of the rate of return studies of Psacharopoulos got a boost from the research about the factors contributing to the high growth rates of East Asian countries. Most of the East Asian countries had achieved UPE a decade or more earlier than other developing countries; early UPE set a virtuous cycle in motion whereby higher human capital along with right economic policies ushered high economic growth rates, which in turn permitted more investment in education leading to further augmentation of human capital and the possibility of boosting economic growth. The new economic belief that primary education was a public expenditure priority was incorporated in the much berated Washington Consensus as well as the Bank's *Educational Sector Policy Paper* (1980). The 1980 Paper laid greater emphasis on primary education than its 1974 predecessor and posited primary education as the foundation of educational development. It called for improving access of girls and rural children to primary education, limiting additional investments in secondary and higher education, enhancing the quality of primary education by providing cost-effective school inputs and teacher training, reducing internal inefficiency, mobilizing community resources and the mass media, and building local institutions. The change of guard in 1986 gave a further impetus to primary education in the Bank's operations. The incoming President Barber B. Conable was eager to revive the poverty focus of his last but one predecessor McNamara. Wadi Haddad, Head of the Bank's Education Policy Division, took advantage of Conable's poverty focus to take a number of initiatives that led to the President embracing education, particularly primary education, as a major element in the development process, and to be in the forefront of the initiative to organize a mega conference on basic education. The Jomtien Conference was the culmination of that initiative. From the mid-1980s onwards, the World Bank had been engaged on 'nothing less than a crusade to shift public monies from higher education to primary education, a position that clashed with the realities in borrowing countries',[7] and this crusade

[7] Phillip W. Jones, *World Bank Financing of Education: Lending, Learning and Development*, 2nd edition, New York: Routledge, p. 222.

was reflected in its lending operations with the share of primary education in the Bank's total educational lending increasing from 14 per cent to 23 per cent during 1985–90.[8] The Bank's message 'investing in primary education is good' was reinforced by the periodic international meetings of central bankers and finance ministers such as the annual meetings of the IMF and the World Bank; the message to developing countries soon acquired the status of conventional wisdom.

It is not unusual in academic discourse for divergent arguments leading to the same conclusion and similar arguments leading to divergent conclusions. It was therefore not surprising that even those economists who were sharply critical of neo-classical economics and of the policy prescriptions of the Washington Consensus were equally articulate in extolling the virtues of universalizing primary education. In the 1990s, Amartya Sen began using his celebrity status to deplore the neglect of elementary education, and urging more investment in, and attention to, elementary education; his associate Jean Drèze, who came to be based in India, began a spirited advocacy campaign for social issues such as UEE and right to food. In his D.T. Lakdawala Lecture (1994), Amartya Sen rued the fact that 'the gap between attention to higher education and neglect of elementary education has, if anything, *grown* rather than shrunk over the last twenty five years' since his Lal Bahadur Shastri Memorial Lecture in 1970. The enrolment in colleges and universities as a proportion of population was about six times in India than in China, while China was far ahead in providing school education. He proceeded to reiterate the cultural explanation he had offered earlier (Chapter IV) and contested the view set out by NPE, 1986, that 'the skew (in educational attainments) set in with foreign domination and influence'. Because of the general social atmosphere in India, even Left parties did not show much interest in reducing educational inequalities. It was therefore imperative to address both ancient and modem biases that shape Indian educational policies.[9]

[8] Adrian Verspoor, 'Lending for Learning: Twenty Years of Support to Basic Education', Working Papers on Education and Employment, WPS 686, May 1991, p. 4.

[9] Amartya Sen, *Beyond Liberalization: Social Opportunity and Human Capability*, The First D.T. Lakdawala Memorial lecture, 29 June 1994, New Delhi: Institute of Social Sciences.

Yet another source of influence which enhanced the salience of UEE was the emergence of human development as an evocative and highly influential concept and advocacy tool. The launch of the UNDP's annual *Human Development Report* came to be a major media event with a customary crop of articles and editorial comments bemoaning the poor Human Development ranking of India. The Human Development Report was first conceived and championed as an antidote to the World Bank's *World Development Report* by Mahbub ul Haq who leaped to fame with his book *Poverty Curtain* (1976) wherein he called upon developing countries to dethrone growth from its high pedestal and launch a direct assault on poverty instead of relentlessly pursuing growth with the expectation that the benefits of growth would percolate to the poor. Human Development is a concept that logically flows from the central message of *Poverty Curtain*, and was detailed by Mahbub ul Haq, Amartya Sen, and a few other development thinkers. As the first report (1990) put it, human development is a process of enlarging people's choices. A person's access to income is no doubt one of the choices, but it is not the sum total of human endeavour. One of the three dimensions of the human development index (HDI), based on which all countries are ranked every year, is knowledge and education; among the values which go into the construction of the HDI are the adult literacy rate and the combined primary Gross Enrollment Ratio. From the perspective of human development, the question was no longer 'How does investment in education promote economic growth?' It was the opposite: 'How does economic growth promote variety and quality in education and human development?'[10]

Yet another personality whose visits to India made waves was Myron Weiner, noted political scientist turned crusader for a compulsory education law. In his much publicized book *The Child and the State in India*—widely distributed by UNICEF as part of its advocacy campaign—as well as in his address at the Rajiv Gandhi Foundation in January 1994, he attributed the failure to abolish child labour in its entirety and compel all children to attend school due to the 'deeply held beliefs that there is a division between people who work with their minds and rule and people who work with their hands and are

[10] Angela Little, Wim Hoppers, and Roy Gardner, *Beyond Jomtien: Implementing Education for All*, London: Macmillan, 1994, p. 2.

ruled, and that education should reinforce rather than break down this division'. Consequently, Indian education had been largely an instrument for differentiation by separating children according to class (Chapter IV).[11]

In the acrimonious debates on structural adjustment during the 1980s, the question whether the obligation to provide primary education to *all* subsisted even during periods of fiscal austerity when governments were compelled to curtail public expenditure loomed large. In the 1970s and early 1980s, the economies of many developing countries in Latin America and Africa were in utter disarray. In order to tide over the macroeconomic crisis, such countries had to secure the assistance of the IMF and the World Bank, and as a condition of securing assistance, they had to adopt policies which go by the name of structural adjustment. Analytically, economic crises which necessitate structural adjustment are different from crises such as the Great Depression and the recent 2008–9 crisis. The symptoms of crises which necessitate structural adjustment are different; so are the causes and policy prescriptions. These crises are characterized by excessive liquidity, high levels of inflation, chronic fiscal imbalances, and chronic trade imbalances. These symptoms are caused by unsustainable subsidies, leakages in revenue collection, bloated public enterprises which were a heavy drain on budgetary resources and in which 'working for profits was almost a sin',[12] a dependent capitalism where private enterprise competes not in the marketplace but in the corridors of power for state patronage by way of licences, distortions in factor and goods markets (prices, wages, and profits), selective implementation of controls and tariff protection, and an artificially pegged foreign exchange rate that discriminates against exports. Keynesian stimulus packages appropriate for the Great Depression would be highly improper for them. Once such a crisis leads to a serious balance of payment situation and inability to service debts, there is no option but to pass through a phase of stabilization that entails economic austerity for restoring through demand management an internal balance between income and expenditure of government as well as an external balance between inflow and outflow

[11] Myron Weiner, *The Child and the State in India*, Princeton, NJ: Princeton University Press, 1991, pp. 5–6.

[12] P.V. Narasimha Rao, *The Insider*, New Delhi: Penguin Press, 2000, p. 290.

of goods and capital. Neither individuals nor societies can chose to be austere without being prepared to bear the pain that austerity necessarily imposes. As stabilization would only cure the symptoms of the crisis but not the basic malaise caused by wrong policies, it would be also necessary to undergo structural stabilization, that is to say complement stabilization by policies which improve the allocation of resources and efficiency by dismantling obsolete and dysfunctional controls and regulations and opening up the economic domestically and externally. Regardless of whether a country opts for credits from the World Bank and IMF, countries such as India in 1991 had little option but to break with the past policy regime unless they chose to be stuck in a denial mode and aggravate the crisis.

As long as the post-Second World War global economic boom lasted, countries which were engulfed in balance of payment crisis could expect support from the IMF to tide over the crisis without being required to commit themselves to structural changes in the economy. This was no longer possible once the boom was over and a global economic downturn manifested itself in the late 1970s, and more and more developing countries landed in acute economic crises. In order to meet the medium- and longer-term needs of countries trying to overcome structural imbalances in their economies, the World Bank and the IMF introduced a number of new credit arrangements to help countries in crisis to stabilize their economies and effect structural adjustment. In many countries, education and training constitute the single largest item of budgeted expenditure; in India for example, education accounts for about 20 per cent of the total budgetary expenditure of state governments. Hence, education was a tempting target for 'big ticket' reduction in public expenditure.

There was much that was wrong with the way that structural adjustment programmes were initially designed and implemented, particularly those in the late 1970s and early 1980s; however, those errors cannot justify glossing over the economic malaise that necessitated adjustment in the first place. The conditionalities that the IMF and World Bank imposed got enmeshed with the sharp ideological strife generated by the demands of developing countries in UN bodies for a new international economic order as well as by the displacement in the 1980s of the state-centric economic paradigm by the market-friendly economic paradigm. In the white heat of ideological strife, a sense of proportion was lacking among the antagonists. Initially, the conditionalities were overzealously imposed with far too much concern for efficiency and far too little concern for equity. In developing countries with hardly any social policies to mitigate poverty, deprivation, and job loss, the short-term costs of adjustment on the poor and basic services such as basic education and primary health care were very high. These hardships came in handy for the old believers to assert that the treatment was worse than the disease, and to challenge the explanatory causes and prescriptions offered by mainstream economists. They had no coherent alternate policy prescriptions to offer and yet they refused to accept the fact that the crisis was the result of inappropriate policies, and there was no way for a country to pull itself out of a crisis by continuing with discredited policies. All in all, in populist discourse, structural adjustment acquired notoriety sufficient to damn anything that could be associated with it.

The praxis of structural adjustment spawned two genres of studies. The first sought to assess how successful the adjustment policies were, and the second explored the social dimensions of adjustment. The results of the first genre of studies were mixed. Only a few scholars were dispassionate enough to try to separate their beliefs from the detachment that serious academic study calls for. Further, it was difficult to establish a cause-and-effect relationship between the policies and the consequences all the more so as few countries persevered long enough or adopted the full panoply of measures because of the political costs of adjustment. The most famous of the second genre of studies was UNICEF's *Adjustment with a Human Face*[13]; it vividly brought out the hardships that adjustment imposed on the short term and had a decisive impact on the policy prescriptions of economists. The UNICEF study recognized that '*the primary cause* of the downward economic pressures on the human situation in most of the countries *is the overall economic situation, globally and nationally, not adjustment policy as such. Indeed, without some form of adjustment, the situation would often be far worse*' (emphasis added). However, adjustment policies should have a 'human face' such that 'the human implications of

[13] Giovanni Andrea Cornia, Richard Jolly, and Frances Stewart, ed., *Adjustment with a Human Face: Protecting the Vulnerable and Promoting Growth: A Study by UNICEF*, Volumes I and II, Oxford: Clarendon Press, 1987.

an adjustment policy' are 'an integral part of the adjustment policy as a whole', and 'not treated as an additional welfare component'. From the start, UNICEF proceeded from the premise that 'practical advance towards adjustment with a human face would only be possible only if it attracted the support of those in the mainstream of economic policy-making, both nationally and internationally' and it sought to win over mainstream economists by anchoring the rationale for human face in development theory. At the request of the IMF and the World Bank, UNICEF started a dialogue in 1984 with those institutions as to how best they could promote adjustment with a human face, and as a result, the idea of adjustment with a human face gained currency, and the terms 'adjustment' and 'with a human face' came to be like a single hyphenated word. On the normative plane, the praxis of structural adjustment now commends that provision of basic education services should not be curtailed during the phase of fiscal austerity. As part of medium- and long-term restructuring of the economy, it commends policy reform in three directions: (*a*) reallocation of expenditure between different levels and types of education; (*b*) an increase in the efficiency of resource use by means such as better use of teachers and facilities, and changes in study programmes; and (*c*) mobilization of new sources of income, and offering incentives to private sector to expand access.[14] However, the UNESCO–ILO case studies on structural adjustment indicated that even when reallocation of resources within education sector took place, it did not always conform to stated priorities, and given the clout of academics, reallocation had often favoured higher education. And furthermore, there were few examples of improved use of resources.[15] Suffice it to say, it is not factually correct to treat the praxis of structural adjustment as if it were invariant; economists like most other professionals do learn from experience and take note of well-reasoned and well-founded criticism. No organization, not even the World Bank or the IMF, can

[14] Klaus Bahr, Lucilla Jallade, and Eddy Lee, in Joel Samoff, ed., *Coping with Crisis: Austerity, Adjustment and Human Resources*, London: Cassel, 1994, p. 11.

[15] Maureen Woodhall, 'The Effects of Austerity and, Adjustment on the Allocation and Use of Resources: A Comparative Analysis of Five Case Studies', in Joel Samroff, ed., *Coping with Crisis: Austerity, Adjustment and Human Resources*, London: Cassell, 1994, pp. 197–8.

survive if it does not learn from experience and absorb advances in knowledge. World Bank policies in education have never been static, and the history of its support to education, to paraphrase Jones, the historian of World Bank educational lending, is a series of yesterday's heresies turning into today's orthodoxies.[16] Once it embraced structural adjustment with a human face, the World Bank began to insist on its lending operations for restoring macroeconomic balance provision of social safety nets so as to protect the poor and basic services during the austerity phase. The lending operations to help India to tide over the economic crisis in 1991 are an example of this policy.

Suffice it to say, by mid-1980s, the Bank preached the virtues of UPE to movers and shakers of the world who control national and international finances, the UNICEF preached evocatively to social activists who could make a dent on public opinion, while UNESCO preached pedantically and rather hesitantly to those who needed no conversion, namely educationists.

Jomtien Conference: A Product of Policy Entrepreneurship

The role of a hero in history has been much debated in historiography. While a hero cannot be the prime mover if the objective conditions and the ideational environment do not permit, he does make a difference in that, to say the very least, get the history turn earlier than it would. From what was narrated above, the idea that primary education was the foundation of development and that it should be sustained even during hard times was acquiring a hegemonic status by the end of the 1980s. However, it would not have, to use a contemporaneous cliché, gone viral and been incorporated into the policies of governments and agencies, and more importantly, acted upon with despatch and resolve but for human intervention. The heroes who made the Jomtien Conference a reality were Haddad and James Grant, Executive Director, UNICEF. In the 'donor world' of those days, the Bank was Snow White while other agencies were dwarfs. Through his initiatives within the Bank, Haddad had prepared the ground to take the lead for organizing a global movement for giving primacy to primary education in development praxis.

[16] Philip W. Jones, *World Bank Financing of Education: Lending, Learning and Development*, 1st edition, London: Routledge, 1992, p. 219.

While financiers are the shakers and movers of the people, they are not exactly popular, and they are better off if they are joined by people and organizations that are universally liked, like mom and apple pie. That was where UNICEF came in. After winning laurels for steering the 'child survival and development revolution' of which mass immunization was the most visible element, Grant was on the lookout for spectacular initiatives that would earn him and the organization he headed more laurels, and he turned to primary education in the belief that the strategy adopted for promoting universal child immunization could be replicated with universal primary education. The moment Grant approached the Bank for organizing a world conference to promote education for all, Conable was more than willing to join Grant's initiative. As soon as Frederico Mayor succeeded M'Bow in 1987, he also joined the Jomtien initiative as it was a golden opportunity to UNESCO to reclaim the standing lost during the M'Bow years and project the impression that, notwithstanding its financial constraints, 'UNESCO crisis' was a thing of the past. UNESCO's institutional interest in the Jomtien was to ensure that there was no erosion in its time-honoured standing as the UN's lead agency in education, and as things turned out, diplomatic sensibilities required that standing to be observed. Consequently, UNESCO was designated as the 'lead agency' for monitoring subsequent progress in attaining conference objectives. UNDP also joined the bandwagon. By February 1989, the heads of the World Bank, UNDP, UNESCO, and UNICEF had announced that a world conference on EFA would be convened at Jomtien in March 1990 at which they and the international community would be invited to commit resources in the hope that universal basic education was assured by 2000.

For India, the timing of the Conference could not have been better; the intensive reflective process preceding and following NPE, 1986, was the best preparation that any country could have had for making its presence felt in such an international conference. What is more remarkable is the fact that the NPE, 1986, praxis for UEE and adult education had neatly anticipated the Jomtien Declaration and Framework for action; it was as if the international community adopted that praxis. With his customary gusto and élan, Bordia plunged into the EFA movement. As happened when he was around, he began to lead the movement from the front.

Negotiation Dance at Jomtien

Managing a coalition, even if it were a coalition of the willing, is quite a task, a fact captured by the quote: 'Lord, protect me from my friends, I can take care of my friends.' The fact that all agencies, international and regional NGOs, and countries were eager to join the EFA bandwagon made securing an agreement on the Declaration and Framework more difficult. In any coalition or partnership the members have some common interests but many of their interests are not congruent, and hence each member would like the common pursuit to be as close to one's interests and preferences as possible. Hence, hard negotiations are needed to define the common pursuit and purse that pursuit. Tensions and contradictions continually and inevitably arise, and if not managed, the coalition or partnership would be torn as under. Multilateral negotiations are often high drama marked by spectacular swing of fortunes. The sequence of events would be such that after a slow start, negotiations move to the brink of collapse and failure. When all hope is lost, a knight in shining armour, or more often a group of knights, miraculously rescues the negotiations, which go on ultimately to a happy ending and conclusion of an agreement. Even when an agreement is reached, it is often not a precise agreement but one deliberately couched in what, in jargon, is called *constructive* ambiguity. Forcing a resolution of one or more of the sensitive issues during the initial negotiation may place unbearable strain on the overall settlement process, and may result in the breakdown of the negotiations. Rather than let the negotiations collapse, the parties agree to deliberately use ambiguous language on sensitive issues in the expectation that they can resolve the other issues and later return to the unresolved issues. There is much truth in the French saying that there could be no treaties without conflicting mental reservations.[17] The Jomtien Conference was no different, for three of the sponsors (UNESCO, UNICEF, and the World Bank) as well as some countries had different perceptions on what is basic education, on whether any particular year should be specified for achievement of the goals and objectives the Conference would agree upon, and on whether basic

[17] David A. Lax and James K. Sebenius, *The Manager as Negotiator: Bargaining for Cooperation and Competitive Gain*, New York: The Free Press, 1986, p. 97.

education should be given an overriding priority as compared to, say, higher education.

What Is Basic Education?

The funding agencies who participated in the Conference were eager to ensure that the concept of basic education adopted by the Conference and the modalities for achieving basic education commended by the Conference were the ones they could financially support without any discomfort. Of the four sponsors of the Jomtien Conference, UNDP strayed into the Conference in a fit of absent-mindedness, and after the Conference, it woke up and was in a tearing hurry to move to an agenda of its own which centred round sustainable human development. No wonder that it had no precise position on the conceptualization of basic education or the optimal modalities for achieving basic education for all. In contrast to other sponsors, UNESCO advocated the most expansive concept of basic education, putting forth the view that no society achieved universal literacy through primary schooling alone, and that all societies require additional means to consolidate and make up the deficiencies of primary schooling. UNESCO could be righteous given its mandate as well as the fact that it was not a funding agency and, as such, not required to make choices and programme priorities that better-resourced organizations are compelled to make.

It was Grant who mooted the idea of the Conference in the first place, and he came to Jomtien eager to secure international validation for his idea that a spirited one-shot global campaign should be launched for getting all children to school, much like the mass immunization programme which eradicated polio and other diseases that endangered the survival of children. For Grant what mattered above all was political will, and he saw the job of the sponsors of the Jomtien Conference to be drumming up the political will. And further, what mattered was getting children to school, and the type of school or the number of years of schooling did not matter. A great favourite of UNICEF those days was the network of alternate schools established by Bangladesh Rural Advancement Committee (BRAC), an NGO originally set up in November to provide emergency relief to people affected by cyclone in a small part of Bangladesh. BRAC diversified rapidly, and among its activities was a network of over 35,000 alternate schools that catered to very poor children. BRAC schools were of two types: three-year non-formal primary education schools for eight to ten-year-old children who never attended primary schools, and two-year *Kishore–Kishori* schools for children in the age group 11–16 who had dropped out of schools and were unlikely to return to schools. The teachers were generally married adults of the locality who had completed 9 years or more of education; they were hired on a temporary, part-time basis, and paid modest wages. Suffice it to say, UNICEF was not inclined to limit basic education to primary schooling. UNICEF's attitude to literacy was ambivalent; on one hand, it had considerable experience of educating women in child care, and on the other, it did not want attention on educating children, its prime constituency, to be distracted by too much attention on literacy and other aspects of basic education.

The Bank was keen that its point of view on educational priorities and modes of delivery be accepted by all the participants of the Jomtien Conference and receive the imprimatur of the Declaration which would be adopted by the Conference. It was convinced that low- to middle-income countries were generally under-investing in basic education, and that many had overestimated the social returns from investments in higher education; the policy implication was that the goals which the Jomtien Conference would set up would require for their realization a shift in the inter se priorities away from higher education towards primary education. Bank President Conable and his delegation in Jomtien convinced that universal primary schooling was the most affordable and realistic pathway to reach the goal of basic education for all. In the Bank's view, universalizing primary schooling and enhancing the efficiency of primary education was the best guarantor of universal literacy and universal basic education. As an intellectual powerhouse, the Bank sought to lend strong support to its position by preparing for the Conference a research study *Improving Primary Education in Developing Countries*,[18] as well as the draft of a new policy paper that would guide the lending operations of the Bank after the Jomtien Conference. Conable himself presided over a Roundtable it organized at the Conference to discuss the research study and draft

[18] Marlaine Lockheed, Adrian M. Verspoor and Associates, *Improving Primary Education in Developing Countries*, New York: Oxford University Press, 1991.

policy. At that Roundtable, Bordia won recognition as 'an influential and highly articulate foe' of World Bank's policy priorities and approach to basic education.[19] Given his ideological disposition and strong commitment to non-formal and adult education, Bordia was quite critical of the study, contending among others that some errors could have been avoided if some case studies relating to the Third World countries were taken into account; that omission led to primary education being treated as an exclusively educational and managerial problem and not as a part of the overall socio-cultural issues, the indispensable need to provide NFE being not appreciated, the possibility of locating instructors by the local community as in Shiksha Karmi being ignored, and the importance of social mobilization being not understood. Even while being critical, Bordia appreciated the fact that ' the document is based on thorough research … the reason for researchers from Third World countries not receiving enough attention could be that they are not sufficiently sophisticated and scientific or their dissemination is not widespread'. He also held that the chapter on content of education was well-written, and that three aspects of the educational crisis (insufficiency of the system, low levels of the learning achievement, and decline and insufficient investment in primary education) were correctly spelt out. Even while asserting that education at primary level could not be confined to the achievement of three 'R's, and that affective issues, character formation, value inculcation, development of scientific temper, and so on were also important, he conceded that the stress on cognitive aspects was justified. All Third World countries, particularly India, need to pay much greater attention to the achievement levels of the three Rs and to the development of problem-solving skills among children. They should also lay stress on measurement of learning. There were many sensitive and justified observations in the chapter on management such as the low status of school principals, need for decentralization, and the involvement of local community. The authors were in the right direction on stressing in-service training rather than pre-service training, and in emphasizing curriculum, text books, and teacher training. He concluded by saying that all in all, although the research study's overall worldview was contestable, it was a solid piece

[19] *World Bank Financing of Education: Lending, Learning and Development*, 1st edition, p. 222.

of research. At the 'Closing Plenary Session', Bordia was one of three delegates chosen to offer 'calls to action', and he spoke eloquently of the need for something substantial being done by everyone, a genuine reordering of priorities in policies and budgetary allocations. We are, he declared, 'asking for a decisive shift in favour of change and fresh look being taken at the way in which the limited resources are reallocated so that basic education receives the priority it deserves'.[20]

Accounts vary as to who should be given the credit for ensuring that an expanded concept of basic education was adopted by the Jomtien Conference; some give credit to Grant and others to Colin Power, UNESCO's Assistant DG for Education. Basic education outlined in the Jomtien Declaration and in the international discourse after Jomtien is education that meets the *basic learning needs* of every person, child, youth, and adult; meeting basic learning needs of all is captured by the much used phrase Education for All (EFA). The Jomtien Declaration expounded an expanded vision of EFA that has two important features. First, even while setting down that the main delivery system for basic education was the school system, the Declaration recognized that the basic learning needs of children, youth, and adults were diverse, and that therefore these needs should be provided by a variety of delivery systems: primary schooling, non-formal education, and adult education. Secondly, irrespective of the delivery systems employed, the learner should achieve and maintain an acceptable level of learning so that provision of basic education is equitable. The Jomtien Declaration graphically presented the magnitude of the challenge. A hundred million children had no access to primary schooling. Of these, at least 60 million were girls. If enrolment rates remained at the current levels, by the year 2000, more than 160 million children would have no access to primary schooling simply because of population growth. More than 980 million adults were illiterate; of these, more than two-third were women. More than a hundred million children and countless adults fail to complete basic educational programmes; millions more satisfy attendance requirement but do not acquire essential knowledge and skills

[20] *Final Report of the World Conference on Education for All: Meeting Basic Learning Needs*, New York: Inter-Agency Commission, WCEFA (UNDP, UNESCO, UNICEF, World Bank), May 1990, p. 35.

(Article 1).[21] The Declaration and Framework called for enhanced international cooperation to support country and regional efforts to achieve EFA goals. They also called upon countries and agencies to develop appropriate action policies and action plans to achieve EFA goals. A mid-decade review was envisaged to take stock of the progress towards the country-specific and global EFA goals; that review was conducted in a conference in Amman, Jordan, in 1996.

Should a Target Year Be Specified for Achieving EFA?

UNICEF was particular that the Declaration should specify a target year, as Grant was of the view that the Jomtien Conference would fail to accomplish its most objective, namely drumming up the political will needed for making EFA a reality, if it did not dare the top leadership of nations and agencies to take up a formidable challenge. Only a Mission Impossible would stir up the animal spirits of leaders who shook and moved the world. However, UNICEF's stand was strongly opposed by many developing countries still far away from UPE and universal literacy. The Bank was inclined to agree with these countries, as UPE could only be achieved when countries could afford it, and UPE was quite a way off for many countries. Eventually the Declaration made no mention of the target year; in fact, it explicitly postulated that 'the scope of basic learning needs and how they should be met varies with individual countries, and inevitably changes with the passage of time'. Over course of time, the scope of basic education was expected to expand further, and eventually, secondary education was expected to be part of basic education. In the face of conflicting views, the Framework of Action resorted to constructive ambiguity. While the countries were left free to set their own targets in the 1990s, they were exhorted not to go solely by 'current trends and resources' but to factor in the possibilities provided by Jomtien Declaration to mobilize external resources from agencies. They were also called upon to fix the targets keeping in mind 'dimensions' set out by the Framework; these dimensions included achieving by the year 2000 universal access to

[21] *World Declaration on Education for All*, Inter-Agency Commission, New York: UNICEF House, April 1990.

primary education, completion of primary schooling by every child, and reducing by the year 2000 adult illiteracy rate to one half of the 1990 level, and while doing so significantly reduce the disparity between female and male literacy. Everyone could go home proclaiming victory; UNICEF and its NGO partners could argue that all governments had committed themselves to achieve EFA by the year 2000 while the countries could argue equally plausibly that there was no such commitment.

Talking of the target year, the personal account of Psacharopoulos on the World Bank's policy one education[22] brings out that this fervent champion of Bank supporting primary education first and foremost was reluctant to attend the Jomtien Conference, and that but for the compulsions of the position he held at the World Bank he would have stayed away. He was uncomfortable with the Jomtien Declaration and Framework which he felt was an 'exopragmatic statement given the available resources', and that the target of UPE by 2000 did not seem feasible in the foreseeable future. He felt vindicated by the fact that the Dakar Conference (2000) extended the target year for UPE to 2015. The UN Millennium Summit (2000) reiterated these targets; however, these targets are likely to be missed. The views of Psacharopoulos raise a host of questions about target-setting by agencies and countries. Should global targets such as the Millennium Development Goals (MDGs) be set up when countries vary widely in their levels of development, resource endowments, and governance structures and capabilities, all the more so as the UN system has consistently shown itself to be 'better at making goals than meeting them' and 'the pledges it mints so readily (at summits and conferences) may become a 'debased currency'.[23] Similarly, in a large country such as India with sharp divergences among states should national targets that hold across different states be laid down? What is the ethics of target setting? Should only a feasible target set? Is it proper to set an 'inspirational' target on the ground that in the real world one has to aim at the stars to shoot the bird on the tree?

[22] G. Psacharopoulos, 'World Bank Policy on Education: A Personal Account', *International Journal of Educational Development*, 26 (2006), pp. 329–38, at p. 334.

[23] 'The Millennium Development Goals: The Eight Commandments', *The Economist*, 5 July 2007.

On a lighter vein, fixing elusive and shifting targets such as the Indian target for UEE is not a monopoly of India.

Priority for Elementary Education: Yes, but Not at the Expense of Higher Education

In the run up to Jomtien, the prospect of basic education getting overriding priority alarmed some countries. At Jomtien, some countries from Latin America, the Caribbean, Africa, and Asia, and IDRC, a public corporation created by the Canadian government, spearheaded efforts to ensure that the priority for basic education did not translate into a lessening of priority for higher education, and that the Declaration provided for explicit safeguards for higher education, research, and access to high technology.[24] These efforts were partly successful, and Article 8 was introduced in the Declaration which called for improving higher education and developing scientific research so as to 'insure' a strong intellectual and scientific environment for basic education. Ironically, secondary education merited no mention in spite of the fact that it was demand for secondary education that would receive an immediate boost with success in universalizing primary education. The reason is not far to seek: secondary education does not have either the political appeal of basic education or powerful constituents like higher education. In operational terms, however, Article 8 was initially of not much consequence as the external agencies including the World Bank gave a higher priority to primary education in their operations. The shift in the lending pattern raised hackles, and there was considerable criticism not only from middle-income countries of Latin America but also from the poorer countries of Africa still considerably away from releasing UPE. There was shrill criticism that external pressures and the neo-liberal agenda were preventing African countries from the pursuit of education for self-reliance.[25]

[24] Kenneth King, 'What Happened at the World Conference in Jomtien?', Norrag News, NN08, 1990, http://www.norrag.org/db_read_article.php?id=297

[25] Birgit Brock-Utne, 'Formulating Higher Education Policies in Africa—the Pressure from External Forces and the Neoliberal Agenda', *Journal of Higher Education in Africa* , 1, no. 1 (2003), pp. 24–56. http://www.netreed.uio.no/articles/high.ed_BBU.pdf (last accessed on 24 May 2015).

The New Focus on Learning Outcomes

An important element of the expanded vision of basic education expounded by the Jomtien Declaration was that irrespective of the delivery systems employed, be it schooling or NFE or adult education, the learner should achieve and maintain an acceptable level of learning. Article 4 of the Declaration postulated that the focus of basic education must, therefore, be on actual learning acquisition and outcome, rather than exclusively upon enrolment, retention, and completion of schooling or learning programmes, and that it was, therefore, necessary to define acceptable levels of learning acquisition for educational programmes and to improve and apply systems of assessing learning achievement. One of the indicative targets laid down by the Framework was 'improvement in learning achievement such that an agreed percentage of an appropriate age cohort (for example, 80 per cent of 14-year-olds) attained or surpassed a defined level of necessary learning achievement'. The new emphasis on learner achievement led Kenneth King, a discerning scholar of 'aid for education', to comment that the Jomtien Conference ushered a *new-style* universal primary education (UPE) which might be 'fittingly renamed as UPPA, universal primary access and achievement', in contrast to the *old-style* UPE which was 'mostly concerned with access, getting enough places for the children to enter'.[26] It is this new emphasis on measuring progress in learner achievement that distinguishes Jomtien. Before the 1980s, there used to be quite a debate about the minimum number of years of schooling that a child should have to be literate without relapsing into illiteracy. In India itself, some felt the number was four, while others felt that it ought to be five. However, study after study had established that not all students who completed primary schooling were functionally literate. Strange but not true, the population of illiterates seemed to be increasing not only because of non-attendance in schools, but also rather in spite of attending schools. In as early as 1958, a group of educational psychologists, sociologists, and psychometricians met at the UNESCO Institute for Education in Hamburg, Germany, to discuss problems of school and student evaluation. They came to the conclusion that discussion of the relative merits of various education systems in the

[26] Kenneth King, *Aid and in the Developing World: The Role of Donor Agencies in Analysis*, Harlow, Essex: Longman, 1991, p. 220.

absence of hard data was futile, and that it was desirable to identify factors that would have meaningful and consistent influences on educational outcomes. Nine years later, the International Association for the Evaluation of Educational Achievement (IEA) was established to promote national and cross-country evaluation of educational achievement. In his classic *The World Educational Crisis* (1967), Coombs highlighted the fact that the impressive increase in enrolment and enrolment ratios recorded in developing countries masked a dark side. The increase did not reveal the 'vast social waste and the human tragedy in the high rate of drop-outs and failures'; nor did they say anything about the nature, quality, and usefulness of the education received.[27] In their seminal study which triggered the 'non-formal fashion' of 1970s, *New Paths to Learning for Rural Education and Youth* (1973),[28] Coombs, Prosser, and Manzoor Ahmed highlighted the need to define essential learning needs in operationally meaningful terms ' so as to provide a clear guide to instruction and learning, and a practical basis for measuring achievement'; such a definition was more useful than vaguely defined objectives such as 'giving every child a good basic education', and using crude proxies such as the number of years spent at school. Increasingly, precision was sought to be imparted to the assessment of the quality of education by laying down benchmarks by way of minimum levels of learning at different stages of schooling in major subjects such as language and mathematics, and those benchmarks being used to evaluate actual learning attainment by students.

The quantitative orientation of assessing the quality of education got a boost from the intrinsic interest of the economists of education in measuring the efficiency of investment in education and of educational systems. To the analysis of education, the economist brings his staple apparatus of production function and cost–benefit analysis. As a production system, the education system should be efficient. Efficiency has two dimensions: external and internal. External efficiency requires that the benefits to the individuals receiving education as well as to the

[27] Philip H. Coombs, *The World Educational Crisis: A Systems Analysis*, New York: Oxford, 1967.

[28] Philip H. Coombs, Roy Prosser, and Manzoor Ahmed, *New Paths to Learning for Rural Education and Youth*, New York: International Council for Educational Development, 1973.

society are maximized through a balance between the supply of skilled manpower by the education system on the one hand and the requirements of the economy on the other. Internal efficiency requires that educational outputs are maximized for a given level of inputs (financial resources, teachers, physical infrastructure, and teaching–learning material). Internal efficiency has two dimensions: the quantitative dimension of expanding the reach of the system for a given level of investment, as well as reducing wastage, stagnation, and dropout, and the qualitative dimension of maximizing the levels of learner achievement for a given level of investment and level of inputs. The economic approach to education lays stress on the visible hand of management to maximize the internal and external efficiency of education system. Most economists subscribe to Lord Kelvin's axiom that 'when you can measure what you are speaking about, and express it in numbers, you know something about it; but when you cannot measure it, when you cannot express it in numbers, your knowledge is of a meagre and unsatisfactory kind'. Given the penchant of economists for quantification, economists suggest the fixation of performance standards for learners, individual institutions, as well as the system as a whole, measurement and assessment of the performance vis-a-vis the standards set. As an organization whose polices are predominantly set by its economists almost all of whom are neo-classical economists, the World Bank, particularly after Jomtien, began to insist on quantitative targets being laid down in education projects financed by it for improvement of learning achievement levels, and the achievement of these targets being assessed through surveys to assess the levels of learning surveys at the commencement, in the middle, and at the termination of a project. Given the belief that the quality of education had a bearing on international competitiveness, in 2000, the Organization for European Cooperation and Development (OECD) started the Programme for International Student Assessment (PISA) to evaluate every 3 years education systems in the participating countries by testing the skills and knowledge of 15-year-old students in the domains of reading, mathematical, and scientific literacy not merely in terms of mastery of the school curriculum, but also in terms of important knowledge and skills needed in adult life. A total of 65 countries participated in the 2009 survey, and in 2010, the states of Tamil Nadu and Himachal Pradesh joined the 2009 survey. Like the ranking in the HDI, the performance of a country in the triennial survey has been receiving considerable media and public attention in the participating countries.

Soon after the Jomtien Conference, UNESCO and UNICEF launched a joint project on learning achievement,[29] which covered 40 countries by 2000. Although India did not join the UNESCO–UNICEF Joint Project, it took steps to lay down minimum levels of learning (MLLs) and conduct learner achievement surveys. In fact, much before Jomtien significant efforts towards specification of MLLs were made by NCERT during 1978 in connection with the UNICEF-assisted projects 'Primary Education Curriculum Renewal' and 'Developmental Activities in Community Education and Participation'. NPE, 1986, declared that MLLs would be laid down for each stage of education; however, it was only in January 1990 during the run up to the Jomtien Conference that a committee was set up under the chairmanship of R.H. Dave to lay down the MLLs for classes III and IV and to recommend a procedure for comprehensive learner evaluation and assessment. As with MLLs, the conduct of learner achievement surveys preceded Jomtien Conference by more than a decade. In 1966, India participated in the cross-country achievement survey on Mathematics organized by IEA. In 1988, P.N. Dave of NCERT conducted an achievement survey in 22 states and union territories as part of his study, 'Primary Education Curriculum Renewal'. His study revealed that in quite a few states children were lacking in basic skills of reading, writing, and numeracy, and that the average learning achievements declined from classes I to IV. In 1990, an achievement survey in Mathematics and language was launched by Snehalata Shukla of NCERT; her framework was adapted for the baseline surveys conducted for DPEP in 1993. A study which received wide attention was the learner assessment study conducted by Sajitha Bashir in Tamil Nadu. What caught the attention of K was her finding that while on an average, the achievement levels in private unaided schools were better than those of government schools, those of government schools were better than those of private aided schools. He was greatly pleased with the finding which rebutted the widely held view that *all* government schools were intrinsically inferior to *any* private school in terms of learning outcomes. To jump the story,

[29] Vinayagum Chinapah, *Handbook on Monitoring Learning Achievement: Towards Capacity Building*, Paris: UNESCO, 1997.

improvement in learner achievement and reduction in disparities of learning achievement among social groups, and conduct of surveys to assess the achievement of the objectives came to be an important feature of DPEP; initially that focus on learner achievement got diluted in SSA for several reasons including the feeling among many educationists that education should not be reduced to a knowledge-delivery system, and that realization of higher-order pedagogic goals such as critical thinking, creativity, problem solving, and 'learning to learn' was more important than acquiring subject matter competencies in a given time.

External Assistance Prior to Jomtien

How should India engage the agencies? This was the million-dollar question that faced India after Jomtien. Having played an important role both in the run up to the Jomtien Conference as well as at the Conference itself, India could not just disengage itself without losing its credibility in the international arena. As home to the largest number of out-of-school children in the world, India's performance was critical to the realization of the Jomtien goals; consequently, the attention of all those associated with the EFA movement was riveted on India. In recognition of its importance in achieving the Jomtien goals, India was chosen to be a member of the Steering Committee of the International Consultative Forum on EFA, a body set up to coordinate the efforts of countries and agencies to implement the Jomtien Declaration and Framework. Other members of this forum were the four organizers of the Jomtien Conference, and a few other countries and agencies. One of the early decisions of this forum was that there should be focus on the nine high-population developing countries, namely Bangladesh, Brazil, China, Egypt, India, Indonesia, Mexico, Nigeria, and Pakistan, which together account for more than 70 per cent of the world's illiterates and more than half of its out-of-school children. A couple of years later, in December 1993, India hosted a summit of the leaders of these nine countries to develop a framework for individual and joint action. The summit was followed by periodic meetings of these nine countries and the sponsors of the Jomtien Conference to take stock of the progress towards Jomtien goals. Therefore, willy-nilly, Jomtien imparted an added sense of urgency to the nation's quest for universal elementary education and universal literacy. Along with the challenge of living up to expectations of other countries and the agencies came new opportunities of accessing financial resources on a scale not imaginable earlier. Even during the run-up to the Jomtien Conference, India, as home to the largest number of out-of-school children, seemed to be the natural destination for agencies eager to demonstrate their commitment to EFA. Once the World Bank emerged as a champion of basic education, it could not afford to miss out India in its efforts to promote basic education. Right from 1987, the World Bank had been a persistent suitor trying to woo the Indian government with offers of substantial soft IDA credit for primary education. In 1989, UNICEF offered to finance a flagship project to demonstrate to the world what an EFA project should be. ODA indicated its willingness to scale up APPEP; UNESCO evinced to support an EFA project in MP and locate additional external financing for another project. Bordia expected large-scale support by UNDP from a special facility supposed to have been created in UNDP headquarters to support EFA. In keeping with the pervading euphoria, India had two policy options to meet the resource requirements of accelerating the pace of its quest: to continue relying on its own resources, or alternately, to take advantage of the new opportunities that the international interest in primary education offered for giving a boost to its national efforts. Some of the offers of assistance were staggering by Indian educational standards. The first option presupposed that abundant domestic resources would be available for accelerating the pace of realization of the goals of universal elementary education and universal literacy. As India drifted into the unprecedented macroeconomic crisis of 1991, the first option turned out to be unrealistic. The second option posed a host of questions: What would be the terms and conditions subject to which funding would be available? Would there be too much meddlesome interference with the design and implementation of policies programmes and curricula? Do agencies differ in the degree of interference? If they were to differ, an attractive intermediary option was available, namely to avail those offers which would not unduly constrict national autonomy.

A perennial question that was posed to K again and again was why the government departed from its past policy and decided to avail external funding for elementary education. Contrary to the popular impression, that decision was not precipitate but one which evolved over a period of 3–4 years. Prior to 1989, modest assistance from UNESCO and UNICEF was availed to finance innovations in elementary education. UNESCO provided cash assistance for organizing training programmes and printing teaching-learning material. India participated in two on-going regional cooperative programmes: Regional Programme of Educational Innovations for Development of Asia and the Pacific (APEID) and Asia-Pacific Programme on Education for All (APPEAL). APPEAL was launched in New Delhi in February 1987, and its overall aim was to promote lifelong learning through the integration of all aspects of educational planning including literacy, universal primary education, and continuing education. However, the activities undertaken under these programmes were, to use jargon, mostly *upstream* activities such as studies and workshops, and few *downstream* programme activities. UNICEF funded five miniscule projects through supply of cash, equipment, and material to strengthen nutrition and health component of elementary education, to assist renewal of curriculum, to foster community participation in elementary education, and to set up a child media laboratory for developing audio-visual material for NFE.[30] In addition to assistance from UNESCO and UNICEF, bilateral assistance was utilized to fund three pilot projects: APPEP with British ODA assistance (1983), the Shiksha Karmi Project in Rajasthan with SIDA assistance (1987), and the NFE Project in UP with Norwegian Agency for Development Cooperation (NORAD) assistance (1987). Before the 1980s, large-scale funding for elementary education was scarce; from the 1980s, such funding could have been availed from the World Bank. However, the central government preferred to avail Bank loans mostly for physical infrastructure projects which had the potential of yielding steady streams of revenue which could be used to repay the loan. When the World Bank began to insist that IDA funds should be used to finance social sector projects, health (disease control programmes) and population control, and early care and child development (ICDS) were preferred as the Ministries concerned were more willing to avail Bank funding.

In contrast to elementary education, aid played an important role in setting up agricultural universities, Indian Institutes of Technology, regional engineering colleges, and state engineering colleges, all of which

[30] C.B. Padmanathan and Jandhyala B.G. Tilak, *External Financing of Education*, New Delhi: National Institute of Educational Planning, 1986, pp. 39–40.

were established to provide the manpower required for planned development. UNESCO and UNDP assistance was utilized to set up centres of advanced study in universities and thereby strengthen the research infrastructure in the country. In the Second and Third Five-Year Plans, technical assistance played an important role in the establishment of agricultural universities which were modelled after American Land Grant universities. The decision to avail external funding for select areas of higher education was not isolated from the overall policy of the government. Till 1991, economic self-reliance was no doubt the avowed policy; however, it did not mean total disengagement from the world economy. It did not preclude soliciting foreign aid till such time as the economy reached a self-sustaining 'take-off' stage. In absolute terms, only a few countries received more external assistance than India; however, relative to the size, population, and GDP of the country, the level of receipts had been low. All the same, till late 1990s when the foreign exchange reserves of the country began to swell, external assistance, particularly the credit from the International Development Agency (IDA, World Bank's soft credit arm), and grants from bilateral agencies, was critical for managing the balance of payments. A major task of the Department of Economic Affairs (DEA), Finance Ministry, was to maximize the flow of external assistance. Likewise, till the end of the Eighth Five-Year Plan (1992–7), external assistance made a significant contribution to the financing of five-year plans in terms of augmenting the investment and, more importantly, financing the foreign exchange component of the investment. The reliance on external assistance was the highest during the Second and Third Five-Year Plans, the high noon of self-reliant development. The contribution of external assistance to plan expenditure increased from 9.64 per cent during the First Five-Year Plan to 23.70 per cent in the Second Five-Year Plan, and reached a maximum of 28.25 per cent during the Third Five-Year Plan. Thereafter it began to decline: the contribution was about 12.75 per cent during the Fourth and Fifth Five-Year Plans, and more than 9 per cent in the Sixth, Seventh, and Eighth Five-Year Plans. It tapered off to 2.2 per cent during the Tenth Five-Year Plan, and the Eleventh Five-Year Plan did not envisage availing external assistance for financing the plan. Thus, strange but true, self-reliance in the financing of the plan was achieved not during the period when self-reliance was the avowed goal but after the economic reforms initiated in 1991 began to impact on the economy, and international competiveness, not self-reliance, came to be the goal. The World Bank was the single largest provider of external funding, and it coordinated the provision of external assistance by the OECD-DAC countries through the Aid-to-India Consortium set up in 1958. The Consortium included thirteen countries such as Japan, Norway, Sweden, United States, United Kingdom, and West Germany. The annual meeting of the Consortium was an important event having a significant bearing on India's balance of payment as well as the Five-Year and Annual Plans.

CABE Parameters for Availing External Funding

In March 1991, CABE was convened to consider the report of the Ramamurti Committee appointed by the V.P. Singh government to review NPE, 1986. Against the backdrop of offers by external agencies to fund basic education projects, Bordia thought it would be appropriate and expedient to get CABE lay down parameters for availing external funding. As was customary, after the first plenary session, CABE broke into thematic groups, and Bordia decided to have the question of external funding considered by the Working Group on Policy and Planning which was chaired by K. Chandrasekharan, Education Minister in the Left Front government of Kerala. As desired by Bordia, K drafted the parameters for accessing external funding, taking fully into account Bordia's views in the matter; after his approval, the parameters were placed before the Working Group for its consideration. The parameters were designed to strengthen the bargaining position of the education department vis-à-vis the World Bank, and to ensure that the projects funded by the Bank would avoid the deficiencies occasionally noticed in Bank-funded education projects. The parameters stipulated that:

- external funding should be an addition to the resources for education;
- the project must be in total conformity with national policies, strategies, and programmes;
- project formulation should be the responsibility of the central and state governments, and of national agencies;
- project formulation should be a process of capacity building;

- project must be drawn up on innovative lines emphasizing people's participation, improvement of quality and equality of education, and a substantial upgradation of facilities; and
- external assistance should be used for educational reconstruction, which should go beyond conventional measures such as opening of new schools and appointment of teachers, and should address issues of content, process, and quality.

The parameters also sought to strengthen the department's bargaining position in the internal negotiations with the Finance Ministry. One of the reasons why Bordia was wary of World Bank financing was that it would induce the Finance Ministry to partly shift the onus of resource mobilization to the Department of Education, and further that the resources mobilized from external funding agencies would substitute the resources that the Finance Ministry would provide in the budget in the normal course. By laying down that external financing should be additional to the resources for education the parameters sought to prevent that shift and avoid the substitution effect of external funding. The parameters were approved by the Working Group and incorporated in its Report. In the plenary, only three members, Adiseshiah, Kanti Biswas (Education Minister, West Bengal), and Saraswati Swain (National Institute of Applied Human Research and Development, Bhubaneswar, Orissa), expressed reservations about securing external funds for elementary education. However, CABE adopted the Report of the Working Group as it was, and with that, the parameters for external funding of elementary education.

Jomtien Conference: A Neo-liberal Conspiracy?

As mentioned earlier, while everyone says education is important, DOE ranks low in status and prestige—not 'sexy'—as a young lady IAS officer once quipped; it hardly makes news, and informed comment is rare in media. No wonder that Jomtien was hardly noticed in India; the EFA Summit of Nine High-Population Countries (New Delhi, December 1993), in contrast, caught the attention of the media basically because it was hosted by India and was relatively a high-profile event. All the same, the Jomtien Conference was subject to scathing criticism by a few academics such as Krishna Kumar, a noted educationist, and Anil Sadgopal, the unremitting champion of the common school. Krishna Kumar labelled Jomtien as 'the venue of a public ceremony at which the poor were introduced into the new nasty world of post-cold war capitalism', that ' for India, Jomtien was the beginning of a structurally adjusted political economy of education', that 'dependence on foreign resources for expansion and improvement of primary education, and privatisation of higher education are two salient features of the emerging education policy', and that 'it is clear that in the years during which the Jomtien conference (March 1990) on EFA was being planned, details of the social safety network were also being worked out to be revealed to the innocent after the announcement of the Structural Adjustment Programme (SAP).[31] In fairness however, it should be said that a few years later when he was in office as Director, NCERT, it would appear that Krishna Kumar had acquired a more nuanced appreciation of the circumstances in which government decided to avail external funding, and perhaps came round the view that there might be 'some visible gains in the first phase' of DPEP.[32] No doubt, the World Bank was a sponsor of the Jomtien Conference and many developed countries with capitalist economies did participate in the Conference. However, to hold that Jomtien Conference unfolded 'the new nasty world of post-cold war capitalism' would be to undertake an exultant flight of fancy defying the gravity of facts and the realities of contemporary multilateral diplomacy . In the late twentieth century, dependency is not the inexorable destiny of *all* developing countries any more than biology is destiny for *all* women. It would be naive to think that all the developing country participants in the Jomtien Conference including China and India were pushovers. There is nothing in the Jomtien Declaration and Framework which makes it mandatory for a country which had not universalized primary education to avail external funding. It was no doubt true that in the past, India did not avail substantial funding for elementary education,

[31] Krishna Kumar, 'Learning and Money: Children as Pawns in Dependency', *Economic and Political Weekly*, XXX, no. 43 (1995), pp. 2719–20, at p. 2719.

[32] Krishna Kumar, Quality of Education at the Beginning of the Twenty First Century: Lessons from India, Background Paper for *EFA Global Monitoring Report 2005*, 2004. Background Paper for *EFA Global Monitoring Report 2005*, pp. 1–25, at p. 16.

and that after the Jomtien Conference, it shed its reluctance not out of compulsion by the World Bank or whoever but because it was in the national interest. Because of the macroeconomic situation, resources for development were under severe pressure, and it made sense to avail external funding as the expanded vision of basic education expounded at Jomtien was wholly in synch with NPE,1986, and funding was offered on terms and conditions which did not, in any manner, infringe on the autonomy of the country to formulate policy and programmes, and further were in synch with the guidelines of CABE (March 1991) designed to ensure that external funding did not impair capacity building or lead to dependency on foreign experts for project formulation and implementation. Uncompromising adherence to ideology is a luxury not available to those in positions of power whether it was the Indian government in the 1990s or to Lenin when he had to retreat from War Communism and adopt the New Economic Policy, not to speak of the Left Front during its long years of rule in West Bengal. As was set out above, it is not factually correct to treat the praxis of structural adjustment as if it were invariant; India's structural adjustment in the 1990s was as different from the initial structural adjustments in Africa and Latin America in the late 1970s and early 1980s as chalk from cheese. Further, as would be set out in great detail in Chapter XIII, Krishna Kumar's assertion that work on social safety nets began in the run-up to the Jomtien Conference was factually incorrect.

The narrative would be incomplete without commenting on Sadgopal's critique of the 'neo-liberal assault on education' which put forth distinctive points relating to primary and adult education. Sadgopal's critique is a good example of what Krishna Kumar described as the use of the term 'neo-liberal' as 'a footloose device to say something forceful and critical' without exploring 'the genealogy of ideas and situate a term in a historical context' on the ground that 'this kind of search for the history of ideas is not regarded as being relevant for the study of education'.[33] Like the expanding universe, Sadgopal's critique kept expanding over time, encompassing more and more points. In 2003, he was critical of the adult literacy programmes organized by the NLM and linked them with the international literacy `conspiracy'

[33] Krishna Kumar, 'Teaching and the Neo-liberal State ', *Economic and Political Weekly*, XLVI, no. 21 (2011), pp. 37–40, at p. 37.

conceived by the World Bank and the agencies of the United Nations. According to him, the market forces believed that literacy skill was all that the masses needed so that they could read the product labels and advertisements. Jomtien Declaration (1990), and the Dakar Framework (2000), were evidence of market forces working over-time to push the literacy paradigm in the global education scenario. The literacy programme was 'akin to "mopping the floor while the tap is on" as it seemed to be waiting for half of the children in the age group of 6 to 14 who are out-of-school to become adult illiterates in the 15–35 age group (the official group for literacy mission) so that the literacy programme can be thrust on them'.[34] In 2008, he claimed that there was a hidden agenda behind the EFA programme and the move towards knowledge economy. His analysis of the Jomtien Conference revealed that its central thesis in the Indian context was threefold. First, the state must abdicate its constitutional obligation towards education of the masses in general and school-based elementary education in particular, and become dependent on international aid for even primary education and work through NGOs, religious bodies, and corporate houses. Second, the people have neither a human right as enshrined in the UN Charter nor a fundamental right to receiving free elementary education of equitable quality as implied by the 86th Constitutional Amendment. Third, education is a commodity that could be marketed in the global market. It followed, therefore, that the education system, from the pre-school stage to higher education, must be, as rapidly as possible, privatized and commercialized.[35] In his presentation to the Indian Academy of Sciences in July 2011, Sadgopal went a step further to argue that NPE, 1986, marked the beginning of the neo-liberal agenda, and that it 'violated the principles of equality' and 'introduced a socio-economic fault [*sic*] for neoliberal forces to promote parallel streams', presumably because it explicitly postulated that UEE could not be achieved in the near future by relying on the school system alone, and that, therefore, schooling needed to be supplemented by an extensive system of non-formal education. He also argued that the Jomtien Declaration and

[34] Anil Sadgopal, 'Education for Too Few', *Frontline*, 20, no. 24 (2003).

[35] Anil Sadgopal, *Common School System and the Future of India*, Posted by *Parisar* (a forum of progressive students) on 24 March 2008, http://parisar.wordpress.com/2008/03/24/common-school-system-and-the-future-of-india/

Framework were a retreat from the constitutional provisions in regard to education. Thus, while the provision of education was a constitutional obligation of early childhood care and education (ECCE), 8 years of elementary education, providing resources for education from internal resources, and guarantee of free education were all given the go by the Jomtien outcome documents. Suffice it to say, a plain reading of the Jomtien Declaration and Framework without interpolating one's preferences and prejudices does not justify the hidden agenda that Sadgopal deciphered in the Jomtien outcome documents. The Constitution has nothing to say about the financing of education, and his claim that ECCE was guaranteed by the Constitution is not warranted from either the drafting history of the Constitution or the history of the demand for free and compulsory education during freedom struggle. Adult literacy and non-formal programmes leave much to be desired but to link them to international neo-liberal conspiracy calls for a fertile imagination of the highest order. Among the intellectual progenitors of literacy and non-formal programmes of the 1990s, the pre-eminent was Naik. In his long, illustrious career, Naik was many things but being a neo-liberal was not one of them. Furthermore, the pedagogy of adult literacy and NFE was much influenced by the radical educationists Freire and Illich whose political philosophy is indeed the ideological antipode of neo-liberalism. Suffice it to say, you see what you want to see.

VIII

GOOD INTENTIONS NOT ENOUGH

'Not what though art, nor what thou hast been, does God consider, but what thou wouldst be'

—*The Cloude of Unknowyng*, English mystical work of the 14th century

The Indian state almost never evaluated policy by consequences, almost always by its own intent.... The state has internalised the message of the Bhagavad Gita: only intentions, and not consequences, matter

—Pratap Bhanu Mehta, *The Burden of Democracy*

Agony and Ecstasy

Tutelage under Bordia was bittersweet—bitter because of Bordia's unforeseeable swings of moods and some of his work methods, and sweet because of his affection for K and special consideration which he extended to K, and because working with Bordia was an educational experience of the highest order. Nowhere was the unity of opposites as evident as during the visits to Bihar, which were very frequent during the last year of his office. As *Mahabhinishkramana* (Great Departure—Bordia's retirement) approached closer and closer, Bordia's passion for BEP grew deeper and deeper. He was not only keen to keep BEP on track but also, as it came out after his retirement, very keen to continue his association with BEP. Once he set his sight on something, nothing, nothing would deter him from relentlessly pursuing his objective. That being so, he descended on Bihar again and again with his standard contingent of deputies who were his favourites and associated with BEP in one way or other. Geeta Verma of UNICEF who, later on, went on to an international career including a stint in war-torn Iraq invariably joined the contingent, for Bordia, being gloriously inconsistent, would not apply to his favourite agencies such as UNICEF the arm's distance relationship he prescribed for dealing with external funding agencies. Visits of such frequency and intensity being unusual for a Secretary to GOI, it was no wonder that his visits drew much attention and Minister Arjun Singh quipped that with so frequent visits of Education Secretary, education of Bihar should no longer be what it used to be. The visits to Bihar were full of visits to innovative NFE centres and meetings of neo-literates, grand parades, visits to historical places, and evenings full of fun and frolic.

It was not uncommon during those visitations for long hectic days to be followed by evenings when Bordia relaxed in the company of his deputies and colleagues from Bihar, enjoying the entertainment offered, playing pranks, and indulging in good-natured banter. In one such, frozen in K's memory, Bordia was holding his durbar in the open area in front of an inspection bungalow. The moonlight was feeble, and the canopy of trees nearby cast long shadows on the place where Bordia and his courtiers sat. Bordia was dressed in a *kurta pyjama* and sat on a cane chair with his legs stretched on a tea table. A couple of feminists dressed in shirts and trousers were smoking away to glory. A seemingly crazy American, an adult educator friend of Bordia, had gone native. A district magistrate who fancied himself to be a poet recited his creations from a notebook as a lackey held a torch to illuminate the pages. His recitation was greeted with *wahvas*—appreciatory sounds *de rigueur* at *mehfils* (recitations of Urdu poetry). The most effusive appreciation was from Bordia who was very eager to co-opt the magistrate for the cause: BEP. Bordia was particular that a collection of the verses should be published, and offered the magistrate his good offices with Rajkamal, a noted publishing house, to bring out the collection. Poetry was followed by a mellifluous rendition of *ghazals* by Geeta Verma who had a trained voice. Good-humoured banter over dinner followed the mehfils. Neither the mehfils nor small talk and banter were to the liking of the buttoned-up Tambrahm that K was. His knowledge of Hindi and Urdu was too poor to follow the verses, and the little he could follow was not to his liking. The protagonists in the verses seemed to be degenerates incapable of taking control of themselves and their lives, and the sentiment of unrequited love oozing out of these verses appeared to be sugary. Further, unlike Bordia who boasted that he was a camel and could work without interruption for long stretches of time—even days—K had poor stamina. He would wilt after a long day of hectic schedule and unremitting drudgery, and looked forward to a good night's sleep, and the enforced participation in contrived entertainment appeared to be yet another chore of drudgery. And no less importantly, he could not turn away his mind from the happenings of the day, and as he brooded over them, iron often filled his soul; the mehfils, far from lifting his spirits, depressed him.

K was often torn by conflicting emotions. Many a time, he was lost in admiration for Bordia, for his superb sense of timing, his meticulous preparation before undertaking a visit to Bihar, his identification of just an objective or two and no more to be accomplished during the visit, the single-minded pursuit of the objectives identified without allowing himself to be distracted by any red herrings that others might insert, his extraordinary ability to conceptualize and articulate even abstract ideas, and his deft management of men and matters. In contrast, there were several occasions when K was exasperated with Bordia who seemed to be carried away by his ideas, persevere with them even when they did not seem to work or were so demanding of financial, human, and organizational resources that they were unlikely to be accomplished, and even if accomplished, were no more than unsustainable flashes in the pan. The long unending *chintan manthans*—talkathons—of BEP seemed to generate a lot of hot air rather than shed any light on how to go about to actualize the grand visions. They served no purpose other than fanning irrational, exuberant expectations. The dysfunctionality of these chinthan manthans validates the observation of *Report of the Working Group on Block Level Planning* (1978) chaired by the eminent economist M.L. Dantwala that

> people could make a contribution to planning only if they are presented with a well-articulated and feasible framework of approaches, objectives, measures, and alternatives. If, however, they are asked to indicate their needs in a vacuum, they are bound to put up a charter of demands which will be far beyond the capacities of Government.

There seemed to be a permanent disconnect between K's visionary plans and the ground reality, and also between his grand plans and actual action. As ever, life was a gateway to literature. During those hectic days, K chanced upon a verse from Adi Sankara's *Vivekachudamani*: '*Sabdajalam Maharanyam Chittabhramana Karakam*' (The mind gets lost in dense forest of words). And that verse seemed to capture the ambience of the chinthan manthans. And then, Bordia often seemed to move from one passion to another without consolidation. K also got the feeling that Bordia was more interested in processes and mobilization for their own sake, and did not lay adequate emphasis on outcomes. While working with Bordia, K reflected a great deal about Bordia's views on educational transformation, programmes dear to his heart, and the strategy and tactics he employed to further his favourite programmes. K anguished a great deal trying to find a rational answer for the questions: Why does he build castles in the air with great artistry even while knowing their true nature and, to compound the folly, seek to disseminate and perpetuate the belief that they were castles with granite foundations? Why does he spend long hours in arcane discussions on the depth of the moats surrounding those castles and the minutiae of the drawbridges that span across those moats? Why does he manufacture illusions? From his reading of Marxist literature, K was inclined to act on the belief that education has only limited ability to alter the social structure in the medium term, and that the design of educational reform cannot therefore be totally out of synch with the social and economic structure. The focus should be on equalization of educational opportunity with the expectation that the transformative power of education would work out itself in the long run. K felt that Bordia was, as Marx said of Augustus von Willich and others, an 'alchemist of revolution', substituting 'idealism for materialism and regard pure will as the motive power of revolution instead of actual conditions'. Once in a way when Bordia was in a jolly good mood, K would give vent to his belief that the transformative power of education was exaggerated, and that his belief stemmed from the historic experience of Jesuit educational institutions turning out in large numbers atheistic French *philosophe*, and, further in recent years, students from developing countries who studied in Paris returning home as Marxists while those who studied in Moscow returning home as anti-communist liberals. Bordia would burst into laughter and quip that K was a Maoist insurgent who came all the way from Andhra. K's own mood swings were no less violent than those of his boss; however, while Bordia gave vent to his feelings without any inhibition unless he chose deliberately to dissimulate, K had to suffer inwardly whenever he was in dark moods. K was too much of a careerist to dare speak truth to authority always and commit *hara-kiri*. In retrospect, he was saved from neurosis by critically reflecting on the events of the day and verbalizing his reflections in his journal which helped him to view the events of the day from a more balanced perspective than his swinging moods would permit.

UNICEF: A Pre-history

UNICEF is a standing proof of Say's law that supply creates its own demand. UNICEF originally stood for United Nations International Children's Emergency Fund, and was created through a resolution of the UN General Assembly in December 1946 as a temporary *emergency* organization that would bring succour to children in war-ravaged Europe and Asia. Ever after its founding mission was completed , it continued to exist by continually discovering new emergencies and expanding the remit of the organization; as Maggie Black, the historian of UNICEF put it, in one form or other, 'the "emergency" continued ... Long may it continue!'[1] As the end of UNICEF's original mandate was winding down and the purpose of setting it up neared its end, there was a campaign in the United States, the country whose government and citizens contributed almost the entire resources of UNICEF, to close it down. Leading the assault against the closure, the Pakistan delegate Ahmed Bukhari told the UN General Committee on Social and Humanitarian Affairs that the notion that the emergency was over was an illusion. In its campaign to mobilize contributions, UNICEF had distributed harrowing photographs of emaciated European children who were victims of the war. Although the photographs were shocking, 'those European children appeared to be a no-worse state than millions of children living so-called normal lives in the underdeveloped countries'. How could children suffering from endemic cholera be

[1] Maggie Black, *The Children and Nations: The Story of UNICEF*, New York: UNICEF, 1986, p. 8.

denied cholera vaccines unless their cholera was the result of a war emergency, he asked rhetorically. The emotional argument eventually prevailed, and in October 1953, the General Assembly agreed to continue UNICEF indefinitely without reference to a time limit, and dropped the words 'international' and 'emergency' from the title of the organization but retained the well-known acronym. On its part, UNICEF never failed to project the needs of children as an emergency which demanded attention *here and now*.

A spirited advocacy and mobilization campaigns had been the major, if not the main, element of UNICEF strategy, particularly during the long Grant years (1980–95); it is its advocacy and campaigns such as immunization, and oral re-hydration therapy (ORT) that UNICEF owes its well-deserved fame and recognition. The heavy reliance on advocacy was a conscious choice, another illustration of the relationship between structure and strategy so admirably explored by the renowned business historian Alfred Chandler.[2] In his detailed study of UNESCO, UNDP, UNICEF, and the World Bank, Jones related the distinct operational style of each organization to its 'Domestic Political Environment' (DPE).[3] DPE comprises the mandate of the organization, its constituency and protagonists, organizational structure, and sources of funding. The mandate of UNESCO is more cerebral and ethical—to build peace in the minds of men; that of UNICEF is more practical. UNESCO's budgetary resources accrue mainly from formula-based contributions by Member States. Therefore, in spite of the paraphernalia of National Commissions and association of experts in an individual capacity, UNESCO has been functioning essentially as an intergovernmental body. Being chronically cash-strapped its

[2] Alfred D. Chandler, Jr. *Strategy and Structure: Chapters in the History of the American Industrial Enterprise*, MIT Press; Cambridge, Mass., 1962.

[3] Phillip W. Jones, *International Policies for Third World Education: UNESCO, Literacy and Development*, London: Routledge, 1988; Phillip W. Jones, "Globalisation and Internationalisation: Democratic Prospects for World Education", *Comparative Education*, 34, no. 2 (1998), pp.143–55; Philip W. Jones, *World Bank Financing of Education: Lending, Learning and Development*, London: Routledge, First Edition, 1992; P.W. Jones with David Coleman, *The United Nations and Education: Multilateralism, Development, and Globalisation*, Routledge, 2005.

comparative advantage lay in reflection, standard setting, and setting agenda for others in its areas of competence. In contrast to UNESCO, UNICEF's mission of providing emergency relief and the compulsion to mobilize voluntary contributions from a number of sources such as governments, private bodies, and individuals imparted a strong inclination to act, act briskly, and demonstrate its activism and the good that flowed from its action. Consequently for UNICEF, advocacy has been a moral as well as operational imperative, and has become second nature. K found that quite a few of its functionaries considered their job to be a calling and not a vocation, and were driven by a sense of being consecrated to a humanitarian mission. Necessity is the mother of invention. Marketing being critical for raising resources necessary for its very survival, UNICEF invented social marketing and, over decades, honed its marketing. It is adept at creating images, shaping perceptions, and banking on endorsements of celebrities such as Peter Ustinov, Audrey Hepburn, Amitabh Bachchan, and Priyanka Chopra in order to create and expand a loyal customer base. It is the UN organization which is most sensitive about its public image, and the most media savvy with an extraordinary capacity to bond with activist groups and mobilize large numbers on its behalf and the causes it espouses. Being the sole UN agency devoted to children, it is free of competition which other agencies such as, say, UNESCO faced and the image of suffering children and of itself as the champion of such children gives its advocacy great potency and gives it formidable strength in dealing with sceptics and critics. On the flip side, however, 'its analyses of need tend to be dramatic, its projections tend to be alarmist and its solutions populist', the annual *State of the World's Children* being a prime example. Furthermore, as K found from his experience some of the UNICEF functionaries were too preachy, and as is common with those wedded to a single cause, unable to see any other point of view except theirs and impatient with the central and state governments for not seeing the truth they espoused and dragging their feet, oblivious to the fact governments are duty bound to represent different constituencies, and must not be driven by passions. UNICEF's country representatives who hailed from the United States were often Innocents Abroad, and often failed to recognize that the Indian system of government was vastly different from the American system and short circuiting senior officials by directly lobbying MPs and chief ministers did not result in primary education securing more funds and higher priority. One such Innocent Abroad provided a few chief ministers with a few thousand UNICEF greeting cards each in the expectation that it would further the cause of primary education.

UNICEF is the UN organization with maximum interface with the public and a vast network of offices; in India itself there are as many as fifteen regional offices. Unlike other UN organizations, it is a quintessential field-based, hands-on organization. Over years, UNICEF has built a strong capacity for procurement and distribution of material supplies such as vehicles, vaccines, and injectors, that is what it does best next only to advocacy and fund raising, and what its functionaries were comfortable with. The fact that supply of materials accounted for a major share of UNICEF assistance gave UNICEF the image of a supplier of material aid. Thus the Director, School Education, Bihar, expected UNICEF to supply all his school inspectors with motor cycles as a component of BEP. But for Bordia firmly putting his foot down, UNICEF functionaries would have been only too happy to concede the request. For all its strengths, UNICEF had a few weaknesses such as lack of concern for outcomes, and inadequate systems and procedures which, among others, led to the financial scandal in UNICEF's Kenya office wherein about $10 million were misappropriated. One of the very first tasks that Carol Bellamy had to address after succeeding Grant was to revamp the organization, and its systems and procedures. Furthermore, UNCEF's extraordinary power to harness media vested its projects with an imagery of effectiveness not entirely deserved.[4] In spite of the vexatious excesses of its advocacy and limitations of its approach, there can be no doubt whatsoever that, on the whole, UNICEF was a force for good, and if did not exist, it ought to be invented.

For the first 13 years of existence, as was expected of it by the UN resolution setting it up, UNICEF was engaged solely in providing emergency relief to children, promoting their health, and improving their nutrition; at best it was willing to assist instructing of mothers and child care providers about child health and nutrition in informal settings. In 1958, some members of the Executive Board suggested expansion of UNICEF activities so as to cover primary education, and in March

4 Jones with Coleman, *The United Nations and Education*, p. 137.

1959, the Executive Board decided to test the waters by deciding to support a few trial projects for supporting training of primary teachers in health and nutrition education. By the time when the Executive Board considered UNICEF financing of education two years later, there was a far-reaching change in the policy environment, and the UNICEF top management made deft use of the launch of the First UN Development Decade and the human capital revolution to advance its agenda of child development by characterizing children as a country's 'most precious resource', and investment in children an investment in country's future. UNESCO began to address all the needs of the 'whole child' instead of addressing only health and nutritional needs. It began advocating that national policies for children should embrace all children and cover all sectors such as health, education, and so on instead of limiting to the welfare of children in special need. In 1972, UNICEF was formally recognized as a development rather than a welfare organization.

When the question of assisting education came up before the UNICEF Executive Board in 1961, many members raised a few seminal questions which cropped up again and again in the 1960s and 1970s. Is it proper for UNICEF to enter the domain of UNESCO, thereby breaching the implicit division of labour among UN agencies? Would it not detract from the primary mission of UNICEF, all the more so because of the conventional wisdom among agencies that, for a number of reasons, it was prudent to stay away from education? The UNICEF Executive Board gave varying answers to these seminal questions from time to time. Jurisdictional dispute with UNESCO did not arise as Maheu, the DG, UNESCO, utilized the opportunity provided by the human capital revolution to persuade other agencies to finance educational development and to avail UNESCO's technical expertise. Like the World Bank, UNICEF also entered into a co-operative agreement with UNESCO; however, while the Bank point blank refused UNESCO's desire to be consulted about the side covenants to education loans, the UNICEF Board decided that educational projects should be undertaken only if endorsed by UNESCO. As years rolled by and UNICEF staff felt that collaboration with UNESCO restricted their freedom of action and flexibility in the design of projects , the UNICEF Board eliminated the power of UNESCO to decide the projects eligible for UNICEF assistance; UNESCO's agreement was no longer necessary, and it was sufficient if UNESCO's advice was sought. During M'Bow years, UNESCO lost most of the field staff. In 1982, the co-operation agreement came to an end, and thereafter UNICEF was on its own without much in-house professional expertise in the field of education till the early 1990s when, after Jomtien, it began to induct more educational professionals at headquarters and in the field. Over time the thrust of educational assistance shifted towards primary education in recognition of the fact that it would not be to support secondary education when millions of children lacked primary education and were growing up into adult illiterates. UNICEF's educational assistance continued to expand; however, that expansion was tempered by the concern that it should not be at the expense of health and nutrition.

The Crusading Pope

James (Jim) Grant with whom K used to occasionally interact during1990–5 when K was in the Department of Education was a restless, crusading Pope leading his legions to slay the demons tormenting children, and to ensure that every political leader in the world acknowledged that 'children (were) first'. His brief interactions with Grant during the period 1990–5 were sufficient to convince K that the tributes paid to Grant as a visionary and missionary were absolutely apt; those interactions also helped K to identify the fountainhead of Grant's dynamism. The grandson and son of medical missionaries in China, the missionary spirit ran in Grant's blood; he had a genuine attachment to India where his wife lay buried. His philosophy of life was captured by the following quotation of Bernard Shaw which was his favourite:

> This is the true of joy of life, being used for a purpose recognized by you as a mighty one. I am of the opinion that my life belongs to the whole community and as long as I live it is my privilege to do it for it whatever it can do for it whatever it can. Life is no brief candle to me. It is a sort of splendid torch which I have got hold of for the moment, and I want to make it burn as brightly as possible before handing over to future generations.[5]

A few months before he died, K had the privilege of meeting him along with Education Secretary S.V. Giri in Geneva, and that meeting

[5] Richard Jolly, ed., *Jim Grant: UNICEF Visionary*, Florence: UNICEF Innocenti Research Centre, 2001, p. 173.

still lingers in K's memory for the truthfulness of Grant. While UNICEF officials in the Delhi Office and in the New York headquarters tried to erect smoke screens to justify the failure of UNICEF to raise supplementary resources for BEP, Grant was candid enough in that meeting to admit that much was expected from Japanese because of the Eimi Watanabe (UNICEF's Country Representative in Delhi) connection but it did not turn out that way. He assured Giri that he would do his very best to spare whatever was possible from the regular budget of UNICEF.

He embodied the American pioneering spirit of *can-do* and *can-change*; he was also a showman who would do Hollywood and Madison Avenue proud. Like every extraordinary chief executive, the moment he took over as Executive Director (January 1980), Grant was on the lookout for spectacular initiatives that would ensure that he left an indelible mark on the organization he now headed and further would earn him accolades for outstanding leadership. His first choice was leading a campaign for unprecedented expansion of primary education so that there would be no child in the world who would not go to school. Grant approached M'Bow of UNESCO, but drawing a blank, he turned to health, sought to build upon the 'health for all' initiative of his predecessor and come up with a spectacular initiative. Whatever, the initiative that Grant plumped for turned was a dramatic reduction in child mortality rates through a package of powerful, doable, low-cost technologies that were christened GOBI, standing for monitoring the **G**rowth of the child, **B**reastfeeding, **O**ral rehydration, and **I**mmunization. Drawing upon the analogy of Green Revolution, Grant visualized a *blitzkrieg*-like assault on child mortality through spirited advocacy of GOBI package and drumming up political will by badgering heads of government. Typical of his salesmanship was his stirring speech to the Executive Board of UNICEF while seeking approval for his trademark GOBI programme. K had the privilege of viewing the footage of a film of the meeting at the memorial meeting organized by UNICEF Delhi office on 6 February 1995, about a week after Grant's death. In that footage, K saw Grant enact a superb performance paying homage to the 40,000 children who needlessly died the previous day and dramatically requesting the members of the Executive Board to rise for a minute in silence. No sooner had the members resumed their seats when Grant repeated the act by paying homage to the 40,000 children who would needless die that day and requesting them to stand in silence once more. By mid-1980s, the GOBI programme was quite successful, leading to what the UNICEF propaganda machine called a child survival and development revolution, and Grant began to be on the lookout for another front where he could replicate the GOBI strategy with the same dramatic success. He returned to his first choice of UPE, and along with the World Bank, gave a push to the idea of organizing a world conference on education which turned out to be the Jomtien Conference. Even while the Jomtien Conference was still in works, the question 'what next after Jomtien' loomed large over Grant and the UNICEF management. It was realized that if UNICEF were to make a mark after Jomtien it would have to go beyond advocacy and its tradition of financing small, local catalytical educational initiatives and would have to go in for large, pace-setting projects, and to foster the perception that UNICEF has much to say at the macro level about education policy. It was against this backdrop that the idea to launch a flagship EFA project in India was conceived, and that project came to be BEP.

Rhetoric No Substitute for Action

To jump the story ahead, in spite of strengthening in-house educational expertise and attracting talent of the highest order such as Aklilu Habte, former Ethiopian Education Minster and later Head of the World Bank's Education Policy Division, and Fay Chung, former Education Minister of Zimbabwe, UNICEF, failed to make a mark. In a sense, it was trying to punch above its weight. Compared with other Jomtien sponsors, UNICEF's education budget in 1990 was small: $57 million compared with World Bank educational disbursements of $1,487 million; it was even less than that of the perennially cash-strapped UNESCO. Higher levels of educational expenditure required reprioritization of the resources of UNICEF and roping in agencies flush with resources as co-sponsors of projects launched by UNICEF. Neither was accomplished, and BEP is a standing example of UNICEF's inability to go big after Jomtien. UNICEF as well as UNESCO offered assistance for EFA projects in the expectation that they could tap resources from other agencies but neither the agencies nor the Indian Government saw any reason why they should have an intermediary when they could deal directly. Even nine years after Jomtien, there was no step-up in the proportion of expenditure devoted to education, and in absolute terms, the total resources earmarked to education were no more than $123 million. No wonder that after retirement, in his reflection on the failure to reflect the programme commitments to education foreshadowed at Jomtien, Habte rued the fact that 'Budgetary allocation did not follow the rhetoric'.[6]

UNICEF's failure extended to advocacy of EFA also. From his experience with UNICEF, K noticed two basic flaws with the advocacy of EFA by UNICEF. The first flaw sprang from the inappropriate analogy between UPE and immunization, and the second from the failure of field functionaries to internalize the expanded concept of basic education that the Jomtien Declaration. The analogy with GOBI, particularly immunization, which inspired Grant, was utterly inappropriate for EFA. In UNICEF headquarters itself, there was realization in UNICEF headquarters of the inappropriateness of the immunization analogy. Just two months after the Jomtien Conference, Grant constituted an ad hoc education advisory group meeting in New York with 26 participants from the World Bank, UNESCO, governments, and NGOs to advise UNICEF on what it could do to advance EFA and review a basic education training package for UNICEF staff. In that group, Nyi Nyi Thaung, Chief of Programmes, UNICEF, who earlier, as Minister of Education, organized the noted mass literacy campaign in Burma reviewed UNICEF's experience with the mass immunization campaigns and brought out vividly the limitations of such a campaign approach to EFA. However, that message did not percolate down to the field, and many functionaries continued to believe that the approach which did wonders with immunization could be replicated with UPE. K had a running row with two successive country representatives of UNICEF, Eimi Watanabe and John Rohde, over the time horizon for achievement of UEE. K was very particular to infuse a sense of realism in the discourse on UEE; he strongly believed that for far too long educational discourse in the country had a penchant for rhetoric and willing suspension of disbelief in the expectation that Hope and Will could create what they desire. In his bully pulpit speeches, K would assert

[6] UNICEF, 'Interview with Aklilu Habte', *Education News*, 6, no. 3, 1997, pp. 19–23, p. 20.

universalizing elementary education was a marathon, and could not be a sprint like, say, TLCs, and that therefore the nation should buck itself for a long haul. He used to highlight the fact that in many states those who are out-of-school belong to very disadvantaged groups, and that getting them to school and retain them till they complete elementary education was a more arduous task than achieving the past expansion in enrolment. Hence, a long and arduous journey was ahead to reach the goal of UEE. K's metaphors of marathon, long haul, and long and hard road were not to the liking of Eimi or Rohde as a long-duration effort was contrary to UNICEF's Party Line. Though well meaning, they would contest K's claim and assert that UEE could be achieved very quickly in two or three years, if only political will could be mobilized. In a speech at a meeting organized in connection with the EFA-9 Summit, in response to the metaphor of marathon used by K in his speech, Eimi responded with Churchillian rhetoric. 'I hate to see an India which failed to universalise elementary education by the end of the 20th century', and followed with more rhetorical lines beginning with the phrase 'I hate to see'. Such rhetorical assertions did little to hasten UEE; they failed to realistically assess the challenge, ignored the historical experience, and failed to recognize that it was not enough to send all children to school and ensure that they complete elementary education, and that as the Jomtien Declaration and NPE, 1992, mandated, it was essential that children learn. What made matters worse in K's view was the efforts of UNICEF officials to organize meetings of Members of Parliament and put forth their simplistic point of view, making it appear that that but, for the apathy of Department of Education and its officials, UEE could be achieved in two or three years. The intensity of such lobbying increased enormously once the imperious Bordia demitted office. K could not help recall the saying 'God, I can take care of my enemies. Please take care of my friends'. Nothing pleased K more than the frank statement of Chitra Naik at one such meeting attended by luminaries such as Atal Behari Vajpayee that free and compulsory primary education was advocated for about a century by eminent nationalists such as Gokhale, that in the year of the Lord 1994 Indians need not be told by foreigners how important was universal elementary education, what was needed was not talk but action, and that the best thing that the MPs could do was to work in their constituencies for UEE. She added that if UNICEF were so anxious about EFA by 2000 it should as well put up below a banyan tree a stone inscription bearing the legend 'EFA by 2000'. Being a venerable old lady and a reputed educationist, she could tell some home truths which *babus* like K could not.

There was yet another serious flaw in the advocacy of UNICEF: the failure to 'educate' the field functionaries about the expanded view of basic education adopted at the Jomtien Conference, a fact highlighted by Habte in his post-retirement confessional. The failure to 'educate' the functionaries was very much in evidence in India. UNICEF was proud of financing a flagship EFA project in Bihar; that project encompassed, among others, adult and NFE comprising about 30 per cent of the projected outlay of BEP. Yet, Eimi Watanabe, the Country Representative, went on harping that attention on educating children, its prime constituency, should not be distracted by too much attention on literacy and other aspects of basic education. While the Eighth Five-Year Plan was being formulated, she wrote to the Secretary, Planning Commission, seeking higher allocations for children's education; that was fair enough as she told a journalist in an interview when she was demitting office 'so far as we are concerned, children are the most important priority, and our job is to keep on making a lot of noise (on behalf of children).[7] However, she would not rest at that and went on to question the allocations to adult education which, in her view, were unduly high. In meetings with Members of the Parliament she made the point again and again that excessive importance given to adult literacy was coming in the way of universalizing elementary education. Her successor, John Rhode, articulated the view that non-formal education was educational apartheid, never mind UNICEF was widely disseminating the BRAC model of NFE in vogue in Bangladesh. It was a classic case of the left hand not knowing what the right hand does. The policy advocacy by UNICEF brings out clearly that it is not only the World Bank or the IMF which tries to influence a country's policy but every agency, and that the policy advocated by an agency might not be congruent with national perceptions or interest. And furthermore, the policy advice offered by agencies with a Good Samaritan image might be more insidious than that of agencies with a negative image

[7] 'The Tuesday Interview: Dr Eimi Watanabe', *Economic Times*, 27 June 1993.

like the World Bank and IMF. Many intellectuals and activists are prone to be taken in by that image without thinking through the relevance or desirability of the advice for the country.

Grandiose Visions

GONZALO

I' the commonwealth I would by contraries
Execute all things; for no kind of traffic
Would I admit; no name of magistrate;
Letters should not be known; riches, poverty,
And use of service, none; contract, succession…
No occupation; all men idle, all;
And women too, but innocent and pure;
No sovereignty;
…

ANTONIO

The latter end of his commonwealth forgets the
beginning.

William Shakespeare, *The Tempest*, Act II, Scene I.

With his customary gusto and élan, Bordia plunged into the EFA movement, and about a year before the Jomtien Conference, he decided it would be opportune to draw up a grand pace-setting project that would cover all the components of EFA. Hitherto, all over the world there had been projects covering one or more aspects of primary schooling or of NFE or of adult education but nowhere was a composite project covering all aspects of primary schooling, and non-formal and adult education ever conceived. Man is a bundle of contradictions; Bordia was no exception. He was a romantic idealist who, if the occasion demanded, was a consummate practitioner of realpolitik. In the initial days of TLCs, Bordia used to say that it was essential to dispel the widely held perception that to attempt to achieve universal literacy in the country in a few years would be futile like chasing a mirage. To that end, it was imperative to create a series of success stories and widely broadcast the successes. Antyodaya, though appealing, is unlikely to create and sustain the momentum necessary for pushing forward a difficult programme such as literacy.

However, being gloriously inconsistent, he did not hesitate to apply the antyodaya principle when a state had to be chosen for the EFA project he had in mind. P. Shiv Shankar was the Minister, MHRD, and L.P. Sahi, the Minister of State. Andhra Pradesh, from where Shiv Shankar hailed had already an externally funded project by way of APPEP. Hence, Bordia chose Bihar for the EFA project.

In February 1990, Bordia had a preliminary discussion with UNICEF, and a month later, he presented to the Jomtien Conference the 'Brown Book'—a document with a brown cover setting out the grand vision of BEP—as an exemplar of what an EFA project ought to be. Reason being a double-edged sword, Bordia offered a brilliant rationale for the choice of Bihar in the Brown Book:

> Its social system is stratified into manifold layers on the basis of class, caste, gender etc., Feudal and *zamindari* values persist, reinforcing social inequalities and the power structure. Gross discrimination is practiced, and atrocities are committed on the "lower classes" and tribal communities. The position of women of poor families is among the lowest in India …
>
> Almost all educational indicators in Bihar are negative. It has one of the lowest enrolment ratios, particularly among women and the poor, and its dropout rates at the primary level are the highest in the country. The educational infrastructure has become degraded; there are reports of large-scale absenteeism, mismanagement of adult and non-formal education programmes, and administrative apathy.

In short, 'Bihar has come to be regarded as a challenge, and it is believed that if you can achieve something in Bihar, you can do anywhere else in India'. However, there were 'some positive indicators'.

> There is a visible disaffection among Bihar's youth with the way things are, leading to the formation of a large number of voluntary agencies and activist groups, which are doing good work. The teachers' organisations have shown vitality, fighting not only for teachers' rights but also evincing interest in improvement of the educations system and the involvement of the masses in educational reconstruction. There is no dearth of dedicated teachers and public-spirited people. The Government of Bihar is willing to meet the situation and bring about necessary changes in the management structure.

The document expressed no doubt whatsoever whether the awesome challenges posed by the ground realities could be met; implicitly, it was considered that the negative features were more than offset by the positive indicators. In keeping with the legacy of 'radical phraseology in education' bequeathed by J.P. Naik, BEP was conceived as a societal mission for bringing about basic changes in the entire scene of social development in Bihar. Educational reconstruction that BEP would undertake would act as driving force which would bring about 'improvement in all spheres', and 'the atmosphere of despair, cynicism, and violence will give way to a firm determination to deal with the environmental, social, cultural, and gender issues'.[8] The document went on to declare that BEP was more than a project and programme; it was the start of a movement—'a movement to question shibboleth, to give new hope and challenge to persons working in the field of education, systematically revamp the entire content and process of education, creating conditions for teachers *to be*, and enable the common man and woman *to be*'.

As he first read the document soon after he joined Bordia's department, K could not help recall the *sampoorna kranthi* (total revolution) movement spearheaded by the legendary Loknayak Jayaprakash Narayan 15 years earlier. Bihar was the epicentre of that movement. Although the ideology of sampoorna kranthi was never defined precisely, from time to time the Loknayak spoke of a total revolution that would redeem the unfulfilled promises of the freedom movement, eradicate corruption and misgovernment, and would overhaul the education system, eliminate casteism and communalism, and usher in a real people's democracy. The sampoorna kranthi did lead to an intense political churning which, 15 years later, led to the collapse of the Congress Party in Bihar and emergence of new leaders such as Lalu Prasad Yadav who strode the political landscape of Bihar like a colossus when BEP began to be implemented. However, the main objectives of sampoorna kranthi fell by the way side, and the state of governance was generally believed to be worse than before. Against that backdrop, the question often cropped in K's mind, would we succeed where the Loknayak did not? At times, he tended to admire the incurable optimism, Promethean spirit of defiance, and grandiose

[8] Government of Bihar, Department of Education, and Government of India, Ministry of Human Resource Development, Department of Education, *Bihar Education Project*, February 1990, pp.1–2.

vision of the BEP document, and at other times, he was put off by the explicit unrealism of the objective as well as the staggering outlay of about Rs 1,600 crore to be expended over half the state over a five-year period, a 15-fold step-up in the project area of the annual plan expenditure on activities covered by BEP. Even in the best administered states, such a step-up would have been a feat that Hercules could not have accomplished but to visualize it in Bihar was sheer fantasy. The document expected external agencies to contribute about 50 per cent of the outlay, Government of Bihar one-sixth, and GOI the rest. About 40 per cent of the outlay was earmarked for primary schooling, about a quarter for NFE, 15 per cent for adult education, and 4 per cent each for early childhood care and development, and women's empowerment. The BEP document presented with broad brush strokes the different programme components and the possible strategies for each of the components. Within five years, all children in the age-group 6–14 were to be enrolled in schools or NFE centres and sufficient number of schools and NFE centres were to be set up within a walking distance of every habitation in the project area. The dropout rate was to be reduced from the aggregate of 60 per cent to 40 per cent in every block and for every group. Adult illiteracy was to be drastically reduced such that at least 80 per cent of the 15–30 age-group population was functionally literate. The education system would be modified so as serve the objects of equality for women and their empowerment, and necessary educational interventions would be made to provide equal educational opportunity to adults and children belonging to the lower castes, 'ethnic communities', and the poorest sections of the society. Education would be related to the working and living conditions of the people, and special emphasis would be laid in all educational activities on science and environment on an inculcation of a sense of social justice. BEP would focus on educationally and economically deprived groups such as women, 'lower castes', scheduled tribes, and scheduled castes. All in all, it was not a conventional project document but a grand manifesto.

The approach to project implementation was equally unconventional, and proceeded on the assumption that the conventional wisdom about education was questionable, and need to be questioned if BEP were to achieve even a modest success. The conventional wisdom held that schooling was the most appropriate form of providing primary education, and that NFE could not provide education of comparable quality. It also held that there was a correlation between the level of educational qualifications and the duration of training of teachers, on the one hand, and the quality of education on the other. It also held that teachers were politicized, and that no significant change could be made in their conduct and effectiveness. It also held that the government alone had the responsibility for educating people, and that since there were only a small number of voluntary agencies, they could not take responsibility for a substantial part of the educational programmes. Lastly, the conventional wisdom also held that the government could not function with flexibility and innovativeness, had little desire to treat voluntary agencies as partners, and could not create means of involving creative individuals and, on the whole, could not instil a missionary spirit among the teaching staff and the society. The entire society—political parties of all hues, teachers and teacher organizations, all government departments and their officials, employers and trade union leaders, voluntary agencies, and all educational institutions—would be mobilized and involved in the implementation of BEP. Improvement of teacher performance and their participation in the planning and management at all levels would be central to BEP; as the document evocatively put it, 'the main effort will be to create conditions for teachers *to be*' (italics in original). Planning, management, and implementation of BEP would be de-bureaucratized, which implied that 'hierarchies must be pulled down', that 'networks need to be built, with symbiotic effect', and that 'all colleagues have to be allowed to understand, absorb, and internalize the tasks and challenges'. In keeping with the cardinal principle of de-bureaucratization, the BEP document envisaged participative management structures to be created from the village onwards to the state level: the Village Education Committee, a District Karyakari Dal (Task Force) headed by the District Collector, and State Mission Task Force organized as an autonomous society (later christened as Bihar Shiksha Pariyojna Parishad [BSPP]). BSPP was to comprise a council headed by the Chief Minister himself, and Mission Task Force headed by the State Education Secretary. In all the structures, voluntary agencies, activists, and teacher representatives were to be associated as colleagues. *Mission not management* was the credo. A mission mode, the document proclaimed, assumes 'sense of urgency, a time-bound scheme of things in which specific responsibility would be attached to institutions, agencies, or individuals, and they would be accountable for the responsibility assigned to them'. However, the missionary management would not rely on 'controls, pressures, and monitoring' but on emotional commitment of the people involved. Efficiency and outputs would be ensured through decentralized, participatory, flexible, and innovative processes. Stock in trade of conventional projects like targets, particularly financial targets, and 'objective verifiable indicators' deny the time and space required for the processes to work out were deemed to suspect in what was labelled an 'evolving project' to contrast it from a 'blueprint project' wherein everything including the pace of attainment of goals and of expenditure is certain. Reminiscent of Japanese quality circles, a rigorous system of review would be put in place 'in which people meet frequently in small, manageable groups, discuss milestones, recall successes and analyse failures'.

What Is Unusual Is Usual

About a month after K joined Bordia, K first heard of BEP. A meeting with Rajni Kothari, Member, Planning Commission, was scheduled later in the day to discuss the note sent by the Planning Commission to MHRD remonstrating about the failure of the department to consult the Planning Commission about externally funded projects, and specifically observing in respect of BEP that the Bihar government was ignorant about BEP. A master of bureaucratic jungle warfare, Bordia decided that the best way to counter was to get the Education Commissioner of Bihar tell Kothari that his government was fully in the picture, that preparatory work was done in the three districts chosen for the commencement of BEP (Rohtas, Ranchi, and West Champaran), and that the state government had committed the requisite financial resources, and was waiting for the response of the central government. As was customary for him, he scripted to the minutest detail what the Education Commissioner had to say, put him through a thorough rehearsal, and coached him to reply to the possible queries. He then announced that the UNICEF Executive Board had conveyed its decision to pledge an amount of US$8 million from its budgetary resources and try to mobilize supplementary funding of the order of $100 million subject to the central and state governments matching the UNICEF contribution. At the prevailing exchange rate, the outlay would therefore be not about Rs 1,600 crore but Rs 360 crore of which half would be provided by UNICEF, one-third by GOI, and one-sixth by Government of Bihar; all the three partners would release their contribution to BSPP as a block grant to jointly finance the activities approved by the Executive Committee of BSPP. He then went on to declare that in relative terms, the shares of the different programme components would remain the same as indicated in the Brown Book. The Meeting with Kothari went on pretty well as the drastic reduction in outlay and the change in the financing pattern required the Cabinet Note to be reworked by the department and no decision was required on the Note earlier submitted by the department. A few days later, Bordia began his preparations for securing the approvals for the revised outlay and revised financing pattern. K expected that a revised detailed project document would be prepared in view of the UNICEF pledge but that was not to be. There never was a project document other than the Brown Book.

About a month later, K joined the contingent that accompanied Bordia to Ranchi, the first of the many, many visits to Bihar that were to follow, and savoured his first experience of such visits. Ranchi was the first district where a district task force was set up. K was surprised to note that even before the financing was firmed up, and even before the visionary document presented to the Jomtien Conference was translated into a concrete plan of action, action had begun in the sense that the Director, Non-formal and Adult Education, began to officiate as the Project Director, BEP, a committee was constituted to sanction micro-projects to be implemented by voluntary agencies, and adult literacy campaigns were launched in three districts, rather strangely districts different from those identified for the implementation of BEP. The literacy campaign launched in Muzaffarpur district had the evocative name of SAMU, and had the ambitious goal of achieving total literacy in four blocks in about a year. A month later, Eimi tipped off K that Carl-Dieter Spranger, the West German Federal Minister for Economic Co-operation, would be meeting Raj Mangal Pandey, the Minister MHRD. She told K that Carl Gustaf Mannerheim, Counsellor of the German Embassy, was keen to fund BEP, and that he was of the view that it would be a good idea if Pandey put in a word for BEP. In fairness to UNICEF, Eimi never failed to mention that only 8 million dollars were pledged from UNICEF's budgetary resources, that the $100 million were contingent on UNICEF's ability to mobilize supplementary resources, and that she expected DOE to assist UNICEF in resource mobilization. She was indefatigable in her efforts to mobilize resources for BEP; she would badger K to follow up with the Department of Economic Affairs and make an effort to transfer the unutilized aid committed by various bilateral agencies to BEP. She tried to work on her Japanese connection to tap funds from Japanese government and Buddhist associations for BEP. For Buddhists, Bihar was a venerated place for it was at Gaya that Prince Siddhartha received enlightenment and became Buddha; Patna was the capital of Emperor Asoka who sent missionaries all over the known world to spread the gospel of the Venerated One. When Eimi spoke of the German Minister, K recalled the observation of David Theobald a few months earlier at Hyderabad when K was still State Education Secretary. K found the long chats he had with Theobald very informative helping him to get an idea of what was happening in the Delhi *durbar* (court) and elsewhere. One day with a mischievous twinkle in his eye, he told K that the Official Development Assistance (ODA) was under terrific pressure to support a project in the making in Bihar, that funding that project required 'far too much courage' to his liking, and that he preferred to leave Bihar to his 'friends', the French who were the ancient rivals of England from the Middle Ages to the beginning of the twentieth century, and the Germans, Anglo-Saxon cousins who turned into deadly enemies in the twentieth century. K admired the prescience of Theobald. Soon after Pandey assumed office, Bordia and K had briefed him on the various external projects in the offing. Hence, Pandey had an idea of the externally aided projects. When K met him at his residence to brief him before Spranger called on him, with a frown he asked K with irritation, 'how many sources would you tap funds?' It was Holi, and K understood from his private secretary that he was none too happy to be disturbed by an official visitor. By the time, Spranger arrived, he was composed, greeted Spranger effusively, offered him a plate laden with a variety of sweets, and introduced his granddaughters colourfully decked in festive dress to the visiting dignitary. The business session was rather brief. Pandey profusely thanked Spranger again and again for assisting BEP, embarrassing the visitor a great deal. Pandey spoke of the poverty, illiteracy, and teeming population of Bihar. In return, Spranger spoke of the great challenge of integrating East Germany with the West, and how it would take decades for the Eastern part of his now unified country to recover from the after-effects of Communism. The unfinished tasks of unification might not be completed in his lifetime. After Spranger left in his limousine, and as they were coming out, K asked Mannerheim about his assessment as to how the interview went. Mannerheim told K that Pandey's request seemed to have been registered by the German Minister; from what followed it did not.

About a month later, the indefatigable Eimi organized a big event—a presentation to donors of BEP. With his customary thoroughness, Bordia made elaborate preparation. He got a video prepared; it was designed to vividly portray the ground realities and the daunting challenges facing BEP. He got prepared a glossy custom-made brochure in two parts, the first summarizing the details of the project and the second detailing the activities already undertaken. He also scripted a slide presentation to be given not by him but by the officiating BEP Project Director outlining the grand vision of BEP, what was accomplished and what were the plans to march ahead. The assistance of UNICEF in preparing the material was invaluable; its forte was media and communications, its procedure for preparing material was extraordinarily flexible, it had an army of media consultants and established links with organizations which produced the material. K saw a new aspect of Bordia's multifaceted personality: he donned the role of a film critic. He watched the video documentary with an Argus-eye, again and again asking the video to be stopped to offer his comments, and giving directions how the treatment should be modified so as to bring out the intended effect more vividly. The turnout for the big event was disappointing—just six representatives from five embassies. As soon as the presentations were over, Mannerheim began to pose incisive questions with logical rigour. It was through Mannerheim's interrogation that K got acquainted with some of the standard questions that constitute the stock-in-trade of 'aid business'. Mannerheim began his fusillade with the questions what would happen after the project ended? Would the Bihar government 'pick up the tab'? No agency would like the project it funds to be a flash in the pan, and would like the benefits of the project to be sustained even after the project is completed. That would require, to say, the least, that the aid recipient has the fiscal capacity to finance the maintenance of the assets created by the project, and of the interventions that ought to be continued. Thus, it makes no sense if at the end of BEP the state government cannot maintain the schools and other institutions created, and pay the salaries of teachers and other staff if the enrolment, retention, participation, and learning levels reached thorough BEP interventions. The state of governance as well as the finances of the Bihar government inspired little confidence about the ability of the state machinery either to implement the audacious programme that the BEP document outlined or to sustain the outcomes of BEP after it ended. As an outstanding professional, Bordia exuded confidence and asserted that Bihar would be so transformed that it could carry on the torch of BEP forever. Bordia's emphatic assertion rattled K for at that very moment he was grappling with the stand taken by the Bihar government on the Memorandum of Association of BSPP which Bordia got drafted by one of his deputies and sent to the Bihar government for concurrence.

The comments of the Bihar government reflected the views of Arun Pathak, one of the brightest officers of Bihar and then Finance Commissioner. The comments, typical , first cut comments of a finance department, made it clear that the state government would not like BEP to undertake any activity which would create a recurring financial liability for the state government. Mannerheim then turned to the question how the village education committees (VECs), which were expected to play a vital role in the educational reconstruction at the grassroots, would be constituted whereupon Bordia launched a long discourse on the process for empowering the local community, and how the empowered community itself would constitute the VEC, and how the process of constituting the VEC would ensure that it was not a rigid bureaucratic structure but a living entity. Never one to give up, Mannerheim then asked how the villages would be selected, and whether the selection would be based on rational criteria or on political considerations. Bordia confidently asserted that the Bihar government was fully committed to BEP, that the process of mobilization would enlist all sections of the society and all the political parties in the implementation of BEP, and that therefore considerations extraneous to BEP objectives and processes would not intrude into the implementation of BEP. On that note, the session ended. A couple of months later, Mannerheim visited BEP to see for himself how BEP was progressing, and assess the prospects of its success. After that visit, Mannerheim, to use the memorable word of Theobald, lost 'courage', and indicated that he would like another state to be suggested for German assistance; the state suggested was Orissa.

Soon after the donors' meeting, Eimi suggested that an action plan for 1991–2 be drawn up, and that the financial requirements for implementing different activities of that plan be estimated. The plan would help UNICEF to put together the financial and material resources that UNICEF would have to contribute to the plan. Further, a plan would infuse a much needed element of concreteness in the thinking about BEP. Successful implementation of the plan would also enhance the credibility of BEP and dispel the scepticism of donors. Preparation of the annual plan brought to the fore the basic dilemmas in the concretization and implementation of the vision articulated in the BEP document. 'Marketing' BEP in Bihar needed to overcome a major mental barrier which gripped Bihar officials as well as the external agencies: near-universal disbelief that any meaningful change could be effected in Bihar. Over the five odd years that K was associated with BEP, in Bihar he heard again and again the refrain 'This is Bihar' meaning 'Don't take for granted that ameliorative measures that are *ex-facie* sound or were successful elsewhere would succeed here.' 'This is Bihar' syndrome is not unique to Bihar; the assertion that 'This is Africa' figures again and again in *Tropical Gangster,*[9] a book which narrates the experience of a bank's consultant while advising the Government of Equatorial Guinea. There is an element of truth in that syndrome, although often it is an excuse for unwillingness to change. To catch the attention of the Bihar government as well as of the voluntary organizations, activists and all others whose enlistment the BEP document had envisaged, it was necessary to project the perception that BEP was not only a grand project but also one financially well-endowed so that finances would not come in the way of implementing the grand vision. Yet ironically, the grander the vision of educational reconstruction and transformative social change, the greater was the disbelief that vision fostered among the funding agencies. If the vision was to be real and not a marketing ploy, it was necessary to make haste slowly. It was necessary to alter the negative features that the BEP document spoke of as well as the ground-level realities which BEP labelled conventional wisdom and sought to question. Such alteration in turn necessitated patiently

[9] Robert Klitgaard, *Tropical Gangsters*, New York: Basic Books, 1990.

working on every element of the Bihar society and polity. The process of ushering such a change was bound to be slow; success would be slow to come by and for a long while it would be difficult to show tangible, demonstrable results on a scale that evokes credibility. The longer it took for tangible results to be shown, the more unwilling would the funding agencies be to pledge funds sufficient to enthuse the Biharis and attain the educational objectives that BEP had boldly proclaimed. All in all, the Grand Vision created a Catch-22 situation. Bordia was extremely hesitant to prepare an action plan lest targets and milestones should deny the time and space processes would require. K made bold to suggest that an action plan be prepared lest the best should be the enemy of the good, and the absence of any action plan give scope to functionaries of Bihar government to take up activities utterly inconsistent with the BEP objectives. With great reluctance, Bordia agreed saying that he would not be around after a few months and K would regret the decision to draft an action plan. After the doctrinal debate was concluded, Bordia prepared an action plan for 1991–2 with the help of Athrayee, a consultant; as a document it was quite impressive clearly specifying the milestones to be achieved in each quarter. Among the activities identified were the constitution of the state and district mission task forces, expansion of BEP to four more districts (Chatra, East Singhbum, Sitamarhi), appointment of staff, delegation of financial powers, orientation of the management personnel, beginning microplanning in two blocks, conference with teachers' organizations, survey of infrastructure of schools in selected blocks, establishing four district resource units and three field centres for training, training of village leaders, education workers and women activists, supply of uniforms to girls from focus group households, and so on.

A few months later, the Expenditure Finance Committee (EFC) approved the implementation of BEP; only an exceptional civil servant like Bordia could have secured that approval. Finance officials are conditioned by their job to be sceptics for whom expenditure is a certainty while benefit is a hypothesis. Yet Bordia could prevail upon the Expenditure Secretary who chaired EFC to literally 'buy a pig in a poker', for while the GOI committed itself to contribute its share of the outlay, UNICEF's firm commitment was only about 7 per cent of the contribution it was expected to make, and the Bihar government was chronically cash-strapped. Except for the Brown Book, and an indicative allocation of Rs 360 crore among a few programme components, EFC had nothing concrete to go by. In a rare burst of generosity, EFC departed from the hoary practice of passing on the aid received as grant to the state governments by passing on an extra two-thirds of a dollar from the GOI budget for every dollar of aid. And further, in another rare burst of far-sightedness, EFC granted an approval in broad terms permitting DOE to pass on the GOI's contribution to BSPP as a lump sum grant, and granting BSPP extraordinary flexibility in planning its activities. The flexibility comes out in bold relief against the backdrop of the rigid schematic pattern of CSS, that is to say schemes drawn up and financed by the central government and implemented by state governments. The representatives of DOE in the BSSP and periodic review by the Union Education Secretary were expected to ensure that the activities were chosen with due deliberation, and that parsimony was observed in incurring expenditure. BSPP was given full flexibility to design the specific activities subject only to the condition that the expenditure on construction should not exceed 24 per cent and that on administration 6 per cent. The ceiling on construction was designed to give a go-by to the much-reviled but hardy perennial 'brick and mortar' approach to education. The most evocative description of the 'brick and mortar' approach to primary education was by Nehru who once rued the fact that building comes to be more important than the people who study, learn, and work in the school, and the first thing that a state government did when funds were available for education was to take up construction of school. From his own experience, K noticed that as compared to construction of school buildings, issues related to quality of education were orphans ignored by most state governments. The ceiling on administrative expenses was designed to ensure that BEP was not afflicted with overstaffing, a common ailment of public sector undertakings. The ceilings on civil construction and administrative expenditure introduced in BEP were extended to other externally funded projects such as Lok Jumbish and DPEP. All in all, in according such an approval for BEP the Expenditure Secretary suspended the customary disbelief of finance officials. After EFC accorded the approval, Eimi was all appreciation for the IAS; in her own organization, it would have been well-nigh impossible for such a creative departure from the past.

BEP and Lok Jumbish: Study in Contrast

With the wisdom of the hindsight, BEP would have been better off if its vision were less grandiose and its outlay less mindboggling. For far too long a time, BEP was considered to be a *kamadhenu*, the mythical 'cow of plenty' which provided everyone everything one desired. The popularization of the messages of the Brown Book triggered irrational, exuberant expectations. Inadvertently perhaps, many voluntary agencies came to believe that BEP would implicitly trust them and generously fund them without any limits. An anecdote, perhaps apocryphal, that K heard from Kenneth King, a noted expert on aid, after visiting BEP in September 1994 is symptomatic of the expectations which prevailed in Bihar. King spoke about a voluntary organization which suggested that it would be useful for it to be supplied with a helicopter to allow it work more effectively in rural areas. The top brass of Bihar expected a massive inflow of resources to spruce up the primary education system; none of them were aware of the contingent nature of UNICEF's promise to raise supplementary resources or of the fact that for a couple of years at least BEP would be in an exploratory phase during which the flow of resources would be a trickle and not a torrential flow. For over a year, BEP was taken to be a programme of non-formal and adult education as few activities relating to primary schooling were taken up. Once primary education began to receive attention, the Director of School Education considered BEP to be a cornucopia that would eliminate all resource constraint. He looked forward to implement with great gusto not only state government programmes which were faltering for want of adequate budgetary support but also any activity which struck his fancy could be taken up. When it was later found that BEP was not free of financial procedures and the scale of funding was modest, there was a backlash so much so it was almost impossible to realistically assess the achievements of BEP. By late 1991, disenchantment set in among the top brass of Bihar government, and they began to consider BEP as Bordia's *shauk* (hobby). Within a few months of being appointed as BEP Project Director, S. Vijayaraghavan was entrusted with additional responsibilities in the Secretariat. Even Eimi began expressing concern about the seemingly unending processes, and the excessive emphasis on mobilization and creating demand for basic education. At a workshop held on the South Orissa Project in April 1992, she gave vent to her feelings that at some point processes should stop and begin yielding concrete, demonstrable outcomes. UNICEF's strategy of mobilizing extra-budgetary resources very much depended on such outcomes to be manifested at the earliest. The international donors would be not carried away by the concept of 'evolving' projects and were prone to believe what they saw. It was imperative to show results without any further delay. She also maintained that even in the villages of Bihar one could not miss the demand for good education among the poor, and that therefore quick 'supply-side' interventions to expand the school network and improve the facilities and quality of instruction in schools should be undertaken as they would yield impressive results. It was only in November 1991 that a relatively coherent approach to primary education fell in place with the beginning of planning exercise to draw up a plan for UPE (classes I–V) in the Sitamarhi district plan; this exercise was a follow-up of the idea of district projects mooted by DOE in its proposals on the Eighth Five-Year Plan which were submitted to the Planning Commission in November 1991. The Sitamarhi Plan, however, was no more than a wish list, and further unlike similar plans drawn up later in DPEP, not subjected to appraisal, and its implementation limped all along because of inadequate resources.

With the wisdom of the hindsight, K feels that BEP would have been better off if UNICEF handled BEP the way SIDA handled Lok Jumbish, and if EFC took note of the fact that the firm commitment of resources by UNICEF was limited to $8 million and accordingly did not extend an unqualified approval for an outlay that took for granted that the supplementary resources of $100 million would be raised by UNICEF and made available to BEP. In tandem with the preparation of the Brown Book, Bordia also began developing an EFA project in his home state of Rajasthan. In November 1989, the GOI submitted to SIDA a note prepared by Bordia entitled *Basic Education for All in Rajasthan by the Year 2000*. The note outlined objectives, strategies, and financial estimates for a 10-year collaborative effort with the overall goal of facilitating 'universalization of primary education and a substantial reduction of adult illiteracy, along with the provision of facilities for post-literacy, continuing education and vocational training'. The project was to be implemented in two phases. In the first phase from 1990 to 1995, approximately half the districts and blocks of Rajasthan would be covered, and the rest of the state in the second phase spanning the period 1995 to 2000. Unlike the Brown Document, the Rajasthan EFA note was not presented to the Jomtien Conference as SIDA insisted that an Indo-Swedish team of consultants should make an initial assessment of the proposal. A modified proposal was presented to the consultants, and it was in this proposal that the term Lok Jumbish made its debut. The modified proposal indicated that the overall goal of Lok Jumbish was the creation of 'a people's movement with a view to providing relevant basic education to all, and to generate a stimulus for human development'. It made no mention about the financing aspects or phasing of the project. In their report in April 1990, the consultants identified a number of issues which needed to be clarified 'in order to move the proposal to an operational framework of collaboration and implementation'. The workshop at Udaipur (August 1990) decided that the project might be started in three blocks on a pilot basis, and a project document for a five-year project would be prepared by a team of consultants by December 1990. A month later, SIDA indicated the possibility of SIDA supporting the project for 3–4 years with about 50 million Swedish kroner (about Rs 15 crore) a year. It also made clear that the preparation of the project document was 'an Indian responsibility', and an SIDA appraisal mission would visit India during March to April 1991. With his customary élan, Bordia embarked on the preparation of the 'Yellow Book' as the project document came to be called because of its cover.[10] Given the tenacity with which SIDA insisted on compliance with the standard project preparation and appraisal cycle, the Yellow Book was less effusive than the Brown Book, yet as a handiwork of Bordia, it could not be totally free from rhetorical flourish.

> There is a postcard view of Rajasthan, of palaces and kings, of sand dunes and camels, of valour and sacrifice. There is yet the same time the other view of Rajasthan, of deteriorating environment, large scale prevalence of child marriage, high infant mortality rate, caste and community stratification.... The overall goal of the Project is to achieve education for all by the year 2000 through people's mobilization and their participation. The Project presupposes that creation of a people's movement would

[10] Government of Rajasthan, Department of Education and Government of India, Ministry of Human Resource Development, Department of Education, *Lok Jumbish: People's Movement for Education for All: Rajasthan*, December 1990.

> generate a stimulus for human development, which in turn, would contribute to basic socio-economic transformation.... Lok Jumbish is also a design of administration of education which will enable people to manage and where necessary, modify the delivery system. This is in contrast to a centrally designed, hierarchically controlled, tradition governed system, with inbuilt flexibility, which eliminates the weaker sections of society from receiving effective access to the opportunities which can improve their lot. The organisational manifestation of Lok Jumbish will be the Village Education Committee, or at some places a Mahila Samooh (women's collective). People connected with the basic education system will be reoriented to perceive *a shift in accountability- from a hierarchical system of Panchayat Raj institutions* and a line of Inspectors, to *an organised forum of the village community*. In turn, the people's organisations begin to ask for the accountability of the basic education system, they will , inevitably, move on to ask for accountability of other systems of basic services, such as cooperative societies, drinking water facilities, health care, etc. It is no exaggeration to say that the proposed strategy of Lok Jumbish comes very close to being an impossible proposition. The aims of the programme are to achieve what no other programme of whatever scale has so far achieved anywhere in India. The aim of the programme is to resuscitate and transform a byzantine educational system which in itself constitutes a major problem. (emphasis added)

It is significant that Bordia's conceptualization of the Panchayat Raj institutions as hierarchical and reliance on a village community disarticulated from the Panchayat Raj institutions to effect educational transformation runs counter to the conventional view that elementary education can be leavened only through decentralization and entrustment of the management of education to democratically elected local bodies. However, the overall goals set out in the Yellow Document were similar to those of BEP; however, given that SIDA was not UNICEF, and that it wanted a greater degree of specificity in the project document, the Yellow Book specified the short-term goals of Phase I covering the fiscal years 1991–2 and 1992–3, and offered detailed financial cost estimates only for that phase. Phase I was to be a period of testing and trial with emphasis to be laid on testing and defining operational modalities in respect of various parameters of basic education, on experimentation with various models and approaches to identify the most efficacious and cost-effective techniques for achievement of the goals of the project, and on institution building, research, and studies. The outlay of this phase was to be Rs 72 crore with SIDA bearing half the outlay, GOI a third, and Government of Rajasthan a sixth. Further, in keeping with the customary practice of project documents, the Yellow Book also spelt out the risks and difficulties in the start and implementation of Lok Jumbish.

> The delay in creation of management teams at the State/District and Block levels, and selection of appropriate persons.
>
> The training system may not materialise. This is an area in which there are few success stories, and numberless resort to shortcuts.
>
> The *vested interests, which include people in Panchayat Raj institutions*, some teachers and others who benefit from the dysfunctionality of primary education and literacy programmes.
>
> A sense of disbelief and cynicism among the people, which is based on the past experience where lofty statements and fine programmes failed at the level of actual delivery, and even when they succeeded they were not sustained. (emphasis added)

In April 1991, SIDA mounted a mission comprising Gordon Tamm, Jörgen Person, and Uno Winblad to appraise the Yellow Book, and to formulate and redesign the project document in such a way as to turn it into an operational document on which implementation and monitoring could be based. The appraisal was stormy. At a meeting of the consultants and representatives of Governments of Rajasthan and India, the consultants suggested, among others, that it was necessary to lay down a set of operational priorities, and that Phase I should cover five years with a 10- to 15-year overall perspective. The appraisal note[11] was remarkable for its candour.

> In almost every respect the proposed Lok Jumbish defies normal standards of appraisal.... The difficulty lies in defining the very nature of Lok Jumbish. As pointed out by the Union Education Secretary, nobody knows what Lok Jumbish is even if one may spell out what it wants to do. Variously called a people's movement, a sector reform, a programme of Education for All, and a gigantic educational experiment, its premise is that the present system of basic education is grossly inadequate.... Assessing the prerequisites of a people's movement is very

[11] Gordon Tamm, Jörgen Person, and Uno Winblad, *Lok Jumbish: Appraisal of Programme Documents*, A Note to SIDA, May 1991.

> different from that for a sector reform or a more clear cut educational programme.
>
> Defining the nature of Lok Jumbish is important for at least two reasons. Unless it is clear what Lok Jumbish stands for and what it is, there is little hope for merging all (the various) actors into a cohesive force. Second, from the point of view of the donor … the character and role of Lok Jumbish will also determine the event and form of collaborative support, financial and otherwise …
>
> The Lok Jumbish concept embodies all three (an investment programme, a development programme, and a socio-educational movement or charter for change) at the same time. From an intellectual point of view this may be a satisfactory view, but it does not augur well from an operational viewpoint. While it may create a constructive happening, it is more likely to end up a Tower of Babel with different actors at different levels talking about different things …
>
> If an attempt is to be made to tackle the entire 'byzantine' education establishment in order to reshape it and make it more efficient, a strong dose of cost awareness is essential. There is little awareness at present … an effort (to promote cost awareness) will have to be made, if the Lok Jumbish would go beyond the mere objective of stirring up people's emotions for a while and/or adding some funds to the State's budget for primary education …
>
> The extremely comprehensive and largely non-determinative Lok Jumbish proposal should be seen as a framework for a possible collaboration, rather than forming the collaboration as such. Consequently most of our efforts have been focussed on how to further develop Lok Jumbish as such.

In conclusion, the consultants recommended to SIDA that it should agree to fund Phase I as modified by them subject to a financial analysis of the basic education sector as a whole, its disbursement and cost-effectiveness over time being done.

The meeting with the consultants on 3 July 1991 was stormy. The consultants rued the fact that their proposal was 'as a whole firmly rejected by the Union Secretary (Bordia)' who stressed 'the inviolate nature of the Draft LJ Document', and maintained that 'our approach was "anti-people and contrary to the spirit of Lok Jumbish"'. In high dudgeon Bordia stayed away most of the time leaving his colleague from Rajasthan, Rajendra Jain, to preside over the meeting, and K to rebut the arguments of the consultants. With his extraordinary skills of managing men and matters, Bordia could persuade SIDA to support the experimental Phase I without insisting on the financial analysis that the consultants recommended. In October, Bordia prepared a 'Pink Book' outlining the Action Plan for Phase I (1992–4) with a total outlay of Rs 20 crore, of which SIDA contributed Rs 10 crore. A total of 25 blocks, about 10 per cent of the blocks in Rajasthan, were to be covered in Phase I. After that phase came to an end, SIDA took stock of what was accomplished and agreed to support Phase II (1994–7) with an outlay of Rs 80 crore; this phase was expected to cover 50 additional blocks. Suffice it to say that the reported achievements of Lok Jumbish are not a little due to the scrutiny that SIDA brought to bear on the Lok Jumbish proposals from time to time, and to its ensuring that rhetoric notwithstanding the Lok Jumbish did not stray too far away from what is do-able; this is a fact that the discourse on Lok Jumbish misses out. Of the various bilateral agencies, SIDA is noted for its empathy to the recipient counties and its willingness to support activities which most other agencies stay away from, adult education being an example. Only an agency like SIDA could have agreed to fund an unconventional project like Lok Jumbish, and persevered with it. Yet even SIDA could not be immune from the accountability of a bilateral agency to its 'masters', namely the government, Parliament, and citizens, and the imperative of discharging that accountability by funding only programmes which are potentially successful and efficient, and to the end, scrutinize the design of a programme and oversee its implementation . As an agency which cultivates the image of a good Samaritan, SIDA might be more liberal than other agencies in its assessment of feasibility and in its eschewal of intrusive oversight. However, it could not abandon altogether considerations of feasibility and oversight. Nor could Swedish assistance be immune from the foreign policy objectives and commercial considerations of the donor country. In bilateral dialogue such as the one in December, the Swedish side was prone to raise issues such as the violation of human rights in the 'Indian-occupied Kashmir' which were unconnected with the issues of development co-operation on the agenda. No wonder that after the Pokhran nuclear test SIDA assistance was unilaterally terminated and DFID stepped in to support Shiksha Karmi and Lok Jumbish.

Like Lok Jumbish, BEP was an open-ended project. The Brown Book itself cautioned that it 'should not be treated as final; it 'was intended to start a dialogue on Bihar's educational reconstruction, for making a start with planning and implementation, and as basis for seeking financial support'. The project was expected 'to evolve as we move', and 'in the meanwhile, even before the project document is finalized and appraised, action will start in all earnest'. If UNICEF were a typical funding agency like SIDA, and its experience of funding education not limited to provision of supplies and financing small, innovative projects, it would have critically examined whether the project outlined in the Brown Book was coherent, consistent, and *prima facie* feasible. With a willing suspension of disbelief, UNICEF came forward with a pledge to fund the grand vision expounded by the Brown Book in spite of the fact the Brown Book was a vision document, pooh-poohed ground realities as conventional wisdom and sought to do in one stroke so many things each of which would have been a daunting project in itself. Even if it had indicated its willingness to support BEP, UNICEF had an opportunity to infuse realism once it firmed up its commitment—8 million dollars from its budget and supplementary funding of 100 million dollars subject to its ability to mobilize resources. It could have insisted on preparation of a revised project document taking into account the funding it had pledged, and insisted on an appraisal. UNICEF left the evolution and detailing of BEP entirely to Bordia, ignoring the fact that none could be infallible, and that without peer reviews even the most well-intentioned ideas could go astray. While an innovative educational project cannot begin as a blueprint project with everything clearly and definitively elaborated, it cannot be totally be open ended all through. To compound its failure, UNICEF naively expected that other agencies with a better knowledge of the 'aid business' would be willing to suspend disbelief like itself. The only way UNICEF could have elicited substantial co-financing was by insisting as SIDA did with Lok Jumbish that BEP go through a pilot phase of a reasonable duration so that the various ideas and possibilities are tested out, and a coherent focussed proposal being developed based on the initiatives proved to be successful in the experimental phase. Agencies would like to go by the adage 'seeing is believing'; instead UNICEF expected them to first believe before they could see something tangible. UNICEF expected even the World Bank, the ultimate 'bean counter', to co-finance BEP, and needless to say, drew a blank. At no point of time did UNICEF functionaries in Delhi office or New York headquarters ever attempt to introspect over the actual reasons for UNICEF's failure to mobilize supplementary resources. A measure of the inadequate financing of BEP comes out from the fact that in June 1994, about half way through the project, a mid-term review-cum-appraisal mission mounted by DOE and UNICEF in June 1994 found that in the first three years (1991–2 to 1993–4) BEP received just Rs 23 crore from UNICEF, GOI, and Bihar government (about 6.4 per cent of the Rs 360 crore outlay approved by EFC), and of this, UNICEF provided only 28.78 per cent as compared to its normative share of 50 per cent. The flow of receipts from the Government of Bihar was erratic from the second year and less than its share. Government of India could have provided its full share of the outlay but for UNICEF failing to provide its share. No wonder that implementation faltered, and BEP never went on scale.

UNICEF was willing to suspend disbelief and finance the Brown Book, and yet it was unwilling to adapt its financing procedures to suit the requirement of an EFA project. All the three partners—GOI, Bihar government, and UNICEF were expected to pool their resources and assist BSPP to implement activities approved by the Executive Council of BSPP in which all the three were represented—or to use an imagery used by Kenneth King to describe the financing of DPEP 'put very large amounts of money into a common pot, and be satisfied with a single set of accounts'. UNICEF was particular that the funds it provided should not be used for payment of salaries or for construction of school buildings. And further, UNICEF was desirous of providing a substantial share of its contribution by way of supplies. These restrictions severely impaired the much needed expansion of access to primary schooling which is inconceivable without opening new schools, appointing new teachers, and constructing new school buildings. Bordia and K made all efforts to persuade Eimi to have the restrictions removed. K argued that if UNICEF were to adhere to its restrictions, a central government minister could as well stipulate that central government funds should be applied only for activities stipulated by him in the districts stipulated by him. Such restrictions and stipulations would distort the implementation of BEP. Bordia argued that in the Executive Committee the UNICEF representative could object to a particular activity on rational grounds such as it being inconsistent with the objectives of BEP or it being not feasible or cost-effective, but it could not object to its funds being applied to an activity which it did not disapprove. As UNICEF favoured expansion of access to primary schooling, it was illogical to object to the application of its funds for the activities without which expansion of access was inconceivable. No amount of reasoning could induce UNICEF to alter its financing policy; the compromise agreed to was to segregate in the accounts the expenditure incurred from UNICEF funds, and not to book the expenditure on salaries and construction of buildings to UNICEF funds.

In statistical theory, there are two types of errors; extending that concept to BEP, UNICEF committed both the types of errors: not doing what a prudent funding agency would do, and by doing what it ought not to do by inadvertently fostering the impression that it was the managing partner. In spite of the inadequate contribution of UNICEF, BEP came to be perceived in Bihar as a UNICEF project. There were many reasons underlying this perception: the colonial mindset still prevalent in large parts of India, the UNICEF office in Patna whose ubiquitous presence and visibility could not be offset by Bordia's frequent and intensive visitations from Delhi, UNICEF being represented in the BEP governance structure and every committee that was set up, and as such being privy to every decision. The functionaries of UNICEF based in Patna toured the districts intensively overseeing implementation of BEP. Because of the colonial mindset, functionaries in the field and voluntary organizations tended to look to those functionaries rather than to the BEP Project Director for guidance, and tended to submit reports to the UNICEF Patna office than to the project office, so much so that Vijayaraghavan quipped that BEP was like the Commonwealth of Independent States formed after the collapse of the Soviet Union; each of the Member States went their own way and were reluctant to recognize any centre. Vijayaraghavan had the mortifying experience of having to rely on UNICEF Patna Office for securing information from state government officers in districts. Compounding the problem arising from the colonial mindset was the fact that UNICEF had considerable powers of patronage such as organizing foreign junkets, a much prized perk those days when foreign travel was a rarity even for GOI officials, and the craze for 'phoren' goods was universal. Chastened by this experience, Bordia decided to exclude SIDA from the governing structures of Lok Jumbish and thereby insulate day-to-day management of the project from the external agency. When SIDA pressed its case, Bordia recounted the historical experience during the British Raj. The British resident had a larger-than-life role in the Native State to which he was accredited; it was he who ruled while the native ruler only reigned. The unhappy experience of BEP reinforced the lessons K drew from ODA having a field office in Hyderabad, and ODA functionaries frequently descending on the state to supervise APPEP. In DPEP, no agency was permitted to have a field office in states; agency functionaries or their consultants were not associated with planning or implementation; they could visit states and interact with programme functionaries in the field only for the purpose of appraisal and later only once in six months as part of the six-monthly joint review missions, and nothing else.

Getting Bihar on Board

In normal course, BEP would have been implemented by the Bihar Education Department. Had it been so, the flexibility that Bordia secured for BEP from EFC would have been rendered nugatory as the state finance department would have had a stranglehold on the release of funds to BEP, and would have had the authority to scrutinize every activity of BEP. The contributions of GOI and UNICEF would have been credited to the consolidated fund of the state government, releases from which would be regulated by the state finance department. State finances being usually precarious, state finance departments tended to regulate the release of funds more in accordance with the maintenance of ways and means than with the needs of the field units implementing programmes. Bordia came up with the idea that BEP should be managed by an entity legally distinct from the state government, the entity being a society registered under the Society Registration Act. Direct flow of funds to BSPP, the legal entity registered under the Society Registration Act, ensured smooth flow of funds for project implementation by short-circuiting the state finance department, and liberating BEP from the 'tyranny of Finance'. It was precisely because state finance department would be short-circuited that Arun Pathak, Finance Commissioner of the Bihar Government, was not initially in favour of BEP being implemented through a society. There was yet another reason for Pathak's unwillingness. Bordia expected BSPP to accomplish two objectives in addition to facilitating the smooth flow of funds. BSSP was expected to distance BEP from the state government and whirlpools of politics, and at the same time, broad-base the management of BEP by enabling the association of voluntary agencies, activists, and teacher organizations. Distancing of the state government raised alarm bells for Pathak as he was worried that in the absence of control by his department, expenditure might not be prudent, activities which could not be sustained or replicated elsewhere might be taken up leading to demands for similar activities to be taken up in districts not covered by BEP, and, more worryingly, the state government might be fastened with the burden of a heavy recurring liability after BEP comes to an end. Needless to say, if BEP were to make headway, it was imperative for Bordia to persuade the state finance department to accept his proposal for the society as it is or to negotiate with that department and secure forge an agreement that would harmonize the divergent positions on BEP implementation. There is a classical axiom that world over in all federations, 'By offering grant, the Federal Government does not buy compliance; It only achieves an opportunity to bargain with states';[12] BEP was no exception. In principle, agreement could be secured either through persuasion or through negotiations, or by imposing one's will through coercive methods such as holding out or actually wielding threats. And Bordia was a past master in creatively employing all the methods of securing the agreement. He built up pressure on the Bihar government by holding out the threat that unless the Bihar government agreed to the establishment of a society and registered the society he would let the budgetary provision for BEP lapse rather than releasing funds to the state government. He got Geeta Verma of UNICEF to categorically inform the Bihar Education Secretary that UNICEF or, for that matter, any donor would be unwilling to fund BEP if it were implemented by the State Education Department, for such an implementation would be too rigid. He also created an artificial deadline by having Geeta Verma announce that if the Bihar government did not register a society within 15 days, UNICEF would withdraw support to BEP. And before the deadline, he landed in Patna with his entourage for a meeting with the Bihar government officials; as ever, he scripted what his deputies would say. He told K that he would find fault with K for drawing upon a Memorandum of Association (MOA) which was far too 'lenient' to the state government, thereby playing the classical bad guy–good guy

[12] Helen Ingram, 'Policy Implementation through Bargaining: The Case of Federal Grants-in-Aid', *Public Policy*, 25, no. 4 (Fall 1977), pp. 499–526.

ploy of negotiations. He was also a past master in *backward mapping*, identifying key players on the other side, and trying to informally work on them, get them soften their stands, and, if possible, hammer out a possible deal so that formal negotiation is smoothened, and, if possible, reduced to a formality where the agreement informally arrived at is ratified. Soon after landing in Patna, Bordia embarked on the job of winning over Pathak, and he entrusted K with the job of similarly winning over Mukund Prasad, Secretary to the Chief Minister and K's friend. Bordia was very confident of his success and, with a smirk on his lips, told K that everything would be sorted out before the meeting, and while Pathak's deputies would mount one objection after another, he would announce a formulation which Pathak would eventually agree after raising objections. Bordia was true to his words, and hammered out an agreement with Pathak whereby Pathak's concerns were fully met. BSPP was required to formulate financial and personnel regulations which would come into effect only after they were approved by state government. BSPP could create posts only if equivalent posts were surrendered by the Directorate of Adult Education; even then such posts could be created only for a period of a year. The MOA would also stipulate that BSPP would observe utmost parsimony in expenditure. These provisions together for representation of the finance department in BSPP were adequate for a strong finance commissioner to exert control; at the same time, they were less stringent than the customary straightjacket regulation of departments by the finance department. As anticipated by Bordia, the meeting with the Bihar government officials went off smoothly. The one issue which caused considerable debate was the representation of teacher unions in the Executive Council of BSPP. Pathak as well as C.R. Venkataraman, Planning Secretary, strongly objected to such a representation on the ground that it would wreck BSPP. They narrated the travails of the officials of the education department in coping with the extortionate demands of the Members of the Legislative Council (MLCs) elected from teacher constituencies. Those MLCs held the officials to ransom by getting the legislative committees in which they were represented to pass ill-considered 'executive orders' favouring teachers, and coercing officers to comply with such orders lest they should be hauled up for contempt of legislature. In Bordia's worldview, the fact that teachers could be politicized and behave in an unprofessional manner was a 'conventional wisdom' which BEP ought to question. Hence, Bordia would not concede the point of view expressed by Pathak and Venkataraman readily; he delivered a long soliloquy on his being the son of a teacher, on teachers being at the centre of BEP, and on the imperative of giving up pre-conceived notions about teachers. Failing to make headway, he settled for a compromise lest the whole deal with Pathak get unstuck.

Once BSPP was registered, Bordia turned his attention to the appointment of a project director, and his choice—S. Vijayaraghavan—was indeed an inspired choice. A thorough professional, a man of few words, and an embodiment of humility, Vijayaraghavan was the ideal person for an unconventional project, and for a job wherein for success the incumbent had had to elicit the cooperation of officials of education department, district collectors, voluntary organizations, and activists, none of whom were under his control. The job was a classic example of *indirect management*—that is to say, manage a situation in which formal authority falls short of responsibilities and success is dependent on actions by individuals and agencies outside the chain command, and over whom one has no direct control. He won laurels in a similar, though less challenging, job as Managing Director of the State Diary Corporation where he had to organize small producers into milk co-operatives and provide them with marketing support. Only a personality like him free of ego could have so masterfully handled the job. Many a time those days, K used to think that Vijayaraghavan ought to be assertive, but in retrospect, K was wrong. Another inspired choice of Bordia was Sister Sujita of the Congregation of the Sisters of Notre Dame. She was a typical *Kerala putri* (daughter of Kerala) with a typical Malayali look, Malayali accent, and Malayali disdain for cant and hypocrisy. Her bony face with protruding jaw used to remind K of Krishna Menon, but in sharp contrast to Menon, she always beamed a charming smile. She was one of the many members of the Roman Catholic orders like Sister Sabina of Rohtas and Father Kurien of West Champaran who used to dress like laity and did stellar social service. She was always dressed in a simple but elegant saree, and lived in a hotel in a Musahar settlement in Jamsoth near Patna. Musahars are among the most deprived communities in India. They were so poor that they reportedly used to subsist on in the grain they collected in rat holes and consuming the flesh of rats they caught. Sujita meticulously practised what later as head of the global congregation of the Sisters of Notre Dame she commended to the congregation: 'we must walk in their shoes, through the mud and the dirt and the filth of their life, and to see the world through their eyes and feel it in their body'. 'Bloom anywhere you are planted' was her conviction, and her conviction was proved right. As already set out earlier, Sister Sujita left her distinctive impress on the MS component of BEP (Chapter V).

In retrospect, and in comparison with K's own experience with externally funded projects in many states, K was amazed by the fact that the Bihar government was utterly indifferent to the specific activities chosen for implementation under the aegis of BEP. Having once tended cattle himself, Chief Minister Lalu Prasad Yadav knew by experience that many poor children could not attend schools as they had to tend cattle, and hence came up with the idea of setting up Charwaha Vidyalayas (schools for shepherds) in government's dilapidated agricultural farms. Children could attend school while their cattle grazed in the farm. Lalu Prasad's vision of Charwaha Vidyalayas was indeed grand. The agriculture department was expected to manage the Charwaha Vidyalayas; the education department was expected to construct school buildings and provide instructors, teaching–learning material, uniforms, and mid-day meal; the forest department was expected to fence the farms and plant trees; the animal husbandry Department was expected to grow grass on the farms and provide fodder; and the fisheries department was expected to dig ponds for pisciculture. During 1991–2, 113 such schools were set up, and during his travels, K came across the name boards of such schools conspicuously displayed on the roads he travelled—so many of them that he used to quip that there were more sign boards of Charwaha Vidyalayas than milestones on the roads of Bihar. Launched with great fanfare as the Chief Minister's dream project, Charwaha Vidyalayas soon languished for want of finances and proper organization, and what all was left were rusting name boards on roads. No teachers were recruited; teachers from neighbouring schools were deputed to the Charwaha Vidyalayas, and in the absence of proper supervision, the teachers deputed did not always turn up in the Charwaha Vidyalayas. In view of the free grazing available in the farms, whoever tended cattle turned up in the Charwaha Vidyalayas even if they were not of school-going age? As a concept, Charwaha Vidyalayas represented sound NFE, and the state government could have insisted that BEP should fund Charwaha Vidyalayas and improve their pedagogic practices. There was no such request. Ram Chandra Purve, the Education Minister, was extremely supportive of BEP, and made it a point to join Bordia and his entourage during as many visits as possible, so much so with the Minister being present, Bordia and his team were often received with great fanfare and led in triumphal processions. R.K. Srivastava, the Education Secretary, always referred to Bordia. However, Purve and Srivastava had no administrative control over district collectors who were expected to play a key role in the implementation of BEP in districts. In the absence of direction from the top, response from district collectors very much depended on the personality of the district collector. Not everyone was suffused with youthful idealism like Jyoti Bhramar Tubid, Ashok Vardhan, and Manoj Kumar Srivastava who plunged themselves in BEP. Bordia as well as Vijayaraghavan had to work overtime to co-opt district officers, and persuade them to take active interest in BEP. In fairness to Chief Minister Laluji, it should be said that he did not pack BSPP bodies with his favourites. Suffice it to say, Laluji adopted a policy of *benign neglect*, leaving time and space to BEP to move ahead as Bordia desired.

The only issue that had to be sorted with the Bihar government was the formation of BSSP, and its MOA and bye-laws. Once Bordia sorted it out with Arun Pathak, Bordia had a free run in the design and implementation of BEP. In contrast, the development of the UP Basic Education Project, which was taking place at about the same time, was highly acrimonious with the three state education secretaries in succession being engaged in a bitter wrangle with Bordia over almost everything: project objectives, programme components, the relative shares in investment of different aspects of EFA such as primary schooling, NFE, and adult education, as well as the modalities of implementation. The flip side of the liberty Bordia had in the design and implementation of BEP was that it sapped the little initiative that officers in Bihar tended to display, and necessitated far too frequent visitations without which nothing seemed to move ahead. These visits are better called *missions*, going by the jargon of international organizations. The word mission has two connotations, the first being an undertaking to achieve a predetermined task, and the second an effort to zealously convert others to one's belief system.[13] World Bank missions are missions in one sense

[13] Kiltgaard, *Tropical Gangsters*, p. 207.

or the other or both. Bank missions strive to complete the specific tasks for which a mission is mounted such as the appraisal of a project or reviewing the pace of implementation of a project or assessing the fulfilment of conditionalities. Bank functionaries are also missionaries in that even while accomplishing its task, a mission also strives to preach the right path to go ahead to achieve the project objectives, sets out blind alleys and promising avenues, and zealously strives to convert the 'borrower' to the true faith. Bordia's visitations to Bihar were similar to World Bank missions in that he had in mind specific objectives to accomplish during each mission, and was also engaged in the task of co-opting key functionaries in government as well as social activists, and of persuading them to contribute their mite to BEP and accept his way of going ahead in the implementation of BEP. Bordia's missions to Bihar were also learning missions for neither Bordia, much less neither his deputies nor anyone in UNICEF had practical experience of planning and implementing a large-scale education project. Groping one's way ahead was unavoidable all the more so because of the scope and nature of the project, and because of the socio-political environment in Bihar which posed special problems for project implementation. In spite of the frequent missions of Bordia, progress was rather slow, and being the cynic he was, K could not help after some hectic visits recall the verse of Matthew Arnold:

The East bow'd low before the blast,
In patient, deep disdain.
She let the legions thunder past,
And plunged in thought once again.

The conventional wisdoms which the Brown Document sought to disprove turned out to be hardy perennials excepting that which posited a nexus between teacher performance and pre-service teacher training; Laluji's government considered that pre-service teacher training would perpetuate the dominance of upper castes in the teaching profession and removed it as a qualification for recruitment. Voluntary agencies participated in large numbers in environment building and in the *talakthons*; however, except for some, most limited their engagement with BEP to securing grants, and could not, as the Brown Book envisaged, 'take responsibility for a substantial part of the educational programmes'. Teacher unionism, motivation, and performance remained unchanged disproving the belief held by the Brown Book that the government could 'instil a missionary spirit among the teaching staff'; nor did most government functionaries willing 'to treat voluntary agencies as partners', and 'create means of involving creative individuals (as individuals)' in the school system. A case in point was the organization of VECs. Bordia set high hopes on the ability of education to build bridges across social divide; the VEC he visualized would bring all elements of the village society together to facilitate the functioning of the school and the teacher, and to improve the reach and grasp of the school. This was not a vision shared by the Director of Education, a Falstaffian character who considered himself close to the Chief Minister. He was not carried away by Bordia's mesmerizing pep talks; nor would he defer to Bordia's seniority either. He was very clear in his mind that teachers should teach and do nothing else, not get mixed up with voluntary organizations and with any activity outside the school. He was certain that if only clear instructions are issued and vigorously enforced, everything would be alright. At a talkathon in West Champaran, an activist from a voluntary agency bitterly complained against the education department for not allowing teachers to interact with his organization and for not allowing his organization to form VECs. The District Superintendent of Education gave a wishy-washy reply, and when the activist protested, Falstaff lashed at him saying that that he would not allow teachers to interact with voluntary agencies. There was a world of difference between government and voluntary agencies—like *jameen aur aasman kaa pharak* (the difference between the sky and the earth). Nothing should happen in schools without orders. VECs should be formed according to government circulars on the subject. Nothing else, he made it clear. Voluntary agencies have no business to organize villagers and set up VECs. When Bordia joked *aap eise baath kar rahe hain ki saakshath sarkar aap hi hai* (You are talking as if you were the State itself). Falstaff remained nonchalant and declared with a hauteur *jee haan* (Yes, I am) making K recall the famous statement of Sun King Louis XIV, '*l'ètat, c'est moi*' (I am the State). From time to time, he would invoke the holy name of Laluji to ward off anything he did not like. Bordia expected VECs to facilitate teachers in the discharge of their duties; in contrast, in quite a few places members of VECs saw themselves as local inspectors entrusted with the power to supervise the teachers. Thus, when Bordia visited a *tola* (habitation) in Sitamarhi district, the VEC members pounced on the teachers as if teachers were their personal servants. In the face of intemperate remarks, the headmaster was dignified and spoke softly with folded hands the problems he had in getting the school function. While Bordia sought to mediate, Falstaff was wild with anger, disbanded the VEC straightaway, and peremptorily ordered a new VEC to be constituted. All this is not to say that VECs could not be a useful mechanism, but that one should eschew exaggerated expectations from them.

As a group, the IAS officers of Bihar were as good as anywhere else in the country. To borrow a typology of D.S. Mukhopadhyay, a colleague of K in the education department and an officer from the Bihar cadre, some were 'affiliative'; they affiliated themselves with an area of work or a cause, say the empowerment of the poor, and preferred to work in areas of their interest. The Sinha duo was a good example of affiliative officers who gave a good boost to BEP in its initial stages. Anil Sinha was Commissioner, Muzaffarpur, and was the prime mover of SAMU, the Muzaffarpur Total Literacy Campaign. Amarjeet Sinha was Director, Non-formal and Adult Education, and officiated as Project Director, BEP, till Vijayaraghavan was appointed as Project Director. Not all affiliative officers were equally enthusiastic about BEP. K.B. Saxena who, all through his career, took up causes such as exploitation of tribals and child labour, and won national renown for taking on the coal mafia of Dhanbad was sceptical about BEP. He was Adviser in the Planning Commission, and during the Annual Plan discussions of 1990–1, he expressed the view that the project was far too ambitious in its scope and expectations of investment; it was unrealistic to expect transformative changes to be brought about on such a large scale and in so short a time. The project was naive in its assumptions about social and political environment, and in its belief that education and development would not generate conflicts, and would bring together different groups in spite of their basic animosities. There was no coherent strategy for bringing about the far-reaching changes the project wished to accomplish. His assessment was proved right by the course of events. Bihar had a fair share of professionals, the second category of officials in Mukhopadhyay's classification. In contrast to the affiliatives, professionals do a good job of whatever job falls by their way; they are the backbone of administration. K noticed that in Bihar, only a few of them persevered with their jobs, ignoring the heavy odds arising from an extremely adverse social and political environment. However, many of them tended to be very wary and cautious. They did not just mark their time in a job like the third category of officers—*chaltha ha is* who believed and practised the creed *theek hai. Kuch bhi nahi kar sakthe* (It is OK. Nothing can be done). Yet the professionals were conditioned to be circumspect, and be less enterprising than they would have been if the environment were less hostile. Circumspection was very justified by the political and administrative environment of Bihar. Symptomatic was a scandalous incident on 27 February 1992 in the Secretariat, the very seat of state power, in which T.C.A. Srinivasavaradan, a senior IAS officer who was Health Commissioner, was assaulted by an MP belonging to the ruling party. The chief minister allotted to a relation of the MP a medical seat in the MGM Medical College, Jamshedpur, from the 'Tata quota'; even before the order of the Chief Minister was received by Srinivasavaradan, the MP arrived in the Secretariat with his followers and demanded that Srinivasavaradan hand him over the order of the government allocating the seat. When Srinivasavaradan pleaded for a little time, Yadav was incensed and reportedly beat Srinivasavaradan with a shoe; the MP's son and others who accompanied him struck blows on the hapless officer. The lynching would have gone on but for the intervention of the office staff. In any place with the rule of law, the MP would have been arrested, but he was not. Srinivasavaradan filed a report with the police; however, D.N. Sahay, the Additional DG of Police, informed the press that action could be taken only if the investigation established prima facie the guilt of the MP. The chief minister described the incident as unfortunate and went on to say that public representatives should behave in a dignified manner and that if the MP had any complaint, 'he should have come to me'. The IAS Officers' Association gave an unprecedented call to its members to go on mass casual leave on 3 March, and demanded arrest of the culprits, filing charge sheet against culprits, and action against Mudrika Singh Yadav, Minister of State for Health, for actively abetting the assailants and giving shelter to the culprits after the crime. The protest by IAS officers evoked no action against the MP who denied the incident and claimed that he met Srinivasavaradan not in connection with a medical seat but in connection with the facilities in a district hospital, that Srinivasavaradan was drunk and had misbehaved with him. What Yadav did was *tayyari* (getting ready), fabricating evidence and manufacturing alibis—a hoary art form in many crime-ridden parts of the country. With passage of time, the incident was forgotten and the efforts of the government to divide the IAS Officers' Association through ingenious tactics were successful. One such tactic was the Chief Minister slotting a meeting of the secretaries to government and heads of department on the evening of 12 March so as to clash with a general body meeting of the IAS Officers' Association. The officers had to wait for several hours as a cabinet meeting was slotted at the same time. *La Affaire Srinivasavaradan* was not an isolated act. During one of his many visits to Patna, K found that life had come to a standstill because of a bandh called by rival gangs swearing allegiance to two MPs with criminal background. In 1994, G. Krishniah, District Magistrate, Gopalgunj, was murdered on the instigation of Anand Mohan, MP, who mercifully was convicted and sentenced to life imprisonment. In 2012, the Supreme Court upheld the conviction and sentence. However, K found most senior officials in Bihar beleaguered with little hope of relief. 'All hope abandon, ye who enter here' seemed to be an apt inscription for the Patna Secretariat. K came to acquire a great respect for officers who strove to do whatever was possible—their efforts were profiles in courage. He would fly into rage whenever broad sweeping criticism was levelled against Bihar and its officer class. Suffice it to say, for a variety of reasons inadequate governance has in Bihar a long history; after Nitish Kumar became the chief minister in 2005, there was a glimmer of hope that governance was changing for the better.

BEP after *Mahabhinishkramana*

Old soldiers do not always fade away. Bordia was keen to continue his association with his creations, the National Institute of Adult Education, BEP, and Lok Jumbish even after his retirement. Lok Jumbish presented no problem; a couple of months before he retired, the Rajasthan government sought the concurrence of DOE to amend the by-laws of the Lok Jumbish Society so that an eminent educationist could be appointed as Chairman instead of the State Education Secretary. The concurrence was conveyed post-haste, and immediately after his retirement, the Rajasthan government identified Bordia as the eminent educationist who should lead the Lok Jumbish Society. Given his relationship with Arjun Singh, the other two goals proved elusive.

Whatever, while his formal association with BEP ceased, Bordia kept a close tab on what was happening in BEP like everything else connected with his former department.

Inadvertently, Bordia gave the best possible parting gift to BEP by providing K an unexpected opportunity to normalize the role of UNICEF in BEP. A couple of days after his retirement, K paid Bordia a courtesy call at his home. Bordia was extremely warm and expansive, outlining his plans and dilating his ideas as to how his successor Giri should go about his work and so on. Suddenly, he interrupted his monologue and disingenuously asked K, 'How did you allow UNICEF to publish such a lopsided report on the behalf of the Ministry?' Then he went on to elaborate how the authors of that report played favourites, exaggerating the achievements of the Muzaffarpur Literacy Campaign and the activities in Jehanabad, and ignoring altogether the stellar work in Ranchi. K had not even the faintest idea of the report Bordia was talking about; as soon as he returned to his office, K ascertained the facts from his deputies and came to know that document was conceived as a *Festschrift* and Bordia was very upset when officials of the UNICEF office met him at his home on the day of his retirement and offered a bouquet and the document. To his horror, K noticed that the Festschrift was brought out as a document of DOE. When K remonstrated with Geeta Verma about the propriety of UNICEF bringing about a document of the Ministry without the knowledge of the Ministry or BSPP, she made matters worse by claiming that the document was approved by the Bihar Education Secretary in his capacity as Chairman, BSPP, and that BSSP in fact had requested for 2,000 copies for wide distribution, K blew his top and, with the extreme rudeness he is given to, demanded to know who the hell did UNICEF or BSPP think they were to authorize the publication of a document purported to be the document of DOE. And furthermore, K peremptorily ordered her to stop distribution of the document and withdraw the copies already distributed lest he should report to the Ministry of External Affairs for exemplary action against UNICEF for breach of diplomatic propriety. It was customary for the highly temperamental K to be given to remorse after an outburst of rudeness; however, on this occasion he had no such remorse, for the action of UNICEF officials was highly inappropriate, and he would have failed in his duty if he had not done what he did. His outburst had a salutary effect and the personnel dealing with BEP in UNICEF's Delhi and Patna offices were changed lock, stock, and barrel, and the shakeup made possible a new beginning that could be made in the relationship between UNICEF and BEP.

By the end of 1992, the management structures were falling in place; after a long process of groping about, a clear outline of how to go ahead seemed to be in sight. The initial emphasis on mobilization *per se* and literacy activities gave way to a sharp focus on primary education; this shift in priorities was facilitated by the stand taken by the DG, NLM, after the retirement of Bordia. Bordia's *panchasheela* doctrine postulated that basic education projects should comprise five elements: provision of schooling of satisfactory quality for all children upto the age of 14 years; non-formal and part-time education for all children who had crossed the stage of enrolment in primary school (namely children in the age-group 9–14) and working children and girls who could not attend schools; functional literacy; women's education; and post-literacy, continuing education and inculcation of skills for survival and general well-being. The design of BEP conformed to the doctrine; so did as Lok Jumbish originally. In the NIEPA Workshop in November 1990, Bordia set out that the UP project document was expected to appropriately incorporate the five elements. The fact that it did not was a major reason for the disagreement between the UP government and DOE. Even as the spat between UP and DOE went on, adult education was quietly dropped from Lok Jumbish once it became clear that SIDA would not provide the order of resources expected from it. The DG, NLM, claimed that he was always opposed to inclusion and was overruled by Bordia, and asserted that TLCs would lose their identity if implemented as part of externally funded projects. In support of his stand that TLCs should not be subsumed in externally funded projects, the DG attributed the unsatisfactory performance of TLCs in Muzaffarpur, Jamshedpur, and Ranchi to the fact that the TLCs were managed by BEP. He claimed that these TLCs would have run a different course had NLM organized them as elsewhere. He would not concede the real reason why the three TLCs faltered, namely the inherent limitations of the Ernakulum model and its inappropriateness to the Hindi heartland with low levels of literacy. What he did not state was the valid reason that the external agencies, particularly the World Bank, would bring to bear on the performance of the TLCs rigorous scrutiny, and such a scrutiny would be figuratively tantamount to 'let daylight in upon magic'. Given the DG's stand, adult education ceased to be a component of BEP; that made sense as BEP chronically faced resource constraints because of the inability of UNICEF to provide its share of funding and NLM was flushed with funds. In due course, it was dropped from projects in the offing such as the UP Project and DPEP.

Major strategies for key components such as district planning, teacher training, MS, school building construction, and NFE began to fall in place. In BEP whatever BEP could achieve should be judged with reference to this context as well as the resource constraint which impaired smooth functioning and efforts to go on scale. BSPP had to organize in-house several functions such as training which, in normal course, it would have entrusted to the State Education Department and resource organizations such as SCERT and DIETs. Consequently, it had to recruit staff on contract or on deputation from other state government organizations. It should be said to the credit of Vijayaraghavan that staff were recruited with meticulous care; it should be said to the credit of Laluji's government that it gave Vijayaraghavan a free hand. It should be said to the credit of BEP that it displayed flexibility in the organization of educational activities and harnessed the co-operation of voluntary agencies wherever possible. Thus, NFE was organized in Ranchi, East Singhbhum, and West Champaran through voluntary organizations, in Muzaffarpur district through regular administrative entities called *tola samithis*, and in Sitamarhi district through a mix of VECs and voluntary agencies. BEP was cribbed in its efforts to improve primary education by the fact that flow of resources from UNICEF was incommensurate with the expectations and, further, due to the fact that UNICEF policies prevented the application of its fund to the payment of teacher salaries or to construction of school buildings. Consequently, it had to limit itself to experimentation by trying out measures to improve primary schooling in *focus schools*. It also took upon the task of setting up DIETs in the project districts, and laying sound foundations for their functioning. It also developed good training modules for teachers and members of the VEC and, for the first time in Bihar, organized good in-service training. The 10-day in-service participatory training programme called Ujala (brightness) won wide appreciation and was commended in the DPEP training literature. With the help of the Society for Rural Industrialization, Ranchi, innovative designs for school buildings were developed, and construction of buildings by local communities and VECs pioneered. For all these accomplishments, BEP could not go to scale because of resource constraints as well as the intrinsic limits to the growth of a fledgling organization which had to do much of the work by itself, and set out to develop an alternate public service culture. Given the resource constraint, BEP could not expand beyond seven districts, and even within those seven districts. geographic coverage was limited to a small proportion of the total villages.

What if UNICEF were able to mobilize the supplementary resources? Would BEP have been able to achieve educational outcomes similar to, say, DPEP? An affirmative answer is plausible. With an officer of the calibre of Vijayaraghavan in charge of the programme, it could have been scaled up; after Bordia's exit, visitations of the officials of DOE were less frequent so that time and space were available to Vijayaraghavan and his team to plan and move ahead. The refinements introduced in DPEP in respect of district planning, appraisal, and monitoring systems could have been extended to BEP with beneficial results. Of course, there is no way of testing the validity or robustness of *what if* speculation. The optimistic prognosis of BEP post-1992 could as well have been derailed if the political economy of Bihar were to impact on BEP; the latitude that Vijayaraghavan had in managing BEP might have been curtailed if the flow of funds were not a trickle but a torrential flow. There is no way to test which of the two prognoses is likely to correct.

BEP's Contribution to India's Quest for UEE

Failure is an orphan. *Children First*, the magisterial history of UNICEF by Maggie Black,[14] makes no mention of BEP even though it was conceived as India's and UNICEF's flagship EFA project, yet it makes a reference to a tiny, flash-in-the-pan teacher empowerment programme Shikshak Samakhya tried out in MP.[15] But then to write off BEP as a failure of no consequence would be utterly wrong. No other project influenced the design and implementation of DPEP as BEP; as the country's quest of UEE mainly relied on DPEP and its successor SSA,

[14] Maggie Black, *Children First: The Story of UNICEF, Past and Present*, Oxford: Oxford University Press, 1996.

[15] Maggie Black, *Children First*.

BEP's contribution to the country's march to UEE is invaluable. K drew many valuable lessons from BEP and incorporated them in the design of DPEP.

First and foremost was the need to moderate the expectations arising from the anticipated flow of substantial financial resources; it should be driven home to everyone concerned, be they functionaries of state governments or NGOs, that money is not available just for the asking with no questions asked. Enthusiasm and good intentions are not enough; they need to be complemented by systematic planning, and rigorous appraisal and monitoring. A vision document cannot be a substitute for a project document however tentative the project document might be. While an innovative educational project cannot begin as a blueprint project with everything clearly and definitively elaborated, it cannot be totally open ended all through. Process cannot be all-and-end-all; process orientation needs to be balanced with concern for outcomes, and mechanisms should be put in place for assessing the outputs and outcomes .These mechanisms include devices such as studies for designing the project parameters, baseline surveys, specifying and monitoring performance indicators, and non-impressionistic and independent evaluation.

Another lesson from BEP was equally profound. Keynes famously wrote that if economists could manage to get themselves thought of as humble, competent people on a level with dentists, it would be splendid. Similarly, rather than talk grandiosely about social transformation, it is better for educationists and educational administrators to humbly stay focussed on education using the curriculum to spread the values and attitudes immanent in the Constitution and hoping that, over time, the transformative effect of education would manifest itself. BEP would have been better off if it set its sights realistically, all the more so as about 90 per cent of the funds UNICEF was expected to provide had to be raised from donors institutional and individual. Expecting the donors to be credulous is not the best way of mobilizing large-scale resources on sustained basis. Few would be willing to fund a programme so grandiose as to stretch credibility. India needed to briskly achieve UEE, and that imperative necessitated design of programmes which were not totally out of synch with the existing socio-economic milieu, and whose implementation did not require supermen. Project objectives and strategy should not stray far too away from what was feasible in the medium term with the best possible orientation and capacity building of functionaries.

BEP had also demonstrated the need to insulate the day-to-day management of the project from agencies; it would be naïve to differentiate among agencies, and hold some to be benign and worthy of implicit trust and others as embodiment of evil. Every agency without exception seeks to pursue its organizational interest and advance its policy preferences through policy dialogue and funding programmes even if they are not congruent with national policies and perceptions. Tensions and dilemmas are intrinsic in the relationship between the provider and recipient of finance, particularly when the provider believes that he is motivated by not commercial or strategic considerations but by benevolent intentions. Ironically, the tensions and dilemmas are greater in dealing with agencies with a strong image of a good Samaritan. APPEP as well as BEP demonstrated the criticality of systematically planning for capacity building. Capacity building would be impaired by hands-on planning and management of the project, and the handholding might as well be by central government officials as functionaries of external agencies. It is imperative to place the responsibility of planning and implementation squarely on the state government instead of descending on the state again and again, and 'mothering' the project development and implementation.

The lesson in respect of the project components was equally clear. Provision of basic education should not be limited to primary education. However, it did not follow that every project should cover all aspects of basic education. As BEP was initially managed by officials in charge of non-formal and adult education, BEP came to be perceived as a non-school programme. In that process, the school education department was alienated; it took a while for it to be brought on board. A year's experience with BEP had established the merit of organizing adult education through separate structures and funding mechanisms instituted by the NLM, and of BEP focusing on primary education and fostering linkages with TLCs. It came to be realized that literacy campaigns were short sprints while UEE was a marathon, and each required efforts and mobilization of a different kind. That apart, unlike literacy efforts, formal structures such as the school education department played a very important role in UEE. There is no way that UEE could be achieved without the active involvement of the formal structures.

A major lesson of BEP that was incorporated in the design of DPEP was the necessity to implement the programme through state societies. The departmental mode of implementation is beset by an acute sclerosis that blocks free flow of finances to the project and insulates the project from other stakeholders in primary education. It was in BEP that the society model was fully developed, and very soon, its potential efficacy was demonstrated; it was later extended to Lok Jumbish and UP Basic Education Project, and eventually to DPEP. The allocation of project outlay for civil construction (24 per cent), administrative overheads (6 per cent), and programme components (70 per cent) which BEP pioneered was followed by subsequent projects. The district planning exercise carried out in Sitamarhi helped flesh out ideas of district planning, and offered valuable lessons of what to do and what not to do. The Sitamarhi experience also influenced the decision in DPEP to concentrate initially on the primary stage (classes I–V). The way MS was implemented in BEP strongly influenced the women's development and girls' education components of DPEP.

Suffice it to say, BEP provided most of the epistemological foundations on which DPEP was erected; the lessons drawn from APPEP, inferences K drew for his study of international relations and negotiation praxis, along with the bitter *ménage à trois* experience of the UP basic education reinforced those foundations.

IX

BIG BAD WOLF

Panini is a renowned grammarian who gave shape to the Sanskrit language. A tale has it that he was one day having a seminar of his students, and that suddenly a tiger emerged from the thickets and headed towards him and his students. The great intellectual he was, Panini thought that the tiger was coming to participate in the seminar and nonchalantly continued his discourse while his students fled. Thereupon, the tiger made a satisfying meal of the great intellectual. The fable about Panini and the tiger was drawn upon by a critic of the World Bank to put his point across vividly.

> We are reminded of the fate of the great Panini by the response of our policymakers and educationists to the blandishments of the international agencies. The World Bank and the IMF having forced the Government of India and other third world countries to slash their budgets on health and education and having made them more inaccessible to the poor, are at the same time showing great solicitude for universal education and health care and inundating the national governments with advice on what to do and not to do.[1]

The anecdote about Panini might be apocryphal but it has an enduring charm that age cannot wither; so are images about the World Bank being a tiger come to breakfast or the big bad wolf in Red Riding Hood's fairy tale. Why did India open up primary education for World Bank lending was a question that had received little attention in our

[1] 'The Tiger Came for Breakfast', *The Vigil*, X, no. 16 (15 September 1993).

country; given the widespread image of the World Bank among many intellectuals and journalists, and the tendency to accept any conspiracy theory involving the Bank, the question was widely deemed redundant. That India opened up because of pressure from the World Bank and that nothing good would come out of World Bank lending was taken as the self-evident truth which needed no exploration. The timing of the lending also seemed to support the pressure-by-Bank theory for the World Bank extended a loan for primary education for the first time during the P.V. Narasimha Rao government while that government was undertaking 'neo-liberal' economic reforms and pushing through structural adjustment of the Indian economy. But then truth is more complex than any theory, and it is easier for many to believe a simple lie than a complex truth.

Once the World Bank emerged as a champion of EFA and decided to co-sponsor the Jomtien Conference, it could not ignore India, home to the world's largest number of out-of-school children. Right from 1987, the World Bank was extremely keen to have primary education in its Indian loan portfolio. Successive Indian executive directors and chiefs of World Bank, Delhi office, and a stream of distinguished visitors from Washington such as vice presidents and President Barber Conable himself tried to persuade the Indian government to include elementary education in the Bank's India loan portfolio. They sought to persuade ministers and senior officials not only in DOE, the Finance Ministry, and the Prime Minister's Office but also in the states. Being always on the lookout for avenues of tapping resources from the central government and external agencies such as the World Bank, state governments were only too happy that the World Bank was willing to finance a new area. In fact, in mid-August 1990 when K paid his farewell call on V.P. Rama Rao, Chief Secretary, AP, before he left the state to join his assignment in DOE, Rama Rao told him that a World Bank delegation had informed him that the Bank would be willing to support a primary education project, and that from his new position K should ensure that a World Bank primary education project materialized in AP. K was to grapple for about three years the baleful consequences of the Bank's lobbying with state governments as some states, particularly Tamil Nadu, were keen to have conventional educational projects which covered the whole state rather than fall in line with DOE's efforts to operationalize a new strategy for UEE and to regulate accessing external funding in accordance with the parameters laid down by CABE in March 1991.

As the country's interlocutor with bilateral and multilateral agencies, and as the department responsible for augmenting net inflow of foreign exchange and maintaining the country's precarious balance of payments, the Department of Economic Affairs (DEA) in the Finance Ministry was supportive of the Bank's efforts. This was all the more so as soft loans from IDA contributed substantially to country's foreign exchange reserves. And furthermore, countries such as the United States strongly objected to India availing soft IDA loans for physical infrastructure instead of tapping private capital flows. They exerted pressure on the World Bank to shift IDA resources away from India to sub-Saharan countries. DEA expected that securing IDA loans for primary and girl's education would blunt the American pressure on the World Bank. DEA's stance was reinforced when, by late 1990, the country's balance of payments deteriorated so badly that the Chandrasekhar government had to send the country's gold holdings abroad as security for raising resources so that an imminent default of international repayment obligations could be prevented. However, till March 1990 because of the strong opposition from DOE the Bank could make no headway. Bordia had the formidable reputation of being 'implacably opposed to Bank activity in Indian primary-level education'.[2] The Minister P.V. Narasimha Rao was caution personified, and did not require much persuasion to support Bordia's point of view as availing World Bank assistance for primary education would have marked a radical departure from the past, and there was no compelling reason to make a departure. DOE was strongly opposed to Bank funding elementary education for two sets of reasons. The first set of reasons related to its concerns about domestic funding of elementary education. After the formulation of NPE, 1986, DOE had high expectations of a steep increase in budgetary allocations for education. DOE feared that if the offer of the Bank were availed it was unlikely to gain as the Bank assistance would substitute rather than augment the resources that Finance Ministry and Planning Commission would

[2] Philip W. Jones, *World Bank Financing of Education: Lending, Learning and Development*, 1st edition, London: Routledge, 1992, p. 222.

allocate to it. Thereby, the Finance Ministry would shift the onus of resource mobilization to it, and DOE would have to take on the responsibility of formulating credit-worthy projects.

The second set of reasons had to do with Bordia's perception of Bank-assisted projects, particularly those in the neighbouring countries of Pakistan and Bangladesh. This was a perception that was shared by the education community in the country. One can discern four interconnected elements of this perception. The first was applicable to all the operations of the Bank, the second to process-intensive social projects, the third to all education projects, and the fourth specifically to primary education projects. Conceptually, a Bank project is a partnership between the borrowing country, the Bank, and other co-financiers if any. The loan agreement sets out the terms of the partnership. However, many felt, and that was the first element of the perceptions about the Bank-assisted projects, that the Bank was a dominant partner, nay a domineering partner so domineering that the sense of partnership was absent in Bank projects. There was an ingrained culture which drove the Bank functionaries to adopt a hands-on management style of project design and implementation, a style that debilitated the borrower's self-reliance. Bank's supervisory missions to bring to bear on the mission to be accomplished the grim determination of fighter pilots or agents of special operations. Disciplined groups parachute in, carry out hectic sorties, sternly review the pace of progress with reference to the milestones agreed upon during the previous mission, scrutinize with a hawk's eye the compliance of conditionality, and depart after delivering an ultimatum spelling out what the 'borrower' government had to do in a specified time frame lest the loan should be suspended.[3] Permeating the style of the Bank functionaries was hubris of 'we know it all', and 'we know from our enormous experience of working all over the world what are the blind alleys and promising avenues'. The style was manifest as the propensity to offer universal prescriptions, to ignore country experience, to induct expatriate consultants regardless of need, and to insist on setting up in the recipient country parallel project structures which debilitate national capacities for project formulation and implementation. The second element held that project components which facilitate fast disbursal of loans predominate in

[3] Robert Klitgaard, *Tropical Gangsters*, New York: Basic Books, 1990, p. 207.

World Bank projects. This is, in a sense, adverse selection in so far as realization of social development goals is concerned. As contrasted with physical infrastructure projects, social sector projects are all about people. With social sector projects, it is not only inputs and outputs but also processes that matter. To give an example, behaviour of key functionaries such as teachers have to be changed if the much needed innovative practices have to be introduced? Social sector projects are not usually 'blue print' projects but 'evolving projects'. What works or not in a particular context has to be discovered through a process of trial and error. Processes take time to evolve, to be tested, scaled up, and to be operationalized. Furthermore, a high degree of risk and uncertainty is associated with them. Consequently, the pace of disbursal of loans would not be as fast with process-intensive components as with 'brick and mortar'. The operational tension between the Bank being a Bank as well as a development agency, and the foreign exchange needs of borrowing countries may put a premium on project components which facilitate fast disbursal. Furthermore, being a bank the Bank's policymaking is dominated by economists whose worldview is much different from that of educators (Chapter VII). And furthermore, given the trial and error nature of projects, flexibility and contingent planning have to be adequately provided for in project implementation. The Bank style of project management does not provide for the requisite flexibility nor the time and space to let processes operate. The third element is an extension of the second element and held that Bank's approach to education was input-output oriented, emphasized excessively managerial interventions, and ignored the criticality of educational processes. Lastly, the Bank looked at the primary schools as the sole engine for UEE and was prone to neglect adult and NFE as it held that there were no 'proven approaches, techniques, and materials' for adult and NFE.

During his visit to India in November 1987, President Conable called on P.V. Narasimha Rao, Minister for Human Resource Development, and offered substantial credit for primary education so that the objectives of NPE, 1986, as well as the Bank's objective of promoting primary education could be realized. He made it clear that the Bank was aware of the sensitivity of the Indian government, and that the Bank had no intention to exert intrusive influence which might be contrary to the tradition and policies of the country. PV responded by saying that the question was not of sensitivity only. There had to be a national commitment to primary education. The recently adopted NPE, 1986, had declared that the nation as a whole would assume the responsibility for providing resources for education; therefore, it would be against the policy to transfer even part of that responsibility to the Bank. Resources for elementary education could be mobilized through central and state budgets as well as through community contributions. Besides, he added that external funding sometimes created imbalances and it was essential to ensure that development of primary education progressed in a more or less uniform fashion throughout the country. He indicated that Bank support could be thought for industrial training institutes (ITIs), polytechnics, regional engineering colleges, and Indian Institutes of Technology (IITs). Bank's support was indeed sought soon thereafter for ITIs by Ministry of Labour, and for polytechnics by the MHRD. The World Bank continued to persevere with its efforts to bring in primary education in its India loan portfolio. During his visit to India in October 1988, Moeen Qureshi, Senior Vice-President, called on Prime Minister Rajiv Gandhi and Finance Minister S.B. Chavan to reiterate the Bank's interest to finance primary education. The Prime Minister gave a broad indication that the government would not hesitate to pose a project on primary education to the Bank; however, no primary education project was posed to the World Bank till Rajiv Gandhi demitted office.

Events moved fast from March 1990 onwards. At Jomtien, President Conable and Vice-President Attila Karaosmanoglu had a meeting with Minister of State M.G.K Menon, and Bordia, and on 13 March 1990, a week after the conclusion of the Jomtien Conference, with Prime Minister V.P. Singh who was also Minister, MHRD. Conable reiterated the willingness of the Bank to support a basic education project with sufficient flexibility built into it. In those meetings, Conable reiterated the fact that in its long dialogue with GOI, Bank functionaries had been stressing the point that Bank was a learning institution and, as such, its thinking, policies, and operations, all of them, were not static. They evolved continuously. The leading role that the Bank played in organizing the Jomtien conference arose from a deep introspection of what primary education was and of what Bank's support to primary education should be. Furthermore, the Bank considered ownership and capacity building to be essential for project effectiveness and sustainability. And furthermore, the Bank was willing 'to be as flexible and accommodating as GOI may consider necessary'. So why not engage the Bank and check for yourself whether the Bank's deeds matched its words was his poser to Singh. The logic underlying the poser was difficult to resist, more so in the context of the fast-deteriorating macroeconomic position, and consequential bleak prospects of adequate budgetary resources for implementing NPE, 1986. About a month later, on 26 April 1990, Heinz Vergin, Director, India Country Department, World Bank, had a meeting with Bordia; in that meeting Bordia indicated that the government might be willing to consider World Bank assistance for a basic education project in UP. The project would include all the elements of EFA covered in BEP and the Lok Jumbish. Bordia told Vergin that later in the year there could be a seminar at which Bank specialists, some international educationists, and officials of the UP and central governments could sit together and acquire clarity regarding the parameters of the project. On 22 August 1990, three days after K joined the department, the Minister of State Chimanbhai Mehta approved the proposal to hold that seminar under the aegis of NIEPA. The approval was hesitant; he noted that 'for the time being proposal to hold seminar is approved'. A little earlier with his typical thoroughness and practice of backward mapping, Bordia worked on Mehta to seek the 'blessings' of Acharya Ramamurti who chaired a Committee appointed by the V.P. Singh government to review NPE, 1986. On 13 August 1990, Mehta told Acharya that 'there was an extreme constraint of resources, from this and also from the point of view securing foreign exchange' it would be advisable to prepare a project on primary and adult education for Bank assistance. Bordia mentioned that the provisional proposal was to take up such a project in 10 districts of UP; the project would strictly be in accordance with the priorities of the country. The Acharya said he 'did not see any objection to the Government going ahead with action in this behalf'. The fact that the state chosen, UP, was that of the Prime Minister V.P. Singh perhaps helped secure the approval of Mehta and the blessings of Acharya.

The Game Begins

Normally in workshops organized by the World Bank, the Bank functionaries and consultants would explain to an attentive audience the Bank procedures for project formulation, procurement, accounting, and reimbursement of expenditure; they would also expound the Bank's view of what works and what does not, what the 'blind alleys and promising avenues' are, a knowledge acquired through its operations all over the world. In this seminar, the roles were inverted; the preachers turned into disciples and disciples teachers. Bordia had *determined* that the Bankers should be educated about his views about what a basic education project should be and how it should be developed and implemented. As is his wont, Bordia meticulously specified to the last detail everything conceivable with the seminar. He decided who should participate, except of course the Bank contingent. He was particular to invite some international educators who were his pals in the international circuit and whom he expected to back him up in his encounter with the bankers. Bordia chose ten such educators; they included R.H. Dave, formerly Director, UNESCO Institute of Education, Hamburg, whom Bordia commissioned to chair a committee for laying down MLLs; Manzoor Ahmad , a renowned educator who became famous for the reports on NFE he co-authored with Philipp Coombs and was then in UNICEF Beijing office; Kasama Varavaran of the Ministry of Education, Thailand, a charming lady who did graduate work at the Graduate School of Education, Harvard University, and justified the saying that 'you can always tell a Harvard man' through her coherent thinking and cogent articulation, and whom K met quite a few times later during his junkets to South East Asia; Youssuf Kassam who was associated with the Tanzanian literacy campaign and was then Executive Director, International Council for Adult Education, Toronto; D.A. Pereira, former Director, National Institute of Education, Sri Lanka; Prem Kassaju, a Nepalese educationist who was then with UNESCO's Principal Regional Office for Asia and Pacific, Bangkok; Minda Sutharia, a specialist in measurement and evaluation from Philippines; and Bernard Horowitz, a specialist in the education of the disadvantaged from New York. Of course, the Bank defrayed their travel and other expenses. Bordia also determined that NIEPA should invite a few Indian educationists chosen by him; they included, among others, Prem Bhai of Vanavasi Sewa Ashram; Anita Dighe, Director Adult Education, Zakir Hussain Centre for Educational Studies; Balquis Fatma; B.K. Joshi, Director, Giri Institute of Development Studies, Lucknow; and Chitra Naik. He also determined what the background documents should be and who should prepare them. The documents pertaining to UP were to be prepared not by the UP government but by faculty members of NIEPA chosen by Bordia. He also determined who should attend from the department, UP, NCERT, and NIEPA, and more particularly those who should not so that dissenting voices were not heard except by design. He also determined the structure of the seminar, what should be the working groups, their composition, and who should chair each group. He also laid down the directors of NIEPA and NCERT and himself should make only occasional appearances and not hang around so that the impression spread that they could not get away from prior commitments and busy schedules. He also laid down that the Indian experts should contradict each other and even be incoherent so that there was utter confusion. 'Play by the ear. Relax, don't be too free and yet don't be too closed. Above all, don't give the impression that you are not free to speak', these were his precise instructions for play-acting that he gave to the participants from DOE and attached organizations. Above all, no impression should be conveyed whatsoever that the government was committed to take up the project with Bank funding. Interestingly, the strategy to discomfit a World Bank/IMF mission by providing conflicting information was earlier used by the United Kingdom when it turned to the IMF to bail it out from a macroeconomic crisis in 1976. The wealth of conflicting expert opinion undermined IMF proposals.[4]

As he supervised the arrangements for the seminar and interacted among others with Richard Cambridge, the Bank's designated pointsman, K gathered that the bankers were wary of Bordia and not comfortable with a seminar in which they had no role and were expected to sit through lectures. He also gathered that the bankers believed that for all his bravura Bordia was under compulsion to move ahead, and that the government, particularly DEA, prodded Bordia to go in for Bank-assisted project. However, not all went according to the game plan that Bordia drafted. Bordia laid down that the hospitality should be frugal, not the customary Indian lavish hospitality. In one of his many

[4] Alastair Fraser, *Aid-Recipient Sovereignty in Historical Perspective*, Global Economic Governance Programme, Managing Aid Dependency Project, Department of Politics and International Relations, University College, Oxford University, 2006, pp.1–61, at pp. 17–8.

table talks that preceded the seminar he posed the question: were not visitors to the Bank headquarters expected to go over to the canteen and buy their food? Why should we pamper the *gore* (white-skinned foreigner)? But then Bordia was inconsistent and prided himself on his inconsistency. There was no departure from the Indian tradition. Lunch at Hotel Qutub was a sumptuous spread on every day of the seminar, and on the last day of the seminar, Bordia arranged passes for the bankers and other foreign guests for a sitar recital by the maestro Pandit Ravi Shankar which was organized by the *Hindustan Times*; he cautioned his guests that they should be in their seats in the concert hall at least 15 minutes earlier, and that they better wear crash helmets to protect themselves from a possible stampede.

The Bank sent a formidable eleven-member contingent to the NIEPA seminar that included educationists Wadi Haddad, Stephen Heyneman, Adrian Verspoor, Marlaine Lockheed, and John Middleton, and economists Cambridge and Sajitha Bashir. From the operational side, the contingent included Richard Skolnik, the Chief of the Human Resources Division of the India Country Department which handled the Bank's education and health portfolios in South Asian countries. Although all members of the contingent participated in the seminar, the role of Haddad and Skolnik was the most significant, for they acted as the spokesmen of the Bank in the more consequential wrap-up meeting that followed after the NIEP Seminar, wherein an agreement was reached on the further course of action regarding the UP Basic Education Project (UP Project in short).

A Lebanese of dual nationality, Haddad's mien and demeanour made it obvious that he was a man of the world; he was an internationally well-known educationist and policy entrepreneur who played a key role in persuading Conable to embrace primary education and ensuring that the World Bank played a prominent role in organizing the Jomtien Conference, and who, as Executive Secretary of the Inter-Agency Commission that organized that Conference, won laurels for his extraordinary organizational capacity. He interrupted his 17-year-long career in the World Bank for being Chief Adviser to the President Lebanon, of all things, on national policy and strategic affairs. After he left the World Bank in 1996, he was Special Adviser to the DG of UNESCO on development issues. After the NIEPA conference, the paths of K and Haddad crossed again in UNESCO while K was a member of the high-level committee set up by DG, UNESCO, to advise him on the establishment of UNESCO Institute of Statistics. Years later, K was pleasantly surprised to find from his book *The Dynamics of Education Policymaking* that Haddad's views on policymaking were similar to his own views, and that Haddad drew upon the seminal work of Graham Allison on decision-making,[5] one of the three canonical texts on decision-making to which K was introduced at Harvard and which heavily influenced his thinking on governance. What Haddad wrote about educational development was divine music to K's ears. Haddad argued in his book that analysis of the education sector focused far too much on content of policy on the mistaken belief that education development involved 'a well-structured field of unambiguous issues, clearly defined objectives, mutually exclusive choices, undisputed causal relationships, predictable rationalities and rational decision makers'. In contrast to this idyllic vision, educational development is actually a series of untidy and overlapping episodes in which a variety of people and organizations with diverse perspectives are involved—politically and technically—in the processes through which the policy is developed and implemented. Hence, education policymaking is not a mere rational technical exercise, and the *how* and *when* of policymaking are as important as the *what* of policy.[6] Haddad's realistic approach was an offshoot of his real-world experience as adviser to the President of Lebanon, and his having had to manage the conflicting demands of agencies and countries as the Secretary General of the Jomtien Conference. In the NIEPA seminar and in the following wrap-up meeting, Haddad played a political role complementing the technical role of his colleagues. He was a perfect foil to Bordia matching Bordia in every respect, wit with wit, and subtlety with subtlety.

K came to know Skolnik, Cambridge, Verspoor, Middleton, and Marlaine more intimately as they were to play an important role in the Bank's engagement with Indian education during K's stint in the

[5] Graham T. Allison, *Essence of Decision: Explaining The Cuban Missile Crisis*, Boston, MA: Little, Brown & Company, 1971; 2nd edition co-authored with Philip D. Zelikow, New York: Longman, 1999.

[6] Wadi D. Haddad with the assistance of Terri Demsky, *The Dynamics of Education Policymaking: Case Studies of Burkina Faso, Jordan, Peru and Thailand*, Washington, DC: The World Bank, 1994, p. 3.

DOE. K's association with them brought out that even an organization such as the World Bank does not homogenize its employees. Individual differences in background and temperament do matter and they shape the style of work. Skolnik was rather short with sharp facial features. After graduating from Yale he specialized in public administration at the Woodrow Wilson Institute, Princeton. He joined the Bank as a young professional, and was one of the youngest division chiefs highly rated for his professional excellence. Though from Midwest, Skolnik was a typical East Coast liberal. He was unusually emotional for a banker, and greatly agonized over the pro-rich policies of the Reagan administration; he brought to bear on his work a passionate attachment to promote the well-being of the people of developing countries. He knew India and Indian bureaucracy very well, was a friend of India, and sought to facilitate interaction between the Bank and the Indian government. Married to a Chinese spouse, he was sensitive to cross-cultural differences. Warm-hearted, he cultivated the friendship of many Indian officials he dealt with. K first got acquainted with him when during a visit to Hyderabad; Skolnik called on K and had a detailed discussion on the Andhra education system and K's perceptions on education. He was much appreciative of the residential school system which catered to meritorious rural children as well as children of disadvantaged groups; he compared it to the *Head Start* Programme in the United States. He was also an admirer of the mid-day meal programme introduced by the government of M.G. Ramachandran in Tamil Nadu. He was fond of cracking jokes—Jewish as well as typical Ivy League jokes. He sought to develop a rapport with K who had briefly studied at Harvard by coming out with staple jokes that Yale students and alumni cracked against their rivals at Harvard. He facilitated a great deal not only Bank's funding of DPEP but also that by European Economic Community (EEC). K still vividly recalls a meeting of his with Almond, a key consultant of EC at which Skolnik happened to be present. EEC was new to funding primary education, Almond a stranger to India and the EEC procedures baffling and ponderous, an inevitable consequence of the multinational character of EEC. Skolnik acted as a *dubashi*—interpreter—translating K-ese as he called K's English into the lingo of international consultants. In his career at the Bank, Skolnik specialized in health; after a stint of 25 years, he left the Bank to take up specialized assignments in health including one at Harvard School of Public

Health, and later as a professor and director of the Center for Global Health, George Washington University. He authored an undergraduate textbook, *Essentials of Global Health*, which was published in 2007. All in all, he is a loveable person.

Bordia set the pace with a magisterial opening speech entitled *Working Together for a New Education*. He extolled the uniqueness of the seminar that was 'aimed at examination of ways in which a new kind of relationship can be formed between the world's most important and most munificent agency and people who are in dire need for help'. This was the first seminar of its kind in India, 'a seminar in which the Federal and state Governments are fully represented, so also are the great academic institutions which support and guide us, namely NCERT, NIEPA, UP State Council of Educational Research and Training (SCERT), as well as eminent educationists from India and overseas and a galaxy of renowned scholars and experts from the World Bank'. He then went on to expound the components a basic education project should have: provision of schooling of satisfactory quality for all children up to the age of 14 years; non-formal and part-time education for all children who had crossed the stage of enrolment in primary schools (namely children in the age group 9–14) and working children and girls who could not attend schools; functional literacy in which self-reliant skills in 3Rs are emphasized alongside education relevant to the needs of the individual, the family, and the community; education of women so that women become the instruments and beneficiaries of the development process; and post-literacy, continuing education, and inculcation of skills for survival and general well-being. He brilliantly summed up divergent worldviews of economists and educators and called up for a grand synthesis that would usher in a new education.

> We (educators) tend to talk about abstract goals about education being related to the soul of the nation, about education's liberating role, about people's mobilization and inculcation of values. Our friends in the Bank, in their tense, hard headed fashion talk about ensuring the minimum achievable goals (essentially literacy and numeracy), they talk about teacher effectiveness, efficient use of resources, cost effectiveness, learning inputs and outputs and so on …
>
> When I mention about the need for a genuine exchange between us, I am hoping that the Bankers can become visionaries and Indian educational planners can become more interested in the efficiency of the educational system.

Bordia closed his opening speech at the NIEPA seminar with self-deprecating humour.

> My 17 year old son chipped in last night, when my wife and I were talking about this seminar, and produced the Murphy's Book of Axioms. The book, it seems, contains John's Collateral Corollary which says: 'If you really need the loan, convince the banker that you don't need it'.
>
> I hope this is not the impression our friends from Washington may go back with.[7]

The concluding session was a bit stormy as Bordia sought to demonstrate to his admirers that Bank was being compelled to modify its stance and respect Indian sensibilities. Haddad was quite a match to Bordia. In his concluding presentation, he clarified that the Bank was not committed to a particular mode of delivery. He also matched Bordia's humour. He asked, 'How can you say that the Bank is a domineering partner? Did we not sit through three days of lecturing?" And then he cracked a joke about a new president of the Bank who laid down the policy for lending. 'Examine the feet of a client', he ordered his officers. 'If he does not wash his feet refuse him a loan right away.' When asked to explain, he said that 'once we give a loan we have no option but to kiss the client's feet'. A truism indeed! The witticism, 'If you owe the bank $100 that's your problem. If you owe the bank $100 million, that's the bank's problem', captures the reverse dependence of a bank on borrowers. Countries can use reverse dependency—the dependency of the Bank on the country to recover the loan and expand its business—as a strategic lever to avoid conditionalities.[8] Once a loan is secured, countries can simply fail to implement the conditions because they understand the Bank's need to keep lending. This applies particularly to the biggest borrowers, who gain significant 'negotiating capital', that is to say bargaining power, because they know they cannot be allowed to default. One can find, 'an inclination in some cases for lender and borrower to conspire to pretend that conditions have been complied with'.[9] The landmark in-house report of the Task Force on

[7] Anil Bordia, *Working Together for a New Education*, Opening Speech at the NIEPA Seminar on Education for All: UP, 6–9 November 1990, National Institute of Educational Planning and Administration, New Delhi.

[8] Alastair Fraser, *Aid-Recipient Sovereignty in Historical Perspective*, p. 20.

[9] Tony Killick with Ramani Gunatilaka and Ana Marr, *Aid and the Political Economy of Policy Change*, London: Routledge, 1998, p. 28.

Portfolio Management, 1992 (generally referred to by the name of its chairman as Wapenhans Report) noticed widespread non-compliance by borrowers with legal loan covenants, especially financial covenants, to be 'gross' and 'overwhelming'. Of the water-supply projects financed by the Bank between 1967 and 1989, for example, only 20–25 per cent of the borrowers complied with their financial covenants. A 1995 review of World Bank lending in South Asia by the eminent scholar-administrator S. Guhan brought out that by and large, the Bank's efforts to enforce financial covenants of various types were not successful; these included cost recovery, tariffs, self-financing, receivables, and repayments. In practical terms, the only option available for the Bank was the exit option and it was rarely resorted to. [10] The reason why the Bank had been generally unwilling to strike, much less wound borrowers, particularly large borrowers, is brought out in the review of Guhan's study by Deena Khatkhate, the intellectual gadfly who, like Socrates, likes 'to sting people and whip them into a fury, all in the service of truth'.

> The lending institution is always prone to be soft for fear of jeopardising achievement of its lending targets. The prospects of promotion and other staff of the bank are closely linked to how much they fulfil their lending targets. If India shies away from a new loan, the careers of the staff will be on the block.[11]

No wonder, with his sardonic wit, Khatkhate gave his review the title *Always a Borrower be*.

But for the sallies of Bordia and Haddad, and his own debut on the international education circuit with a presentation on externally funded projects, K cannot recall much of the deliberations in the working groups and plenary except that they were laced with long-winding speeches—Niagaras of words and Saharas of content—and as Bordia had intended and planned, they lacked a sense of purpose and direction. By design, Bordia was away much of the time on 'affairs of state' as he told Haddad leaving K to be in charge of the seminar. However, he did not expect K participating in, much less guide, the

[10] S. Guhan, *The World Bank's Lending in South Asia*, Washington, DC: The Brookings Institution, 1995, p. 68.

[11] Deena Khatkhate, 'Always a Borrower be', *Economic and Political Weekly*, XXX, no. 52 (December 30, 1995), pp. 3361–2.

discussions. That being so, K spent part of his time walking around the Qutub nearby and savouring the warmth of the balmy winter sun. One evening when Bordia asked K how the discussions were going and K conveyed his true feelings, Bordia burst into a hoarse laughter and said that he was happy that the discussions were going 'merry-go-round'. However, while the discussions in the working groups did not lead to any conclusions, Bordia's intention of confusing the Bankers was not fulfilled because, like programmed robots, some of them relentlessly raised questions about minutiae of education, never hesitating to come back again and again to the same issue if they were not satisfied with the answers provided by the Indian participants. However, the Bankers were not any wiser in spite of their tenacity. Nor was Bordia's intention of keeping the Bankers in suspense about the project fulfilled for in the discussions on management. Hardeepak Singh, a Director of DEA, spilled the beans by saying that the government had already decided to pose a project. When he came to know of it, Bordia was upset but he could do little but remonstrate with a colleague of Singh in DEA.

Before meeting the Bank contingent for the wrap-up, Bordia had a meeting with officials of DEA, Planning Commission, and the state government. M.R. Kolhatkar, Educational Adviser, Planning Commission, and Bordia were not the best of friends. Bordia considered Planning Commission to be a *jatrani*—a meddlesome aunt—while Kolhatkar in turn resented Bordia's domineering attitude and was contemptuous of Bordia's castles in the air. Kolhatkar said that the background document prepared for the Seminar did not adequately cover primary schooling. Furthermore, he doubted the ability of the state government to implement a far-reaching project that Bordia had in mind; it was better that the project were initiated in one district and then extended to other districts based on the experience gained. Hardeepak Singh, the DEA representative, had exactly the opposite view. He felt that the massive funds likely to be offered by the Bank could be absorbed only if the whole state were covered. He was a UP IAS officer, and in retrospect, it was he and not the state education secretary who echoed the state government's view. The state education secretary, a NLM aficionado, seemed to think that what was best for Bordia was best for all, UP included. Strangely, Bordia was moderation personified. He countered Singh's views by saying that the size of the project was not yet certain, and hence apprehension about absorption capacity was premature. He countered Kolhatkar by saying that a project required a critical minimum mass, and that a single district was too small. Management problems should be addressed and attended to. There was no question of there being an imbalance between NFE and primary schooling; both would definitely get their due place. He suggested that the project should cover ten districts with the option of ten reserve districts to absorb any unutilized funds. Once the Cabinet approved the proposal to approach the World Bank, project formulation would commence.

The wrap-up meeting with the World Bank contingent was stormy. Bordia expounded his litany of the shortfalls of Bank projects. The UP Project would be something that the Bank had not seen before; it would be a unique educational document. It would be a test case project to probe the earnestness of the Bank, to ascertain whether the assurances given to him by the Bank functionaries would be fulfilled or not. It would cover all the five components of basic education: primary schooling, NFE, adult education, women's education, and post-literacy. He demanded that all the five components should be financed. He demanded the right to prepare a project without the visitations of Bank functionaries, without having to comply with any checklist from the Bank. Project formulation was a process of capacity building. In the course of project formulation, people who would be responsible for implementation in UP would acquire a better understanding of the project. To this end it was imperative that Bank functionaries keep away from the state while the project was being formulated as many in India, Pakistan, and Bangladesh still had colonial, unliberated minds, and provincial officers such as the district education officers were likely to treat Bank functionaries as if they were God Almighty. The responsibility for project preparation should be left entirely to the UP government with the central government extending such assistance as might be necessary. No consultant should be appointed by the Bank unless specifically asked for by the Indian side. It might be necessary to appoint Indian consultants. The central government would take a decision regarding their selection and arrange payment at rates which were comparable to Indian experts who were engaged by external funding agencies in India. Overseas experts might be selected by Indian authorities but they would not be paid any consultancy fees but only travel expenses and per diem at the

World Bank rates; in effect, they would have to *karaseva* (make votive offering) for the project by offering their services gratis. The Bank may place in Delhi such experts as it might consider appropriate, but their help would be taken by the state and central governments only as they considered necessary. It might be difficult to prepare the complete project at one time. At the initial stage, a detailed outline of the project could be prepared, followed by preparation of a few sub-projects. As the implementation of these sub-projects proceeded, a few more sub-projects could be taken up for implementation. What he had in mind was an evolving project. Bordia also indicated that 10–15 districts would be taken up in the first instances but some activities outside these districts would also form part of the project. If the experience with the project was satisfactory, the whole of UP would be covered in more than one project or more. He also indicated that a number of pre-project activities would be taken up in a district or block which would provide inputs for better implementation. Over time, the list of pre-project activities grew longer and longer. The list included developing a modified form of MS linked with NFE; improving the system of educational statistics; microplanning for basic education; reorganization of management of education from village to district level; and locality-specific curriculum reform, material development, and improved methods of teaching.

Haddad and Skolnik formed a wonderful good guy–bad guy combination. Point by point, Haddad sought to rebut the Bordia critique. The five components of which Bordia spoke of were part of the basic education approach adopted at the Jomtien Conference. The Bank had no reservation whatsoever in the incorporation of all these five components in the proposed project. Bank projects were not repetitive, and there were many success stories. Skolnik questioned the knowledge of Bordia about Bank projects. The Bank had no objection whatsoever to finance non-formal and adult education. The question was not whether they would be financed but what the relative shares of investment and what the feasibility of project proposals were. Cambridge enquired whether ECCE would not be included in the project. Bordia clarified that ECCE was not viewed as a part of the basic education concept, although its importance as preparatory change for primary education was appreciated. Furthermore, ICDS programme, for which the government had decided to seek Bank support, was intended as a nation-wide programme to provide ECCE. Haddad intervened to say that the community needed to be fully involved in ECCE; otherwise it could greatly burden the basic education system. Regarding project formulation, Skolnik said it was always the responsibility of the borrower government, and that the Bank would give all possible assistance in project preparation. The Bank's anxiety was to ensure that from the point of view of fiduciary acceptability, the project should meet the Bank's requirements. Ordinarily the Bank and the borrower work together so that the project satisfied the Bank's requirements. For this purpose, ordinarily Bank project teams visited the borrower country from time to time to facilitate project formulation. Bordia observed that the Bank's requirements regarding project formulation could be taken care of if the Bank could furnish a detailed list of points to be kept in view while formulating the project. Skolnik said that such a list could be furnished, and that the Bank had no objection to leave the responsibility of project formulation to the Indian and UP governments. It was for Bordia to lay down the pace; if he wanted to go ahead on a war footing, he had his best wishes. The Bank would respond to his pace whatever be it. However, it would help if Bordia could indicate the possible schedules so that he could arrange for the manpower required to appraise the project. He had also no objection to the idea of an evolving project. However, generally speaking, implementation would be delayed if preparations were not completed. Bordia clarified that the way the sub-projects would be drawn up there would be no difficulties in implementation. Once an outline was drawn up, it should be possible to organize a pre-appraisal consultation with a few Bank staff members. As words were being bandied, an attendant turned up with tea. Bordia himself served the tea and regretted that he could not serve whiskey. Skolnik said sharply that he did not drink liquor. As he sipped tea, Haddad quipped that it looked as if after all it was whiskey that was served. Concluding the meeting, Bordia said that the approval of the Cabinet for seeking Bank funding for the project would be sought, and if the Cabinet accorded approval, UP government would prepare a project outline in consultation with the central government and initiate surveys. Thereafter, there could be a pre-appraisal consultation in Lucknow followed by an appraisal of the project and commencement of the project during 1991–2. The offer of the World Bank to retroactively finance pre-project activities and of a Japanese Grant facility for project preparation was accepted. The day after the wrap-up meeting with the Bank team, Bordia assigned S.C. Behar, an IAS officer with experience in education, and an acolyte of his who shared his vision, the task of assisting UP in the preparation of the project. A little later, Bordia drafted Vivek Oberoi, an IAS official who worked in the Fund-Bank Division of DEA and had considerable experience in handling Bank projects, to help the project document being formatted in a manner that would pass muster with the Bank management. With his customary zeal, Behar surged forward to prepare a unique educational document.

Within a month of the wrap-up meeting, detailed guidelines for the preparation of the UP Project arrived in the department. Prepared by Cambridge, it was a formidable document calling for voluminous information which was in stark contrast to the requirements of UNICEF in regard to BEP and of SIDA in regard to Lok Jumbish. In those guidelines, Cambridge referred to Bordia's observation that in due course the whole of UP might be covered by more than one project. In an internal meeting, Bordia faulted K for not lodging a protest that the purported observation was not factually correct. Bordia chided them saying 'The document was lying with you for a month. Yet you did nothing.' K just pocketed the admonition even though it was not warranted, as Bordia did say at the wrap-up meeting what Cambridge mentioned in the guidelines. K was often petrified in the presence of his superiors, particularly Bordia; furthermore, knowing Bordia so well through close observation and interaction, K knew that he did not like his deputies to contradict him in public. Later in the day, when they were alone and Bordia was in an amiable mood, K mentioned that Cambridge was not in the wrong. Bordia burst into a laughter and said '*yar*, when it comes to the Bank I am paranoid'. From his experience, K would like to say that while there was no need for paranoia, it was imperative while dealing with external agencies to be on guard all the time. For handling a project, agencies had more qualified dedicated staff than governments. While the Bank had several persons exclusively dealing with the UP Project, UP Project was only one of the many tasks K and his deputy dealing with that project had to attend to. K used to quip that DPEP took only 10 per cent of his work, and that within DPEP dealing with functionaries of external agencies only 10 per cent of his time. Compared to any government in India, central or state, the institutional memory of the agencies is enormous. Even a slip of a tongue by the borrower becomes part of the record to be retrieved and used when necessary. This was all the more so with the Bank as there is a measure of truth in the Hegelian dictum that quantity becomes quality. By virtue of its size, range, and scope of operations, financial, intellectual, and managerial resources the Bank is *sui generis*. Among the agencies, it is like the elephant among animals, and as it used to be said of IBM and others among computer manufacturers in the pre-PC age, Snow White among dwarfs arousing envy and resentment bordering on hatred. Without giving up all the attributes of a bank, it had been for nearly seven decades *the* leading development agency of the world. The salience of the World Bank used to be enhanced by the fact that when countries such as India were in dire need of foreign exchange and aid was an important source of foreign exchange. The World Bank used to be the prime mover of donors clubs such as the Aid India Consortium (renamed as India Development Forum in 1994). The Country Economic Memorandum prepared by the World Bank formed the basis for the annual discussions in the Aid India Consortium where aid pledges were made to help meet the foreign exchange needs of the country. Functionaries of the Bank take great pride in the prevalence of evidence-based decision making in their organization. It is part of the Bank's deep-rooted organizational culture to collect and analyse every conceivable type of information about the borrower and the project financed; the process of collection begins even in anticipation of a proposal for funding being received. A plausible explanation for this practice is that the Bank is steeped in American official culture as the headquarters of the Bank is located in Washington, DC, and by convention the Bank's President so far continues to be American, and the Bank professionals, though drawn from all over the world, are mostly educated in the graduate schools of the United States, and would have imbibed in those schools the belligerently questioning frame of mind and the belief that a problem without a solution could not exist. On the flipside, readiness for action is often combined with naiveté and a tendency to underestimate just how complex the situation is. A quip of S. Bhoothalingam, the legendary ICS officer, about Americans crisply captures the obsessive gathering and analysis of information. During the Second World War, Bhoothalingam was in the supply department in GOI, and one of his major tasks was to procure supplies from the Americans. He concluded from the exhausting trivia that the Americans demanded in any 'justification' for a request for supply, that Americans wanted to prove even the obvious, and to *know everything* about something *before they did anything at all*. For instance, if the supply of timber was requested, the 'justification' for request should begin with an elaborate exposition of what timber was, how many varieties of timber were there, what the characteristics of the each of the variety was, what purposes they were used for, and so forth, even though most of the information was hardly necessary for a decision on the request.[12] The information collected and analysed together with its strong institutional memory gives the Bank enormous power in dealing with countries. At the end of a mission, it is customary for the mission to draft a document called in the Bank's jargon as aide-memoire, and finalize the draft after consultations with the 'client'. Thanks to the admonition of Bordia, it became second nature for K to minutely pore through every word and even punctuation marks in the draft aide-memoire, search for layers of meaning which might not be apparent, and fight over every questionable word with the mission as if dear life depended on victory.

[12] S. Bhoothalingam, *Reflections on an Era: Memoirs of a Civil Servant*, New Delhi: Affiliated East-West Press Private Limited, 1993, p. 24.

X

TEST CASE PROJECT BECOMES TESTING

Problem of Maria

How do you solve a problem like Maria?
How do you catch a cloud and pin it down?
…
Many a thing you know you'd like to tell her
Many a thing she ought to understand
But how do you make her stay and listen to all you say
How do you keep a wave upon the sand?

—Nuns in the film *Sound of Music*

Soon after the NIEPA seminar, the question of coverage popped up much like King Charles' head. Behar and S.R. Tayal, a deputy of K, visited Lucknow on 19–20 December 1990, and during discussions, some officials of the state finance and planning departments expressed the view that the unit costs in the project should not be excessive and that the project should not be limited to ten districts only. By then, the NLM aficionado gave way to K.K. Bakshi as UP Education Secretary. On 7 January 1991, Bordia, with K in tow, made a flying visit to Lucknow to apprise Bakshi of what the test case project was about and win him over to his point of view. K knew Bakshi very well; he was an archetypal *bhadralok* (belonging to Bengali gentry), soft spoken, cerebral, and reflective, a Renaissance Man with eclectic tastes ranging from Persian to Malayalam script to the music of M.L.Vasanta Kumari, the Carnatic music maestro. In response to Bordia's exposition, he crisply replied that he understood the gravitas of NFE. In his exposition, Bordia referred to the views of the state finance and planning department officials, and said that the UP Project was expected to have a bearing on basic education all over the country, and hence it would be ensured that the unit costs in the UP Project were feasible not only with reference to the situation in UP but also with reference to the national context. Regarding coverage, he reiterated what he said during the NIEPA seminar that depending on the experience with the proposed UP Project, a second phase might be taken up that would cover the whole state. The question of coverage would not go away. Two months later, Bakshi sought to reopen the scope of the project by conveying the view of the state government that the project should cover 20 districts straightaway and not 10. Bordia informed him that the Union Cabinet having approved the proposal to seek Bank funding for ten project and ten reserve districts, it would not be desirable to reopen the question of coverage. In another development, someone suggested to Cambridge that some districts from one or more other states could be added to the UP districts. Cambridge reported this possibility to his management. In a communication to Tayal, he mentioned that the Bank always looked positively on the idea of a project where two distinct strategies would be explored. In the proposed project also, there could be two strategies, one addressing districts where access and equity were major issues and NFE and literacy programmes were emphasized. The other could address districts where quality, and not access, was the issue; this strategy would concentrate on curriculum, learning materials, teacher training, and evaluation. A project covering two or more states provides an opportunity to try out distinct strategies, and hence was welcome. However, this possibility never materialized, as that idea on his own without the approval was not acceptable to Bordia as well as the UP government. To jump the story ahead, the idea of testing multiple strategies within a single project became a reality only three years later with DPEP which covered districts with wide variations in demography, educational development, and patterns of governance. To illustrate, Kerala is one large village with a high density of population, near-universal participation, a high proportion of female teachers and large schools with hardly any multigrade teaching, that is to say a single teacher simultaneously teaching many grade levels (for example, classes I–V) in a single class. The quintessential challenge is quality, as baseline studies indicated that learning levels were low and dropped significantly after class II. In contrast, MP is sparsely populated with thousands of remote tribal populations too small to support a full-fledged school, making multigrade teaching, if not informal teaching, unavoidable. Participation was as much a major issue as quality. However, it is a commentary on the functioning of the Bank that the idea of a multi-state project which was welcomed when the UP Project was under discussion was objected to when DPEP was under consideration, and K had to 'sweat' a great deal to win over the opposition. Suffice to say, even in a well-knit organization such as the World Bank, the managers have considerable discretion, and the use of that discretion impacts the contours and management of a project.

From time to time, Bordia closely reviewed the progress of project formulation; however, the pace of formulation was glacial. Project formulation appeared to be like the burden of Sisyphus—a futile, never-ending task. A document of sorts was prepared by April 1991; it was heavy on rhetoric and jargon and very short on specifics. Strangely for a document to be posed to a bank, it did not project costs, the implementation schedule, or the flow of funds required. And furthermore, for every solution it posed more than one problem; it passionately spoke of bureaucratic rigidities and obstruction by politicians and Panchayat Raj institutions. In vagueness, it was close to the BEP Brown Book. The document was discussed in a workshop held in NIEPA on 24 and 25 April 1991. By this time, Madhukar Gupta had replaced Bakshi as State Education Secretary. Gupta was an extremely competent officer, exuded self-assurance, spoke with a stentorian voice, walked with a swagger, and rose to be the Union Home Secretary. Among others, Cambridge attended the workshop. In his introductory remarks, Bordia observed that the document was not 'even a preliminary or pre-preliminary document'; instead, it was only 'reflecting on various educational issues' and raised a host of policy issues. During the exhausting discussions, Cambridge suggested that if detailing the specifics of the project was difficult, the government could opt for a sectoral investment project instead of a specific investment project. In a sectoral investment project, it would suffice if the government and the bank agreed on the areas of intervention and the policy for each area of intervention. To illustrate, in the matter of school building construction, what all was necessary was to agree on policy issues such as the type of schools to be constructed and the modalities of school building construction It was not necessary to specify how many school buildings would be constructed and where. Bordia was not in favour of a sectoral investment loan, as in his view the bank dictated policy in countries which opted for a sectoral policy loan. Responding to Bordia's views, Cambridge drew a distinction between a sectoral adjustment loan and a sectoral investment loan; with the latter the government could insist that certain policies would not be examined by the bank and interventions covered by such policies would not be financed by the bank. Bordia responded by saying that a sectoral investment loan could be agreed to if the bank went on record that it would not question any of the government's policies, and would not leave out any project component from funding. Figuratively and to mix metaphors, Bordia was asking for the moon, for as a financial institution which relied on financial markets for most of its funding, the Bank could buy a pig in the poker; to do so would be to abdicate its fiduciary responsibility. Bordia had a point in that many of the unconventional things he had been talking about required testing and trial; yet in such a case the proper course would have been to opt for an experimental phase as was done with APPEP or Lok Jumbish, and after the completion of that phase to draw up a specific investment project including all interventions which were proved to be feasible through testing and trial and such a project posed to the bank. After following the due process of appraisal and so on, the bank could have financed it and limited its oversight to the specific activities covered by the project and not foray into policy issues. If, on the other hand, Bordia wanted the bank to approve a huge loan without detailing the project components, he could have opted for a sector investment loan in which case the bank would not have minded testing and trial of the programme components, financing those components which pass muster in evaluation with which it would be associated. To be honest, Bordia did not have direct experience of developing a large-scale project with substantial investment and posing such a project to agencies for funding; hence, his demands were impractical. Bordia could not have his way even with SIDA, one of the most recipient-friendly agencies, as SIDA insisted on small experimental phase before committing substantial funds for Lok Jumbish. Whatever, the workshop concluded with the decision that the project document would be handed over to the World Bank by 15 June 1991.

June 1991 came and went by without a project document in sight. The April workshop, far from settling matters, turned out to be a prelude to the widening of the chasm between the thinking of Bordia and that of the state government. On 12 May 1991, the State Level Project Committee met under the chairmanship of the Chief Secretary and decided to totally change the scope, duration, and parameters as well as the type of lending. Gupta met Bordia on 7 June 1991 to persuade Bordia to accept the views of the state government. The state government felt strongly that the project would result in severe imbalances and grave political and administrative problems, as the level of investment envisaged in the ten project districts would be unduly high in comparison with the plan expenditure on basic education in the state as a whole. Oberoi, the IAS official drafted by Bordia to help the project document being formatted in a manner that would pass muster with the bank management, gave the State Finance Secretary to understand that the bank would be willing to pick up part of the ongoing non-plan expenditure on basic education and provide substantial additional resources for basic education. Consequently, the state government wanted to cover the state as a whole right from the beginning, with a sectoral loan extending over two five-year plans. In the state government's view, the main challenge was lack of access to schooling and inadequate facilities. There were about 11,000 habitations without a primary school within a radius of 1 kilometre. Many of the schools did not have proper buildings and infrastructure. Therefore, in the first 5 years, the project should concentrate on improving access to primary schooling, school infrastructure, and facilities. In the second five years, issues of quality and alternative systems could be considered. What the state government suggested was phasing of project components, while Bordia suggested phasing of coverage—ten project and ten reserve districts in the first phase and the rest of the state in the second phase. What the state government proposed was heresy to Bordia for what the state government proposed proceeded from the archetypal 'brick and mortar' approach to education. After Gupta said his piece, Bordia theatrically picked up his phone and told his secretary not to let anyone or a phone call interrupt his meeting with Gupta. He pointed his finger at the photograph of J.P. Naik embedded on a wall of his room and began to speak nostalgically of his association with Naik *Saheb* and of what he learnt from him. He wistfully recalled the informal training sessions that Naik Saheb conducted in Srinagar for young officers like him, P.K. Umashankar, and Anjali Dayand who were then in the Ministry of Education. Naik spoke of the elusive triangle of quantity, quality, and equity, and stressed that educational planning was not divisible and that one cannot distinguish between access and issues such as content, process, and levels of learning. One cannot attend to access issues alone in one plan and quality in another. From a larger perspective, access to schooling and school buildings were relatively smaller problems, while the main problems were low levels of retention and learning attainment, poor teacher performance, and an improperly functioning school system. The most difficult aspect of access is to set up and operate a really good NFE system for working children and girls who cannot participate in the school system. UP officials should understand that the project design was not a matter for the state government alone; the project was envisaged as a test case project to test the real intentions of the bank and establish a new type of relationship that would blaze a trial for the whole developing world. It appeared to him that the UP officials were only relaying the signals of the bank. The competent officer that he was, Gupta stood his ground and suggested a compromise. In the first phase, issues of quality along with access to schooling would be addressed in all the districts, and 'alternative systems' tried out in ten districts. In the second phase, alternate systems would be scaled up. Bordia would not relent; he reiterated that this was a test case project, and given the sensitivity attached to bank financing of basic education, it was better to make haste slowly. If the state government felt that the outlay was too high for the ten project and ten reserve districts, the outlay could be reduced. What the state government proposed was a project similar to that implemented in some South Asian countries such as Pakistan and Bangladesh; he was bound by the Union Cabinet decision as well as the CABE parameters for external financing of basic education. Financial considerations could not dictate project parameters. He closed the meeting theatrically declaring 'If you do not consider me too rude, your recipe is recipe for destruction. I would not be instrumental in destroying the education system in the country. I am sorry that my arguments do no convince you. The project is frozen till you revalidate our approach. Do not be guided only by those who know only how to draw money from the Bank. I have my educational blinkers, and I care two hoots about country getting resources.' So saying, he picked up the phone and asked his secretary to send in Athreyee, a consultant of BEP.

About a week later, on 13–15 June 1991, Bordia and Skolnik discussed the project framework again. Both were in Shanghai attending a seminar on 'Basic Education and National Development' organized by the Shanghai Institute of Human Resource Development and the UNICEF to discuss 40 years of Chinese experience in promoting primary education. As is common with such events, Bordia and Skolnik used the occasion for a side meeting. The *Shanghai communiqué*, the epithet K gave for the aide-memoir that Bordia superbly crafted to document his discussions with Skolnik, makes an interesting reading. It reiterated the conclusions of the wrap-up meeting held after the NIEPA seminar. Skolnik made a pitch for a sector policy loan instead of a specific investment project loan. Among the many advantages of the policy loan was the fact that it could finance a larger project with faster disbursals. Given the foreign exchange situation, a sector policy loan would suit DEA better. The whole of UP could be covered straightaway. A sector policy loan proposal was easier to formulate, as all the components and the *inter se* allocation of the investment among different programme components need not be detailed to the last point. Sector policy lending was resorted to augment the resource base of Industrial Development Bank of India (IDBI) and Industrial Credit and Investment Corporation of India (ICICI), and no problems were faced. This argument had no appeal to Bordia. In his view, efforts to secure fast reimbursement by the bank might lead to distortions and poor educational outcomes. The state government might be tempted to take up investment in areas where expenditure is easy such as construction of school buildings and appointment of teachers. And then, a test case project is better tested initially at a lower scale. Proper relationship has to be established between the three parties—DOE, state government, and the World Bank structures, and processes for programme management have to be developed. All in all, it makes sense to hasten slowly. Continuing his pitch for a sector investment loan, Skolnik added that the bank saw no difficulty in accepting the policy of the Indian Government in respect of the various components of the project. Technically the bank would have the right to raise policy issues; however, such a contingency might not arise at all. Here lay the rub. The very contingency of a policy dialogue with the bank, however remote, was not acceptable to Bordia. The CABE parameters came in very handy for Bordia to clinch the argument. A policy loan was incompatible with those parameters. As it was, there was considerable opposition to bank financing a primary education and the CABE parameters embodied a very fragile consensus. Bordia distinguished between refinancing of credit institutions and financing primary education. There the matter rested and the suggestion for a sector policy loan was never again broached by the Bank. At Shanghai, there was some sparring on project components other than primary schooling such as ECCE, NFE, adult education, post-literacy and continuing education, and women's development. Starting from the premise that there may not be enough clarity on some of these programme components, Skolnik suggested that a part of the project funds, say about 20 per cent, be set apart for these components whose detailing may evolve over time. Bordia contested the premise; there was reasonable clarity, and in fact, these components would require a good deal more than 20 per cent of the total project cost. If that were so, Skolnik had again no difficulty.

At the time Bordia met D in Shanghai, momentous political changes took place in India. The General Elections, which were concluded on 15 June 1991, brought in a new government in Delhi as well as Lucknow. The Congress Party, under the leadership of P.V. Narasimha Rao, Bordia's former Minister at MHRD, formed a minority government at the centre. Arjun Singh assumed office as Minister, MHRD. In UP, Mulayam Singh's government was replaced by a BJP government with a diametrically opposite political ideology. Bordia saw the possibility of new openings with these political changes. He briefed his new Minister Arjun Singh about the status of the UP Project and sought the good offices of Ramu Damodaran to similarly brief the Prime Minister. He was hopeful that he could work his charm on Kalyan Singh, the new Chief Minister of UP, and the new Education Secretary of that state, Karan Singh who replaced Gupta, all the more so as Karan Singh worked with him earlier. In a meeting taken by him to review the project on 27 July 1991, Behar reported to Bordia that project formulation had ground to a halt. Not to worry, Bordia told Behar and K. So confident was he that he asked Behar not to wait for the response of the state government but instead go ahead with the preparation of the project document, drawing upon the assistance of NIEPA faculty and the data available in NCERT and the statistical division of DOE. K was not that sure that UP could be persuaded to fall in line; his apprehensions were confirmed when Cambridge met him 3 days later to take stock of the project development. Cambridge was aware that not much happened after the workshop in April 1991 in view of the General Elections and the general expectancy in UP that change of the state government was imminent. He volunteered the information that two BJP functionaries, Ved Prakash Goel who was in charge of UP and Ramdass Keswani who worked earlier in the Asian Development Bank (ADB), met him and a few other bank officials in the New Delhi branch of the bank. He got the impression that the new government in UP might not go along with the approach suggested by DOE. He felt that the project might not be posed in the bank's fiscal year 1991, and expressed concern that funds earmarked for the project in 1991 might not be utilized. He suggested that alternatives to utilize the amount could be explored. He suggested three alternatives, they being an *ad hoc* loan for UP, formulation of projects in states which might have a better rapport with the central government, and a loan directly to the central government to finance on-going schemes such as Operation Blackboard. K appreciated his concern but reiterated that the UP Project would definitely be posed in the bank's fiscal year 1991.

In retrospect, Cambridge was right in his assessment while Bordia was not. Karan Singh proved to be a thorough professional who, like a tough lawyer, would do everything possible to further his client's interests. He refused to concede any role for DOE in externally funded educational projects, tenaciously interpreting to the advantage of the state government every agreement that was reached between DOE and UP government and did not hesitate to use the bank's appraisal process to reopen settled issues and thwart DOE. Till Bordia demitted office, K was under the mistaken impression that Singh played the no man's role because of the bitter memories of his earlier association with Bordia in the Labour Ministry. Even after the amiable Giri succeeded Bordia, and the differences appeared to have been sorted out in a meeting between Giri and V.K. Saxena, Chief Secretary, UP, the finalization of the UP Project dragged on and on like a running sore till the very eve of the negotiations with the World Bank, 11 months after Bordia's retirement . In retrospect, a resolution of the differences was not possible not only because of the clash of personalities of key players but also because of sharp contest over the project design, and more importantly over the role of DOE in project formulation and implementation. Whatever, after the BJP government was formed, Bordia visited Lucknow once again, with K in tow, to win over Kalyan Singh and his secretary, Nripendra Mishra. He returned from the visit full of hope which turned out to be false. Yet another version of the project document was received in February 1992; it was more of the same. It proposed that 40 per cent of the project outlay to be expended in the very first year on school building construction.

As the stalemate continued, and the retirement of Bordia drew nearer, UP officials bade their time looking forward to the day, not far off and fast approaching, when there would be no more hurdles to cross in accessing bank funding. As the macroeconomic situation worsened, there were desperate attempts to scrounge for foreign exchange. In February 1992, DEA floated a note for the consideration of the Committee of Secretaries on the possibilities of utilizing external assistance for social sector projects. In that note, DEA expressed the view that it was in national interest to expedite the preparation of the UP Project and pose more state basic education projects as a number of states had already evinced in accessing bank funding for primary education. Ever on the move for openings, Bordia thought that the meeting of the Committee of Secretaries would be an opportunity to avert the possibility of UP officials having their way once he exited from the scene. He was confident that he could prevail upon the Cabinet Secretary Naresh Chandra who was his friend, to get the UP officials fall in line. He suggested that the UP Chief Secretary be invited to the next meeting so that the differences could be resolved. The meeting 'took a wondrous turning' as Naresh Chandra had to rush to a meeting in the Prime Minister's house on conferring Bharat Ratna on Ambedkar leaving the meeting to be handled by the Secretary (Coordination). Irrespective of who the incumbent is, the post of the Secretary (Coordination) is invariably an officer kicked upstairs, a fifth wheel in the coach. Therefore, he was in no position to sort out the divergent points of view of DOE, DEA, and the UP government. As soon as his friend moved out, Bordia too got up and left after making an impromptu remark, perhaps intended as a negotiation ploy but more likely the offshoot of his self-avowed rashness, that if UP continued to be intransigent he would shift the project to

MP. After he left, K was left to face trial by a kangaroo court, arrayed against the representative of DEA who was from UP cadre, and UP officials. Others could not understand why so much fuss was being made by DOE in an innocuous area such as education. The conclusion of that meeting was of no consequence. Bordia's remark shifted the battle to the political arena. It reinforced the belief of the UP officials to believe that the project document was not accepted for ulterior motives; after all Bordia's Minister Arjun Singh was from MP, and was more and more relying on the anti-BJP plank to settle scores with the Prime Minister and give a boost to his career. The innumerable queries that Bordia's department raised seemed to be politically motivated, much like the 58 queries that the central government posed to the state government on Ayodhya. The response of the state government was similar—Kalyan Singh had declared that he was not central government's *patwari* (village official), and would not answer any more queries. Kalyan Singh wrote to his party MPs seeking their intervention. Viswanath Sastry, a BJP MP, raised the matter in the Parliamentary Consultative Committee attached to the Ministry. On 24 April 1992, two BJP MPs, Mahadeepak Singh Shakya and Atal Behari Vajpayee (later Prime Minister), raised the matter in the Lok Sabha during the zero hour. Arjun Singh fully supported Bordia and made a statement conceding nothing to the UP demand and reiterated that a basic education project cannot emphasize solely school building construction and appointment of teachers to the exclusion of substantive educational issues. In his statement, he also referred to the externally funded basic education projects under implementation (BEP, Lok Jumbish), and those in the pipeline (MP and South Orissa); he also announced the intention of the government to eventually cover all states with such projects. Given the political configuration in the centre and state, the signal was loud and clear to the UP government: you cannot have your way defying DOE. K wondered what the turn of events would have been if UP were ruled by the same party as at the centre, and if the Minister were someone other than Arjun Singh who had a visceral dislike of BJP. Whatever, the test case project emerged as an unfinished business of Bordia's helmsmanship of the department. After the failure of the political assault, UP officials waited for the change of guard just about a month away.

Understanding the Behaviour of UP

a. A Little Bit of Theory

i. Looking at Agencies through the Prism of Negotiations

Till the very last moment before K boarded the plane to New York for negotiations with the World Bank in Washington a year later in May 1993, UP and DOE had sharp differences of opinion, and consequently, uncertainty hovered over the project. As discussions between DOE and the UP government failed to resolve the differences, the matter moved again up to the Cabinet Secretary for 'adjudication'. Had the state been not under President's rule, it is possible UP Government might not have accepted Cabinet Secretary's award without any further ado. The UP stalemate is a good illustration of the challenges which arise in a federal polity which seeks to access external funding for a project which would be implemented by a state government. K tried to understand the deeper meaning of the prolonged fracas with the UP government by drawing upon the knowledge he picked up from the most meaningful course that he took at Harvard—a course on negotiations offered by James Sebenius. K's attempt to view the UP project from a larger theoretical perspective and generalize its lessons enhanced the educational value of his experience in handling the UP Project, and helped him to understand the dynamics of dealing with agencies and state governments.

Among the seminal truths K picked up from Sebenius was that contrary to the general impression, negotiations are not limited to explicit bargaining situations, such as that between union and management, or between nations in bilateral or multilateral forums. Yet another is that an organization is not a homogenous, monolithic entity. Hence, in parallel to the external negotiations, that is negotiations with parties external to the organization, there are internal negotiations within each of the organizations (parties) engaged in negotiations. It is necessary to have negotiations within each organization for selecting the negotiating team for external negotiations; defining the issues to be negotiated; choosing the goals of negotiation; choosing the negotiation strategy; reviewing the progress of external negotiations; aligning the negotiation strategy and tactics to the evolving situation; and; deciding whether to clinch the deal or break off negotiations. The internal negotiations are likely to be more bitter and acrimonious than the external negotiations. The internal and external negotiations are not usually insulated from each other; together, their interplay drives the negotiation process. And yet another was that in every negotiation, there is tension between cooperation and conflict. The very rationale for a negotiation is that the agreement that could be secured is preferable to other alternatives. There is, therefore, figuratively a commonality of interest in trying to augment the size of the pie one secures through negotiation through cooperation and joint pursuit of gains. At the same time, there is a conflict of interest in that each party seeks to maximize his share of the pie. Opportunistic behaviour being intrinsic to negotiation, the course of negotiation is zigzag and often acrimonious. Parties engage in activities outside the negotiating forum in order to enhance their bargaining strength. Even in negotiations that culminate in agreement there could be occasions of bitter acrimony when the negotiations seem to be on the verge of collapse. And yet another was that strategic thinking ahead of negotiations enormously enhances barraging power and its importance cannot be stressed enough. While preparing for negotiations, it is imperative to *know oneself*, identifying one's interests, whether all the interests are congruent, and if not, the trade-offs among the interests, what are the non-negotiables, how essential it is secure an agreement in the negotiations, whether one can walk off from the negotiations, what were the alternatives to negotiations, what is one's bargaining power, how much elbow room one has negotiations, and how could one's bargaining power be improved. It is equally imperative to *know the other*, knowing everything about the opposite side.[1]

Having internalized the seminal truths taught by Sebenius, once he began dealing with agencies it did not take long for K to recognize that accessing and utilizing external funding by any mode—be it specific investment loan or sectoral policy loan—was a process of negotiations

[1] Howard Raiffa, *The Art and Science of Negotiation*, Cambridge, MA: The Belknap Press of Harvard University Press, 1982; David A. Lax and James K. Sebenius, *The Manager As Negotiator: Bargaining for Cooperation and Competition*, New York: Free Press, 1986; David A. Lax and James K. Sebenius, '3-D Negotiation: Playing the Whole Game', *Harvard Business Review*, November 2003, pp. 65–74; James K. Sebenius, *3-D Negotiation: Powerful Tools to Change the Game in Your Most Important Deals*. Boston: Harvard Business School Press, 2006.

from the beginning to the end, and that being so, every interaction with an agency is to be better handled the way negotiation ought to be. The formal commitment to fund a project, the terms and conditions of funding, and the contours of the project to be funded are the outcomes of a formal negotiation; however, the formal negotiation comes at the end of a long informal negotiating process stretching for over a year, if not more with stages such as an indication to fund a project, project preparation, pre-appraisal, and appraisal. What appears to be project development process is also a long-drawn-out process of informal negotiations. During this long process, agencies attempt to come to an agreement with the recipient of funding almost every aspect of funding so that as few contentious issues as possible are left to be settled at the final formal negotiation. In fact, an agency would normally not agree for final formal negotiation unless it is confident that agreement is highly probable, if not certain. Thus, the design of the content of the project or policy reform and design of implementation come out from the long informal process of negotiations. There is an American saying 'it ain't over till it is over'. In actuality 'it ain't over even after it is over' as during the process of implementation the agency monitors the compliance with the terms of the formal agreement; it is quite possible that differences arise between the agency and the recipient of funds as they might interpret the agreement differently. The principle *caveat emptor* is equally applicable to the process of implementing a project funded by an agency; unless the recipient is vigilant, the agency functionaries might interpret the terms of agreement in a manner different from what was intended. Furthermore, quite often the balance of power between the parties to negotiation might change once an agreement is entered into, and the party in whose favour the balance of power might have tilted might not comply with the letter and spirit of the agreement. This development is captured by the concept of *Obsolescing bargaining* developed by Raymond Vernon to explain the shift in the relationship between a multinational corporation (MNC) and the host country.[2] Once an MNC invests heavily in a country, its fixed assets

[2] Raymond Vernon, *Sovereignty at Bay: The Multinational Spread of American Enterprises*, New York: Basic Books, 1971; Richard E. Caves, *Multinational Enterprise and Economic Analysis*, Cambridge: Cambridge University Press, 1982.

become hostage to the host country. The latter can alter to its advantage the terms and conditions of the agreement subject to which the MNC invested in the country. For example, it can levy higher taxes than what was assured prior to investment. Similarly, if the economic situation of the recipient country deteriorates and the country is more dependent on external funding, the agreement to fund a project may obsolesce. All this is not to say that engagement with agencies should be avoided, but that deftly negotiating with agencies is an essential aspect of accessing external funds. Therefore, the recipient should not perceive accessing external funds to be only a question of designing a good project which is sound educationally and cost-effective.

From personal experience, K noticed that agencies in general and the bank in particular view project development as a process of negotiation; that explains the meticulous attention to documenting the project development process and anchoring the discussions at a given stage in the agreements reached at the previous stage. To give an example, an important aspect of the appraisal stage of project development is scrutiny of the compliance with the agreements reached at the pre-appraisal stage. The bank is also an avid, almost obsessive, practitioner of the principle *knowing the other*. One day while he was in the bank's headquarters for negotiations, he came to know from his office in Delhi that his father-in-law had died; he wanted to immediately talk to his wife, which he was not able to do as she was disconsolate and would not pick up the phone. He wanted to speak to his neighbour, K. Dharmarajan who was his colleague in the Ministry of Urban Development and was handling a World Bank project on water supply, and request him to pass on a message to his wife that K was eager to speak to her. However, K did not have Dharamarajan's telephone number and he was distraught; however, Skolnik came to K's rescue by handing over to K the bank's compilation on the officers of Delhi. K was startled to find that the compilation had information about every district education officer of UP as well as his own personal secretary, Arjun Bhatia. K had no clue where Bhatia lived but the bank had full details of his coordinates. Suffice to say, when one is dealing with the bank one is dealing with a formidable institution, or to use the Biblical imagery Goliath. K realized from personal experience that David could prevail, but for that one could not always depend on pluck and luck. K internalized that lesson and *knowing the other*, getting to know all about the agencies and the functionaries of the agencies he had to deal with became a lifelong obsession. If economic strength is the muscle of bargaining strength, knowledge is the brain which guides the use of the strength. The asymmetry that one often notices in international economic and business relations is partly derived from the asymmetry in information. To their country operations agencies bring in their rich experience in operating in different countries fortified by close interaction with other agencies. More often than not for conducting the operations they have more qualified dedicated staff than the recipient of finances. Countries which wish to ensure that resources are fungible need to match the knowledge of agencies. Apart from deep knowledge of the sector, ministries of developing countries dealing with agencies require a deep understanding of the operations, operational styles and mindset of providers of finance, and the analytical capacity to weigh options and make intelligent choices. Often, education ministries of developing countries lack the understanding necessary. Only then can they embark on donor coordination which is much talked about in literature but so little practised.[3]

Adapting the powerful imagery of Weiler, external agencies march to the three sets of drums: one set played by the agency's domestic policy environment, the second by the leadership of the recipient country; and the third by the regnant conventional wisdom of the international development and finance community.[4] Analytically, bilateral agencies are distinguishable from development banks such as the World Bank and the Asian Development Bank (ADB). The funds that a bilateral agency provides are voted by the Parliament of the donor country, and it is expected to further the national interest as set by its government. Most of the aid disbursed by bilateral agencies is offered as grant without any obligation to repay. Bilateral aid differs from lending by World Bank, ADB, and other development banks in a few significant respects. Bilateral aid is an arm of the public diplomacy of the country offering aid and is expected to predispose the recipient in favour of the donor.

[3] R.V. Vaidyanatha Ayyar, 'Educational Policy Planning and Globalisation', *International Journal of Educational Development*, 16, no. 4, 1996, pp. 347–53, p. 351.

[4] H. Weiler, 'The Political Economy of International Cooperation in Educational Development', in R.M. Garrett, ed., *Education and Development*, London: Croor Helm, 1984, pp. 123–56, p. 142.

It is not unusual for development concerns to be tempered by foreign policy or commercial considerations. Thus, after the Pokhran nuclear test in May 1998, Japan and Sweden suspended aid to India as they considered that testing the nuclear devices infringed non-proliferation, a cornerstone of their foreign policy. Sweden used to raise frequently in its annual aid dialogue with India the question of human rights violations in Kashmir. Among others, inadequate patent protection in India invariably cropped up in the dialogue between India and countries such as the United States and West Germany.

Compared to multilateral financial institutions, bilateral agencies are in general more 'particularistic' in regard to the countries to which assistance is directed and the activities they support. Thus, the distribution of World Bank funding is more widely spread than, say, French assistance almost all of which goes to former colonies of France. In a large country such as India, bilateral agencies wish to concentrate on a few states; thus, the Dutch preferred funding activities only in the states of Gujarat, Karnataka, and UP. In the late 1990s, DFID shifted from a geographically dispersed approach to one that concentrated on four 'Focus States': AP, MP, Orissa, and West Bengal.[5] In 1996, even the World Bank sought to depart from its policy of having no focus states and be selective in funding, giving preference to states such as AP which undertake to adopt economic reforms and restructuring of their economy. The new Country Director Edwin Lim could persuade P.C. Chidambaram, the finance minister in the United Front government, that the new policy of the Bank would foster reforms in the states that Finance Ministry wished to promote but could not because of political compulsions. The Bank was permitted to directly engage the states and advance adjustment policy loans to states without the intermediation of GOI. The development of a closer relationship with AP and the 'iconization' of Chandrababu Naidu, Chief Minister of AP, was an offshoot of the Bank's new policy.[6] However, the policy did

[5] John Heath, *An Evaluation of DFID's India Programme 2000–2005*, Evaluation report EV 670, London: Department for International Development, August 2006.

[6] Jason A. Kirk, 'Remaining Relevant: The World Bank's Strategy for an India of States', Chapter II of *India and the World Bank: The Politics of Aid*, New York: Anthem Press, 2011.

not last long as Jaswant Singh, the finance minister in the incoming National Democratic Alliance (NDA) government, had reservations about a policy that attenuated the intermediary role of DEA.[7]

While the World Bank has a long tradition of supporting a sector or sub-sector as a whole based on the analysis of that sector or sub-sector, before the 1990s bilateral aid also used to be characterized by a *tradition of assistance* supporting only some areas of a sector or sub-sector; the areas to be supported were largely determined by the experience back home or in countries where that agency operates. Thus, Japanese aid used to be predominantly tied aid comprising equipment which had to be imported from Japan. K's first experience of an externally assisted project was APPEP; from a reading of King's classic on aid and education K discovered that there was a 'method in the madness' of the way APPEP was designed and managed by ODA. The tradition of assistance heavily influences research and evaluation. Thus,

> British aid to in-service teacher education, to supportive forms of inspection and supervision, or to school-based curriculum development, do not emerge as hypotheses to be tested against other forms of possible intervention; they appear more as 'givens', as areas which can draw on relatively rich layers of British expertise. In respect of these areas of comparative advantage, the specific role of research has been more confirmatory than exploratory.[8]

The tradition of assistance also influences evaluation. Even when a programme is of limited success, that success is often exaggerated by the functionaries who developed the programme as they have a vested interest to show that what they managed is a success. This is but human; human nature is reinforced when that programme is one which conforms to the tradition of assistance. If the outcome of such a programme is not that expected *a priori*, the judgment often is that the programme is good but that implementation is poor. That conclusion is unlikely to be questioned even in external evaluation as

[7] Jason A. Kirk, 'Economic Reform, Federal Politics, and External Assistance: Understanding New Delhi's Perspective on the World Bank's State-Level Loans', in Rahul Mukherji, ed., *India's Economic Transition, The Politics of Reform*, New Delhi: Oxford University Press, 2007.

[8] Kenneth King, *Aid and Education* in *the Developing World: The Role of Donor Agencies in Educational Analysis*, London: Longman, 1991, pp. 196–7.

the consultants chosen by an agency for evaluation are drawn from a known pool of experts who are usually aware of the agency's tradition of assistance, and are generally unlikely to question the tradition. The World Bank had a strong division for internal audit which directly reports to the Board—the Internal Evaluation Group; most bilateral agencies have no such unit. K found that the tradition of assistance was a formidable barrier in his attempts to secure external assistance in a manner different from what the agencies were accustomed to in the past.

Donor countries expect even their own bilateral agencies to fund efficient programmes and further ensure efficient implementation of such programmes. In theory, a developing country is expected to formulate its development priorities, and if domestic resources are not adequate, approach an agency with a proposal for funding, and in turn the agency is expected to appraise the proposal, and if found satisfactory, finance it and oversee the implementation so that funds are applied as agreed between the country and the agency, and efficiently. A corollary of this proposition is that provision of financial resources is driven by demand from developing countries. The reality, however, is more complex. Countries differ in the degree of compulsion they face to access external funding, and their capacity to formulate and implement policies and programmes. Given the pressure to finance well-designed projects and ensure efficient implementation of such projects even in countries which do not have adequate indigenous capacity to develop and implement projects, many functionaries of agencies develop the habit of adopting a hands-on-management style or 'mothering' the countries, at different stages of a project—conceptualization, design, start-up, implementation, and evaluation. The habit soon becomes second nature for many functionaries who seek to adopt the same approach even in countries which are capable of managing their affairs well. Offering technical assistance through consultants is an important component of the aid. It is not unusual for an agency functionary or a consultant to offer advice based on his comparative experience of working in different countries and on different projects and shy away from expending time and effort to understand the distinctive context of the recipient country and to offer advice rooted in the context. Such practices by agency functionaries and consultants aggravate the dependency on outside advice for project development and implementation with the result that the donor rather than the country is in the driver's seat, activities such as donor coordination are taken over by the donors, and donors call the shots. If, in addition, a country is in desperate need of external finances, the dependency syndrome is aggravated and projects offered by donors are willingly accepted even if such projects are unrelated to the developmental priorities of the country. Thus, instead of demand by the recipient country determining the choice and profile of projects, supply of 'projects' by external agencies emerges as the determining factor.

The idea underlying capacity building has been for long an important component of project assistance; the agency functionaries and consultants were expected to teach how to fish and not give fish. Yet successful teaching–learning is a long-drawn process; no learning can take place except by doing, committing errors, and learning and internalizing appropriate lessons from such errors. No child learns to walk without faltering and stumbling. Yet an error-prone project development and implementation process runs counter to the objective of financing an efficient project efficiently implemented. And furthermore, if capacity development were to be seriously addressed in a project, it would be necessary to draw up realistic schedules for project development and implementation that provide for the country's learning by doing; such prolonged schedules might militate against the criteria by which functionaries are judged, namely fast disbursal of aid and rapid approval of new projects. In practice, however, capacity building had taken place only when the government of the country and its functionaries make determined and concerted efforts to acquire the skills and competencies required for formulating and implementing policies and programmes. Without demand, the supply is not likely to be forthcoming. Historically, capacity building had been substantial only where it is a country preoccupation and not just an agency preoccupation, and only when, as with Meiji Japan, contemporary China, or India, technical assistance is perceived to be not *receiving* from the donor's expertise for specific tasks but as *acquiring* technical resources to develop one's own capacity to do specific tasks. As negotiations are an important aspect of accessing funds from agencies, capacity building should encompass the negotiation skills needed to handle the external agencies. 'Don't forget to build up your capacity to negotiate' was the message that K consistently delivered whenever he had the bully pulpit, be it the

Third Oxford Conference on Globalisation and Learning (1995),[9] the NIEPA-IIEPA on Design of Development Programmes/Projects in Basic Education (1996), or the capacity building workshops that the World Bank organized in Cape Town and Tunis in 2007.[10]

ii. How Do Governments Decide?[11]

Sebenius's course also offered valuable insights into the decision-making process in the government; of the three canonical texts prescribed by Sebenius, the one with most direct relevance for understanding decision-making by governments is that of Graham Allison.[12] It is common for many insiders impatient for action, not to speak of those outside government and the media, to feel that government decisions are 'irrational', motivated because they tend to subserve vested interests or the political interests of the ruling party, that the process is exasperatingly tortuous, and that decisions are transient likely to be reversed by the same government or its successors. Many a time the feeling is legitimate, but more often than not, such a feeling emanates from a lack of understanding of the way organizations function, of the distinctiveness of government as an organization, and of the ineluctable fact that people have divergent views on how the economy, polity, and society should be organized and the consequential imperative of a democratic government having to reconcile divergent, often conflicting, views on major policy issues. The first element of distinctiveness comprises the fact that sole organizing principle of a business or not-for-profit

[9] R.V. Vaidyanatha Ayyar, 'Educational Policy Planning and Globalisation'.

[10] R.V. Vaidyanatha Ayyar, *Donor Harmonization and Alignment—Organizing to Take Leadership: The Experience of India*, 2nd Africa Region Education Capacity Development Workshop, 'Country Leadership and Implementation for Results in the EFA FTI Partnership', Tunis, Tunisia, December 3–6, 2007, http://www.fasttrackinitiative.org/library/moduleIIIcoordination.pdf; *Country-Agency Relationship: The Indian Experience*, Background paper prepared for the Education for All Global Monitoring Report 2009, UNESCO, 2009/ED/EFA/MRT/PI/02, 2008.

[11] For elaboration, see R.V. Vaidyanatha Ayyar, *Public Policymaking in India*, New Delhi: Pearson Longman, 2009.

[12] Graham T. Allison, *Essence of Decision: Explaining the Cuban Missile Crisis*, Boston: Little, Brown & Company, 1971.

organization is effectiveness. Considerations of effectiveness guide the allocation of power, functions, and responsibilities among different units and functionaries of an organization. On the other hand, the structure and process of a democratic government are deliberately designed to disperse power and prevent abuse of power and tyranny. Checks and balances among and within the three branches of government (executive, legislature, and judiciary) are intrinsic to democratic functioning. In a vibrant democracy with effective competition among political parties, the government of the day is like a business under potential, if not imminent, threat of hostile takeover. Consequently, governments are under constant compulsion to consolidate power and please important groups and the electorate at large. This compulsion does impact on governmental policies and actions. The second element comprises the fact that no business or not-for-profit organization can match either the central or even most state governments in the scale and scope of operations. Scale itself introduces complexities and challenges. In view of the vast scope, sweep, and impact of its policymaking, it is incumbent on the government to make policy with due deliberation, taking into consideration the diverse, and often conflicting, interests of all the citizens and groups. Consequently, the structure of a democratic government (separation of powers and checks and balances) and the seemingly tortuous policy are intentionally designed to ensure hasty and intemperate decisions and provide opportunities for citizens and groups to influence the policy process. The seeming lack of decisiveness is set off by the fact that a democracy avoids policy catastrophes such as *The Great Leap Forward* of China.

A decision can be said to be rational if the underlying issues are correctly identified and rigorously analysed, all alternative solutions comprehensively identified, the implications of each alternative rigorously evaluated, and the best chosen. Rationality is bounded; no one, not even the most rational person, can escape from the cognitive limitations on the human mind—its limited ability to gather all the available information and perfectly process the information gathered. Consequently, analysis can never be comprehensive and perfect. In reality, instead of analysing all the characteristics of a problem, only some are analysed; the search procedures are not exhaustive but limited, and they identify only some and not all the options; evaluation is not absolute but, in comparative terms, limited to a comparison with the existing policy as the referral point. In fact, life would be unbearable if one has to wake up every day and attend to every task as if it were utterly new and attended to after exhaustive *de novo* deliberation. Instinctively, every individual categorizes the tasks he has to attend to frequently and develop routines to attend to each category of tasks; similarly, it is common to develop a standardized approach to issues which have to be resolved frequently. These routines develop into tendencies, are ingrained in conscious and unconscious memory, and constrain behaviour and thinking when a new task or issue has to be addressed. As organizations are groups of individuals, their behaviour and decision-making process, though more complicated, are not much different from those of individuals.

The feeling that government decisions are irrational often proceeds from the premise that organizations can be rational in the sense individuals ought to be. In actuality, governmental decision-making is not the outcome of the rational calculations of a single actor but of reconciling the different points of view of the departments that together constitute the government. Each department has primary responsibility for a few tasks, and that responsibility constitutes its mandate and conditions its functioning, be it analysing an issue or performing a task. Most issues span several departments, and therefore resolution of an issue requires consideration by more than one department. Over time each department would have acquired a distinct identity as well as a distinct way of functioning, the distinctiveness being an offshoot of its mandate and the experience it gained in fulfilling its mandate. From a department's point of view, its distinctive way of analysing an issue is rational as it might help it to fulfil its mandate. However, from the point of view of the government as a whole, the department's point of view , or to use jargon its *angle of vision*, might be no more than tunnel vision, and as such not rational. In exceptional situations, a department might readily give up its solipsism and be a willing team player; however, exceptions prove the rule that disagreements, dissensions, and conflicts are the breath of life in any organization, a hierarchy of bodies such as the Committee of Secretaries (COS), Cabinet Committees, and the Cabinet exist to reconcile the differences, and consequently, the mills of government grind slowly as the divergent viewpoints have to be reconciled. Lest the conclusion should be drawn that the tussle among departments is unique in the government, it should be said that other types of organizations are no different; yet disagreements and conflicts in business organizations come out less frequently into open as compared to the government.[13] No less importantly, other types of organizations are driven by the pursuit of one or two objectives, say profit maximization or increasing market share in case of business organizations. In case the government often has to pursue many, often conflicting, objectives simultaneously.

It is impossible for an individual or a single branch of knowledge or a single department within the government to look at a complex policy problem from all possible points of view and to visualize all the possible policy options. Working in groups can, in principle, stretch the boundaries of bounded rationality. The whole is occasionally larger than the sum of parts. A group, particularly if it is diverse, can be more rational than the individuals that comprise the group. The multiple interactions that take place in groups within the government along with the interaction with the 'players' outside the government can be considered to be a *social method of analysis* that helps overcome, to some extent, the constraints imposed by bounded rationality. Furthermore, these interactions enhance the acceptability of decisions. The merit of democracy lies in its being a government by dialogue. Human beings disagree about almost everything; there is no satisfactory "rational" analytic method for resolving disparate perceptions and priorities into collective choices. Only through the multiple interactions built into the public policy process can disagreements be resolved—never fully though. It is said that for the great problems of life there are no solutions, only adjustments. The same can be said of public policies. All policymaking is, in a sense, about trade-offs. Interactive adjustment facilitates a weighing of trade-offs, something that is usually impossible using analysis alone. However, having to balance many considerations, public policymaking is arduous.

Given that the policy process has the potential to generate more "rational" policies than what any individual could, the question arises what are the conditions necessary to ensure that the potentiality

[13] Organizational (office) politics is intrinsic to every organization. Those who believe that organizational politics does not impact on business decision-making are advised to read the witty play by Anurag Mathur, *Scenes from an Executive Life*, New Delhi: Penguin, 2000.

becomes a reality. First, the decision-making mechanisms should facilitate free exchange of opinion. Second, they should provide for groups outside to canvass their viewpoints; third and most importantly, there should be a strong mechanism for reconciling competing viewpoints, duly balancing the time needed for due deliberation and the need for a timely response. Although democracy means government by discussion, it is rightly said 'it is only effective if you can stop people talking' at some point of time;[14] India 'it seems, will never reach the point'.[15]

b. The UP Fracas from a Theoretical Perspective

The basic issue underlying *l'affaire UP* was the question whether the bank's offer of IDA credit for basic education should be availed or not, and if so, on what terms.

DEA as the department responsible for the macroeconomic management of the economy and for maintaining the balance of payments and, to that end, mobilizing foreign exchange, particularly foreign exchange available on soft terms such as grants from bilateral agencies and soft IDA loans from the bank, was extremely keen that the UP Project be as large as possible, posed to the World Bank at the very earliest, and concentrate on programme components which facilitate fast disbursal of IDA loan by the bank. Yet given the allocation of business among different departments of governments, project development was the responsibility of the line ministry concerned, say DOE in respect of education. Given the opposition of DOE, DEA could have taken the matter to the Cabinet, but it was unlikely that given the strong objection to bank financing by many academics, the Cabinet would have overridden DOE. Only after Bordia settled the terms of engagement with the bank, a decision to avail bank funding was taken. However, by deciding that the bank funding would be slotted for a state project in UP, Bordia brought a new actor in the 'play', and DOE unwittingly got into a trilateral negotiation between GOI, the UP government, and the World Bank; the negotiation unexpectedly turned out into a messy *ménage à trios*.

Bordia was accustomed to prepare drafts for his deputies and project documents for the states. He found UP to be utterly different. UP was

[14] Attributed to Clement Atlee, British Prime Minister (1945–51).

[15] 'Survey of India and China, *The Economist*, March 5, 2005.

not Bihar or Rajasthan for several reasons. For Bihar, BEP was a bonanza by the grace of Bordia. Bihar was never an attractive investment destination; its financial position was parlous. The promised outlay was staggering by Indian standards; the contribution of UNICEF and the central government, about 83 per cent of the outlay, was grant, and unlike a loan from the World Bank, not repayable. As to Lok Jumbish, Bordia hailed from the state of Rajasthan, and was a son of the soil with an extensive network of kinsmen, NGOs, officers, and ministers. And then the outlay was too meagre to elicit close scrutiny by the state government. As later events showed, the harmonious relationship between Bordia and the state government, particularly the State Education Department, did not persist forever. Eventually, Bordia was eased out of Lok Jumbish. In contrast to BEP and Lok Jumbish, the UP project was a state project financed by a loan, a different ball game altogether. Conceptually, a state project is a project designed by the state in the light of its own priorities and developmental strategy albeit within the national framework. It is only because the bank's charter prohibits a state from directly accessing loans that the central government gets into the picture. It would be natural for the state government to consider the central government as a conduit, as an agent helping it to access external resources and, as such, having no overriding right whatsoever to lay down what the project should be. Between November 1990 and May 1992, UP saw the turnover of four state education secretaries, and of the state government. With every change, Bordia worked his charm on each new arrival: education secretaries, education ministers, Chief Minister, and even those who were in a position to influence ministers and Chief Minister. But all to no avail. With the stalemate, there was bitterness among the parties to internal negotiations, namely DOE, UP government, and DEA. The UP government and DEA felt that DOE was unreasonable and obstructive, and that the area of divergence was limited and did not warrant not posing the project to the bank. The bank was more than willing to lend; DEA was very keen to get the loan through as bank projects in social sectors such as health and education were critical for India accessing adequately the concessional IDA funds; the faster the disbursal of bank funds, the better for the foreign exchange situation. DEA was very conscious of its position as the *malik* (Lord) of foreign assistance. Laying down the framework of cooperation with bilateral agencies and multilateral financing institutions was its turf. Every organization is extremely possessive of its turf, and DEA is no exception. Furthermore, there is weighty rationale for its nodal role. It was expedient for the country to have a single focal point for interaction with agencies. That would enhance its bargaining power and the ability to get foreign aid on the best possible financial terms. From its perspective, DEA had no difficulty with the state determining the project parameters, so long as its gatekeeper role was duly acknowledged and so long as the project design facilitated fast disbursal; that being so, it was felt that DOE seemed to be mindlessly intrusive in project design by the state. On their part, the UP officials bitterly resented the domineering attitude of DOE. In dealing with the World Bank, UP was no babe; on the contrary, it had experience of negotiating and implementing several World Bank projects, and standard operating procedures for the design and management of Bank projects were in place. The key players in UP just could not understand how an education project could be different from, say, an agriculture project, and quite a few wondered what could be a policy angle in an area such as basic education. The State Education Department and its professional functionaries themselves did not fully share the vision Bordia had for the basic education project; they had different views on the strategy to universalize elementary education, relative priorities of project components, coverage, and organizational arrangements for implementation. Within the State Education Department, NFE and adult education were viewed as Cinderella who, unlike in the fairy tale, did not go to the ball and later marry the Prince. Domestic funds were available for adult education and NFE. It was primary schooling, particularly construction of school buildings that faced resource shortage. They could not understand Bordia's insistence that the project should be managed by a new society even though primary education was already being looked after by a body called *Basic Siksha Parishad*. Furthermore, the conviction of the key UP players that the education project was no different from other Bank projects was reinforced by the fact that its financial terms were no different from others financed by loans from the Bank, wherein the state had to repay 70 per cent of the loan. And then, in a departure from the past precedent, Bordia sought to micro-manage a project for which the central government did not extend any financial assistance. What Bordia demanded was not consistent with the tradition of either Bank projects or CSSs.

On its part, DOE felt that it was UP, which was unreasonable, and that its functionaries did not adequately understand the nature of the project. It would cease to be a test case project if there was no adequate probing of the Bank's willingness to finance components other than primary schooling. Also at stake was the role of the DOE, its responsibility to enforce the CABE parameters for external financing. However, it had a weak hand as it had no policy lever to prod the UP to fall in line. From the negotiation perspective, a test case project seeks to probe the outermost limits of the other side's willingness to give in. A test pilot tests the endurance of an engine; a negotiator, in a game of testing the wills, tests the endurance of the other side. A negotiation in that condition is more likely to be testing than to exude hail-fellow-well-met-bonhomie. When a stalemate results in any negotiation, it is customary to blame the other side for lack of bona fides, and for its abrasive negotiating style, and to lose sight of the intrinsic complexity of the substance of negotiation. Likewise, if the UP project turned out to be a testing than a test-case project, it was not solely due to the personalities of key players—although the personalities did aggravate a difficult situation. Substantive divisive issues existed. By yoking the test case to a single state, DOE became a hostage to that state. Invoking the imagery of the test flight once again, there were two, not one, pilots at the cockpit and there was a tussle between them as to who should be in the pilot's seat.

Even CSSs which are substantially funded by the central government from its own resources and implemented by the states with the grant provided by the central government are enmeshed in a complex web of negotiations at three levels—within the central government, within each state government, and between the central government and state governments. If a CSS is to be launched and effectively implemented, it is necessary to reconcile divergent perceptions on whether there should be a CSS at all, and if so, what its design and parameters should be. Within the central government itself, there would be divergent views on these issues, with the Planning Commission being generally averse to the launch of new CSSs and opposed to any proposal of an administrative department to launch a new CSS. Within the state governments themselves, opinions differ on CSSs. Administrative departments have been very keen to have more and more of them so that they can have more resources. On the other hand, chief ministers and the state finance and planning departments have been persistently demanding that the centre should transfer the funds it expends on the CSSs to the states as a block grant and should leave it to the states to develop and implement programmes anchored in the local context. It has been rightly said that by offering grant, federal government does not buy compliance, and that it only acquires an opportunity to bargain with the states.[16] The CSSs are no exception. A CSS creates a principal-agent relationship between the centre and the sates; the centre releases fund to the states in the expectation that states would implement the scheme in accordance with the scheme parameters. Principal-agent relationship is beset with the *agency problem*, that is to say the agent may not always act according to the interests and instructions of the principal. The central and state governments are mutually interdependent to an exceptional degree, and are evenly balanced in their power. The states no doubt need central funding; however, the centre needs the states no less for implementation of the policies the CSSs seek to implement. Alternative modalities such as enlisting NGOs for implementation may be of limited utility as the operations of NGOs are unlikely to reach the scale that implementation of these schemes necessitates. The instruments that private parties take resort to, in order to avoid the agency problem (for example, MOUs and contracts that lay down clearly performance standards, performance-linked incentives, and penalties for non-performance or underperformance) are likely to be less effective with constitutional entities such as the central and state governments being the principal and agents. Stoppage of funds or excluding some states from the purview of the scheme for non-performance or underperformance defeats the very purpose of such schemes, for many of the schemes seek to reduce inter-state disparities in levels of development, and the states which generally underperform are often the very states with low levels of development. Suffice it to say, effective implementation of a CSS requires not only good design and intense monitoring but also continual dialogue and bargaining with state governments. Suffice to say, tensions are thus intrinsic to the implementation of these programmes, and departments such as DOE have to get involved in continual dialogue with the states,

[16] Helen Ingram, 'Policy Implementation through Bargaining: The Case of Federal Grants-in-Aid'. *Public Policy*, 25, no. 4 (Fall 1977), pp. 499–526.

cajoling and coaxing the state finance departments to ensure timely release of funds, and prodding the state departments of education to effectively implement the schemes in accordance with the scheme parameters and guidelines. Banks do roll over overdue loans. Likewise, offering more funds may be sometimes the only way to prod utilization of funds already released!

Accessing external funding adds additional dimensions of complexity, transforming an *as-it-is* complex relationship between the central and state governments into a more complex triangular relationship of the agency, centre, and states. The complexity of the triangular relationship is further accentuated if more than one agency funds a programme. Legally an agency can provide financial resources only to the central government which is legally liable for repayment if the funding provided is a loan and for fulfilment of all the conditions subject to which the funding is provided. Support by an agency is conditional on an agreement being reached with the central government on the content of a project, and the modalities of implementation including phasing of the financial flows, monitoring and evaluation, verifiable benchmarks, and performance indicators. In order to ensure the accountability of the states, agencies associate the states concerned with in formal negotiations and agreements. However, legally the centre alone is responsible for compliance with the terms of agreement. Consequently, the centre has to wrestle with the tensions and challenges of *indirect management*. Generally in 'state projects' funded by agencies, the central government just plays the role of a conduit for flow of funds from the agency to the state; the triangular relationship functions in effect as a bilateral relationship between the state and the agency, with the task manager of the agency being closely associated with the implementation of the project, if not the development of the project itself. Consequently, the burden cast on the central government by the compulsions of indirect management is mitigated to some extent. If, however, the centre wishes to be more than just a conduit for flow of funds from an agency to the states, a triangular relationship between the funding agency and the central and state governments is put to severe stress and strain.

The preparation of the UP Project document was not just a rational technical exercise of deciding the project objectives and components, identifying the best approaches to achieving project objectives, costing the components, and identifying the implementation modalities.

DOE and the UP government had sharply divergent perceptions and interests. No project document could be posed to the Bank unless DOE and the UP government reached an agreement either through successful negotiation or one side being able to coerce the other side to surrender. Contrary to Bordia's expectation, UP was not a passive spectator, nor a pushover. The acrimony in the discussions between Bordia and the bankers—external negotiations—was nothing comparable to that in the internal negotiations between DOE and the UP government, proving the proposition that internal negotiations could be more acrimonious than the external negotiations. Given its organizational interest in posing a large, fast-disbursing project at the very earliest, DEA was an ally of the UP government. DEA's organizational interest was reinforced by the fact that the key officers dealing with the project in the Fund–Bank Division of DEA were IAS officers from the UP cadre. However, those officers could not clinch the issue on their own without going to the Cabinet; because of the political interests of the ruling party as well of the key players such as Prime Minister P.V. Narasimha Rao and Arjun Singh, the Cabinet was unlikely to support them and override DOE. As a former Minister, MHRD, the Prime Minister was fully aware of the political salience of the Bank lending to basic education and had, in 1987, declined President Conable's offer. And it was a well-known fact that Arjun Singh was out and out a challenger who wanted to wrest the office of the Prime Minister by opposing economic reforms and claiming that, unlike PV who was soft on BJP, he was a relentless crusader against the BJP and Hindutva forces. PV was a *jujutsu* wrestler preferring to manipulate the opponent's force against himself rather than confronting it with one's own force. He would be the last person to give his rival a *cause celebre* and an opportunity to criticize him for 'selling off' Indian education to the World Bank and favouring a BJP-ruled state. It is no wonder that the Cabinet Secretary was unwilling to use the authority of his office and resolve the differences between DOE and the UP government.

Every Dark Cloud Has a Silver Lining

As the stand-off with UP continued, Middleton and Cambridge would often visit K to ascertain the status of the project preparation. Occasionally, Skolnik would come over from Washington and his meetings with Bordia were stormier than usual for no particular reason except perhaps that Bordia wanted to sublimate his frustration with UP officials by lashing at Skolnik and his colleagues. In fairness to the Bank functionaries, it should be said that they stayed aloof as the spat between Bordia and UP officials continued; maybe they expected that other interested parties would pull the chestnuts out of fire for them. Given the dire need of foreign exchange, DEA could not be a passive spectator for far too long. Many state governments were eager to have projects of their own like the UP Project. It was reasonable to expect that it was only a matter of time before DOE gave in to the pressure of DEA and the state governments. Whatever, in one of his many meetings with Bordia, Skolnik was incensed when Bordia called him and Cambridge as mere technicians. Skolnik, Middleton, and Cambridge would follow K to his room after these encounters where over a cup of tea they would try to recover their composure. K's soothing words helped build a personal rapport with them. K began to work on a contingent plan to get out of the impasse, to enable DOE to test the earnestness of the Bank without being a hostage to a state government as in UP. The lesson that K drew from the UP fracas was that if external funding were to be accessed on a large scale without infringing the CABE parameters, external funding should not be utilized for 'state projects'. The brick and mortar approach to educational development was deep rooted in the states, and it was extremely difficult for the central government to wean the states away from that approach in 'state projects'. In their eagerness to secure as large a flow of resources as possible in the shortest possible time, the state governments were unlikely to stand up to the agencies and categorically insist that agency functionaries would not 'mother' the project impairing the development of capacity to autonomously develop and implement the projects. If external funding were accessed for a central programme, and the central government funded the state governments for the formulation and implementation of district projects, the cosy bilateral relationship between the agency and the state government would give way to a set of two discrete bilateral relations, one between the centre and the agency, and another between the centre and states. DOE would acquire a fiscal lever to forcefully wean the states away from the brick and mortar approach; in addition, DOE could also take advantage of the deep-rooted tendency of states to unquestioningly accept and abide by the terms and conditions of externally aided projects. For developing a programme he had in mind, he drew upon a nascent idea of district projects mooted by DOE in its proposals for the Eighth Five-Year Plan which were submitted to the Planning Commission in November 1991, and which was being tried out in Sitamarhi. He also drew upon a chance remark of Bordia in the April 1991 workshop of crafting a loan that would lie in between a specific investment loan and sectoral investment loan. It appeared to him that the analogy cited by Skolnik in the Shanghai Communiqué, of the Bank refinancing IDBI and ICICI, could serve as the basis for crafting such a loan. Why not try to secure refinancing from the World Bank within the framework of a specific investment loan instead of a policy loan? That would be the best of all worlds, the flexibility of a policy loan without policy conditionalities and Bank oversight. By February 1992, K conceived of an India Primary Education Fund set up by DOE by pooling resources, both domestic and external. The fund would be managed by DOE and used to implement the district-based strategy proposed in November 1991 by DOE in its proposals for the Eighth Five-Year Plan. The fund would offer technical support to the states to develop district plans; like the Bank, it would appraise, finance, monitor, and evaluate the projects. States which accept the parameters set by the fund would be eligible for support. Preference could be given to educationally backward districts. Before supporting the fund, the Bank and other agencies supporting the fund would examine a few district projects appraised by the fund to satisfy itself that the fund has the technical competence to appraise the projects, and that the appraisal by the fund was rigorous. In effect, DOE would be the Bank as far as the states are concerned in that apart from disbursing funds, it would perform many of the management and supervisory functions normally associated with the Bank. Competition among the states was in-built in the fund idea. The message to states was loud and clear. Abide by the framework laid out by DOE and perform, and you would be rewarded by approval of more and more district projects. Conversely, if you play the Prima Donna, you would be left high and dry. During his exploratory informal talks, K found that the idea of fund appealed to Skolnik, Middleton, and Cambridge on several counts, particularly its holistic, context-based strategy to achieve UEE. Chance favours the prepared mind. In retrospect, this contingent planning came in handy to creatively respond to unexpected developments which appeared 4 months later and convert a potential threat to the department's strategy of engaging the Bank into a great opportunity to launch DPEP and hasten the country's march to UEE. The new relationship that DPEP sought to establish imposed a heavy burden of unlearning on established agencies as well as on the states, most of whom had a long experience of implementing externally funded projects in the traditional bilateral pattern of relationship between the agency and the state government. Unlearning could take place only after bitter struggles in which DOE prevailed; those struggles are interesting episodes in the DPEP saga which would be narrated later.

K mooted with Bordia the idea of utilizing the India Primary Education Fund as a vehicle for tapping Bank funding for primary education. However, he did not respond to K's idea, and seemed in no mood to entertain any alternative to the test case project. Bordia was in a farewell mood, trying to consolidate whatever he initiated rather than explore new avenues. His heart was more in BEP and Lok Jumbish, and if the test case project did not go ahead, he was not unduly concerned. His unstated feeling seemed to be that if the Bank funding did not come through because of the intransigence of UP, all the more better. K was not sure that the Bank could be warded off; UP or no UP, constructive engagement with the Bank seemed unavoidable because of the macroeconomic situation and increasing pressure from states to permit them to access bank funds for education. The decision to develop a test case project was akin to opening Pandora's box, which once opened cannot be closed.

XI

CHANGE OF GUARD

Even for an obsessive workaholic like Bordia, the last few months before retirement from government service on 31 May 1992 were unduly hectic. As an extremely astute civil servant, he worked overtime to bring to fruition the tasks he had undertaken and ensure that his favourite creations were not uprooted once he left the stage. The frequent hurricane-like visitations stirred up such a frenzy of activity in Bihar, and he spent the last month in office giving finishing touches to the Sitamarhi district plan. In retrospect, it was his Last Hurrah in service. When he was not in Bihar, he was spending long hours in office, working on the revision of NPE, 1986, and on the design of Lok Jumbish. He was also prodding the UP government to fall in line and design the UP Project in the manner he wanted. He was successful in steering the revision of NPE, 1986, to a happy ending. About 20 days prior to his retirement, the revised policy was placed before the Parliament. Bordia undertook three measures to ensure that his creations outlasted his tenure. First, through headhunting he sought to spot younger officers whom he can mould and place in important positions in the education system, so that there would be more like him within the system, and his innovative creations would survive his retirement from the government. K himself was one such officer. Second, he sought to create a halo of success and phenomenal innovation around his programmes by engaging friendly consultants to evaluate the programmes, co-opting media, and working through his network of friends in the national and international arena so that his successors as well as the government dare not disband his creations. Third, he expected that his programmes would create a sufficiently critical mass of active and competent activists who could exert pressure on the central and state governments and ensure that the programmes continued to be implemented strictly in accordance with the principles he laid down while designing the programmes. TLCs and MS are good examples.

In spite of his superhuman effort, Bordia did not succeed in accomplishing whatever he wanted to. UP was obviously an unfinished business; but it was emblematic of the fact that his grand design of basic education projects appeared to be on the verge of collapsing like a proverbial house of cards. In the aftermath of the Jomtien Conference, Bordia envisioned the prospect of all the educationally backward states to be covered by one basic education project or other. Andhra Pradesh had APPEP, Bihar the flagship EFA project BEP, and Rajasthan SIDA funded Lok Jumbish. The mighty World Bank appeared to have been tamed and was desperate to fund primary education on Bordia's terms, and UP was strategically chosen for World Bank funding. In pursuance of its strategy to emerge as an actor in its own right with an identity of its own transcending the identities of the nations that constituted it, the European Economic Community (EEC) also was eager to join the EFA game and offered to fund a project, and fourteen districts of MP were chosen for EEC funding of a project with the picturesque name of Roopantar (transformation). The choice of MP was strategic, for Arjun Singh hailed from MP and had been its chief minister thrice. UNESCO offered to assist an EFA project; five tribal districts of MP were chosen for the project which was given another picturesque name of Dhumkuria (youth dormitory in tribal areas). Bordia was under the impression that UNDP, one of the sponsors of the Jomtien Conference, had set up a special facility at its headquarters for funding EFA projects, and wanted to access it for a project in South Orissa. The German Embassy also showed interest in funding the South Orissa Project. Thus, Bordia's plans covered all the educationally backward states except Assam, Arunachal Pradesh, and Karnataka. Given the political and strategic salience of the North East, external funding did not seem expedient. It did not seem difficult to cover Karnataka soon.

The best laid plans of mice and men, it is said, often go awry, and Bordia's plans did. It was clear when he demitted office that BEP, the flagship EFA project, was not majestically sailing towards its destination. The wind appeared to be inclement. There were enough indications that UNICEF could never mobilize the supplementary resources that were anticipated for BEP and looked to DOE to prevail upon DEA to divert unutilized funds allocated by bilateral agencies to it so that it could fund BEP. It could not depart from its financial and accounting procedures, and its functionaries seemed to run amok as if BEP were their fiefdom. SIDA accorded approval for funding only a pilot phase of Lok Jumbish with a modest outlay. Not even in his dreams did Bordia imagine that his intention of subjecting the World Bank to an *agni pariksha* (the test of fire) would be thwarted by the obduracy of the UP officials, and that all his blandishments would fail. The other projects appeared non-starters. For whatever reason, he evinced little interest in the two MP projects. The ever-cash-strapped UNESCO had only plenty of advice—much of it of little practical utility—to offer. It eventually turned out that what UNESCO had in mind was assistance to prepare a project for being posed to a funding agency. It was a help which India did not need all the more so as the experts deputed from UNESCO headquarters, to put it charitably, did not have expertise that would have complemented domestically available expertise. That apart, associating expatriate agencies and consultants would have fallen foul of the parameters approved by CABE in March 1991 for availing external finance for primary education; it would have been odd to permit UNESCO to participate in project preparation while stoutly denying a similar role for the World Bank. Roopantar was going nowhere as neither the donor not the recipient had any idea of how to go about. There were enough signs that it was difficult to deal with the Germans. In March 1992, without any prior consultation with K, they got DEA to agree during bilateral discussions to organize a workshop on the South Orissa Project with two moderators. K was worried that he would get a rap on the knuckles for not keeping a tab on the bilateral discussions. To his utter surprise, Bordia was rather avuncular, and said it was time to deliver farewell sermons. He said, 'We should stick to our positions, even though they were unpopular.' He declared, 'we want their money and not their directions or foreign personnel'. He said he conveyed 'our position' to the German Minister for

Development Cooperation in a meeting in Paris. He cautioned K that Germans would be very difficult to deal with as their procedures were very rigid, and they were particular about associating their personnel with the project development and implementation. His observations were indeed prophetic; the Germans were the donors with whom K could make no headway, and eventually K had to close the discussions saying enough was enough. During the tête-à-tête, he told K that he was no longer interesting in taking up new ventures such as the MP and Orissa projects, and would be happy to tie up loose ends of BEP, Lok Jumbish, and UP projects.

UNDP proved to be a broken reed. John Lawrence, the key functionary at the UNDP headquarters dealing with education, called on Bordia on 2 April 1992. It came out that, contrary to Bordia's expectation, UNDP did not have at its headquarters any special facility which could be drawn to finance an EFA project in South Orissa. It was also apparent from the meeting with Lawrence that the UNDP Governing Council had decided to shift the allocation of resources from technology transfer to human development; however, Lawrence made it clear that the conception of human development went far beyond Jomtien goals, and envisaged an emphasis on linkages between different sectors such as education and health. Thereupon Bordia delivered Lawrence a long sermon on the Jomtien Conference, the pledges given by UNDP and other agencies to fund EFA, and the indication given by the sponsors that resources would not be a constraint on the achievement of the Jomtien goals. Lawrence made it clear that what all UNDP could do was to provide seed money and try to rope in agencies having substantial funds such as the Bank. Pitching for a non-available UNDP support while not being able to access the deep pockets of the Bank was the stuff of which tragi-comedies are made. Whatever, Bordia bluntly told him that there was no need for an intermediary for India to tap funds from the World Bank or other agencies. Ironically, while UNDP looked at the Bank to provide substantive funding, UNESCO looked at UNDP for funding. Frederico Mayor, DG, UNESCO, wrote to the Administrator, UNDP, seeking $10 million for the Dhumkuria. The hopes for domestic funding of district projects were no brighter. In its eight Five-Year Plan proposals (November 1991), DOE made substantial provision for district projects in the expectation that domestic and external funding would be available in large measure. However, the domestic resource scene was forbidding.

The calibrated strategy of accessing Bank funding seemed to be on the verge of collapse. If man's difficulty is God's opportunity, a country's macroeconomic crisis is a God-sent opportunity for the Bank and the IMF. With the country precariously dependent on IMF and Bank support for not defaulting on its obligations, DOE gave the impression of being a dog in the manger by dilly-dallying forever on accessing Bank funding for primary education, and coming in the way of accessing much-needed foreign exchange. The decision to pose a test case project to the World Bank was figuratively like opening the Pandora's Box which, once opened, could not be closed. State governments, particularly finance secretaries, are always on the lookout for new ways of accessing funds from the central government and funding agencies such as the Bank. That being so, while the UP project did not make any headway it whetted the appetite of other states to access Bank funding for education. From early 1991, several states began to press for Bank-funded education projects. At a meeting taken by Mira Seth, Secretary, Department of Women and Child Development, K was besieged like Abhimanyu (tragic hero of *Mahabharata*) in *chakravyuha* (a labyrinth-like military formation which is difficult to penetrate, and once penetrated, is almost impossible to exit). Mira was discussing in that meeting her grand design of empowering all the women of Haryana in a record period of just five years and exploring the possibility of tapping funds from various departments and United Nations Population Fund (UNFPA) to implement that design. The Education Secretary, Haryana, who was one of the participants, began to wax eloquent about the imperative of mounting a Marshall Plan of sorts for constructing school buildings and appointing teachers. There was no need for any advocacy for girl's education; the state was bulging with demand for education for girls, and what all was needed was providing access and school facilities. K questioned his claim and informed that DOE had no budgetary provision for school building construction or for appointment of teachers unless such appointment conformed to the parameters of Operation Blackboard. Tevia Abrahams of UNFPA, who was on his way to Bali to attend a meeting, said that UNFPA could not finance school infrastructure; however, he had it from the Bank that it would finance a massive educational infrastructure project. K had to put forth his department's line that education was more than access and infrastructure, and that DOE would not support any project unless its experience of the UP test case project was satisfactory. And furthermore, he firmly added that his department would not support an infrastructure project only to elicit the derisive remark, 'Mr K, what would you support?' K went on to say that the functionaries of the Bank were going round states offering assistance for primary education and egging them on to pose projects, and that this could not be countenanced. However, it was well-nigh impossible to be an Abominable No-man forever, and resist the pressure from DEA and from the states far too long on philosophical grounds and by contending that other states should wait till the test case project ran its natural course. It seemed that all was lost, and that DOE could no more persevere with its strategy of engaging the Bank.

It is only with passage of time can one discern the outcome of events, a fact captured from the purported reply of Zhou Enlai to the question about the impact of the French Revolution that 'it is too early say'. When one looks back, one realizes that what then seemed to be happening was not what happened. If the measures of success in regard to EFA projects are quantitative indicators such as the number of projects firmed up, the coverage of the projects, the financial resources pledged, and so on, the period from Jomtien to Mahabhinishkramana does not have much to show. But if, instead, the measure is contribution to future developments and the impact on the course of future events, the period comes out to be momentous. During this period, great clarity emerged on many critical strategies: the strategy for hastening the march towards UPE, the strategy for harnessing external assistance in a mode of equal partnership, and the strategy for being in the driver's seat and effect donor's coordination, which is spoken about but little practised. The impression of this period can be seen on DPEP, SSA, and all other subsequent developments in the field of elementary education.

In September 1993, 15 months after his retirement, Bordia expounded his worldview of dealing with the external agencies in his presentation at the NIEPA workshop on planning and management of educational improvement programmes for basic education. His presentation, entitled *Adjusting to a New Culture*, was implicitly a rudimentary negotiation analysis which K learnt from the course of James Sebenius at Harvard. The presentation had much to say on who are they, what do they want, and what our negotiation strategy and style should be. Bordia began his presentation with the observation that for EFAs (external finance agencies, a typical Bordia play on words, a play on the acronym EFA, which usually stands for education for all) education is a new area in India. Therefore, it was necessary to establish new relationships and build mutual confidence. EFAs accepted India's special capability, but that recognition needed to be reconfirmed in education. We should be on guard against EFA's tendency to determine project parameters as in countries such as Pakistan and Bangladesh. We would have to learn from the experience of other projects where India determined parameters. We should maintain dignity and cordiality with aloofness, show self-confidence and humility, and demonstrate our professional excellence. We should convert the interest of EFAs into an opportunity. Whether we like or not, we would have to meet certain demands of EFAs. These include target setting in quantitative terms, accountability, adoption of a systemic approach, use of modern techniques of project management, crisp documentation, MIS, and clear channels for flow of funds. Most things that would seem unreasonable are indeed negotiable. Thus, it should be possible to set process targets along with quantitative targets and do away with the contractor system for construction of school buildings. Further, these demands could be used as an opportunity for capacity building in the states, strengthen the effectiveness of the education system at the district and block levels, introduce a management system at the sub-block cluster level, operationalize village-level participatory planning, which was so far a mere idea, and rejuvenate resource institutions. Thus, it is an opportunity for systemic change, decentralization, and capacity building. Although Bordia's exposition was 15 months after his retirement, K had intuitively absorbed Bordia's vision by observing him closely and conflated that vision with his own views on international economic relations and the precious lessons he learnt from Sebenius and the experiential wisdom he gained from a reflection on the frustrating experience of getting the UP officers on board in designing the test case project, and of BEP; they constituted the conceptual underpinnings of his development of DPEP and engagement with external agencies. To be honest, however, the normative negotiating vision that Bordia put forth in the NIEPA workshop did not always inform his engagement with agencies. However, to draw upon the life of Buddha, after Mahabhinishkramana (the Great Departure), when the Master exited the official world, Ananda (K the disciple) was ready to face the world.

Old soldiers do not always fade away. While his formal association with DOE, TLCs, and EFA projects except for Lok Jumbish ceased, Bordia kept a close tab on what was happening in ERP projects like everything else connected with his former department much like Stasi, the East German secret police, whose creed was 'to know everything'. It was said of Sir Robert Morant, the legendary British civil servant renowned for landmark contribution to education at the beginning of the twentieth century, that 40 years later James Chuter Ede, the Permanent Secretary in Education Department, found himself grappling with Morant's ghost when piloting the 1943 Bill through the House of Commons. Like Morant, even after retirement Bordia remained a highly visible live presence on the education landscape in the country and on the international scene, and took excessive interest in the affairs of his erstwhile department. He spread the impression among agencies such as UNESCO that it was he alone who mattered, and some functionaries in UNESCO believed and acted as if it were true. That annoyed Giri and infuriated Arjun Singh. Bordia's friends in the media made matters worse by publishing reports that after the exit of Bordia programmes such as Operation Blackboard and TLCs were collapsing, and that Arjun Singh was all the time politicking and neglecting his charge. There were rumours among the feminists active in MS that the programme was collapsing; all of a sudden the Director of that programme decided to resign at short notice giving the impression that the decision to resign was at the behest of Bordia and designed to ensure the collapse of that programme. On the spur of the moment, K suggested to Giri that Vrinda Sarup better be appointed Director, MS, straightaway so that the programme was not disrupted. The appointment of an outstanding lady officer with sharp gender sensibility as Director provoked a media friend of Bordia to come up with a story about the bureaucratization of MS; never mind that eminent social activists and feminists such as Ela Bhatt, nationally and internationally renowned for the stellar role she played in labour, cooperative, women, and microfinance movements, were associated with the National Resource Group of MS which guided the programme.Vrinda's appointment proved to be an inspired choice indeed as she steered the programme splendidly winning the admiration of the feminist fraternity. She brought bear on her work a rare mix of extreme sensitivity to the uniqueness of the programme and administrative capability of the highest order.

K was not happy with what Bordia was doing, for he strongly believed that, like death, moving out of a job was a certainty and that once an officer moves out he should not haunt his erstwhile arena of action and should instead let his successor manage affairs according to his own light. K believed that, like Bhisma in *Mahabharata* who would fight for whoever ruled Hastinapur (the capital of his kingdom), his *dharma* (duty) lay in being loyal to Bordia's successor, however much highly he esteemed Bordia. That seemed to annoy Bordia; in turn, his feeling annoyed K. His trying to practise what he learnt from Bordia got K into deep trouble with Bordia. As Education Secretary, Bordia would not brook any state government directly dealing and settling matters with agencies; yet, as Chairperson of Lok Jumbish, he precisely did the very opposite, treating the central government as if it were no more than a jatrani at best to be kept in good humour, and presenting DOE with one *fait accompli* after another. K was caught in the middle: Bordia was annoyed that K was reading the rule book while Govindarajan of DEA and Arjun Singh the Minister faulted K for letting Bordia run amok. Bordia's relations with Arjun Singh are best characterized as a Cold War about to flare up into a hot war; given the wide impression in the department that K was Bordia's blue-eyed boy, K was as it is suspect in the eyes of the minister and his factotums. Office politics being an ineluctable condition of any organization, in their conversation with the minister, quite a few colleagues of K would try to run down K by flaunting K's connection with Bordia. An incident in K's office aggravated matters. Around the time when newspapers carried reports of Arjun Singh and his acolyte Digvijay Singh, Chief Minister of Madhya Pradesh, falling out, K was having a chat with his friend from MP cadre who was Secretary to Digvijay Singh. Bordia dropped in, and as was his wont, began to banter and, in the course of conversation, told Digvijay Singh's aide that he was happy that his boss was standing up to Arjun Singh. Somehow this remark reached Arjun Singh, and a thunderous minute descended on K for slack supervision of Lok Jumbish and for letting Bordia get away with whatever Bordia wanted to merely because he was K's former boss. Like Morant, Bordia was prone to unleash a vendetta against everyone who disagreed with him, and it was now K's turn to be at the receiving end of a vendetta for going by the rule book. What hurt K most were Bordia's efforts to throw a spanner in K's efforts to constructively engage the external funding agencies in difficult circumstances, to develop DPEP, and to ensure that states conform to the DPEP frame. Freed from the burden of office and, consequently, under no obligation to engage the World Bank he was more critical than ever of the Bank and its operations, oblivious to the fact that the terms of engagement were exactly the same as those he laid down while in office. Bordia had many admirers who occupied important positions in State Education Departments. With his indefatigable energy, Bordia toured the states and encouraged his acolytes not to fall in line with the DPEP frame which he derided as a Cambridge–Middleton matrix. K would not have been hurt so much if Bordia came out in the open and squarely criticized the engagement of agencies as many critics did. Again and again, whenever they met either alone or along with Giri, Bordia would compliment K for the way K engaged agencies and for steadfastly adhering to the path 'we together' laid down. K was human, all too human incapable of practising Christian forbearance. He developed a pathological aversion to Bordia and his activities; perhaps he let transient emotions influence his actions. In that mood, Mark Antony's one-liner in Julius Caesar, 'The evil that men do lives after them; the good they is interred with their bones', came true. K would often recall with bitterness the ordeal of coping with Bordia's work style, the swings in his moods, his occasional cussed behaviour, as well as the angst arising from ideological and temperamental differences. Given his current moods, Bordia's extraordinary ability to manage men and matters appeared to be unscrupulous scheming and manipulation; quite a few imageries would come to his mind—a spider weaving webs, and lying in wait to entrap and exterminate all opposition, an unscrupulous enemy sneakily planting booby traps and landmines to blow away opponents, and an Orwellian Big Brother .

For several years, K reflected again and again on his intellectual differences with Bordia, and sought to view them from a larger context. It seemed to him that an apt analogy was the battle between Plato and his disciple Aristotle over 'universals'. Plato was a visionary so 'devoted to generalities that they began to determine his particulars, so devoted to ideas that they began to define or select his facts'. In contrast, Aristotle's 'is a matter-of-fact mind' and 'he sees the root of endless mysticism and scholarly nonsense' in the Platonic worldview. K would conjure up imaginary conversations with Bordia in which he would repeat the famous saying of Aristotle, *Amicus Plato, sed magis amica veritas*— 'Dear is Plato, but dearer still is truth'. Admiration for his master notwithstanding, K reacted to what he perceived as the excesses flowing from Bordia's romantic streak. He was put off by Bordia's excessive attachment to processes such as mobilization and environment building, his shying away from specification of outcomes, and his tendency to fib, manufacture illusions, and build castles in the air with great artistry even while knowing their true nature, and to compound the folly seek to disseminate and perpetuate the belief that they were castles with granite foundations. At a meeting of Lok Jumbish Executive Committee, after hearing a passionate declamation by Bordia about environment building in Lok Jumbish, a teacher member disingenuously asked, *Dar asal yeh vatavaran nirman kya hotha hai* (What exactly is this environment building?). K was not inclined to dismiss the question as a cynical remark; like the question of the Jesting Pilate, 'What is Truth?' The teacher's question seemed to unintendedly raise a valid question: is educational orientation only about process with no questions to be raised about outputs and outcomes? K's reaction to the seeming excesses of Bordia explains K's obsession with rigour outcomes, efficiency, and sustainability in DPEP.

With passage of time, bitterness fades away; even erstwhile enemies on the battlefield come together to commemorate in a spirit of camaraderie yesterday's battles in which they fought against each other. In the evening of one's life, one comes to have a more objective and less solipsistic view of men and matters. K's re-reading of Will Durant's *The Story of Philosophy* brought home to him that he was sharply critical of Bordia precisely because there was so much of Bordia in him, and that he too remained 'a lover of abstractions and generalities', repeatedly betraying the simple fact 'for some speciously bedizened theory',[1] excepting that his abstractions and generalities were different from those of Bordia. He realized that, like Bordia, he too was rash, intolerant, and authoritarian—it was a matter of difference in degree and not kind. He had no hesitation to admit that in their chosen career, Bordia was infinitely superior; Bordia was a *un homme de government* which he

[1] Will Durant, *The Story of Philosophers: The Lives and Opinions of Great Philosophers*, New York: Simon and Schuster, 1926, p. 70.

was not. Whatever, over time, his bitterness faded away and admiration for Bordia surfaced again. Nothing gave K greater pleasure than to recall what Bordia once told him: 'K, in guessing what I think about a matter, you are right not nine out of ten, but nineteen out of twenty. The one time you are wrong, you go wrong because I act impulsively.' It is this streak of unpredictable behaviour that made Bordia a great visionary, innovator, and path-setter. There seemed no other explanation than malicious destiny which could explain why deep bonds of affection between K and Bordia were torn asunder. However, K owes Bordia an immense debt of gratitude for making him a better officer and a better writer, and launching him on an exacting voyage of discovery of education. And there is no better way to acknowledge that debt than falling back on the traditional Hindu salutation *Om Gurubhyo Namah, Harihi Om* (Salutations to the Teacher who is God himself).

Transitions—change of top bosses such as the Minister or the Secretary—are anxious, even perilous moments for officers in ministries. Incoming presidential administrations observed Richard Neustadt, the great scholar on American Presidency, bring into the White House and Executive Mansion their special blend of ignorance—ignorance of men, roles, institutions, policies, and nuances—and hopefulness, and of innocence and arrogance.[2] It is a rare successor who would not like to erase the impression of his administrator in the ministry, and make his mark by breaking with the past as far as possible. This trait, human all too human, unleashes the full fury of office politics. Many who feel aggrieved with the previous boss and feel that they were wrongly sidelined see in the transition a splendid opportunity to settle scores, topple the favourites of the previous regime, and catapult themselves to prized positions. In normal course, K would have been a target of vicious office politics as he was perceived to be the blue eyed boy of Bordia who was handling an enviable portfolio which had the potential to provide many opportunities of frequent foreign travel. However, as his great luck had it, the transition in fact strengthened his position as S.V. Giri, his senior colleague from his own state IAS cadre—Andhra Pradesh—succeeded Bordia C. Giri was exceptional in that he did behave like any other senior office in a similar station. Far from going

[2] Richard E. Neustadt, *Presidential Power: The Politics of Leadership*, New York: Wiley, 1960, pp. 254, 356.

out of the way to keep K at a distance and thereby seek to avoid the criticism that he was partial to an officer from the same cadre and community, he had no hesitation to be seen as close to K. He banked on K to settle down in his job by briefing him on various aspects of the department, and all through his stint in DOE, bank on K to give him dispassionate advice, even if it were contrarian. K's advice was a major but not the sole input, and he was master of his own mind. K came to be his Man Friday, and in contrast to the extremely tense environment of working with Bordia, working with Giri was like working as a sub-collector in an Andhra district with a collector and his wife who treated the young sub-collector and his wife as members of their family and took extra efforts to guide the youngsters and make them feel happy in all respects.

Giri did not have the overarching visions of Bordia, or his suave urbanity, or his gift of communication skills, or his extraordinary ability to manipulate men and the system. But then, he had many assets. Like Trotsky, Bordia had only disciples and enemies, and no colleagues. In contrast, Giri was free of any ideological baggage, had no angularities, was not imperious, was willing to listen to a wide variety of opinions, and patiently tried to build a genuine consensus than peremptorily impose his views or manipulate men. K admired the way Giri sucked like a vacuum cleaner the information and analysis that were provided to him, and reached sound conclusions. Giri was a sound administrator, result-oriented, and mastered the art of working on the machinery of government gently but effectively. He had a tremendous ability to get the best out of his deputies and heads of the organizations attached to his department. In order to enlist the co-operation of the state governments he used to have periodic meetings with education secretaries and heads of departments, not in jumbo All-India meetings but in more cosy regional groupings. Like a professional and conscientious civil servant, he never tried to subvert the wishes of his minister. He was not as passionate as Bordia, but then unlike Bordia who did only what he liked, Giri did everything he had to do with professional rigour. It would be fair to say that Bordia concentrated almost exclusively on elementary and adult education, and education policy. Not that he was uninitiated in higher education; in his first stint in DOE for a while, he looked after higher education. He had also written about the initiatives in Indian higher education, and the linkages between higher education and adult education. His heart, no doubt, lay with his areas of concentration; he told K more than once that there is no fun in doing what one does not like. However, smart as he was he would have realized that it is more expedient to try reaching those unreached by the earlier stages of education than governing the ungovernables of higher education. After Giri took over, for the first time in several decades, the secretary of the department began to bestow attention on all areas. The change of guard and Giri's affable personality facilitated the resolution of the deadlock over the UP Project, and change of gears in the management of BEP. It should be said to the credit of Giri that he did not let affability come in the way of safeguarding the department's interests as well as its duty to ensure that externally funded projects adhere to the parameters laid down by CABE in March 1991. He was willing to heed the advice of K and ensured that DOE was not reduced to being a conduit for flow of funds to the state governments. The change of guard was also a moment to change the style of managing BEP and move from a hand-held style of management to one which placed the responsibility of managing BEP on the Bihar officers themselves. In K's view, Giri's accomplishments were no less substantial than those of Bordia because of his sterling personal qualities and broad range of action. Giri imparted a new thrust to TLCs by instituting systems and procedures; hitherto approvals were highly subjective being dependent on the personal impression of Bordia and the DG, NLM, about the district collector. Subjective approvals often blindsided the state governments which often had no idea that without their knowledge their own district collectors made a proposal to the NLM, and that the proposal was approved saddling them with the burden of providing matching funds. The system of monitoring was weak; there were no details of the millions who were reportedly made literate and the millions more who reportedly participated in the campaigns. What Giri silently and subtly accomplished in the matter of financing higher education was remarkable.

The 41 months during which Giri was K's boss constituted a happy stretch of K's career with K's creativity in full bloom and tremendous opportunity being available to K to display his initiative, creativity, and administrative abilities and bring to bear on his work the skills and competencies he acquired from Sebenius and Bordia. K was hitherto playing second fiddle, and now he could conduct an orchestra under the benign eye of his boss who acted more like the manager of the orchestra allowing the conductor full rein. Giri was an extraordinary officer who acted on the hoary principle that the best way to administer was to delegate powers to the fullest extent possible to deputies who are adjudged to be competent and worthy of reposing confidence. There is this anecdote of a commissioner during the Raj who, when a riot was about to take place left the headquarters for hunting, leaving the district collector to handle the situation in his own light without being cribbed by the presence of his superior. Giri could have been that commissioner. K was no doubt the Chief Co-coordinator of the EFA-9 Summit but the Summit would not have been the resounding success it was but for Giri's masterly way in which he guided the organization of the Summit, co-opting and enlisting everyone need for the organization. Giri was a splendid example of an officer and gentleman, and K owes him gratitude which can never be redeemed for giving him a free hand in dealing with agencies and developing programmes such as DPEP, for throwing the full weight of his office and deploying his immense experience and administrative skills to support K, and most importantly for saving K from himself and his impetuousness, and yet giving K full credit for achievement. Few are as generous as Giri and make such full use of deputies.

XII

NEW LAMPS FOR OLD

1992 Revision of NPE, 1986: Elementary Education

With the formation of anti-Congress governments at the centre, opportunities arose in 1977 and 1989 to attempt a paradigm shift in the education policy. As in 1977, in 1989 the National Front (NF) government sought to make a break with the past and constituted the Ramamurti Committee to review NPE, 1986. However, before the NF government could revise NPE, 1986, it fell, and the eventual revision that was done in 1992, after the PV government came to power, was marginal. If the Ramamurti Committee had its way, the elementary and secondary education systems would have changed beyond recognition; they would have been stripped of dualism and rigidity, and infused with infinite flexibility in the organization, content, and process of education. There would have been no separate programme of NFE, and the elementary school itself would have be *non-formalized* with flexible timings and curricula appropriate for the local community, and with ungraded classes that would allow students to learn at their own pace. Each school would have had a network of para-schools which would serve habitations without schools as well as boys and girls engaged in domestic chores or wage labour. In discussing the problems of child labour, the Ramamurti Committee had come to the conclusion that there were three categories of children, and that only a three-pronged strategy could meet their educational needs. Thus, out-of-school children in the age group 6–10 years who were not working for wages should be brought back to school. The strategy for out-of-school children in the same age group of 6–10 who were in the labour market would have to be based on the principle that such children could not be disassociated from work. Such children should be put through a programme which 'educationalizes work' and promotes skill formation. The strategy for educating out-of-school children in the age group 10–14 who were in the labour market should promote skill formation equip those children with a minimum level of knowledge. The Ramamurti Committee recommended that the Constitution should be amended so that the right to education is included amongst the fundamental rights, and all socio-economic measures necessary for ensuring that all children realize the right to education undertaken. It should be said that the Committee's recommendation to enact a right to elementary education was precocious, for it was only three years later that the Supreme Court in the *Unnikrishnan* judgment declared that the right to elementary education was a fundamental right[1], and it was only a couple of years later that the demand to enact a right to education began to be articulated by civil society groups following the Convention on the Rights of the Child being adopted by the UN General Assembly in 1989, and UNICEF launching a vigorous advocacy of the children rights. The Ramamurti Committee took the view that Constitution-makers envisaged that the constitutional directive (Article 45) of providing free and compulsory education for all children till they reach the age of 14 would include children in the age group 0–6; it therefore recommended that the state should provide free ECCE. The revision of NPE, 1986, was required to fix a new target date for achieving UEE as by the time the Ramamurti Committee was constituted in May 1990, it was obvious that the target fixed by NPE, 1986, for UPE was missed, and that the target date for UEE was bound to be missed. The Ramamurti Committee recommended that there should be no targets for achieving UPE or UEE for the country as a whole; instead targets should be fixed only for individual habitations through a participative mode of disaggregated planning.

On 6 March 1991, over two months after the Ramamurti Committee submitted its report, CABE met and decided to set up a

[1] *Unnikrishnan, J.P. & Others v. State of Andhra Pradesh & Others*, AIR 1993 S.C. 2178.

committee to examine the report. Four months later, in July 1991, after the government headed by P.V. Narasimha Rao assumed office, the committee that CABE wanted to be set up to review the Ramamurti Committee was constituted with N. Janardhana Reddy, Chief Minister of AP, as the Chairman of the Committee, and K as Member-Secretary. The Committee included Chitra Naik, Member, Planning Commission in charge of education, and G. Ram Reddy, Chairman, UGC, and was evenly balanced between experts and ministers. And furthermore, the education ministers were purposively chosen so as to represent the entire political spectrum and the different regions of the country. The committee was constituted, with his customary thoroughness and penchant to orchestrate every event and every meeting, to clearly lay down the role and script for his deputies, to specify who would do and say what, and to plan ahead the stratagems to thwart those who may oppose.

The text prepared by DOE under Bordia's direction assailed the Ramamurti Committee's approach to UEE and its specific recommendations with a sharp logic that would make a dialectician proud. It turned on its head the recommendation that the Constitution should be amended so that the right to education is included amongst the fundamental rights guaranteed by the Constitution, and that all socio-economic measures necessary for ensuring that all children realize the right to education should be undertaken. It was not lack of a constitutional guarantee that came in the way of UEE; the problem lay in taking 'all the socio-economic measures'. If all such measures are undertaken, a constitutional guarantee is redundant. If such measures cannot be undertaken, the constitutional guarantee would be ineffective. One had to only look at the enormity of the prevalence of child labour to realize the limitations of a legalistic approach to deep-rooted socio-economic problems. The record of implementation of fundamental rights did not give the confidence that a constitutional guarantee to education would make any difference. What was important was political will and sustained measures to expand access to education, to improve the quality and relevance of education, and to break down the socio-economic taboos and barriers that dissuade parents from sending their children to school. This stance very much reflected Bordia's views which K had an opportunity to find out during his many interactions with Bordia. His views were conditioned by the implementation of compulsory primary education laws which were enacted in many states during the 1920s and 1930s; he used to cite J.P. Naik's views that if those acts were vigorously implemented and parents prosecuted for not sending their children to school, there would be more parents in jail than children in schools. All in all, the text came out against a legalistic approach to achieve UEE. The text pointed out that the debates of the Constituent Assembly as well as the history of freedom struggle did not support the contention of the Ramamurti Committee that the Constitution-makers intended to include children in the age group 0–6 in Article 45.

The text put forth the argument that the uncompromising stand against a separate programme of NFE was inconsistent with the committee's own analysis of child labour, the strategy it commended for educating child labourers out-of-school, and the para-schools it advocated. The text also categorically stated that the committee's prescription of a 'fluidly flexible non-formal school, with extended arms of para-schools' which is 'expected to provide universal education to all children irrespective of their age, occupation or habitation' was just impractical. In spite of the different strategies it proposed for the three categories of child labourers, it proposed just one type of non-formalized school. The text sharply commented that 'one is struck by the rigidity of a recommendation that supports only one type of educational model for all even while talking of the need for flexibility, and the inconsistency between analysis and solution'. The text went on to observe that even while coming out against a separate programme of NFE, the para-schools that the committee recommended were just one variant of NFE, namely the Shiksha Karmi model in vogue in Rajasthan. The text went on to elaborate on the impracticability of the various features of non-formalized school that the Ramamurti Committee effusively proposed. Thus, an important feature of the non-formalized school was adjustment of school timing and calendar to local needs in consultation with the VEC. Such an adjustment is feasible if the learner group is homogenous. Such adjustment is possible only in NFE centres which have only 20–25 learners. In a formal school, such an adjustment might not always be possible because the number of learners was large, the backgrounds and needs of learners were heterogeneous, and the school curriculum stipulated a certain minimum time for each subject. Flexibility in the school system had always been recommended but never actualized. The changes required in a massive schools system could be attempted only over a long period, and till then, the necessity for NFE had to be acknowledged. Similarly, the idea of introducing ungraded classrooms where the children could learn at their own pace was a doubtful venture. Education was a process of learning that moved from one stage to another higher one. As such, gradation of stages would indicate to the learner the level attained by him and also would motivate him to move to higher and higher levels of learning. Obliterating grades not only would ignore that very content and process of learning, but also might reduce the motivation for attaining higher levels of learning. Besides, there would be practical difficulties in dealing with different levels in an ungraded classroom of undefined size, which the committee did not discuss. It is only in NFE that ungraded classes are feasible. All in all, the departures which the Ramamurti Committee would like to make in the policy were unrealistic and ill-conceived.

The CABE Committee accepted the stance of DOE that there was no need to amend the Constitution and make elementary education a fundamental right; it also accepted the view of DOE that Article 45 of the Constitution does not include pre-primary education. Regarding NFE, during the deliberations of the CABE Committee, all the members except Satyasodhan Chakrabarty felt that, for a long time to come, there was no alternative but to have a large and systematic programme of first-rate NFE. The CABE Committee recommended the target for UEE should be before the advent of the new century. During internal discussions, Bordia suggested going by the report of the Eighth Five-Year Plan Working Group on Elementary Education, which suggested separate targets as NPE, 1986, did for providing free and compulsory education for primary education (UPE covering age group 6–11) and elementary education (UEE covering age group 6–14). Arjun Singh sharply expressed the view that the question was not which formulation to choose, that of the Working Group or of the CABE Committee. Neither of them seemed to be based on a realistic assessment of the magnitude of effort and the resources required. Unrealistic targets aroused false hopes and cynicism and dejection when those hopes were belied. When Bordia persisted with his view that separate target dates should be fixed for UPE and UEE as suggested by the Working Group, Arjun Singh interjected to say, 'How can we break away from our habit? Words are there; intentions are there. But is there anything specific? There is enough hope for everything in the country'. Arjun Singh's observations were pearls of wisdom, for a consistent feature of educational discourse in the country has been a penchant for rhetoric and willing suspension of disbelief in the expectation that Hope and Will could create what they desire.

At the very last minute just before CABE concluded its deliberations, CABE accepted without discussion the suggestion of Arjun Singh prompted by Bordia to incorporate in the revised policy the intention of the government to constitute a National Elementary Education Mission (NEEM) even though it was neither suggested by the Ramamurti Committee which reviewed the 1986 policy, nor deliberated upon in the CABE Committee on Policy. Looking back, the NPE revision missed out a very significant development which gave a new direction to the nation's quest for UEE. In November 1991, six months before the revision was completed DOE pitched on a district-based planning and implementation as the optimal way to achieve UEE and proposed it to the Planning Commission for implementation during the Eighth Five-Year Plan. The most significant aspect of the 1992 revision was the linkage of quality with learning achievement. NPE, 1986, postulated that in addition to universal access, enrolment, and universal retention of children up to the age of 14 years, substantial improvement in the quality of education should receive emphasis. The salience that learner achievement acquired in the wake of the Jomtien Conference led to the improvement in quality ceasing to be a standalone provision and being linked with learning achievement. Substantial improvement in quality was no longer an end in itself but an instrument to enable all children to achieve essential levels of learning. The linkage with learner achievement enables claims about improvements in quality of learning to be reliably assessed.

New Strategy for UEE

Soon after development planning began in 1950, there was recognition of the need to decentralize planning as there were wide physical, geographic, and economic variations within every large state, and a single, one-size-fits-all development strategy might not be adequate to promote balanced development of all regions. For long, there was considerable debate on what should be the unit of decentralized planning. In 1969, the Planning Commission issued *Guidelines for District Planning* and agreed to assist the states in the setting up of planning machinery in districts. K can still recall the gusto with which district agricultural plans were prepared in the later 1960s in the districts he served. Similarly, after nationalization of 14 banks in 1969, the designation of a lead bank in every district, and the direction given to nationalized banks to give emphasis to 'priority lending', district credit plans used to be prepared. However, it be would be fair to say that these plans were no more than litanies of wish lists. Efforts were made to further decentralize planning, and the 1978 *Report of the Working Group on Block Level Planning* chaired by M.L. Dantwala was a landmark. The report identified the remoteness of planning agencies at the district level from the actual scene of action as the cause of mismatch of actual financial allocations with location-specific needs. The Working Group forcefully argued that the Community Development Block would be the most appropriate planning unit. Thereafter, guidelines were issued regarding the formulation of block-level plans. At about the same time, a committee headed by Asoka Mehta was appointed to go into the working of Panchayat Raj institutions. It advocated that developmental efforts should be in tune with the needs of the poor and should be marked by a high degree of coordination; it was not possible to achieve these objectives solely through planning at the state level. Panchayat Raj institutions should be made to develop into agencies for planning schemes which were of immediate necessity. The committee considered the village to be too small a unit for planning, and argued that block-level planning would be desirable. However, even while commending block-level planning, the committee suggested that district should be the first point of decentralization, and that district officials should be properly qualified and placed under the control of the *zilla parishad*. Suffice to say, there was considerable discussion in literature about multilevel planning and integration of the plans developed at different levels from the village to the nation. However, it would be fair to say that planning below the state level was much talked about but little practised mainly for three reasons: lack of resources, absence of a planning machinery, and lack of planning competencies. Planning without resources was an illusory exercise. Districts did not have worthwhile resources of their own; therefore, unless the state governments provided them adequate untied grants which they could expend at their discretion, the plans they drew up were either a litany of wish lists or a disaggregation of the targets fixed by the state government for different programmes to be implemented in districts. District administrations were mostly geared for implementing various programmes initiated by central and state governments rather than initiating programmes of their own; they had little technical expertise for either development planning or programme development.

Planning for UEE was no different. The idea of district planning of UEE was, figuratively speaking, hibernating since it was articulated by as early as 1941 by D.R. Gadgil, the eminent economist and a deputy chairman of the Planning Commission (September 1967 to March 1971). Gadgil prepared plans for reforming primary education in Wardha and Satara districts of Maharashtra.[2] The Kothari Commission Report suggested that each state and even each district should prepare a perspective plan for fulfilling the constitutional obligation of UEE as early as possible, that each state and district should be assisted to go ahead at the best pace it can, and that the 'progress in no area shall be allowed to be held up for want of essential facilities or financial allocations'.[3] Like almost everything that the Kothari Commission recommended in regard to elementary education, the recommendation in regard to district plans was not acted upon. In 1969, J.P. Naik wrote about the modalities of preparing district plans for improving elementary education.[4] Yet, planning for UEE continued to be an arithmetic exercise. As part of the Five-Year and Annual Planning exercises, the Planning Commission used to estimate the gap between the population of the age group 6–14 and the number of children in elementary schools in each state and set the estimated gap as enrolment targets for states. Each state made a similar exercise and apportioned the state enrolment target among lower-level administrative units. At the beginning of an academic year, teachers used to organize enrolment drives going round the habitations which a school catered and enrolling the children in the

[2] D.R. Gadgil and V.M. Dandekar, *Primary Education in Satara District: Reports of Two Investigations*, Pune: Gokhale Institute of Economics and Politics, 1955; Nilakantha Rath, 'D.R. Gadgil on Planning at the District Level', *Economic and Political Weekly*, 37, no. 23 (June 8, 2002), pp. 2219–22.

[3] Ministry of Education, *Education and National Development: Report of the Education Commission, 1964–66*, 1966, Volume II, pp.199–200.

[4] J.P. Naik, *Educational Planning in a District*, New Delhi: Asian Institute for Educational Planning and Administration, 1969.

school. However, enrolment, as POA, 1986, observed, was 'by itself of little importance if children did not continue education beyond even one year, many of them not seeing the school for more than a few days'. Opening of primary and upper primary schools were guided by national norms; notwithstanding the literature on school mapping and limited training on school mapping by NIEPA, opening of schools was largely driven by demands from villagers and public representatives.

An area focus appeared in 1977 when nine states which accounted for 75 per cent of out-of-school children were identified as educationally backward and targeted for focused attention. In practice, this meant priority to the nine states by GOI in the National Adult Education Programme (NAEP) and in the rather modest NFE programme and a sympathetic consideration by the Planning Commission of plan proposals of these states to expand access with their resources. All the same, this prioritization came to be questioned by states which were left out by the classification as well as by academics, particularly votaries of district and block-level planning. NPE, 1986, made significant advances in the thinking about UEE, and the educational advancement of educationally backward states. The focus of the expanded NFE scheme launched in the wake of NPE, 1986, was on the educationally backward states. The scheme of Operation Blackboard had a tilt towards educationally backward states as it was in such states that most of the single-teacher schools were located. Lizzy Jacob, Kerala Education Secretary, had a valid reason to be aggrieved for a state like Kerala which was ahead of the curve and invested its own resources to provide adequate access and achieve near-universal participation: did not receive funds under Operation Blackboard while laggard states were rewarded. NPE, 1986, and its POA also spoke about microplanning and social mobilization. As already set out earlier, these high-sounding provisions made little headway and remained pious intentions, and as a cynical State Education Secretary observed at a CABE meeting, they amounted to generously distributing advice without offering resources. Persuasion is a poor policy lever indeed. And furthermore, the provisions took for granted that district education officials had the technical competence to undertake planning. Even now, in most states, educational officials do not receive any induction or in-service training, and the B.Ed. qualification many of them possess does not equip them with managerial and planning skills and competencies.

Systematic district-level planning for attaining an educational objective was first attempted with TLCs. Among the defining features of TLC, as originally conceived, were taking an entire district in one go for organizing a TLC, and meticulous spatial and temporal planning for the deployment of human and material resources and for organizing mobilization and learning. As district after district declared that it was totally literate, the thought crossed the minds of many including Bordia and K that, as with TLCs, the district should be the arena for a systematic planning and implementation of UEE, and that the methodology of planning used by TLCs could be extended to UEE?. These cogitations awakened interest in the idea of district planning of UEE, an idea that was, figuratively speaking, hibernating since it was articulated by as early as 1941 by the eminent economist Gadgil, and later by the Kothari Commission (1968), and Naik in 1969.

The intellectual leap to district-based projects was effected during mid-1991. The department's Eighth Five-Year Plan proposals were first formulated in September 1990, and they did not mention district-level planning at all. Following the General Elections and a new government assuming office, it was decided to reschedule Eighth Five-Year Plan so that it began in April 1992 instead of April 1991. DOE reworked its plan proposals which were submitted to the Planning Commission in November 1991; these proposals commended disaggregated target setting and decentralized planning as a strategy to achieve UEE and, to that end, preparation and implementation of district projects. These proposals observed that an analysis of educational indicators revealed that even within educationally backward states there were districts which were almost within reach of universalization while, conversely, even in educationally advanced states there were districts which were still farther away from UEE. Hence, they postulated that the district should be the unit for determining backwardness and planning for UEE. Attempts would be made to prepare and implement district-specific, population-specific plans. The document visualized that by 1993–4, the second year of the Eighth Five-Year Plan, state plans would become a compilation of district plans. The document classified districts into four categories: (*a*) high-literacy districts; (*b*) districts covered by TLCs; (*c*) low-literacy districts; and (*d*) externally funded project districts. A distinct strategy would be developed for each category of districts. Soon after the submission of the Eighth Five-Year Plan proposals in

November 1991, the concept of district planning was field tested in Sitamarhi district in November 1991 to May 1992 (Chapter VIII).

After the revision of NPE, 1986, was completed and the revised version placed in the Parliament, revision of the POA, 1986, began. The process for revision of POA was similar to that followed for the preparation of the POA in 1986. A total of 22 thematic task forces were constituted to develop a programme of action for the various areas covered by the policy; the members of the task forces included senior officials of the central and state governments as well as noted educationists. A steering committee was constituted to harmonize the reports of the 22 task forces set up to draw up action plans for different areas of education, and coming up with a consolidated action programme for consideration by CABE. As head of the Policy Planning Division and Member Secretary of the Steering Committee, K had to attend the mammoth task of co-ordinating the functioning of the task forces, ensure that they complete their task in a manner within about one and half months, and further that the reports of the task forces do not transgress the policy parameters. K also had the burden of editing the disparate reports and weaving them into a seamless fabric that conformed to the conceptual underpinnings of the revised policy.

K took the opportunity of incorporating the district-based strategy in the revised POA as the Sitamarhi planning exercise indicated that it was a feasible strategy; that strategy was given the imprimatur by CABE at its meeting on 3–4 August 1991 when it approved the revised POA. It is this home-grown strategy that DPEP sought to operationalize, a point K used to drive home again and again to ward off criticism of DPEP as a project inspired by the World Bank.

Financing of Higher Education

This is an issue which would not have been ordinarily discussed in a book on UEE; however, as it cropped in critiques of DPEP, it needs to be dilated upon. In its treatment of the financing of education, the Ramamurti Committee broke new ground, surpassing even the Kothari Commission's report not to speak of the Challenge of Education. NPE, 1986, did talk, in a matter-of-fact tone, of raising fees to the extent possible fees at higher levels of education, effecting some savings by the efficient use of facilities, and levying a user fees on government departments and entrepreneurs who utilize research, and scientific and technical manpower. The POA did not detail the measures that could be taken to translate the NPE hopes about raising non-budgetary resources such as fees. Where the NPE was hesitant, the Ramamurti Committee was forthright. Without any equivocation, it drew the right policy conclusions from its analysis of the trends in the expenditure on education. It highlighted the fact that the share of elementary education in plan expenditure had come down from 56 per cent in the First Five-Year Plan to 29 per cent in the Seventh Five-Year Plan. The Ramamurti Committee drew the logical conclusion that the down-trend of the share of elementary education was not consistent with the constitutional mandate of achieving UEE, and that the mobilization of resources and their deployment should take into account the need to correct the distortion of investment priorities in education. It emphasized the imperative of categorically assigning a high priority to UEE and adult education and, to that end, recommended that all technical and professional education should be made self-financing. The committee presented data to establish that the disparity between the cost of higher education and the tuition fees was quite high, and that the proportion of fees to the total income of higher education institutions had come down from 20 per cent in 1950–1 to 5 per cent as the tuition fees remained unchanged. Therefore, it was of the view that it was necessary to increase the tuition fees such that at least the cost of recurring expenditure was recovered, and that while doing so it was essential to take into account the levels of income of the parents. The committee accordingly suggested a differential fee structure which provided for the richest first quartile to bear 75 per cent of the cost of education, the second quartile 50 per cent, the third quartile 25 per cent, and the fourth bottom-most quartile to receive education free. The committee further recommended that increase in tuition fees should be supplemented by an effective system for provision of scholarships and loans, and that institutions should be encouraged to mobilize non-budgetary resources through consultancy and other measures in order to decrease their reliance on budgetary support. If the Kothari Commission was a product of its time, the Ramamurti Committee also was a product of its time. The Ramamurti Committee's analysis and recommendations have an added significance in that they antedate the 1991 economic reforms and its members were all educationists of political persuasions (Gandhian, Marxist, radical, and apolitical) least inclined to support the 'neo-liberal' worldview.

In its analysis of educational finances and in putting forth its recommendations, the Ramamurti Committee drew heavily on a background paper on the financing of higher education furnished to the committee by the noted economists of finance Tilak and Varghese of NIEPA; they later published this background in *Higher Education*, a scholarly journal. About three years later, in 1993 Tilak published a more elaborate article on higher education in the same vein.[5] The externalities of higher education are not as high as those of primary education. This fact explains why the primary demand for primary education is weak while there is excess demand for higher education. In short, 'while primary education can be viewed as a pure public good, higher education can be viewed only as a quasi-public good'. Since higher education is quasi-public good, cent per cent public financing may not be economically unjustified. These articles also refer to the rate of return studies, and observe that it was universally found that 'of the different layers of education, investment in primary education carries higher returns and higher education the least'. Tilak's own research confirms that this finding was of relevance in the case of India. The financing of higher education needed to be critically examined in this context as well as the following considerations:

> Basic needs like education like universal elementary education, and universal literacy are not yet fulfilled. Targets that were to be achieved about half a century ago may remain unfulfilled even by the turn of the century. It is also realised that higher education could expand only at the cost of mass education programmes. Only those economies that check the growth of investment in higher education are found able to achieve universal primary education Secondly, the number of educated unemployed is bulging year after year, resulting in huge wastage of investment made by the society in higher education.[6]

[5] Jandhyala B.G. Tilak and N.G. Varghese, 'Financing Higher Education', *Higher Education*, 21, no. 1 (1991), pp. 83–101; Jandhyala B.G. Tilak, 'Financing Higher Education in India: Principles, Practice and Policy Issues', *Higher Education*, 26, no. 1 (1993), pp. 43–67.

[6] Tilak, 'Financing Higher Education in India', p. 44.

The share of private financing of higher education had declined over years, and it appeared that the private share in funding higher education needed to be increased on efficiency as well as equity considerations. While the social rates of return on higher education are high, they are lower than the private rates of return. While the rapid growth of higher education resulted in the democratization, a majority of students in higher education were from relatively better-off sections of the society and their ability to pay was higher than what they actually pay. Relative to the expenditure per pupil, the cost recovery from fees was the least in the faculty of business management and the highest in the case of arts and science faculties. The recovery of costs was very small in all professional courses and was negative in medical courses. This inequity was aggravated by the fact that the tax system was regressive in that government revenues were largely made of indirect taxes predominantly paid by the poor. All in all, huge indiscriminate public subsidization may be highly inequitable, with serious regressive effects on income distribution. Since private benefits of higher education were high and they accrued to the individuals more than to the society, there was a strong case for recovery of costs from the students in the form of fees and from the users of graduates in the form of a graduate tax. It was desirable to have a discriminatory fee structure based on (*a*) the cost-fee disparity; (*b*) the share of the fee to the expenditure per student across disciplines and levels, and (*c*) the family income of the students; and (*d*) the likely benefits for a given type of education.

It is pertinent to point out that about hree years after the Ramamurti Committee submitted its report, the report of the Education Commission established by the Left Front government of West Bengal and chaired by Ashok Mitra, noted economist and Finance Minister of West Bengal for a pretty long time, called for correcting the anomalous tuition fees in higher education.

> These [college and university] fees have more or less remained unchanged since before the Second World War. In the course of the past six decades, the general price level must have gone up at least thirty times; the direct and indirect costs per student must have also multiplied by the same order. Little reason exists for exempting affluent households from bearing a part of the excruciatingly heavy financial

burden the Government has been enduring on account of the educational outlay.[7]

While noting that it would be absurd to propose the fees so as to fully compensate the increase in the cost of higher education, the Ashok Mitra Commission pointed out that it would be pointless to effect only a marginal increase in fees; that would serve the cause of tokenism and little else. Besides, since resistance to annual increases may be expected, it would be prudent to plan for the present for a once-ever rise in prices; it should be of a reasonably sizeable magnitude. The increase in fees was not to be a once-and-for-all exercise. Like the Ramamurti Committee, the commission recommended that students not particularly well placed economically should be exempted from payment of fees; it estimated the proportion of such students to be about 30 per cent of the total students. The commission suggested that the tuition fees should be Rs 50 a month at the undergraduate level and Rs 75 a month at the graduate and postgraduate levels. The increase in fees suggested by the commission was hefty considering the then-prevailing levels of Rs 120–216 a year for undergraduate education, Rs 140–240 for postgraduate education a year in central universities, Rs 500 a year charged by IIMs, and Rs 100–150 a term charged by IITs. The analysis as well as recommendations of the Ramamurti Committee and the Ashok Mitra Commission highlights the fact that neo-classical economists (or neo-liberal economists, going by poplar usage) were not alone in calling for an increase in fees as part of the reform of the financing of higher education. It is wrong to contend that higher education institutions were compelled to raise more of their own resources only because of the hegemony of neo-liberal economic policies and of the World Bank.

The CABE Committee on Policy endorsed the recommendations of the Ramamurti Committee in regard to educational finances. It made clear the fact that given the competing demands and resource constraints, budgetary resources for education could never be adequate, and that higher budgetary allocations for education should be complemented

[7] Government of West Bengal, *Report of the Education Commission*, 1992, p. 305.

by a number of other measures to mobilize non-budgetary resources and to promote the efficient utilization of resources. UEE, adult education, and vocationalization should be accorded a clear priority in the matter of allocation of resources. Higher education should be progressively made largely self-financing by appropriate support to the needy students by way of student loans. Incentives should be provided to academic institutions to augment income by way of consultancy and research. Efficiency and effectiveness of expenditure should be promoted. Implementation of programmes should be judged not only with reference to expenditure or coverage in terms of geographical area or number of beneficiaries but also in terms of outcomes.

DOE strangely took the view that the recommendations of the Ramamurti and CABE Committees on education financing had no policy implications, and were no more than a re-statement of the existing provision of NPE, 1986, relating to finance, this too at a moment when the budgetary resources were under severe stress. When the P.V. Narasimha Rao (PV) government assumed office in June 1991, the economy was on the verge of collapse; about a month earlier, the caretaker government of Chandra Sekhar had to pledge the entire gold reserves of the country and fly the reserves out as security for an emergency loan without which the country would have defaulted in meeting its debt obligations to foreign creditors. The slew of measures undertaken by the PV Government during the financial year 1991–2 saved the economy from collapse; however, as the finance minister explained in his budget speech of February 1992, it would take at least two to three years to bring the economy back to a path of rapid and sustainable growth provided 'we persevere with the process of stabilization and economic reforms begun in the current year'. The finance minister also stated the obvious when he said that stabilization and structural adjustment were never painless or quick, and that all efforts should be made to ensure that the burden of adjustment on the poorer and weaker sections should be ameliorated. The grim macroeconomic situation inevitably impacted on government expenditure. All in all, the resource position was aptly captured by the comment made by the Prime Minister during the presentation by DOE about the modifications proposed to the NPE: *das rupya bhi dekhna padega* (have to scrounge even for a dime). In contrast to the past trend, the difficult resource position forced the government to curtail budgetary support for the central plan. The financial year 1992–3 was the first year of the Eighth Five-Year Plan, and it was important that a good start should be made by stepping up investment; however, the resource availability and macroeconomic situation were such that the government was severely constrained. The government had no option but to maximize the plan expenditure that the macroeconomic situation would permit by containing the non-plan expenditure as much as it could. The government expected all government departments and organizations funded by it to make do with the non-plan budget provided. Even then, the provision for the central plan in the budget of the fiscal year 1992–3 was 2.7 per cent less than that in 1991–2; consequently, allocation of resources to different sectors including education suffered severe cuts. The plan allocation for elementary education in 1992–3 was only Rs 232.24 crore, about 85 per cent of the plan expenditure in 1991–2. The impact on Operation Blackboard was very severe as the plan allocation in 1992–3 was only about 55 per cent of the expenditure in 1991–2. Higher and technical education accounted for much of the non-plan expenditure on education, and consequently, the maintenance grants to central government institutions such as central universities were frozen. In such a grim situation, one would expect the better-educated sections of the society to set an example to others by asking 'what you can do for the country' instead of asking 'not what your country should do for you'. The sharp budget cuts imposed by the 1992 budget loomed large when the NPE was adopted by CABE. The sharp resource crunch made it imperative to briskly act on the recommendations on resource mobilization of the Ramamurti Committee and the CABE Committee on Policy with expedition and resolve. Having taken the stand that the recommendations of the Ramamurti Committee in regard to financing of higher education and the priority which needed to be accorded to UEE and adult education were no more than re-statements of the policy postulates of NPE, 1986, Bordia stuck to the stand that the relevant provisions of NPE, 1986, needed no revision. It was not that he was unaware of the acute economic crisis which began to grip the nation from late 1990. In his note to the Minister Chimanbhai Patel, he cited the crisis as one of the reasons why the World Bank's offer to finance elementary education should be accepted. He attended quite a few meetings in the Cabinet Secretariat where the crisis was discussed, and ministries encouraged to avail external funding. On the top of it, in February 1992, for the first time ever a budget for the next financial year reduced the plan allocations for education below the current year's allocations, and even reduced the maintenance grants to universities. It was obvious that business as usual would not do, and resource mobilization by universities could not be wished away. Yet, to recall a Sherlock Holmes story, why did the dog not bark? The only explanation that K could surmise was that being an ace realist, Bordia knew that any attempt to reform higher education financing would stir a hornet's nest, and that he better use the few months he still had before he retired to revalidate NPE, 1986. CABE went by the advice of Bordia and DOE. The prevailing macroeconomic and resource position were such that mobilization of non-budgetary resources was a categorical imperative not dependent on a person's inclination, and revision of NPE, 1986, was a unique opportunity to sharply articulate the categorical imperative and make the government's compulsions more explicit to the 'education community' and public at large. The opportunity was missed; in the deliberations of CABE, there was not even a whisper about the macroeconomic situation and much less how the education system should help the nation overcome the crisis.

While the policy discourse in CABE could dodge a serious discussion on financing higher education among the policymakers of the Department of Education, the Chairman of UGC and the vice-chancellors of central universities could not avoid responding to the budgetary cuts imposed by the 1992–3 budget. The vice-chancellors of the central universities which compared to the state universities were well funded chafed at the cuts in non-plan budget. Over the next year or so, all efforts were made by the central universities and the UGC to insulate the grants given by the government from budgetary cuts while DOE was equally keen to prod the central government institutions to act on the recommendations of the Ramamurti and CABE Committees. Giri could persuade G. Rami Reddy, Chairman, UGC, as well as Chairman of the Task Force on Higher Education to agree to mention in the POA Chapter on Higher Education that UGC would constitute a high-power committee 'to consider steps for the mobilization of resources for higher education, to bring about a better balance in the funding of institutions for higher education, and to improve the cost efficiency of the higher education system'. Compared to the Task

Force on Higher Education, there was less resistance in the Task Force on Technical and Management Education to the CABE Committee's recommendations on revenue generation. It was proposed to set up a high-power committee with the same remit as that of higher education; the Task Force also declared that 'efforts will also be made to streamline the scheme of educational loans with a view to make it more customer friendly'.

Soon after the adoption of the POA by CABE, DOE took prompt steps to revise the fees charged by the Indian Institute of Science (IISc), IIMs whose students secure lucrative jobs in the private sector, and IITs a high proportion of whose undergraduates used to migrate to the United States. The fees charged by these institutions were ridiculously low in comparison with the cost of providing education or the stream of income that flowed to the graduates of these institutions. Along with an increase in fees, a new system of grants was introduced whereby incentives were provided to those institutions to be cost-effective and generate their own resources. The block grants system had a built-in disincentive to mobilize own resources, for any effort by an educational institution to mobilize own resources would reduce the deficit and, consequently, the block grant provided by the Government. The new patterns of grants eliminated the disincentive by permitting the institutions to deposit savings from the grants given by the government in a corpus fund instead of being required to surrender the savings to the government. Apart from removing the disincentive, the new pattern also provided a strong incentive to the institutions to raise their own resources by providing that the government would match every rupee raised by an institution with a rupee of its own. The revised pattern was so attractive that IIMs straightaway effected a substantial increase in annual tuition fees from Rs 500 to Rs 6,000, and IITs from Rs 100 to Rs 150 per term to Rs 750–1,000. The fee increase had a rationale which is often lost sight of. When the IIT, Kharagpur, was established in 1950, the annual cost per student was estimated to be Rs 1,800. It was decided to recover 10 per cent of the operating cost as fees from students, and the principle was adopted by the other three IITs set up a few years later. By 1992, the annual cost per student increased to Rs 55,000; however, the fees remained more or less the same. Adopting the principle of recovering 10 per cent of the operating cost, IITs increased the fees to Rs 6,000.[8] From 1992 onwards, IITs and IIMs began to periodically revise fees, taking note not only of the cost of providing education but also of the stream of income that graduates could expect after completing the course. By now the fees per semester charged by IITs had risen to about Rs 50,000, and the fees charged by the older IIMs (Ahmadabad, Bangalore, and Kolkata) for the two-year MBA programme had risen to about Rs 15 lakh. Although precise data are not available, IITs now recover a fifth of the cost providing undergraduate education and the older IIMs wholly.

In spite of the steep step-up in fees, admission to these primary institutions remains highly prized, and there are no reports that any student had declined admission. The availability of student loans from commercial banks together with the high levels of income earned by graduates had ensured that no student who secured admission was prevented from studying at these prized institutions for want of means. The level of fees as well as regular increase has elicited no opposition except from scholars who believe that higher education is a public good which the government should make available free or by charging tokenistic fees. To say that 'it can certainly be expected the demand of middle and lower classes for highly professional education would be highly fees elastic', and that high levels of fees and steep increases would keep the students of middle and lower classes away from IITs and IIMs because of fees,[9] is no more than asserting something based on preconceived notions without any empirical evidence. The revised financing pattern helped these institutions, particularly IIMs, to build up hefty corpus funds, attract substantial donations to open new areas of study, and acquire a considerable measure of self-sufficiency. If they chose, the older IIMs in particular can now give up government funding. The new financing pattern proved to be so attractive to IIMs that when later Murli Manohar Joshi, Minister of Human Resource Development (HRD), attempted to get the IIMs to slash their fees, the

[8] N.C. Nigam, 'Report on National Colloquium on Right to Education as a Fundamental Right', Organised by the UGC and Association of Indian Universities (AIU), September 1992, *Journal of Higher Education* , 18, no. 1 (Autumn 1992), pp. 1–139, at p. 48.

[9] Jandhyala B.G. Tilak, 'Fees, Autonomy and Equity', *Economic and Political Weekly*, XXXIX, no. 9 (February 28, 2004), pp. 870–3, at p. 871.

faculty as well as the institutions fiercely and successfully resisted his move as an assault on the autonomy of IIMs. Apart from assisting Giri in developing the new financial pattern, K also chaired a committee to review the pattern of financing three years after that pattern was introduced; that committee included all the directors of IITs, Indian Institutes of Management (IIMs), and the IISc, which suggested a few refinements.

Following the adoption of POA, AICTE set up an 18-member high-power committee headed by D. Swaminadhan, Member, Planning Commission, to study and make recommendations for the mobilization of resources by technical and management institutions. Among others, the committee recommended an increase in tuition fees such that at least 20 per cent of the recurring cost per student was recovered, levying an education cess on industries for funding technical education as well as research in technical education institutions, the establishment of an Educational Bank of India (EBI) for providing soft loans to technical education institutions as well as for extending soft educational loans to students, and the setting up of a national loan scholarship scheme to assist needy students. Central government institutions such as the RECs and state government engineering colleges had no difficulty whatsoever in acting upon the recommendation of the committee to enhance fees as they offered education generally of a better quality than that of most private unaided engineering colleges, and that too at far lower fees.

The UGC constitute a high-level committee under the chairmanship of Justice K. Punnayya; however, the scope of committee's study was limited to the financing of central universities, Delhi colleges, and deemed universities which were financed by UGC. It did not extend to the study of the financing of higher education as a whole as would be expected from the facts that the NPE is national and not limited to the central government, and that the UGC is a national body with an All India jurisdiction vested with powers (Section 12A of the UGC Act) to fix the fees any college in the country could collect in respect of any course. The appointment of the Punnayya Committee came in handy to Rami Reddy, Chairman of the UGC, to advance his view that the freezing of maintenance grants should be revoked and additional maintenance grant provided till such time as a rational formula for determining maintenance grants was evolved and put into effect. In regard to resource mobilization by universities, he conceded that universities could raise resources; however, in keeping with the tradition of the UGC, he preferred a gradualist approach which relied on persuasion and nothing else. Rami Reddy was exceptionally savvy politically and capable of gravity-defying feats that even the very best trapezium artists are incapable of, such as being on very good terms simultaneously with arch-rivals, Arjun Singh and Prime Minister P.V. Narasimha Rao. That being so, he had no difficulty in persuading Arjun Singh to take the opportunity provided by the constitution of the Punnayya Committee to request the Prime Minister to direct the Finance Ministry to provide an additional maintenance grant of Rs 42 crore to central universities; his request was conceded. Ironically, while additional maintenance grant was provided to central universities through domestic resources, the cut in allocation to elementary education was restored only through the external funding offered by the World Bank under the Social Safety Net Adjustment Credit operation.

The Punnayya Committee was more specific about what the government should do in the matter of grants to central universities and Delhi colleges than what those institutions should do to raise their internal resources.[10] However, the committee recommended that universities should mobilize at least 15 per cent of their total recurring expenditure at the end of the first five years and 25 per cent at the end of ten years, fees should be increased keeping in view the rate of inflation, scholarships should be provided to at least 20 per cent of students, and the nationalized banks should provide soft educational loans. The implementation of the report was slow and faltering. The recommendation of the Punnayya Committee regarding fees was eminently reasonable. As the distinguished economist of education Tapas Mazumdar put it, there was no way one could support the proposition that the common man should be asked to pay for such a basic commodity as food, a price in 1996 50 times what one had to pay in 1946, but college or university education should continue to charge the same as in 1946. There was nothing wrong with a rise in fees that would cover 25–30 per cent of the cost of education rather than 10–12 per cent as was prevailing then.[11] Yet the implementation of the Punnayya Committee

[10] University Grants Commission, *Report of Justice Dr. K. Punnayya Committee-1992–93*, 1993.

[11] Tapas Mazumdar, 'Financing Higher Education: Beyond 'Public vs Private', *The Observer of Business and Politics*, March 26, 1996.

recommendation by the central universities was lackadaisical. To wit, a distinguished vice-chancellor of JNU, when asked about student fees, replied that student fees that accounted for a very small proportion in the total expenditure did not constitute vital aspect of university finance.[12] An NIEPA study of the finances of 39 universities (including four central universities) revealed that in the late 1990s the contribution of fees to the total recurring expenditure of central universities (other than Indira Gandhi National Open University [IGNOU]) was lower than that of state universities. Thus, the contribution of fess was less than 5 per cent in Hyderabad and Viswa Bharati, and about 8 per cent in the Delhi University, much lower than the norm laid down by the Punnayya Committee of 15 per cent by the end of 1998.[13] Even in 2013, the Delhi colleges were charging tuition fees of Rs 240 a year compared to Rs 180 in 1990 and a pittance compared to what most students paid when they were at school. What comes out loud and cleaner from the NIEPA study is that the underfinanced and 'famished' institutions financed by state governments were more willing to raise fees and offer 'self-financing' courses than relatively well-financed central universities.

It is often alleged that the higher education institutions were compelled to raise more of their own resources only because of the hegemony of neo-liberal economic policies and of the World Bank; the enhancement of fees was reportedly 'a direct outcome of the introduction of market reforms in higher education institutions'.[14] As one closely associated with the events in Indian education following the Jomtien Conference, K could vouch for the fact that the Jomtien Conference had no impact on the domestic financing of education. While access to external funding helped elementary education overcome the acute resource crunch arising from the macroeconomic crisis of 1991, higher education could not. It is no doubt true that India was undergoing structural adjustment, and beginning to earnestly attempting to meet

[12] Y.K. Alagh, 'Financing Higher Education: State must Bear the Major Brunt', *The Observer of Business and Politics*, March 27, 1996.

[13] National Institute of Educational Planning, *University Finances in India* 2000 (mimeo), cited in Central Advisory Board of Education, *Report of the* CABE *Committee on Financing of Higher and Technical Education*, 2005, pp. 32–5.

[14] Tilak, 'Fees, Autonomy and Equity', p. 870.

the basic learning needs of children and illiterate youth as enjoined by the Jomtien Declaration and Framework. It is equally true that in its policy advocacy as well as in its Social Safety Net Credit Operation (1992), the World Bank advocated increase in fees and higher priority to elementary education in budgetary allocations. However, association is not causation, and to attribute the increase in fees of central and state government general and technical educational institutions and shift in inter se priority between elementary education, on the one hand, and higher education, on the other, is unhistorical. As narrated at great length earlier, the Ramamurti Committee and the CABE Committee on Policy made a strong case for priority in budgetary expenditure to be given to elementary and adult education, progressively ensuring that all technical and professional institutions are self-financing, putting an end to the absurdly low tuition fees in colleges and universities, and put in place an effective system of scholarships and bank loans to assist students in need of financial support. The Ramamurti Committee's analysis and recommendations have an added significance in that they antedate the 1991 economic reforms and its members were all educationists of political persuasions (Gandhian, Marxist, radical, and apolitical) least inclined to support the 'neo-liberal' worldview. Nor could the members of the CABE Committee be accused of being neo-liberals. In fact, as early as 1974, in his K.G. Saiydain memorial, Naik attributed the much more rapid expansion of secondary and higher education at the expense of primary education to 'the class-base of political power'; this had led to 'the worst crisis in the post-independence period' and that 'the major tasks of educational reconstruction ... are still unfinished' and had become a lot more difficult.[15] And furthermore, economists spread over the entire ideological spectrum—neo-classical economists, equity-focussed economists such as Amartya Sen and Mahbub ul Haq, and leftists such as Ashok Mitra—bemoaned the neglect of elementary education'. Suffice to say, there is no need to invoke a 'foreign hand' to explain the changes which occurred in higher education in the 1990s.

Contrary to the belief of those who have no direct experiential knowledge of how the government functions, the government is not a monolith; it is a constellation of different entities such as ministries

[15] J.P. Naik, *Policy and Performance in Indian Education 1947–74*, Dr K.G. Saiydain Lectures, 1974, New Delhi: Allied, 1975, pp. 11, 16.

and it is rare for all these entities to act in concert driven by a common purpose, vision, and ideology (Chapter X). It is no doubt true that the Finance Ministry took the view that higher education was non-merit goods;[16] so did a minority of economists such as M. Govinda Rao.[17] However, it is common knowledge that the spirit of economic reforms did not extend to most Bhavans housing GOI ministries and to most of the states. Most ministries and states went ahead as if it were business as usual. For nearly four years, from May 1991 to December 1994, the period during which the Punnayya and Swaminadhan Committees were appointed and fees were increased by central government higher and technical education institutions, MHRD was presided over by Arjun Singh. In fact, between them Arjun Singh and Murli Manohar Joshi presided over MHRD for 14 of the 19 years from June 1991 to May 2009; for over 20 months (June 1996 to March 1998), the country was ruled by United Front governments of which the Communist Party of India was a constituent. By no stretch of imagination can Arjun Singh or Joshi be considered to be neo-economic liberals; nor were they push-overs in the governments of which they were ministers. While Arjun Singh went out of the way to flaunt his opposition to the economic policies of the government and did everything possible to embarrass the government, Joshi was the ultimate votary of *swadeshi* ideology. Suffice it to say, DOE did not plan any grand retreat of the state in the field of higher education nor did the state governments.

[16] Ministry of Finance, Department of Economic Affairs, *Economic Reforms: Two Years After and the Task Ahead*, 1993, pp. 26–7.

[17] M. Govinda Rao, 'Some Proposals for State-level Budgetary Reforms', *Economic and Political Weekly*, XXVII, no. 5 (February 1, 1992), pp. 211–21; 'Subsidies in Higher Education', *Economic and Political Weekly*, XXVII, no. 28 (May 1, 1993), pp. 891–2.

XIII

OPPORTUNITY KNOCKS AT THE DOOR

> There is one thing stronger than all the armies in the world, and that is an idea whose time has come.
>
> —Victor Hugo

To recapitulate, the revised POA gave its imprimatur to the new district-based strategy for UEE (Chapter XII). In view of the continuing macro-economic crisis and acute resource constraint, the expectations of domestic resources did not materialize, and given the unfinished tasks of the Seventh Five-Year Plan and the requirements of on-going programmes such as Operation Blackboard and teacher education there seemed little scope for new programme initiatives in the Eighth Five-Year Plan. All in all, the idea of district projects seemed to be an idea the time for which had not yet come, for innovations of all types require, among other things, adequate resources to operationalize the seminal idea underlying the innovation. In the rich literature on the technical innovation, the schema proposed by Norbert Weiner stands out.[1] Weiner proposed that innovation takes place only when there is a confluence of four elements. First, before a new idea can be applied, some person must have thought about it and preserved his thoughts in accessible records. Second, proper techniques should exist in the absence of which an idea, like the many precocious visualizations of

[1] Norbert Weiner, *Invention: The Care and Feeding of Ideas*, Cambridge, MA: the MIT Press, 1994.

Leonardo da Vinci (for example, the submarine), would remain trapped in the realm of abstraction. Third, there should be an environment which makes it possible, to paraphrase Plato, for philosophers to become artisans and for artisans to be philosophers, and finally an economic climate which provides the wherewithal to produce and distribute the product in large volume. The genesis of DPEP neatly fits in the Wiener scheme. The idea of district planning for improving elementary education was mooted by D.R. Gadgil as early as the 1930s and suggested by the Kothari Commission as well as J.P. Naik. NIEPA had a tradition of training education functionaries in various aspects of educational planning and had the generic skills which could be used to develop the specific technical tools of district planning for UEE (Chapter VI). Hence, the first two elements of the Weiner scheme existed when the idea of district planning for UEE became topical. The third and fourth elements were missing; these could be provided only by a well-funded programme to finance district planning for UEE. In this context, it is worth mentioning that microplanning spoken about by NPE and POA, 1986, remained a concept, at best occasionally tried in isolated pockets, in the absence of a scheme which extended financial assistance to conduct microplanning. It follows that only a well-funded programme would encourage the state officials to go in for district projects and look out for planning tools, and at the same time provide an incentive for the experts of NIEPA to develop, test, and disseminate district planning tools sought by the states. In other words, only a well-funded programme would prod the philosophers to move from the realm of ideas and teaching to practice. When Bordia demitted office in May 1992, it appeared to K that there was no way for the innovation of district planning to be operationalized on a substantive scale unless the UP Project was abandoned which because of the politics involved was easier thought of than done. But then opportunity knocked K's door as a threat. On 1 June 1992, the day after Bordia demitted office, K was surprised to receive a note asking him to attend a meeting of the National Renewal Fund (NRF) to be taken by Secretary, Department of Industrial Development, the next day. The subject of the meeting, NRF, did not seem much to do with education. Like a reluctant kid going 'towards the school with heavy looks', K went to the meeting grumbling. That was how an opportunity presented itself to operationalize the district-based approach to UEE.

As he was about to leave for the meeting, K was informed that he should attend the meeting in the office of the Health Secretary R.K. Mishra, and not that of the Industry Secretary. K was given neither a brief nor background papers. It came out in the meeting that soon after the new government assumed office in June 1991, it approached the World Bank for a structural adjustment loan (SAL) to avert the impending international default in 1991, and had informed the Bank that, in addition to SAL, it would seek the Bank's support for its medium-term strategy to meet the transitional social costs of adjustment. In pursuance thereof, the Industry Ministry sought funding from the World Bank for NRF which was designed to alleviate the problems of workers who might be affected by the restructuring of industry, and provide retrenched workers retraining and redeployment. The Secretary and Economic Adviser of that Ministry had discussions with the Bank staff in Washington in 10–14 April 1992. During the discussions in Washington, they were given to understand that, in addition to financing the NRF, the Bank was willing to extend what in jargon is called a Social Safety Net (SSN) credit which would help India meet the 'social dimensions of adjustment' through a package of policies and programmes which would mitigate the short-term negative effects of the on-going structural adjustment programme on the poor. The Bank would extend a policy loan which would be disbursed in foreign exchange in two tranches. The foreign exchange would come in handy to finance essential imports, and the counterpart funds in Indian rupees could be used to finance the ameliorative measures covered by the operation. For securing approval of the Bank, it was necessary to go through the customary sequence of discussions with Bank missions at the preparation stage, pre-appraisal, appraisal, and finally formal negotiations on the terms and conditions of the credit. In addition, the government was required to write to the Bank a *Letter of Development Policy* so as to provide a policy background for the loan, justification for a social safety net, and a description of the actions it proposed to undertake to ameliorate the social costs of adjustment.

In the meeting attended by him, K realized in no time that without his knowing, in the last week of April 1992, within a few days of Arjun Singh's statement on the UP Project in the Lok Sabha, the strategy of testing the intentions and good behaviour of Bank through a test case project got a quiet burial. To recapitulate, Skolnik tried to persuade

Bordia to go in for a sector policy loan instead of a specific investment (project) loan and mentioned that the Bank was satisfied with the education policy and that, therefore, while technically the Bank would have the right to raise policy issues it might not raise policy issues at all. On its part, UP was keen to go for a sector loan as project preparation would be faster and the whole state could be covered at one go. Bordia, however, stood his ground as he was dead set against giving any opening to the Bank to enter into a policy dialogue with DOE (Chapter X). It now appeared that because of macroeconomic compulsions, the government might have no option but to go in for the fast disbursal credit being offered by the Bank among others for primary education and enter into a policy dialogue with the Bank for improving the delivery of primary education. DOE's carefully calibrated strategy of engaging the World Bank appeared to be on the verge of collapse. The course of subsequent events proved the sayings that every threat is an opportunity and that fortune favours the prepared mind.

It came out that when the Industry Ministry and DEA held discussions with the Bank's Preparatory Mission for NRF (25 April to 9 May 1992) DOE was not involved, perhaps because it was felt that it was not as yet necessary to bring DOE into their discussion with the mission. During the discussions, it was agreed that *in the short term* NRF would be operationalized, the Public Distribution System (PDS) would be strengthened in specially targeted blocks with large population of the poor, and the matching rupee resources of the credit disbursed in foreign exchange used to restore the cuts made in the financial year 1992–3 in the allocations to programmes in social sectors such as primary education, basic rural health, child development, and employment generation. It was also agreed that *in the medium term* pro-poor programmes would be better financed, better targeted towards the poor, and made more cost-effective. Financing of social sectors would be reviewed so that adequate arrangements could be made for the long-term financing of social sectors; as a corollary, cost recovery, where appropriate, would be made in higher and technical education, medical education, and hospital services. Efforts would be made to enhance the efficiency and effectiveness of social sectors by better targeting and better attention to logistics such as supply of drugs. Efforts would also be made to promote the convergence of services in the villages, thereby harnessing the synergy between services such as ECCE, primary schooling, maternal and child health, and nutrition. The government had second thoughts about including PDS and employment generation schemes such as Jawahar Rozgar Yojana in the SSN operation and excluded them from the scope of the operation. In support of its stand, the government claimed that the issues pertaining to these two areas were of a very special nature and study of these issues would require more time than what the time frame of SSN operation would permit. The government's stand was prudent as these two sensitive areas would have been subject to the Bank's conditionalities even though what the Bank would have offered by way of assistance would have been a pittance of what the government itself expended.

It was only about a decade later that K came to know from a doctoral thesis of Moushumi Basu that the exclusion of PDS and employment generation schemes and inclusion of primary education generated considerable controversy within the Bank.[2] The design of the SSN operation significantly differed from similar operations previously financed in Africa and Latin America; those operations only sought to mitigate the short-term pains of adjustment and did not attempt to improve in the medium term the financing and delivery of services such as primary education and basic health. To many within the Bank, the proposed Indian SSN operation suffered from Type I as well as Type II errors, failing to do what ought to be done and doing what ought not to be. In their view, by failing to address the inequities and inefficiencies in PDS and employment generation programmes, SSN did not protect the poor adequately during adjustment. And furthermore, while not doing what ought to be done, the SSN operation was also erroneously attempting to use a short-term fast-disbursing programme such as the SSN to promote medium-term developments in the social sectors such as primary education and basic health. The time span required for systemic changes in the delivery of services such as primary education and basic health extends over several years—may be even a decade—while the SSN operation would not extend beyond a year or two. That being so, the logical doubt that arose was how could

[2] Moushumi Basu, 'World Bank's Lending to Social Sectors in India', Jawaharlal Nehru University thesis, 2003; Moushumi Basu, 'Negotiating Aid: World Bank and Primary Education in India', *Comparative Education Dialogue*, 3, no. 2 (Spring 2006), pp.133–54, at p. 145.

the Bank monitor and ensure that the changes initiated by the SSN operation were sustained for several years after the SSN operation ended. Many in the Loan Committee, our Cabinet as Cambridge the task manager of the SSN operation described it, had reservations about including primary education in SSN operation. Vergin and Cambridge who steered the SSN operations were interested in assisting India at a critical stage, if not for any other reason because of *localitis*, a syndrome which afflicts ambassadors and foreign correspondents. The saying that if one 'has lived long in a country where a thousand ties, a thousand sympathies, attach you to it one's judgement of that country is falsified' is not untrue.[3] Vergin and Cambridge were also eager that the SSN operations should be used to 'leverage' changes in delivery of social services so that their scope, reach, grasp, and effectiveness were enhanced; they were willing to take the risk that after the end of the SSN operations the changes initiated might not be institutionalized as they were optimistic that the Indian Government would realize that the changes were in the country's own interest and would sustain them. K is of the firm belief that Vergin and Cambridge were right and their critics wrong. The policy disagreements within the Bank prove the universal validity of the seminal truth he picked up from Sebenius and Allison's classic *Essence of Decision*: *Explaining the Cuban Missile Crisis*,[4] namely that no organization can be free of disagreements and groups. Contrary to the widely held view, the World Bank is not a monolithic organization with an inflexible 'Party line' which it seeks to forcefully impose on borrowing countries; nor are all the units and functionaries of the Bank like the sheep of Orwell's *Animal Farm* mindlessly bleating 'four legs good, two legs bad', or whatever is the policy laid down by the top management. As in every large organization, individual divisions have their own interests and priorities, and individual personality matters a great deal in the dealings between the Bank functionaries and officials of the borrowing countries. Three forces drive decision-making: the 'rationality' of policy analysis, dynamic interaction of divisions and other sub-units that together

[3] William Shirer, *The Collapse of the Third Republic: An Inquiry in the Fall of France in 1940*, Simon & Schuster, 1969, p. 449.

[4] Graham T. Allison, *Essence of Decision: Explaining the Cuban Missile Crisis*, Boston: Little, Brown & Company, 1971.

constitute the organization, and organizational politics. If this ineluctable fact is internalized, many of the blips which one encounters during the zig-zag course of interactions with the agencies such as the World Bank and within the government are easily explicable, and cease to be shocks. However, the way Cambridge went about ensured that the changes were precisely those that the policy documents of the Indian Government had commended.

K was already well acquainted with Cambridge who was a principal economist in the Bank's India Country Department and was the task manager for the UP Project. A big burly person from Guyana ever exuding warmth, he brought to bear upon his work the perspective and empathy of a citizen of a developing country. When K visited his office in the Bank headquarters in November 1992 during the SSN negotiations, K was amazed to find a framed poster of Lenin in a hectoring mood. A poster of the scourge of capitalism in the citadel of world capitalism was rather startling. Cambridge was a consummate task manager who could resolve with finesse the tensions intrinsic to any interaction between two organizations or individuals, cut through red tape like a sharp knife through butter, and improvise solutions that neatly harmonized the requirements of the Bank and the preferences of the country seeking Bank's financial support. In his approach to SSN negotiations, he was reasonableness personified. It is difficult to say how much of the reasonableness was due to the directions issued by his management and how much was due to his own inclination. It is well known that the Bank is eager to use loans as a policy lever to further its brand of reform in recipient countries, loans being explicitly understood as a means of 'buying a seat at the decision-making table'. It is also well known that the Bank is eager to continue its lending operations in large countries. A country could take strategic advantage of the Bank's eagerness to use by convincing the Bank that internal political conditions were such that attempts by the Bank to impose stiff conditionalities would not be tolerated.[5] Weakness, as K learnt from Thomas

[5] Alastair Fraser, *Aid-Recipient Sovereignty in Historical Perspective*, Global Economic Governance Programme, Managing Aid dependency Project, Department of Politics and International Relations, University Colleges, Oxford University, 220–6, pp. 1–61, at p. 20.

Schelling's *Strategy of Conflict*,[6] one of the three canonical works that K was introduced to by Sebenius at Harvard, could indeed be strength in negotiations. K was to put to great use Schelling's great axiom in his dealings with agencies. K was not alone in his deft use of limited mandate—little flexibility in negotiations. Thus, in the 1980s, there was

> no macroeconomic conditionality on Bank loans to China, and sparse conditionality on programme lending to Mexico and Indonesia, not because of any explicit ultimatum by those recipients but because of an unspoken understanding that their governments will not welcome detailed programmes of policy reform being imposed on them, coupled with an awareness in the Bank of the importance of maintaining a lending programme in these countries.[7]

Whatever, Cambridge was an excellent person to work with. K believed that the inclusion of primary education in the SSN operations owed much to Cambridge; he was associated with the UP Project right from the beginning. He attended the NIEPA seminar in November 1990, witnessed the stalemate over the preparation of the UP Project document, and was aware of the contingency proposal drawn by K for setting up an India Primary Education Fund with Bank funding. He was greatly impressed by the idea underlying district projects for primary education, and said it was one of the best ideas he had ever come across. K's surmise is that he would have convinced Vergin of the merit of district projects, and the opportunity that inclusion of primary education in the SSN operations would provide the Bank to the operationalization of a great idea as well as the fulfilment of the long and deeply held aspiration to include primary education in the Bank's loan portfolio in India. K owes him a huge debt of gratitude for strongly supporting DOE in the negotiations with EC on the co-financing arrangements; that support went a long way in ensuring that the financing arrangement fully conformed to DOE's views.

In order to develop the response of GOI to the Bank's offer of a SSN credit, GOI constituted a Core Group of Secretaries under the

[6] Thomas C. Schelling, *The Strategy of Conflict*, Cambridge, MA: Harvard University Press, 1960.

[7] Paul Mosley, Jane Harrigan, and John Toye, *Aid and Power: The World Bank and Policy-Based Lending*, 2nd edition, Volume 1, London: Routledge, 1995, p. 78, cited in Alastair Fraser, *Aid-Recipient Sovereignty in Historical Perspective*, p. 20.

chairmanship of R.L. Mishra, the Health Secretary; a representative of DEA, as well as secretaries of all departments whose programmes were to be covered in the SSN operation were members. The group was required to recommend the relative shares of health, basic education, and nutrition in the SSN programme. Mishra was a go-getter *extraordinaire* with rich experience of dealing with agencies and sensitive to the political implications of engagement with agencies. He was Minister (Economic) in the Indian Embassy, Washington, and his present ministry had for long extensive dealings with many multilateral and bilateral agencies. The first meeting of the Core Group was of an exploratory nature. Mishra elegantly outlined in general terms how the different departments could go about. Although the impact of the adjustment would be felt on both central and state budgets, it would be expedient to consider only the central plan budget. There was no clarity as yet about the quantum of funding that would be available to social sectors. However, it was clear that the funds would be received in two instalments, the first instalment of which could be used to restore the cut made by the 1992–3 budget in the allocations to the four Departments associated with the SSN operation: Education, Family Welfare, Health, and Women and Child Development. It was necessary to conceptualize the manner in which the SSN funds would be operated; they could be used for an ongoing programme or to start a new programme. If the funds were used for an existing programme, it would be necessary to demonstrate how the programme would be made more cost-effective and how it would target the beneficiary groups better. If a new programme is chosen, it would be necessary to take into account the sustainability of that programme as the prospects for domestic funding were not bright because of the resource situation. It was possible that the Bank might finance such programmes through separate loans; however, it might not, and therefore using the SSN funds for a new programme was risky. Whatever be the option chosen, the basic idea was that the departments would propose what they themselves would like to do even if Bank assistance were not forthcoming. Mishra also indicated that it was also necessary for the four departments to come to an agreement about the modalities of distributing the additional funds that would be available. DEA should estimate the notional budgetary allocations Health, Family Welfare, Education, and Women and Child Development departments would have received in the financial year

1992–3 if there were no fiscal compression due to structural adjustment. Each of the four departments would be entitled to the difference between the notional and actual budgetary allocation.

Soon after the Core Group meeting chaired by Mishra, Cambridge met K along with Middleton and Odeh to take stock of the developments in the preparation of the UP Project. By then K knew Middleton fairly well because of Middleton's association with the UP Project. His appearance—erect figure and carefully trimmed beard—and his being from the South—Georgia—reminded K of General Lee of American Civil War fame. He was an alumnus of Harvard, did his graduate work at the Harvard School of Education, and acquired a doctorate in educational planning. He was a Peace Corps teacher in the Republic of Korea in the mid-1960s. Before arriving in the Delhi office of the World Bank, he did policy research at the Bank headquarters on school reform, educational planning, and vocational and technical education and training. The World Bank's Policy paper on Vocational and Technical Education (1991) was largely based on his research. Apart from the UP Project, he was also the task manager for the first DPEP Project, and was quite helpful to K in fleshing out many ideas. He managed DPEP during its formative phase and left for the headquarters in August 1994 after the negotiations were successfully concluded. However, it was the first time that K met Odeh, a short sprightly Bank functionary from the Bank headquarters; K was to run into Odeh many times during the next few years in the country and in Washington, DC. K remembers Odeh mainly for his narration of how he tested the structural soundness of school buildings constructed by local communities themselves in UP without engaging contractors. Odeh was visiting that state as a member of the Bank's pre-appraisal mission. In every village he visited, he would get on to the roof of a school building, and jump again and again on the roof like a jack in the box. He told K that he expected to fall crashing down from the roof; instead he found that the roofs were intact and that one of his legs was sprained.

Cambridge took advantage of the meeting to brief K about SSN. From Cambridge, K got a good understanding of the Bank's expectations from the operation, as well as the likely conditionalities. Cambridge explained that for the operation as a whole as well as for each of the areas covered by the operation such as primary education, the Bank identified a few issues and the corrective steps that it expected the government to take to address these issues, some by November 1992 (when the first tranche was expected to be released) and others by July 1993 (when the second tranche was expected to be released). These steps would emerge as conditionalities for the release of the first and second tranches. The Bank identified three general policy issues. First, the budgetary outlays on several social sector programmes (primary education, primary heath, endemic disease programme, ICDS, and Jawahar Rozgar Yojana) were reduced in the financial year 1992–3. In order to address this issue, by November 1992, the government was expected to restore in real terms the budgetary allocations for these sectors which prevailed in 1991–2. It was also required to specify the programmes to which the additional funds provided would be applied (or to use the jargon SSN programmes), and further to commit that 'all donor assistance to safety net programs would be 'additional to the plan outlays'. That is to say that contrary to the general practice, the assistance received from the SSN operation would be over and above the plan outlay and be not subsumed in the outlay earlier fixed. It was clarified that the SSN programmes could be one of the existing programmes or a new programme. By July 1993, the government was expected to provide in the 1993–4 budget satisfactory allocations to SSN programmes. The second issue that the mission identified was underfunding of social sector programmes. In order to address this issue, by November 1992, the government was expected to review the allocations to be made to the Minimum Needs Programme during the Eighth Five-Year Plan, and to initiate a study of the financing of social sectors, with terms of reference jointly agreed by the government and the Bank. The study was required to make recommendations on how resources could be mobilized to meet agreed goals and targets. By July 1993, the study was required to be completed. The third issue was weak coordination among different social sector programmes, which led to waste and inefficient use of resources. In order to address this issue, by November 1992, the government was expected to set up a Social Sector Coordination Committee to review programme design and implementation at national, state, and panchayat levels. The committee would examine convergence of social services, duplication and redundancy in service provision, and staffing and management. By July 1993, the Committee was expected to complete its review and come up with recommendations.

Coming to the specifics of education, Cambridge informed K that his management was fully satisfied with the revised NPE and the strategies that DOE proposed during the Eighth Five-Year Plan, and that therefore there were no major issues to be resolved. He was much impressed by the proposal of the department to rely on district projects for achieving UEE; it was more focussed than across-the-board programmes such as Operation Blackboard. The Bank was eager to facilitate the operationalization of the revised NPE and the Eighth Five-Year Plan strategies through the SSN operation as well as basic education projects which could be back-to-back to the SSN operation. What Cambridge said was confirmed soon thereafter by Heinz Vergin, Director, India Department, and Oktay Yenal, Chief, Bank's country office, when they met Giri and K. In SSN operation, the Bank proposed that by November 1992 the government should (*a*) restore in real terms the budgetary allocations for primary education which prevailed in 1991–2; (*b*) get the ongoing evaluation of Operation Blackboard completed and discuss the findings with the Bank; (*c*) establish a task force to develop an action plan for the development of basic education in targeted states and districts; and (*d*) establish a task force under the aegis of the UGC to prepare guidelines for phased increase in tuition fees and compensatory scholarship programmes with effect from the financial year 1993–4. The proposals of the Bank were based on a few premises, the first being that primary education was underfunded in spite of being a priority area and should therefore get preference in budgetary allocations. Second, as higher and technical education was highly subsidized, fees should be progressively raised and non-budgetary resources mobilized more and more so as to recover the cost of providing education. To the extent that higher and technical education was less dependent on budgetary resources, more resources would be available for the priority area of primary education. Third, higher allocation of budgetary resources to primary education should be complemented by measures to enhance cost-effectiveness of programmes. Operation Blackboard should be revamped in the light of the on-going evaluation of the programme by five agencies, Operation Research Group, NCERT, National Institute of Rural Development, Giri Institute of Development, and Sandhan. The strategy of universalizing primary education through district projects should be operationalized so as ensure that educationally backward districts received focussed attention. As the proposals of the Bank were based on what was implicitly or explicitly stated in NPE, 1986, as well as DOE's Eighth Five-Year Plan proposals, the contention of the Bank that it was only assisting the government to implement its own policy was true. He also indicated that once the first tranche was released in November 1992, there would be no further monitoring by the Bank either of Operation Blackboard or of increase in tuition fees for higher education, and establishment of compensatory scholarships. It was sufficient if the *Letter of Development Policy* indicates a reasonable time frame within which Operation Blackboard and tuition fees for higher education would be revised.

A few days after the first meeting of the Core Group chaired by Mishra, K came to know that the loan would be of the order $500 million, and that the share of DOE in the first tranche of SSN would be just Rs 67 crore, a rather modest sum, about 28 per cent of the plan expenditure on elementary education in 1991–2. On 18 June 1992, a few days after that meeting and his discussions with Cambridge, K formulated a strategy note outlining the implications of the SSN operation, the options available for DOE, and the department's possible response, and submitted the note to Giri and Arjun Singh for a decision. Over the next month, the note was continually refined in the light of more information obtained during inter-ministerial meetings; however, the core elements of the strategy remained intact. Basically, there were two strategic questions: should DOE avail the assistance offered under SSN operations, and if so, should the assistance be utilized for an existing activity or a new activity? Declining the SSN assistance with a 'No, Thank you' would be the preferred option if the government permitted DOE to plough a lonely furrow, and if DOE could live with curtailment of the budgetary allocations for elementary education during 1992–3, and the limited plan allocations during the Eight Five-Year Plan which preclude any new initiatives such as district projects. Furthermore, the outlay of Rs 7,800 crore that Planning Commission provided for education during the Eighth Five-Year Plan was contingent on an inflow of external funds to a tune of Rs 1,500 crore. Only the Bank could provide financing of this magnitude.

In principle, the Bank's offer was welcome, for what the Bank suggested was generally in accordance with what the government itself had been advocating, namely that structural adjustment should have a human face, that social sectors should receive a higher priority in public investment, that within education primary education should get preference in budgetary allocations, and that strategies for universalizing primary education should be cost-effective and better targeted towards girls and educationally backward regions. But then, God is in details. Clarity was necessary on a number of questions: What would be the final terms and conditionalities? Would the operation be a Faustian bargain, too little funding for too much scrutiny? What would a policy loan mean in terms of oversight and monitoring? How much of a leeway the country would have in the policy dialogue? Would the Bank be too prescriptive? Can we persevere with policies which, we feel, are the right policies in the Indian context? These were questions which concerned the government as a whole and require consideration at the highest level. The gamut of activities and programmes impacting upon the poor is vast, and many of their problems are intractable in the short and medium terms. Hence, it was imperative, from the government's point of view, to narrow the focus and coverage of the SSN operation and, in turn, the scope of the conditionalities and the extent of monitoring. This is all the more so given the volume of lending expected was insignificant in relation to the central and state government expenditure on social sectors. In addition to questions which concerned the government as a whole, there were particular concerns for the DOE. Given the macroeconomic imperative, would DOE be stampeded into accessing Bank credit? Whatever, it seemed that DOE's carefully calibrated strategy of accessing Bank credit for primary education was in grave peril. In its dialogue with the Bank since 1987, the consistent stand of the department had been that policy was beyond the purview of the Bank's scrutiny. Accepting the SSN assistance would in effect mean abandonment of that stand. One should not underestimate the formidable ability of the Bank to gather information as well as its equally formidable institutional memory—the proposals of the Bank vouch for this fact. It was obvious that the Bank was closely following the revision of NPE, 1986, and its POA, the dialogue between the UGC and the vice-chancellors of central universities about the freezing of maintenance grants by the Finance Ministry, and the formulation of the Eighth Five-Year Plan. Therefore, while the SSN operation itself would not monitor the implementation of the revised Operation Blackboard scheme or revision of tuition fees by central universities, it would be prudent to expect that the Bank would be following what was happening, and raise these issues in its annual policy dialogue with DEA or in its lending operations either in the education sector or in the economy as a whole. There was force in the argument that sooner or later it was in the country's own interest to push through reform in the education sector and a certain degree of compulsion was helpful. However, our perception of the desirable pace and specifics of policy might differ from those of the Bank. The Bank's insistence on raising tuition fees effective from the financial year 1993–4 was politically sensitive. As it is, the vice-chancellors had been restive about the freezing of the maintenance grants to central universities. K put forth the view that on the whole it would not be prudent to go as fast as the Bank would like and to commit that the tuition fees would be revised with effect from 1993–4, unless we wished to use the Bank's insistence to hasten action by UGC and face the political fallout of such an action. Furthermore, conceptually, the principle of cost recovery through enhanced tuition fees could not be delinked from optimization of cost through rationalization of expenditure and prudent financial management. Time and space would be necessary for a proper study of reforming higher education finances and making efforts to get the universities on board before implementing the recommendations of that study. It would not be prudent tactically to commit to a deadline. If declining the assistance were not possible, DOE should strive to whittle down the conditionalities so that they are limited to the programme funded by SSN operations. In his strategy note, K also highlighted the fact that SSN credit would have political implications; for example, raising tuition fees or levying user charges in public hospitals would have political costs. Yet at the same time, not availing SSN assistance would also impose costs, as good relationship with the Bank was important given the precarious macroeconomic situation and dependence on the Bank and the IMF in the medium term. Availing or not availing the SSN assistance was therefore a political decision, and not solely an economic decision. K therefore suggested that DOE should propose that the SSN credit be considered by the Cabinet Committee on Political Affairs (CCPA), and not the Cabinet Committee on Economic Affairs (CCEA) which usually considers such issues.

Coming to the next question of whether the SSN assistance should be utilized for an existing activity or a new activity, K put forth the view that the balance of consideration lay in utilizing the assistance for drawing up district plans and posing them as a project for funding by IDA. Utilizing the assistance for an existing programme such as the Operation Blackboard was relatively easy, as all the systems and procedures were in place; however, that option rendered the entire programme spread all over the country being subjected to the supervision of the Bank even though it funded only an infinitesimally small part of the programme. Using the assistance to draw up district plans would enable the Eighth Five-Year Plan strategy to be operationalized; the Bank's assistance would be limited to the district projects it would fund.

The strategy suggested by K was accepted fully by Giri well as Arjun Singh. The latter wrote to the prime minister suggesting that the question of accepting SSN assistance be considered by the Cabinet Committee on Political Affairs; he also wrote to the Finance Minister setting out the stand of DOE. SSN assistance would be utilized to start preparation for district-specific projects for primary education which would eventually be posed to IDA for assistance. It was necessary to ensure as few policy conditionalities as possible. The Department's proposal to utilize SSN assistance was conditional on monitoring by IDA being limited and not extending to the whole education sector or a subsector of it. The UGC and AICTE had set up committees to study the entire range of issues related to financing of higher education; AICTE could take a similar step in respect of technical and management education. These steps should satisfy IDA, and no commitment need be given as to when the tuition fees would be revised in the light of the reports of the UGC and AICTE committees. Operation Blackboard was being revised in the light of the findings of the evaluation reports. As what IDA was seeking was already being done, a further discussion with IDA on Operation Blackboard was not necessary.

Being a fast-disbursing credit, one of whose objectives was to give balance of payment support to a government in acute need of foreign exchange, the project cycle of SSN was much shorter than that with specific investment loans such as the UP Project. One stage after another of the project cycle was reached in quick succession: discussions with the preparation mission (25 May to 8 June 1992), pre-appraisal mission (24 July to 9 August 1992), appraisal mission (23 September to 25 October 1992), and negotiations at the Bank headquarters on 16–20 November 1992. Like Beatrice benignly guiding

Dante in heaven, Mishra guided his flock with deftness through the internal and external negotiations that together drove the process. While all the departments had a common interest in securing as soft terms from the Bank as possible, they had at the same time conflicting interests and viewpoints. A bone of contention was the share each department would receive from the funds that SSN operation would provide; the representatives of the Departments of Family Welfare, and Women and Child Development pitched their demands high putting forth specious arguments. The politically savvy Mishra readily picked up the demand of K and Giri that it would be expedient to secure the approval of the Cabinet Committee on Political Affairs; the Secretary, DEA, however, pooh-poohed the suggestion saying that that CCEA had already approved the proposal to secure funding from the IMF and the Bank for balance of payment support. In a light-hearted banter, he wondered what all the fuss was about, since ministers, after all, followed the advice of secretaries.. The ever-earnest K replied that Arjun Singh could not be taken for granted by any secretary; having Arjun Singh as a minister was a bargaining asset of the highest order, yet another proof of Schelling's axiom that weakness is strength and that limited mandate in negotiations was a bargaining asset. Invoking the holy name of Arjun Singh clinched the issue. Preparatory to the consideration of the Cabinet Committee, Mishra got the Cabinet Secretary into the act by getting the decisions of the Core Committee chaired by him approved by the Cabinet Secretary through the medium of the Committee of Secretaries. It was also necessary to get the Planning Commission on board, for many of the issues arising from the SSN operations fell in the domain of the Commission. A couple of meetings in Yojana Bhavan which housed the Commission satisfied the *amour propre* of the Commission. The Commission agreed to come on board the SSN operations subject to the condition that after the SSN operation ended it was not bound to provide additional plan allocations to programmes covered by SSN operations; that was the rub. With the funds expected from SSN operations, district plans could be formulated and a few pre-project activities could be taken up in the chosen districts. Those funds could be used for field testing the methodologies and organizational arrangements for preparation of the district plans but were utterly inadequate to implement the projects drawn up unless plan funds were provided or, alternately, the Bank funded them. Giri and K betted on the assurances given by Vergin and Cambridge that Bank could approve loans for projects drawn up back-to-back the SSN operation for implementing the district plans drawn up under the SSN, and also to cover more and more districts with the new strategy for achieving UEE. It was a risk to go by verbal assurances as in formal settings Cambridge took the stand that the new programmes started under SSN operations would require to be continued by the government without any insistence that continuance would be dependent on the Bank loans. But then 'No Risk, No Reward'. However, not making an issue that the new district-based programme would have no additional plan support was figuratively skating on thin ice. Eventually, as the project cycle moved forward, it became necessary for the government to indicate how it would finance the new activities that would be financed once SSN operations ended, and in the Letter of Development Policy, the government indicated to the World Bank that during the Eighth Five-Year Plan, 110 districts with an outlay of Rs 1,950 crore would be covered by the new programme, and that of this outlay, *all but* Rs 230 crore would be externally funded. Technically, the government was obligated to implement the programme in 110 districts irrespective of the availability of external funding; while Vergin and senior functionaries did assure Giri and K that the Bank would provide the requisite resources they could not be expected to give a written undertaking as it would amount to a 'cross-conditionality'.

K could persuade Cambridge to accept the stand of DOE in its entirety when he visited the country again later for the appraisal mission. Cambridge agreed to treat the actions which the Bank proposed in respect of the UGC Committee on financing of higher education, as well as Operation Blackboard as already acted upon and completed for the purpose of SSN Operation. The substantial increase in tuition fees by IIMs and IITs came in handy for K to convince Cambridge about the earnestness of the government to prod higher and technical educational institutions to raise more and more of their own resources and to rely less on budgetary resources. Involved as they were with the zigzag course of the UP Basic Education Project, Cambridge and Middleton were very much appreciative of the sensitivity attached to the Bank funding of basic education, and had empathy with K's argument that far too rigorous condtionalities would compel DOE to spurn SSN assistance altogether. Mishra was similarly successful in whittling down the conditionalities that the Bank suggested in respect of the government hospitals and medical education. The Bank's preparation mission in June had suggested freezing of government expenditure on hospitals and medical colleges. The pre-appraisal mission agreed with the averment of Health Ministry that it had undertaken action to reduce the dependence of hospitals and medical colleges on budgetary support. However, at subsequent stages of the project cycle and during the formal negotiations the Bank did raise the issue of higher education and medical education institutions relying less on the budgetary support by the government. It did not elevate the issue to the level of a 'make or break issue'. Initially, the Bank team insisted that before the second tranche was released, the government was required to complete the review of the financing of social sectors, and to adopt comprehensive cost recovery policies for tertiary health and higher education, and increase charges for medical care and fees for higher education. The government was in no mood to bind itself. As a result of hard negotiations, the conditionality for the second tranche was diluted, deleting the provision to adopt comprehensive cost recovery policies; it was sufficient if the government acted on the recommendations of the committee it constituted to conduct the review. The committee could as well recommend that given the opposition to the on-going economic reforms it was advisable to proceed cautiously and, therefore, the question of cost recovery be deferred to a more opportune time. Technically the government acting on such a recommendation was fulfilment of the condition attached to the release of the second tranche. To jump the story ahead, higher education financing was never again raised in any of the nine credits that IDA offered to basic education in India after SSN credit: two UP Basic Education Projects, six DPEP projects, and the AP Economic Restructuring Project. All in all, this indicated that, like the American Supreme Court following 'th' illiction returns', the Bank is quite aware of political sensitivity associated with its operations, and that countries, particularly large developing countries such as India, can take strategic advantage of the Bank's eagerness to use loans as a policy lever by convincing the Bank that internal political conditions were such that attempts by the Bank to impose stiff conditionalities would not be tolerated.[8] Another plausible reason why the Bank was

[8] Alastair Fraser, *Aid-Recipient Sovereignty in Historical Perspective*, p. 20.

not far too rigid on the cost recovery issue could be the judgment of the Supreme Court in the Mohini Jain case[9] delivered on 30 July 1992 while the pre-appraisal mission was engaged in dialogue with different departments concerned. The judges who delivered that judgment discovered an unconditional right to education in the penumbra of Article 21 of the Constitution. The government could legitimately argue that the judgment constricted the freedom of the government to raise fees as enhancement of fees might be successfully challenged as an encroachment of the right to education; it needed time to study the judgment and take steps if need be to overturn the judgment. However, the Mohini Jain case acted as a damper on any overzealousness that some Bank functionaries might have exhibited in regard to cost recovery in tertiary health care and higher education. K could, in good humour, joke to Cambridge that he ordered the judgment to serve as a bargaining asset.

The fact that Cambridge agreed to treat the issue regarding Operation Blackboard as closed induced K to rethink about utilization of the SSN releases. He now proposed that the first tranche release in 1992–3 be used for Operation Blackboard instead of preparation of district plans, and that the second tranche release in 1993–4 be used for development of district plans and pre-project activities in the districts chosen. The new proposal would ensure that the pressure to utilize finds before March 1993 would not force abandoning the salutary principle of making haste slowly, all the more as the new strategy was as yet not fleshed out, and more importantly, the new strategy called for lot of dialogue with the states to convince them that business as usual would not do. It was necessary to abandon the 'brick and mortar' approach to education, to break the traditional pattern of relationship between the World Bank and the state governments, and to replace the expenditure-oriented implementation of CSSs by a new culture of implementation which laid strong emphasis on processes as well as outcomes. K's new proposal provided more time and space for developing the methodology and guidelines for preparation of district plans, building capacity in the states for drawing up district plans, and undertaking the dialogue needed with the states.

[9] *Mohini Jain, Miss v. State of Karnataka & Others*, AIR SC 1858.

It Never Rains but Pours

Cambridge was greatly enthused by the idea of district planning for UEE, and said again and again in many forums that that the idea was the best to come out of SSN operation. The SAR of the operation presented to the World Bank Board in November 1992 described the new district-based programme as the 'centrepiece policy change and instrument' in the area of primary education; that programme was named DPEP around March 1993 and till then was called by different names such as the National Primary Education Development Programme. The SAR's laudatory description of the new programme was repeated by the Implementation Report of the SSN operation (1995). It noted that:

> One of the more significant and probably long-lasting contributions of the SSN was the basis that it set for increasing investment in primary education. It facilitated the rapid development of the DPEP in India, which is quickly becoming an umbrella for both national and international assistance to the development of primary education in India. The DPEP is now the main vehicle for encouraging universalization of primary education in India.... Furthermore, it has been prepared in an exceptionally participatory manner, with extensive involvement of key Indian educational policymakers and research institutions, further contributing to its likely sustainability.[10]

SSN was the centrepiece of the Bank's presentation at the Aid India Consortium in Paris in June 1992, and the participants were very much appreciative of the new initiative in primary education with emphasis on most backward districts rather than general countrywide programmes which dissipated the country's efforts to universalize primary education. It was this meeting that persuaded the European Economic Commission (EC), as the European Union was known prior to 1993, to piggyback on SSN to support the district planning strategy for UEE with the largest grant it ever offered to primary education. The decision of the EC was literally a *deus ex machina*, an utterly unexpected divine intervention that suddenly and abruptly solved the seemingly unsolvable problems associated with Roopantar and Dhumkuria, the

[10] World Bank, *India: Social Safety Net Sector Adjustment Program: Completion Report*, 1995, pp. iv, 19.

MP projects in which Arjun Singh had a personal interest. Roopantar was expected to be financed by EC and Dhumkuria by UNESCO. On 10 June 1992, before the Aid India Consortium meeting and 10 days after C retired, an EC delegation landed on K. Erich Müller, Deputy Head of the Directorate dealing with aid, was visiting Delhi and he wanted to carry further the offer of EC assistance to Roopantar. He was accompanied by W. Almond and two functionaries of the EC delegation in Delhi, H. Østerby and Shanti Jagannathan. It was immense pleasure to work closely with Østerby and Jagannathan without whose solid support the EC support would not have materialized. Østerby was a Dane with a tremendous sense of humour. Shanti came to be a dear friend and comrade-in-arms in the development and implementation of DPEP. She was a professional par excellence with a rare blend of academic expertise, cogency of conceptualization, clear articulation, practicability, sensitivity and integrity, and had, among others, published a case study of six NGOs which won widespread recognition for their work in the field of primary education: Bodh Shiksha Samithi, Centre for Education Management and Development, Ekalavya, M.V. Rangayya Foundation, Pratham, and Rishi Valley Education Centre. She also authored a path-breaking article on programme-based approach (PBA) to education in which she brought out that DPEP was an embryonic PBA, and SSA was a full-fledged version. Apart from being EC's anchor for DPEP, she also played a lead role in developing the EC's multisector state partnership programmes in Chhattisgarh and Rajasthan. In 2010, she moved to ADB and co-edited a volume, on Skills for Inclusive and Sustainable Growth in Developing Asia-Pacific. She was the Convener of the ADB International Skills Forum series from 2011 to 2013, and is currently engaged in a study on Asia's Knowledge Economies. Prior to joining ADB, she worked with the European Union on development cooperation in South Asia and with an economic research think tank in India. All in all she was a pillar of support.

For good order's sake, for the meeting with Müller, K invited the MP State Education Secretary as well as the Commissioner of Public Instruction to join the discussion. The members of the EC delegation seemed to be a divided lot, emblematic of that organization, a constellation of twelve (as of 1992) fractious members. Müller appeared keen about the project, while Almond was hesitant and cautioned against a tight time schedule emphasizing that EC was venturing into a new area. The moment Müller and Almond made their observations the Commissioner of Public Institution sought to have a broad indication of the assistance likely to be made available. Müller seemed inclined to present a ballpark figure but Almond struck a contrary note saying that a coherent project document should first be prepared, and financing issues should come later. The State Education Secretary pitched in like Oliver Twist pleading, 'Please Sir, give me more,' and said, 'We expect so much from you. Ours is a very poor state with a huge tribal population. *Jab tak suraj chand rahega* [so long as the sun and moon last] the people of our state would remember you with gratitude'. The plea did not move the visitors who maintained that it was too early to commit the quantum of assistance. As ever, the choice of project components cropped up, and sticking to the stance of Bordia, K maintained that being a post-Jomtien project all the components of the Jomtien Declaration should be covered, and it would be expedient to go by the precedent of BEP, Lok Jumbish, and the UP Project. Almond was particular that the project should focus on a few components lest the management of the project should be overstretched. Thereupon K passionately delivered the dissertation on basic education which he heard Bordia deliver again and again. While Müller returned to Brussels, his colleagues went to MP to acquaint themselves with the MP educational scene. About 20 days later, on 29 June, there was yet another gruelling meeting on Roopantar. K first met with the MP officials before Almond joined them; the Commissioner wanted the project to be limited in scope and focus on the construction of school buildings as EC was daunted by the comprehensive basic project that K insisted. What he said was *déjà vu*; K was fed up with hearing the same litany being recited by the State Education Secretary after another: 'school buildings, buildings, buildings'. Given his authoritarian streak and rudeness, K read the riot act and lashed out at the 'brick and mortar' approach to education. In the full meeting, Almond's stance was no less frustrating; he asserted that at least 18 months would be required for approving the project proposal. This was understandable given that before EC could make up its mind on any issue it was necessary to reconcile divergent interests and opinions through a tortuous process. K concluded the meeting saying if the project cycle was so prolonged there was no point in having a project with limited scope, and that it was better to go with a comprehensive project. K gave up hope on EC and began to toy with the idea of MP being covered by one of the projects which could be back-to-back to the SSN operation.

About seven months later, on 20 August 1992, a UNESCO mission landed on K. Arjun Singh had high expectations from the offer of the DG, UNESCO, to assist an EFA project; he was confident that given his stature the DG has only to say 'Open Sesame' and the door to a treasure trove would open. Given that UNESCO was the specialized UN organization for education, K also had high expectations from the mission; he looked forward to the mission providing unique inputs for carrying forward the design of EFA projects. In his introductory remarks, K highlighted the fact that the mission had a significance that went beyond Dhumkuria and expressed his confidence that the mission's endeavours would benefit the nation's quest of UEE as whole. To maximize the spin-off effects, K associated four NIEPA faculty with the mission and organized a workshop on EFA projects at Bhopal to which education officials from several states such as AP, Bihar, Orissa , Rajasthan, and UP, as well all the external agencies which have been supporting and were expected to support basic education projects were invited. So many officials turned up that Giri joked that Bhopal had become the Mecca of basic education projects. Of the three NIEPA faculty associated with the UNESCO mission, N.G. Varghese had conducted a path-breaking study of the MP primary school system,[11] Yash Aggarwal was an educational statistician of distinction, and K. Sujata was a distinguished expert on tribal education, an apt choice given that MP had a high tribal population. Varghese was a precious member of the inner circle which collaborated with K and shared with him the agony and ecstasy of a maiden voyage in unchartered seas that translating the strategy of district planning for UEE was. His distinctive contribution lay in developing capacity for district planning in several states. Looking back, all the three were among those who played an important role in launching DPEP. Along with Arun C. Mehta of NIEPA, Yash Aggarwal developed the remarkable nationwide school-based *District Information System for Education*, which collects

[11] R. Govinda and N.V. Varghese, *Quality of Primary Schooling in India: A Case Study of Madhya Pradesh*, Paris: International Institute of Educational Planning, 1993.

all conceivable information on access to, facilities in, and enrolment in government-managed elementary schools. Sujata made significant contribution by way of tribal studies and as a member of the various review missions that periodically visited the states where DPEP was being implemented to take stock of the progress or lack of it.

K was in for great disillusionment; it did not take long for him to realize that, to put it charitably, the members of the mission had little to offer which was of any practical utility. The mission suggested studies and more studies, and surveys and more surveys. A couple of years later, as he interacted more and more with UNESCO functionaries and read more and more about agencies, K realized that he was naive in expecting so much from that UNESCO mission. He came to know that more than a decade earlier, UNESCO ceased to be an intellectual powerhouse; UNESCO was no longer the organization of the 1960s to which the new entrants to the area of education such as the UNICEF and the World Bank turned to help them navigate the untested waters of a new area. The politically disastrous M'bow period in UNESCO (1974–87) saw a rapid decline in UNESCO's educational expertise',[12] a fact which came out in the damning assessment in 1988 of UNESCO's external auditor of the capacity of UNESCO's education sector staffing capacity: 'UNESCO's professional capacity and expertise in education policy development, research and technical capacity has gradually declined'.[13] Apart from the limited technical competence of the members of the UNESCO mission, it also came out that UNESCO would not be offering any resources of its own. UNESCO's strategy was to piggyback on agencies with substantial resources which were interested to fund primary education in India, and get brownie points; or to use another imagery, UNESCO wanted to play a 'catalytic role' and provide technical support to draw up a project that would attract donors with substantial resources . UNESCO's efforts to tap resources from other agencies created problems. Frederico Mayor, DG, UNESCO, wrote to

[12] Philip W. Jones, *World Bank Financing of Education: Lending, Learning and Development*, 1st edition, London: Routledge, 1992, p. 110.

[13] UNESCO, *Report of The External Auditor*, Executive Board Document155 EX/27 Addendum, para 126; *Report by the DG on The Progress Made in the Implementation of the Recommendation of the External Auditor*, Executive Board Document 156 EX/31.

the Administrator, UNDP, seeking $10 million for the *Dhumkuria*.. But then from the meeting Bordia had with John Lawrence of UNDP headquarters just about three months earlier, K knew that what all UNDP could do was to provide seed money and try to rope in agencies having substantial funds such as the Bank. The as-it-is meagre assistance of UNDP having already being slotted for the South Orissa Project, UNDP support to Dhumkuria would entail withdrawing commitment to Orissa. In all honesty, K informed Arjun Singh that not much could be expected from UNESCO, and that it was better that MP be covered by SSN operations and by the back-to-back projects that were proposed to be posed to the World Bank. None loves the bearer of bad news, and Arjun Singh was no different. He was apprehensive that if MP were included in SSN operations, it would have to share with other states the resources that would be available. He entrusted Nina Sibal, India's Permanent Representative to UNESCO whom he handpicked for the job, to follow up with the DG. Nothing came of it. K did not know then that UNESCO was so cash-strapped that DG, UNESCO, had to order a 60 per cent cut in programme expenditures and had to borrow from a German Bank to pay salaries. Had he known he could have proved his point and convinced Arjun Singh. Truth to be told, he came to know later of the acute financial crisis from an article in the *Newsweek* and not from the Indian delegation.[14]

On 19 October, a communication was received from Neeraj Jain of DEA that an EC mission would be descending three days later. Soon enough Østerby and Shanti met K to get his reaction to the mission being mounted. Having been Bordia's understudy, K knew that occasionally it is a good ploy to be on the offensive; hence, he began the conversation saying 'you have surprised us. What's all this about?' They were apologetic and said they themselves had no clue about the genesis of the mission; however, they said it would be awkward if the mission were not received. K requested them to come back with more information about the mission and its background, and that in the meanwhile he would make his own inquiries. K rung up Jain to check what the mission was about; Jain was surprised that K did not receive communication sent on 13 October by J. Broadhurst, Charge d'Affaires of the EC delegation. The communication addressed to Jain was copied

[14] 'Back to UNESCO: Renewing Old Ties', *Newsweek*, June 14, 1993.

to K. K asked him to send a copy of it to him so that he could study it and take a view. When he received the communication, he noticed that it bore no address of DOE, symptomatic of the fact that EC was as yet a novitiate in the field of diplomacy; for all that he knew the communication might have reached DOE, Delhi Administration. From Broadhurst's letter, K came to know that the ambassador of the EC Delegation met Jain before she left for Brussels, that Jain indicated to her that the government were agreeable to the possibility of EC supporting primary education within the framework of SSN, and that the mission was an offshoot of the government's willingness conveyed by Jain. K was incensed by the failure of DEA to consult DOE before conveying the government's willingness. K came to know Jain intimately over the course of the next year when they interacted often over the EC support and travelled together to Brussels to conclude the agreement with EC. He was a gentleman, and unusual for a deputy secretary or director in DEA, he was quite deferential to a senior officer of another department like K. However, the very fact that even he conveyed the government's views without consulting DOE, the department concerned, is symptomatic of the high and mighty attitude of DEA officials, and their tendency to take officials of other departments for granted.

Later in the day, Østerby and Shanti came back and informed that the EC assistance was likely of the order of 150 million ECUs (about $184.5 million, Rs 480 crore)—a mind boggling figure. The EC assistance was nearly as much as the funding provided by the Bank under the SSN operations for the government as a whole, and about five times the amount DOE was receiving under the SSN operations. Half the assistance was scheduled to be released by June 1993, about eight months hence, and the rest released in tranches of 10–20 per cent of the assistance committed subject to the fulfilment of conditionalities. The counterpart rupee funds of the releases could be deposited in a commercial bank and drawn for the DPEP projects as and when required depending on the pace of implementation. The meeting with Østerby and Shanti lifted K to the seventh heaven; the offer was manna from heaven as it resolved at one stroke the acute dilemma facing K in getting the MP projects going and the embarrassment he faced in his relations with his minister, Arjun Singh. K savoured the sweet feeling of being able to inform Arjun Singh, 'I told you so, SSN is good from MP'.

By then the dialogue with the Bank had reached a stage when one could feel comfortable with the SSN operation and its terms and conditions. The fact that EC offered assistance under the SSN framework was a good augury that the terms and conditions were likely to be acceptable. There was, however, a major problem: the mismatch between a fast-disbursing assistance and the rather slow pace of utilization of funds by a social sector project which, unlike building a dam or a hydroelectric project, was mainly about people: changing the attitude, motivation and improving the competency of teachers and educational administrators, building the capacity to bring about change, develop and implement the district plans, and so on. Although the tranche releases would be deposited in a bank account, the fact that money was lying idle might tempt the state government to short-circuit the planning process and go in for programme components, which facilitated fast utilization of funds; in short, there was a danger that the 'brick and mortar' mania would be reinforced. The problems arising from the mismatch were not hypothetical; over the next 18 months or so, dealing with MP officials was a prolonged nightmare.

Østerby and Shanti also informed K that EC was in a hurry to get the mission through before the negotiations with the Bank scheduled for mid-November in which EC was expected to participate. The EC entrusted the task of organizing a mission to the British Council, and the mission was being led by David Theobald with whom K was familiar from the time he was State Education Secretary and Theobald was the anchor-person for APPEP. The choice of Theobald was deliberate as he was an astute India hand and could complete the task much faster than those who were strangers to India, the Indian educational landscape and the Indian bureaucracy. The other members of the mission were J. Watson, an educational economist, and Juliet McCafferty, Social Development Advisor. K's reaction to the choice of Theobald was rather mixed. K had a very good rapport with Theobald, and Theobald could plunge into his task straightaway. But K had also deep concerns. There was the danger that the MP Project would become a fertile ground for British consultancy and bear the deep impression of APPEP as it was not unusual for the choice of consultants to affect ex-ante the design and technical criteria that a project adopted. His apprehensions were not unwarranted. About a year earlier, before leaving India back home, Theobald had met K, and after the discussions about APPEP, he turned to another theme. Saying that he was now wearing a different hat, he said he heard that the Bank had fixed up a Japanese Grant Facility to help DOE and UP government to formulate the UP Project, and requested K to draw upon British expertise which was quite varied and strong instead of drawing upon solely on IIEP. While the professional support by ODA and its consultants for APPEP had a few admirable features, there were also severe limitations of which the most important was the handholding style of managing the project and insignificant association of the 'locals' and Indian resource institutions in the design and detailing of programme components. K carried with him to Delhi his concern that capacity development should not be impaired by continuous 'mothering' by a local agency office and by hordes of expatriate consultants and officials descending on the states and districts at short, or no notice.

For good order's sake, at K's suggestion Giri wrote to the Secretary, DEA, suggesting a meeting to discuss the instrumentalities for financing a medium-term project with a fast-disbursing grant. What DOE got in response was a cryptic reply saying that DEA would support the EC proposal and would like DOE to receive the mission. Obviously, the fact that financing a medium-term education project of five to seven years with relatively slow absorption of funds through a fast-disbursing loan was an anomaly, and that if the EC offer were to be availed it was necessary to think through the implications and modalities, was lost on the mandarins of DEA. Strange but true, in K's experience, while DEA's management of aid at the macro-level was admirable it was indifferent to the design, implementation, and outcomes of a project. It would not be unfair to say that quite a few of its senior functionaries did not mind even if an agency micromanaged a project so long as disbursement by the agency was as scheduled in the project and financing agreement. Three challenges are intrinsic to the management of external assistance. First, how does one ensure, figuratively speaking, that the tail does not wag the dog? How does one prevent the availability of assistance and the priorities of agencies from determining the overall national priorities? Or in other words, how does one ensure that the assistance received matches national priorities and not the other way round? Second, how does one ensure that a project funded by an agency is in synch with the relevant sectoral policy and promotes the attainment of those policy objectives?

Third, how does one ensure that an agency does not micromanage the development and implementation of a project precluding indigenous capacity development? The first challenge was met by centralizing major decisions regarding external funding and vesting them in DEA; the Planning Commission played a complementary role. It was DEA which decided the agencies from which the assistance was to be tapped, the purposes for which the assistance was to be tapped, the inter se priorities among the different purposes, and the terms and conditions relating to financing, accounting, and procurement subject to which the assistance was to be availed. Important functions were also centralized; thus, it was DEA which led the negotiations with the agencies, maintained the 'aid accounts', provided the documentation necessary for reimbursement of the assistance utilized, and monitored the utilization of assistance. DEA also operated procedures which sought to stabilize project spending in the face of fluctuations in the flow of assistance. The Planning Commission complemented the efforts of DEA by ensuring that the size and composition of investment programmes funded by agencies are in sync with plan priorities; to this end, the standard practice was to insist that the outlays of projects funded by external assistance were adjusted within the outlay fixed for a given sector and for planning entities such as central government departments and state governments. The central government departments such as DOE have to play a pro-active role if the second and third challenges are to be meaningfully addressed, and their task would have been easier if DEA were empathetic to the challenges faced by them. Suffice to say, DEA's management of aid was conditioned by its angle of vision and mandate; it tended to view projects through the finance prism and more concerned with augmenting aid flows and their utilization than the compatibility of projects with sectoral objectives, project outcomes, and capacity building.

Again at K's suggestion, Giri invited his batchmate Nirmala Buch, Chief Secretary, MP, for discussions before the Theobald Mission so that the state government was brought on board, and DOE and the state could speak to the mission with one voice. A remarkable civil servant with a strong sense of social commitment, Nirmala Buch had no difficulty in agreeing that it was imperative to avoid unseemly haste in utilizing funds without going through a rigorous process of preparing district plans, that all aspects of UEE should be covered without an excessive focus on buildings, and that there was no need to engage expatriate consultants for project formulation and implementation. With BEP and the pilot phase of Lok Jumbish as reference points, K had by then already worked out the broad financial parameters for implementing the district plans. The ceiling of 24 per cent on civil construction and 6 per cent on administrative overheads laid down in BEP would continue so that all aspects of UEE were addressed, and aspects such as quality and learner achievement would not be orphans. However, it was not possible to sustain the financing arrangement of BEP wherein half of the outlay was provided by the agency, a third of the outlay by the central government, and a sixth of the outlay by the state government as the central government did not have the resources required to match the hefty funding expected from the Bank, and now the EC. Hence, K came up with a new financing formula wherein 90 per cent of the outlay would be provided by the central government and 10 per cent by the state with the entire share of the central government being raised from agencies. The financing arrangement proposed by K was approved by Giri and acceptable to Nirmala. Giri and K also made it clear that with EC in a terrific hurry to provide resources, there was no need whatsoever for the state government officials to make a pitch for funding. Nirmala was also taken into confidence that UNESCO might not be able to provide funding and that being so the districts which were to have been covered by UNESCO would have to be financed by EC. Respected for her professional abilities and integrity, she had no difficulty in finalizing the districts which would be covered to the satisfaction of the state government which was then ruled by BJP as well as Arjun Singh, the sworn enemy of Hindutva forces. All in all, it was an excellent start for the MP Project; however, in keeping with the American saying 'it ain't over till it is over', Nirmala soon moved to GOI as Secretary, Rural Development, and after her exit, the relations between DOE and the MP officials were to pass through a stormy patch before they became perfectly harmonious.

The mission neatly accomplished its task of reconnoitring the MP educational scene, and the wrap-up discussions were extremely cordial. Almond also joined the discussions. Before the formal meeting wrap-up presided over by Giri, K had informal discussions with the mission members, Østerby, Shanti, Almond, and the State Education Secretary and Commissioner of Education. The Commissioner sought to reopen the financing pattern even though it was accepted by the Chief Secretary herself; he wanted the ceiling on civil construction to be removed altogether, which if agreed would result in the thrust of the MP Project being on construction of school buildings and expansion of school facilities. It is a standard practice for interest groups and idea brokers not to concede defeat but to continually look for new opportunities to push their preferred option, and to package their preferred option from time to time in sync the changing context. Or to put it figuratively, they are on the lookout for a new peg to hang their preferred option or, to mix metaphor, a new bottle to pour their old wine. Thus, in the United States, when a federal programme for mass transit was first proposed, it was sold as a straightforward traffic management tool. When the proposal did not fly, the proponents waited for the next opportunity to push their proposal. Once the environment movement gained salience and pollution was in everyone's mind, urban mass transit systems were put forth as *the* answer for curbing pollution as mass transit would get people out of their cars while commuting.[15] Similarly, the Commissioner hitch-hiked on the idea of decentralized planning to argue that there should be no *a priori* ceilings, that local communities should be free to decide what they want, that district plans and the MP Project should be an aggregation of the felt needs. *A priori* ceilings would make a mockery of decentralized planning. Watson supported him even though earlier he observed that the local conditions were as yet not ripe for 'bottom-up' planning, and that planning should be done at the district or sub-district levels and the plans finalized after extensive consultations with local communities. Personalities and interests apart, fundamental issues underlay the Commissioner's stand, and they kept cropping in the initial years of DPEP: Would not a national programme to support districts undercut the states? How legitimate is central direction by way of a national framework and broad financial parameters in a programme whose avowed objective was to decentralize the planning and implementation of UEE? If a national framework and broad financial parameters were unavoidable, how much flexibility should be provided to the state governments and districts? These were

[15] John W. Kingdon, *Agenda, Alternatives and Policies*, 2nd edition, New York: Longman, 1995, p. 175.

questions that came up during the dialogue with the bank on the SSN operations as well as with the state governments when they began to get district plans prepared.

The view that broad financial and programme parameters were incompatible with decentralized planning was as much of an immaculate conception as the idea that DPEP undercuts state governments. Ideally, a plan should be 'bottom up', and originate in the felt needs of local community. The ideal assumes that all citizens are well-informed and rational human beings fully aware of the choices, and are willing and able to choose the option that is best for them individually and collectively. However, the real is different from the ideal. If officers like the Commissioner who had worked with Bordia and was aware of the limitations of the conventional approach to UEE could not give up the 'brick and mortar' mania, it would be naive to expect that educational functionaries in the field and local communities would view educational development as something more than opening schools, appointing teachers, and construction of school buildings. Letting the planning process go on without a framework or parameters would be counterproductive, as the plans would be no more than a long charter of demands far beyond the capacities of the government. Such a freewheeling process also carried the danger of being captured by interest groups such as civil contractors who would see in the massive funding of education a business opportunity. The best could be the enemy of the good, and if the Commissioner's argument were accepted the MP Project might turn out to be a civil construction programme making a mockery of educational planning. As compared to the rigid schematic pattern of CSSs, DPEP offers greater flexibility. Within the broad parameters laid down by DOE, states and districts would have considerable flexibility to plan and design their programme interventions. Raising the argument to a more abstract level, uncompromising thought is the luxury of the closeted recluse. At the cost of being dubbed politically incorrect, it should be said that in the real world, planning or policy or, for that matter, governance itself has to deftly balance responsiveness to citizens on the one hand and doing what was good for citizens on the other. To take an example cited by Chief Justice Kapadia had there been a referendum in 1947 on the question whether untouchability should be abolished, the majority would not have agreed to abolish untouchability. In spite of the extant predominant public opinion, Article 17 of the Constitution abolished untouchability.[16]

In the meeting K had with the state government and the EC functionaries, K tried to convince the Commissioner why the broad financial parameters were not antithetical to decentralized planning. K was happy that Østerby supported his point of view. However, the Commissioner dogmatically stuck to his stand and insisted that the ceiling of 24 per cent on civil construction be removed, whereupon K rudely told him, much like his mentor Bordia, that settled issues could not be reopened, and that if the state government believed that the MP Project should be a construction programme and not an educational programme, he would like to close the discussions. Quite a few eyebrows were raised including those of Neeraj Jain of DEA. That settled the matter of financing parameters once and for all. However, an editorial in the *Economic Times* entitled 'Schnorrer Syndrome' around that time captured K's feelings in the dialogue with the MP officials. Schnorrers are a special class of persons in the European Jewish community who accepted gratuities not as a dole but as a right. The editorial referred to the story of a schnorrer's encounter with Baron Rothschild, philanthropist and financier of nations and empires. The Baron told the schnorrer that he would invariably receive his weekly gift and should not be grouchy. In high dudgeon, the schnorrer shot off a rebuke: 'I don't teach you how to be a millionaire. Please don't teach me how to schnorr.' Then came the illuminating lines

> If senior officials and India-based representatives of (funding) agencies had heard the story, they would probably chuckle over it when they return from exasperating negotiations with Indian officials. For all along, India had been a schnorrer, approaching such negotiations with a gifted pompousness, ill-concealed sense of superiority and righteous rigidity.... The attitude was give us the money; don't tell us how to use it; who else would know our requirements better?[17]

Once the 'mutiny on board' was squelched, K could afford to be a genial chairman of the meeting. K praised EC for pragmatism and observed that the innovation of clubbing rapid disbursal assistance

[16] 'Parliament Is Supreme: CJI', *Times of India*, 26 August 2102.

[17] 'Schnorr Enough', *Economic Times*, 15 November 1992.

with a specific medium-term project would go down as a landmark in the history of development assistance. K contrasted the frustrating meetings with EC in the recent past with the satisfactory outcome now achieved because of the latest EC initiative. Østerby quipped that the earlier meetings were frustrating because 'you wanted soap and we were offering you toothpaste'. K noticed a sneaking concern among the EC functionaries that the identity of the EC would be submerged by that of the Bank. K made it clear that EC would fund a national programme with multiple sources of funding, that in fact EC stole a march over the Bank in providing substantial funding, that systems and procedures would be put in place after due discussion with all those who funded the programme, and therefore there should be no apprehension that EC would be saddled with Bank procedures. In the formal wrap-up meeting, Giri reiterated this point.

It was only much later that it came out that while the Theobald Mission supported the extension of EC assistance to MP there was a sting in the tail. Noting that there was little capacity in MP for district planning and implementing a project of such a magnitude, it recommended establishing by EC of a strong monitoring unit as well as appointment of consultants to assist MP to go develop and implement the project. At one level, the recommendation could not be faulted as the mission was duty bound to inform EC, its employer, of the position on ground and the need for strong institutional arrangements for monitoring and capacity building. At the other level, the recommendation of the Theobald Mission failed to take cognizance of the fact that much water had flown down the Thames since ODA decided to extend assistance to APPEP in 1984, that the March 1991 CABE parameters for availing external assistance had changed the rules of the game altogether, and that any arrangement proposed by an external agency should not detract from the paramount objective of building national and state capacity for the design and management of UEE projects. Before making its recommendation, the mission ought to have raised the issue of institutional arrangements for addressing the problem of inadequate capacity during the wrap-up discussions. Truth to be told, the Theobald Mission did not even give a hint of its concern. The question of monitoring was the most vexatious issue to be resolved in the dialogue with EC. Whatever, all is well that ends well, a circle squared, and an unprecedented financial innovation was made.

Soon after the EC Mission completed its task, yet another UNESCO Mission landed in Bhopal without even touching base with DOE as is customary, began demanding massive information, and suggesting some more studies to be made. Nirmala rang up K with irritation, demanding to know what the mission was about and why more and more studies were needed. K consulted Giri and suggested to Nirmala that the mission should be requested to first consult DOE before taking further action. Having come to know that EC had decided to fund the MP Project, the UNESCO headquarters began to lobby the EC to involve UNESCO in the MP Project. Colin Power visited the EC headquarters at Brussels and went over to Manchester to plead with Theobald. However, neither DOE nor EC was keen to have an intermediary between them; K came to know that the British who were members of EC but not of UNESCO spiked UNESCO moves. Sure enough, Dhumkuria was cast in the limbo of history.

SSN and Organizational Politics within the Bank

K came to know from Cambridge when he turned up to lead the Appraisal Mission that there were reservations within the Bank about the new district approach, and that among those who felt that the new programme of DOE in the making (or DPEP as it was to be known later) would undercut the state governments was Rajagopalan, Vice President in the Bank President's office and the President's Special Adviser. Looking back, the then nomenclature of the new programme—National Primary Education Development Programme—was a culprit to a considerable extent, for mankind, as Gibbon observed, is governed by names and most are prone to be guided by words and symbols, positive or negative, rather than by the realities behind them. Mohan Gopal, a Harvard educated lawyer from Kerala who was then working for the World Bank and was a member of the Appraisal Mission, also echoed Rajagopalan's reservation. K told him that one should judge the new programme-in-the-making not by abstract notions such as decentralization but by what it actually would do. DPEP proposed to keep the state governments fully in the picture in that they were free to choose districts so long as those districts fulfilled the criteria laid down by the programme. The funds would be released by the central government to a state-level society created by the state government whose governing organs were presided over by government functionaries and included representatives of all the departments concerned. It was the state-level Society which released funds to the districts, and organized and oversaw the implementation in the districts. In contrast to the rigid schematic pattern of CSSs, the new programme-in-the-making allowed considerable flexibility to the states to decide what they wished to do subject to the feasibility and cost-effectiveness of the measures they proposed passing professional scrutiny organized by DOE. Furthermore, the district-based approach was set out in the POA, 1992, which got the imprimatur of CABE in which all the state governments were represented. The new programme-in-the-making was not a unilateral decision of DOE but was anchored in a federal consensus on the new strategy to be followed for universalizing elementary education. This explanation satisfied Mohan Gopal and came in handy to persuade the sceptics within the Bank.

SSN Negotiations (16–22 November 1992)

With the EC Mission and the Bank's Appraisal Mission concluding their tasks to the satisfaction of DOE and the government, the road to Washington for negotiations with the Bank was clear by early November.

While taking leave of K after concluding the Appraisal Mission, Cambridge alerted K that he wore two hats, and that across the negotiating table in Washington, he would wear the other hat; he would no longer be the amiable Big Boy but a Baddie, a tough, relentless negotiator. He did his very best to act as Baddie but K felt he was not wholly successful, and the Big Boy in him popped up once in a while. The negotiations took place in the Human Resources Division of the India Country Department which was headed by Skolnik and was temporarily located in a building close to the Bank headquarters. When K arrived in the building, he came across in the foyer a steel sculpture of Don Quixote riding on his horse Rocinante and charging at something invisible, perhaps non-existent. Looking back, the sculpture neatly captured the spirit of the negotiations; like Don Quixote, Cambridge and his team appeared to be relentlessly tilting at the windmills of cost recovery in higher education and tertiary healthcare. When a couple of days later, K entered the foyer along with Mohan Gopal and told him that the Bank seemed to be fond of tilting at windmills, to elicit the reply of the precise lawyer that Mohan Gopal was that the building was not owned by the Bank but leased. Once the Indians settled down at the negotiating table, he wore the other hat and surprised K and his colleagues saying that the Bank's senior management had not yet approved the negotiations and was upset about the lack of clarity about many issues. 'Beware, a tough negotiation awaits you,' was his message. The negotiations were scheduled to be concluded by 20 November; it now appeared that they might stretch beyond 24 November. Till the management approved the negotiations, only technical discussions could be held. Vergin was away on a mission and was expected to be back only on 20 November. Co-financiers such as USAID, the Dutch, and the Germans would join the negotiations on 18 November; as it would be necessary to finalize the terms and conditions of co-financing, the negotiations have to be more prolonged than expected earlier. He clarified that the EC would not be joining the negotiations; however, it was understood that the EC Mission had a satisfactory visit. The documents circulated earlier in the morning—the latest 'policy matrix' and the report and recommendations of the President to the Executive Board—did not seem to indicate that what was agreed to with the Appraisal Mission was being reopened. But then God is in fine print, and then the next five days were spent on the question of non-budgetary resources for higher education and healthcare, with the Bank team insisting that the Indians should more precisely commit themselves to raise more non-budgetary resources and the Indians arguing that more precision was precluded by the uncertainty arising from the on-going review by the Supreme Court of its judgment in the Mohini Jain case, and the necessity to ensure that the Committee on Social Sector Financing which both parties had agreed to constitute was free to go about its work without being constrained by a specific agreement between the Bank and the government. As it always happens in such negotiations, the drudgery eventually ended in a mutually acceptable text with built-in constructive ambiguity which committed no one definitively and which allowed everyone to go home claiming victory. It was agreed that before the second tranche was released a committee of secretaries would be constituted to review the financing of social sectors, and its recommendations regarding timely availability of funds for the programmes covered by the SSN credit and enhanced mobilization of non-budgetary resources for higher education and tertiary health-care would be implemented. This was almost the same as that agreed with the Appraisal Mission, for the agreement now concluded did not preclude the Committee from saying that it was not opportune to go in for more non-budgetary resources.

The negotiations began with fireworks. Ashok Khurana of DEA, the designated leader of Indian delegation, was expected to join the negotiating team only on 18 November, and in his absence, B.S. Lamba, Mishra's deputy, had appropriated for himself the position of leader. In reply to Cambridge's introductory remarks, he dropped a brick by saying that Mishra would meet Earnest Stern, Managing Director, and would settle all contentious issues. A pin-drop silence followed; Cambridge said with indignation that 'the negotiation occurs here. It does not work out that way'. Mohan Gopal also joined him in voicing his indignation. A day later, during the discussion on non-budgetary resources Cambridge said that during the recent visit of President Preston to India, Vergin had further discussion on the issue, and that Ashok Khurana might come up with an acceptable proposition. It was now the turn of K to whip himself into a fit of anger. He said that he was not a free agent; his Minister, Arjun Singh, was away in China when Preston visited India, and that he could not be a party to any formulation other than that approved by CCPA which was attended by Arjun Singh. Cambridge as well as Skolnik who was sitting on behalf of Vergin was appreciative of his stand; Skolnik said that the Bank is aware of the political sensitivity, and would not like to be instrumental in triggering riots and students burning buses. By 19 November evening, the formulation agreed to during the Appraisal was accepted by all.

The discussions on primary education were very smooth because everything was already settled with Cambridge back home, and Cambridge was a great fan of the new district-based approach to UEE. What was already agreed was formalized in the Development Credit Agreement and the agreed minutes of negotiations. Before the second tranche was released, it was agreed that detailed action plans would be prepared for at least 20 districts, that at least 20 per cent of the 1993–4 budgetary provision for implementing the action plans would be released, and that in each state where the programme would be implemented a project director would be appointed, and in each of the districts covered a district project officer. At the least, the plans were to contain an assessment of 'the current status of primary school facilities, the enrolment in primary schools by boys and girls, and the number of teachers and facilities for teacher training'. In addition, the plans were required to outline the strategy of a number of matters such as increasing enrolment particularly of girls, enhancing community participation, pump priming demand for primary education, and improving retention, learning achievement, quality of teacher training, and the logistics of providing text books and teaching learning materials. The plans were also required to outline the activities proposed to be undertaken in 1993–4, financing arrangements, and the system for implementing and monitoring the plans. The compliance with these conditions was not at all difficult, and eventually action plans prepared in 23 districts spread across the six states of Assam, Haryana, Karnataka, Kerala, Maharashtra, and Tamil Nadu formed the basis for the first DPEP Project posed to the World Bank in early 1994 and approved by the Bank in November 1994. In addition, 19 districts of MP were covered by EC funding.

True to the nomenclature of the proceedings of the first two days, during the technical discussions, considerable time was spent on 17 November to discuss a bright idea of a consultant that all the programmes covered by SSN operation should be implemented in a single set of districts which were backward in all respects such as primary education, health, and income levels. Indicators such as educational backwardness, high maternal mortality rate (MMR), high infant mortality rate (IMR), and high poverty ratios should be used to choose the districts. In his view, that alone would ensure that the programmes targeted the poor, and that convergence of basic services actually took place. He also came up a table showing the districts and the indicators, and a map showing the spatial location. K explained that the best was often the enemy of the good, and that if the consultant's suggestion were accepted DPEP would have to be implemented in Hindi-speaking states, and that it would be inexpedient to limit a national pace-setting programme to a single category of states. In many states, there were educationally backward districts which had to a long way to UPE and yet they might not have high MMRs and IMRs. The choice of districts as suggested by the consultant would be too prescriptive and smacked of the planning rationality of command-control economies. K reminded the Bank team about the concern of many in the Bank that

DPEP would undercut the states and run counter to the federal principle. The consultant's suggestion would further restrict the choice of districts by the states. It is important to promote convergence of the delivery of basic services all over; convergence cannot be limited to spatial convergence. Therefore, each of the SSN programmes might choose relevant criteria to decide backwardness, and in all the districts covered by SSN programmes, attempts should be made to promote convergence. This view was readily accepted by all; however, the consultant's work was not in vain, for it set K thinking about the criteria for choice of districts for coverage. A month after the conclusion of the SSN negotiations, he could make up his mind. While proposing a strategy of disaggregated target setting and decentralized planning for the achievement of UEE, DOE's Eighth Five-Year Plan proposals as well as POA, 1986, classified districts into four categories and proposed a distinct strategy for each category. These categories were high-literacy districts, total literacy campaign districts, low-literacy districts, and externally funded project districts. Those documents did not lay down any criteria for choosing the externally funded project districts. In the dialogue with the Bank on SSN operations, it was proposed that the new district-based strategy would give priority to districts which were educationally backward as well as districts where total literacy campaigns have been successful resulting in increased demand for primary education. While reviewing the criteria for selection of districts, K felt that the best indicator of educational backwardness would the female literacy rate as reported by the 1991 Decennial Census; it would be simpler than the multiple indicators that have to be used to determine educational backwardness, and at the same time would be free of the subjectivity inherent in a criterion like 'a district where total literacy campaign was successful resulting in increased demand'. In order to enhance the spread of the programme, it was laid down that in every state, districts with female literacy rate lower than that of the state average female literacy rate would be eligible for coverage by DPEP.

With the perspective that Time provides it should be said that the SSN negotiations were cordial and ratified the agreements arrived at during the various stages of the project cycle. K believes that the attempt to reopen some issues such as cost recovery was a 'made-up' act designed to convince those in the Bank who had reservations about the agreements reached with the Appraisal Mission that everything possible was done to force the Indians to be more precise about their commitments, and that given the intransigence of the Indians and the imperative of not alienating a large borrower like India who seemed to move in the right direction, nothing more could be done. Although it contradicts conventional wisdom, Deena Khatkhate's observation that 'it is not so often that the government gets bought by the donors; it is the other way round' has a kernel of truth. The SSN negotiations seem to be one of a piece with the aid negotiations India was engaged during 1992–3 which, according to Ashok Desai, Chief Economic Adviser, were 'cozy to the point of incest'.[18] In retrospect, what appeared to be a major threat to the carefully calibrated strategy of DOE was turned into an opportunity to strike a new path to UPE.

Is External Funding for Elementary Education Warranted?

The eminent economist of education Tilak noted that the most important consequences of DPEP were 'relaxation of resource constraints in planning education', and restoring to a' respectable place' district planning in primary education. Hitherto educational planning under austerity had been the characteristic feature of planning education in India. Furthermore, 'while there has been much talk about the need for district planning in India ever since Independence', planning was generally undertaken from above and expertise was consequently concentrated at national and state levels. Under DPEP it had become imperative to train and develop local-level manpower for planning, project preparation, and execution of the plans and projects. And DPEP met the challenge of district planning by building capacity at local levels and gradually filling the demand for trained middle-level personnel. Yet, he concluded that:

> While the contribution of DPEP has to be acknowledged, it must be emphasized that the fact that revitalization of district planning and capacity-building has taken place under an externally assisted programme also reveals the inability and failure of the government in these

[18] Deena Khatkhate, 'Always a Borrower Be', *Economic and Political Weekly*, XXX, no. 52 (30 December 1995), pp. 3361–2.

areas during the last fifty years ... a clear and sound rationale for external assistance for primary education does not exist.[19]

Tilak put forth four arguments in support of his contention that there was no rationale for external assistance for elementary education. First, UEE being a fundamental right, the government should fund it with its own resources rather than rely upon insecure external funding. Second, external funding might substitute rather than complement domestic resources, so much so that it might not contribute much to enhancing total resources. Third, external assistance for education might increase 'donor dependence'. Fourth, external assistance might lead to external influence on domestic educational policies, which might not be necessarily desirable.[20] Tilak's concerns are well founded, and they highlight the risk inherent in accessing external financing. However, a policymaker has no option but to act in accordance with concrete circumstances rather than absolute propositions. Life would have been easier and more comfortable for K and DOE if the funds for DPEP were available domestically but they were just not available. 'Reality' cannot be ignored; the Prime Minister was not exaggerating when he said, *das rupya bhi dekhna padega* (have to scrounge even for a dime). As already detailed above, in a climate of unavoidable fiscal austerity the domestic resources were not available to operationalize the new district-based strategy for UEE. In fact, the requirements of on-going elementary education programmes such as Operation Blackboard and teacher education could be met only if compressing the plan outlay for higher education. DOE had only two options: to wait for better times to operationalize the new strategy for UEE or to seize the opportunity provided by the willingness of agencies such as the Bank, EC, and ODA to fund DPEP, and strive to minimize the risks associated with accessing external financing. The second option was availed, and the relations with agencies managed deftly so that education policy, the content and

[19] Jandhyala B.G. Tilak, 'Development Assistance to Primary Education: Transformation of Enthusiastic Donors and Reluctant Recipients', in Kenneth King and Lene Buchert, *Changing International Aid to Education: Global Patterns and National Contexts*, Paris: UNESCO, 1999, pp. 307–17, at pp. 310, 313, 315.

[20] Jandhyala. B.G. Tilak, 'Education in the UPA Government Common Minimum Programme', *Economic and Political Weekly*, XXXIX, no. 43 (October 23, 2004), pp. 4717–21, at pp. 4719–20.

process of education, and the planning and implementation of DPEP were insulated from the agencies, a fact which, among others, is confirmed by the study of the impact of aid on India's education policy by the distinguished economist of education Christopher Colclough. The study concluded that aid to primary education in India had little impact on the establishment or change of Indian policy objectives. Some might argue that aid to primary education might have brought some negative consequences for India, in that GOI was less likely 'to consider the non-primary/elementary subsectors as priorities for reform and expansion'. However, 'the substantial unmet needs of the poorest families in India, very many of whose children had had no access to schooling prior to DPEP/SSA, were certainly served better by the application of India's priorities to universalize primary/elementary schooling during the past two decades'.[21] The insistence of the agencies on target setting in quantitative terms, accountability, adoption of a systemic approach, use of modern techniques of project management, crisp documentation, MIS, and clear channels for flow of funds was used as an opportunity to attempt building capacity in the states to plan and implement programmes, strengthening the training infrastructure and programmes, operationalizing local area participatory planning, and putting in place strong monitoring and evaluation mechanisms. DPEP did not achieve what it all set out to do. Far from it; yet, there is one thing which it had unequivocally achieved and established, namely that like biology being not destiny, donor dependency need not be destiny if a country has the capacity to autonomously design and implement policies and programmes as well the capacity to negotiate the best possible deal in given circumstances. For such a country it is indeed possible to exercise leadership in its relations with agencies and access external resources without compromising its autonomy in the matters of policymaking, programme design, and development. And yet ironically, that achievement of DPEP is not well recognized. Yet another fact that receives little recognition is the fact that unlike quite a few developing countries, on the whole India accessed external resources judiciously. If one looks at the trend of educational expenditure over the last two decades

[21] Christopher Colclough and Anirudha De, 'The Impact of Aid on Education Policy in India', RECOUP Working Paper. 27, University of Cambridge, London: DFID, March 2010, pp. 20–3.

it would come out clearly that availing external funding did not lead to donor dependence. Once the economic reform process augmented the fiscal capability of the government the contribution of external funding to the central government's plan expenditure on elementary education sharply declined from a peak of about a third in 2001–2 to 7.83 per cent by 2006–7, the level that prevailed prior to the launch of DPEP, and further to 3.37 per cent by 2013–14. As already set out, at a more aggregate level, the contribution of external assistance to plan expenditure continued to decline from the peak level of 28.25 per cent during the Third Five-Year Plan off to 2.2 per cent during the Tenth Five-Year Plan; it was of no consequence for the Eleventh and Twelfth Five-Year Plans. The Indian planning experience demonstrates that accessing aid does not always lead to 'donor' dependency (Chapter VII).

So deep rooted was the East India Company syndrome that a section of academics, activists, media, and public would not accept the plain facts that DPEP, though externally funded, operationalized a home-grown programme, that foreign expertise was not at all utilized for planning and implementation, and that curriculum was beyond the pale of the agencies. No one could argue with prejudice. K's belief that he was on the right path was also fortified by his study of international relations and negotiation theory. K's study of international relations led him to believe that the bargaining theory of international relations is more valid for large developed countries such as India and Brazil than the *dependencia* theory which holds that developing countries were invariably bound to lose in their engagement with advanced capitalist countries and MNCs. The outcome of engagement of a developing country with an MNC is not invariant; the terms by which an MNC operated in a country and the distribution of benefits between the country and the MNC were very much dependent on the results of negotiations and the balance of bargaining power between the country and the MNC. Developing countries could negotiate to their advantage all aspects of the relations, not just peripheral issues, or as Bordia used to put it, most things that would seem unreasonable are negotiable. K felt that interaction with agencies such as the World Bank was no different. If a country is prudent, it could use the financial resources it secured on fair terms and conditions to augment the pool of investible resources, frontload investment, and accelerate development. His feelings were vindicated by his experience of mobilizing resources from external agencies. China's experience with the World Bank also validates K's views. In China, which had both the domestic capacity and size always to come up with mutually agreeable projects, projects began to flourish, and with very few exceptions, the intimacy and rapport between the Bank's Beijing Resident Mission and the Chinese authorities were unmatched in the Bank's history. The Bank facilitated China's integration with the global economy after about three decades of isolation by educating a cadre of senior Chinese officials in new economic ideas and technical systems, and putting together comprehensive reports on the Chinese economy. The Bank's first comprehensive report on the Chinese economy, *China: Socialist Economic Development*, released in 1981 became a primer for senior Chinese officials and went a long way in establishing the Bank's credibility in China. The early Bank loans were used for rebuilding higher education system which was still recovering from the ravages of the Cultural Revolution. In agriculture, the Bank played an important role in accentuating the reforms that had been well under the way in the late 1970s before the Bank appeared on the scene. While almost all private foreign investment concentrated in the coastal provinces, the Bank's lending covered poorer interior provinces. At the behest of the central authorities, much of the Bank's lending was at the provincial level; unlike in India, provinces were also responsible for repayment of loans, and had clear-cut ground lines for engaging the Bank. Yet China was not a pushover. The ground rules for engagement with the Bank came out in a statement of the Chinese Finance Minister in October 1984. The Chinese official position was that the Bank assistance to developing countries should be unconditional; this, however, did not mean that the Bank could not offer advice and ideas. They would be accepted if found useful. However, the Bank should not impose its ideas and advice. The Bank scrupulously adhered to those ground rules.[22]

K was convinced that the East India Company syndrome, the fear that any interaction with the West and institutions dominated by Western countries would lead to loss of autonomy and endanger national interest, was a phobia which the country needed to get over. K's belief was

[22] Devesh Kapur, John Prior Lewis, and Richard Charles Webb, eds., *The World Bank: Its First Half Century*, Volume 1: History, Washington, DC: Brookings Institution Press, 1997, pp. 24, 45, 538.

fortified by a study of the contest of ideas in which the Mahatma and the Gurudev were engaged. For nearly three decades, through letters, articles in the press, and personal discussions, the two giants sparred with each other on an intellectual plane. Their dialogue is a fascinating tale of the contest of competing ideas, and an exemplar of the civilized manner in which a dialogue should be conducted. In spite of their differences, they respected each other and sought each other's opinion on every important occasion; in fact they owed their mutual respect to the candour with which they expressed their views.[23] Among the many issues on which Gurudev differed from the Mahatma were the economic rationality of the *charkha* programme and the burning of foreign clothes. Tagore was critical of economics being bundled out and a 'fictitious moral dictum' of foreign cloth being impure being dragged in place of economics. Gurudev wondered how long it was possible 'to hide ourselves away from commerce with the outside world'.[24] Further, unlike the Mahatma, Gurudev did not reject Western civilization; one of the explicit objectives in founding the Viswa-Bharati (which means communion of the world with India) included:

> To seek to realise in a common fellowship of study the meeting of the East and the West, and thus ultimately to strengthen the fundamental conditions of world peace through the establishment of free communication of ideas between the two hemispheres.

During the Non-cooperation Movement in 1921, Gurudev was hurt by 'the cry of rejection ringing loud against the West in my country with the cry that Western education can only hurt us', and went on to say that when we had 'the intellectual capital of our own, the commerce of thought with the outside world becomes natural and fully profitable'. To say that such commerce was inherently wrong was 'to encourage the worst form of provincialism, productive of nothing but intellectual indigence'.[25] In defence of his view, the Mahatma made it

[23] For an excellent documentation of the dialogue, see Sabyasachi Bhattacharya, ed., *The Mahatma and the Poet: Letters and Debates between Gandhi and Tagore, 1915–1941*, New Delhi: National Book Trust, 1997.

[24] Sabyasachi Bhattacharya, Introduction, *The Mahatma and the Poet*, pp. 10–11.

[25] 'Tagore's Reflections on Non-cooperation and Cooperation', in Sabyasachi Bhattacharya, *The Mahatma and the Poet*, pp. 55–62, at p. 62.

clear that Non-cooperation was neither with the English nor with the West; it was with the system the British had established, a refusal to cooperate with the English administrators on their own terms. He went on to assert:

> We say to them, 'Come and co-operate with us on our terms, and it will be well for us, for you and the world'. We must refuse to be lifted off our feet.[26]

He also clarified:

> I hope I am as great a believer in free air as the great Poet. I do not want my house to be walled in on all sides and my windows to be stuffed. I want the cultures of all the lands to be blown about my house as freely as possible. But I refuse to be blown off by any.[27]

By happenstance, during the seven years he spent in DOE, a life-size batik painting of Tagore stood behind the huge desk of K in his office. K was wont to spend long evenings in the office; the world outside would be totally dark and the lighting in the office subdued—an ambience conducive to dreaming. He would conjure imaginary debates between the two Greats; the painting behind his chair would come alive, and the Mahatma would materialize in front of him. One such evening, it was hot and stuffy; because of power cut, the air-conditioning was off. In his dream-world Great Conversation, K once intervened and posed to the two Greats the questions, 'What should I do?' and 'Is it proper to engage the World Bank and other agencies?' As if in a séance, with his eyes closed, Gurudev slowly whispered, 'Open the window to the world outside so that fresh breeze can waft through.' With a mischievous grin, the Mahatma cautioned, 'But K, do not let your feet be blown off by the breeze.' K thought that together both were right and together they illuminated the path he should follow.

[26] Mahatma Gandhi, 'The Great Sentinel', in Sabyasachi Bhattachrya, *The Mahatma and the Poet*, pp. 87–92, at p. 91.

[27] Mahatma Gandhi, 'English Learning', in Sabyasachi Bhattachrya, *The Mahatma and the Poet*, pp. 63–4, at p. 64.

XIV

MUDDLING THROUGH

> 'Well, go on,' he continued, returning to his hobby; 'tell me how the Germans have taught you to fight Bonaparte by this new science you call "strategy".... What science can there be is a matter in which, as in all practical matter, nothing can be defined and everything depends on innumerable conditions the significance of which is determined at a particular moment which arises no one knows when?'
>
> —Leo Tolstoy, *War and Peace*

Analogous to Tolstoy debunking the pretensions of 'military science' in *War and Peace,* in his seminal articles 'The Science of Muddling Through' and 'Still Muddling, Not Yet Through', Charles Lindblom questioned the claim of policy scientists and analysts that policymaking was an entirely rational exercise and claimed that real-world policymaking comprises *taking a few small steps at a time* without being guided by any grand strategy.[1] The course of developing externally funded projects was no different.

Within a month after the successful conclusion of the SSN negotiations, preparations began for the formulation of the first DPEP Project to be funded by the World Bank. Fifteen days later, in the first week of January 1993, Arjun Singh approved the proposal to cover Assam, Haryana, Karnataka, Kerala, Maharashtra, and Tamil Nadu. Kerala was included to allay the grievance of that state that it was being penalized

[1] Charles E. Lindblom, 'The Science of Muddling Through', *Public Administration* Review, 19 (1959), pp. 79–88; Lindblom, 'Still Muddling, Not Yet Through', *Public Administration Review*, 39 (1979), pp. 517–26.

by schemes such as Operation Blackboard for having invested its own resources to provide adequate access and achieved near-universal participation, and that its requirement of resources for improving quality and enhancing learning achievement was being ignored. This decision incidentally ensured that the first set of 42 districts (including the 19 in MP funded by EC) was a better testing ground for probing the premises and strategies. These 42 districts varied widely in demography, educational development, and patterns of governance. As was Bank's wont, there were divergent views on including Kerala in the first DPEP project funded by the Bank (Chapter X). Some were opposed to include Kerala in a programme which addressed educationally backwardness. In contrast, many others looked positively on the idea of a project where distinct strategies would be explored: one addressing districts where access and equity were major issues, and the other addressing districts where quality and not access is the issue. In Kerala districts, the strategy would concentrate on curriculum, learning materials, teacher training, and evaluation; the experiences in implementing these districts could appropriately extended to other states. Ayes prevailed.

Following the decision to cover them in the first DPEP Project, these six states joined MP, Orissa, and UP where external funded projects were already on the drawing board; taking into account the on-going projects of APPEP (AP), BEP, and Lok Jumbish (Rajasthan), external funded projects now covered 12 of the 17 major states in the country. As the first DPEP Project was expected to be the harbinger of many more DPEP projects, it appeared that within a couple of years the new strategy for UPE would be implemented in many districts spread all over the country except for UP and Rajasthan. Unlike the DPEP projects, the UP Project was a state project, and even though Cambridge suggested revisiting the parameters of that project and fit it in the DPEP frame, Giri and K felt that it would be inexpedient to change the parameters and ask the UP government to begin working on the project *de novo* just when the dark clouds of misunderstanding between DOE and the UP government appeared to have been cleared. They also felt that it would be inexpedient to foray into Rajasthan, Bordia's fiefdom. K believed that given the intrinsic superiority of the DPEP idea, it was a matter of time before UP and Rajasthan fell in line. K was vindicated, for UP was one of the states covered by the second DPEP project and the Rajasthan government decided in May 1999 to implement DPEP with World Bank funding.

In *Divine Comedy* Dante did not ascend to *Paradiso* without first travelling through the depths of *Inferno*; likewise, K could not savour the heady and intoxicating feeling of success and achievement without undergoing a fiery ordeal of overcoming several seemingly insurmountable problems. In 1993, many things were happening at the same time: the regional workshops that Giri organized to enthuse the states to implement the POA,1992, the battles over the 'ownership' of the UP Project, attempts to impart a new direction to BEP, the see-saw negotiation dance that culminated in the Financing Agreement with the EC, the exasperating dialogue with the Germans and UNDP about the South Orissa Project (SOP), the development of DPEP which involved more feats than the 12 labours of the legendary Hercules, the Sixth Meeting of the Ministers of Education of the Asia Pacific Region (MINEDAP-VI), the hosting of the meeting of the International Consultative Forum on EFA (September 1993), and organizing the EFA-9 Summit of Nine High-Population Countries (December 1993) which necessitated dancing a quadrille with UNESCO, UNICEF, and the Ministry of External Affairs. All these events with the exception of MINEDAP-VI were interconnected, and the developments in one area influenced the others. Figuratively, it was as if like, an inept magician, K was clumsily juggling with the several balls up in the air, with the trajectory of one ball influencing the trajectory of other balls and thereby compounding the complexity of juggling with several balls up in the air. Or to mix the metaphor, moving ahead seemed to be an unending hurdle race, or more accurately, running through one gauntlet after another.

Launching the new district-based strategy with external funding was metaphorically a voyage in unchartered seas, something similar to the progress of India towards self-rule.

> Seen from six thousand feet above her, the tiny ship seemed to gain a little on almost every tack and slowly pass one marked reef or buoyed mud flat after another. But from the deck it was not so easy to discern the progress, and ... it looked from close quarters as though the captain and the crew were thoroughly confused about the whole affair.[2]

[2] Philip Woodruff, *The Men Who Ruled India*, Volume II: *The Guardians*, London: Jonathan Cape, 1954, p. 244.

If the crew and captain appeared confused, it was because of two reasons. Neither K nor his associates in DOE or resource organizations such as NCERT and NIEPA had practical experience of designing and developing a large-scale externally funded project; for that matter, even the masterly Bordia had none. Neither did his training at the IAS Academy, Mussoorie nor his 27-year experience in the government prepared K to cope with the tasks to be started from the scratch, detail the parameters and guidelines of a major programme, design the management structure for implementing and overseeing the programme, and secure the necessary approvals from the government and the World Bank. And furthermore, self-reliance was preferred to the easy option of relying on the agencies to provide technical support; self-reliant learning meant that at every stage as and when a problem or issue arose, those associated with DPEP had to improvise and respond through trial and error. On the plus side, the learning was a gruelling experience but it built national capacity to design, develop, and implement in a way that reliance on outside technical support would not have. And furthermore, the programme did not become a hostage to agencies and the predilections of agency functionaries and consultants. On the negative side, the process of trial and error meant that it was quite some time before K and his associates could offer clear, flip-flop-free. A consequence of prickly self-reliance was that the infusion of good international experience was less than optimal. Whatever, the defining feature of DPEP in its initial stages was continual improvisation rather than rolling out a grand well-thought-out plan.

There was yet a reason why the crew and captain appeared confused. Every stage of the journey called for multi-party and multi-stage negotiations about the further course of action: negotiations within GOI, negotiations within each of the seven state governments participating in DPEP, negotiations between the DOE office and State Education Departments, and negotiations between DOE and funding agencies. Some of the funding agencies were eager to command the ship lest the funds provided by them should not be put to good use. More importantly, what was moving ahead was not a ship but a motley fleet of ships, with quite a few ships (state governments) led by self-willed captains who were not subordinates of the commanding officer of the flagship and were unwilling to follow the lead of the flagship . Furthermore, the crew in all the ships were either indifferent or quarrelsome and prone to questioning the authority and wisdom of the captain. True to this imagery, moving forward with DPEP was inextricably intertwined with parallel developments in regard to the UP Project, the SOP, the dialogue with the EC, and the tenacious efforts by Tamil Nadu to secure World Bank funding for secondary education that would cover the whole state. Moving forward with the SSN operation, and after the SSN negotiations were concluded, the development of DPEP necessitated doing many things not all of which were directly connected with SSN operations or DPEP. These included (*a*) getting the Bank to accept wholeheartedly the idea of a multi-state DPEP Project; (*b*) definitively getting the six states proposed to be covered by the first DPEP project to accept that DPEP was the 'only game in the town' and that however much they might try a state project was out of question; (*c*) vanquish the efforts of UP state government to deny any role for DOE in the design and implementation of the UP Project; (*d*) persuade the EC that its proposal for supervision and monitoring was too intrusive to be accepted; (*e*) put up with unrelenting rigidity in the matter of SOP and keep the dialogue going instead of breaking it off lest the all-too-important Germany should veto the EC proposal to support the MP Project; (*f*) cope with the mindless advocacy by UNICEF in the context of the not-yet-firmed EFA-9 Summit; and (*g*) keep Arjun Singh in good humour even as the tortuous negotiations with EC dragged on, and in the face of the maladroit effort by the MP government to hog credit for the MP Project through huge advertisements in the media even before the funding was firmed up and even as it appeared as if the EC dialogue might collapse.

In his darker moods, K felt that the decision to avail external funding proved to be a Faustian bargain. UP seemed happier to hobnob with the Bank functionaries than abide by NPE, 1986, and its understanding with DOE. Against the backdrop of the demands by EC and the Germans, the developments in UP seemed to be a portent of what was in store with each state turning out to be a sphere of influence, or more accurately, a privileged enclave, of the agency which funded primary education in that state. K was reminded of the saying he came across as a student that while India was the colony of the British, China was the colony of many countries with whom it had concluded treaties. To the middle-aged K, it appeared that the externally funded projects were figuratively driving India towards China of the colonial era; it was a denouement which worried him a lot. More through luck than pluck by end July 1993, the nightmare of DOE being reduced to a hapless spectator of agencies running amuck in the states passed away. To use the popular imagery of 'aid business' DOE was firmly in the driver's seat; an observation of Eimi Watanabe captured the fact—'K tells each one of us, well You, You go here, and You, You go there; we all go where he wants us to go.'

UP Project: *plus ça change, plus c'est la même chose*[3]

The meeting between Giri and UP Chief Secretary Saxena on 25 June went off smoothly, for he was reportedly instructed by the Chief Minister to settle the matter; he agreed to every suggestion of Giri: implementation of the project through an autonomous society similar to that of BEP Society, augment non-formal and women's education, establishment of a state-level educational management institution analogous to NIEPA, Bank funding to be an additionality as mandated by the CABE parameters, staggering the investment, and so on. In retrospect, Karan Singh sought to raise a very valid point which cropped up rather vexatiously later in the appraisal process: the need to reconcile the proposed management structure and the UP Basic Shiksha Parishad which managed the elementary schools in the state. Saxena brushed him off saying that the issue raised by Singh could be easily sorted out. He was so keen to ensure that the project made smooth progress that while concluding the meeting he advised K that he should ring him up should any problem arise. When Giri and K broke to Arjun Singh the news of the impasse with UP being resolved, he significantly posed the question, *on whose terms?*

And what followed was the operation of the seminal concept of *obsolescing bargain*. Soon after the meeting with the UP Chief Secretary, K had a meeting with Middleton, and made it clear to him that DOE still considered the UP Project to be a test case project, and that therefore DOE should be fully kept in the picture at all times. The DOE representatives would participate in the visits of the Bank teams to districts and in all meetings between the UP government

[3] The more it changes, the more it is the same again.

and the Bank. The wrap-up meetings with the Bank missions should be held only in DOE. As events unfolded, it became evident these arrangements did not prevent the UP State Education and Finance Departments to renege on the understanding reached between Giri and Saxena and to use the Bank's process of appraising project proposals to reopen settled issues. In his meeting with Middleton and later with Skolnik, K requested compression of the project clearance cycle by doing away with the customary preparation mission as there had been a long dialogue with the Bank on the UP Project. K also suggested shortening the interval between the pre-appraisal and appraisal missions. While assuring that he would do what all he could, Skolnik indicated that some within the Bank had reservations about the UP Project. A little later, Vergin informed Giri and K that the Bank was apprehensive about a project with whose preparation it was not associated. By then, the SSN operation was being appraised, and as came out subsequently, the reservation within the Bank had more to do with the UP Project which did not fully fit in the DPEP framework. Now that the Bank and GOI had agreed about the modalities of revamping social sector programmes so that they target the poor better and are cost-effective, the sceptics posed the question as to how the Bank could fund a pre-SSN project.

All agreements tend to obsolesce; however, K did not expect that the agreement reached with the Chief Secretary (CS), UP, the highest official of the state government, would be disregarded by his deputies (Chapter X). But that was what exactly happened. When the Bank's pre-appraisal mission visited UP in September 1992, the geographical scope of the project, the implementation of the project through a society, and the additionality principle were reopened. The Finance Secretary wanted the whole state to be covered; as if this were not enough he put forth the bizarre idea that the counterpart funds to be provided by the state government could be met through grants released by the central government under CSSs, never mind that the grants were tied grants to be used exclusively for the implementation of designated schemes and could not be diverted to other purposes. And as to the additionality principle, he had no absolutely no intention to commit that the funds received by the state government from the Bank would not be used to substitute for resources the state government would have provided for primary education. In short, he saw World Bank funding purely through the finance prism, and as a means to augment the state plan outlay without the state government being required to raise the requisite resources for a higher plan outlay. He as well as Singh were opposed to the setting up of a society to implement the project and came up with ingenious legalistic arguments. How could the state government undertake to repay the loan when the funds were released not to it but to a society? Would not release of funds to the society circumvent the accountability to the State Legislature as the Legislature would not vote the budget of the society? Singh could prevail upon Middleton to include a paragraph in the aide memoire that the main rationale for the society was smooth flow of funds to the project-implementing units and that if UP government could come up with a satisfactory alternative arrangement the mission was agreeable to reconsider implementation through a society. When K objected to the paragraph, Middleton pleaded helplessness saying he could not help reflect the factual discussions. K believes that Singh banked on the Bank to spike the society proposal, and that Middleton conveyed to the headquarters the objections to the society in greater detail than what that crisp paragraph conveyed. Sure enough a few months later, in March 1993, Middleton came back to K with the bad tidings that Mohan Gopal, counsel in the Legal Department of the Bank, was opposed to society.

Given that Singh had managed to reopen settled issues, K requested Giri to have a meeting with CS, UP, once again to discuss the parameters of the UP Project as well as matters relating to the UP MS society. In the meeting on 12 October 1992, Saxena once again appeared to be very helpful. K could not be sure whether he and Singh played a good guy–bad guy combination; however, short of asking Singh to keep quiet he overruled the objections of Singh and agreed with everything that Giri and K had to say. He came up with a pretty good solution for the legalistic problems raised by Singh. The release of funds to UP would be routed through the state budget; however, they would be immediately transferred to the UP Project Society as a lump sum without examination of details. He assured that basic education would receive its due share in the State Plan, and that during the annual plan discussions DOE could examine whether basic education was adequately provided for. Saxena's formulation on additionality did not offer an iron clad assurance; however, in a spirit of give and take it was accepted. When the discussion turned to the programme components,

Singh nonchalantly told Giri that the UP Project was a state project and hence the state would have the right to choose the project components. To the historically minded K, it appeared that Singh's stance was like that of legendary Senator Calhoun in pre-Civil War American history. Singh would not brook any encroachment on what he perceived to be the rights of the state. Even the mild-mannered Giri was provoked to say that it was wrong to treat the UP Project solely as a state project, and that right from the beginning the project was treated as a tripartite project in which DOE had vital stakes. Saxena intervened to say that he understood the political sensitivity and agreed to go by what Giri said. However, true to the American saying *it ain't over till it is over* the confrontation with the UP government did not end with that meeting.

Things Falling Apart? Can the Centre Hold?

Hardly had the New Year arrived when it appeared that DOE's strategy of accessing external funding for primary education for DPEP would be wrecked by the tenacity with which Tamil Nadu lobbied for Bank funding of a secondary education project and the hesitation by the Bank to commit itself to a support to a multi-state DPEP project. By early February 1993, these challenges were resolved and the modalities of the Bank's support to education in the foreseeable future were definitively settled and conveyed to the state governments. However, it was not yet the final curtain call, and a long play with many twists and turns lay ahead.

After returning from the successful SSN negotiations in Washington and identifying the states which could be covered in the first DPEP Project, K had a meeting with Middleton on 18 December 1992 to set out his thinking on the next steps to be taken. K recalled the fact that even while the SSN operation was being discussed, DOE made it clear that during 1993–4, district plans would be drawn up the and a few activities carried out, and simultaneously a DPEP project would be developed and posed to the Bank for funding. Ideally, the Bank should approve the project by June 1994 so that the actions under SSN operation would smoothly be dovetailed with the launch of the DPEP Project. K suggested a schedule which worked backwards from June 1994 so that the Bank, DOE, and the states participating in the first DPEP project can plan their actions appropriately. Middleton was guarded in his response. He told K that a six-state project, as K had suggested, might involve an outlay of Rs 800 crore which was far in excess of any education project so far approved by the Bank. Being so, it would be better if the six states were covered by two separate projects of three states each instead of one project. At K's insistence, he agreed to consult his headquarters and come back to K.

K scheduled an 'initiation meeting' with the education secretaries of the six states on 19 January 1993; prior to that meeting he scheduled a meeting with the four sponsors of the Jomtien Conference—UNDP, UNESCO, UNICEF, and the Bank—and the EC to explain about the new strategy for UPE. In a strict sense, it was not necessary to take into confidence those who had not expressed willingness to fund DPEP. However, K deliberately opted for a policy of inclusion and co-option, as by then K was well aware of the deep rivalry among all the agencies interested in education, particularly the multilateral agencies, and their tendency to make carping comments about the activities and work styles of their rivals. Leaving out UNICEF would have aggravated the insecurity and deep-rooted 'Bank-envy' of many of its functionaries. In the 'donor' jungle, the Bank was the elephant dwarfing others in terms of resources and the scale of its operations. Yet, in spite of deep rivalry among them, the agencies met periodically to exchange notes, and on occasions, did not hesitate to gang up against the host country in which they operated. Paraphrasing the raunchy remark of President Johnson, K though it was better to have them in one's camp and put up with their gratuitous remarks than let them loose outside and demonize the programme, all the more so as some of them such as UNESCO and UNICEF had a good Samaritan image. Ted Palac of UNICEF who used to attend most of the meetings was a pillar of support with his frank and useful observations and comments. In the first meeting, he was honest to admit that DPEP placed UNICEF in a predicament. UNICEF had limited resources and its accounting rules did not permit its funds to be used for the construction of school buildings and payment of teacher salaries. Consequently, district plans could not be implemented through UNICEF contribution alone. In BEP, this problem was circumvented by the fact that the central government provided matching funds and such funds could be used to finance activities which UNICEF could not. He could understand that the central government would not provide matching funds in DPEP as the area of operations would soon extend to the whole country and as agencies such as the Bank could provide the resources needed. So far, in most states UNICEF was popular because of the support it gave by way of free UNICEF cards, support to workshops, and other such small activities. Now it stood to lose that standing because of competition with agencies with deep purses such as the Bank and EC. K told him that there was room for everyone in DPEP, and agencies such as UNICEF could support the states and districts by way of technical support for planning, social mobilization, and building up media support. Eventually ODA was also included in all the meetings with agencies and missions connected with DPEP once it expressed its willingness to support DPEP in AP and West Bengal; UNDP opted out. While the policy of inclusion was the right policy and largely successful, it did not prevent some UNICEF functionaries from giving in to their old habits and making snide comments about DPEP merely because it was funded by the Bank, and to exaggerate the achievements of other projects even though their scale was puny in comparison with DPEP and comparing them with DPEP was like comparing apples with oranges, or to mix metaphor with peanuts. But then it is all part of the game.

The meeting with the state education secretaries was disappointing for three of the states—Assam, Karnataka, and Tamil Nadu—were not enthusiastic about a project that covered only a few districts of each state. And they were keen to engage a consultant to expeditiously draw up the project document; one secretary was very keen to engage the renowned consultancy firm Price Waterhouse, never mind that that firm was as much acquainted with education as Martians with the rites of passage of Toda tribals in the Nilgiris, and further that the CABE parameters for accessing external education had specified that project formulation should be the responsibility of the central and state governments and of national agencies, and that it should be a process of capacity building. Given the rapid turnover of state education secretaries few of them had a ghost of an idea about NPE, 1986, itself, much less the CABE decisions. Why settle for a spoon when one could have the whole pot was the underlying motivation of the state secretaries; they believed in the repeated averments of Bank functionaries that the Bank would only be too happy to assist a state project if only the central government gave the green light. K was quite upset with the Bank for its stirring up the state governments against DOE.

The Bank's lobbying the states before DOE agreed to pose the UP Project as a test case project was understandable, though not excusable; yet to continue the seduction—much like the serpent in the Garden of Eden—even after a good working relationship was established with DOE in general and K in particular it seemed to be outright dishonesty.

As he recapitulated the sequence of events since the NIEPA Seminar on the UP Project in November 1990, he recognized a pattern. Once word about the NIEPA seminar spread among states, enterprising states such as Assam and Tamil Nadu made a bid for similar projects in their states. In January 1991, K conveyed to the chief secretaries of these two states as well as DEA which espoused the cause of these states that the decision to avail Bank funding for basic education was not open ended, that after considerable hesitation DOE decided to probe the bona fides of the Bank by posing a test case project, and that the question of enlarging Bank support to primary education would be considered only after some experience was gained with the implementation of the test case project. The campaign abated for the time being, but as later events showed, it was not terminated. In August 1991, Iravanan, Tamil Nadu Education Secretary, dropped in K's room and began to lobby for a Tamil Nadu project on basic education. K told him that it was not opportune to consider another World Bank project as the test case project itself ran into difficulties, and DOE had the impression that the Bank was trying to twist its arms by egging on the state governments to float projects. Iravanan was not satisfied with K's explanation, and began to lecture K about the unreasonableness of DOE; he wondered why DOE should shy away from the assistance of the Bank. 'What conditionalities could the Bank lay down in an education project?' he demanded to know. To be honest, he was not alone in posing that question; it was a refrain that K heard again and again in his interactions with many officials in DEA as well as State Education Departments. K wanted to persuade Iravanan by quoting chapter and verse in support of DOE's contention that it was imperative to make haste slowly, and took him through the proceedings of the meeting of CABE in March 1991 which considered the question of external financing of basic education. K highlighted the fact that the decision to go in for external funding was based on a fragile consensus, and at that CABE meeting an eminent educationalist such as Malcolm Adiseshiah expressed opposition of to the idea of taking loans from the Bank for basic education. Iravanan was not one who would not take a 'no' for an answer, and came up with a counter proposal. If basic education was problematic, he was willing to develop a project for funding secondary and vocational education. His patience exhausted, K rudely told him that such a project stood less chance of being supported as CABE did not approve accessing external funding for secondary education, and that it would be a travesty when the country and Tamil Nadu were so far away from UEE one should think of massive loans for investment in secondary education. As ever, after a few months Iravanan moved out and K thought he had heard the last of a secondary education project. K was mistaken and he forgot his own experience of working in an economic ministry during the evening of the licence-permit-control raj; those days while Gujarat aggressively courted private investment and deftly used its lobbying prowess to secure industrial licences for entrepreneurs, Tamil Nadu tenaciously lobbied with the central government for securing central projects.

K was in for a surprise—a shock—when on 24 July 1992 he received a letter from Neeraj Jain, Deputy Secretary, DEA, forwarding a set of three letters: the first from the chief minister of Assam to the Finance Minister indicating the interest of his government in the development of a primary education project for World Bank funding, the second from DEA to the Assam government expressing its general support to the proposal of the Assam government, and the third from Skolnik to P.C. Sharma, Assam Education Secretary, conveying the Bank's support to the Assam government. DEA's advice to DOE was unequivocal; in so many words DOE was told, 'by agreeing to pose the UP Project you have opened up primary education for the World Bank involvement; the Bank is likely to support at least one project a year. So get moving'. However, Prasad's letter was not devoid of the usual official ploy to shift responsibility. DOE was advised to pose at least one project a year 'subject to the NPE, 1986, and the norms evolved by DOE for projects/State coverage'. In his letter to Sharma dated 24 June 1992, Skolnik spoke of Sharma's discussions with Humphrey and Middleton and then he reiterated the 'interest of the World Bank in collaborating with the Government of Assam in formulating (a basic education) project'. He also referred to Sharma's intention of seeking the support of UNICEF for preparing the project document, and went on to say 'we have worked very closely with UNICEF in a number of projects in India and we would, of course, be very pleased to do it again'. He further mentioned in his letter that he wrote to Neeraj Jain expressing the interest of the Bank in the matter, and expressed the hope that 'we will hear soon from DEA on this matter and that project preparation could proceed expeditiously'. He took 'the liberty of copying 'his letter to Neeraj Jain and Eimi Watanabe, UNICEF Country Representative'. Neither Skolnik nor Middleton nor Eimi nor her minions whispered even a word to K, notwithstanding they were in continual contact with him; Skolnik and Middleton were aware of the frustrations DOE had with the UP Project and K's determination to come up with a new project design that would not let DOE be a hostage to a state government. They owed him consideration, if not gratitude, for consoling them after their stormy encounters with C. K raged in anger shouting inwardly, 'You cannot do this to me', yet he realized that DOE was in no position to call off the engagement with the Bank. DOE had travelled a long way down the road of engagement, and further the macroeconomic environment did not permit the luxury of freedom to act as one wished. People in high positions have to play with the cards they are dealt with. This incident reinforced his experience of dealing with ODA in APPEP, UNICEF in BEP, and of the Bank with the UP Project. He was determined to prevent agency functionaries roving across the length and breadth of the country and act like 'loose cannons' by erecting an iron wall between the states and the agencies in the new programme (DPEP) he was developing. For the moment, the proposal of Assam was spiked by conveying to DEA the-by-then standardized position of DOE that it would not like to consider another state project till its experience with the UP Project proved to be satisfactory, and indicating that a few districts of Assam would be included in the project that DOE would propose to develop back-to-back to the SSN operation. When he was free from bouts of rage and coolly thought over the matter, it appeared possible to K that Skolnik and DEA went overboard as Manmohan Singh, the Finance Minister, was an MP from Assam and owed his election to the Parliament to the support of the Assam government. K could not help think that Assam might have succeeded if the Chief Minister had directly approached Arjun Singh; compared to Arjun Singh, Manmohan Singh was a political lightweight, and could not afford to override Arjun Singh. K still recalls his accompanying several ministers of HRD going over to the North Block to meet the

Finance Minister; in contrast, Manmohan Singh used to come over to Arjun Singh whenever the latter had an issue to discuss with him.

Tamil Nadu went one step further. In the first week of August 1992, a bulky school education project document with a gargantuan outlay of over Rs 1,200 crore (about $461 million) landed on K's table. It was a typical brick-and-mortar project with a huge programme construction of school and office buildings, and massive procurement of equipment such as televisions and computers; every classroom in Tamil Nadu schools was to be provided with a television. The proposal was also sent to DEA as well as to the New Delhi office of the Bank itself. The launch of the weighty project document synchronized with a massive lobbying campaign headed by Chief Minister Jayalalitha herself. The Chief Minister took up the matter with the Prime Minister, Finance Minister, and Arjun Singh; the Education Minister C. Aranganayagam met Arjun Singh to press his state's case; the Chief Secretary took up the matter with the Finance Secretary and Giri who was from Tamil Nadu. K was given up as a contrarian hopelessly opposed to the proposal. Shortly after the proposal was received, a factotum of Arjun Singh's office rung up K to say that the Minister was on his way to Madras to meet Jayalalitha, and that the Minister desired that the Tamil Nadu proposal should be cleared. As was not unusual, the factotum was speaking for himself and not the Minister; it turned out that what the Minister wanted was only a brief and not clearance of the Tamil Nadu proposal. Arjun Singh wanted the matter to be taken to the Cabinet so that the he did not have to take the blame for turning down the Tamil Nadu proposal, and in compliance with his direction, K prepared a note for the Cabinet. With his infinite patience, Giri tried to persuade the TN officials not to press the proposal, offering to include a few districts of Tamil Nadu in the multi-state DPEP project that was proposed to be developed. He even invited the State Education Secretary to attend a meeting on EFA in Bhopal organized on the occasion of the visit of the UNESCO Dhumkuria Mission, so that 'participation in the Workshop would facilitate the state government officials to understand the thinking of multilateral agencies for assistance in the field of education'. Giri thought he had succeeded in weaning away the Tamil Nadu officials from the state project and wanted K to hold the Cabinet Note in abeyance. He was as much surprised as K when the education officials of Tamil Nadu repeated the demand for a state project in the initiation meeting on DPEP on 19 January 1993. K gave vent to his irritation by telling Giri that it appeared as though the State Education Secretary and his minions wanted to secede from India in keeping with the original creed of the Dravidian movement that Dravidians were a separate nation and should strive for a Dravida Nadu, a sovereign nation independent of India.

Come April 1993, another wave of lobbying emerged. The Gujarat Chief Minister wrote to the Finance Minister conveying the interest of his government in preparing a project for elementary education and post-literacy for World Bank funding. The World Bank had indicated its willingness to support the project, and was prepared to offer a technical assistance grant of $50–70,000 for project assistance. He wanted the clearance of the Finance Ministry to go ahead. As ever, K played the role of a 'no' man; in addition to the point about a test case project being as yet not through, it was also pointed out that Gujarat, being not an educationally backward state, could not be given priority in the matter of external funding. Help came from an unexpected quarters; the Education Secretary was shifted a couple of months later, and R. Balakrishnan, the new State Education Secretary, rung up to say that he would not prefer the Bank funding and would instead prefer UNICEF support for DPEP. Of course, UNICEF did not have the resources required to fund DPEP and Gujarat was one of the states covered by the second DPEP Project funded by the Bank.

Turn of the Tide

It so happened that a week after his disappointing meeting with the state education secretaries, K had a series of momentous meetings with Skolnik, Cambridge, and Middleton during the period from 27 January 1993 to 11 February 1993, and an equally momentous visit of Earnest Stern, Managing Director of the World Bank. The meetings covered the UP and DPEP projects, and the relationship between the SSN operation and DPEP.

The Bank was keen that the parameters of the UP Project should be revisited, and the project document reformulated as DPEP project. As it came out in the next few days, DEA was also keen to treat the UP Project as a project coming within the purview of the SSN operation purely as an accounting ploy that would facilitate GOI claiming that it had provided Rs.1,950 crores to district projects as agreed during the SSN negotiations; if this accounting ploy was accepted by the Bank, the DEA functionaries cared little about the content of the UP Project. K's first impulse was to agree with Cambridge and settle scores with his UP colleagues, but better sense prevailed. In a trice he realized that one should not let personal pique dictate the stance of a senior civil servant. Reopening the UP Project would trigger a firestorm of protest, and would embarrass the central government a great deal as it was now directly administering UP after the demolition of the disputed Mandir-Masjid structure in Ayodhya on 6 December 1992 and the imposition of President's rule. K told Cambridge and Middleton that one should not lose sight of history, that the formulation of the UP Project began about a year before DOE came up with the new strategy for universalizing elementary education, and that but for the intransigence of the UP officials the UP Project would have been negotiated with the Bank before the SSN operation and implementation of the project begun. As it was, the project was delayed and it would be inappropriate to further delay the project all the more so as the specifics of DPEP were yet to be developed. Further, the UP Project and DPEP had a few common features; most of the interventions would be common, most of the investment would be in districts, and both would be implemented by autonomous societies. DOE's position was that the UP Project should go ahead without being linked with SSN operation and yet at the same time DPEP should be recognized as the only vehicle for further Bank funding of primary education.

K came to know that Stern and Vergin were due to visit India very soon, and would meet among others Jayalalitha. K worked on Middleton to use the Stern visit to convey unequivocally to Jayalalitha that the Bank would support primary education only and nothing else. Middleton was good enough to admit that 'the Bank should clear the mess it created'. In retrospect, his willingness to help was also motivated by eagerness to avoid embarrassment for his colleagues. When K met Stern on 8 February, K found that he was every inch a grandee, a Big Boss. K found Skolnik quite tense as he waited in the Minister's office for the meeting between Stern and Arjun Singh. In the meeting, he sat on the very edge of the chair as if he were a nervous student facing a dreaded headmaster. K was startled to find even N.K. Singh, the supremo of the Finance Ministry, waiting in the Personal Secretary's office to participate in the high-level meeting. NK told K that Stern was a Managing Director with a capital 'M'; Presidents might come and go but Stern ruled the roost. Like all top American executives, Stern expected to be fully briefed about every major meeting, that too with a brief which did not exceed a single page. As Jayalalitha would definitely seek the support of Stern for the school education project and would claim that the state was assured of support by the local Bank officials, it was imperative for Bank officials who encouraged Tamil Nadu to develop the school education project to cover their tracks lest Stern should come down heavily on local Bank functionaries who encouraged Tamil Nadu to develop a secondary education project when the Bank's avowed policy was to promote primary education in India. Whatever, Middleton was good enough to show to K the brief proposed to be given to Stern, and it brought out crisply that Tamil Nadu was exerting political pressure on Arjun Singh to undo the priority the central government and the Bank extended to primary education.

In the meeting with Arjun Singh, Stern made a strong pitch for primary education, and what he said was music for K's ears. He said primary education was truly fundamental and whether in agriculture or industry it had a pivotal role to play. Primary education was the truly neglected area of economic reforms. Responding to Stern's pitch, Arjun Singh told him that 'we have evolved strategies', referred to the literacy campaigns, and said that from 'this year on we are implementing primary education in a mission mode'. Thereupon Stern observed that while literacy was important primary education was the foundation without which adult education campaigns would go on forever and forever. And then, rather tactless for a worldly wise man like him, so thought K, he went on to make an appreciative reference to the Prime Minister's interview in the BBC's 'phone-in programme' the previous day. He was all praise for the strong commitment that the Prime Minister pledged to primary education as well as for the emphasis he laid on retention of children, particularly girls, in the schools. One of the persons who rung up the Prime Minister in that programme was Myron Weiner, the eminent political scientist turned crusader for a compulsory education law. Stern wondered why a person of the eminence of Weiner with so many channels to reach the Prime Minister should have used an occasion like the 'phone-in programme'. Five days earlier the Supreme Court delivered the landmark *Unnikrishnan* judgment and held that free and compulsory education till the age of 14 years was a fundamental right. Stern wanted to know whether the compulsory education Weiner championed and the compulsory education the Supreme Court judgment spoke of were one and the same. Being the resident expert, K explained that they were not, and that Weiner spoke of compulsion on parents to send their children to school while the Supreme Court spoke of the compulsion on the government to provide free education to all children till the age of four years. Then, Stern delivered the line which K was eager that he should deliver, namely that secondary and higher education tend to take away resources from primary education, and that the concentration should be on primary education. He wanted to know from Arjun Singh the resource support to primary education. In reply, Arjun Singh spoke of the UP Project, EC support to MP, and the new multi-state DPEP project in the making. He added that the strategy was clear, the states were eager, and the new approach would deliver goods. Stern chipped in to say that with the right kind of approach, funds should not be a problem. K intervened to say that a higher proportion of plan outlay was earmarked for primary education, and that resources were necessary but not sufficient; it was imperative for programmes to be cost-effective and for efficiency of expenditure to be enhanced. K believed sincerely in what he said, and at the same time what he said was what would please a banker. Stern looked at K and said with a smile, 'I am happy that it is you and not we who are speaking about effectiveness.' On that note, the meeting ended, even as Arjun Singh was impatiently looking at his wrist watch and asked for his secretary.

As he moved to the escalator with Giri, N.K. Singh, K, and Skolnik in tow Stern asked Skolnik about the projects in the pipeline. Skolnik enthusiastically told him that every year DOE can come up with at least a project. Stern turned to Giri and K and said it was hard to believe that 'you are succeeding' and advised them 'to proceed fast but not too fast'. K thought 'once a banker always a banker'; after delivering his line the grey eminence left in the lift en route to Madras. There was no doubt that he delivered the signal that K wanted him to deliver to Jayalalitha, for the next day State Education Secretary rung up Giri to inform him that in the light of what 'MD *Saar* told Madame' project proposals were being revised by engaging a consultancy organization to give priority to primary education, retention of the girl child in primary schools, and teacher training. Even while participating in the various events of the multi-state DPEP Project, Tamil Nadu would not give up its attempts to pose a project covering the whole state to the Bank. At a meeting of the DPEP Project Lekka, the consultant engaged by Tamil Nadu turned up; at coffee break, he wanted to know from K *Saar* whether World Bank consultancy rates would be applicable to him. The *Saar* rudely told him to get lost as he did not want busybodies like Lekka to come in the way of field functionaries developing the much needed capacity to plan for UPE and implement the project. For quite some time, Tamil Nadu did not give up. As late as August 1993, the Tamil Nadu CS was still lobbying Giri; in a communication he informed Giri that he would not mind if DOE went ahead with a multi-state national minimum needs project; however, given the stage of education development of Tamil Nadu, he wanted Giri to find out some way of permitting the whole State of Tamil Nadu in one stroke. The amiable Giri hesitated to say 'no', and with efflux of time, the tenacious but worldly-wise officials of Tamil Nadu found that their unremitting efforts to push through a project covering the whole state would not succeed; they gave up its efforts, perhaps because Tamil Nadu did not, as in the past, receive any encouragement from World Bank functionaries. All through the three subsequent years that K steered DPEP, no state or Bank functionary ever spoke of a state project. For agencies eager to fund primary education, and for states which wanted to have primary education projects, DPEP was the only game in the town. While K was jubilant with the dénouement, he could not help feeling sad that it a foreigner succeeded in conveying what the priority ought to be where a central government minister and secretary could not.

Later in the day on 11 February, K had a long meeting with Skolnik and Middleton. They agreed with everything K had to say in that meeting. K told him that the purpose of accessing external funding was to put into practice the new strategy of universalizing elementary education; it was from this perspective that DOE saw the SSN operation as an opportunity. DOE was required to have 20 district plans to be prepared as a condition for the release of the second tranche. DOE stood to lose its credibility if it got the states to prepare plans without the ability to finance their implementation. It was imperative to field test the new strategy in as many states as possible. A single state project would not serve the strategy DOE had in mind for universalizing

UEE. A multi-state project has the additional merit of infusing competition among states and ensuring that DOE did not become a hostage to a state as in a state project. Skolnik wholeheartedly accepted the rationale for a multi-state project and added that there was no magic number of states to be covered in a project, and that the number of states to be covered would depend on the response of the states. K outlined his vision of expanding the coverage of DPEP. The states covered or proposed to be covered by external funding such as AP, Bihar, MP, Orissa, and Rajasthan would not be covered by Bank-assisted DPEP projects. Similarly, West Bengal would be covered by ODA assistance, a strategic decision by K which took note of the special affinity Bengali bhadralok had for Britain as vouched by the fact that every year even Jyoti Basu spent some time in Blighty. While the Left Front government might be disinclined to accept World Bank funding, it would not mind ODA funding. DPEP in Jammu and Kashmir and North-Eastern states would be funded domestically. Gujarat had reservations about Bank funding. Progressively all other states and union territories would be covered by one DPEP project after another even though the source of funding might vary. While appreciating the rationale of shifting the unit of educational backwardness for the state to districts and the fact that even in Kerala much needed to be done to improve quality and enhance levels of learning. Skolnik offered the useful suggestion that data should be collected to show that even in Kerala there were pockets where participation was low, and that levels of learning achievement were not high. K emphasized the importance of capacity building and spoke of his vision of forging strong linkages between national and state resource institutions and the university system. K informed Skolnik that very soon a core team of experts would be assembled and deployed by DOE to assist the states in the preparation of district plans and organize training workshops. He agreed with the schedule proposed by K for the appraisal and approval of the first project: preparatory mission in June 1993, pre-appraisal mission in August–September 1993, appraisal mission in December 1993, and approval before June 1994.

Skolnik was also in agreement with everything K had to say about the UP Project. K told Skolnik that CABE approved accessing external financing subject to rigorous parameters. It was stipulated that projects should go beyond conventional measures such as opening of new schools and appointment of teachers, and should address issues of content, process and quality, and enlist people's participation. Apart from facilitating smooth flow of funds to the implementing units, the society structure would ensure that implementation was more effective as 'deadwood' in the traditional administrative structures could be short-circuited. While agreeing with K, Skolnik observed that it should be ensured that the deadwood did not sabotage the society. K conveyed to Skolnik the apprehensions of the National Resource Groups about extension of MS to seven of the project districts. After explaining the salience and uniqueness of the Mahila Samakhya programme, K sought assurances that the Bank would respect the parameters and process orientation of MS, the full autonomy of the MS society, and would develop norms for monitoring and evaluation that took into account the fact that MS was process oriented, and that time and space had to be given for the empowerment process to yield results. Skolnik wholeheartedly agreed to accept the terms and conditions appreciative of the programme that they were extremely happy at the inclusion of an MS component in the project, and they would be 'up in arms' against any attempt to tinker with the letter and spirit of the programme. All in all, all is well that ends well; the meeting on 11 February 1993 led to a clear understanding between K and Skolnik.

UP Project: Policy Battle Ends in Victory

One of the major initiatives which Giri undertook was to organize regional meetings of educations secretaries and other senior officials of State Education Departments in places outside New Delhi to consider in detail the operationalization of the POA, 1992 so that the central and state governments could work together to achieve the goals and objectives of the revised NPE, 1986. Giri's initiative stirred the enthusiasm of the state education officials with the lone exception of Singh who did not attend even a single meeting. K could not help recalling the Unilateral Declaration of Independence from Britain by Rhodesia in 1965 designed to maintain white supremacy. The year 1992 ended with a tiff between Singh and DOE over two ordinances issued by the Bharatiya Janata Party (BJP) government before it resigned in the wake of the demolition of the disputed Mandir–Masjid structure at Ayodhya. The ordinance in respect of universities provided for the vice-chancellors holding office at the pleasure of the chancellor

(Governor), a provision that was not in conformity with the *Report of the UGC Committee towards New Educational Management*, popularly known after its chairman as Gnanam Committee. The other ordinance made a travesty of the concept of VEC elaborated by the POA, 1992, approved by CABE just three months earlier; the BJP education minister from UP participated in that meeting and was a party to the decision. The POA postulated the constitution of the VEC by the elected panchayat and envisaged the local community and teaching community not as opposites but partners in the common cause of facilitating better functioning of schools and ensuring that every child in every family participated in the school and completed elementary education. In contrast to the POA postulates, the UP ordinance provided for members of the VEC to be appointed by the government, and cast the VEC in the mould of inspectorate culture. It appeared as if the ordinance was designed to pit the teachers against the VEC rather than forge partnership, for it placed the teachers under the control of the VEC; thus, without the recommendation of the VEC a teacher would not receive his annual increment in salary. As the State Legislature was dissolved and the state was under President's rule, the ordinances would have lapsed if the replacement bills were not approved by the Parliament before it was prorogued after completion of the Winter Session a little before Christmas. In the Cabinet Note prepared by the UP government justifying the replacement of the ordinance by an act, it made out that the World Bank would not approve the UP Project if VECs were not constituted as provided for by the ordinance. Nothing was farther from the truth. Giri had by then completed six months in office as Education Secretary and had a clear sense of what was right and what was not. He was categorical in his view that empowerment of the village community was not a legal issue only, and that pitting the teachers and the VEC against each other was utterly counterproductive. Arjun Singh who was deeply suspicious of BJP felt that the ordinance was designed to politicize the administration of schools, and demanded to know whether the Bank indeed was behind the move to set up such VECs.

The Bank's Appraisal Mission descended on UP in March 1993, and the indefatigable Singh began to work on the mission members to reopen a few settled issues and twist the arms of DOE. He was successful in persuading Fledgling, a mission member, that NFE ought to be excluded from the project; not much persuasion was required given the Bank's line was that universal primary schooling was the most affordable and realistic pathway to reach the goal of basic education for all, that that from equity point of view there should not be two systems at the primary stage, one for the have-nots and another for the haves, and that NFE should not be a dead end but a bridge end. Middleton brought Fledgling to K for discussion before the aide-memoire was drafted; he was worried that one more round of disagreement would wreck the project and earn him a black mark as task manager. Fledgling breezily demanded to know why DOE should insist on an intervention which neither the Bank nor the 'borrower' desired. One thing that K picked from Bordia was that one should give as good as one gets. K began by saying that his stay at Harvard made him appreciate the candour of Americans, and he was happy that Fledgling did not equivocate and came straight to the point. K asked him how long he was with the Bank, and when he received the answer '10 years' he told Fledgling that while he was an eminent educational expert, he did not appear to have learnt much about the covenants the Bank entered into with borrowers. Legally, it was GOI which was the borrower while the UP government was only a project-implementing agency. Nor did he seemed to have learnt that trust was key to banking business, and that one does not breach deals voluntarily entered into with others. As back as November 1990, it was agreed by the Bank mission headed by Wadi Haddad that NFE would be a part of the project. The Bank was entitled to question the costs and effectiveness of the particular model of NFE proposed in a project document. He then turned to Middleton and wanted to know why rather unusually the Appraisal Mission was reopening issues settled during previous missions. And then K delivered his standard dissertation on the provisions of NPE, 1992, and the CABE parameters, UP Government being a party to the deliberations of the CABE meetings which approved NPE, 1986, and CABE parameters. Singh, a mere official, was not competent to question decisions of CABE. Fledgling changed his tack and suggested that NFE could be imparted wherever there was *manifest demand* for it. K told him that it appeared that he did not adequately appreciate the fact that in countries such as India elementary education was afflicted with deficient demand, and that there was no way elementary education could be universalized if the government catered only to manifest demand and did not pump-prime demand and provide children how might not be able to attend schools to learn in a non-formal setting. K then went on to say that the Badhoi-Mirzapur region of UP was famous for its carpets, and that children were engaged in making of carpets in large numbers. How did the UP government propose to provide them education? The project document spoke of achieving 95–100 per cent participation and 95 per cent retention. Eminent experts such as Victor Ordonez who examined the UP project document at Bordia's behest considered this objective to be overly ambitious. How did the UP government expect these goals to be achieved by relying on only schools? At the end of the tirade, Fledgling conceded that K had a point and left along with Middleton. NFE was one of the themes to which Giri was deeply attached, and he wanted to put an end to the discussion on NFE once and for all by having a clear action plan for NFE to be prepared.

What Eid Dib, the mission member in charge of civil construction, had to say about classroom design was music to the ears of the UP Education Department. Dib was of the view that the standards of classrooms to be built in the project districts should conform to the standards in countries such as the United States. Every child should be provided a space of one square metre as compared to the national norm of 0.7 square metre laid down in the Operation Blackboard scheme, never mind the costs, and criteria such as sustainability and replicability. When K remonstrated with Singh, he sought to justify by arguing that safer designs were warranted because of the recent collapse of an old school building in Moradabad; how more area per child would enhance safety was left unsaid. The technical argument that Bank missions should not flip-flop and that which was settled pre-appraisal should not be reopened by the appraisal mission clinched the issue.

The UP Education Department had high expectations that it could shoot down the society from the shoulders of the Bank as Mohan Gopal, the Legal Counsel, had reservations about the idea of a society implementing the project. However, in his meeting with K, Mohan Gopal made it clear that he was not opposed to the society as such but was keen to ensure that the society did not dilute the fiduciary responsibility of the state government to implement the project in accordance with the agreement, and provide an alibi to the state government to shirk its obligation by claiming that the society, an autonomous organization over which it had no control, took up actions which were not in conformity with the project agreement. K took Mohan Gopal through the MOA and bye-laws of the BEP Society, and explained how given the composition of the governance structures his fears were without any basis. Mohan Gopal then recalled that a similar structure was created for the Sardar Sarovar Project, and the concern about fiduciary responsibility of the state government could be got over by having the society itself participate in the negotiations with the Bank and have a formal agreement between the society and the state government legally binding the former to implement the project in accordance with the project agreement between the Bank and the state government. He also touched up the BEP bye-laws so that his concerns were met; as drafted by him the bye-laws provided for the central and UP governments to issue joint directives to the society, and further for the central government's views to prevail should the central government and UP government differ over the joint directive. The suggestion that the society should participate in the negotiations eminently suited K. A day earlier, Middleton requested K to hurry up saying that if the formal negotiations were not concluded by 15 May 1993 the project would not be cleared in the 'current' Bank financial year and funds earmarked for the UP Project would lapse. K curtly told him that if the funds lapsed 'let them be'; the matter of the society had to be thrashed out. K thought that deadline for the negotiations together with Mohan Gopal coming on board would get Singh to accept the inevitable. He shot a letter to Singh to accept the MOA and bye-laws drafted by Mohan Gopal and have the society registered so that the final negotiations could be fixed in the Bank headquarters wherein the society would also participate. Although K settled the matter with Mohan Gopal, Singh did not give up. To jump the story ahead, Mohan Gopal himself revisited the matter of the society about a year later during the appraisal of the first DPEP project. Not without reason is it said that it ain't over till it is over, and that it ain't over even after it is over.

Did Napoleon lose the vital Battle of Waterloo which ended the Napoleonic campaigns because he was unwell on the day of the battle? This is a question which occasionally crops up in historical debates. Similarly, looking back K is intrigued by the question whether Singh being away on a junket to Seoul affected the decisive meeting taken by the Cabinet Secretary which put an end to the intransigence of UP. A little later, Middleton turned up to say that Singh had suggested to the state government that Montek Singh Ahluwalia, the Finance Secretary, should be requested to convene a meeting with the UP government, the Bank, and DOE to iron out the differences lest the negotiations should be stalled if disagreement continued between DOE and the UP government. The suggestion was like letting the fox inside the chicken's coop; DOE would be cornered if the Bank agreed with the stand of the UP government. K could not help recalling that the British could conquer India with *sepoys* (Indian soldiers) and with Indian allies as Indian rulers did not mind allying with foreigners to discomfit their rivals. K told Middleton that enough was enough, and that he should inform Skolnik and Vergin not to be in a hurry to fix the negotiations. K also contacted N.K. Singh of DEA whom he had been badgering to get UP on line and informed him of the latest move of UP, and cautioned him that if UP had its way DOE would reconsider its decision to pose projects to the Bank and he should look to other social sectors to utilize the IDA allocation to India. The move of Singh which Middleton spoke of did materialize by way of a letter from T.S.R. Subramanian, Chief Secretary, UP, himself. In that letter, TSR set out that the UP government reconsidered its decision to accept the society and now felt that the UP Basic Shiksha Parishad was good enough, and that if necessary the UP government was willing to set up a separate structure for NFE. K and Giri decided to shift the forum of adjudication to the more neutral ground of the Cabinet Secretariat. At Giri's direction K drafted a note for consideration of the Cabinet Secretary which was a riposte, figuratively a mailed fist in a velvet glove. Though couched in cold seemingly objective prose, it was implicitly a sharp polemical tract and hit at the opposition like a sledgehammer. No wonder the moment Giri and K turned up in the Cabinet Secretariat for the meeting, Sanjiv Mishra, the Joint Secretary in the Cabinet Secretariat, complimented K for a note which was refreshingly free from officialese, and had literary qualities, and wished 'we have more of these'. The note made out that the issue raised by the UP government was not an isolated issue of management but one inextricably intertwined with education policy and the prospects for absorbing IDA allocations to India through basic education projects. To consider education to be an exclusive state subject was an immaculate misconception, for constitutionally education was a concurrent subject, and NPE, 1986, had defined concurrency as a meaningful partnership. It was in keeping with the spirit of meaningful partnership that DOE fully involved the state governments in the revision of NPE, 1986 and its POA, and in the evolution of the parameters for accessing external funding for basic education; a national consensus was forged through the deliberations of CABE. The centrality of NFE in universalizing elementary education was clearly set out by the NPE; being so, it was not open to a state to question the utility of NFE. DOE was bound by the CABE parameters to ensure that externally funded projects conform to national policies. The decision to avail external funding was based on a fragile consensus, and there was considerable apprehension that Bank funding would lead to the country losing its autonomy to frame educational policies and curriculum. It was expedient for the central government to be closely associated with the management of the project as the UP Project was conceived as a test case project and DOE was eager to apply the lessons learnt from the implementation of the UP Project to the other projects which would be posed to the Bank and other funding agencies; society was an instrument that permitted that association. Unfortunately, all along a section of the UP government conducted itself as if the central government could have no role in the design or implementation of the project. From time to time, DOE made earnest attempts to amicably resolve the differences. Twice in his meetings with DOE, Chief Secretary Saxena agreed to go by the views of DOE in regard to NFE and the society. It is understandable if for well-considered reasons the state government seeks to reopen the understanding it reached with DOE. However, propriety demanded that the state government takes up the matter with DOE and seek an amicable resolution of differences. Rather than follow such a legitimate procedure, the UP government raised these issues with the Bank's missions and took positions that infringed its understanding with DOE. If news of the UP government acting in concert with the Bank comes out in the open, DOE would be in an untenable position and would have to give up its attempt to access external funding. This would have a bearing on the strategy of DEA to utilize the IDA allocation through the new avenue of basic education projects. Without DOE chipping in the prospect of IDA allocation being utilized would be rather dim. Thus, the issue raised by the UP government should not be perceived as a simple issue of management or through the prism of centre–state relations. Given that DEA's own interests were threatened, Montek Singh Ahluwalia endorsed the views of Giri that the Cabinet Secretary should take a meeting to resolve the issue as the stand taken by the UP government would jeopardize the project.

The meeting was held on 24 April 1993, and it was indeed a miracle that the meeting was held at all, for an Indian Airlines aircraft was hijacked; it appeared damn silly that the Cabinet Secretary should divert his attention to a petty matter akin to the spat of school children. TSR, a future Cabinet Secretary himself, made his points very cogently. He said that the divergences were rather minor. He wanted less emphasis on NFE not because 'I do not believe in it but because it was unchartered'; however, he would give in to Giri. It was no doubt true that Saxena agreed to the society, but later thinking, made the UP government to reconsider, as a society might create complications. The apprehension seemed to be that funds would not flow to the project in time; however, he claimed 'our batting record is good', eliciting the quip from S. Rajagopal, the Cabinet Secretary, that 'you don't play at all'. The society was redundant in view of the fact that there was a separate body called the UP Basic Shiksha Parishad which managed the schools very well. Given the UP political climate, society might not be just a redundant, harmless body; there would be jockeying for positions and conflict of interest. If the idea was to promote efficiency in the release and utilization of funds and to ensure that the funds received by the project were additional he would not mind amending the Basic Shiksha Parishad Act suitably. He went on to say that he had detailed discussion with Middleton who seemed to be 'greatly impressed' by the functioning of the Basic Shiksha Parishad, and that it would have been a different matter if the central government shared with the state government that part of the outlay which was not funded by the Bank. This observation provoked Rajagopal to say that he did not relish the Bank functionaries directly dealing with the states. Concluding his submission, TSR said that as the state was under the President's rule, he would accept whatever was the decision of the Cabinet Secretary; however, there was no guarantee that the new government headed by the Samajwadi Party or the BJP which came to power after elections might reopen the issue. Rajagopal said that we could 'cross the bridge when we came upon it', and asked Montek about the views of the Bank. Montek's observation was very supportive. The society was no doubt an ugly structure; however, the Bank seemed to be of the view that 'whatever we might say about UP things are pretty bad in that part of the country; we are short of evidence about the efficiency of existing structures', and further, the Bank seemed to be happy with the idea of the society. That clinched the issue. Obviously, Mohan Gopal's supportive stance seemed to have prevailed in the internal discussions of the Bank about the society. Thereafter, TSR objected to the provision in the society bye-laws which provided for the issue of a joint directive to the society, and the views of the central government should prevail. Rajagopal, however , not only wanted that proviso to remain intact but also stipulated that the Society should submit its accounts to the state government which in turn should forward them to the central government for acceptance. Touché! It was the Delhi Mughal *durbar* (court) asserting its primacy over a *subedar* (vassal)!

Strange but true, reasoned argument was only one of the factors which clinched the issue. Earlier in the day, newspapers carried a report about a speech of the Prime Minister at a meeting of secondary school teachers at Kamala Nehru Nagar in Ghaziabad, a district of UP which abuts Delhi. In that speech, the Prime Minister said:

> Education now being on the concurrent list, concerted efforts have to be made by the Central and State Governments for furthering education. The Central Government is now earmarking funds for specific use so that these could not be diverted to other programmes as in the past.... Attempts to alter textbooks to 'remake' history will not be tolerated.

Rajagopal referred to the statement and wondered who the Education Secretary was during the BJP rule, to receive the reply it was Singh. He wanted to know where he was, to be told that he was away in Seoul attending a World Bank workshop. So, he is off on a junket having thrown a mighty spanner in the works, Rajagopal remarked and directed TSR to keep Singh away from the negotiations so that he did not complicate matters. Truth to be told, while Singh rigidly sought to protect his state's interest as he saw them he was not a political animal like quite a few IAS officers and his professional integrity was exemplary.

In Robert Southey's famous poem, *The Battle of Blenheim*, little Peterkin poses the question 'But what good came of it at last?' only to receive the reply 'Why, that I can't tell, but 'twas a famous victory.' Insofar as the limited objective of smoothening the flow of funds to the project-implementing units was concerned, nothing good came of the 'victory' for the reason that the Finance Ministry did not wish to depart from its standard practice of passing the loan it received from the Bank only to the consolidated fund of the state government; consequently, the flow of funds to the society would be regulated by the state finance department whose pressing concern was balancing the ways and the position of the state government. It was only in DPEP, technically a CSS, that DOE could release from its budgetary provision funds straight to the DPEP societies without intermediation of the state finance departments, and submit claims to the Bank for reimbursement of funds expended by the societies. However, just as making salt was a symbol for a larger purpose, namely asserting the right of Indians to be free of British rule, the society was a symbol of the right of DOE to be associated with the design and management of the DPEP; it was also a symbol for repudiation of the Schnorrer attitude of 'give us the money; don't tell us how to use it; who else would know our requirements better?' Judged by its contribution to the advancement of the larger purpose, 'twas indeed a famous victory for DOE. Had the UP government prevailed in the contest, DPEP would have come unstuck and gone the way of a conventional CSS. In the formative phase of DPEP, there were tensions galore between functionaries of the state government education departments and of those of the DPEP Bureau in DOE. The fountainhead of these tensions was the fact that DPEP departed from the past in several respects. First, the relationship between the external financing agency and the state government was vastly different from the past. To begin with, there was not much understanding of the difference between DPEP and other CSSs, and of DPEP and other externally funded state projects in different sectors such as agriculture, irrigation, and health. Many education secretaries thought that it was the Bank which called the shots, and that so long as the Bank did not raise any objection, DOE would not quibble about the proposals of states. They were surprised to find that it was K and his deputies who did all the quibbling. It was but natural that quite a few equate the insistence on work plans, appraisal, and so on with too much of unwarranted centralization and control. Second, though a CSS, DPEP was not to be implemented in the customary way; it sought to usher a new culture of outcome orientation and accountability by laying down targets for enrolment, retention, learning levels, and reduction of educational disparities, by specifying processes such as preparation of annual work plans, appraisal of plans, joint review missions to assess implementation, and putting in place a strong MIS and periodic as well as terminal evaluation. Third, without decentralized planning and implementation the DPEP strategy for UPE would have been no different from the strategy hitherto followed, yet a certain amount of uniformity, standardization, and rigour were imperative to ensure satisfactory outcomes and meet the demands of the agencies funding the programme as well of the Finance Ministry. What DPEP was attempting to accomplish was *organized decentralization* rather than decentralization without a national framework and without the programme being steered at the national level by DOE. Without such steering it would have been impossible for the new culture of outcomes to be introduced and for weaning away the external agencies from their tradition of hands-on management of the project preparation and implementation process. When DPEP was introduced, there were two concurrent and apparently opposite streams, one of more centralized direction of a CSS and the other of devolution of planning and implementation functions for the first time to local levels. The central paradox of the DPEP strategy was that in order to foster decentralization it was necessary initially for DOE to exercise more centralized control and direction. An analogy is President Nixon's attempts to usher in a new federalism wherein the federal government provides grants to states for resolving social issues without being prescriptive allowing broad discretion to the states for how the programmes are implemented, and yet at the same time closely monitoring outcomes. Paraphrasing Nixon's blunt comment on the strategy followed to usher in a new federalism 'bringing power to the DOE in order to dish it out'. It is a matter of record that over time DOE loosened its control and devolved on the state DPEP societies many functions it was initially discharging by itself such as the appraisal of the annual work plans. More importantly, the control was so exercised as to let the states and districts display initiative and, if they choose, innovate. Without the initial centralization, decentralization which is at the heart of DPEP would have been disorganized decentralization and reduced DPEP to a conventional CSS. It is but natural that what appears so lucidly in retrospect would appear differently in the initial phase of DPEP. Perceptions were bound to differ on what constituted the right balance between decentralized planning and implementation on the one hand and the need to ensure uniformity, standardization, and rigour on the other, and reconciling the multiple perceptions called for sensitive negotiations between DOE and the states. The larger the number of parties in a negotiation, the greater is the complexity of the negotiation process and the greater the uncertainty of the outcome. Even the addition of a single party to a two-party negotiation introduces coalition dynamics. Two or more parties might act in league to enhance their bargaining power against those who are outside the coalition. Thus, with the UP Project, Singh was consistently trying to enhance his bargaining power vis-á-vis DOE by trying to rope in the Bank and DEA wherever and whenever he could. In the multi-state DPEP project the prospects of two or more states upsetting the regime that K was trying to introduce by coming together and roping in the Bank were far higher. The 'famous' victory in the UP Project obviated such a possibility as other states which were watching the developments in UP did not fail to take note of the outcome of the cocky defiance of UP. That apart, the UP standoff was a defining experience for Middleton; he drew the right conclusion from the decisive victory of DOE in the UP standoff that in a confrontation with a state DOE would prevail, and that he better not play on both sides of the road as he did in UP. He scrupulously stood aloof from any disagreement between DOE and a state, making it clear that the Bank had nothing to do with such matters.

Compared to the SSN negotiations or the negotiations of the first DPEP project, the UP Project negotiations in Washington, DC, were smooth with most of the discussions centring round the project agreement. It was during this visit that K came to get acquainted socially with Marlaine Lockheed who played an important role from the Bank side in DPEP. Marlaine Lockheed was from California and a scion of the illustrious family which set up the aviation firm that manufactured Lockheed aircraft. Like Middleton, she was an educationist, but she did her graduate work at Stanford, Harvard on the West Coast. An exceptionally gifted researcher, she was strong in evaluation having been associated with Education Testing Service at Princeton, where her home was and to which she returned from Washington DC every weekend. She was the principal author of two documents which were the Bank's core contributions to the Jomtien Conference: the World Bank's draft policy paper *Primary Education*, and the book co-authored with

Adrian Verspoor and others, *Improving Primary Education in Developing Countries*.[4] The book was discussed at a Roundtable in the Jomtien Conference, presided by no less than Barber Conable, President, World Bank (Chapter VII). Marlaine Lockheed saw in the engagement with Indian primary education a great opportunity to embark on a voyage of discovery, collect precious data, and test hypotheses on improving primary education. She took great interest in the studies conducted as a part of the preparation of the first DPEP project for Bank funding—more interest than K liked, as insistence on more and more data and analysis seemed to delay the posing of the project for the approval of the board. She also played a key role in the DPEP research conferences organized by NCERT at the behest of the DPEP Bureau. Like a good American academic, she quickly put together a book *Primary Education in India*,[5] copiously drawing upon the various studies and published research duly acknowledging the 'debt owed to the various institutions and many scholars whose work made the preparation of this report possible'. She attended to the education and evaluation aspects of DPEP in the Education and Employment Division in the Bank, and as such K came to develop a good rapport with her, and appreciated her graciousness and warmth.

Coming to the 'famous victory' in the policy battle over the UP Project, history tells us that the outcome of victories, however famous and decisive, are likely to be challenged by unexpected developments. To jump the story, the 'famous' victory established the right of DOE to have a say in the management of the programme which in turn necessitated DOE significantly contributing to the implementation of the UP Project; this fact brought forth new tensions given that divergent perceptions and views are intrinsic to any continuing, close relationship. Resolution of these differences got a little complicated because of the work style of the new task manager who succeeded Middleton. It is common to come across the perception of the Bank as a monolithic organization driven by power elite encompassing the interests of the US and global financial markets, and manned by

[4] Marlaine Lockheed, Adriaan M. Verspoor, and Associates, *Improving Primary Education in Developing Countries*, New York: Oxford University Press, 1991.

[5] World Bank, *Primary Education in India*, 1997.

zombies who enforce the Party line mechanically. In K's experience, the reality is different from that perception. The Bank functionaries 'come in all shapes and sizes', and their personalities and work styles significantly impact on their task. Being so, the Bank's oversight of the UP Project by Verspoor, the new task manager, was vastly different from what it was when Cambridge and Middleton were the task managers. It appeared to K that he believed that it was for the state government and the Bank to manage the project, and that DOE had little role. His main conclusion from his acclaimed study of World Bank lending for basic education was that flexibility, community involvement, and adaptation of programmes to local conditions are critical elements of successful educational programmes, yet it appeared to K that he did not apply to his task as task manager the conclusions of his own study, and that he was overly keen to bring to bear on the UP Project his rich international experience without much regard for local conditions and national sensitivities. K was not amused when, in a review meeting, he suggested that UP outsource its requirements for academic support rather than draw upon national resource organizations such as NCERT. In offering that suggestion, K felt that he viewed the UP Education Project in isolation without recognizing the fact that the project was part of the national effort to universalize elementary education, build national capacity for developing and implementing projects, and strengthen national resource organizations. In all fairness to him, it is possible that K's assessment is perhaps too harsh, and is based on miscommunication and misperception. To him, the UP Project was one of the very many education projects he had dealt with as an educationist in the Bank. However, for K, the UP Project was not just an education project; it was a test case to probe the earnestness of the Bank and ascertain whether the assurances given by the Bank functionaries regarding country ownership would be fulfilled or not. It was about to use contemporary vocabulary of aid discourse the country being in the driver's seat, exercising 'leadership in developing and implementing national development strategies', and taking 'the lead in coordinating aid at all levels'. More importantly, the seven states which were developing DPEP district plans were watching closely how the UP Project was being implemented, and any marginalization of DOE's role or of national strategies would have a domino effect. Consequently, K asserted all the time the 'paramountcy' of DOE never failing to remind the state government and the Bank whenever the situation warranted that, unlike in a typical 'state project' funded by the Bank, the central government was not a mere conduit for flow of funds from the Bank, and that implementation was not a matter for the task manager and the state government officials alone. As it is, K has an authoritarian streak and is intolerant of any conflicting opinion. Given the imperative of asserting DOE's role, K was pricklier in his dealings with Verspoor than he would have been even with his authoritarian streak. In retrospect, K feels he ought to have had a frank talk with him, much as he used to have with other functionaries of the Bank such as Skolnik or Cambridge or Middleton, shared with him his concerns and perceptions, and sought his cooperation for what K sought to achieve.

Set in Concrete

Compared with many other activities which were happening at the same time, the SOP was a tiny sideshow; however, it acquired an unusual salience given the hint the Germans gave in the bilateral discussions between India and Germany that they intended to link the SOP with the Financing Agreement with EC. The implicit message was 'better accept our terms with SOP lest we should make things difficult for you in your negotiations with the EC'. There was no reason to disbelieve the German threat, for it was common knowledge that the EC was a Franco-German project, and that not a sparrow could fall in the EC without Germany's acquiescence. K took full advantage of the fact that EC offered assistance to primary education in India as a co-financier of the Bank's SSN operation, and fully harnessed Cambridge's willingness to work on the EC. Unlike K the memorialist, the K who was negotiating with the Germans and the EC had no way of knowing that the negotiations with EC would conclude so well. Consequently, he had to play safe, and with patience unusual for him, K kept the dialogue with Germans going even when it became clear that the Germans offered too little and their demands were impossible. SOP has the distinction of being the only project in which K failed to secure an agreement with the funding agency; after the negotiations with the Germans were formally called off, SOP was subsumed in the second DPEP project financed by the Bank.

Like the UP and MP projects, SOP was one of the unfinished tasks which Bordia left behind. The dialogue with Germans did not move beyond the agreement to hold a workshop; before Bordia demitted office in May 1992, a workshop was scheduled on the SOP. Even though his meeting with John Lawrence of UNDP brought out that little funding could be expected from UNDP for SOP, regardless of the damper of the discussions with Lawrence, Bordia decided to go ahead with the workshop as scheduled (Chapter XI). Nothing came out of the workshop except for reinforcing K's belief that he would have an uphill struggle in weaning the states away from the brick-and-mortar approach to education development, and a deep-rooted culture of being excessively deferential to donors. A 'Discussion Paper' prepared by the State Education Department projected the requirement of funds at Rs 425 crore spread over a five-year period for the four districts covered by SOP. A measure of the hefty investment projected is brought out by the fact that if SOP were approved as proposed, about Rs 85 crore would have been expended each year in the four project districts as compared to the Rs 69 odd crore of plan funds spent on elementary education in all the 13 districts of Orissa during 1993–4. Obviously, while projecting requirements of funds to the funding agency, critical parameters such as sustainability of the investment and reliability of the programme interventions in other districts were not taken note of; 85 per cent of the outlay was earmarked for opening of schools and hostels, construction of school and buildings, and teacher salaries. While a meagre amount of Rs 10 crore was provided for strengthening DIETs, no provision was made for training costs or quality improvement. The one feature of the project outline which was very commendable was the proposal to prepare bilingual primers; in a state with large tribal populations and many tribal languages, the essentiality of such primers cannot be stressed enough. The CS wanted a commitment by UNDP of the funding it would provide then and there, and the State Education Secretary was ready with a list of blocks where school building construction could begin straightaway. The Orissa government was ready to provide its share of the outlay for 1992–3 to get the project going. When so pressed, Lawrence had to disappoint the Orissa officials by saying that issues of quality, training, and curriculum were too important to be ignored; he also evaded any commitment of resources by UNDP. Lawrence was to visit India a couple of times later in connection with the SOP, and K came to be better acquainted with him. Like most Englishmen, he was a cricket buff; he turned up once in K's office for a meeting straight from the airport. He was in an ecstatic mood having travelled along with the Indian cricket team from Calcutta. He was thrilled that he could get the autograph of Kapil Dev. K came to know that he had quite a chequered career. An Oxford alumnus, he began his career as a Royal Marines Commando; after a decade in uniform, he turned to the academia, consultancy, and international civil service. He dropped out of sight once UNDP association with basic education projects in India did not materialize. K's interactions with Lawrence did not help K to understand the real agenda of UNDP or of Lawrence. It was only about a dozen years later when he read a book by Phillip Jones that he got a clear indication that UNDP strayed into the Jomtien Conference in a fit of absent-mindedness, and after the Conference, it woke up and was in a tearing hurry to move to an agenda of its own which centred round sustainable human development.[6] It appears that

> what excited Lawrence was not the focus of UPE as evident in the World Bank priorities, as are girls' and women's education as embraced by UNICEF, or the comprehensive or balanced development of formal and non-formal systems by the UNESCO. Rather, it was opportunity to shift the focus within UNDP from education as a specific, freestanding, sector to something broader and inter sectoral.

Once UNDP had a new administrator Lawrence James Gustave Speth in 1993, and Speth embraced Sustainable Human Development (SHD) agenda as a single rallying point for all that UNDP was to undertake over the next five years, Lawrence saw his primary task as steering UNDP away from Jomtien agenda towards SHD.

Whatever, at the workshop held in April 1992, Bordia advised Orissa officers to revisit the project parameters, take note of the Sitamarhi district plan, and come up with a more balanced proposal. Little progress was made even by 1 December 1992 when the Germans organized another workshop. Once bitten twice shy; going by his experience with BEP, K did not wish to get a project proposal prepared for Orissa by DOE and its consultants the way the BEP Brown Book or BEP's annual

[6] P.W. Jones with David Coleman, *The United Nations and Education: Multilateralism, Development, and Globalisation*, New York: Routledge, 2005, pp. 213–16.

plan for 1993–4 was. He was particular that Orissa officers should go through the burdensome and yet educative experience of thinking through and coming out with a project proposal which would address all the challenges of UEE. Another valuable lesson of BEP which led him not to force the pace of project formulation was that plans and project documents made no sense without resources being firmed up. On 19 October 1992, Carl Gustaf Mannerheim, the Counsellor in the German Embassy, Mannerheim's Deputy Rosenberg, and Rosencratz of GTZ (Deutsche Gesellschaft für Technische Zusammenarbeit, German Society for Technical Cooperation) met K to discuss the terms of reference for organizing the workshop. The terms of reference made it clear that the Orissa proposal was no good, and that it was necessary to develop project parameters. This was not an unreasonable proposition by itself, but the next term of reference made it utterly unreasonable. It was made clear that no assurance of assistance could be given even if the workshop was successful and clear project parameters emerged from the workshop. It passed K's comprehension why DOE and Government of Orissa should take the trouble of organizing a workshop if the Germans shirked from offering even a faint assurance of assistance. And further, the Germans issued a *diktat* that the workshop was to last for five days and was to be 'conducted' by a German moderator with absolute freedom to organize it as he wished. Mannerheim and his colleagues were unwilling even to discuss the structure of the workshop, its organization, and the outcomes expected from it lest the deliberations of the workshop should be 'rigged'. They were equally inflexible in regard to the dates on which the workshop was to be held. K suggested a date later than what Mannerheim suggested as the State Education Secretary was on leave but Mannerheim would not relent. Left to him, K would have read the riot act and called off the workshop but he was not a free agent as he did not wish to jeopardize the sensitive negotiations with EC. K suggested to Mannerheim to emulate the EC and offer assistance under the framework of the SSN agreement so that the seemingly endless rigmarole of clearances is done away with. Mannerheim did agree that the SSN framework would expedite matters; he admired the EC for getting the old India hand Theobald into the act and expediting the decision-making process. However, Mannerheim expressed helplessness as the German Minister for Development Co-operation was unlikely to approve a fast-disbursing grant for primary education; German support for assistance under the SSN operation was sought only for National Renewal fund and not for primary education. It was too late to make a request for bringing in primary education within the SSN assistance that the German government was considering. Being so, there was no option but to pass through the traditional German process for approving developmental projects. Unlike other countries, Germany did not have a single agency for technical and financial 'co-operation'. It is customary for technical assistance being first provided GTZ for developing projects, and thereafter for substantial investment in the project being made by Kreditanstalt für Wiederaufbau, a development bank.

Looking back, the SOP workshop organized by the Germans was a Gilbert and Sullivan opera. The project area covered many tribal tracts in which schools were managed by the Tribal Welfare Department. The Minister and officials of that department stayed away from the workshop as they felt that the workshop was the show of the Education Department, and that they were not given due importance in the organization of the workshop. The state had no regular Education Secretary, and the officiating Education Secretary was an enterprising IAS officer who spoke eloquently at the inaugural session. The new just-then-promoted Director, Primary Education, was disingenuous enough to say during the course of his speech that the Education Department would have preferred postponement of the workshop but for the fax from K that unless the state government bucked up and organized the workshop on the dates indicated by the Germans the project might be delayed by at least a year. During the couple of days K spent at Bhubaneswar, K came to know that further progress after the April workshop was stalled because of departmental politics. The former Education Secretary wanted a consultant to be appointed and his proposal was not approved by the Minister of State for Education who was engaged in a cold war with the Cabinet Minister for Education, and insistent that he should hold independent charge of school education. The moderator was a Canadian of German origin who came from faraway Canadian prairies with little idea even of India not to speak of Orissa, and with no idea either of the Indian educational scene or the Indian educational policy and strategies for UEE. However, he was proficient in the stock in trade of 'facilitating' workshops, in adeptly steering the deliberations so as to force the participants to think through and come up with creative solutions for the problems they wished to solve. As he saw him in action, K recalled the case method of teaching with which he became familiar at Harvard. The techniques that the German moderator adopted shared a few common features with the case method. Socratic questioning is the model that the case instructor tries to emulate. Socrates, the midwife of critical thinking, was also the unlovable Socrates, the gadfly who takes delight in 'to sting people and whip them into a fury, all in the service of truth', and 'projecting an image of arrogance'. Hence, the jeering and intimidating style of the case instructor is not wholly inappropriate to the method that goes by the name of Socrates. The German moderator was very much acting the role of the gadfly. However, the case method by itself cannot elevate the thought process of the participants beyond the frontiers of their experiential knowledge or innate intuition; it needs to be supplemented by the teaching of concepts if the students are to acquire a good grounding in the praxis of management or policymaking. The method of facilitation adopted by the German moderator is no different. None of the participants had any experience of project design and implementation or a proper understanding of what it takes to universalize elementary education. Leadership could have been provided by senior officials of the Education Department if they were at least *au courant* with the latest thinking on UEE. However, because of the turnover in the key positions of State Education Secretary and Director, Primary Education, the new incumbents were not familiar even with NPE, 1986, and POA as revised in 1992.

The UNDP had appointed a troika of Indian consultants to analyse the status of elementary education in Orissa and recommend what needs to be done. The German moderator was good enough to K's request that the troika be permitted to make a presentation soon after the inaugural session to set the pace for the deliberations of the workshop. The troika went on and on for about a couple of hours with cluttered slides, lost themselves in a mass of information, and failed to focus on the key issues and connect with the listless audience. They ought to have started from the basics keeping in mind the audience they were addressing instead of prefacing every sentence they spoke with phrases that would have befitted an academic audience such as 'we believe' and 'we are of the view'. Sitting through the presentation K could not help recalling a witticism about the reaction of a bored audience to a longish speech: we forgot the beginning, sat through the middle of it, and nothing was more pleasing than its end. Whatever, the workshop began to drift from its second day; on the third day a high functionary of the state government announced dramatically that a SOP society was registered at Rayagada, a town in the project area, and introduced the Project Director designate who was considered to be the blue-eyed boy of the Chief Minister. Two days later, the workshop wound up without serving any purpose except reinforcing the innate belief of the Germans that they should tightly manage every project they finance. In his follow-up meeting with K, Mannerheim pronounced that the workshop arrangements were 'lousy'; K had half a mind to tell him that he had to blame himself as he would not deign to discuss the structure and organization of the workshop. He proposed a long pilot phase of three to four years which could be financed by GTZ and UNDP; however, he would not commit to substantial funding even after the conclusion of the pilot phase. He then put forth the demand that a GTZ representative should be posted in Bhubaneswar to monitoring the Project. Accustomed as he was to 'thinking in time' and recall historical analogies, Mannerheim's demand reminded K of the grant in 1765 by Emperor Shah Alam II of *diwani* (right to collect revenue) to the East India Company that paved the way for Orissa being ruled by the Company. Mannerheim was also worried that the officer appointed as the Project Director was not senior enough and might not have enough clout to get the Education and Tribal Welfare Departments work together. K sought to allay his apprehensions by telling him that as the Chief Minister's blue-eyed boy he would have enough clout to get everyone on board. However, K's reply far from assuaging Mannerheim's worry sowed fresh doubts in his interlocutor's mind. Would not the project be jeopardized when a different government comes to power? K could not help recall in his mind the famous observation of Hitler about his meeting with General Franco at Hendaye in October 1940, 'I prefer to have three or four of my own teeth pulled out than to speak to that man again!'. K kept his cool and refrained from grinding his teeth lest the EC negotiations should be jeopardized. Once the Financing Agreement with the EC was signed in December 1993, K ignored the advice of the Joint Secretary in DEA dealing with Germany to give in to the demands of the Germans, and put an end to his agony by calling off the dialogue with Germans and

UNDP, and including Orissa in the second DPEP project funded by the Bank.

National Core Group: An Inspired idea

Although the SOP workshop was frustrating, it had an unintended consequence for it set K think deeply about the reasons underlying the German demands, and explore what the literature of development co-operation had to say about the behaviour of bilateral and multilateral agencies. As he reflected on his conversation with Mannerheim again and again for the next few days, the conversation began to appear in a different light, and K came to be more understanding of Mannerheim's position. What Mannerheim offered was similar to what SIDA offered to Bordia in regard to Lok Jumbish excepting that SIDA gave up the demand to position a representative in Jaipur while Mannerheim was obdurate. But then as Bordia, a native of Rajasthan, made it explicitly clear to everyone who mattered that he would continue his association with Lok Jumbish even after his retirement, and that SIDA could bank on him to ensure that Lok Jumbish would be managed well. In contrast, there was no such assurance with SOP. To say the least the Orissa scene did not inspire confidence and DOE had not put in an institutional mechanism in place to assist Orissa in the design and implementation of SOP. Placing himself in Mannerheim's position, K realized that what he was demanding of Mannerheim was a departure from the German tradition of assistance. That being so, the natural questions that arose were: Why should Germans depart from their tradition? Was there a compulsion or incentive to change? K realized that there was none because, unlike the World Bank, the Germans were not overly eager to include primary education in their India operations; nor were they like the EC which was eager to make it big in the 'aid business'. That apart, K recognized that Mannerheim was obligated to ensure that assistance was used well. To generalize, agencies are accountable to their 'masters': governments, parliaments, and citizens in case of bilateral agencies, governing bodies and Member States in case of multilateral and regional agencies, and governing bodies and Member States as well as financial markets from which they raise resources in case of multilateral and regional financial agencies. In order to discharge this accountability, agencies are obligated to fund only efficient programmes and further ensure efficient implementation of such programmes. Where capacity of the recipient country to design and implement a project is inadequate, an agency has three options: (*a*) giving up the project; (*b*) patiently building the capacity of recipient country; and (*c*) engaging foreign consultants to design and implement the project either on a turnkey basis or in close association with local professionals so that even while design and implementation proceeds briskly capacity is built. Enhancing the capacity of recipient countries to develop and implement projects is a time-consuming process. It is difficult to resist the temptation to adopt a hands-on-management style or 'mother' a project at different stages—conceptualization, design, start-up, implementation—so that the project supported is well designed, takes off briskly, and is well implemented, and credit could be taken for a successful project. It is also difficult to resist to offer advice based on comparative experience of working in different countries and different projects without much consideration for the relevance of the advice to the specific context of the recipient country, and also to put in place excessively tight monitoring systems. Tensions arise because the recipient country has a different perception of the actions of the agency. The recipient of advice might consider such advice to be irrelevant to their context, and even unwarranted. The attitude is: Who else would know our requirements better than us? Monitoring may be considered by the recipient to be far too intrusive; such a feeling evokes in turn a feeling in the agency functionaries that the recipient is indifferent to the accountability that the recipient owes, and that the recipient is in the grip of a schnorrer syndrome. Compounding the intrinsic tensions of agency–country relationship are the hazards of cross-cultural communication so vividly in E.M. Foster's *A Passage to India*. Unless the key functionaries of the agency and the recipient country conduct themselves with maturity, the relationship may go down the slippery path of incomprehension, misperception, confrontation, and collapse of the relationship. As Barbara Tuchman has vividly illustrated in *Guns of August*, a classic work on the First World War, even experienced statesmen might sometimes not exhibit maturity, leading them to situations which they never desired and even strove to avoid. The scope for tension is all the more with education projects, which, by their very nature, are hard to fit to the standards and criteria of accountability, and which, notable exceptions notwithstanding, tend to be particularly difficult to administer, implement, complete, and assess.

As he thought more and more, K's stream of thought moved from analysis of the problem to the question as to what could be done to resolve the problem. Divergence of perceptions was at the root of the problem, and unless an agency and DOE reach a common ground, there was no way for that agency to offer assistance on mutually acceptable terms. About three months after the SOP Workshop, like a flash of lightning the thought crossed K's mind that if an agreement were to be reached it was not sufficient to flaunt the CABE parameters for availing external assistance for basic education and assert that they were not non-negotiable; it was necessary to identify and address the interests and concerns of the agency. K recognized that it was necessary to demonstrate and convince the agencies that DOE could professionally organize the design and implement projects in a manner that would fully meet the fiduciary responsibility and accountability of the agencies to their 'masters'. It was this epiphany that inspired the constitution in February 1993 of a National Core Group (NCG) comprising 50 odd faculty members of NIEPA and NCERT to assist the states in project design and implementation and to build the capacity of state and district functionaries. Over time, it became self-evident that the requirements of technical assistance and capacity building were so vast that NCG by itself could not meet the requirements, and that it was necessary to build up a larger pool of technical expertise. This recognition led to the constitution of a DPEP Technical Support Group of Indian consultants, putting in place a network of academic and training institutions such as universities, IIMs, and the Lal Bahadur Shastri National Academy of Administration and enlisting academics of the networked institutions for various tasks such as training in various aspects of project design and implementation, pedagogy, conduct of appraisals, and supervisory missions. Most of these academics were engaged in teaching and 'pure' research, and had no experience hitherto in the tasks associated with program development and management; to be enlisted for project work they had to be oriented to do 'applied work'. Their association with DPEP created a large national pool of educational programme professionals that fully met the concerns of the World Bank, EC, and later ODA, but not the Germans, proving the point that it is a fallacy to believe, as the titles of a few potboilers convey, that anything and everything could be successfully negotiated.

The constitution of NCG was followed about two months later by the publication of the document *District Primary Education Programme* which outlined the basic framework of DPEP and the broad guidelines. Like the basic structure of the Indian Constitution, this seminal document set out cardinal features of the programme which were built upon but never altered; they formed the core of SSA. Among others, it brought out cogently that DPEP was a home-grown programme anchored in the NPE and its POA, 1992; it highlighted the elements of the new strategy that DPEP wished to implement as well as the salient features of DPEP. The districts selected would be educationally backward districts with female literacy below the state average; the programme would focus on the primary stage (classes I–V and its NFE equivalent), with stress on education for girls and socially disadvantaged groups. In states where enrolment and retention were near universal in the primary stage, support could be considered for the upper primary stage. The document drew upon the lessons K learnt from his tutelage under Bordia, his historical study of Indian education, and the experiential knowledge derived from APPEP, Shiksha Karmi, Lok Jumbish, BEP, and the UP Project. For the first time for any educational programme it spelled out the educational outcomes it wanted to achieve in concrete terms instead of vague formulations such as universal participation and universal attainment of at least minimum levels of learning (MLLs). The programme implicitly expected that universal enrolment in the primary stage (classes I–V) would be achieved by the end of the programme cycle of seven years. To that end access was to be provided according to national norms for all children to primary education classes through primary schooling wherever possible, or its equivalent NFE. In regard to reduction of dropout rates and enhancement of completion rates, DPEP had two interrelated objectives: overall primary dropout rates were to be reduced for all students to less than 10 per cent and concomitantly increase the completion rates to 90 per cent of the children enrolled; and disparities in dropout rates among gender and social groups were to be reduced to less than 5 per cent. The DPEP objectives in regard to learner achievement were threefold: all children should achieve a minimum average score of 40 per cent in language and mathematics; the average primary learning achievement in language and mathematics was to be increased by 25 per cent over measured baseline levels; and disparities in learning achievement gender and social disparities were to be reduced to less than 5 per cent. The DPEP document also set out that the programme would strengthen the capacity of national, state, and district institutions for planning, management, and evaluation of primary education. The document stipulated that the programme would be implemented in a mission mode through registered state autonomous societies, and spelled out in broad terms the structure and functions of the society and its organs. It also outlined the planning process, the criteria for appraisal of the plans, and the programme components. The criteria for appraisal would be equity, participative processes, feasibility, sustainability, and replicability. It also spelt out that while the quantum of funding would depend on the district plan and its appraisal, the ceiling on the overall investment per district would be Rs 40 crore. The guidelines provided that funds would be released by DOE to state societies. DOE contribution was expected to be about 85 per cent of the outlay required for implementation of DPEP, and the state governments share the balance. And further, construction would be limited to 24 per cent of the investment, and management cost to 6 per cent. The recurring liability at the end of the programme would be the responsibility of the state government.

DPEP Framework and Guidelines

The logic underlying the decision to generally limit the coverage of DPEP to the primary stage needs an explanation. As K conceived it, DPEP was not a programme or an enclave project that addressed a few aspects of the elementary education system like, say, Operation Blackboard which addressed the question of facilities or Teacher Education which sought to improve pre-service and in-service teacher training. Instead it sought to address all aspects at the same time so as to enhance the reach, grasp, and quality of and equity in primary education. It had the ambitious objective of transforming the entire elementary education system and build up the institutional capacity to effect such transformation: it sought to transform the way the states planned for UEE, wean the states away from the brick-and-mortar approach to elementary education, and instil an outcome orientation such that the focus moves away from mere instrumental objectives such as opening of new schools and construction of school buildings towards outcomes in regard to enrolment, dropout reduction, learning achievement, and reduction of disparities in outcomes. It also sought to enhance the capacity of the State Education Departments and functionaries to improve school effectiveness as well as the content and process of education. It was not an objective amenable to quick fixes, and called for steady and prolonged effort, and moving forward with a spirit of inquiry and perseverance. Given as he was to think in terms of imageries, K visualized DPEP to be a beachhead. A beachhead strategy focuses on a small area, achieves success, and gradually expands the beachhead to achieve the larger strategic objectives by applying the lessons of the success achieved on a large scale and scope. It is in keeping with this line of thinking that DPEP was started in about 10 per cent of the total districts in the country spread over seven states, and as a matter of conscious decision, it covered only the primary stage (classes I–V). With the exception of Kerala, the challenges in the primary stage were awesome in the states initially covered by DPEP. In those states the dropout rates in the primary stage were significant—the reported dropout rate varied from about 20 per cent in Tamil Nadu to over 50 per cent in Assam. Ensuring universal participation, enhancing teacher competency and motivation, improving school effectiveness, operationalizing MLLs and introducing competency-based textbooks and teaching, and building the institutional capacity to turnaround the primary stage required extraordinary effort, learning, and unlearning. The challenges at the upper primary stage were more awesome; even the initial steps needed for enhancing learner achievement such as laying down MLLs were not yet taken. That being so, to simultaneously take on the upper primary stage would be audacious to a point far beyond practical; there was nothing to be gained by dissipating the effort on the upper primary stage. As an exception, the guidelines did provide for the upper primary stage being covered in states where enrolment and retention were near universal. Kerala was an ideal candidate for application of that provision. However, giving Kerala a special dispensation would have made it difficult for DOE to resist the pressure being brought on it by Tamil Nadu to accept its demand for being treated differently from other states and allowed to go ahead with a 'state project' covering secondary education. Once the demand of Tamil Nadu was conceded, the floodgates would have been opened, and flood of demands from other states for state projects would have washed away the inchoate DPEP. Government is the art of the possible, a truth critics ignore. However, DPEP made several departures from the past, and one such was not fixing unrealistic objectives without assessing the magnitude of effort and the resources required, and willingly suspending disbelief in the expectation that Hope and Will would create what they desire. In its espousal of district planning and focus on primary stage, it drew inspiration from the Kothari Commission which advocated preparation of district plans, the central government providing resources for the implementation of the district plans, and pragmatically recommended a staggered fulfilment of the constitutional obligation to provide free and compulsory elementary education: Five years of good and effective education (classes I–V) all over the country by 1975–6 (10 years from the submission of the report), and seven years of such education by another ten years hence in 1985–6. Even while deciding to limit the initial coverage to the primary stage, DPEP always expected that once the programme got a good grasp over the primary stage, it would be extended to the upper primary stage; that was exactly the trajectory followed by DPEP and its successor SSA which was built on the DPEP frame and covered all districts and the entire elementary stage.

Lest it should be construed that by April 1993 everything connected with DPEP was set in concrete, it should be stated that the document *District Primary Education Programme* was all about *what*: What DPEP was about, what it sought to achieve, and what could be done. The document was like the beam of a lighthouse; it provided a sense of direction but not much guidance on how to navigate to the preferred destination. The vital *how*: How to go about to achieve the *what*, had to be discovered over the next two years year through a tortuous process. While it was easy to decry the brick-and-mortar orientation, the search for alternatives was painful and taxing. The hastily assembled NCG provided invaluable support in individual functional areas but what the field functionaries were looking for was a blue print which could be replicated. Such a blue print, apart from being just non-existent, was incongruent with the idea of a contextual process project which expected the district plans to reflect the variations among districts and to be home grown. To many field functionaries, the DPEP Bureau appeared to be issuing diktats of what is *verboten*, detailing what not to do but not what to do. At an initiation workshop for starting the DPEP process in West Bengal, in reply to a demand for a planning template which the field functionaries could follow, K quipped that 'Bengalis should develop Bengali solutions to Bengali problems'; it was no doubt sparkling wit but poor solace and plain insouciance. And then there was the very vexatious task of coping with the inevitable dilemmas of a process of exploration which excludes *ab initio* definitive detailing, but yet without sufficient detailing, it is not possible to secure an investment approval. By late 1994, almost all the elements of the how were discovered and incorporated in the revised edition of the document *District Primary Education Programme* in November 1994; the definitive edition was published in May 1995.

EC Support: Sublime Mutual Incomprehension

The British Empire, it was said, was founded in a fit of absent-mindedness; the EC assistance to DPEP seemed to be no different. As the dialogue with EC proceeded, it became apparent that EC's decision to finance DPEP under the SSN framework was based on inadequate knowledge about the SSN operations. In the best of circumstances, crafting an agreement with EC would have presented a grave challenge, for what was attempted was innovatively reconciling two conflicting objectives of providing fast disbursal of assistance to provide the short-term balance of payments support, and providing time and space to DOE to utilize the counterpart rupee resources such that the best possible educational outcomes are realized. What compounded the challenge were factors such as the EC's misperceptions of the SSN operation, EC being a new entrant into the 'aid business' and the strong tradition in many of its Member States of micromanaging projects they fund. In October 1992 when EC mounted a mission to explore the possibility of supporting primary education within the framework of the SSN operation, DPEP was just a *la grande idée*—a grand idea but an idea all the same. The ideas were fleshed out to a considerable extent only in April 1993 when K and his deputies brought out the document *District Primary Education Programme*. The functionaries in the European Commission harboured the immaculate misconception that all the arrangements for the financing, implementation, supervision, monitoring, and evaluation of DPEP were already in place and EC had to just to jump on a bandwagon on the roll. Come to think of it, when the new year 1993 arrived, even the name of the programme was not finalized. It bore the clumsy name of *National Primary Education Development Programme* and the state societies which were to implement it bore the clumsy name *Primary Education Improvement Initiative Authorities*. Hence, once the reality dawned rather late on the EC functionaries, the dialogue with EC went into a tailspin. The dialogue with EC was also complicated by the conflicting motivations towards the co-financing arrangement within the Bank and the intense jockeying for power and influence among the Member States of the EC. The EC was keen to piggyback on the Bank's experience and institutional arrangements for supervision and monitoring; however, at the same time it was eager to protect the identity of its assistance by having monitoring arrangements of its own. Whatever, two main issues which dominated the dialogue: should the EC assistance be slotted for a single state, namely MP? What should be the arrangements for ensuring efficient utilization of the assistance? A host of further questions sprung from the second question. Should the EC be associated with the management of the project? Or would it be adequate for EC to insist on credible and rigorous mechanisms for monitoring and implementation?

A month after the Theobald Mission concluded its task, on 5 January 1993, Østerby of the EC Delegation in Delhi shot a note to the EC headquarters strongly supporting the case of DOE for EC support; K could not have made the department's case better. Østerby's note covered, among others, the merit of concentrating EC assistance in MP, the sustainability of the new programme, the implication of the funds provided by EC being an 'additonality', and the importance of setting up monitoring mechanisms in a manner that would not detract the autonomy and initiative necessary for effective implementation. He made it clear that a 'geographical concentration of EC's assistance would not convert the proposal into a traditional project set up'; further, GOI had all along had the understanding that the EC grant would be applied to districts in MP, and had given MP that impression. GOI would be 'at extreme pain if it should retreat from this commitment, especially because of the given political situation', and a retreat 'might even have a negative political bearing on the entire Safety Net Program'. Geographic concentration was also in keeping with the strategy of the Indian Government to have no more than one donor to fund the new programme in any state. Further, geographic concentration had merit of its own in that it would help EC to put in a specific monitoring system for ensuring that the assistance it provided was additionality to investment in primary education and created a real impact. Østerby's communication was followed by a letter from the EC Ambassador in Delhi to EC headquarters strongly supporting DOE's proposal. The Ambassador pointed out that MP was large enough to be a country that DOE proposed to follow an area-specific strategy, all along DOE wanted to slot EC assistance to MP, and objecting to the DOE proposal would have political implications. Although K did not know at that time, the EC assistance to the new programme was 'the first practical example applying the concept of sector programme financing which was written into the ALA Council Regulation 473 of 1992', 'ALA Council' being the competent body in the EC to approve EC assistance to countries of Asia and Latin America. Like many other agencies at that time, the EC veered round the view that traditional standalone projects, however well-conceived, would not accomplish their objectives unless the larger policy environment was supportive of the project objectives. As sector programme assistance was conceived as 'a new channel' of assistance, the Commission Services (a unit in the EC which provided policy and administrative advice) was particular that the new approach to aid should not in any way be compromised; it harboured the concern that earmarking EC assistance to a single state might be no more than 'old wine in new bottles', a traditional project in the garb of a sector programme. Østerby and the Ambassador came out in support of DOE's position and against the views of the Commission Services.

Østerby's note and the Ambassador's communication did influence the key decision-makers in the EC, for when on 12 February 1993, E. Fossati, Director, Asia, EC, and his deputy Erich Müller met Giri and K, they made it clear that DOE could utilize EC assistance to fund the new programme in MP so long as the districts chosen fulfilled the criteria agreed to in the SSN agreement. They handed over to Giri a document *Basis for an EC financing to the Education Sector Programme* which outlined the broad features of the proposed EC assistance. EC financing would be provided over a four-year period, and the EC was eager to accord approval by end May 1993; as EC procedures for project assistance were long drawn out, the assistance was being crafted as 'programme assistance'. EC would monitor broad outcome indicators such as enrolment and retention and not specific activities such as construction of school buildings. The meeting ended on a happy note; however, that feeling turned out to be ephemeral and K's meeting with Müller four days later turned to be exasperating, and it came out that the arrangements for the management and supervision of the programme were not as simple as those put across by Fossati and Müller in the meeting on 12 February. Müller was under an erroneous impression that a Steering Committee was set up to oversee the implementation of the SSN operation; he wanted the constitution of a sub-committee of the Steering Committee for overseeing the implementation of the new programme. The Sub-Committee was to include representatives of agencies supporting the new programme. He was inflexible refusing to listen to what K had to say, namely that, contrary to his impression, there was no Steering Committee and that what he proposed went far beyond what established agencies such as the World Bank insisted for the supervision of programmes funded by them; K also made it clear that the arrangement he insisted was inconsistent with the CABE parameters on accessing external funding for basic education. The take-it-or-leave-it choice that Müller presented galled K a great deal; however, he restrained his natural impulse to give as good as he gets lest the funding of the MP projects should be jeopardized. The meeting ended with K informing Müller that he would revert back after consulting Giri. After the meeting, K contacted Middleton to ascertain the Bank's position on the EC stance as EC intended to provide assistance through a co-financing agreement with the Bank. What Middleton had to say was music to K's ears. Middleton expressed the view that the rigidity of Müller emanated from his ignorance of the specifics of the SSN agreement, that the arrangements demanded by EC departed from the Bank's standard arrangements for monitoring and management and hence were not acceptable to the Bank, and that he would request the Bank's headquarters to convey this position to EC. K decided to go ahead with getting the district plans prepared for the districts which would be covered by the EC assistance with the expectation that the Bank would prevail upon the EC to accept its standard arrangements. Should this not come through, he decided to include the MP districts in the first DPEP project that was being drawn up for financial support by the Bank.

A further opportunity to work on the EC through the Bank presented when Cambridge turned up a few days later to participate in the SSN supervision mission, and informed K of his impending visit to Brussels to carry forward the co-financing arrangement. He was more than willing to 'educate' EC about the SSN agreement, the new programme, and the standard arrangements of the Bank for monitoring and supervision during the visit. When K contacted Cambridge in late February about the outcome of his visit to Brussels, he sought to assure K that the differences between DOE and EC were of a minor nature, and enthusiastically told K that 'you guys have won the battle'; later events were to show that Cambridge's assessment was over-optimistic. On 2 April, K received a discussion draft of EC's *Technical Assistance and Administrative Procedures* (TAPs) from Neeraj Jain; TAPs were the provisions in the Financing Agreement which were specific for the programme assistance to DPEP, the other parts of the Financing Agreement being general provisions common to all projects and programmes funded by the EC. Like the SSN documents, it was appreciative of the new programme which it called National District Primary Education Programme, and the Programme's objective of 'establishing an improved, well-tested system of education targeted especially at girls in selected, educationally deprived, and disadvantaged districts'. The assistance was to be disbursed in four equal annual tranches beginning from 1993 to 1994 subject to a staggered coverage of 95 districts: 20 in 1993–4, 20 more in 1994–5, 25 more in 1995–6, and 30 more in 1996–7. EC assistance was subject to the conditions of the SSN agreement remaining in force; the second tranche release of EC was linked with the fulfilment of the conditions prerequisite for the release by the World Bank of the SSN credit. Thus, even if DOE fulfilled all other conditions regarding EC assistance, the second and subsequent releases would not be released if any of the other departments failed to fulfil the conditions for release by the Bank of the second tranche of SSN credit. The draft proceeded under the wrong premise, that of the estimated investment of 531 million ECUs (Rs 1,950 crore) during the Eighth Five-Year Plan, the Bank and other donors had committed 318 million ECUs under SSN programme and the state governments 63 million ECUs. The EC assistance of 150 million ECUs would fill the gap between the requirement and the amount pledged. In actuality, the Bank's pledge to the new programme was just 15 odd million ECUs.

It was obvious to K that the facts should be brought to the notice of the EC, as an agreement could not be crafted on an erroneous premise; however, telling the truth carried the risk for EC withdrawing its offer, as the basic premise of its decision to extend assistance was non-existent. The EC proposal for supervision was very intrusive and based on the implicit belief that DOE reports needed to be cross-checked by independent investigation. EC's supervision proposal had three elements. First, the EC would participate in 'the review missions to be coordinated by the World Bank for the monitoring of the SSN programme'. Second, the EC would mount its own missions every year to monitor whether the conditions for the release of a tranche were fulfilled or not. Third, sample districts would be jointly identified by the EC and DOE to check whether enrolment, commencement of the programme in identified districts, retraining of teachers, building and renovation of classrooms, and training of female teachers were being 'accurately recorded'. As a matter of record, the belief that the Bank would mount supervision missions even after the second tranche was released and the SSN operation came to an end was based on an extended reading of an obscure statement in an annex to the report of the Bank President recommending to the Executive Board approval of SSN credit. That statement mentioned that 'the Bank staff will continue to monitor progress with specific policies and programs, particularly the adequate funding of the new initiatives and commitments made by GOI to do so until at least the end of the Eighth Five Year Plan period (1997)'. It also stated that IDA would regard the SSN operation 'as an 'umbrella' under which 'new investments would be made, project preparation and appraisal of specific investment operations in each of the core social sectors would closely relate to the progress being achieved by GOI in implementing the Program beyond 1993–94'. This statement was ambiguous enough to allow Cambridge to inform EC that a full-fledged 'supervision plan' was in place to monitor the progress of the new programme even after the disbursal of the SSN second tranche in spite of the fact that he had informed K that after the disbursal of the second tranche the Bank would not monitor the physical progress of the new programme unless DOE sought Bank funding of the new programme. However, so deep rooted was the EC's yearning for supervision that it was not satisfied with participation in the missions co-ordinated by the Bank. Under the guise of technical assistance, the

EC Draft proposed appointment of an EC expert in DOE to 'work exclusively on planning and management aspects and training assessment for the first 18 months'. That EC expert would be supported by consultancies as deemed necessary during the development of the programme. It also proposed provision of 'field management resources' to 'ensure the timely delivery down to the district level of technical inputs, to monitor the impact of the program activities', and 'scrutiny of the program accounts at district level and assist with the preparation of expenditure forecasts'. It appeared to K that whoever drafted the draft incorporated the highest common denominator of the hands-on management practices adopted by some of the EC Member States to deliver aid, and had little knowledge of the Indian political and administrative system, and of the fact that, unlike many developing countries receiving aid, India was not bereft of the human resources needed for the design and implementation of programmes. Even as a discussion draft, the draft was utterly inadequate.

A few days after K received the draft, Shanti Jagannathan and Østerby met K to convey to K the keenness of the External Economic Relations in EC that the EC supervision should not be limited to the districts in MP where the funds would be applied but to all the districts in the country where the new programme would be implemented lest the assistance should acquire the character of traditional project assistance. K assured them that he had no problem in conceding their request, for he realized that the assistance being extended was sector programme assistance and not project assistance; however, the proposals for supervision and technical assistance were utterly unacceptable. They both assured K that proposals in the draft emanated from an inadequate understanding of India, and that satisfactory arrangements could be worked out during the forthcoming visit of Almond, an EC consultant who was primarily responsible for design of the assistance. In a large government office, be it the Count's in Kafka's *Castle* or the EC, 'one Department ordains this, another that; neither knows of the other, and though the supreme control is absolutely efficient, it comes by its nature too late, and so every now and then a trifling miscalculation arises'.[7] On 8 March, K was woken from his sleep by

[7] Franz Kafka, *The Complete Novels: The Trial, America, The Castle*, London: Vintage, 1999, p. 309.

a 'mid-night knock' on the door of his home by a courier from the Prime Minister's Office (PMO); the communication delivered to him sought the views of his department on an unsigned note of the EC Ambassador to Bhuvanesh Chaturvedi, Minister of State, in the PMO wherein the Ambassador conveyed her impression that at the behest of Arjun Singh DOE was pushing the case for utilizing the EC assistance in MP while the EC was in favour of supporting the programme in the country as a whole. To say the least, the Ambassador's move was baffling. The Theobald Mission that EC mounted visited only one state, namely MP. Just two months earlier, she herself made out a strong case for utilizing EC assistance in MP, and about a month earlier, the officials concerned with EC assistance, Fossati and Müller, concurred with DOE's proposal to apply the whole of EC assistance to MP. Her missive was like a bolt from the blue, a rude volte-face. Far worse was the mode of communication she adopted. Though rare, a party to a negotiation reversing its stand is not unknown; however, if, for whatever reason, the EC were to reverse its stand it was only proper for the Ambassador to convey its latest position to DEA, the organization responsible for coordinating all external assistance to the country, or to DOE, the agency responsible for utilizing the proposed assistance. To resort to handing over an unsigned communication to PMO, casting aspersions on DOE for the stance it took was to say the least bizarre. When K consulted Neeraj Jain and Østerby the next morning, K came to know that the Ambassador occasionally went 'off on a tangent'. Hardly had his consultations with Østerby and Neeraj Jain finished when Nishi Kant Sinha, K's batchmate and a key official in PMO, rung up K regarding the communication from PMO. K informed him of the facts as well as the internal politics of EC, and followed it up with a factual note to the PMO approved by Giri. K did not hear of the Ambassador's letter again. Although the Ambassador's *demarche* failed to accomplish its objective, the apprehension that the proposal to utilize EC assistance for the programme in MP might be reopened always lurked in his mind. K and Giri were particular that till the Financing Agreement was formally concluded, the fact that EC assistance would be utilized in MP should not be given undue publicity. Yet that was precisely what the MP government did when, on 22 April, it went to town with a press note claiming credit for an EC-assisted primary education mega project covering 14 districts of the state; the press note even spoke of release of funds by the EC at a time when the negotiations with EC were passing through a rough patch. Arjun Singh was upset that K kept him in the dark about the EC approval of the assistance and allowed the MP government to hog the credit. However, he was good enough to accept K's explanation as well as K's suggestion that the negotiations were at a delicate stage and overt eagerness on our part to secure assistance would erode our bargaining strength. K quoted Murphy's Axiom that he picked from Bordia's speech to NIEPA's UP Seminar in November 1990, namely that 'If you really need the loan, convince the banker that you don't need it'. When he heard that Axiom, Giri burst out laughing and even the generally staid Arjun Singh could not help beam a sly smile. The state was under the President's rule, and it was therefore decided that Arjun Singh should write a letter to the Governor remonstrating with the state government for the premature, inopportune, and erroneous publicity. The letter crafted by K brought out clearly it was the initiative of DOE to tap EC assistance and ended with a homily to the state government not to take any action in regard to the project without prior consultation and coordination with DOE.

In the first week of May 1993, K had a series of meetings with Almond and Skolnik separately as well as jointly; it was of great help that by happenstance Skolnik was visiting Delhi when Almond turned up for discussions with K. When consulted, a senior functionary of DEA dismissed off Almond as a minor functionary of no consequence and that K better palm him off on his deputy J.P. Prakash. However, Skolnik strongly advised K to enter into a serious dialogue with him, as in his view, senior EC functionaries would bank on a consultant to come up with formulations which would be acceptable to them as well as the Indian government. Almond would be eager to clinch a deal as 'he would be out of a job if he fails'. He also offered the tip that K should stand firm on issues that were important for him, state, and restate his position. His tips were very useful; so was his assertion at the joint meeting K had with Almond and Skolnik that DPEP was an exciting programme and that the Bank was aware of the management and technical challenges faced by DOE in implementing DPEP. However, the Bank was also aware of the determined and unprecedented efforts being made by DOE to build technical and management capabilities in the states and districts for developing district plans and implementing DPEP. The Bank would trust DOE to deliver results and did not believe in going beyond the customary supervision through missions. On his part, K explained the arrangements being made by DOE to build capacity and implement DPEP. He also made clear that given that DPEP would be funded by more than one agency it would be expedient to build common systems and procedures that would meet the fiduciary responsibility of all the agencies funding DPEP without in any way detracting from the autonomy required for the management and implementation of the programme and capacity building. His own experience with APPEP had convinced him that capacity development would be impaired by continuous 'mothering' of a project by a local agency office and by hordes of expatriate consultants and officials descending on states and districts at short, or no, notice. He would not like agency functionaries or their consultants to be associated with planning or implementation; they could visit states and interact with programme functionaries in the field only for the purpose of appraisal and later as part of the six-monthly joint review missions and nothing else. DOE was confident that it could mobilize the resources required for implementing DPEP in 110 districts during the Eighth Five-Year Plan. K also assured Almond that DOE would ensure a rigorous appraisal of the district plans of MP and would be happy to associate EC with the appraisal. He and his boss Giri strongly believed that the planning, implementation, and management should be rigorous, that programmes should be cost-effective, that the efficiency of expenditure needed to be enhanced, and that external funding was an opportunity to improve systems and management of education. Skolnik's observations were very supportive of K's stand; he later told K jocularly that he acted well as an interpreter translating K's In-glish into English only to elicit the jocular repartee from K that Skolnik's American English was as incomprehensible to the British Almond as K's own In-glish, and that what actually helped was Skolnik's body language exuding assurance and empathy. As expected by Skolnik, most of the issues were resolved during the discussion with Almond. Almond gave up the idea of EC experts being part of DOE or NCG or of the state management structures of DPEP. He agreed that EC's fiduciary responsibility could be discharged by participating in the joint review missions, securing all the documents periodically prepared by DOE to appraise the different agencies, and appointing an educational functionary in the EC delegation in New Delhi. The educational functionary, however, was to be supported by two national experts who would visit the states and districts for 'spot checking'. K made it clear that the role of the EC education functionary should be no more than being a counterpart of Middleton in the World Bank office in Delhi, and the proposal to engage two national experts for spot checking in the states and districts was utterly unacceptable as it would undermine the autonomy of project authorities in states and districts. Field visits of EC functionaries should be limited to joint supervision missions; these missions could follow the time-tested procedures of the Bank missions. Joint evaluation of the outcomes could be built in as with some projects such as MS. Almond indicated that the EC might go by K's suggestions. Skolnik's assessment which he shared with K at the end of the prolonged meeting was that Almond would do his very best to sell the new package that was developed during the discussions, and the million dollar question was how successful he would be and how the political dynamics within EC would work out.

K did not have to wait long, for on 2 June the ALA Committee decided to approve assistance to DPEP which, it noted in EC officialese, would be 'established' in the ' most deprived areas', and would 'enable education to be decentralized and community oriented to address the constraints of the rigidity and impractical nature of the present system'. The DPEP strategy would 'improve access to primary education and the quality of education for deprived children, particularly girls'. K's jubilation was short lived, for about 10 days later Shanti Jagannathan and Østerby turned up to say during the discussions in the ALA Council the Danish delegation raised a few doubts about implementation by state societies which were parallel structures instead of existing administrative structures, and they wanted a reasoned note to remove the doubts of the Danes. Like King Charles's head, the merit of establishing state societies cropped up again and again in the interaction with the states and the agencies. It was a bone of contention in the acrimonious dialogue with UP during the development of the UP Project, and was raised by Mohan Gopal during the appraisal of the UP Project, again during the appraisal of the first DPEP Project by Danes during the dialogue with EC, and later by Kenneth King, an internationally well-known expert on aid to education when he visited India in July 1994 to acquaint himself with the developments in primary education projects funded by agencies. Even during the development of the first

DPEP project, a few states such as Maharashtra and Tamil Nadu were not inclined to establish a state society and preferred to implement through the State Education Departments. If the dialogue with such states was not as acrimonious as with UP, it was because DPEP was a different species: it was not a state project like the UP Project. DPEP being a multi-state project, the central government could reward a state government with more coverage if its performance was good and penalize it if it did not abide by the parameters of DPEP. While the reservation about, if not opposition to, implementation through a state society arose from different quarters, the reasoning and motivation underlying a common stand were different. Opposition from state governments emanated from the state finance departments which felt that the society was a redundant structure performing the functions of the State Education Departments and wasteful in that their constitution entailed creation of staff and incurring of other avoidable expenditure. In addition, officers of the UP government thought that the society was a Trojan horse which would curtail their right to design and manage the UP Project as they choose without reference to national policies. The reservation of Mohan Gopal arose from the concern that implementation by a society might dilute the fiduciary responsibility of the state government to implement the project in accordance with the agreement. The reservation of Danes arose from managerial concerns as well as the new thinking on the effectiveness of aid. Implicitly, they viewed the State Education Department and the society as independent and unconnected entities. Such a perception spawned a number of organizational questions. What would be the relationship of the society and the traditional administrative structures at the state, district, and sub-district levels? A whole host of further questions arise from this question. Who would do what? In a district covered by a project would the administration of primary education be transferred to the society? If the schools were transferred to the society, the questions arise of how the services of the existing teachers in schools were to be treated, how new teachers would be recruited, how the promotion prospects of teachers recruited by the society would be brought in line with those of teachers appointed by the government, and what would happen to the services of the teachers at the end of the project. If the administration of primary education in a project district were not to be transferred to the society then arise the questions as to what would be the roles of the society and the department, and how the society would ensure that its project inputs are integrated with the normal departmental schemes and operation. Is the society not a parallel structure whose functions overlap with those of the State Education Department? Would not the society undercut the education department? As DPEP expands, would not the overlap extend? These questions have obvious implications in terms of budgets, costs, and administration of primary education. What would happen to the society at the end of the DPEP? Would the society be wound up? Or would be it the education department that would be wound up?

The managerial concerns about a parallel structure implementing DPEP were also intertwined with the emerging thinking about improving the effectiveness of aid. The new thinking held that if standalone projects without supporting policy environment were bad enough, enclave projects in which projects were protected from the hostile administrative and political environment by a project implementation structure sequestered from the government were worse.[8] Project outcomes using such structures were unlikely to be satisfactory; even if there were any satisfactory outcome, it was likely to be a flash in the pan not likely to be sustained after the end of the project. Furthermore, parallel structures attenuated rather contributed to national capacity building. The emerging orthodoxy held that educational reform should be attempted through the main system itself, or to use the imagery of King, the reformer should use the *front door* leading to the system and not the *back door*. King did note that DPEP societies had some key linkages at a very high level into the State Education Departments. However, he opined that avoiding the front door of the State Education Department 'raised for many analysts concerns about how these alternative or shadow systems of implementation can eventually be reintegrated with the educational mainstream'.

The necessity to repeatedly address the question of the appropriateness of implementation through a society compelled K to think through the whole question rigorously and iteratively, come up with imageries that could effectively communicate the rationale underlying the choice of the society mode of implementation, and write and speak about the

[8] Kenneth King, 'The External Agenda of Aid in Internal Educational Reform', *International Journal of Educational Development*, 12, no. 4 (1992), pp. 257–64.

conceptual underpinnings of the society mode of implementation on many occasions. A major strand of K's defence of the society mode was that while there could be no two opinions about the undesirability of enclave projects having sequestered project structures, it was facile to argue that the front door, namely implementing the project through the mainstream Department of Education, was the one and only alternative. It was necessary to avoid the dead burden of uniformity, and of 'urging one and all to talk in the same strain, to work at the same mill', an urge against which Gurudev Rabindranath Tagore cautioned.[9] Governments are known to employ a variety of organizational models to implement state policy and these models are vested with varying degrees of autonomy, for example administrative departments, state-owned enterprises, boards, commissions, and agencies. Firms are known to promote *intrapreneurship* by setting up independent units within the corporate structure and later hive off the 'intraprise' as a separate entity or, alternatively, mesh it into the corporate structure. The DPEP society could be considered an *intraprise*.

The second strand of K's argument was that the decision to implement DPEP through a society was a strategic choice. State Education Departments were in a state of utter disarray, and steeped in an introvert, inspectorate culture. To implement the new strategy for UEE, they needed to be professionalized. They needed to be more open and inclusive by being willing to accept good advice and practices even from outside and to work in partnerships with NGOs, local communities, and others interested in the achievement of UEE in letter and spirit. They also needed to become outcome-oriented. In effect, the reform that is needed is far-reaching, a veritable cultural revolution. Even while recognizing the need for comprehensive reform, it was considered strategically more expedient to adopt an incremental, staggered approach. The society model of implementation was more than creating a conduit for free flow of funds from GOI to the project-implementing entities in the field. Far from being a valve, a graft to bypass the choked arteries of financial flows, it was designed to usher a new form of managing primary education. The changes that were needed in the system at large were to be developed and tried out in a parastatal structure such as the state society which was part of

[9] Rabindranath Tagore, "The Call of Truth', *Modern Review*, October, 1921.

the system but could function autonomously and be more professional, inclusive, and outcome oriented. Over the course of time, the new managerial practices would percolate to the main education departments. That was the strategy. To use an imagery of those years, the society was separated from the department and not by a Great China Wall, but by a permeable membrane. This membrane facilitates osmosis of the good practices and thereby transformation of the department, the system itself. It was not a question of implementation *either* through a separate project implementation unit *or* by the education department. The mode selected was expected to be part of the education department but yet be different—a lotus in the pond.

The third strand of K's argument was that it was an immaculate misconception to consider that the DPEP society was a project implementation structure sequestered from the main education department. The DPEP society was a parastatal organization embedded in the education department and yet designed to function autonomously. Thus, the General Council, the policymaking body of the society, was chaired by the Chief Minister or the Education Minister, and included all the top officials of the state government connected. The Executive Committee was chaired by the Chief Secretary or the Education Secretary and included key officials of the state government. The structure of the DPEP society was not exclusionary, an attribute that characterizes enclave project structures. In fact, it attempted to forge an 'alliance' between the State Education Department and other stakeholders such as teachers and experts. In states such as the UP, the Director-in-charge of elementary education was ex-officio Project Director of DPEP. At no time was DPEP sequestered from the State Education Department. The strategy of decentralized planning and district-specific projects was evolved through the mechanism of CABE which was anything but the back door. The planning process was expected to be participative, enlisting not only the functionaries of the mainstream education department but also other connected governmental functionaries, teachers, and public representatives. DPEP was expected to draw on the resources of DIET for planning and in-service teacher training. Initially in BEP, there was an idea to hand over schools in districts covered by BEP to the society; however, on deeper consideration that thought was given up because of the operational problems it would create. Implementation in the districts was not envisaged through cadres segregated from the mainstream department; the district-level staff of the society was to be a mere handful designed to support the implementation of the programme through the departments of the state government. Functionaries of the education department were to be fully associated with the implementation. Implementation at the district level was expected to be co-ordinated by the District Collector who was the pivot round which all development programmes in the district revolved. At the village level, a crucial role in programme implementation was envisaged for the VECs. Given the way the implementation of DPEP was envisaged the host of operational questions implicit in the doubt expressed by the Danes did not arise at all. Suffice to say, the imagery of front door versus back door was irrelevant to DPEP, as the DPEP society was not a sequestered structure.

At the macro level there was a conscious design to incorporate the positive features of DPEP into the primary education system as a whole; DPEP was envisaged to become a beachhead for transforming the entire primary education system by enabling participating states to introduce changes in pedagogy, in teacher training and textbook development, to strengthen their institutional capacity in technical areas and to reform policy. Figuratively, the permeable membrane that separated the DPEP society from the mainstream education department was expected to facilitate the osmosis of the good practices developed in DPEP and thereby effect the transformation of the education department itself. Given the way DPEP was designed, the question of integration of the project structure and the mainstream education system was unlikely to be a matter of serious concern. It is only in projects small in relation to the State Education Department with norms for programme activities far above the levels the main system could sustain that the questions of integration would be problematic. That was not the case as fiscal sustainability was proposed to be built in the design of the programme components and DPEP was eventually expected to cover all the districts in the country. Hence it could be reasonably expected that eventually the society would get subsumed within the mainstream education department; even if it were to retain an identity it was as a development wing of the education department.

The justification that K offered to Shanti Jagannathan and Østerby satisfied the Danes and EC never raised the question of the society ever again. However, K was aware that unless the dialectical interplay between the society and the department is delicately managed, the society structure may tend to function in isolation as it did in BEP initially or be reduced to an appendage of the department without an identity as initially in the UP Project, and that either way the objectives underlying the DPEP strategy and structure would be defeated. For that reason, in 1994–5, the very first year of implementing DPEP, K got the DPEP Technical Support Group to undertake a diagnostic and formative study of the new management structures introduced by DPEP so that 'all deformities, disorders or signs of sclerosis should be flagged at the very outset', and DOE and states could take corrective steps. K was to address the question whether the DPEP societies functioned in the manner expected of them in an article he co-authored with Sajitha Bashir for the *Encyclopaedia* in 2001 and again in an address to a seminar on the impact of DPEP in primary education in 2003.

EC Support: Negotiations in Brussels

The society was relatively a minor issue compared to that of the arrangements for supervision of the utilization of EC assistance. The communication from EC conveying the decision of the ALA Committee indicated, in an inscrutable sentence that was *officialese* at its worst, that 'it is important to note that the positive support of the Member States is linked with close coordination and information of the Member States during the programme implementation, a contribution to common effort which had been welcomed by the Commission'. The import of this intriguing sentence was brought out by two provisions of a revised version of the TAPs which K received on 2 July 1993. The provision which stated that 'the advance of tranche release, EC Member States will be advised that India has justified payment of the next tranche' was unobjectionable; however, the other which stated that 'the EC supervision, monitoring and evaluation activities will be carried out in close co-ordination with EC Member States' bothered K a little bit, for the provision seemed to indicate that the Member States would be closely overseeing the release and utilization of EC assistance and such oversight might be influenced by the state of bilateral relations with ODA and the Germans. As it is, DPEP, being a multi-state programme financed by more than one agency organizing and dealing with joint supervision and review missions, was more complex than such missions or projects financed by a single agency; K was absolutely opposed to any arrangement whereby representatives of countries who would not finance DPEP by themselves would have a right to participate in such missions and have a seat at the table in the dialogue between DOE and the funding agencies by virtue of being a Member State of EC. An occasion to sort out these vexatious issues presented soon when the Indian Embassy in Brussels suggested that K and Neeraj Jain visit Brussels for final negotiation with EC officials.

K always looked forward to foreign tours with pleasant anticipation. However, this was one trip which he did not look forward to because the customary pleasant anticipation was overwhelmed by the apprehension that the talks might not be productive and that he might have to face an irate Arjun Singh on return and face the accusation that he wangled a junket. When he thought deeply about the negotiating strategy, he was to adopt K hit upon the idea that in a negotiation where he had so much personal stake, he better adopt a nonchalant attitude conveying the impression to the EC negotiators that TAPs were very satisfactory and that only a few minor points remained for clarification. It turned out that it was absolutely the right strategy, and contrary to his expectation that the negotiation would be yet another encore of the exasperating meeting he had with Müller on 16 February 1993, the negotiations were very productive and proceeded smoothly like a well-oiled engine; furthermore, they yielded unexpected outcomes far beyond the best K hoped for.

K and Jain arrived in Brussels on 18 July by when the EC headquarters had already acquired a deserted look; EC staffers had already begun to leave for the summer vacation which, in France and Belgium, is a sacred ritual. Müller himself was a *juilletiste*—one who takes vacation in July as contrasted with *aoûtiens*, those who take their vacation in August; he was scheduled to go on leave on 21 July, immediately after the conclusion of the negotiations. Most the negotiations were conducted with Almond and Müller; it was at this negotiation that K met Le Ruyet, a tall, pleasant Frenchman with whom K interacted in the two years that followed. K came to know that once the agreement was finalized he would 'take over' and would be responsible in the EC for handling the assistance. The meetings with Fossati were the high-point of the negotiation and yielded unexpected bonanza. K played on the eagerness of EC officials to be as free as possible from intrusive oversight of the Member States, and act as an independent entity in their dealings with the recipients of aid. K made it clear to Fossati that he understood the sensitivity of the relationship between the EC and its Member States, recognized the fact that in no other intergovernmental body were the Member States so keen to assert their interests, identity, and sovereignty, and understood the eagerness of the EC not to ruffle the sensitivities of the Member States. However, a line should be drawn somewhere; it was one thing to keep the Member States fully informed of the progress in the disbursal and aid of assistance; it was absolutely a different thing to directly associate them in the operations that an intergovernmental organization had to get involved as a funding agency. EC's quest to be a major player in the 'aid business' in its own right was inconceivable if in its interaction with aid recipients it did not function autonomously; K's clinching poser was whether the Member States of the World Bank had a right to participate in the Bank's missions. It was agreed that joint supervision missions would be carried out with DOE and 'other donors' supporting the programme, and that 'the Commission will be responsible for coordination of the interests of Member States in the implementation of the programme'. The final version of TAPs also made it clear that it was DOE which would be responsible for adequately monitoring as well as for the overall coordination of the planning, implementation, and financing of DPEP. The guidelines for operation would be DOE's document *District Primary Education Programme* dated 15 April 1993, or an updated version of that document. The concept of sample districts was modified such that it was a sampling and not an audit device. The choice of the sample districts was left to DOE; they were 'to represent a range of social and physical conditions'. It was specified that they would be used 'to assist Government of India to monitor intensively the development of DPEP, to generate the information needed to evaluate progress, and test indicated modifications'. A satisfactory agreement was also reached in regard to the Education Programme Coordinator (EPC) and the National Education Specialist (NEC) to be appointed in the EC Delegation. As the assistance was sector programme support, these functionaries would interact only with DOE officials and not with the state government functionaries. K took advantage of Müller's penchant for precision by specifying in the TAPs the EPC's 'direct contact in the DOE will be at the Deputy Secretary level and will be defined by the

Joint Secretary responsible for DPEP'. The role of NES was limited to providing technical support to the visiting missions. Even in the wildest of his dreams he did not expect that DOE would have a say in the selection of the EPC and NES but then truth is sometimes stranger than fiction.

During K's follow-up discussion with Müller, the latter confirmed that DOE would be consulted at all stages of the selection of EC Programme Coordinator and the National Education Specialist as consultants. Thus far from being a *lat sahib* (a liege lord) lording over the programme the EC Programme Coordinator was a functionary who owed his employment to the concurrence of DOE. The extraordinary voice DOE acquired in the EC's management of assistance is brought out by the fact that the Indian Government cannot even imagine to have a say in the appointment of the task manager dealing with DPEP in the World Bank's Delhi office, or for that matter, of the functionary dealing with education in the Delhi office of any agency. As suggested by Jayant Prasad, Counsellor, Indian Embassy, K sought to consolidate the gains by setting out his understanding of the discussions and requesting Fossati to confirm the mutual understanding arrived at during the meeting through exchange of letters. In his reply, Fossati confirmed what K set out in his letter, and went on to categorically state that the 'Commission and the Government of India share the view' that 'much of the implementation of DPEP, its monitoring and capacity building DPEP proposed to undertake could be undertaken with local expertise'. The need for expatriate assistance if any would be decided jointly by EC and DOE. DOE would be consulted for short-listing appropriate European and Indian companies and individuals for supplying technical services. A representative of DOE would be associated with the technical evaluation of offers received. Financial control, supervision, and evaluation would be jointly undertaken, and DOE would be consulted on the planning, preparation of the terms of reference, and the composition of joint missions.

'I Have Seen the Future and It Works'

All is well that ends gloriously well. Everyone in EC associated with the EC assistance as well as K and his deputy J.P. Prakash were immensely gratified with the outcome of the dialogue. Müller was jubilant; at a dinner later in the evening, he claimed credit for the original idea of harnessing a fast-disbursing grant to finance an education programme. He recalled that few believed him when he claimed that programme assistance was simple, and that funds would flow without detailing to the last degree the physical targets such as the number of classrooms to be built. Of course, his claim was not free of exaggeration; however, there were many including Skolnik who wondered how a fast-disbursing credit could be used to finance a basic education project. Müller also put forth the view that it was better to finance a big project through sector programme assistance rather a large number of tiny projects. Østerby chimed in and recalled his anecdote that before the idea to offer sector programme assistance came up EC was offering soap while K wanted toothpaste. K intervened to say that all was well that ended well, and that eventually Østerby sold not just toothpaste but a toothpaste factory.

There was every reason to be jubilant. In spite of the chequered course of the dialogue with EC and its rough patches, the EC agreement was pace setting in more than one respect. The agreement figuratively squared a circle, and was very creative in that it provided for short-term balance of payments support through fast disbursal of assistance, and at the same time, provided time and space to DOE to let the full operation of the planning and implementation processes over a period of seven years so that the best possible educational outcomes are realized. EC was the first agency to pledge substantive support to DPEP, and it was followed by the Bank, the Netherlands, ODA, and UNICEF. The Financing Agreement had a far-reaching impact on DPEP as a whole. As a matter of deliberate choice, project lending was availed from the World Bank instead of sector investment loan so as to preclude altogether even the remote possibility of the Bank raising policy questions. As a seasoned and prudent civil servant Giri was extremely particular to avoid any possible criticism, and that being so was sensitive to any expression that included the word 'sector', be it sector analysis or sector investment lending. The Dutch offered modest co-financing under the SSN agreement, the ODA offered project assistance, and the meagre assistance provided by UNICEF went largely for conduct of studies, publications, and media support. In spite of the Bank and ODA offering project support, in actuality the procedures followed for supervision and monitoring were almost identical to those provided for in the Financing Agreement with EC. The joint supervision arrangements were such that the messy *ménage à trios* of the UP Project was avoided, and capacity development was not impaired by continuous 'mothering' by a local agency office and by hordes of expatriate consultants and officials descending on states and districts at short, or no, notice. Agency functionaries or their consultants were not associated with planning or implementation; they could visit states and interact with programme functionaries in the field only for the purpose of appraisal and later only once in 6 months as part of the six-monthly joint review missions and nothing else.

The Financing Agreement is a splendid example of development partnership in the true spirit of partnership; this spirit continued to inform all the dealings between DOE and EC thereafter. It was only a year after the Financing Agreement with the EC, and that too after quite a few hiccups were negotiations with IDA for the first credit for DPEP concluded. EC took a great risk in extending support; in a sense, the EC support was 'a willing suspension of disbelief'. It placed implicit trust in the verbal assurances of K that the embryonic DPEP Bureau in DOE that K headed would effectively deliver and implement the programme. The risk for EC was mitigated to some extent by the fact that when it decided to finance DPEP, there were clear indications that the Bank would fund DPEP, and consequently the Bank could be expected to ensure rigour in the monitoring and review of DPEP. To jump the story, the Financing Agreement and the DPEP's approach to access external funding anticipated by 12 years the Paris Declaration on Aid Effectiveness (2005). DPEP pioneered many of the normative practices and principles which received an imprimatur from that Declaration. Thus, DPEP precociously introduced many practices commended by the Paris Declaration such as the recipient country taking a lead in developing a strategy for achieving goals and objectives in a given sector and developing a programme for implementing that strategy, pooling of domestic and external resources of different agencies for implementing the national programme, the country exercising leadership in coordinating the contributions of different donors, and developing joint review and reporting mechanisms.

In her seminal Reith Lecture of 2002, the Cambridge philosopher Onara O'Neill deplored the tendency to carry to the extreme the culture of accountability. Incessant attempts to make business, public servants, and politicians more and more accountable in more and more ways to more and more stakeholders—looking for cast-iron guarantees—have not succeeded except in spreading more suspicion , more complaints, and more demands for more controls, more regulations, and more transparency. For in the ultimate, suspicion can only have a debilitating effect, and trust is necessary precisely when we cannot be certain.[10] Truth to be told, EC would not have blazed a trail in development partnership but for the implicit trust it placed in DOE to develop and deliver a programme with little expatriate technical assistance. From that perspective, the series of meetings that K had with Almond and Skolnik in May 1993 was the turning point in the dialogue between DOE and EC. Almond went back from the meetings confident that DOE could be trusted, and thereafter the conclusion of Financing Agreement did not have to wait long.

The EC considered DPEP as a model of donor coordination and sector programme assistance that it could apply in many other developing countries. While reporting his impressions of a visit to MP in February 1994, Raymond Le Ruyet observed in trademark Cartesian prose:

> The DPEP is setting its sights extremely high, since its resolution depends on the resolution of a range of particularly complex administrative, pedagogical and sociological problems. To face this challenge, the programme luckily has … a programme design based on a triple approach characterized by realism, imagination and flexibility: no central master plan, but rather a philosophy and methodology … The programme has set in motion a descending hierarchy of approaches in various respects, leading from
>
> - the centre to the periphery;
> - administrative authority towards the school;
> - the school towards society in general …
>
> The initiative may be characterized by comparing it with the form of a three tier ladder, consisting of an administrative ladder, a pedagogic ladder and or a social (community-based) tier …
>
> The vast 'educational building site' opened in India by this programme may also be rich in terms of the elements of feedback for the donor agencies which have a significance far beyond the specific confines of the programme itself.

[10] Onara O'Neill, *A Question of Trust*, BBC Radio, 2002, http://www.bbc.co.uk/radio4/reith2002/lectures.shtml.

It was not Le Ruyet alone who thought DPEP would offer valuable insights for agencies which they could apply elsewhere. Lavinia Gasperini, a specialist in education and training who represented the Ministry of Foreign Affairs, Italy, at the EFA Summit of Nine High-Population Countries held in Delhi in December 1993, was much impressed with DPEP and suggested that an Indian Government representative be invited at the periodic consultation meetings of Member States to improve the effectiveness of aid. Accordingly, K was invited to give a presentation on DPEP to 'Horizon 2000 Education Experts Meeting' in Brussels on 14 November 1994, about a year after the implementation of DPEP had begun. The purpose of the meeting was to follow up on the decision of the EC that the EC and its Member States 'must endeavour to provide coordinated support, in a limited number of developing countries, for strategies and support programmes consistent with the educations systems concerned', and the endeavour 'should lead in the longer term to an enhancement of the ability of the respective Ministries of Education to manage external assistance'. The experts assembled in the meeting were expected to propose a list of countries where coordinated support was to be provided, and to 'define consistent support methods' for better management of assistance. Johan Leestemaker of the Dutch Ministry of Foreign Affairs summed up the response of the participants to K's presentation by saying that 'here was programme by a Government which knows its mind, and coordinated "donor" effort, and was the ideal "donor" coordination which EC and member States should pursue'. Along with K's presentation, a video film on DPEP was screened; the video however drew a mixed response. Tony Krasner of the EC described it as pure Hollywood. The experts concluded that DPEP could be 'a marker for coordination exercise elsewhere'.

XV

BUILDING NEW JERUSALEM

I will not cease from Mental Fight,
Nor shall my Sword sleep in my hand:
Till we have built Jerusalem

—William Blake

In April 1993, when the document *District Primary Education Programme* was published, DPEP had, in the words of Le Ruyet, only a philosophy and a broad methodology; before planning and implementation could start, considerable detailing had to be done, and the approval of the World Bank taken. K could not have steered the development of DPEP without the Rock of Gibraltar–like support that Giri and K's comrades-in-arms extended. Giri took personal pride that a great programme was being launched under his watch, and strongly believed that DPEP along with the successful organization of the EFA-9 Summit, the pledge that the Prime Minister made at that summit to boost public expenditure on education to 6 per cent of GDP from the Ninth Five-Year Plan onwards, and the outcome orientation he tried to instil in the TLCs would make a significant difference to the country's quest for UEE and universal literacy.

K's comrades-in-arms were his five deputies in DOE (Vrinda Sarup, J.P. Prakash, Seema Khurona Patra, and Sibani Swainand Sadhana Rout), the supporting staff in DOE such as Savita Prabhakar, K.S. Chib, and P.S. Chakraborty, A.K. Sharma, N.K. Jangira and N.V. Varghese of NCG, and Sajitha Bashir and Shanti Jagannathan. K's five deputies were precious assets with distinctive qualities and they complemented each other. Their deft handling of problems in the functional areas and states assigned to them was invaluable, for K was basically a 'Big Picture' man averse to going into details. God, it is really said, is in details, and without minute attention to details and minutiae, nothing is possible in administration, all the more so in the matter of programme innovation and entrepreneurship. In addition, his deputies constituted K's War Cabinet and their counsel was equally invaluable. Vrinda was a born administrator and diplomat who often reminded K of FDR; she was utterly unruffled and could handle the most sensitive situations with aplomb. She could charm her way through with any disagreement or opposition. 'Oh, John, come on, be reasonable' would disarm Middleton, and 'Ma'm, please understand our helplessness' would mollify a State Education Secretary 15 years her senior. There could be no greater tribute to her skills than the way she endeared herself to the social activists and feminists who played a lead role in MS. To jump the story, of the four, it was Vrinda who happened to have the longest stint in education in UP and at the national level (Chapter XI). It was she who carried forward the torch of DPEP and UEE as envisioned by the 1992 revision of NPE, 1986, and rescued SSA from being a brick-and-mortar programme and put it on the right track. J.P.Prakash was Mr Systems and a computer buff. It was he who chiselled the programme components and steered the development of the MIS. Above all, he was the ideal person to deal with the problematic BEP and the determined obstructionism of MP. There are situations when diplomacy does not work, and one is required to dig in, repulse assaults, and then overwhelm the opposition. A penchant to comprise regardless of the value of outcomes may jeopardize long-term strategic goals. 'Conviction politicians' such as Margaret Thatcher had ushered in far-reaching reforms by refusing to compromise easily and insisting that 'the lady is not for turning'. From January to July 1994 DPEP was in grave jeopardy in MP, and if it were not to lose its essence and go the way of 'Give, Give, Give' driven programmes, it was imperative to take a principled position and stand up for the integrity of the DPEP processes not being infringed. J.P. was the person for such a job.

DPEP being an investment programme, the financial dimension was as important as its planning and implementation processes all the more so because of the new culture of outcome orientation that DPEP wanted to usher. Seema from the Income Tax Service was the quintessential finance person; her skills were honed in the Internal Finance Division of the Ministry where she worked prior to her joining K. Initially she was puzzled by the work culture of the DPEP Bureau into which she moved; 'too much of English' was her comment on a work culture that placed high premium on precise expression in drafting, a premium necessitated by the fact that that there could be no ambiguity in communication with the agencies unless the ambiguity was deliberate. It was imperative while dealing with external agencies to be on guard all the time, as their institutional memory was enormous and even a slip of a tongue becomes part of the record to be retrieved and used when necessary. Very soon she came into her element when the financial parameters of DPEP had to be drafted, approvals of the Expenditure Finance Committee secured, and the plans received from districts and states appraised. She was more than a match for the officers of the Expenditure Department, Ministry of Finance, whose job was to play the role of the abominable no-man. Impressed by the capacity of the DPEP Bureau to guide the preparation of plans and scrutinize them, the World Bank decided to depart from its standard practice of appraising all project proposals by itself. As the Bank's Pre-appraisal Mission (February 1994) decided put it, 'the GOI (that is to say, the DOE) will assume principal responsibility for continuing appraisal of State and district plans. IDA's focus will now shift to the national program and proposed mechanism for implementation, monitoring and evaluation. IDA will review a sub-sample of State and district proposals during appraisal'. The World Bank's Appraisal Mission (March–April 1994) was fully satisfied with the appraisal of the plans by DOE; credit for this achievement should largely go to Seema. Like the legendary Nachiketa of *Kathopanishad* who, in his quest for the Truth, did not hesitate to relentlessly put searching questions to his father and even to Yama, the Lord of Death, Seema would never relent but would keep on probing and insist on loose ends to be tied up before she accepted the proposals; no wonder the proposals were refined so as to meet exacting standards. Later, once implementation began, she put in place procedures for ensuring that claims were put up to the Bank for disbursal.

Another salient aspect of DPEP was the attempt it made to promote action research, anchor programme activities in research, and conduct international research seminars in education. The anchor persons for this activity were Sibani from the Indian Economic Service and Sajitha

Bashir (after she joined the DPEP Technical Support Group [TSG] and steered it). Working in a bureaucracy, it is said, consumes intellectual capital and dampens the inquisitive spirit. Sibani was an exception. Coordinating with academics, quite a few of whom are high strung, is no easy task. But Sibani went about her job with aplomb and distinction. Apart from the preparatory studies conducted before the launch of DPEP and several initial, mid-term, and terminal evaluations, over two hundred and fifty research studies on primary education were conducted in the first five years of DPEP. In 2005, the DPEP TSG published the abstracts of 491 studies supported by DPEP.[1] Never before did any educational programme spawn so many studies and evaluations, and never before did any programme enlist so many organizations spread across the country. The most notable DPEP research study was *Budgetary Resources for Education, 1951–52 to 1993–94* (1995), which was a historic publication that documented the public expenditure on education by states and sub-sectors of education right from the beginning of planning in 1951–2 to 1993–4. No other sector of the Indian economy had such a treasure trove of information. The credit for compiling the voluminous data goes to S.C. Sahay who was associated with the Planning Division of DOE from 1984 till his retirement in 1994. He was a veritable encyclopaedia on Indian educational statistics, and the publication *Budgetary Resources* was, as K wrote in the preface, was the legacy Sahay left behind to Indian education. Sadhana Rout looked after NFE, and was not directly associated with DPEP. However, her help was invaluable in managing the media, or more accurately the press; however, the BBC 24×7 TV channels had not yet made their appearance. An officer of the Indian Information Service, she was extraordinarily media savvy and good at networking. She was a close associate of Narendra, Principal Information Officer, GOI's official spokesperson, and a confidant of Prime Minster PV. Courtesy Sadhana he became a dear friend of K, and between him and Sadhana, the media was deftly managed in regard to not only the DPEP but also EFA-9 Summit of Nine High-Population Countries. Again thanks to Sadhana and Swagat Ghosh, the Ministry's Information Officer, K developed

[1] Research, Evaluation and Studies Unit, Technical Support Group of DPEP, EdCIL, *Research Abstracts in Primary Education (1994–1997)*, 1999; *Research Abstracts in Primary Education (1997–2000)*, 2002.

good contacts with journalists, and came to be well cued into the political happenings, for no one is more cued about those happenings than the media. Generals cannot win battles without lieutenants and soldiers; DPEP would not have moved ahead without the dedication of people such as Savita Prabhakar, K.S. Chib, P.S. Chakraborty, and other staff members who attended to their tasks beyond the call of duty. K feels privileged to work with such people.

Till the TSG was established as a unit in Educational Consultants India Limited (EdCIL), DPEP had to rely exclusively on NCG for technical support to assist the states and districts in formulating plans and programme interventions, organize capacity building training workshops, and conduct the preparatory studies intended to get a precise idea of the tasks to be attended to and to fine-tune the programme interventions (Chapter XIV). The studies were also expected to convince the Bank management that the programme was well designed and worthy of support. NCG comprised over 50 academics drawn up from NCERT, NIEPA, and the School of Planning and Architecture, and spanned 13 functional areas. The preparation studies comprised baseline studies of the levels of and the factors affecting enrolment, retention, and learning achievement; the educational context and needs of girls and scheduled caste and scheduled tribe students in the districts covered by DPEP; textbook production and distribution; state finances; and teacher education, training, recruitment, and motivation in the states as a whole with focus on the districts covered. In addition to reviewing the literature, these studies were also expected to conduct field studies. The learner achievement studies aimed at assessing the achievement level of students who were nearing the end of the primary cycle and collecting relevant pupil background and school factors that could explain differences in the learning achievement of pupils belonging to different groups such as boys and girls, rural and urban students, and scheduled caste and scheduled tribe students. Jangira, Varghese, and Yash Aggarwal supervised the conduct of learner achievement studies; J.B.G. Tilak State Finance Studies; Usha Nayyar and Anjana Mangalagiri, Gender Studies; Kusum Premi and K. Sujata, education of scheduled castes and scheduled tribes; C.N. Rao, textbooks; and Jangira teacher training. Never before was such a diverse set of studies undertaken; the faculty of NCERT and NIEPA organized research teams in states and districts and trained over 250 researchers; many institutions in the states were associated with the data processing and analysis. The whole exercise went a considerable way in improving the capacity in states and districts to conduct action research. Among others, Bordia was sceptical of the ability of the NCERT faculty to undertake the studies and prophesied that the Bank would conduct the studies and prepare the reports. The prophecy did not come true. Middleton also was sceptical of the ability of NCERT and NIEPA faculty to undertake baseline studies and suggested downsizing the scope of the project and staggering of the states. His scepticism proved to be unfounded.

The very qualities which go to make an academic of distinction—intellectual autonomy, 'independence of mind on all occasions, thought free from obligation to any authority save the authority of "reason"',[2] honest doubt and a mind trained to identify lacunae in facts, analysis and reasoning as well as to make subtle distinctions, refusal to defer to authority and be pressurised by deadlines—are qualities which often preclude a person from being members of a team or appreciate the requirements or compulsions of a man of action, much less be a man of action. Most academics strive to conform to the ideal, normative values of academic life. It would have been well-nigh impossible to maintain the coherence of NCG and secure the active co-operation of the 50 odd members without the solid support of an academic of the standing and personality of Sharma who was Director, NCERT. His support was particularly valuable in MP; the missions had to function against very heavy odds, and it is a tribute to his leadership that all members of the mission, Indian as well as European, save an Indian consultant based in Paris held together in spite of the blandishments. The professional integrity and commitment of Sharma was all the more admirable given that his tenure was uncertain, and 'flexibility' might have been advantageous for his career.

Among members of NCG, Jangira and Varghese stood out by virtue of their extraordinary commitment as well as the range and value of their individual contribution. K and his deputies relied so heavily on Jangira for pedagogic aspects of DPEP and on Varghese for planning that it is apt to describe them as academic counsellors of the DPEP in its initial stage. Jangira was an expert in teacher training, school effectiveness,

[2] Michael Oakeshott, 'Rationalism in Politics', in *Rationalism in Politics and Other Essays*, Indianapolis: Liberty Press, 1991, pp. 5–42, at p. 5.

and special education. He was a rare academic who worked in remote places such as the villages of Manipur bordering Myanmar and Sikkim bordering China trying to improve classroom practices. An important feature of DPEP was the expansion and deepening of in-service teacher training. Jangira played a key role in the design of the in-service training programmes in DIETs, block and cluster training centres. The baseline learner achievement studies brought out that the achievement levels in language and mathematics were uniformly low, and strong corrective measures were needed. Jangira played a key role in developing cost-effective strategies for implementing MLL standards through improved textbooks and in-service training of teachers, and development of programmes for enhancing language and numeracy skills. K was in for a great shock when after about a year's stellar contribution Jangira decided to prematurely retire from NCERT and join the Delhi office of the World Bank. He was terribly upset with Jangira for deserting him, and with the World Bank for stealing one of his crown jewels. It took a long while for him to reluctantly accept Jangira's explanation that he was due to retire shortly and he had little else to look forward to. But then Jangira was not alone in migrating from the government to agencies. Many IAS and Indian Foreign Service (IFS) officials took advantage of their position to wangle assignments in agencies they were dealing with in spite of rules prohibiting accepting such assignments lest conflict of interest should compromise public interest.

Varghese was an economist of education of distinction; however, his oeuvre was not limited to the study of the financing of education. Apart from making significant contributions to educational planning and the measurement of learner achievement, areas which are natural extensions of the economics of education, he also grappled with issues of quality bringing to bear on his study methodological approaches which went beyond those adopted by the economic profession. Along with R. Govinda, he conducted a path-breaking study of the Madhya Pradesh primary school system;[3] his insightful knowledge of the school system in MP proved invaluable in the appraisal of the DPEP plans in the state. Varghese left a deep impression on the planning process which lay at

[3] R. Govinda and N.V. Varghese, *Quality of Primary Schooling in India: A Case Study of Madhya Pradesh*, Paris: International Institute of educational Planning, 1993.

the heart of DPEP (Chapter XIII). It was he who designed and detailed the planning process, field-tested the design in states such as Kerala, developed a manual, and organized extensive training of field functionaries drawn from all the DPEP states. His article, which was presented at the Third Oxford Conference on Globalisation (1995) and later published in *International Journal of Educational Development*,[4] crisply outlines the salient features, distinctiveness, and limitations of the DPEP planning process. The baseline learner assessment survey he conducted in the DPEP districts of Kerala was remarkable for the policy questions it raised. Soon after K moved out of DPEP, Varghese moved to IIEP, Paris, and to an international career in education. In IIEP, he made pioneering contributions to advancing the frontiers of research in higher education, addressing among others globalization of higher education, GATS and higher education, cross-border migration of students, and governance reforms across Asia and Africa. In 2013, he returned to India to build a new Centre for Policy Research in Higher Education (CPRHE) located in NUEPA. The mission of CPRHE is conceived to become a 'knowledge warehouse and a cutting-edge centre of research on higher education policy' at a moment higher education was expected to undergo large-scale transformation.

District Planning: Operationalizing an Idea

The BEP experience brought home to K that a preliminary technical exercise needed to be made before presenting the proposals to the people for their views. DPEP attempted to harmonize the technical and participatory aspects of decentralized planning by having a core group in each district to attend to the technical aspects, assisting the core groups to acquire the requisite competencies and skills, and requiring the core groups to interact closely with teachers, parents, elected representatives of local bodies such as zilla parishad and panchayat samithis, and functionaries of other departments providing services which need to be converged with primary education such as ICDS, basic health, and so on. The composition of the core group varied from state to state;

[4] N.V. Varghese, 'Decentralisation of Educational Planning in India: The Case of the District Primary Education Programme', *International Journal of Educational Development*, 6, no. 4 (1995), pp. 355–65.

in some states such as Kerala, staff of DIETs played a key role, and in other states district officials of the education department played a key role. In Maharashtra with a vibrant system of Panchayat Raj bodies, the chief executive officers of zilla parishads played a key role in the planning process. The DPEP planning process incorporated the idea of an 'evolving project' in that there were two sets of plans: a medium-term seven-year perspective plan and annual work plans. While the medium-term plan was indicative, the annual plans were expected to be specific and elaborate. The medium-term plan was expected to outline the present state of primary education in the district, assess the tasks required to achieve the objectives of DPEP, elaborate the strategies and indicate programmes and costing of the plan. The annual work plan was expected to offer a review of the activities undertaken in the previous year, set out the specific activities proposed to be taken up during the year, the milestones of the activities, performance indicators, and costing of those activities. The mechanism of annual plans enabled the lessons of implementation to be incorporated in the planning process; they also enabled new ideas and programme interventions to be tried out and taken up for large-scale implementation if they passed the test of rigorous evaluation. To use jargon, the annual plans were conceived to be rolling plans entirely in keeping with the idea of an evolving project. DPEP differed from basic education projects which claimed to be 'evolving projects' such as BEP and Lok Jumbish in the concreteness of its work plans, the rigour of the process it followed to appraise the plans, and rigorous monitoring of milestones and evaluation of outcomes.

From a technical point of view, the challenge to operationalization of the idea of district projects essentially lay in (*a*) logistics; (*b*) working against entropy and pooling the resources that lie dispersed among different resources institutions such as NCERT and its affiliates, NIEPA, universities, management and social science research institutions, and NGOs; and (*c*) deepening and widening skills of various types, particularly in the states and districts. More than anything else, DPEP was all about capacity building and spreading technical competencies. Capacity building in DPEP covered the five areas of planning: research, pedagogy, programme management, monitoring, and evaluation. As Varghese said in one of the workshops, the objective was to 'make ourselves redundant' by strengthening the institutions in the states such as SCERT and developing a corps of professionals in the states and districts who could attend to all aspects of DPEP. The weakest links of the planning process were the lack of technical competencies, and more egregiously, a mindset which conditioned the officials and public representatives to do whatever is required to secure the maximum funding possible. Repairing these weak links, particularly the mindset, proved to be very difficult. No wonder that it is said that in management, particularly management of change, the big issues are mindset issues. Without attitudinal change, planning would be a resource-driven calculation. Thus, Varghese was not joking when he said in a training workshop that the first cut of the three district plans received from Kerala proposed an outlay of Rs 400 crore over seven years, about a seventh of the plan outlay on elementary education for the country as a whole during the Seventh Five-Year Plan (1985–90). Once it was made clear that DPEP was not a cornucopia and that the investment should conform to the ceiling of Rs 40 crore, the focus shifted to somehow reaching the magic figure of Rs 40 crore. When he came across a plan with an outlay of Rs 39.99 crore, K caustically commented that the outlay reminded him of the Bata pricing and that Bata was not the best exemplar for planning. Suffice it to say that for quite some time the planning process left much to be desired; it took a long time for the functionaries to realize that planning was a process of exploring answers to the question of what needs to be done to realize the DPEP objectives in a particular district. No wonder that a few learned critics scoffed at the banality of the planning process in the field. A visiting expert on aid for educational development was sceptical of the attempt to develop highly contextual plans; planning might 'end up being a formula which had to be filled precisely according to the Guidelines, in order to secure the external funding. Good district plans could begin to have a currency in the DPEP marketplace like good examination answers in the school and university systems'.

Given that it took a long time for the field functionaries to acquire the necessary technical skills and to internalize DPEP, the critics were not wholly off the mark but where they were amiss was their failure in not recognizing that the administrative system was resilient enough to cope with a challenge, that there can be no learning except by doing, that no child learns to walk without faltering and stumbling, and that what was being witnessed was the initial stages of a learning process. Repeated training and learning till the plans conformed to the stringent requirements laid down by the appraising team were the main means by which the capacity was built and the mindset changed. It took over a year and several revisions of the plans before the plans were accepted by the appraisal group. The hastily assembled NCG provided invaluable support in individual functional areas but what the field functionaries were looking for was a blue print which could be replicated. Such a blue print, apart from being just non-existent, was incongruent with the idea of a contextual process project which expected the district plans to reflect the variations among districts and to be home grown. Truth to be told, to many field functionaries the whole process of planning appeared to be exasperating, and the DPEP Bureau issuing diktats of what is *verboten*, detailing what not to do but not what to do. All in all, for everyone associated with DPEP was as much a process of learning as of unlearning, a painful process of catharsis, of excising deeply held fixations about education and externally financed projects. All this is not to say that the planning process was perfect, far from it. Yet the idea of district planning was sown, some hands-on experience with planning gained, and an enabling frame with adequate resource base created to facilitate universalization of primary education in all its dimensions.

There was yet another aspect of DPEP development which created a great deal of angst among the field functionaries. The DPEP planning process started with no more than broad principles and no clear roadmap; it also laid down three norms, namely that the investment in a district should not exceed Rs 40 crore, that the expenditure on administration and management should not exceed 6 per cent of the outlay, and that the expenditure on civil construction should not exceed 24 per cent. Nothing else was stipulated; the first cut plans which were received and discussions with the World Bank brought out that further 'blue sky' planning would be counterproductive, and that laying down certain broad norms were expedient. Thus, the plans received from Haryana proposed expansion of ICDS to all the villages in the districts covered as the State Education Secretary was an ICDS enthusiast. ECCE was one of the six elements of ICDS. While ECCE no doubt was beneficial and facilitated a smooth transition of the child from home to the school, its expansion had to be done with a sense of proportion. It is only now, nearly two decades later, that ICDS is on the verge of becoming universal and covering all villages in the country. Expansion of ICDS, as proposed by Haryana, would have curtailed more important educational interventions, and would have run counter to the criterion of sustainability as the state was unlikely to have the resources needed to continue the programme at the end of the seven years of DPEP project. It was therefore considered prudent to let the ICDS expand on its own steam and lay down that DPEP would finance the expansion of ECCE only in habitations not eligible to be covered by ICDS. Likewise, a number of states proposed a long list of incentives for fostering participation in the schools; it was decided to limit the financing of only the provision of textbooks to girls and children of scheduled castes and tribes wherever the state government did not have a scheme for free distribution of textbooks. The rationale for limiting the incentives was once again the sustainability of the incentive as well as the principle that only activities which have a direct educational impact should be funded. The DPEP norms needed to be refined so as to secure the approval of the Planning Commission and the Finance Ministry for implementing the programme; it was also imperative to ensure that they were aligned with the reimbursement norms of all the agencies which funded DPEP. Rarely do major policies and programmes majestically move from a grand, comprehensive, and definitive design to implementation without being tainted by modifications necessitated by second thoughts or new information. No one can escape from the cognitive limitations on the human mind—its limited ability to gather all the available information and to perfectly process the information gathered; therefore, all the information necessary and the analytical prowess required for grand design are not available in actuality. Therefore, there is an element of truism in Lindblom's maxim that 'the mind flees from comprehensiveness'. Major policies and programmes often evolve incrementally by disjointed or uncoordinated processes, and at each stage of the evolution, further movement arises from human choices. The DPEP Guidelines were issued on 16 April 1993 and the financial parameters on 27 April 1994. What is distinctive about the financial parameters was their flexibility; unlike a conventional CSS, the DPEP financial parameters did not rigidly stipulate the cost for each and every programme activity; they stipulated cost ceilings for a cluster of related programme activities. However, the iterative evolution of the programme parameters imposed an element of uncertainty on an even otherwise arduous planning process. Field functionaries were baffled by what they perceived to be varying versions of what was grossly but perhaps accurately called, "what is permitted and what is not". While the DPEP Bureau had to do what it had to do, the angst and frustration of the field functionaries were genuine and understandable. The right perception of any matter and a misunderstanding of the same matter, as Kafka pointed out, do not wholly exclude each other. In spite of the norms designed to ensure a certain degree of uniformity and sustainability, the DPEP framework continued to be broad permitting a great deal of flexibility and creative innovation.

Design of Management Structures

Even before the programme was launched, it was necessary to firm up the national, state, and district structures which would implement and manage the programme so that approval of the Finance Ministry could be secured for the staff the programme would require, and the Bank's Appraisal Mission convinced about the adequacy of the arrangements for implementing the programme. Being so, a proper design of management structures assumed urgency. Implementation through the state DPEP society being sacrosanct, and the bye-laws of the UP society having been drawn up in accordance with the decision of the Cabinet Secretary who 'adjudicated' the disagreement between DOE and the UP government over the UP Basic Education Project, K and his deputies needed to do no more than persuade the states to adapt the UP Society bye-laws and ensure that the society did not function as a sequestered enclave but was organically linked to the State Education Department. The state governments were given considerable flexibility in the design of the district-level structures subject to the organizing principle that those structures should be fully implanted within the existing educational administration system as well as within the general administration of the district. Slim district project offices were established in all states more as co-ordinating bodies and preparing the documentation required by the state society. Following the successful enlistment of district collectors in the TLCs, DPEP sought to harness the positional power of the district collector by organizing a district advisory committee headed by the district collector. However, in Maharashtra with its tradition of a strong Panchayat Raj system, the

Chairman, zilla parishad, headed the district advisory committee. The association of the district collector or of the Chairman, zilla parishad, in Maharashtra was expected to promote the convergence of services as well as facilitate the construction of civil works which was generally organized in most states by engineering departments of the state government. In most states, the district education officer was the DPEP programme co-ordinator, and he was assisted by an assistant programme co-ordinator drawn from the education department or from the tribal welfare department in the tribal districts of MP. Except Assam and MP, other states did not create any structure at the block level. Another aspect of institution building undertaken by DPEP was the establishment of block and cluster resource centres to impart in-service training and foster the bonding among teachers. As DPEP laid emphasis on community mobilization, VECs were expected to play a pivotal role in enlisting community support for primary education through awareness campaigns, enhancing the effectiveness of schools and NFE centres, improving school facilities, and administering the grant of Rs 2,000 that DPEP provided for each school for discretionary spending on various activities such as preparation of teaching aids, improvement of school environment, health check-up of pupils, and so on. By happenstance, a CABE Committee was appointed in February 1993 to formulate guidelines for the management of education at district, block, and village levels in keeping with the 72nd and 73rd Amendments to the Constitution which accorded a constitutional status to Panchayat Raj and urban local bodies. The Committee was chaired by Veerappa Moily, Chief Minister of Karnataka, and as is customary, with CABE Committees well balanced with state education ministers drawn from different regions and political parties, a few educationists, and officials of the relevant ministries as members. K was Member Secretary of the Committee. Among the members was P.K. Umashankar, an illustrious senior of K who spent long years in the education field in Kerala and DOE, was Director of the Indian Institute of Public Administration, chaired a committee which reviewed the functioning of NIEPA, and for whom educational management was the passion of his life. He virtually acted as the Member Secretary of the Committee and wrote the report of the Committee. The report suggested that every panchayat with a single village in its jurisdiction should set up a standing committee on education which would discharge all the functions which the POA,

1992, and the DPEP Guidelines expected of a VEC. In a panchayat with more than one village in its jurisdiction, VECs should be set up in each village as a standing committee of the panchayat. Truth to be told, few states were keen about devolving primary education on panchayats, and the VECs set up were standalone bodies not linked with the panchayat. In some states such as Tamil Nadu, Parent Teacher Associations or Mothers' Councils discharged the function expected of VECs.

Unlike earlier externally funded programmes such as APPEP, BEP, and the UP Project, DPEP was not a standalone project programme which covered a single state; hence, it was necessary to have adequate arrangements at the national level to steer the programme. The contribution of P.K. Umashankar and J.P. Prakash to the design of the national management structure was invaluable. Two factors which would have normally been extraneous to the design of the national management structure impacted a great deal on the decision-making process: the constitution of NEEM as proposed by the revised NPE, 1992, and the interface between DPEP and TLCs (Chapter XII). As already set out, on 6 May 1992, at the very last minute as the meeting of CABE was winding up, Bordia floated the idea of NEEM and it was readily agreed to by Arjun Singh; thereupon CABE accepted without discussion. This off-the-cuff decision is an exemplar of the spell of buzzwords, and the disconnect some Western observers see between rhetoric and behaviour in India and their impression that 'Indians see mantras as potent, that if they say the right words often enough they will change the world'.[5] No wonder that soon after the CABE decision there were demands from some columnists that NEEM should be established 'here and now'. Given the short time for the formulation of the new POA, the details of NEEM could not be fleshed out before the POA was finalized; consequently, the POA, 1992, did not go beyond a general formulation that NEEM would be operationalized in 1993–4 after extensive consultation and that its central objective would be 'mobilizing all the resources, human, financial, and institutional, necessary for achieving the goals of UEE'. As the POA had advocated a district-based strategy for achieving and DPEP came

[5] Myron Weiner, *The Child and the State in India*, Princeton, NJ: Princeton University Press, 1991, p. 71.

to be *the* programme for operationalizing the district-based strategy, it was logical that DPEP would constitute the core of NEEM. However, being prudent, Giri decided to make haste slowly, and wait for DPEP to take off before constituting the NEEM. It was a sound decision because of conflicting views articulated by TLC enthusiasts about the interface between NLM on the one hand and NEEM and DPEP on the other. Some were of the view that as the quest of universal literacy and UEE had to go together, there was no need to set up NEEM and that the same structures could manage TLCs as well as programmes for achieving UEE at all levels. Thus, the remit of the NLM, state literacy societies, and the *zilla saksharatha samithi*s could be expanded to encompass elementary education. Some, however, recognized the apparent incompatibility between a 'volunteer-rich' TLC programme that relied on volunteer instructors and 'cash-rich' DPEP, and put forth what could be called a stage theory of educational development. If DPEP and TLC were to be implemented simultaneously, the volunteer instructors of TLC might be lured away by the higher remuneration which DPEP might offer to part-time instructors in NFE centres and schools. Further sequencing DPEP after TLC would also benefit DPEP; the mobilization of the community and the enhanced demand for education would give a boost to the implementation of DPEP. K, of course, had to partly disabuse these proponents by paraphrasing Philip Coombs[6] and clarifying that 'organised education systems do not run on slogans and good intentions but run on money' and that while 'not all the problems of education can be solved by throwing money at them' without resources reform of organized educational systems would be an empty rhetoric, and that while DPEP was definitely resource-rich as befitting a programme designed to transform the primary education system it was no more finance driven than TLCs. DPEP was aware of the imperative that the infusion of additional resources should synchronize with the creation of the capacity for proper utilization of resources. It was for that reason that the scheduling of activities under DPEP was so designed that intense planning and rigorous appraisal precede the approval of district plans, the first year of the programme would concentrate on mobilization, capacity building, and putting the

[6] Philip H. Coombs, *The World Crisis in Education: The View from the Eighties*, New York: Oxford University Press, 1985, p. 137.

system and processes in place for effective implementation of DPEP, and that substantial investment would start only from the second year onwards. The third school of literacy enthusiasts did not believe in the stage theory. A number of ideas were afloat. One such idea advocated funding the NLM funding 'mini-DPEPs' in districts covered by TLCs. Another advocated handing over primary education in chosen blocks to NGOs capable of ushering educational innovation and mobilizing the community for educational transformation. Yet another idea suggested the launch of *Taleem* (Total Elementary Education Movement).

K's stance was that while promising innovations, whatever be the source, should be encouraged it would be expedient to keep the structures for NLM and UEE separate. He expounded the rationale first in an internal note titled 'What is the mission of the Mission', later published in *DPEP Calling*, a widely circulated in-house magazine of DPEP which K launched as a forum for exchange of information on elementary education in general and DPEP in particular.[7] In brief, the article set out that TLC and DPEP had different target groups. There were significant differences in content and process such as syllabi, curricula, instructional material, and their transaction. That apart, the time spans of DPEP and TLC were different. The learning cycle in DPEP spanned five years of schooling or its non-formal equivalent, and was much longer than the nine-month instruction cycle in TLC. Consequently, DPEP would have a longer gestation period than TLC; figuratively, TLC was a sprint while DPEP was a marathon. Given the different time spans, the mobilization strategies had to be different. Mobilization for a period of one to two years in a district in order to achieve total literacy was qualitatively different from the mobilization required over a decade or more in order to achieve UEE in all its aspects. DPEP therefore called for more durable institutional arrangements for sustained community participation. Only the post-literacy phase of TLCs called for the permanency of institutional arrangements which DPEP required. Yet another major distinction between DPEP and TLC lay in the different environments in which they had to operate. TLCs could operate totally outside the traditional educational structures. In comparison with the State Directorates of

[7] 'Placing DPEP and NLM in Perspective', *DPEP Calling*, January 1995, pp. 8–11.

Education which existed for about a century, State Directorates of Adult Education were late entrants and lower in terms of status and influence. Adult education instructors and inspectors were, likewise, no match for their counterparts in elementary education such as teachers, teacher unions, and the school education bureaucracy. In spite of the relatively weak bargaining power of the adult education staff, the states had found it difficult to do away with the services of the temporary instructors who had been operating night adult education schools even though in the wake of the TLCs such centres were no longer needed; DOE found it difficult to disband the staff of the Directorate of Adult Education in spite of it creating a new institution, the National Institute of Adult Education, to better discharge the functions the Directorate was hitherto discharging. Being so, it was inconceivable for DPEP to replicate the strategy of NLM of short-circuiting established structures and bureaucracy, and operating only through volunteers. DPEP had to operate a strategy of largely working through the system to transform the system.

K's article also brought out that conceptually there should be no problems for DPEP and TLCs coexisting in a district. Conceptually there could be three types of sequencing of DPEP and TLC: Type A in which TLC would be followed by DPEP, Type B in which TLC would be started during the implementation of DPEP, and Type C in which TLC would follow DPEP. During the Eighth Five-Year Plan, TLCs and DPEP were expected to cover 345 and 110 districts, respectively. Given that the TLCs were expected to expand faster than DPEP, Types A and B were more likely than Type C. However, it would not be proper, *a priori*, to exclude Type C altogether. Such exclusion would be inversion of the policy that TLC and UEE had to go together; or figuratively, the policy should be not dual track but mono-track with adult literacy preceding UEE. In Type A districts, the mobilization process of TLC could be a good launching pad for DPEP. In Type B districts, the only area where there could be duplication was in the area of NFE. However, the scope for duplication would be limited as DPEP would be financing NFE centres only in districts which were not eligible to be covered in the Centrally Sponsored Scheme of NFE. Under DPEP, the main thrust would be development of a variety of effective and scalable NFE models. If the synergies of DPEP and TLC were to be maximized, the mobilization process of TLC should draw in more intensely primary education teachers, teacher unions, VEC, panchayat raj, and urban local bodies. That is to say, TLCs would have to collaborate more with the existing education system than had been the practice so far. The article also pointed out that of the 42 districts where DPEP was being first started, TLCs fully cover 31 districts and partially two districts. In these districts, all efforts would be made to ensure that DPEP and TLC would operate in unison.

In the article, K did not spell out yet another substantive reason why it would be expedient to keep the structures for NLM and UEE separate. Suffice to say, given the close association of leftist inclined activists with the TLC structures at different levels it was inconceivable that DPEP could be implemented by structures common to it and TLC unless it ceased to be funded by external agencies; at the same time, given the resource constraint there was no way that DPEP could take off without external funding. K had an encounter with the mindset of those viscerally opposed to Bank funding of primary education at the meetings of an expert group DOE appointed to evaluate the TLCs. Although DPEP was not in the remit of the expert group, it was brought in by the standard ploy of the Adult Education Bureau those days to drag DPEP in the ambit of any discussion of adult education, be it a parliament question or a meeting, with the expectation that the foreign funded DPEP would act as a lightning rod and deflect criticism away from adult education. The Chairman of the Expert Group was Arun Ghosh, an economist who had a long career in the government. A self-confessed 'rebel' in the government, he worked in the IMF also; he was, however, one of the economists like Ashok Mitra, Finance Minister of the Left Front West Bengal government, K.S. Krishnaswamy of the Reserve Bank, and more famously, Joseph Stiglitz who, in spite of working in Bretton Woods institutions, were hostile to those institutions, thereby proving that 'there is no isomorphic mapping between working with the Bretton Woods institutions and support for liberalization'.[8] Ghosh was such an uncompromising critic of the new economic policies that he was critical even of the modernization of offices by Rajiv

[8] Devesh Kapur, *Diaspora, Development and Democracy: The Domestic Impact of International Migration from India*, Princeton, NJ: Princeton University Press, 2010, p. 151.

Gandhi government.[9] It is fair to criticize computerization without attempting to change the 'antediluvian' systems and procedures; it is no doubt true that to begin with, personal computers in the offices of senior officers such as secretaries to GOI and members, Planning Commission, were no more than adornments. However, to attribute as Ghosh did personal computers being provided to secretaries to the government and not to section officers as a desire to keep the veil of secrecy over the misdeeds of companies and help the lower officials who had knowledge of such misdeed to continue exercising power is, to put it mildly, rather farfetched. It is in the nature of things for the dissemination of any new technology to begin on a modest scale and to falter before it spreads widely. From K's experience, personal computers made their appearance in central government offices around 1984, and to begin with, they were provided to the topmost officers who were mostly computer illiterate. However, by 1990 they were quite numerous and many enterprising stenographers were proficient in the use of personal computers; a decade later, personal computers replaced typewriters, many officers were proficient in the use of personal computers, and e-mail, e-services, and computerized databases made their appearance. Suffice to say, secretaries to the government being first provided computers was an example of Deng Xiaoping's slogan 'let some people get rich first' and had little to do with any conspiracy theory.

To come back to the meeting of the Expert Group, at the behest of Giri K submitted to the Chairman the DPEP guidelines and a brief note spelling out what DPEP was about. In the meeting he explained in considerable detail the genesis and salience of DPEP. K's explanation would not satisfy the Chairman who maintained that there was an objectionable Bank guideline with the states with which UNICEF found problems. His source was a high UNICEF official. Giri told him clearly that there were no Bank guidelines on DPEP, that the guidelines were those prepared by DOE, and that the planning was process intensive and wholly indigenous in which the NIEPA and NCERT staff were fully associated. K added the point that far from being unhappy with DPEP, UNICEF was supporting the preparatory studies and was keen that the Bank should support BEP within the DPEP frame. The Chairman still

[9] Arun Ghosh, 'Darkness at Noon', *Economic and Political Weekly*, 22, no. 18 (2 May 1987), pp. 769–70.

stuck to his piece of information, and to add insult to injury, insisted there could be a document with the states of which Giri and K were not aware of, and that he should have asked Oktay Yenal, former Chief, Bank's Country Office about the Bank guidelines before Yenal left India. K was wild with anger that a person who held high positions in the government should prefer to go by hearsay and trust the word of foreigners in preference to Indians who would have been his colleagues had he still been in the government. Of course, as official decorum required, K restrained himself and decorously requested the Chairman to request his UNICEF informant to provide the guideline he was speaking of, and to share that guideline with DOE so that he and Giri could take appropriate action. Needless to say such a document was never made available as it did not exist in the first instance. As was his wont, K brooded long on the episode, and in his reveries, he imagined himself to be a victim of witch hunting in a parallel universe of McCarthyism in the reverse. In that universe, anyone who was not against LPG, the acronym they used for liberalization, privatization, and globalization, was invariably un-Indian and anti-people as one could not secure funding from the Bank without giving in to every diktat of the Bank, Strange but true, critics of the liberalization process did not hesitate to attribute anything untoward to the policies of economic liberalization being followed by the government. As he thought more and more, he realized that what was played out in the meeting was the refusal of many intellectuals to accept facts which were incompatible with their ideology or with theories in whose development they had invested a great deal of time and effort. However, the incident is emblematic of the suspicion and hostility that DPEP had to face in some quarters; no matter whatever be the evidence adduced many continued to be incredulous that a Bank-financed project could be home grown, have no policy conditionalites, and associated no foreign consultants. All is well that ends well, and the report of the expert group made no reference whatsoever to DPEP, perhaps because the discussion on DPEP was a foray in a matter which was not within the remit of the group.

Genesis of the Technical Support Group

Technically, the DPEP TSG was a unit of EdCIL, and was financed by the credit from the World Bank. In practice, it was an outfit of DPEP overseen by the K as Joint Secretary and managed from day to day by K's deputies in the DPEP Bureau. It was K and his deputies who chose the consultants and assigned duties to them. The key technical services to be provided by the DPEP TSG span the three areas of programme delivery, academic guidance, and capacity building. The activities in regard to programme delivery covered technical assistance for appraisal of medium-term plans and annual work plans, organizing DPEP supervision missions, coordination of biannual joint supervision missions with external funding agencies, assisting DPEP Bureau in scrutinizing the proposals for procurement, submission of claims to the World Bank for disbursement of funds, supervision of civil works, development of improved school construction designs, and monitoring and evaluation. The MIS that was developed was distinctive in that it kept track not only of fund flows and programme activities as the MIS of every project and programme does but also of the outcome objectives of DPEP. The project indicators were monitored through a specifically designed Project Management Information System which kept track of funds flows, construction of civil works, appointment and training of teachers, training of other educational personnel, research, and evaluation studies. The appraisal of the educational statistics brought out that the existing system was not adequate. Consequently, NIEPA was entrusted with the task of developing a school education system which came to be widely known as District Information System for Education (DISE). DISE reports on key variables and performance indicators at the school, cluster resource centre, block, and district levels, and brings out state and district report cards of performance. Among the variables monitored are number of schools, teachers, and school facilities as well as enrolment by gender, and social categories such as scheduled castes and scheduled tribes. The design of MIS also provided for the progress towards achievement of the outcome objectives being derived from reports of the supervision missions, research and evaluation studies, and special surveys to examine different aspects of programme delivery and implementation as well as impact of programme activities. To jump the story, with the change of the government in 1996 a view was taken that with its 'entire focus' on DPEP, NEEM as constituted did not function as the NEEM which the POA envisaged; the existing NEEM was re-designated as DPEP Mission. In January 1998, a committee under the chairmanship of the Education Secretary recommended the reconstitution of

NEEM as an autonomous society. However, nothing came of the report. In 2001, SSA, the successor programme of DPEP, was launched as a CSS. Unlike DPEP it was predominantly funded domestically; DPEP as well as other CSSs in the field of elementary education were subsumed in it. A National Mission for SSA was launched for managing SSA more or less on the lines of the DPEP Mission.

TSG also undertook academic activities such as development of prototype in-service teacher training designs and materials including those required for multi-grade teaching (that is to say, a single teacher handling at the same time more than one class because of the small number of pupils in each class), development of research-based, field-tested prototype packages of textbooks, auxiliary learning materials, and teacher guides based on MLL, integrated and active learning techniques for enhancing reading and mathematics skills in classes I–III, and development of training material for educational planning and management. The TSG also made concerted efforts to promote the networking of institutions all over the country such as Lal Bahadur Shastry National Academy of Administration, NCERT, SCERTs, NIEPA, universities, Social Science Research institutions, and the IIMs, and utilize the network for conduct of research and evaluation relevant to primary education, and for capacity building.

The TSG was privileged to have Sajitha Bashir as the first Chief Consultant and many persons who made a mark later in the academia and consultancy field such as Jyotsna Jha and Subir Shukla. Shukla was TSG's mainstay in the area of pedagogy; he was an invaluable link between DPEP and SSA as he worked in the TSG of SSA also. Sajitha Bashir is an institution by herself. Agencies require 'local' staff to complement their expatriate staff, and they are well known to 'poach' staff from the government offering emoluments several times higher than those government offers. DPEP itself was the victim of such poaching when Jangira who contributed a great deal to DPEP was lured away from NCERT by the local office of the Bank. Soon thereafter, K could do a bit of 'reverse poaching'. All agencies, the Bank included, pay lower emoluments to those recruited locally for work in their 'country offices' than 'international' staff recruited for deployment all over the world in spite of the fact that the academic qualifications of 'locals' might be as good as, if not better than, the international staff. Sajitha resigned in protest, and after a few months, readily accepted K's offer to be the

Chief of the DPEP TSG at emoluments just a fraction of what she drew in the Bank. Though educated abroad, with schooling in Geneva and doctoral work in the London School of Economics, she is an archetypal daughter of Kerala proud of her Malayali identity and heritage. She has the typical Malayali temperament of being brutally frank and outspoken. Her professional integrity is impeccable. She never hesitates to call a spade a spade, and declare vehemently that the emperor had no clothes. Sajitha came to be K's comrade-in-arms, bringing to bear on her new assignment her exceptional capabilities; many aspects of DPEP, such as organization of studies, evaluation, synthesis of the findings of studies and evaluation, application of the findings of research studies and evaluation to programme activities, MIS, and joint review missions, owe a great deal to her. The appellation, Lord Root-of-the-Matter that FDR jovially applied to his Man Friday, Harry Hopkins, could aptly be applied to her. She had an uncanny ability to spot the essential, offer unusual insights, a rare ability to look at the trees without losing sight of the wood, and a fine felicity of expression. Sajitha's doctoral thesis was about learning achievement in Tamil Nadu schools. K was thrilled by what she established, namely that private schools were not *per se* superior to government schools. What makes the difference to learner achievement in schools is not ownership but the level of per student investment, the quality of teaching–learning material, classroom processes, the degree of supervision, and the home environment. The learning achievement in well-endowed private schools was better than that in government schools, even though many of these private schools paid most of their teachers far less what government schools paid. However, the learning achievement in government schools was better than that of poorly endowed private schools which received grant-in-aid from the government; many such schools were in the business of securing grants from the government rather than imparting education. She brought to bear on the DPEP baseline learner achievement studies her expertise on learning achievement and enlisted Snehalata Shulka, formerly of NCERT, who pioneered learner achievement studies in India. As she crisply put it, few even in NCERT, not to speak of educators in India and abroad, knew of the pace-setting work of Snehalata, a senior professor in NCERT, while many educators abroad and in the Bank knew about the findings of a doctoral student merely because the work was carried out under the aegis of the London School of Economics.

Sajitha also pioneered a managerial evaluation of the structures and processes that were critical to the success of DPEP such as the village education committees, state-level societies, and the planning process. Right from the beginning, she perceived the challenges facing DPEP as well its limitations. The initial coverage of DPEP was small, and in terms of size, the new management structures were insignificant in size compared to the existing state administrative structures for education, the education department in every state constituting the single largest entity. As she put it in the synthesis study of the managerial evaluation in different states:

> The realization of the ambitious objectives and goals of DPEP rely quite heavily on the new management structures and processes that have been introduced as part of the program. Yet, these new structures and processes operate in an environment that is indifferent, if not hostile, to these innovations. Given the relative size of the new structures, there is every possibility that the larger environment and its inertia may overwhelm the nascent processes, or that the new processes may themselves become encased in petrified forms, which prevent invigoration of the content. Furthermore, while management reforms are seen as crucial to the success of DPEP, these reforms are being introduced only in a small part of the system and are expected to gradually diffuse through the system. At the same time, the objectives of universal enrolment and retention, raising achievement levels and reducing social gaps are to be attained within a relatively short time span.[10]

She was no armchair theorist, and she did not rest content by articulating her concerns. As the Chief Consultant of the DPEP TSG, she took it to be her primary task to be taking all possible steps to put in place monitoring tools to continually scan the managerial structures and processes so that the dangers she foresaw were identified in time and preventive steps taken. It was to this end that she instituted a diagnostic, formative managerial evaluation of the managerial structures and enlisted well-known organizations and experts to undertake the evaluation. As she put it:

[10] *Evaluation of Managerial Structures and Processes under DPEP – A Synthesis Study*, New Delhi: Research, Evaluation and Studies under Technical Support Group of DPEP, EdCIL, 1996, p. 18.

> (In contrast to friendly and co-opted consultants drafted for evaluation of most externally funded projects) the research agencies were asked to be candid and critical in conducting the evaluation and in presenting their conclusions and the evidence on which these were based. In preparing the synthesis volume, a decision had to be taken regarding the manner in which the findings were to be presented. It is possible to take the stand that many shortcomings are likely to occur in the first year and hence, implicitly, underplay them. Since this evaluation is a diagnostic and formative study, it was necessary to highlight the issues in as unambiguous manner as possible. Furthermore, as DPEP has aroused high expectations on being a programme 'with a difference', it was felt that all deformities, disorders or signs of sclerosis should be flagged at the very outset, rather than waiting for them to engulf the whole body, so that at least further investigation can be undertaken if necessary. It is hoped that the systematic study and presentation of issues … will serve to provide (the State and national managers of DPEP) another perspective and deeper insight into the operation of the programme. If this report can serve to stimulate further analytical discussion and concrete steps to address issues, it will have served the purpose. (Text in parenthesis added by K).[11]

The purpose she set out was fulfilled to that extent DPEP spawned a large number of studies and evaluations. Noteworthy among the managerial evaluations was the one by Jyotsna Jha, Saxena, and Baxi.[12] Truth to be told, however, one is not sure how far the studies and evaluations were made use of to address issues better. Sajitha was rather impatient with simplistic evaluations of DPEP and the facile conclusions drawn from such evaluations. However, she was not the one who would be blinded by any emotional attachment to the programme she was closely associated with. She never failed to highlight the limitations of DPEP, and the possibility of the innovative processes and structures that DPEP introduced being overwhelmed in a manner akin to the jungle creeping and engulfing an unattended clearance or structure in its midst. It is rightly said that *spartha vridhathe vidya* (learning

[11] *Evaluation of Managerial Structures*, p. 6.

[12] Jyotsna Jha, K.B.C. Saxena and C.V. Baxi, *Management Processes in Elementary Education: A Study of Existing Practices in Selected States in India*, European Union, New Delhi, 2001.

advances through strife); that being so, K owes Sajitha an immense debt for being an formidable intellectual sparring partner who sharply challenged his beliefs, assumptions, and inferences not only when they were comrades-in-arms steering DPEP but also later.

XVI

DON'T COUNT YOUR CHICKENS

Much Ado about Nothing? Education for All-9 Summit, December 1993

By the end of 1993, it appeared to K that all the troubles and travails were over, and that he could look forward to a smooth implementation of DPEP and its progressive extension to all the states in the country. The year 1993 ended with yet another feather in K's cap. The Education for All Summit of Nine High-Population Countries (EFA-9), of which K was the Chief Co-ordinator, was a grand 'success' acclaimed by the media and appreciated by the Prime Minister himself as well as leaders such as Chief Minister Lalu Prasad Yadav who participated in the pre-Summit events (Chapter VII). Along with his bosses, Arjun Singh and Giri, K also came in for praise, but far from being exhilarated, he was dejected, as he could not help recall the question of little Peterkin in the famous poem *Blenheim* 'What good would come of it?' and seek answers. As an idea, organizing the summit was not bad. The basic concept was that if the Jomtien goals were to be achieved, special attention needed to be paid to nine high-population countries (Bangladesh, Brazil, China, Egypt India, Indonesia, Mexico, Nigeria, and Pakistan) which had approximately half of the total world population, some two-thirds of the illiterate adults and over a third of out-of-school children, and faced the greatest challenges in meeting the Jomtien goals. It was not much of an intellectual leap to draw the inference that collaboration between the nine countries for sharing of information, ideas, and best practices would be expedient. It was also logical to take the view that there was no better way to promote collaboration than getting the heads of the state/government to sit together in a summit. However, the logical fallacy lay in the simplistic belief that the mere fact that the nine countries shared similar problems would bring them together into a partnership and, more importantly, sustain that partnership. What was needed was a strong incentive by way of priority treatment in development assistance or a well-funded programme of collaboration. Financing institutions such as the World Bank were unwilling to give such an undertaking, as it detracted from their policy of giving priority to least developed countries (LDCs); of the EFA-9 countries, only Bangladesh qualified to be an LDC. So much so, the World Bank did not sponsor the EFA-9 Summit, the way it sponsored the Jomtien Conference. UNDP, which strayed into the Jomtien Conference, chose not to let its focus on sustainable development be distracted by the EFA-9 initiative. Even within UNESCO, sub-Saharan countries, which were a strong group by virtue of numbers, opposed a special treatment for EFA-9 countries. So much so, UNESCO and UNICEF came to be the prime movers of the EFA-9 initiative, neither of whom had the financial resources needed to finance anything other than advocacy and *upstream activities*, that is to say organize meetings, workshops, and studies. UNFPA, which was a co-sponsor of the Jomtien Conference, chose to be full sponsor of EFA-9; however, it was a minor player and its financial resources were no better than UNESCO and UNICEF. No wonder that, in spite of vigorous lobbying by emissaries of UNESCO, UNICEF, and the Indian Government, only President Suharto of India chose fit to travel to India for the Summit; other countries were represented by education ministers or officials. Hence, the very name Summit was a misnomer. The follow-up mostly comprised meetings and more meetings providing opportunities to ministers and officers like K to travel and see the world. There was one seemingly concrete initiative though: a collaborative distance education project. Nothing came out of it except 'Words, Words, and Words'—documents which were not acted upon. Not everyone saw the Summit as K did. Encomiums in the media are manna from heaven for any politician; no sooner had the Summit concluded when the minister's office and the minister's trusted lieutenant Sudip Banerjee began preparation for a similar summit of BIMARU states in Bhopal. The Bhopal Declaration, like the Delhi Declaration, had fallen into the limbo of history little noticed and unmourned.

Every cloud has a silver lining; while the collaboration between the EFA-9 countries did not take place, India by itself was benefitted. The Delhi Summit popularized the term EFA, if not the idea underlying it, in the Indian media and among the political leaders who attended many meetings organized back-to-back with the Summit in a way no conference abroad could do be it Jomtien or its successor at Dakar or the Millennium Development Summit. This popularization triggered the creative inspiration which gave birth to the evocative expression of SSA and SSA's equally evocative logo.

No Smooth Sailing

In December 1993, the CCEA accorded an in-principle approval for DPEP. With Skolnik brought on board, he expected World Bank's approval of the DPEP project to be smooth sailing. K also expected that the interaction with the seven states chosen for the implementation of DPEP in the first phase would be equally smooth; the era when the states, with the encouragement of Bank functionaries, floated project proposals which did not fit in DOE's scheme of priorities faded into oblivion. Even with a state project such as the UP Project, DOE had successfully established its right to have a legitimate role in project design and implementation; that being so, with a CSS in which DOE provided 85 per cent of the outlay as grant, the question of a state government questioning the programme parameters or cocking a snook at DOE appeared to be inconceivable. When the New Year began, the six-state project seemed to proceed smoothly, much like a well-oiled machine; it appeared certain that the approval process would culminate in presentation of the case to the Bank's Executive Board in June 1994, and the loan becoming effective soon thereafter. Once in December 1993 CCEA approved DPEP in principle, Finance Ministry had no objection to make adequate budgetary provision for the expenditure expected to be incurred in the financial year 1994–5. K expected to begin implementation of DPEP in the six states in June 1994 itself as the Department of Expenditure should have no objection to release funds already provided for once the Bank's Board cleared the proposal. The Bank's Pre-appraisal Mission (February 1994) was appreciative of the ongoing preparatory studies as well as of the planning, and had such confidence in the ability of the embryonic DPEP Bureau that it wanted the DPEP Bureau to 'assume principal responsibility for continuing appraisal of state and district plans'. In a departure from the past practice, the Appraisal Mission would only review a sub-sample of state and district proposals. The focus of the Appraisal Mission would be on the national programme and proposed mechanism for implementation, monitoring, and evaluation. K thought that DPEP could get going without any further hurdles, and that he could go full steam ahead on the launch of DPEP and its effective implementation thereafter. He saw his task as mainly managerial: ensure rigour in planning, get all the systems in place in DOE and the seven participating states, build the capacity of state and district functionaries to develop and implement the plans, enhance the motivation and competence of teachers, foster and disseminate innovations of various kinds including pedagogic innovation, and instil a culture of outcomes. K was mistaken, the appraisal of DPEP by the Bank faced unexpected troubles, and getting MP on board was tortuous. During this challenging period, K often thought that *The Pilgrim's Progress*, the famous theological work which allegorizes the Christian doctrine of salvation, vividly captured the pangs of angst and despondency which gripped him often as well as the travails of DPEP. Like the dark, narrow path Christian, the protagonist whose journey to the City of Light *The Pilgrim's Progress* describes, had to traverse in the Valley of the Shadow of Death, DPEP had to traverse an equally parlous path with a deep trap on the right of failing to secure Bank assistance, and deep slough on the left in which DPEP might slip, sink, and disappear because of the failure of MP to abide by the DPEP framework and guidelines.

Vagaries of the Bank's Appraisal

After the Bank's Pre-Appraisal Mission concluded its task, John Middleton, the Bank's Task Manager based in Delhi, and Marlaine Lockheed, Middleton's counterpart based in Washington, expressed happiness with the way the project was developing. As Task Manager, Middleton was primarily responsible to ensure that the project was of a standard which met the management's high expectations, well designed in all respects, and potentially successful. A good design was expected to ensure clear objectives, a strong nexus between the objectives and the interventions proposed, adequate institutional mechanisms for implementation, and sustainability of the project outcomes. The design was expected to be evidence-based offering proof to the maximum extent possible of whatever is proposed by way of objectives, interventions, and implementation mechanisms. The Washington-based Marlaine was Middleton's collaborator, and one of her main tasks was to 'defend' the project and its preparation process during consideration by the internal mechanisms of the Board; a project is placed before the Executive Board only after it passes muster with those mechanisms.

Do not count your chickens before they are hatched, so goes a famous proverb. True to that saying, the prospects for an early clearance of the project suddenly turned dim. A few days after the visitation of the Pre-Appraisal Mission, Middleton turned up in K's office, and during chit chat, casually mentioned that he was asked to broach with K an idea of Vice President Joe Wood that an investment proposal of the magnitude of DPEP (a loan of about $260 million) should not be brought before the Board in the fag end of the Bank's financial year, and that it is better presented two months later in August. Wood, 'probably the most powerful man in South Asia' as the column of an environmental activist put it, was the boss of Heinz Vergin and supervised the Bank operations in the South Asian countries; he was the one to decide if and when any project from India should be presented to the Executive Board. K was to learn later that Robert Drysdale, adviser in Wood's office, was doubtful whether a project with such an ambitious design like DPEP could be implemented; he might have been the one who sowed the seeds of doubt in the mind of Wood. Middleton tried to win over K by claiming that a three-month delay in consideration by the Executive Board should not make any difference as the project was 'budgeted' by the Bank. K would not, however, 'buy' Middleton's argument and told him categorically that he saw no reason why there should be any delay when the preparation was going as scheduled and the Pre-Appraisal Mission expressed satisfaction with the progress. Any delay was unwarranted and would affect K's credibility as well as that of the Bank. Having made his position clear, K thought that the matter would rest but it did not, and unwittingly the path ahead turned into a gruelling obstacle race. As it was, the officers of the six participating states were chafing at the unwonted rigour that K and his deputies demanded from them in the preparation of plans; they were like doctoral students frustrated with a perfinicky research guide, going crazy at being called upon to do umpteen revisions of the plans. If still they complied with what they considered to be the whims and fancies of K and his minions, it was because they expected that at the end of it all they would receive hefty funding for a long time to come. The Bank's volte face confronted K with the prospect of being dubbed a sadistic fool who led so many up the garden path.

To begin, studies seemed to the epicentre of problems. Middleton expressed unhappiness with a few studies particularly that belonging to indigenous people, the Bank's jargon for schedule tribes. It was only a few months later during negotiations that K could understand Middleton's anxiety about indigenous people. K was dismayed when a representative from the unit dealing with indigenous people turned up to demand that no indigenous people should be displaced by the school building construction programme that the Bank would fund. K knew that in the wake of the controversy over the Bank's funding of the Narmada Valley Project, the Bank management had become overly sensitive to the displacement of indigenous people by large infrastructure projects such as construction of dams. K, however, did not expect Bank's functionaries who had a high reputation for professionalism to lack a sense of proportion, for the construction of small structures such as classrooms was qualitatively different from dams, and displacement of indigenous people was not an issue in a basic education project. The very term indigenous people smacked of cultural insularity. It might make sense in a country like the United States with a history of a few hundred years and where everyone except Native Americans were immigrants. But not in a country like India with thousands of years of recorded history; any attempt to identify indigenous people was bound to be entangled with bitter historical controversies like that on the authenticity of Aryan invasion. However, Middleton's demand for improving the quality of studies was accompanied by the demand for a few more studies such as decentralization and school effectiveness. Particularly obnoxious was a mysterious condition in the initial aide memoire of the Appraisal Mission (30 March 1994) obligating the lender 'to provide to IDA on computer discs the complete data files for baseline beneficiary studies conducted in Assam, Haryana, Karnataka, Kerala, Maharashtra, and Tamil Nadu together with the related code books'. K rejected that condition outright as it would amount to unfair appropriation of the 'fruits of labour' of the NCERT and NIEPA faculty and their associates. While assuring that the studies would completed on schedule, would be of good quality, and widely disseminated among the state and district functionaries associated with DPEP, K gave vent to his irritation with the excessive preoccupation with studies and the tendency to demand proof of even the obvious and know everything about everything before doing anything at all. K told Middleton that he saw the merit of evidence-based design and implementation; however, it was an epistemological fallacy to believe that one could know everything before implementation could begin. K had the uncanny feeling that overemphasizing these studies had little to do with gathering the information needed to convince the Board of the soundness of the project and had more to do with the publication mania of World Bank researchers. That his feeling was not off the mark was borne out by the fact that from March onwards, Middleton began to downplay the studies and focus on the implementations aspects. About a decade later, K came across in a book on World Bank lending by an ex-staffer a corroboration of K's intuitive surmise about the overemphasis on studies; the ex-staffer wrote:

> *An axiom of Confucius is that the essence of knowledge is, having it, to apply it.* Are they (studies like the one on how much older people are willing to pay to reduce their risk of dying) for real? What does this have to do with anything? ... Multiply this by thousands of reports produced by the Bank staff each year, and you will understand how this endless intellectual self-gratification distracts the Bank from its mission. What we need then, and now, is to take Confucius's advice and apply what we need know sensibly.[1]

Hardly had the issue of studies been satisfactorily resolved, K received the tiding that the project encountered serious objections in an internal review within the Bank. The critics considered the project to be too risky to be approved, expressed reservations about the state of preparedness for implementation, and floated an alternative of downsizing the project and splitting it into two separate projects one following the other. They refused to take note of the track record of DOE, of it being the only department which fulfilled all the conditions for the

[1] Steve Berkman, *The World Bank and the Gods of Lending*, Sterling VA: Kumarian Press, 2008, pp. 35, 39.

release of the second tranche of SSN credit and of the Bank's review mission being appreciative of the manner in which the UP Project was proceeding. Compared to the UP Project, more preparatory work was done for DPEP by way of the studies, design of the national component, forging institutional linkages, and decentralized planning and community participation. DPEP was ready with the model financial regulations for the state societies, while several months after the loan became effective and implementation began, the UP Society Financial Regulations were not ready. K could not help feeling that obsolescing bargain was at work; before DOE agreed to pose the UP Project as a test case project, the Bank wooed DOE hard; thereafter it was acting high and mighty. K was indignant that new conditions which were not even hinted at during pre-appraisal or mooted for the UP Project were being suggested. There were suggestions that in order to convince the Bank management of the state of readiness to implement DPEP, funds be released for implementation and staff appointed in all the states and districts. This placed K in a Catch-22 situation. The Department of Expenditure would not permit funds to be released till appraisal would be completed, and the Appraisal Mission would not be convinced about the state of readiness unless funds were released. In keeping with the idea of downsizing the project, Middleton expressed the view that the preparation in Haryana and Assam was inadequate, and suggested that these two states should be dropped from the first phase of the project funded by the Bank and shifted to the second phase. K strongly opposed the suggestion for a variety of reasons. He strongly believed that Middleton's views were not borne out by facts, and that he was influenced by a point of view in the Bank DPEP project was too ambitious in scope and risky. K strongly believed that launching a truncated project was politically not feasible and would badly hurt the image of DPEP as a 'happening' project. Selja, the Minister of State with whom K had an excellent rapport, was from Haryana and her constituency Sirsa was one of the districts covered in DPEP. Realistically, it would have been impossible for K to persevere with DPEP if he were to alienate either Selja or Arjun Singh. K told Middleton in no uncertain terms that if the Bank continued to be unreasonable, he would as well go ahead with the implementation using the EC assistance and meanwhile mobilize resources domestically. EC would be more than happy to have its assistance applied to more than one state, and once implementation began, pressure could be mounted on the Finance Ministry and the Planning Commission to provide resources. As Task Manager he would have to offer a lot of explanation to his management as to why a promising relationship with DOE went sour. Irritated about the seeming foot-dragging by Middleton, K wanted to raise the matter with Skolnik, Middleton's superior. However, this was not necessary as K could sort out with Middleton who quipped that he was 'eccentric', and dropped his insistence to truncate the project. K's informal conversations with Middleton brought out that he was as much upset as K by the headquarters trying to change the 'rules of the game' and raise a series of questions about the implementability of the DPEP Project and the state of readiness of the central and state governments to implement the project. He was hurt that his professional judgement was being questioned by people with little experience in planning and implementation of educational projects, and he was being accused of having gone 'native'. He attributed his predicament to politics within the Bank, and the reservation of some in the Bank about yet another massive loan for a primary education project in India when it was too early to assess how the first project, the UP Project, was faring. And further, it did not help that a few projects such as the Blindness and Population Control projects were stuck in the Ministry of Health. The challenge imposed by the politics within the Bank was a blessing in disguise as it compelled K and his deputies to review and bolster the systems for appraisal of the district plans as well as those for implementation. Conflict with difficulty, Edmund Burke had rightly said, 'makes us acquainted with our object, and compels us to consider it in all its relations (and) it will not suffer us to be superficial'.

The state society emerged as a break or make issue in the standoff between DOE and the UP government. As if to prove the adage that history repeats itself, the society popped up again as an equally contentious issue during the appraisal of DPEP. A list of ten questions on the society mode of implementation was formally communicated to K as preliminary questions with a caveat that 'additional questions may be forthcoming'. K was required to furnish answers to these questions so that the appraisal could be completed. Quite a few questions covered familiar ground which was extensively trod over the previous two years while considering the SSN operations, the UP Project, and DPEP itself. Given the formidable institutional memory of the Bank as well as of the fact that quite a few Bank functionaries were common to the processing of the SSN operation, the UP Project, and DPEP, a question like 'why is DPEP requiring use of societies as a required agency for project implementation (please provide specific advantage in using societies)' reminded K of the *babu* (clerical) mentality that some of the lower-level functionaries in the government displayed. Some were questions similar to the loaded question when did you stop beating your wife? The main objection revolved round the view that implementation by a society might dilute the fiduciary responsibility of the state governments to implement the project in accordance with the loan agreement, and consequently pose a grave risk to the Bank. DOE's rejoinder was ably drafted by Vrinda and Naved Masood. Masood was a colleague in DOE who was from the Manipur–Tripura cadre of the IAS, and endowed with a brilliant mind and exceptional legal prowess. He won encomiums from the Supreme Court for his order in a land revenue matter in Manipur which he decided on first principles relying on Baden Powell's classic manual of land revenue systems and land tenures of British India (1882). K and Vrinda solicited his help to ensure that the rejoinder was a legal document rebutting in legal language the view that use of society was a grave risk.

Masood, note quoted chapter and verse to establish that the extant legislations provided a robust legal framework to ensure that the societies implemented the project with fidelity and that any apprehension that GOI and state government did not have adequate legal power to prevent misapplication or misappropriation of funds was unwarranted. The Societies Registration Act, 1860, was a central legislation that is applicable all over the country except in the Telengana region of AP and six other states. Even in states which have laws of their own, the state legislation is modelled after the Central Act. These legislations provided a comprehensive framework regulating the formation of societies and broad aspects of their functioning; they also mandated the management of the societies be done with due diligence, and specified the penal consequences that followed any infringement of the legislations. These legislations had withstood the test of time, the Central Act having been on the statute book for more than 130 years, and it could be safely asserted that the legislations had ensured orderly transaction of business by societies. The functionaries of the DPEP Society were accountable for acts of omission and commission. Offences of misappropriation, cheating, and criminal breach of truest are punishable under the specific provisions of the Indian Penal Code, and the culpability of the society officials is specifically established by Section 11 of the Societies Registration Act, 1860, as well as the corresponding provisions of the state acts. A special feature of the DPEP societies was that the major office bearers of the DPEP societies were officials of the central and state governments who were required to conform to the rigorous provisions of conduct rules. In the event of their being found guilty of illegal pecuniary gains while discharging their functions in the society, they were liable for punishment not only under the provisions of the Societies Registration Act and the Indian Penal Code but also of the Prevention of Corruption Act. As substantial government funds were involved, the functioning of the DPEP societies was subject to audit by the Comptroller and Auditor General who is a constitutional authority; that audit is not limited to audit of accounts but of performance. In view of all these, there was no reason to doubt that DPEP would not be implemented in accordance with the loan agreement to which the central and state governments were parties. One has to take note of the long history of involvement of societies registered under these legislations to undertake activities on behalf of the central and state governments with funds provided by governments. The example par excellence was that of the district rural development agencies which were constituted under the legislations governing societies and had been involved in the implementation of various poverty alleviation and employment generation programmes which were sponsored by GOI. The experience gained in the working of these agencies had established that established norms of financial propriety in dealing with government expenditure and personal accountability of functionaries dealing with government funds could be ensured satisfactorily within the provisions of the Societies Registration Act, even while cutting red tape and eliminating bureaucratic rigidities associated with government departments.

When Mohan Gopal visited him, K suggested to him that he visit Bihar and see for himself how the BEP Society functioned. Seeing is believing indeed. Mohan Gopal returned convinced that normal mode of implementation through State Education Departments would be inadequate, and the use of societies represented an important experiment by GOI to overcome critical hurdles to project implementation such as lack of adequate institutional capacity of State Education Departments to manage the project, severe limitations in engaging and utilizing specialist expertise required for project implementation, prolonged delays in funds being passed on to project implementing units on a timely basis, and prolonged delays in decision-making required for effective project implementation. And further, the early experience of the BEP Society indicated that the objectives of establishing DPEP societies were achievable in significant measure. He also suggested careful drafting of the personnel, finance, and procurement regulations of DPEP societies with those extant in the BEP Society as a model. After Mohan Gopal's visit, the society issue faded away as abruptly as its appearance. And so did the bank's hesitancy after the visit of Vergin a fortnight later.

Vergin's meeting with Giri and K on 15 April 1994 was one of the turning points in the evolution of DPEP, for he not only signalled the removal of hurdles for the negotiation but also reiterated the Bank's commitment for funding a succession of DPEP projects and conveyed its recognition that India was a happening place in so far as primary education was concerned. He was appreciative of the process employed for development of the DPEP project, and of the state of preparedness to implement DPEP. In his experience this was one of the very few projects in which the borrower was ahead of the Bank. In his April meeting, Vergin was appreciative of the fact that in anticipation of Bank's approval, the Planning Commission had agreed to treat DPEP as a CSS and the funds received from external agencies as an additionality to DOE's plan provision, that CCEA had accorded in-principle approval of DPEP, that adequate budgetary provision was made for implementation in the financial year 1994–5, and that it was proposed to release funds immediately after negotiations were concluded in advance of the loan becoming legally effective. These measures would facilitate approval by the Bank's Executive Committee. He also reiterated the fact that all expenditure on project activities undertaken after appraisal would be reimbursed by the Bank. He appreciated the fact that delay in negotiations would delay the launch of the programme and dishearten field functionaries. He would do all he could to ensure there were no delays. He directed Middleton to complete his preparatory work and assured him that he would direct the concerned staff in the Bank's headquarters to bestow the necessary attention and priority so that negotiations were not delayed. 'Let me tell you bluntly,' he told Giri and K, 'we are committed to DPEP. It was not a matter of Big Bang with not much happening thereafter'. He foresaw Bank financing in the new few years at least one DPEP project a year, and he suggested beginning of preparations for the second DPEP project. He had another offer to make. The Aid India Consortium was reorganized as India Development Forum and its annual meetings would henceforth consider social sectors. The Ministry of Environment was making a presentation at the forthcoming meeting of the Forum in Madrid. It was be a good idea if at the June 1995 meeting DOE made a presentation on primary education. Vergin's meeting cleared the way for the negotiations.

Why all of a sudden did the processing of the first DPEP project face hurdles and why did they suddenly disappear is a mystery which K tried for long to decipher. He could never definitively decipher the mystery given that 'there will be always dark and tangled stretches in the decision-making proves mysterious even to those who may be most intimately involved'.[2] Yet he had a fairly good picture of what might have happened. Being human, all too human K's first impulse was to blame the task manager Middleton, and Marlaine Lockheed his counterpart in Washington for the turn of events. They were good researchers; however, unlike the veteran Cambridge they were not loan operatives. It appeared that instead of getting K and his colleagues to address matters which would help convince the management of the bankability of the project, they pushed through project preparation studies which were more useful for them to publish scholarly publications. K vaguely heard from Middleton that an internal report in the Bank was making waves and that the management was now laying greater emphasis on implementability of projects. It was only much later that he came to know the details of the landmark Wapenhans Report (1992),[3] the report of

[2] John F. Kennedy, 'Preface' to Theodore Sorensen, *Decision-Making in the White House: The Olive Branch and the Arrow*, New York: Columbia University Press, 1963, p. vi.

[3] Task Force on Portfolio Management, named after its chairman, the recently retired Vice-President Willi Wapenahans. The World Bank, *Effective Implementation: Key to Development Impact: Report of the World Bank's Portfolio Task Force*, Washington, DC: World Bank, 1992.

an internal review of the Bank's portfolio commissioned by President Preston, and the deep turmoil it triggered within the Bank. The report highlighted the fact that a third of the projects completed in 1991 were failures, that this was not an odd outcome. There was a dramatic 150 per cent rise in failures over the previous decade, and deep-rooted problems were at the root of the malady. The main culprits were a managerial culture and incentive structure which rewarded project design and lending at the expense of implementation and follow-up. The report also brought out that many Bank staff perceived appraisals as marketing devices for securing loan approval as well as personal recognition, and that the management valued conceptual and planning activities higher than implementation and project management. The report sent many in the Bank into a tizzy, and snag hunting suddenly became the flavour of the season. Discovering any traces of 'pervasive appraisal optimism' in the projects in the pipeline came to be a hot pursuit. The Wapenhans Report came in handy for those who were of the view that one should make haste slowly and wait to see how the UP Project fared before funding another primary education project—that too one with the largest outlay so far funded by the Bank. In such an environment, even seasoned loan managers would have gone slowly for a while till the dust raised by the report settled down. It is quite possible that as Director, India Country Office, Vergin bade his time till it was opportune to give a push to the processing of the DPEP credit. Suffice it to say, in keeping with the seminal schema of Allison, the Bank was no different from any other large organization. Vergin put it all when he told K by way of advice before K left for negotiations that in a large bureaucracy one has to live with Doubting Thomases and senseless queries, and that he was confident that satisfactory formulations could be found for the few unresolved problems.

XVII

CRUCIBLE OF FIRE

Madhya Padesh was different in many respects. Figuratively, in MP the cart was put before the horse; a hefty grant was assured even before the planning process was completed. Consequently, government functionaries of MP felt that the question which faced them was, 'Now that hundreds of crores of rupees are available what would we do with it?' None in MP bothered about the fact that EC assistance was technically for DPEP in the country as a whole and not specific to MP, that many in EC including the Ambassador in the EC Delegation in Delhi were averse to the EC assistance being applied exclusively to MP, and that it was quite a task for K to persuade the EC to slot its assistance exclusively to MP. While officials of the MP government were associated with the discussions with the preparatory mission led by David Theobald in December 1992 to January 1993, they were not associated with the subsequent negotiations for the reason that their presence would have aggravated the suspicion of EC officials that they were being trapped into providing project assistance in the guise of programme assistance. Had they participated in the negotiations they would have had a better sense of the reality than oral communication by K could convey; however, K was in no position to associate the MP functionaries in the sensitive negotiations. Even otherwise, once EC agreed to the proposal of DOE to apply the funds exclusively to MP, negotiating history was of little relevance to 'practical men'. Adding to the treacherousness of the MP slough was the fact that it was well known that it was DOE which was responsible for appraising the district plans and giving the necessary clearances. Figuratively, it was DOE which regulated the tap from which funds flowed. It appeared inconceivable to many in the state that a department which was headed by a formidable minister from the state itself—one who, like Margaret Thatcher, was one who 'must be obeyed' by civil servants, and was the mentor of Digvijay Singh, the new Chief Minister, would stand firm on procedures and parameters so rigidly as to come in the way of an immediate start without any ado or taking up whatever the state government fancied. It was only humane to believe that the visitations of the missions, appraisals, and so on were mere facades set up by DOE to convince EC that there was hunky-dory. A nasty confrontation was inevitable given the pervasive state of that mind in MP among those who mattered and given that K felt that he was honour bound to live up to the trust that the EC functionaries reposed in him to effectively design deliver and implement the programme, and thereby help them fulfil their fiduciary responsibility to the Member States of EC.

Aggravating the problem was the *scale* of DPEP in MP. Nineteen districts were covered in MP as against 23 districts in all the other six states put together. The scale and outlay of the programme were too hefty to miss the attention of the top political executive. The formal signing of the agreement was almost co-eval with the Congress Party gaining power in the state, and no minister or government anywhere in the world would have failed to capitalize on such a significant 'achievement' as firming up of financing of a mega-programme. The new state government launched the State DPEP Society with fanfare christening it as Rajiv Gandhi Shiksha Mission; the mission was to manage also TLCs in the state. The constitution of the Mission was a welcome move and signified the state government's commitment to promote literacy and primary education in a missionary mode. But then the law of unintended consequences struck with vengeance. The structure of the DPEP societies for managing externally funded projects was designed to broad-base decision-making and implementation, secure good advice and practices from 'outside', and forge partnerships with NGOs, local communities, and others interested in the achievement of UEE in letter and spirit. Thus, the General Council of a society was not expected to comprise only ministers and officials. In the early days of DPEP, when it was still an idea, Ted Palac of UNICEF presciently observed that the society structure carried the danger of politicization as well as of a conflict between the functionaries of the society and the State Education Department. The starry-eyed K dismissed Palac's prognosis; however, the events in MP were an eye opener. Three active members of the Congress Party, known to be Arjun Singh loyalists, were nominated as members of the General Council by virtue of being 'distinguished voluntary agency workers', and another as a 'woman'. These nominations were in keeping with the explicit strategy of Arjun Singh to fully use official patronage at his disposal in order to build up his political strength. It is significant that one of these General Council members resigned when Arjun Singh resigned from the Council of Ministers and left the Congress Party in December 1994. As if these nominations were not enough to shock a politically naïve K, indications were given to the newly nominated members of the General Council that they would manage the development of primary education in the state and that each one of them would be assigned the management of the programme in a district assigned to them. And worse, demands began to be put forth which ran contrary to the basic spirit of DPEP. There were demands to cover more districts straightaway in spite of the fact that, as it was, the scale of DPEP was unduly large in relation to the existing capacity to manage a radically innovative programme. The trajectory of DPEP in MP would have followed that in the six other states but for the fact that EC had offered project assistance to a basic education project in MP before offering sector programme support, and no less importantly, K as well as Giri were keen not to upset, if not please, Arjun Singh. In the six states funded by the Bank, three to five districts were chosen in the first phase, with the assurance to the states that the programme would expanded in phases, and that expansion would be guided by the principle that states which perform well would be rewarded with accelerated expansion and the laggards penalized. Whatever, the Bank and EC functionaries would not have liked the expansion of DPEP before there was clear evidence that DPEP was on the right track in the first phase of 42 districts. Covering straightaway more districts in MP would definitely have been construed as clear evidence that all the talk about the distinctiveness of DPEP was no more than empty rhetoric or worse cant. As it was, the decision to start DPEP in all the 19 districts at one go surprised the EC as well as the Bank. H. Østerby, who strongly supported K on the issue of applying the EC funds exclusively to MP, expected that as in the other six states,

DPEP would start in five or six districts, and would be expanded in subsequent years. He expressed concern that MP being the state from which the minister heading DOE hailed the process would be compromised, and that the appraisal would not be as rigorous as in the other states. K frankly told him that the decision to start the programme in all the 19 districts was never concealed; as early as April 1993, even while the discussions with the EC on the Financing Agreement were going on, the department's *District Primary Education Programme* made it clear that to begin with DPEP would cover 42 districts including the 19 districts of MP. He also made it clear to Østerby that he was as much committed to the sanctity of the process as the EC, and would not let the process be compromised on any score. In order to ensure the credibility of the appraisal he would mount a large mission comprising national and European experts, and it was for that mission to decide how many districts were ready for implementation. The Bank's draft Staff Appraisal Report covering the other six states mentioned that DPEP would begin in five or six districts of MP, and K had to prevail upon Middleton to drop that mention on the ground that the Bank had no business to comment on matters belonging to a state it was not funding. The demand to cover more districts died down as K and Giri could convince Arjun Singh that conceding the demand would jeopardize EC assistance itself because the first tranche was yet to be released by EC and the suspicion that DOE was grabbing project assistance under the garb of programme assistance was still harboured by some in EC.

The immaculate misconception that each district was allocated Rs 40 crore and that it could be utilized for any activity that could plausibly be linked with the development of primary education took root deeply in MP. The 'jingle of money', a phrase K heard from Ted Palac, clangoured loudly; the expectation that money was easy to secure lured many hawkers of quick fixes and there was a great clamour to get on to the DPEP bandwagon. The feeling that the allocation of Rs 40 crore for every district discriminated large districts gained currency and spawned a spirited campaign to revise the allocation. The demand had a ring of plausibility in that districts varied widely in terms of area and population, and it was unfair that all of them should be entitled to the same allocation. How could Bilaspur, a district with 17 blocks have the same allocation as puny Dattia, a district with three blocks was the question that was posed to clinch the argument. When the Commissioner and Secretary, Education, raised the issue with K, he explained to them that ceiling could not be equated with allocation, and then went on to explain the rationale for the ceiling. The planning exercise in Sitamarhi, a large, educationally very backward district in Bihar, had indicated that the outlay required was about Rs 30 crore over five years; on that basis, Rs 40 crore was a reasonable ceiling for the districts covered by the first phase of DPEP, which spanned seven years. Proportionately, even in Bilaspur the outlay would not be much different from that estimated for Sitamarhi; it was fallacious to think that Rs 40 crore would automatically be allotted to Dattia without planning and assessment of needs. K also emphasized the imperative of taking note of the problems besetting of efficient absorption of funds; the ceiling laid down represented a step up of about 20 times the average plan expenditure in a district. Not satisfied with K's explanation, the Commissioner of Education, MP government, put forth the theoretical argument that the investment needed should be determined solely with reference to the needs and that there should be no ceiling at all. K told him that the best could be the enemy of the good, and that in the absence of any ceiling parsimony, sustainability and replicability of programme interventions might be given the go-by. He attempted to sound conciliatory and indicated to his interlocutors that any revision of the ceiling at this stage would send the wrong signals to EC and the Bank, and that after a couple of years the matter could be reconsidered in the light of experience. His attempt had an unexpected consequence; the interlocutors drew the inference that if pressure was mounted and EC persuaded, the ceiling could be down away with. Soon thereafter, the Education Minister raised the matter in a meeting of CABE; in a meeting of the General Council, some members raised the question and the Chief Minister expressed the view that the block should be the unit for allocation and not the district, and promised the members that the matter would be taken up with the Appraisal Mission which was due to visit the state soon. K, who was present, once again recited his litany and submitted to the Chief Minister that the Appraisal Mission was a technical mission and was not concerned with policy issues. He came away with the impression that his views were accepted. He was mistaken. A few days before the appraisal mission was to arrive in Bhopal, the *Statesman* carried a report criticizing sharply the DPEP guidelines in general, and the ceiling in particular.[1] The Chief Minister did raise the matter with Theobald leader of the mission only to draw a blank. Theobald confirmed that the question of revising the ceiling was beyond the remit of the Mission, and candidly added for good measure that the EC was worried that the programme in MP was finance driven. The demand for revising the ceiling was never again raised. In retrospect, the whole controversy about the investment ceiling was utterly uncalled for, as it turned out later that average expenditure in each of the 134 districts covered by DPEP including 34 districts of MP was about Rs 25 crore.

Tennyson immortalized the charge of British cavalry at the Battle of Balaclava during a battle of the Crimean war through his celebrated poem *Charge of the Light Brigade*. The 600 who charged through the Valley of Death found cannon to right of them and cannon to left of them all of which 'volley'd and thunder'd'. Likewise, from one end, K was being sharply criticized by the state government functionaries for rigidly enforcing the DPEP framework; at the same time, he was also being criticized with equal vehemence for needlessly spearheading an externally funded programme which flooded the districts with money and opened the floodgates of corruption. The foremost and most tenacious critic on the other side was Krishna Kumar, a noted educationist; at least twice he wrote critical pieces in the *Times of India* which ruffled K a great deal not only because of what K thought to be uninformed and unfair criticism but because of the timing. The publication of the articles coincided with the visit of EC officials to the state and put K to a great deal of embarrassment. K could understand Krishna Kumar's visceral opposition to external funding. K could also not fault Krishna Kumar for being critical of the actual manner in which planning was being done in MP; he was saying in public what K was expressing in official forums. Even though he was from MP and was close enough to Arjun Singh to be appointed a member of the NIEPA Executive Committee during Arjun Singh's first term as Minister of HRD and later as Director, NCERT, during Arjun Singh's second term he pulled no punches in assailing what was happening in the MP districts. In his view, the scale of financial inputs envisaged under DPEP was staggering, and the system did not have the capacity to spend resources of such

[1] 'Controversy over Revised Guidelines', *The Statesman*, 31 March 1994.

magnitude judiciously. It was difficult to believe that a system which could not train teachers in any effective manner or ensure that schools actually opened and worked could work just because new funds have become available. A handful of officers and local politicians were drawing up plans, focusing on ways to spend the new, opulent funds. In many districts, the local politicians and officers involved in the planning of DPEP were people who had a reputation for financial corruption. Even these few people have had no opportunity to do any thoughtful homework, for they were told to fill in the format prepared at higher levels. The key message of the articles was 'restructure the system first before you pump in money'.[2]

While Krishna Kumar was right on the dot in his criticism of what the MP officials sought to do in the name of decentralized planning, he missed out the imperative of boosting investment in primary education as well as how DPEP attempted to make a break from the past in order to ensure that it was not finance driven. Krishna Kumar continued to be a sharp critic of DPEP, and in an article published in 2001, he asserted that contrary to its claim of being a national programme, DPEP was a 'smokescreen', 'a vivid story of the roll-back of the state, of contracting commitments for formal education, of the dismantling of the existing structures of formal education, proliferation of "teach anyhow" strategies, a thrust on publicity management, and a neo-conservative reliance on the community'.[3] Given the continuous barrage of criticism from a section of the academia and activists, K thought a great deal about the criticism. As was his wont, K would fall into reveries and conjure dialogues. In his imaginary dialogues, K would quote the famous saying of Marx that philosophers have only interpreted the world in various ways while the point was to change it. What was at issue, he would contend, was not whether the education system needed to be radically

[2] Krishna Kumar, 'Myopic Education: Foreign Aid to No Purpose', *Times of India*, 30 April 1994.

[3] Kumar Krishna, Manisha Priyam, and Sadhna Saxena, 'Looking Beyond the Smokescreen: DPEP and Primary Education in India'. *Economic and Political Weekly*, XXXVI, no. 7 (February 17, 2001), pp. 560–8; 'The Trouble with Para-teachers', *Frontline*, 18, no. 22 (October 27 to November 2009, 2001). http://www.frontline.in/navigation/?type=static&page=archive (last accessed on 20 January 2016).

restructured but what was the best way to effect the restructuring. What exactly do you suggest to bring about the restructuring, he would challenge the critics. What is the incentive for state governments to restructure the system? Why do you fail to see the bait of substantial funding might act as an incentive to the state governments to modify the system? K would recall Bordia's say that the plea for total revolution is an alibi for inaction, and hold the plea for restructuring first and resource infusion later akin to the call for total revolution. In a polemical mood, he would distinguish himself, a civil servant, from arm chair thinkers and critics. Well, you have the luxury of being able to go by *Gesinnungsethik* (the ethics of conviction) whereby good intentions and mouthing uncompromising thoughts are good enough and one is not bound to act, and much less take the responsibility for the consequences of actions by others based on thoughts one espouses. In contrast, I have to go by *Verantwortungsethik* (the ethics of responsibility), and I am judged not by my ideas but by what I accomplish. I have to play by the cards dealt with to me; given the current state of economy the country has no option but to engage the Bank and others. I am trying to convert a challenge into an opportunity, and you do not understand. As Henry Kissinger once said, a journalist or academic did not practise foreign policy but had abundant, publicly expressed views on the subject. He could pick his topic, can work on it as long as he wanted, could choose the best possible vision of it, and had the option of changing his mind. If they err, they have the option of writing another book or article. Statesmen do not have such luxuries, and are squarely held responsible for errors they commit.[4]

It appeared to K that the criticism of DPEP was carping and flew in the face of facts. However, in retrospect, such criticism proved to be greatly beneficial in two respects. First, it enhanced the bargaining power of the DPEP Bureau in its interaction with agencies, for domestic contest over policy (for example, whether or not to access external funding) can be a useful lever in negotiations with external actors. Schelling's axiom 'Weakness is strength' may sound paradoxical but it has a great deal of truth in the matter of negotiations. A party to negotiation who tries to push his weak counterpart (with a limited mandate) to the wall

[4] 'Kissinger Returns', *Harvard Magazine*, March–April 2012.

may fail to secure any agreement.[5] Using domestic political constraints to tie one's own hands and thereby strengthening one's bargaining position in international negotiations is a subtle and often effective negotiation ploy.[6] Second, vulnerability to criticism acted as a deterrent against uncritical acceptance of inappropriate comparative experience. On the flip side, however, the vulnerability might have inhibited a pro-active exploration of comparative experience in pedagogy and school effectiveness, and adaptation of relevant experience. Over the course of time, some of the critics have come to acknowledge, though with qualification, the 'visible gains of DPEP'. Public intellectuals who are sharp critics of the pathology of the state acquire different perceptions once they constructively engage the state. Krishna Kumar was no exception. Once he was Director, NCERT, he had a more moderate perception of DPEP. He credited DPEP with the development 'of new approaches and procedures in successive, rapidly covered stages … (in areas such as) administrative decentralization, creation of local-level structures for planning, decision making and monitoring, a massive drive to improve school buildings, reorganize the monitoring, and the involvement of non-government organizations,' with the launch of 'massive drive to improve school buildings, reorganize curriculum and recruit and train teachers at the local level', and with the conduct of large-scale surveys of children's learning achievement carried out mostly in accordance with the NCERT curricular document. There is also a more nuanced appreciation of the circumstances in which the government decided to avail external funding.[7]

Given the highly politicized environment in which DPEP began in MP, only exceptional civil servants endowed with professional integrity as well as the skills needed to manage the political bosses could have deftly steered DPEP without compromising the spirit of DPEP and at

[5] Thomas C. Schelling, *The Strategy of Conflict*, Cambridge, MA: Harvard University Press, 1960.

[6] Conversely, it is useful to enter into international agreements in order to achieve domestic objectives which otherwise cannot be realized. Robert Putnam, 'Diplomacy and Domestic Politics: The Logic of Two-Level Games', *International Organization*, 42, no. 3 (1988), pp. 427–60.

[7] Krishna Kumar, 'Quality of Education at the Beginning of the Twenty First Century: Lessons from India', 2004, Background Paper for *EFA Global Monitoring Report 2005*.

the same time keeping the political bosses in good humour. After the departure of Nirmala Buch to GOI, DPEP in MP was not fortunate to be guided by such civil servants, particularly at a critical moment when the appraisal process had to be completed and approvals given for the implementation of DPEP. Overall management of DPEP rested with the Secretary, Education, and his deputy the Commissioner of Education attended to the nitty-gritty of planning. While the Secretary was new to the job, the Commissioner had a long stint in DOE and in his current job, and was associated with the preparation of the Roopantar document. He was absolutely earnest; however, he failed to recognize that once EC offered programme assistance for DPEP in lieu of project assistance for Roopantar, the rules of the game had changed altogether. All in all, his attitude offered proof of the fact that knowledge could sometimes be a burden in a radically new context, and that unlearning is always more difficult than learning. Both the Secretary and the Commissioner failed to take note of the fact that DPEP in MP was not a standalone project and had to conform to the parameters and guidelines of DPEP, a national programme. They also failed to recognize that in DPEP the role envisaged for the senior education officials in the state headquarters was one of guiding the planning process rather than producing documents themselves. Right from the beginning, the Commissioner was averse to accept the DPEP guidelines as he strongly believed that the guidelines developed for the development of the *Roopantar* project document were more specific than those of DPEP and superior. Had the state guidelines been adopted instead of DPEP guidelines, the critics within the EC of the entire assistance being applied to MP would have been vindicated. Even though the state government accepted the DPEP guidelines, the Commissioner never did, and used every opportunity to question the guidelines, thereby complicating the planning, pre-appraisal, and appraisal processes, and embarrassing K a great deal with the visiting EC functionaries and members of the missions. The participation of MP officials in the various DPEP training workshops was rather patchy. The members of the National Core Group who visited MP to assist the preparation of plans noticed the reluctance of MP officials to accept their suggestions. K had a feeling of *déjà vu*, of having to once again savour the frustration of developing the UP Project. UP officials at least had a semblance of justification in that the UP Project was a state project and the UP government was liable to repay 70 per cent of the amount GOI passed on to the state. DPEP was a CSS in which the amount passed on by GOI was a grant; to cock a snook at the parameters and guidelines subject to which the funding was provided and to ignore the conditions subject to which the EC provided assistance was to say the least unreasonable.

Reason being a slave of passion, the Commissioner always could find reasons for his actions. He construed decentralized planning which DPEP swore to mean that districts and states were free to plan and decide what should be done without any binding norms such as the ceiling on investment in a district or the ceiling on the outlay which could be earmarked for civil construction. To illustrate, people in the districts associated good education with a good school building and good teachers; that being so, to prevent the construction of all the school buildings needed would be centralization and not participative decentralized planning. The people in the field are the best judges of needs as well as what works; questioning the assessment of the people in field was centralization. It was another matter that he would not extend to the district functionaries the freedom to decide and judge which he demanded from DOE. To make matters worse, the Commissioner was upset that norms seemed to be 'shifting'; they were not so much shifting as evolving and getting more detailed. The transition of DPEP from an idea to a programme with clear guidelines and norms was a painful, iterative process of trial and error which occurred over about a year, and much of the transition was already accomplished by the time the planning process began in MP, and the element of uncertainty that the evolution of norms was much less in MP than in the six other states. The Commissioner who never reconciled to the DPEP guidelines was plain irritated with the seeming inconsistency of DOE in general and K in particular. Complementing the intransigence of the Commissioner was the protean flexibility of means the MP Education Secretary employed to secure fast financial approvals without having to follow either the DPEP planning process or its guidelines. A man of the world, he strongly believed that there was nothing that could not be accomplished by 'managing' the key men. He tried hard to win over K by talking as one civil servant to another, speaking about the enormity of political compulsions weighing on him, and pleading with K to be considerate. When this ploy did not work, he began to work on the members of the missions and do his very best to make them happy and massage their egos. Every mission to Bhopal was greeted by a welcome dinner at which liquor freely flowed like water. The meetings of the appraisal mission were organized in a star hotel which threw the puritanical K into a paroxysm of rage; to assuage the feelings of K, the venue was shifted to the Regional Engineering College. A Paris-based Indian consultant was bowled over, and began to lobby with fellow members of the mission to accept the plea of the MP government to do away with the 'unreasonable' ceiling on the investment in a district. However, all other members of the mission, Indian as well as European, held together in spite of the blandishments. Thereupon, the Secretary took another tack and began 'playing the man, not the ball', a tactic immortalized by *Yes, Prime Minister*, namely, of discrediting the person who was coming in the way. A campaign of *Suppressio veri, suggestio falsi* (suppressing truth and suggesting what is false) and spreading canards about K was launched, and the Education Minister and the media were enlisted in the campaign. But for the solid support of Giri and the intervention, though belated, of Arjun Singh K's standing would have been undermined, and DPEP would have collapsed even before it took off. It goes without saying that the future of DPEP was at stake; what was happening in MP was being closely watched by other states as well as the agencies. If MP were allowed to go its way, the other states would also have insisted that they be provided the same leeway as MP, and DPEP would have been reduced to being yet another CSS. K can still recall the wry remark of Middleton that it looked as though K was on the verge of being replaced by the MP Education Secretary and that, therefore, it was imperative that the Bank funding should be anchored in firm contractual arrangements rather than personal understandings which were contingent. The developments in MP were also being closely watched by the EC as well as ODA, and if MP had its way, EC would have stopped further release of funds.

The obstructionism of MP could have been nipped in the bud if Arjun Singh had been persuaded to send a clear message to the Chief Minister that he should direct his officials to extend full cooperation to K and not be obstructive. However, securing the intervention of Arjun Singh was no easy task, all the more so as the matter pertained to his own state, he had full confidence in the Chief Minister and the Education Minister who were his acolytes, and he preferred to work through his confidants and granted access rather grudgingly even for secretaries like Giri. K did from time to time submit crisp notes outlining the developments happening and the problems he was facing, and the methodical Giri used to strongly endorse K's views. However, a senior minister with heavy responsibilities and intense political involvement cannot be expected to pore over official notes, and would rely on his aides to keep him posted of the happenings in the Ministry under his charge and clear the files. From time to time, Giri did bring to the notice of the minister the problems whenever he had an opportunity to discuss matters with him, and sought his intervention. At Giri's behest, he might have spoken to the Chief Minster but perhaps not with the directness that the situation demanded. Whatever, the inevitable happened: K was put 'in the dock' not once but twice and pulled up by the Minister. Though emotionally searing, these encounters did bring home to the Minister the problems in MP in a way that no note or briefing could have, and the second encounter did bring in his decisive intervention which put an end, once and for all, to the intransigence of MP.

The Appraisal Mission (April 1994) was led by A.K. Sharma, Director, NCERT, and had 30 members, including two experts from UNESCO, ten European, and 18 Indian experts jointly chosen by DOE and EC. The Indian experts were drawn from a number of institutions such as NCERT, NIEPA, IIMs, and included practitioners such as Sister Sujitha of BEP and a DIET principal from Kerala who did splendid work in drawing up the district plan of Kasargode district. A large Indian contingent was deliberately drawn up so that the skills of project appraisal were widely disseminated and a pool of project appraisal expertise was created. Such expertise was rare but much needed as even the Bank expected the DPEP Bureau to appraise the district plans and annual work plans. As a team, the mission brought to bear on the appraisal every relevant functional expertise such as planning and management, civil works, finance and costing, tribal education, curriculum and textbooks, teacher training, NFE, and gender and early childhood education. The EC entrusted the British Council with organizing the logistics; however, it was the EC and not the British Council which chose the experts. Raymond Le Ryuet who looked after the assistance in EC headquarters was keen that the choice of experts should be diversified and not limited to those chosen by the British Council. Making a strong sales pitch, Theobald made the point that European experts who did not know much English and were strangers to India would not be as effective as British experts. Le Ryuet was keen not to ruffle the other Member States by exclusively assigning the 'business' to the British. His sensitivity to the concerns of the Member States also suited K, as he was apprehensive that DPEP-MP would be a hostage to the 'knowledgeable' India hands, and that it might be 'mothered' by British consultants the way APPEP had been. However, Theobald was a precious asset, and along with A.K. Sharma, Sajitha Bashir and J.P. Prakash did a stellar job in guiding the appraisal. J.P. Prakash was K's Man Friday who stayed put all the ten days that the Mission spent in Bhopal, keeping a close tab on the happenings with a hawk's eye and keeping K posed of the happenings as and when they occurred. Because of his quiet but dignified personality, Sharma ensured that the Mission was not a European show. Ten days prior to the arrival of the Appraisal Mission, the story 'Controversy over Revised Guidelines' appeared in the *Statesman*; the story, obviously a plant, assailed the 'astounding guidelines'. To the literary-minded K, the *Statesman* report was an opening salvo of the cannons on either side of the Valley of Death through which the Mission should plod as in *The Charge of the Light Brigade*. Unlike the British generals who ordered the charge, Theobald was very astute, and he offered the members of the Mission eminently practical advice. In the briefing session, he told the members that there was a conceptual gap in the approach of MP officials to DPEP, which was an exceptional programme, and it was very important that it made a good beginning and was well grounded. The members of the Mission should not accept vague ideas, assurances, or explanations, but would have to probe, and pose searching questions with a smile on lips. They should not give the impression that they were critical and censorious; therefore, the more difficult the question, the broader should be the smile on their lips. Any suggestion made should be SMART—specific, measurable, achievable, realistic, and time bound. Sajitha Bashir's role was no less important; with her matchless rigour and ability to get to the root of the matter in a trice, she meticulously consolidated the reports of all the members of the Mission and put together the appraisal report which pulled no punches. Among others, the report noted that appraisal could only be based on detailed plans and not ideas, and that most of the recommendations of the pre-appraisal mission were not followed to a level of detail required for full appraisal and were still at the idea stage. The state plan and district plans appeared to have been produced by a small team of very hard-working administrators without involving even senior officers of the Department of School Education, not to speak of district teams. It was important to honestly evaluate the planning process and revise planning procedures.

Even while concluding that it was unable to complete its tasks as the proposals presented did not contain sufficient detail on needs, strategies, and activities for a full appraisal, the Mission offered several concrete suggestions in each of the programme areas. With K's concurrence, it offered a practical solution to the impasse in MP. MP should give priority to the formulation of a detailed work plan for the year 1994–5 so that, in a couple of months, the plan could be appraised and a green signal given to the commencement of activities for building up the systems. Simultaneously, efforts should be made to rigorously formulate the seven-year medium-term plan within about six months. The willingness of the Mission to be practical and reasonable did not mollify the MP government functionaries who saw the 'hand' of K in the Mission failing to approve their proposals as they were. And to use a colourful phrase, they decided to go thermonuclear. After the Mission returned from the state without clearing the district plans, K was summoned to the Minister's office one late evening and given a tough dressing down by Arjun Singh. He demanded to know why K was holding back the clearance of the MP plans. When K told him that the Appraisal Mission in which foreign experts participated was not satisfied with the plans, he shot back, 'Don't tell me all that. Who are these experts? You appoint them and they raise all objections as you wish.' And then he conveyed to K the innuendo purveyed to him that K was holding up clearance as he was from AP, the state to which his arch-rival PM belonged. K feelingly replied that he was a professional, and did not play politics. As it was, he was feeling deeply hurt that Arjun Singh never even faintly acknowledged the extraordinary efforts K made to mobilize EC funding for MP; his barbed comments aggravated the deep feeling of hurt K nurtured. Figuratively, the comments were much like ripping open a raw wound and rubbing salt into the wound. K muttered within himself the Sanskrit saying *Sevadharmaha parama gahano yoginamapyagamyaha* (To serve is extremely difficult, it is difficult even for ascetics). Having administered the dressing down, to K's great surprise, Arjun Singh suddenly changed his tack. Like a good actor, he cleared his throat and asked K to help the MP officers to prepare proper plans instead of being a stern critic all the time. He did not leave it at that; he called for the MP officers who were waiting outside, chided them for carrying tales against K, and directed them to comply with K's advice. K was inclined to attribute Arjun Singh's 'hot and cold treatment' to his being a seasoned administrator as well as his being a realist who realized that K was held in such high esteem by EC and other agencies that stripping K of the DPEP charge was the surest way to jeopardize EC grant. Within a few days, support came from an unexpected source—an article by Krishna Kumar highly critical of foreign funding in general and of DPEP in MP in particular. This critique by an academic who was the Minister's favourite came in handy for Giri and K to rebut the insinuations of the MP officials. However, the decisive intervention that they expected from Arjun Singh did not occur, and K had two other emotionally searing encounters with him in June 1994 when the annual work plans came for appraisal.

So desperate were the MP government functionaries to secure the clearance that they would leave nothing to chance and mounted political pressure on the eve of the June 1994 Mission beginning its work. A few days before the Mission was to commence its work, the Chief Minister and the Education Minister met Arjun Singh and the latter came up with a long litany of complaints accusing the department, and K by implication, of prejudice. He accused DOE of applying higher standards to MP than the six other states and demanded that a comparative evaluation of all the seven states should be done. He also derisively referred to the composition of the Appraisal Mission and highlighted the fact that it included a DIET principal from Andhra. K was much hurt by the accusations, and with more emotion than desirable, replied that there was no reason why having secured the EC grant for MP, he should come in the way of it being utilized. It was preposterous to suggest that a team of 30 could be influenced by him, how, like other states, it was incumbent on the MP government to act on the recommendations of the Appraisal Mission rather than whine and whimper over the insistence that rigorous planning process should precede issue of clearances and release of funds; other states also had to undergo the same process before their proposals were approved by DOE and the Bank. Arjun Singh was naturally annoyed that, like a running sore, the matter was coming up to him again and again. However, in all likelihood, he was apparently satisfied with K's explanation, as he cryptically observed that nothing much could be expected so long as the incumbent remained the Chief Secretary, implying thereby that matters ought to be sorted out by the state government. Looking back, K should have come away from the meeting satisfied; however, being what he was, he greatly agonized over the accusations and the failure of the Minister to come put openly in his support. By happenstance, K was re-reading *War and Peace*, and given his existential condition, he readily identified himself with General Kutuzov, architect of the Russian victory against Napoleon, who stoically went about his job in spite of the emperor being dissatisfied with him, and in spite of the machinations all-around and the baseless criticism he was subjected to.

The shenanigans of the MP government functionaries were unwarranted as the June Mission went about its job of appraising the annual work plan for 1994–5 in its customary professional and objective manner. The 12-member Mission which appraised the work plans included Theobald and Sajitha Bashir and ten others who were members of the Appraisal Mission. Theobald was so much taken in by the DPEP process that when the Appraisal Mission concluded its task, he expressed his keenness to join the next mission even though he was 'exhausted by the experience but willing to try again'. The Mission did note significant progress in the formulation of the work plans and cleared specific activities with an outlay of Rs 31.5 crore; it also offered precise advice on the formulation of the medium-term perspective plan. However, the Mission was a turning point that drastically changed for better the course of DPEP in MP. Even a play with a happy ending is not free of twists; the turning around of DPEP in MP was no different. Before the Mission commenced its work, K met the chief minister at the latter's insistence; may be the meeting was at the behest of Arjun Singh. The meeting lasted about an hour, went off exceedingly well, and all air was cleared. K brought out clearly that external funding had its consequences, and that everything, including the obvious, had to be proven, more so in the case of the polyglot EC. He also established that other states had to go through the same drill and, in fact, were in a less advantageous position as the funds were not yet pledged and would be firmed only after negotiations. K showed him the aide-memoire of the World Bank's Mission (March 1994) which came out harshly on

Maharashtra and Assam. K also showed him the plan of Kasaragod with the caption eighth draft. The Chief Minister quipped, 'You say we have got off lightly'. K told him that he would not say that, but others had a tougher time. K also showed him the summary of the baseline studies conducted in other states. He was much impressed and went on to say that such studies are important, and when the learning achievement levels were so low even in Kerala, MP faced an awesome challenge. Complimenting the chief minister for the state being the first state in the country to conduct elections to the Panchayat Raj bodies after the 73rd Constitution Amendment, K told him that association of the panchayat with DPEP would go a long way in providing the much needed community support to DPEP. The real knock-out came when K pointed to him that six other states together had 23 districts as compared to the 19 in MP, and that together those states had at least six times more staff dedicated to DPEP than MP. It was therefore important that DPEP should be adequately staffed.

After the Mission completed its task, it met the Chief Minister again. A new Theobald was in action. In the meeting in Bhopal after the Appraisal Mission concluded its task about two months earlier, he preferred understatement, allusion, and ellipsis. Now his words were precise, hitting like a sledgehammer. He made it clear that his comments were not couched in diplomatic terms, and they were nonpersonal and issue based. He mentioned that the annual work plans were acceptable to the Mission; however, a lot of work had to be done in regard to the medium-term plan. He went on to say that the comments of the Appraisal Mission hit sensitive spots and touched raw nerves and were being contested; the attempt was to get locked in small details and small criticisms. The task of the mission was to scrutinize and not to please and that 'we would go with the job as is expected of us'. He made two vital points. Long stay in India convinced him that costs were often inflated, and that a detailed scrutiny was needed. He appealed to the Chief Minister not to judge the officers by the level of funding cleared, by the pot of gold, and went on to observe that 'this is not a money-squeeze programme'. He also said that with the large number of districts MP was different from the other states. The risk factor was higher. If only he could turn the clock back by seven months, he would have insisted the programme start with a manageable number of districts. However, he realized that it was too late and that 19 was a magical and historic number. In his reply, the chief minister sportingly said that he appreciated the brutal frankness and constructive criticism of Theobald. For every action, there was a reaction, so goes Newton's Law; however, unlike in Physics, it was not Theobald but K who received the flak for Theobald's candour. From the meeting, the Education Minister, the state education secretary, and K went over to the office of Arjun Singh. While travelling in the car, K told the Education Minister how he could clinch the EC funding, and how, in spite of its reluctance, he could get EC to agree for its assistance to be applied. The clearance of the 1994–5 work plans was a happy augury. However, he did not respond and was withdrawn. As soon as they reached Arjun Singh's office, the MP Education Minister and Education Secretary were ushered in while K stood outside. After a while, K was asked to meet the Minister, and as he entered the room, Arjun Singh turned to K and said with a great deal of irascibility 'your EC does not want to fund the nineteen districts'. K was taken aback as he was not prepared for the verbal assault. K told him that what mattered was the fact that the Mission cleared the work plans, that Theobald was only giving vent to the opinion prevailing in the EC that far too many districts were chosen, and that the state government seemed to be more eager to access and utilize the funds rather than implement DPEP earnestly. However, EC would not mind now all the 19 districts to be funded at the same time. K's explanation did not satisfy Arjun Singh. He wanted to know why the MP proposals were being objected to, and harshly observed that K disavowed all responsibility for pushing through the MP project and that little had happened in the previous six months. When K told him that the 1994–5 work plans could be got cleared, he said that the seven-year perspective plan was not through and demanded to know when it would be cleared. K told him that if everything went well, it could be cleared in December. Thereupon he sniped at K and wondered whether K was planting ideas in the mission. K replied that at no point did he try to influence the professional judgement of the Mission members; however, he was all along defending the decision to commence DPEP in all the 19 districts of MP. As K's inquisition was going on, he was impatient that the Chief Minister did not turn up; when he was told that the CM was held up elsewhere, he sternly asked his Private Secretary to ensure that he spoke to the Chief Minster before he left for Bhopal. Before the audience ended, he darkly observed that he would review DPEP personally a few days later after he returned from his visit to Israel. K was shell shocked and felt as if the earth gave way under his feet.

In a tightly woven play with a happy ending, there are often long-drawn-out episodes when it appears that all is lost, when the unpredictable happens. A couple of days after his traumatic encounter with Arjun Singh, K was pleasantly surprised to hear that a full-fledged director of the Rajiv Gandhi Shiksha Mission was appointed, and that the state education secretary would be moved out. The choice of the director was splendid—Amita Sharma, a highly refined lady officer with a deep interest in de-constructionist literary criticism and immense professional competence. After Arjun Singh returned from Israel, Giri met him and made it clear to him that K should not be faulted, that he was being set up as a fall guy for the acts of omission and commission of the state officials, and that but for the high professional standing of K among the agencies and his good offices the EC would have revoked its pledge to provide assistance. Giri informed K that Arjun Singh cryptically told him that he knew how to tackle the problem. Tackle, he did. K accompanied Arjun Singh to Bhopal with a great deal of trepidation, and he had a rocking headache before the meeting of the General Council on 2 July—a sign of his angst. His angst gave way to jubilation once the Chief Minister began to speak. In his address, Digvijay Singh specifically referred to K, his discussions with K, and said that planning process was important as it ensured that faults were removed at the planning stage itself and did not vitiate implementation. He said it was important to plan from below. *Yatha raja thatha praja* (As the King, so the subjects). The Education Minister said financial resources alone were not important, and that participation, proper planning, and implementation were essential. Over lunch, he thanked K for bringing out the point clearly that compared to the other states there were few officers for DPEP-MP. When he ran into K, the CS kindly inquired 'I hope we are on the right path.' If misery loves company, so does happiness. Later in the day, Arjun Singh addressed a press conference; so many turned up—to draw upon a Telugu proverb—that it appeared that the earth spawned countless journalists. He was asked whether the delay in approvals and only a meagre sum of Rs 31.5 crore being allotted for 1994–5 was not due to some misunderstanding or lack of clarity in his Ministry. He replied that what was important was the process, and that there was no mathematical formula that the entire amount of Rs. 600 crore should be equally spent over seven years. He also dismissed as canard the allegation that every district was allotted an equal amount. Of course, he was also called upon to explain why so many of his loyalists were nominated to the General Council of the Rajiv Gandhi Shiksha Mission. He replied with a square face that being a Congressman did not mean that one could not be an educationist. Soon thereafter Sumit Bose, an outstanding officer, was appointed as the Education Secretary, and R. Gopalakrishnan, Chief Minister's Secretary and one of the finest officers of his generation with an uncanny ability to manage the interface between politics and administration with professional integrity, began to be the Guardian Angel of DPEP in the state. B.V.R. Subrahmanyam, a young, brilliant officer who was hitherto assisting the Commissioner and felt cramped, could get into his own and ably assist Amita Sharma. With the change of guard, MP came to be one of the states where DPEP was very well implemented and became a pioneer in educational innovation.

Setting Record Straight

To set the record straight, it should be said that of the many ministers and chief ministers K had the privilege of working with, Arjun Singh was the minister in dealing with whom K was always tense. Even with imperious Caesar-like personalities such as N.T. Rama Rao and Channa Reddy, there were many occasions when K could feel free but there was no such occasion with Arjun Singh. Although K always did and said what he ought to, he was always on the guard in dealing with Arjun Singh. Except perhaps with his Chosen Few from MP, Arjun Singh always kept a steely reserve and his visage impassive most of the time. There were moments when irritation was writ large on his face; a sly smile was rather rare. He hardly unwound himself. His body language left no doubt that he was the boss; yet he was an active listener, rarely interrupting an officer who was saying something except when he wanted to pose a question and probe further. His preparation for the Parliament or a media session was meticulous and thorough.

It is not always true that 'The evil that men do lives after them; the good is oft interred with their bones.' With the past becoming a hazy memory, the warts get smoothened and one gets to have a more rounded and balanced assessment. What K remembers now is not so much the fact that Arjun Singh treated him differently from the Chosen Few but the fact that Arjun Singh supported him in everything that he did. It was well known that Arjun Singh sharply disagreed with the economic perspective of the PV–Manmohan Singh team and remained ill-adjusted to the liberalization initiatives of the PV government. Opening up elementary education to the World Bank was perceived by old believers opposed to economic liberalization as of a piece with the 'accursed neo-liberal policies' of the PV government. Yet Arjun Singh steadfastly supported K and the department at every step on file, in media, and in the Parliament. Thus, he refuted in the Lok Sabha on 3 May1994 a 'common point' made by some MPs that 'for externally aided projects we have accepted conditions which are totally untenable and which compromise our freedom in the sphere of education'. He quoted chapter and verse from the resolutions of CABE at its meetings of 8–9 May 1991, and 6 May 1992, and asserted that the parameters those resolutions laid down for tapping external resources were being meticulously complied with, and that this ensured that external funding did not lead to dependency syndrome. When Prem Dhumal, an MP (and later Chief Minister of Himachal Pradesh), claimed that the EC imposed a condition that a a certain percentage of the grant should be spent on staff and consultants, he bluntly told Dhumal:

> I am sorry that somebody had misinformed you. That is the point. We have laid down for ourselves—not by them—a condition that in the amounts available for this aided project not more than six percent should be spent on administration. That is our condition. They did not lay down any condition.

Dhumal was gracious enough to say, 'We are happy.'

Arjun Singh might have extended support due to his realism and for the same reason why as Chairman of the group of ministers to consider the question of accession to the World Trade Organization (WTO) treaties he did not come out against accession. Whatever be his personal views on the accession, realistically there was no alternative to accession. Likewise, given the macroeconomic situation, and given that the government banked on the World Bank and the Western countries to bail it out of the dire economic straits, there was no alternative to conceding the World Bank's long-standing desire to include elementary education in its loan portfolio in India. It was said of Sir Olaf Caroe of the ICS who was the British Raj's last Foreign Secretary that he would not take even the security provided by the Himalayas for granted; likewise Arjun Singh would not take anything on trust. It was only after ensuring that whatever K was doing was the best deal possible and in country's interests would he extend support. However, in the ultimate what matters are decision and action and not the motive. Civil servants should expect no more from a minister than his having a clear head, being decisive, and supporting them from unfair attacks. They cannot demand that they be liked and admired for doing what is their duty however well they do it. By that measure, Arjun Singh was an outstanding minister, and K is beholden to him for his kindness.

XVIII

GANGA DESCENDS FROM HEAVEN

Figuratively, the transformation of DPEP from an idea to a programme ready for implementation was like the descent of the Ganga (Ganges) from the heavens. Legend has it that Bhagiratha vowed to bring Ganga down to Earth so that her waters could cleanse the souls of his ancestors and release them to heaven; he had to face so many hurdles that, in Indian languages, *Bhagiratha Prayatna* has come to be a renowned metaphor for denoting superhuman effort to achieve one's objective without being deterred by countless seemingly insurmountable hurdles. The ordeals of DPEP were no less arduous. The agreement with EC which blazed a new trail of development cooperation and spawned a financial innovation necessitated battling against heavy odds. Decision-making by EC was necessarily cumbersome given that it was new to the 'aid business', and had inadequate understanding of the SSN operation in spite of the fact that it sought to provide assistance as a co-financier of the Bank's SSN operation. Many in the EC were doubtful about the ability of DOE to properly utilize the assistance EC offered, and consequently insisted that EC consultants should be placed in DOE and in the field to manage DPEP, and to check whether enrolment, retention, and pace of project activities were being truthfully reported by undertaking audits in the sample districts. Accepting assistance on such terms would have been a Faustian bargain and detracted from the objective of capacity development. Many in EC were unhappy at DOE's insistence that the EC funds be applied only to the implementation of

DPEP in only one state, namely MP. The EC Ambassador in Delhi went out of her way to thwart DOE by trying to play on the rivalry between Arjun Singh and the Prime Minister. It was imperative to keep the Germans in good humour and not break off the dialogue with them in spite of the unacceptable conditions they insisted for assistance to the South Orissa Project lest they should use their formidable clout in the EC to thwart a deal. A multi-state programme with multiple sources of funding necessitated pioneering of institutional and process innovation such as joint review and reporting mechanisms, and getting the funding agencies accept the innovations. Getting the states to accept DPEP was not easy; some such as Tamil Nadu exerted enormous pressure on DOE to let them avail bank assistance for 'state projects' for areas such as secondary education which had lower priority than primary education. Given that DPEP was a home-grown programme which sought shunned expatriate technical assistance altogether, and field functionaries lacked the skills of planning, programme development, and implementation, it was necessary to work against entropy, pool the academic resources that lay dispersed among different resource institutions across the length and breadth of the country, and orient the academics to the specific requirements of DPEP. Tackling mindset issues was more formidable than technical aspects such as instilling the technical capacity to develop district plans and implement them. The bitter conflict with MP vividly brings out the challenge K and his colleagues faced in convincing their colleagues in the states that DPEP was not yet another CSS, that 'business as usual' would not do, that funds would be released only on the basis of work plans that passed the test of appraisal, and that planning could not be a resource-driven calculation. The turmoil in the Bank that the Wapenhans Report triggered threatened to derail DPEP. To get the EC, the Bank, and the states to accept the society mode of implementation was a *Bhagiratha prayathna* (Herculean task) in itself. As if these tribulations were not enough, there was an unending chorus that the 'sky is falling' and a fusillade of criticism the future of Indian education was being mortgaged to foreign agencies. Or to mix the metaphor, getting DPEP to move ahead was like the voyage on Noah's Ark. The Bible itself does not describe the problems Noah had in getting on board the different species of living beings. However, with DPEP getting everyone concerned—the agencies, states, Planning Commission, Ministry of Finance, GOI, and the faculty of NCERT and

NIEPA—on board was an awesome task. Designing and developing the Ark was far simpler. In July 1994, negotiations with the World Bank were concluded in Washington, funds for the six DPEP states were firmed up, and DPEP was ready for implementation. In retrospect, the flip flop of the Bank delayed the launch of implementation in June 1994 by just a month. Unexpectedly, however, the launch was delayed by three more months to get the Department of Economic Affairs (DEA), Ministry of Finance, to relent and accept DOE's request that irrespective of the source of funding funds should be released to the states for implementation of DPEP only as grant. Thus, the organizational dynamics within the government contributed more delay than securing external funding.

Wheels of Government Grind Slow

Nowhere is the famous American saying 'it ain't over till it is over' more valid than in the Indian Government. Rather strangely, there are two antithetical dimensions of the 'indecisiveness' of senior functionaries in the government. As experienced lobbyists know the system has infinite flexibility, and that given tenacity and perseverance there is nothing one could not secure from the government, a fact that is crisply conveyed in a remark of K.B. Lall, an ICS officer with enormous experience in industry and international trade, to a corporate executive:

> You may find us indecisive and dilatory, but compared with the British civil servant, you enjoy an advantage that is most worthwhile. When my counterpart in Whitehall makes up his mind, it is made up; there is no further argument. But when we decide, if the decision does not suit you, you can always come back, and the door will be open.... We remain indecisive even when we have decided.[1]

The other dimension of 'remaining indecisive even when we have decided' is that securing a final clearance for any programme particularly if off the beaten track is often excruciatingly tortuous. Once the Cabinet Committee had accorded an in-principle to DPEP, one would not expect the basics of the programme such as the rationale of the

[1] Prakash Tandon, *Return to Punjab*, Berkeley: University of California Press, 1981, p. 29.

programme and broad features to be questioned, but they were not once but time and again.

Neither his bookish knowledge nor his previous administrative experience could erase entirely K's belief that administrative decision-making and implementation ought to be predominantly exercises in rationality which do not allow subjectivity and that if all the information necessary is collected and the analysis is rigorous, there could only be one rational decision or one way of doing things. From his perspective, DPEP was anchored in a better strategy to achieve UPE than the extant approach, and its design was robust and cost-effective. Being so, consideration by the Finance Ministry and the Planning Commission should focus on examining whether the strategy underlying DPEP was indeed better and, if so, whether it could be further improved, whether the design was robust and cost-effective and, if so, how the design could be further improved, and whether the planning and implementation mechanisms could be further improved. The meetings in the Department of Expenditure and Planning Commission totally skipped consideration of these basic questions, and centred on procedural questions and an attempt to downsize, if not scuttle, the programme. The functionaries of the Department of Expenditure viewed it as yet another proposal for expenditure with no regard for its distinctiveness or what it might do to hasten UPE. To their mind, the fact that the resources were mobilized from external agencies was of little consequence as the Bank loan cast an obligation on the government to repay the loan, however soft the terms might be. And further, after funding by the Bank ceased, the programme might create huge liabilities which had to be discharged from budgetary resources. The questions they posed were routine questions which would have been posed in regard to any other proposal for the central government funding the state governments. The whole exercise of scrutiny was driven by the belief that benefit was a questionable hypothesis and cost was an understated certainty. The proximate objectives of the scrutiny were to downsize the programme and pare down costs; the ultimate objective was to curtail public expenditure and maintain a strong ways and means position. To some extent, K could understand the routine examination by 'bean counters' (the functionaries of the Department of Expenditure), for the highest priority of Finance was to avoid illiquidity, not being able to meet financial liabilities that cannot be avoided and postponed.

However, the approach of the Project Appraisal Division (PAD) of the Planning Commission totally baffled K. K expected that PAD's analysis would be informed by methods of project appraisal and economic reasoning. K himself considered economic reasoning to be precious and strongly believed that it should inform every aspect of administration, and at Harvard, he acquired a good grounding in methodologies of project appraisal. He eagerly looked forward to the findings of the appraisal of DPEP. To his dismay, the comments of that division were the very antithesis of what a sound appraisal ought to be; the focus was on expenditure without any consideration of the strategy underlying DPEP or its design. However, administration was warfare, not campaigning on the large scale in which you annihilate the enemy or at least his capability to fight but a series of skirmishes in which you have to prevail. As he reflected on his experience, K recognized that there was a 'method behind the madness' of the 'organized obstructionism', and 'tyranny' of Finance. World over an organization, every established organization, be it a private company or a government department, has a standardized routine approach to fulfil its mandate, to ensure regular and coordinated action, to achieve minimum acceptable levels of performance, and, more importantly, to avoid serious failure. Actions based on such an approach constitute precedents, and as the eminent jurist Benjamin Cardozo put it, 'What has once been settled by a precedent will not be unsettled overnight, for certainty and uniformity are gains not lightly sacrificed'.[2] What distinguishes a senior officer from his subordinates is his willingness and ability to recognize a situation in which standard routine approaches are not adequate, grasp the larger picture without being conditioned by a tunnel vision and act as the larger picture required. While many mature civil servants do act according to that norm, their first impulse is to stick to the conventional approach of the department in which they work. B.P.R. Vithal, a veteran state finance secretary, used to say that he wanted in his department cultivated and not congenital idiots who, after subjecting proposals to the test of attrition, would, at the end of it all, discover reasons to approve a proposal if it is really meritorious or if politically it cannot be helped.

[2] Benjamin N. Cardozo , *The Paradoxes of Legal Science,* New York: Columbia University Press, 1928, pp. 29–30.

The mother of all issues which delayed internal approvals was the manner in which DOE would pass on the funds to the state societies. The consistent policy of DEA had been that the central government would pass on to the states as a grant the funds it received as a grant from an external agency; in case of loan received from an external agency, it would pass on only 30 per cent as grant and the rest as loan to be repaid by the state government. The rationale for differential financing norms was that the state government should share with the central government the burden of repaying the loan as well as the foreign exchange risk. That rationale could not be faulted if the project funded was a 'state project' which, in principle, the state government was expected to finance from its own resources. However, DPEP was not a 'state project' but a CSS wherein the central government funded the state governments in a uniform manner. It would have been odd if MP were to receive funds for DPEP as a grant merely because the EC assistance slotted to that state was a grant while six states wherein DPEP was financed by raising a Bank loan had to repay to the central government 70 per cent of the funds. Had DPEP been a domestically funded programme or financed by similar types of agencies, namely either from those providing assistance as a grant or from those providing assistance as a loan, DEA could have persevered with its policy. The problem arose because DPEP was funded by multiple sources. It was not as if DEA was unaware of DOE's stance; at every stage of processing of the Bank credit for the first DPEP Project, DEA was associated; its representatives who attended the wrap-up meetings of the Bank missions were aware that the DPEP guidelines as well as the project proposal clearly stated that funds would be passed on to state societies as a grant, and further that Bank appraised the project and assessed the fiscal sustainability of the project on the basis that the states would not be required to repay any part of the assistance received to the central government. And further, DEA had given population control a special dispensation whereby IDA loan was passed on the states wholly as grant. It was plain common sense that DEA should treat the loan secured for DPEP on par with that for population control. This was all the more so as DEA pushed DOE all along to avail Bank funding for primary education so that the IDA allocated to the country on soft terms could be fully availed and the fast-disbursing EC grant could be availed. But then common sense is uncommon, and does not usually guide the functioning of organizations and of functionaries. It was therefore nothing unusual for the DEA functionaries to act according to a narrow perception of their mandate. Their job was to maximize the inflow of concessional foreign assistance flows by encouraging other departments to pose projects to funding agencies, critically examine the financial aspects of flows such as procurement, and financial and economic conditionalities, and prevail upon the departments to utilize the assistance as rapidly as possible so that the external agency disburses the assistance as fast as possible; anything else was not their business. The DEA officials did not bother to examine the implications of DOE implementing DPEP with two types of external assistance, a grant as well as a loan. Worse, they took quite a few months to realize that DOE's request was the logical consequence of going by their advice and availing two types of external assistance. K was struck by a similar obtuseness in the matter of utilizing the fast-disbursing EC grant for a medium-term educational programme. The manner in which that issue was resolved offers a good case study of the decision-making process when a department has to depart from a past practice. In order to secure a favourable decision before the impending negotiations with the Bank in Washington, Arjun Singh was prevailed upon to take up the matter with the Finance Minister. A 'summit meeting' was held on 15 July 1994 which was inconclusive as Manmohan Singh was not as yet prepared to concede DOE's request to treat IDA loans for DPEP on par with loans for population control. When Arjun Singh strongly pressed his department's case, Manmohan Singh told him that he was not disinclined to treat primary education on par with population control; however, more discussion was needed before the matter was brought before CCEA for a final view. As the negotiations in Washington were just a few days away, it was decided that the government representatives would not raise the matter.

Negotiations in Washington: 20–25 July 1994

In contrast to the previous two negotiations with the Bank in which K participated, he was now the elder statesman, much like R.K. Mishra, Health Secretary, at the SSN negotiations. He left the nitty-gritty of negotiations to Vrinda who preceded him to Washington. Apart from dealing with the bankers, her hands were full keeping happy the six state education secretaries who joined the negotiations but had little role. There were hardly any serious issue to be negotiated and the negotiations would have been a non-event but for Murphy's Law (Anything that can go wrong will go wrong). At the negotiations in Washington, K found that truth was stranger than fiction, and that the DEA's representative was not aware of his minister's decision not to raise the matter of how the state societies would be funded. K's game plan for the negotiations was to get on with negotiations, and at some stage, he would casually mention to Middleton that the issue was unresolved and that he expected to secure a favourable decision from CCEA soon, well before the Bank loan became effective. It is axiomatic that the first casualty in a battle is the battle plan, however well drawn the plan might be. True to that saying, on 20 July, as soon as K reached Washington for negotiations, Vrinda met him and told him with a bit of concern that the previous day the DEA representative, *suo motto*, raised the question of pattern of assistance to the states. As expected, this pushed Middleton and Marlaine into a tailspin; Middleton hinted that given the stance of DEA a fresh appraisal was necessary, and that there was no purpose in carrying on with the negotiations. K was put in a tight spot. The DEA representative's bloomer sent Kumud Bansal and Jayanthi—education secretaries of Maharashtra and Tamil Nadu—also into a tizzy, rightly so, for they legitimately felt that the states were taken for a ride. However, K could persuade Middleton to complete the negotiations on the assurance that the issue would be resolved to the satisfaction of DOE.

Waiting for Godot

August went by, and September was about to pass by without the issue being resolved. The consideration of the project by the Bank's Executive Board was on hold, and the implementation stalled even though the six states were ready to begin with implementation by June itself. K came to know that DEA was still unwilling to concede DOE's request in the mistaken belief that the Bank would not like the IDA credit to be passed on to states as grant, and that even if the DPEP funding was passed on part as loan and part as grant, there was no need for any further reappraisal and exchange of side letters would do. It turned out that DEA's assessment of the Bank's view was incorrect.

After a few weeks, without much ado DEA conceded the request of DEA that irrespective of the source of external funding the central government would finance 85 per cent of the outlay as grant and pass on that grant to the state societies. A few weeks later, CCEA formally approved DPEP. Needless to say, if DPEP were domestically funded it would have been far more difficult to secure approvals, particularly on the scale with which it began. With DEA conceding the request of DOE, the *Sturm und Drang* (storm and stress) phase of DPEP was over.

Skirmishes Continue

From the perspective time provides, November 1994 was the turning point for DPEP, as all things fell in place. In October 1994, the Finance Ministry came round and accepted the principle that irrespective of the source and pattern of funding by an agency which supported DPEP, the central government would release funds to the states only as grant. On 22 November 1994, the Board of the World Bank approved an IDA credit of US $260.3 million for implementation of DPEP in six states; three months earlier, in August 1994, the European Community released the first tranche of its programme assistance in terms of the Finance Agreement negotiated in July 1994. Consequently, in November 1994, DOE could issue all the necessary approvals and release funds for the implementation of DPEP in the seven states of Assam, Haryana, Karnataka, Kerala, MP, Maharashtra, and Tamil Nadu. With that DPEP has entered a new phase, moving from one of planning and pre-project activities to implementation of the 1994–5 work plans. The squashing of unilateral declaration of independence by MP, the very state from which Arjun Singh hailed, sent the message loud and clear to each and every state that they had no option but to fall in line with the DPEP framework and guidelines if DPEP were to be implemented in a state. Even though it was not realized then, it is now clear that the war was won and the period of struggle was over; a few skirmishes here and there were unlikely to significantly take away the fruits of the war won. In retrospect, the skirmishes which seemed so large then were inconsequential. To use imagery used earlier, by end November 1994 the Valley of the Shadow of Death was traversed, a snare here or there and the gnawing Giant Despair of which K could not be free because of his temperament did not endanger DPEP (Chapter XVI). As K looks back, there were two major snares which threatened to trap DPEP and stall its progress: a new poverty alleviation initiative of the Bank which was warmly espoused by DEA, and ODA's conditions for funding DPEP in AP and West Bengal.

It is natural for every organization as well as a unit of an organization to try to expand its activities, and the India Country Division of the Bank is no exception. The officers of the Division such as Vergin and Skolnik were much taken with DPEP and saw in it a valuable model for poverty alleviation which was the core of Bank's operations ever since poverty was discovered by the Bank during the McNamara presidency. They conceived a new operation which went by the name of District Poverty Initiative Program (DPIP), and Ashok, an IAS officer of the UP cadre who was with DEA earlier and now a consultant with the Bank in Washington, was chosen as the anchor of the programme. As set out earlier about 30 months earlier, during the SSN operation, the World Bank suggested inclusion of like employment generation programmes in the SSN operation (Chapter XIII). But the government did not agree for the inclusion. This did not prevent DEA from embracing DPIP, and with its concurrence, the Bank mounted a mission to some states. When K heard of DPIP, he was initially happy as imitation was the best form of flattery; however, his mood swung to the other extreme when he learnt that primary education would be one of the components of DPIP, and that component would be independent of DPEP. It appeared that DOE might not have a role in the development and implementation of DPIP, and that the herculean efforts taken to ensure that the Bank financed only DPEP and not conventional brick-and-mortar primary education projects would turn out to be futile. The threat did not last long for the failure of DEA to consult the Ministry of Rural Development (MORD)—the nodal Ministry for alleviation of rural poverty—before mounting the Mission turned to be the undoing of DPIP. K was present at a high-level meeting in DEA which turned out to be a slanging match between the representatives of DEA and MORD. B.N. Yugandhar, Secretary, MORD, was dead set against DPIP; he made it clear that it made no sense to subject oneself to an intrusive supervision by the Bank when the Bank would contribute only a small proportion of the expenditure incurred by the government. He would not buy the argument that engaging the Bank would help improve the efficiency of the poverty alleviation programmes; he contended that agency functionaries were inclined to pass sweeping judgements based on limited experience. He illustrated the hubris of agency functionaries by referring to the imperious demand of a UNICEF functionary who demanded to know from Yugandhar why a hand pump installed by UNICEF in a remote village of Orissa was not functioning. He would not mind if the Bank supported promotion of rural industries which was central to the strategy of industrialization set out in the Second Five-Year Plan, and which, according to him, played an important role in the development of China. He bemoaned the fact that after Mahalanobis there was no coherent thinking on development strategy, and after the Second Five-Year Plan rural industries were neglected. Bimal Jalan, India's representative on the Bank's Executive Board and a distinguished economic administrator, who was present in the meeting, told him that there was no longer any constituency for rural industry. Soon after the meeting, Yugandhar became the Secretary to the Prime Minister, and with that, DPIP was still born, and the threat that DPIP posed to DPEP gone. DPIP is an example of the fact that ideas might fade away but not die for ever, and might stage reappearance in a different incarnation. It was revived in 2001 as a vehicle for supporting self-help groups of women to improve their livelihoods and community infrastructure. DPIP projects were launched in a few states such as AP, MP, and Rajasthan. Looking back, the Bank did not finance any primary education programme other than DPEP and its progeny SSA, even when occasions arose when it could get away by financing primary education differently. DPIP was such an occasion; yet another occasion was the development and approval of AP Economic Restructuring Loan (APERL) (Chapter X). In 1996, with the agreement of the Finance Minister P. Chidambaram, the Bank's new country Director, Edwin Lim, put in place a new strategy to directly engage states and offer loans for adjustment and sectoral reform, and Chandrababu Naidu, Chief Minister of AP, became the public face of the Bank's new strategy. APERL with a hefty loan of $543 million was the first of the series of Bank loans extended to AP over the next six years. From 1995, DPEP was being implemented in five districts of AP with ODA assistance, and APERL financed the coverage of 14 more districts. This project incorporated *in toto* the DPEP objectives and parameters, and turned out to be no more than an additional financial line for DPEP. The Bank's attempt to have a more direct policy dialogue did create some tensions but it mattered little as the dialogue had no impact on the design or modalities of implementation or the nodal role of DOE in regard to DPEP. Presumably, the Bank was, on the whole, too happy with DPEP and the education reform that DPEP promoted to upset the apple cart. So were the state functionaries; if they were not, they could have insisted that APERL finance primary education in a different way, and given the extraordinary clout Chandrababu Naidu with the NDA government and the World Bank, there was no way that DOE could have stalled the demand of AP. It might have been requiem for DPEP as other states which wished to secure privileged access to Bank funds might have emulated AP in the matter of primary education also. It is because of this possibility that the negotiations with ODA on funding DPEP in AP and West Bengal acquire a salience of proportion to the quantum of funds extended.

With the imminent end of Phase II of APPEP in about a year, in mid-1993 ODA expressed its firm interest in supporting DPEP in five districts each of AP and West Bengal. Support to West Bengal by ODA was particularly welcome as it came in handy to extend DPEP to West Bengal ruled by the Left Front government who might not have been willing to come into the DPEP fold were the Bank to support DPEP. In retrospect, getting ODA and the ODA-assisted states on board was far less taxing than getting EC, World Bank, MP, and Tamil Nadu on board; however, back in 1995 it did not appear so and there were tense moments during the interactions with the state government and ODA. It was easier to handle West Bengal despite the fact that the teacher unions as well as administration of primary education were highly politicized, the main reason being that unlike AP the state was new to external funding of primary education; figuratively it was a clean slate on which DPEP framework and methodology could be neatly written without wiping out the undesirable features of any earlier project funded by an agency. In contrast, APPEP was under implementation for about a decade; thanks to APPEP in-service teacher training was systemically planned, DIETs became functional earlier than in other states, the training infrastructure was deepened by the establishment of sub-district resource centres, and activity-based learning was introduced on a large scale. DPEP sought to mainstream these good features of APPEP all over the country, or to use a neologism coined by Kenneth King, an internationally renowned scholar on aid to education who visited different externally funded projects in July 1994, promote the *APPEP-ization of DPEP*. However, at the same time APPEP had to be *DPEP-ized* if UEE were to be achieved, for the scope of APPEP was limited to construction of school buildings and teacher training, and more importantly, if the planning and implementation capacity of the State Education Department were to be developed. Conditioned by his APPEP and BEP experiences, minimizing the interface between the agency funding a programme and the state government, functionaries came to be an article of faith for K; he was convinced that otherwise the functionaries in the field could not develop their capacity for planning and implementation of basic education projects. Ever since ODA evinced its interest to fund DPEP, K's single-point agenda was to close down ODA's Hyderabad project office and ensure that the interface between the state government and agency functionaries did not deviate a bit from the DPEP frame and guidelines which limited the interface to biannual joint review missions with functionaries of agencies and GOI nominees working together as a team. It was the interface which emerged as make or break point in the negotiations with ODA.

Right from the day ODA expressed its firm interest in funding DPEP, K brought ODA into the DPEP consultative process and supervision mechanisms in the belief that DPEP had so much to show that those who came to scoff might remain to pray. K's belief was proved right as the Delhi-based education officials of ODA were much impressed and willing to fall in line. The association of David Theobald with the missions to MP was a big bonanza, for he could send a clear message that ODA could live with DPEP framework and guidelines, and the message conveyed by a senior functionary of ODA like him had great weight. However, old habits die hard, and it was not that easy to break the cosy relationship that ODA developed with the state government over a decade, and quite a few within ODA who were keen on that relationship, thereby ensuring—adapting the famous maxim of Clausewitz—that DPEP in AP was APPEP by another means. Consequently, the negotiations were prolonged and had many tense, bitter moments as ODA insisted on retaining its Hyderabad office and not limiting field visits to biannual joint review missions. Around that time the British left Hong Kong; referring to that historic event, K would tell his deputies that 'we should liberate AP from the British' and that 'we should break the spell the British cast over the officials of the APPEP project office'. Eventually British pragmatism prevailed, and ODA accepted DPEP parameters as it recognized that DPEP was the only game going in the town and that an agency which seeks to join the EFA bandwagon in India should either join DPEP in accordance with the DPEP framework for agency support or else opt out from assisting primary education in India. By February 1995, negotiations with ODA were satisfactorily concluded. By then, preparations for the massive second DPEP project funded by the Bank and covering 92 districts had begun. It was as clear as day light that by the end of 1995, the objective of covering all major states with one externally funded basic education or other would be fulfilled. Given the sensitivity of the areas, K toyed with the idea of funding DPEP in the Northeast and Jammu and Kashmir with domestic funding. With the possibility of a DPEP project being posed to the Bank every year, he was sure that in a few years of time all the districts in India would be covered by DPEP, and that sooner than later DPEP would be extended to upper primary stage. Figuratively, Noah's Ark could steadily and majestically move forward without being caught in whirlpools as the Ganga had descended from the hills to the plains.

Proof of the Pudding Is in Eating

Once implementation began in November 1994, DPEP acquired a new focus. Hitherto DPEP had three foci: (*a*) project development in a self-reliant mode; (*b*) accessing external funding for a home-grown national programme on terms which would avoid dependency and ensure that the programme was driven by DOE and not the agencies; and (*c*) all the necessary approvals of the central government were obtained. Hereafter implementation became the primary focus. In the beginning, the implementation of any programme calls for meticulous attention to details such as staffing, financing, and orientation and training of the functionaries. Further as it rightly said, the first casualty of a battle is the battle plan; assumptions go awry, and unanticipated challenges appear. That apart, World Bank–funded projects face special challenges, the most important of which is to get state and district functionaries make a sense of the arcane procurement policies. In addition to all these challenges, DPEP faced two special challenges arising from its distinctiveness. First, it had to put in place a communication system which would promote a shared vision of DPEP among all the functionaries at all levels of administration in all the participating states, convince them that the DPEP's strategy of organized decentralization provided them not only flexibility in planning and implementation but also a great opportunity to innovate and experiment, and facilitate wide dissemination and adaption all over the country of good practices and innovations tried anywhere in the country (Chapter XIV). The basic concern was whether the essential concepts of DPEP have been internalized adequately by all the functionaries concerned so that they continually inform implementation and DPEP did not degenerate into yet another programme of the government with 'more of the same' and 'business as usual'. Central to the communication strategy adopted was the use of umpteen workshops and meetings as bully pulpits to expound a clear message that the distinctiveness of DPEP should not be lost sight of in implementation, and the publication of a monthly newsletter *DPEP Calling*. The second challenge was to put in place systems for supervision and monitoring which would fulfil two objectives. The first was to design systems for supervision and monitoring which foster a new culture of accountability and outcome orientation, and at the same time, meet the satisfactions and requirements of each and every agency funding the programme.

It should be said to the credit of Adrian Verspoor who succeeded Middleton as Bank's Task Manager and considered within the Bank to be a *mahaguru* of supervision that he agreed to treat Bank funding of DPEP as Sector Investment lending, and with that for all purposes there were no hurdles left to the development of a unitary supervision system. He also agreed to the principle that while the supervision missions of agencies would do a few spot checks in the field, they would be concerned mainly with the delivery by the DPEP Bureau and the state societies. It was agreed that every six months a joint supervision mission (JSM) would review the progress in implementation of DPEP by analysing the various progress reports and by visits to the field; among others, the JSM would review the project outputs, progress toward educational outcomes, institutional development, and financial flows as compared to the goals set in the annual work plans. Each joint review mission (JRM) would comprise representatives of the agencies funding the programme and DOE; by turns, the agencies and GOI would nominate leaders of the JRMs. For the first time in the world, a country was associated with the agencies in the supervision missions as an equal partner; it was yet another recognition by the agencies of the fact the DPEP Bureau would play almost exactly the role of the agencies in traditional projects, undertaking much of the detailed appraisal and supervision work typically carried out by them. DOE decided that other agencies that are likely to support DPEP such as ODA and UNICEF should be invited to join the JRM. Association with JRMs proved useful in convincing ODA about the merit of DPEP. It was also helpful in enlisting UNICEF for communication and advocacy, areas in which it had a strong comparative advantage. Not every agency functionary was happy with this arrangement, a fact captured by a remark that the joint supervision mission was not supervision but review mission. In 1999, the reality that the joint missions reviewed the progress and did not supervise was acknowledged in 1998 by the re-labelling of the missions as JRMs. Supervision was recognized to be the job of DOE, while the agencies participated in the JRMs to confirm and verify the supervision results. In order to discharge its supervisory role, DPEP Bureau initially mounted supervision missions of its own for every quarter intervening between one JSM and the next. In view of complaints from states that these internal supervision mission cast a heavy burden and interfered with programme implementation, after a few years they were given and replaced by mid-year reviews of progress and despatch of ad hoc missions to problematic states. Over the course of time, the procedure for the conduct of JRMs got standardized. In a calendar year, the first JRM made field visits as well as analyses the documents provided to it and the second did only *desk review*, that is to say, did not make field visits and relied only the documents provided and presentations made. Before the draft aide-memoire of the JRM was discussed with the states, it was reviewed by the DPEP Bureau; as elaborated above in connection with the UP Basic Education Project, it became second nature for K to minutely pore through every word and even punctuation marks in the draft aide-memoire, search for layers of meaning which might not be apparent, and fight over every questionable word with the mission as if dear life depended on victory (Chapter IX). The process initiated by K became custom as his deputies and successors followed that process. When K introduced the process, his objective was not to whitewash any inadequacy in implementation or any failure to fulfil a commitment given to the previous JRM but to ensure that there were no factual inaccuracies, and that the basic understandings with the agencies were not subtly diluted through formulations. However, a discerning observer such as Shanti Jagannathan, who was K's comrade-in-arms in the development of DPEP and later continued to be associated with DPEP as well as SSA, was of the view that the preview process 'somewhat limited the scope of critical assessments of programme developments.[3] K has to plead *mea culpa*.

Au Revoir

For about a year after the implementation of DPEP began, K continued to steer DPEP; he ensured that all systems were put in place, the Bank agreed to finance a mammoth second DPEP Project covering 92 districts in 11 states of Assam, Gujarat, Haryana, Himachal Pradesh, Karnataka, Kerala, MP, Maharashtra, Orissa, Tamil Nadu, and UP, and that the planning process for that project went on stream smoothly. K was promoted in DOE itself in December 1995, and with that elevation, K ceased to steer DPEP. And 21 months later, he was further promoted and bid goodbye to DOE itself. As he was about to leave, K penned his farewell message *Let Not the Dead Seize the Living*; in that, K offered his assessment of what was accomplished, and the challenges and threats ahead:

> What has been accomplished is a marvellous *tour de force* but history is replete with many examples where a battle has been won but the war has been lost. Let there be no illusion that we have touched anything but the fringes of the complex problem that DPEP is set to solve. There is the perennial danger that at the end of the day nothing but the brick and mortar approach would prevail. There is need to collectively work, evolve and practice the praxis of improving the content and process of education.
>
> Programmes no less than individuals and nations cannot inhabit too long in their rarefied air of idealism. Rather than counting on

[3] Shanti Jagannathan, 'Programme-based Approaches and International Collaboration: Experiences and Lessons from Education Sector', paper presented to LEPNA Forum, 'Programme-based Approaches to Diversity: Adapting to Diversity', Tokyo, 1–3 June 2004, p. 9.

heroes and heroic efforts a long and arduous process like DPEP calls for institution building and rejuvenation. The management structures at all levels, national, state and district are still inadequate; strategic planning on the future of the national structure should commence. In the Ninth Five Year Plan more domestic resources are expected to be provided for elementary education as a result of the Prime Minister's announcement on the six per cent GDP norm; it is legitimate to expect that considerable domestic resources would flow into DPEP and over 300 districts, including all the low female literacy districts, would be covered. What are its implications for the national structure? Should it be hived off as an educational trust or bank? What would be the long term arrangements for technical support of the programme? These need to be worked out and necessary approvals obtained. Rather than emerge as a leviathan it should emerge as a lean and effective organisation working with other organisations in a matrix network, promoting a variety of approaches and cross fertilisation of ideas and experiences in a country which is the microcosm of the developing world. Similar exercises need to be carried out in states and districts.

While a beginning has been made to work with local communities, we are still far away from the task of grappling with the task of training and orienting the communities. Then there is the huge inert land mass of educational administration; it needs to be stirred up. The training strategies to improve the functionality of educational administration need to be worked out and implemented.

There can be no academic renewal unless SCERTs are rejuvenated and DIETs operationalised; in many states DIETs are not fully and properly supported, the facilities have not been established as envisaged and there are no plans for staff development. It appears as though the brick and mortar approach is engulfing the institutional innovation of DIET. Openness should be the cardinal principle of institutional reform. Instead of being inward-bound and inward-looking institutions should work in co-operation with other institutions and NGOs. Networking is still in the realm of ideas; concrete plans have to be drawn for networking. One should not minimize the organisational complexities or the intricacies of coalition or alliance building.

While thinking on academic aspects has begun, the enormity of the tasks cannot be minimised. We have not yet touched earnestly, except perhaps in MP, alternatives to schooling; the nitty-gritty of gender and tribal education has to be detailed and the special needs of physically handicapped needs to be addressed. Now that NCERT has revised the

MLLs, the pedagogic and teacher training tasks need to be addressed with dispatch and resolve.

The praxis of planning continues to be weak; while the impact of the learning experience on the planning in the three new States gives us hope, the need to document the learning experience and be in a position to advise the States what to do rather than what not to do is crucial. There should be greater rigour in the preparation of the annual work plans.

While much has been accomplished in the conduct and analysis of baseline achievement surveys, the methodologies, conduct of surveys and analysis need to be honed. The quality of the data so far collected is such that inter-state comparison cannot be robust. More importantly, there is need to develop a macro-analytic frame linking these surveys with classroom observations and equally importantly extract and disseminate the findings that have a bearing on quality and achievement to practitioners. The connection between research and action is weak. While quantitative indicators are important, qualitative indicators and assessment are equally important. The management of external finances is a sensitive area; bargains tend to obsolesce. Apart from vigilance, reversal of the knowledge asymmetry is paramount. Apart from deep knowledge of the education sector, we should continue to acquire a deep understanding of the operations, operational styles and mind-set of providers of finance, and the analytical capacity to weigh options and to make intelligent choices. Only then can we effectively continue to coordinate the activities of agencies.

To paraphrase the UNESCO Constitution, it is in the minds of men that failure begins and it is in the minds of men that safeguards against failure should be built. DPEP is as much psychological struggle with uncongenial mind sets of which the brick and mortar approach is only one. One has to combat cynicism in all its manifestations. There is the low brow cynicism exemplified by the witticism that teacher can be transferred but not transformed. One has to disregard worldly-wise men, the 'voice of reason'. More pernicious is the high-brow cynicism which masquerades as idealism, which posits that nothing can change unless the total system changes. Totalism is often an elegant alibi for inaction, or worse the royal road to totalitarianism. There is some merit in attempting a change for the better in one's limited domain.

Inaction also springs from the lure of buzz words which abound in pedagogy as well as educational planning and management. The meaning of buzz-words needs to be explored in specific contexts and translated into actionable plans.

Basic to the praxis of process projects like DPEP is the belief in the virtues of incremental action as opposed to the comprehensive and definitive, but elusive choice. Incremental action in turn presupposes abandoning the deep-rooted oral tradition and instead documenting the processes, willingness to evaluate action with an open-mind and without possessiveness and to institutionalise change, breaking with the deep-rooted generalist tradition of 'before me the chaos and after me the deluge.'

The praxis of DPEP calls for shunning the attitude of business as usual, of having done it all and of being ever right. Evolution is the law of nature. Even 'God changes'. 'Today's achievement is only tomorrow's confusion' and 'possessiveness cheapens the thing that was precious'. Reform is change, creative destruction. We should be ready to abandon what was developed in DPEP should the context change. To impede natural selection is to cohabit with death. 'If the dead shall live, the living die'. The dead, as the French say seize the living (*Le Mort Saisit le Vif*); we should not let that happen.[4]

[4] R.V.Vaidyanatha Ayyar, 'Let Not the Dead Seize the Living: The DPEP Saga', *DPEP Calling*, December 1995.

XIX

WINDS OF CHANGE

Looking back, during the early 1990s winds of change began to waft across all areas of education, and by 2005 these winds acquired so much force that they swept away quite a few of the defining features of the India education system. The educational system ceased to being an almost exclusively public funded system and it also ceased to be a closed system with hardly any institution having linkages with institutions abroad or foreign organizations providing education or training. While these changes were more conspicuous in higher and technical education, elementary school system was not immune to these changes. In the 1990s, the accelerated march towards UEE was taking against a backdrop of increasing salience of private unaided schools as well as of increasing civil society activism in the areas of elementary education and child labour. The late 1970s and early 1980s witnessed the formation of a few NGOs (as civil society organizations were known then) and institutions which attempted to factor in ground realities and pioneer new models of pedagogy. Notable among those voluntary agencies were *Ekalavya* in MP, *Digantar* and *Bodh* in Rajasthan, Rishi Valley Rural Centre in AP, and *Srujanika* in Orissa, and notable among such institutions was the Centre for Learning Resources in Pune. While some of them such as Ekalvaya and the Centre for Learning Resources attempted to engage the larger educational system, none of them were engaged in policy advocacy and pressuring the central and state governments to adopt policies they preferred; they limited their activities to pedagogy. Policy activism in the area of education could be discerned only from the late 1990s. Thus, it was only in 1995 that *Pratham*, which is now a prominent actor in the educational landscape and whose *Annual Status of Education Reports* had acquired a canonical status, came into existence. It was established as a Public Charitable Trust by the Commissioner of the Municipal Corporation of Greater Mumbai, UNICEF, and several prominent citizens of the country to provide education to children in the slums of Mumbai; for quite some time, its activities were confined to the Bombay Municipal Corporation. When the 1990s ended, a large number of groups and networks of groups had come into existence. Thus, the Azim Premji Foundation, which is now a major important educational NGO and had established the Azim Premji University noted for its pace-setting development and education programmes, was set up in 2001.

A Modern Maharaja

On X-mas eve 1994, Arjun Singh threw a surprise on the nation by changing his tactics in his duel with the Prime Minister P.V. Narasimha Rao (PV). Ever since the duel began, he practised calculated brinkmanship discomfiting PV on every possible occasion shooting off censorious letters and releasing them to the press, and voicing spicy comments in the media. He perhaps expected PV to overreact by throwing him out of the Cabinet so that he could openly rally the opposition to PV within the Congress Party. But then he was up against a Great Master in *jujutsu* who preferred subtly manipulating the opponent's force against himself rather than confronting it with one's own force. So much so, the brilliant manoeuvrings of Arjun Singh came to naught, a fact evocatively captured by a Telugu newspaper which labelled him *Uttara Kumara,* a play on the word 'Uttara'; he was a past master in hurling 'uttaras' (letters), and was also Uttara Kumara of *Mahabharata* who boasted of his prowess as a warrior only to panic in the battlefield. On the X-mas eve of 1994, he did not tarry to remain in office after hurling his letter bomb—a long litany of commissions and omissions of PV. With his resignation from the Council of Ministers , his helmsmanship of the Ministry of Human Resource Development came to a sudden end; he was to return in 2004, but by then K was no longer in the government.

About a month later, on 8 February 1993 to be precise, Madhavrao Scindia became the Minister, MHRD. Scindia's entry in the Ministry was like a powerful current of fresh air; for a politician, he was young, just 50 years, and had all the élan of youth. He was an exotic blend of feudalism and modernity. He was proud of his royal lineage and wealth, and never allowed others to be oblivious of that fact. K remembers Scindia not for his foibles which no human being can be free of but for his sterling qualities such as modernity, a managerial approach, strong result orientation and determination to leave a mark on everything he touched, his generosity of heart, charming manners, and social graces. He was cast in the mould of Maharajas who modernized their states. Before arriving at MHRD he had been Minister of Railways and Minister of Civil Aviation, acquiring reputation as a great reformer impatient with conventional way of doing things. His tenure was abruptly cut short 11 months after as his name cropped up in the Hawala (money laundering) scandal that rocked the country in January 1996. His tenure was too short to leave a mark; it was during his stint that national programme of school mid-meals was launched and national open debates on key educational issues were organized; an off-shoot of these debates was that legislation for free and compulsory primary education secured national attention.

Mid-Day Meals

As 1995 rolled on and elections due in early 1996 began to loom large, the Prime Minister's Office became hyperactive in developing pro-poor initiatives. One of the ideas mooted by the PMO was to launch a new initiative for UEE by providing students in elementary schools with vouchers for foodgrains and to transfer the implementation of all CSSs such as Operation Blackboard to the District Rural Development Agencies (DRDAs), and transfer central grants to DRDAs directly without the intermediation of the state governments. This idea was partially dropped when Giri convinced the functionaries who toyed with that idea that DRDA was not a suitable agency for universalizing elementary education. However, the idea of *Food for Education* survived and surfaced in the Budget Speech of 1995–6. In that speech, the Finance Minister observed that some of the state governments have been operating school mid-day meals schemes, and that such schemes had a beneficial impact not only on child nutrition but also on school attendance. As part of the emphasis being laid down on elementary education by the government and taking into account the comfortable food stocks with public sector agencies, the government had decided to 'participate in the phased expansion' of school mid-day meals schemes. He also announced that the modalities of the participation of the central government would be worked out by a committee and the scheme would be started in 1995–6 itself. A few weeks later, in April 1995 DOE constituted a committee with Giri as Chairman and K as Member Secretary. Apart from the representatives of the central government departments concerned, the committee had four state education secretaries and the Director, National Institute of Nutrition, as members.

As early as 1925, mid-day meal was provided to poor school children by the Madras Corporation; however, it was in the 1950s that many state governments introduced school mid-day meal programmes with the assistance of agencies such as UNICEF, FAO, WHO, and CARE. As of 31 December 1994, variants of the mid-day meal programme were being implemented in as many as 13 states and 4 union territories; about 2.5 crore children, or roughly one in every seven elementary school children, were covered by these programmes. The most well-known of these programmes was that in Tamil Nadu which offered a hot cooked meal to all children in classes I–X; the scheme was introduced by Chief Minister K. Kamaraj and later expanded and vastly improved upon by Chief Minister M.G. Ramachandran. Cooked meal was provided to all elementary school children in Pondicherry and all primary school children in Gujarat. West Bengal provided all primary school children a mix of cooked and pre-processed food. All children of primary classes were provided bread and biscuits in Delhi and ready-to-eat processed energy food in Karnataka. Tamil Nadu (with 36 per cent of the total children provided mid-day meals in the country), West Bengal (17.5 per cent), Kerala (13.6 per cent), Gujarat (12.7 per cent), and Karnataka (6.3 per cent) together accounted for 86 per cent of the school children who were provided mid-day meals in the country. The cost of providing a meal to a child was generally Rs. 1.5 a day in most states while it was as high as Rs 5.4 in Bihar where 23,000 children in Charawaha Vidyalayas, the flagship programme of Chief Minister Lalu Prasad Yadav, were being provided sumptuous meal which included meat once every week (Chapter VIII).

In the 1980s, GOI toyed with the idea of starting a National Mid-day Meal Programme; thus, in 1982 a Food for Learning programme targeting SC and ST girls was proposed to be launched with FAO support but the programme was not launched, as states such as Rajasthan made it clear that they could not continue the programme if WEP support was withdrawn. The stance of Rajasthan was influenced by Bordia who was then Development Commissioner; then as well as later as Union Education Secretary he had grave reservations about the utility of a school mid-day meal as an educational intervention. He strongly felt that the expenditure on mid-day meals would be heavy and cut into the allocations for elementary education; as the burden of procuring the material, organizing the cooking of meal, and its distribution would fall on teachers it would distract teachers from their primary task of teaching. The distraction would be greater in small schools with one or two teachers. Paraphrasing what is said about old soldiers, popular ideas do not even fade away but crop up again and again. Being so, in 1984–5, and again 1988–9, proposals for providing school mid-day meals were mooted with domestic funding; however, apparently due to resource constraints they did not materialize. However, in 1995 the school mid-day meal was an idea whose time had come for two main reasons: Food Corporation of India (FCI) being saddled with mounting stocks of foodgrains, and the programme finding a champion in K.R.Venugopal, Secretary to the Prime Minister. FCI was increasingly being saddled with mounting stocks for the same reason that the European Union was saddled with wine lakes and butter mountains. One of the key elements of the policies which fuelled the Green Revolution was eliminating the risk undertaken by farmers when they opted for the new high-yielding varieties and new agronomic practices. Lest the higher production of wheat and rice should lower their prices and consequently the income of farmers, the government guaranteed procurement of whatever was marketed by farmers at a price which fully covered the costs of production and a decent return on capital. What was envisaged as an insurance against a fall in income due to increase in production eventually turned out to be a voracious subsidy-guzzler as year after year the government increased procurement prices beyond what increase in cost of production would warrant, and did not commensurately raise the price of foodgrains issued by the public distribution system. More often than not, the procurement price was higher than the open market price; as FCI went on procuring whatever was offered without regard to its storage capacity and the off-take by the public distribution system, the stocks had to be stored in makeshift storage facilities leading to huge storage losses. Good economics not always being good politics, the government would not rationalize the irrational procurement policies. As the government procured the entire marketable surplus of wheat and rice without regard to the mounting stocks and lack of storage space, a food for education programme in which wheat or rice is issued to children as an incentive for attending school would not cast an additional fiscal burden on the government.

In its report, the Giri Committee[1] felt that mid-day meals should not viewed in isolation but as part of the efforts to relate elementary education with nutrition, health, and early child care and education (offered by ICDS). It held that it was necessary to foster linkages between ICDS and schools on the one hand and the public health system and schools on the other so that the country could move towards a comprehensive child care. Ultimately, the objective should be to provide a hot meal to all elementary school children; however, given that the organizational arrangements necessary for attaining the ultimate objective would take time, the state governments should be given the option to decide the modalities of delivering the school mid-day meal. They could provide hot meal or pre-cooked food or only foodgrains. The central government would provide the wheat or rice required at the rate of 100 grams per child a day to states which would provide hot food or pre-cooked food; the supply would be for 200 school days. Where a state government opted to provide only foodgrains, the central government would provide 5 kg of wheat or rice a month for each family for 10 months. Children in classes I–VIII would be covered in a phased manner beginning with 10 per cent of the blocks in each state and union territory. The state governments were required to bear the charges for transport from the FCI warehouses where foodgrains would be issued. The government accepted the recommendations of the committee, and the programme was launched on Independence Day, 1995. It is noteworthy that during the deliberations of the committee, the Rajasthan Education Secretary, an acolyte of Bordia, conveyed the reservation of the state government on the utility of the mid-day meal programme and that the expenditure on such a

[1] Ministry of Human Resource Development, Department of Education, *Report of the Committee on Mid-Day Meals*, 1995.

programme was better invested on programmes having a direct bearing on elementary education such as supply of uniforms to girls and free textbooks. While the state government would go by the decision of the central government on mid-day meals, it would prefer distribution of foodgrains with the freedom to the state government to use the proceeds of the foodgrains to an educational scheme approved by the central government.

To jump the story, the move towards supply of hot cooked meal was hastened by the emergence of a Right to Food Movement, and directions of the Supreme Court in a public interest litigation (PIL) filed by the People's Union for Civil Liberties. These judgments covered not only the mid-day meal programme but also seven other food-related programmes such as targeted public distribution scheme and ICDS. In its interim order dated 28 November 2001, the Supreme Court directed all the state governments to provide a hot meal with a minimum content of 300 calories and 8–12 grams of protein each day of school for a minimum of 200 days. Every state government which had been providing only foodgrains was required to provide hot meal by 28 February 2002 in half the districts of the state; these districts were to be selected in the order of poverty. Within another three months, the rest of the state was to be covered.[2] In its order dated 8 May 2002, two retired civil servants N.C. Saxena and S.R. Sankaran were appointed as commissioners to review the implementation of the court orders by the state governments and report to the Court; later Sankaran was replaced by Harsh Mandir. On May 2003, the Court noticed that many states, particularly Bihar, Jharkhand, and UP, failed to comply with the interim order, and directed all the states to make a meaningful beginning in at least a quarter of the districts which were the most poor. In its order dated 20 April 2004, the Court observed that some state governments did not even make a beginning despite lapse of so many years, some had only made a partial beginning, some had made a token beginning, and only few had fully implemented the Court's order in respect of hot meals. The Court directed all the state governments to comply with the order latest by 1 September 2004, and held the chief secretaries personally responsible for the implementation of the direction. It

[2] *People's Union for Civil Liberties v. Union of India and Others,* Civil Writ Petition No.196/2001.

further directed that preference should be given to scheduled caste and scheduled tribes in the appointment of cooks and helpers. In drought-affected districts, cooked food should be supplied even during holidays. It directed the central government to make provisions for construction of kitchen sheds and to allocate funds to meet with the conversion costs of foodgrains into cooked mid-day meals. It also directed the central government to submit an affidavit within 3 months stating when it would be possible for it to implement the Prime Minister's announcement that the mid-day meal scheme would be extended to classes IX and X. It would appear that all states had complied with the Court directive by 1 January 2005. Thirteen years after the PIL was filed and the Court issued its first interim order, the Court is yet to dispose of the matter through a final order. The Commissioners continue to oversee the implementation of the programme by state governments.

The Supreme Court's intervention in the PIL filed by the People's Union for Civil Liberties is a good example of the new jurisprudence underlying PIL in which the subject matter of litigation is not a dispute between private individuals about private rights or a judicial review of governmental decisions and actions but a grievance about the operation of public policy.[3] In the specific case of mid-day meals, it is a moot point whether, given the wide variation in the administrative capacity of the states, all states ought to have been required to provide hot meal by the same date. The fact that the date for providing hot meal had to be extended by nearly two and half years indicates that the target date fixed in the first directive of 28 February 2002 might not have been based on a realistic assessment of the time required to putting in place the arrangements necessary for serving hot . As subsequent events bring out, it is also a moot point whether the state governments should not have been provided with an option to serve an equally good alternative to hot meal. India is a vast country, and a 'one-size-fits-all' approach might not always be optimal.

In January 2004, soon after the states began to implement the Supreme Court directives on providing hot meal, the Right to Food Campaign brought out a brochure which sought to allay apprehensions

[3] Abraham Chayes, 'The Role of Judges in Public Law Litigation', *Harvard Law Review*, 89, no. 7 (1976), pp. 1281–316; Mamta Rao, *Public Interest Litigation*, Lucknow: Eastern Book Company, 2002.

about preparing and serving cooked hot food in schools.[4] The brochure conceded that in the initial stages cooked hot meals might be a health hazard as they might not be prepared in hygienic conditions. However, the brochure expected that over time the situation would improve with the introduction of quality safeguards. The brochure brought out that field visits indicated that cooks were appointed in all the sample schools visited and nowhere did teachers double as chefs. While organizing mid-day meals would certainly disrupt classroom processes when the infrastructure was inadequate, mid-day meals had positive rather than negative effects on classroom processes as they made it easier to reconvene the classes after the lunch break. In short, if adequate facilities were available, classroom activity can be readily insulated from the cooking process. Contrary to such hopes in August 2013, eight-and-a-half years after Bihar complied with the Supreme Court directive, 23 children in Gandamal school in Bihar died after eating the school mid-day meal. Following a PIL filed by an NGO, Manav Adhikaar Nigraani, and an advocate, Sanjeeb Panigrahi, the Supreme Court issued notices to the centre and 12 states seeking their response on preventing such incidents and providing hygienic food to children. Responding to the tragedy, N.C. Saxena, the Commissioner appointed by the Court, observed that the mid-day meal scheme could not be blamed for the tragedy, and that it was a question of professionalizing the administration and everyone doing his duty. He implicitly brought the limits of judicial intervention and oversight by Court-appointed Commissioners to improve administration by saying:

> Monitoring mechanism is ... very weak to the point of being defunct. Government schools are marred by high indiscipline, teacher absenteeism, and corruption. It is not something we can improve by passing a law or through a court order. It is a question of ... everyone doing their duty. Here, teachers don't do their duty, there is no discipline.... All are concerned only about making money.... It is a known fact that quality of food served is bad in the scheme, besides being insufficient.[5]

[4] Jean Drèze and Aparajita Goyal, 'The Future of Mid-day Meals', in *Mid-day Meal in Primary Schools*, http://www.righttofoodindia.org/data/wsfmdm.pdf, pp. 24–6 (last accessed on 28 May 2015).

[5] Sreelatha Menon, 'Mid-day Meal Monitoring Is Defunct', *Business Standard*, July 2013.

The Gandamal tragedy once again raised the question whether serving pre-cooked meal or processed food is a better option in states with inadequate capacity such as Bihar. However, activists tend to see such proposals as floated by business lobbies who eye an attractive market; they are also upset about media coverage of the tragedy as well as on reports of the poor quality on the food served in a few other states. In their view, the lessons to be drawn are that administrative and monitoring systems need to be reorganized and improved in line with what is seen in the leading states, action needs to be taken in a timely manner against all those responsible for the children's deaths, and there is a need to correct the imbalance in media coverage of rural issues in general, and social security programmes (such as the mid-day meal scheme) in particular.[6]

In retrospect, Bordia's concern that the expenditure on mid-day meals would be heavy and cut into the allocations for elementary education proved to be right. The Cabinet approved the proposal of DOE that the expenditure on mid-day meals should not be reckoned as expenditure one education and should be excluded while implementing the declaration of Prime Minister P.V. Narasimha Rao at the EFA-9 Summit that from the Ninth Five-Year Plan onwards, education would be provided adequate budgetary resources such that the public expenditure on education would be 6 per cent of GDP. The 6 per cent norm is yet to be achieved; from the Tenth Five-Year Plan onwards, a third of the central government plan expenditure on elementary education is incurred on mid-day meals, and this expenditure is taken into account in calculating the expenditure on education as a proportion of GDP, thereby inflating the spending on elementary education by the central government by about 30 per cent and of total public spending by central and state governments by at least 10 per cent.

Child Labour and Compulsory Primary Education Law

As the 1990s progressed, child labour began to increasingly engage the attention of the government because of civil society activism as well as the missionary zeal with which Myron Weiner began to advocate the

[6] Reetika Khera, 'Mid-day Meals; Looking Ahead', *Economic and Political Weekly*, XLVIII, no. 32 (10 August 2013), pp. 12–14.

enactment and enforcement of a compulsory primary education law. Among the first to spiritedly advocate the abolition of child labour was Kailash Satyarthi who founded the Bachpan Bachao Andolan. A constant presence at international forums such as the UN Human Rights Commission, he continually criticized Indian legislation for being inadequate and exorcised the Indian Government for not enforcing even the limited legal provisions. His advocacy induced some members of the US Congress to push for punitive measures such as a ban on imports of carpets from India on the ground that child labour was employed in the manufacture of carpets, an activity forbidden by the Child Labour (Prohibition and Regulation) Act of 1986. A similar move was also launched in Germany. Satyarthi's activities embarrassed the government a great deal and irritated the officials, K included, as they were as yet unreconciled to Indian citizens and organizations conducting their struggle against the government and its actions of omission and commission in foreign countries and forums.

Broadly speaking, two approaches were suggested to abolish child labour. The first approach commended a frontal attack by legally abolishing child labour in its entirety, forcefully enforcing the law, rehabilitating and educating the erstwhile child labourers, and compensating the families, if any, of the child labourers for the income forgone by the abolition of child labour. There were as many eight legislations dealing with child labour; however, even taken together they laws did not abolish child labour in its entirety, and they only prohibited children being employed as wage labourers in over two dozen occupations such as mining, motor transport, plantation, and so on. The legal minimum age for employment varied from occupation to occupation, and was mostly 14 years. In a strict sense, the laws as they stood were in conformity with the Constitution as well as international instruments to which India was a party. Thus, the Constitution did not explicitly prohibit child labour in its entirety; in the chapter on Fundamental Rights, Article 15(3) enables the state to make special provisions to restrict employment of children in certain areas on the ground of the nature of the work, and Article 24 prohibits employment of children below the age of 14 years in any factory or mine or in any other hazardous employment. Article 39(f), a Directive Principle, makes it obligatory for the state to ensure that children are 'given opportunities and facilities to develop in a healthy manner and in conditions of freedom and dignity and that childhood and youth are protected against exploitation and against moral and material abandonment'. However, the Supreme Court never interpreted this article or Article 21 (right to life) to hold that child labour prevented children to develop in a healthy manner and in conditions of freedom and dignity, and were as such unconstitutional. Even when the Supreme Court considered the question of child labour in *Bandhua Mukti Morcha* case[7] it did not altogether prohibit wage employment of children altogether. It only gave certain directions regarding the manner in which children working in hazardous occupations were to be withdrawn and rehabilitated as also the manner in which the working conditions of children working in non-hazardous occupations were to be regulated and improved upon.

It is significant that none of the six ILO conventions to which India was a party in the 1990s prohibited child labour altogether. Even the Convention Number 182 adopted by ILO in July 1999 only related to prohibition and elimination of the worst forms of labour, and not elimination of child labour altogether. The worst forms of labour were defined to include all forms of slavery, commercial sexual exploitation of children, bonded labour, use, procurement, and offering of children for illegal activities such as trafficking in drugs, and work by its nature that was likely to harm the health, safety, or morals of children. The Convention left it to the member states to determine in consultation with organizations of employers and workers what constituted work likely to harm the health, safety, or morals of children. To borrow the phraseology of economic reforms, activists were in favour of a big bang reform of outright abolition while governments of developing countries were in favour of a gradualist approach. While arguing for complete eradication of child labour, activists contended that school was the only place where the child should be, and that accordingly every child out of school should be treated as a child labourer. In contrast, governments of developing countries such as India considered child labour to be a complex, multidimensional problem, and were cognizant of the grim reality that for many working children and their families the alternative to work was starvation, and that because of resource constraint the government could not rehabilitate all the working children straightaway. Consequently, they preferred a gradualist legal-cum-developmental

[7] *Bandhua Mukti Morchav. Union of India and Others*, AIR 1984 S.C. 802.

approach to the eventual eradication of child labour. The gradualist approach comprised prohibiting employment in hazardous occupations, improving the working conditions in non-hazardous occupations, and progressively expanding the list of occupations where employment is prohibited. Simultaneously, attempts were made to rehabilitate children working in hazardous occupations and provide opportunities to working children for learning through alternatives to schooling. Suffice to say, the Convention shied away from eradicating child labour in all forms, not surprising at all given that ILO could not go beyond the mandate developing countries that constituted the majority of its Member States were willing to bestow on it. Even the Convention on the Rights of the Child (CRC), 1989, only recognized 'the right of the child to be protected from economic exploitation and from performing any work that is likely to be hazardous or to interfere with the child's education, or to be harmful to the child's health or physical, mental, spiritual, moral or social development' (Article 32).

One of the reasons why activists were strongly opposed to NFE was that it provided an escape route to the government to get away from its obligations under CRC; the government could argue that children could enrol in NFE and learn at their own pace at their own time, and consequently as long as children were not engaged in non-hazardous occupations, there was no infringement of international obligations (Chapter II). A year after the *Bandhua Mukti Morcha* judgment, the National Child Labour Policy (NCLP), 1985, came into effect. The Child Labour (Prohibition and Regulation) Act, 1986, which was enacted in the wake of the NCLP, expanded the list of hazardous industries; to jump the story, that list was expanded in 2006 and again in 2008. NCLP put in place three complementary measures: (*a*) stringent enforcement of child labour and other child-related laws; (*b*) development programmes for providing NFE, healthcare, and nutrition to working children, bridge programmes for children withdrawn from work so that they could join the school system, income and employment generation programmes for parents; and (*c*) area-specific projects focussing on areas known to have high concentration of child labour and adopting a project approach for identification, withdrawal, and rehabilitation of working children. Such areas included Bhivandi (Maharashtra, power looms), Sivakasi (Tamil Nadu, match and fireworks), Surat (Gujarat, diamond cutting), Jaipur (Rajasthan, gem polishing), Aligarh (lock making), Markapur (AP, slate making), Mandsour (MP, slate making), and Firozabad (UP, glass manufacturing). With the wisdom of hindsight, K feels that the gradualist policy would have carried more conviction if a time-bound plan were put in place for the eradication of child labour specifying the sequence in which child labour would be eradicated in occupation after occupation. A law akin to The Fiscal Responsibility and Budget Management Act, 2003, would have been a credibility-enhancing mechanism.

Against this backdrop Myron Weiner came out with a novel way of eradicating child labour by putting forth the proposition that it was easier to eradicate child labour through enforcement of a compulsory primary education law than of child labour laws because powerful economic interests would not oppose a primary education law the way they would oppose child labour laws. He argued that no country could eradicate child labour without enforcing a compulsory primary education law, and further that the experience of some countries showed that education system might improve after, and not before, a compulsory primary education law (Chapter VII).[8] Weiner's book appeared just at the moment when UEE began to acquire great political salience, and was widely noticed and commented upon. From a historical perspective, the publication of Weiner's book and the debate it triggered is a milestone in the sequence of events that give a big boost to the nation's quest for UEE: NPE, 1986, TLCs (1989), CRC (1989), Jomtien Conference (1990), BEP (1990), Weiner's book, DPEP (1994), and SSA (2001). The wide distribution by UNICEF of Weiner's book *The Child and the State in India* as part of its advocacy campaign, his address to Delhi's power elite at the Rajiv Gandhi Foundation in January 1994, and the articles he wrote in magazines such as *Frontline* convinced many in the media that Weiner offered an efficacious solution to the seemingly intractable problem of child labour, and that if his prescription was not accepted it was because of bureaucratic resistance. Thus, in her column styled 'Open Letter to Scindia' the noted journalist Tavleen Singh called upon Scindia to 'take note of the fact that we are running out of time' and enact compulsory primary education 'legislation' whatever 'your bureaucrats tell you'.[9]

[8] Myron Weiner, pp. 5–6.

[9] Tavleen Singh, 'Open Letter to Scindia', *Indian Express*, 19 February 1995.

As elections were due to be held in May 1996, right from day one in MHRD Scindia knew he was racing against time. Soon after he joined MHRD he realized that in MHRD the technocratic and managerial solutions such as those undertaken during his stint in the Ministries of Railways and Civil Aviation were unlikely to acquire for him the name and fame he craved for, and that it was important to project the image that he was set to address topical educational issues in an unconventional way. To that end, he took up three initiatives: (*a*) a bill to regulate the establishment of private universities was introduced in the Rajya Sabha in August 1995; (*b*) four synergy groups were set up to suggest new approaches to primary education and literacy, vocational education, IITs, and IIMs, and (*c*) organizing a 'national debate' on topical issues. Unusual for DOE, the synergy group on primary education and literacy was headed by Abid Hussain, a distinguished administrator and known proponent of liberalization, that on vocationalization by Sam Pitroda, that on IITs by industrialist V.K. Modi, and that on IIMs by the Hindustan Lever Chairman S.N. Dutta. The national debates were to be organized in different regions of the country through interactive sessions to which a cross section of teachers, academics, parents, and students were to be invited to discuss issues. He hoped that unconventional ideas might emerge from these interactions; even if the hope was not fulfilled, the interaction would provide opportunities for photo-ops and media coverage, and also act an insurance against the possibility that he might not succeed in giving a new direction to education given the short time and the need to carry most if not all the states. He zeroed in on for topical issues: compulsory primary education legislation, vocational education, value education, and reducing the 'load of the school bag', a catchy expression for reducing the curricular load of school education. Not to speak of acting on the recommendations emanating from the regional meets, Scindia could not even complete them as his tenure was abruptly cut short in January 1996 by the *hawala* (money laundering) racket.

Legislation for compelling the parents had to confront a sharp dilemma; if the legislation is bereft of penal provisions, it would be no more than a statement of pious intentions, and if it were to incorporate penal provisions, it would be vesting lower echelons of bureaucracy with powers of enforcement against a considerable segment of population, predominantly poor and illiterate. When this dilemma was brought to the notice of Weiner when he gave an address at the Rajiv

Gandhi Foundation, he argued that compulsion did not necessarily imply prison sentences or heavy finances. Local officials, teachers, and members of the school committees could visit the houses of parents whose children were not at school to inform them that school attendance was compulsory. Weiner expected that such efforts, if carried out for some time, would lead to a norm being established that all children must attend school, and such a norm could then be enforced by the local community than by authorities.[10] In effect, Myron Weiner envisaged the legislation as a strategic deterrent much like the nuclear arsenals in the Cold Warera with the fond hope that the deterrent need not and would not be used. The wisdom of enacting a legislation as a strategic deterrent is a moot point in the face of the reality that child labour itself was not banned except in hazardous industries, and that the system has not found it easy to properly enforce criminal laws that are intended to be enforced without jeopardizing the human rights of those prima facie suspected of infracting the law. The way Weiner intended the law to be enforced was no different from the enrolment drives which were organised in many states from time to time. All in all a law was no law if it was not enforced. Promoting voluntary compliance with law was eminently desirable but it could never be sufficient. As it was, there were many laws which were neither enforced nor obeyed, and there was no point in having yet another law which would not be enforced.

The Indian experience with the enforcement of compulsory primary education laws was no different from that of many other developing countries. Christopher Colclough, an internationally renowned economist of education, explored the question whether there was any relationship between the non-enactment of a compulsory primary education laws and the incidence of low enrolment ratios caused by low demand for schooling. His conclusion was that across developing countries, the existence of compulsory schooling regulations often seemed to have had little impact upon the proportion of children actually enrolled. The evidence from industrialized countries suggested that compulsory primary education laws become important when the net enrolment ratio (percentage of children enrolled to population of

[10] *Compulsory Education and Child Labour*, RGIC Proceedings, no. 4, New Delhi: Rajiv Gandhi Institute for Contemporary Studies, 1994, pp. 47–8.

children in the relevant group, 6–14 years in India) moves towards 90 per cent and school facilities are created to enrol all school-age children because compulsion sustained high levels of enrolment[11] All in all, the excitement caused by the Weiner prescription is an example of the flutter caused by simplistic solutions to complex problems espoused with a moralistic zeal.

In 1996, compulsory primary education law faded away from media and activist advocacy, and child rights stepped in its place. It was perhaps just not coincidental that this development was coeval with the change of guard at UNICEF headquarters; Carol Bellamy who succeeded James Grant as UNICEF Executive Director in May 1995 embraced CRC and unequivocally declared that CRC was UNICEF's mandate (Chapter VII).

Constitution Amendment: Right to Elementary Education

After the General Elections in April–May 1996, and the formation of the United Front (UF) government on 1 June 1996, S.R. Bommai came to be the Minister, and K was to serve him in DOE as well as Department of Culture. Like Arjun Singh he was a political heavyweight but they were poles apart. Bommai had been the President of the Janata Dal which was the major constituent of the United Front and the Chief Minister of Karnataka. His judicial challenge to the dismissal of his government and imposition of the President's rule immortalized his name because of the landmark decision of the Supreme Court which held that the imposition of the President's rule was justiciable, and that the Court could strike down the imposition if it was found to be *malafide* or based on wholly irrelevant or extraneous grounds.[12] He had a long political career having risen from grassroots to the national level; having been in and outside power he had a good understanding of the ephemeral nature of power as well as of the human nature to court those in power and then cast them aside once they lose power. He started his career as a follower of M.N. Roy, and continued to be a great admirer of Roy and his thoughts.

[11] Christopher Colclough with Keith M. Lewin, *Educating All the Children: Strategies for Primary Schooling in the South*, Cambridge: Cambridge University Press, 1993, pp. 260–2.

[12] *S.R.Bommai v. Union of India*, AIR 1994 SC 1918.

On 5 June 1996, a Common Minimum Programme (CMP) was unveiled by the constituent parties of UF government; in so far as education is considered the most significant component of the CMP was the commitment to make the right to free and compulsory education a fundamental right and suitably enforce that right. The million dollar question is why the constituent parties of the UF government thought it necessary to amend the Constitution when the Supreme Court had already held in *Unnikrishnan* judgment that free and compulsory primary education was a fundamental right. At best legislation was required to spell out the modalities of implementing the *Unnikrishnan* judgment. It is equally inscrutable why civil society organizations sought to push through a Constitution Amendment instead of approaching the Court to issue directions to the central and state governments to comply with the judgment. During the run up to the enactment of a constitutional amendment, quite a few civil society organizations such as the National Alliance of Fundamental Right to Education contended that the Amendment Bill withdrew some of the rights conferred by the *Unnikrishnan* judgment. If that judgment were acted upon, legislation like the RTE Act would have come into force about 5 years earlier. To be honest what was at play was the *politics of appearances*, managing the public image acquiring greater salience than governance itself. Whatever, it should be said to the credit of the UF government in general and Bommai in particular that in spite of the short tenure of the UF government the commitment made in the CMP was fulfilled, and the 83rd Constitution Amendment Bill was introduced in the Rajya Sabha in October 1997.

All through his tenure Bommai's priority was amending the Constitution to make elementary education a fundamental right. He spelt out his priority right in the very first meeting P.R. Dasgupta (who succeeded Giri) and K had with him; he wanted to convene a meeting of chief ministers early to discuss the issue. He was of the view that once elementary education was a fundamental right, the Courts would ensure that the central and state governments provided the necessary resources. He went full steam ahead with the move to make elementary education a fundamental right. Within two months of his assuming charge he had a series of meetings with chief ministers, state education secretaries and ministers, and educational experts to consider the issue. Going by the consensus of those meetings he constituted a group of state education ministers to consider the financial, administrative, legal, and academic implications of the proposal; the group was headed by Muhi Ram Saikia, Minister of State, MHRD. In its report of January 1997, the group came to the conclusion that the Constitution should be amended to make the right to free elementary education a fundamental right, and that simultaneously, an explicit provision should be made in the Constitution to make it a fundamental duty of every parent to send children to school. The group, however, came to the conclusion that there was no need to enact a central legislation to enforce the new fundamental right and duty in view of the facts that India was a diverse federal polity with wide disparities in provision of school education between and within states, and that states who were the main providers of elementary education varied widely in their fiscal capacity and levels of development. To jump the story, the question, where there should be a central or state legislation for enforcing the fundamental right was one of the vexatious issues which cropped up before the Right of Children to Free and Compulsory Education (RTE) Act, 2009, was enacted. Even while holding that central legislation was not desirable, the Saikia Group suggested that the central government might in consultation with state governments issue guidelines providing a broad framework for enactment of state legislations. While the states should have the freedom to precisely define what constituted free education, free education should generally include exemption from tuition fee, provision of free textbooks, provision of free essential stationary, and free mid-day meals to all primary school children; for girls, however, free textbooks were to be provided at the upper primary level also. State governments might provide other incentives such as free school uniforms, cash incentives, and scholarships in accordance with their economic capacity and priorities. The norms for establishment of primary and upper primary schools were the same as the then prevailing norms: a primary school within a walking distance of 1–1.5 kilometres from a settlement of 250 people, and an upper primary school within a walking distance of 3 kilometres from a settlement of 250 people. States could relax norms for locating schools in hilly, desert, tribal, and inaccessible areas so as to ensure that the schools established are viable. Minimum infrastructure and teachers, as envisaged under Operation Blackboard, were required to be provided in all primary and upper primary schools preferably during the Ninth Five-Year Plan itself. However, provision of such facilities should not be made a statutory obligation right away. Furthermore, the norms prescribed under Operation Blackboard would not be applicable to alternative schooling and NFE programme. Provision of recurrent teacher training and quality textbooks, besides introduction of MLLs, should be given due attention. The group made it clear that the primary responsibility to promote elementary education should remain with the state governments. It suggested that the state governments should consider levying an educational cess and encourage local bodies to raise revenues for improvement of facilities in schools in their jurisdiction. The group suggested that in consultation with the state governments the Planning Commission and Ministry of Finance should evolve an appropriate formula for providing additional finances required to implement the proposal to amend the Constitution. The formula so evolved should provide for transfer of more resources to educationally backward states, districts, and blocks. The group estimated the requirements of funding to comply with the obligations arising from the Constitutional Amendment to be of the order of Rs 40,000 crore over a five-year period. However, the group also suggested that the estimates of additional funds required should be carefully examined in consultation with experts who may also identify the possible sources of financing the additional requirements. The additional expenditure to implement the proposal should be phased out preferably over a period of five years coinciding with the Ninth Five-Year Plan. As could be expected of a group of state education ministers, the group did not want the autonomy of states to be impaired by a central legislation. It did not want the finances of the state government to be overstretched by adopting norms beyond those which were prevailing; it also wanted assured central financial support for fulfilling the obligations arising from the Constitutional Amendment. In January 1997, an expert group was set up under the chairmanship of K to study the financial implications of the Constitutional Amendment. K could prevail upon Tapas Mazumdar to join the group. By August 1997, K moved out of DOE, and as he moving out, he prevailed upon Dasgupta to reconstitute the expert group with Tapas Mazumdar as Chairman. The expert group submitted its report in January 1999. Given his belief that what was important was to get the Constitution amended and that once the Constitution was amended governments would be compelled to provide adequate resources, Bommai did not wait for the Mazumdar

Expert Group to submit its report, In October 1997, he introduced the 83rd Constitution Amendment Bill to make elementary education a fundamental right.

All in all, in spite of his relatively short tenure, Bommai left an imprint on Indian education by introducing the 83rd Constitution Amendment Bill; figuratively, he let the genie out of the bottle, for no successor of his could fail to carry the Amendment Bill forward. The introduction of the Bill gave fillip to civil society activism, and from then onwards, a large number of groups and networks of groups such as the People's Alliance for Right to Education and the Right to Education Forum were extremely active in advocating the most expansive Constitutional Amendment possible and enabling central legislation possible.

The 1998 General Elections brought to power the first truly non-Congress Party government at the Centre. All the previous governments including the Janata government had significant numbers of erstwhile members of the Congress Party. In fact, before A.B. Vajpayee every non-Congress party Prime Minister—Morarji Desai, Charan Singh, V.P. Singh, and Chandra Sekhar—had been an erstwhile member of the Congress Party. In contrast, the BJP, which was the main constituent of the new NDA government, carried forward a legacy of dissent from the mainstream freedom movement led by Mahatma Gandhi. With NDA coming to power in March 1998, Murli Manohar Joshi came to be Minister, MHRD. Like Arjun Singh, Joshi was a political heavy-weight and a solid minister who decisively presided over the Ministry throughout the nearly six-year-long NDA government. Joshi carried forward the initiative of Bommai to amend the Constitution and make free and compulsory education till the age of 14 years a fundamental right. He wanted to leave his imprint on the Constitution Amendment, and to that end, in November 2001 he withdrew the bill introduced by Bommai, and about six months later in May 2002, he introduced in the Lok Sabha the 93rd Constitution Amendment Bill which took note of the recommendations of the Parliamentary Standing Committee on the Bommai Bill and the 165th report of the Law Commission (1998). The 93rd Constitution Amendment Bill was passed in Lok Sabha on 28 November 2001, and by Rajya Sabha on 14 May 2002, and the Constitution Amendment came into force on 12 December 2002. This amendment inserted Article 21A in the Chapter on Fundamental Rights; Article 21A obligated the state to provide free and compulsory education to all children of the age of 6–14 years 'in such manner as the State may, by law, determine'. At the same time, Article 45 in the Chapter on Directive Principles was amended to make it obligatory for the state to endeavour to provide early childhood care and education for all children until they complete the age of 6 years (Chapter XIII). However, the enabling legislation, RTE Act, 2009, came into effect only on 1 April 2010, thereby setting a record for the period intervening between enactment of a Constitution Amendment and its effectively coming into force. Joshi got drafted an enabling legislation to give effect to the right guaranteed by Article 21A, and began discussions with political parties and the state governments and build a consensus on the draft bill so that it could be rapidly enacted short-circuiting the process of the bill being referred to the Parliamentary Standing Committee for MHRD. The Free and Compulsory Education Bill, 2003, could not be enacted because before the consultative process was completed the NDA government decided to go in for elections prematurely with the expectation that with *India Shining* it would come back to power. The electorate had other ideas and NDA's bid was lost.

Right of Children to Free and Compulsory Elementary Education (RTE) Act, 2009

Even though the incoming UPA government and Arjun Singh who returned to MHRD as minister were keen to enact the enabling legislation, five more years were to pass before the RTE Act, 2009, could be enacted. It was no easy task to harmonize the competing concerns of the Finance Ministry, Planning Commission, state governments, and educational activists, some of whom were members of the newly constituted CABE and close to Arjun Singh. As they were primarily responsible for implementing the legislation, the state governments were averse to take on commitments which, in their view, were difficult, if not impossible, to fulfil and expose them to the vagaries of PIL litigation. They expected the central government to fully meet the additional expenditure required to fulfil the obligations arising from the constitutional amendment and its enabling legislation. Given its mandate of maintaining the ways and means position, the Finance Ministry could not absolve itself of worrying about financing the additional burden the implementation of the bill would cast on it; it was therefore wary of being saddled with heavy financial liability which, in its view, was a legitimate charge on state governments. In the existing scheme of things, plan outlays were determined by the funds the Finance Ministry placed at disposal of the Planning Commission; unless the Finance Ministry provided it commensurate additional resources, the Planning Commission was wary that implementation of the enabling legislation would distort the *inter se* sectoral priorities of the Tenth and Eleventh Five-Year Plans. Furthermore, the Planning Commission, under the watch of Montek Singh Ahluwalia, was trying to break away from the beaten path and began to assume an activist policy role. Thus, the draft Approach Paper of the Eleventh Five-Year Plan (June 2006) expressed concern about the poor quality of learning in government schools and advocated parental choice to promote teacher and school accountability. Parents should be allowed to 'choose between available public or private schools (by giving them suitable entitlements reimbursable to the school) and thus creating competition among schools'.[13] This approach of the Planning Commission was anathema to educational activists who were bitterly opposed to private high-fee-charging schools which, in their view, resulted in a dual educational system which segregated children of common people from those of elite and perpetuated social and economic inequalities. Furthermore, in their view of the activists free and compulsory education of children in the age group being a fundamental right guaranteed by the Constitution cast an irrevocable obligation on the central and state governments, and consequently financial considerations were irrelevant and the worries of the Finance Ministry, Planning Commission, and the state governments misplaced. They strongly believed that the main reason why UEE was elusive so far was the lack of commitment to UEE by central and state governments; the logical conclusion of the belief was that only an irrevocable binding legal obligation and a Damocles' sword of judicial disapprobation would compel the governments to do the right things necessary to ensure that UEE moves from the plane of dreams to that of reality. As governments could not be trusted, it was necessary to cast in legal stone every aspiration of theirs. And further, they believed that enactment of the enabling legislation was a historic opportunity to

[13] Planning Commission, *Towards Faster and More Inclusive Growth: An Approach to the Eleventh Five Year Plan*, June 2006, pp. 46–7.

reconstruct the elementary education system in its entirety: its philosophical underpinnings, content and process, its positioning in society, and its accountability. In the face of conflicting concerns and viewpoints, and the miasma of mistrust prevailing between Arjun Singh on the one hand and the Prime Minister, Chidambaram, and Ahluwalia on the other, the UPA government could make the final call only in December 2008, when its tenure was about to end, and introduce a bill in Rajya Sabha. It was left to Kapil Sibal, Arjun Singh's successor in the second UPA government, to get the bill enacted; the Act came into force on 1 April 2010.

The RTE Act, 2009, mandated formal school system being the sole vehicle for providing free and compulsory education and cast an obligation on the state to provide enough neighbourhood schools so as to admit every child who demanded admission. It also cast an obligation on every private school to earmark at least 25 per cent of its seats to students from weaker sections living in its neighbourhood even though it received no grant from central or state governments. It also specified the norms and standards which every school is required to comply with. Among others, the norms and standards include teacher–pupil ratios, specifications for school buildings, minimum number of working days and instructional hours, and the principles which should guide the curriculum to be transacted as well as evaluation; these principles conform to the constructivism as spelt out in National Curricular Framework, 2005. Given the educational philosophy of the activist members the draft bill altogether abandoned the very idea of laying down essential levels of learning and assessing how much progress was achieved in the attainment of those levels. It laid down that curricular transaction should build on the child's knowledge, environment, and cultural identity, particularly linguistic, and develop the child's personality, talents, and mental and physical abilities to their fullest potential, and rely on activity, discovery, exploration, and understanding. And further, curricular transaction and evaluation should make the child free of fear, trauma, and anxiety, and help the child to express his views; no child should be required to appear in any public examination at the elementary stage; and a system of continuous and comprehensive evaluation (CCE) should be put in place in schools to evaluate a child's understanding of knowledge and his ability to apply that knowledge

After the enactment of the RTE Act, the NCTE Act was amended in 2011 vesting in NCTE the power to prescribe the qualifications required for appointment as a teacher at all stages of school education; following this amendment, a Teacher's Eligibility Test (TET) was introduced on the lines of the National Eligibility Test for college lecturers. In other words, to be a teacher one has to possess not only academic qualifications and a pre-service training diploma or degree but also a licence to teach, and that licence is to be acquired by qualifying in TET. NCERT was notified as the academic authority to lay down the curriculum and the evaluation procedure for elementary education; the NCERT in turn notified the National Curricular Framework, 2005, as the framework for the states to develop their curricula, and issued guidelines for CCE.

The Act was welcomed by most as a historic milestone in the nation's quest for UEE; however, many activists were discontented dubbing the Act as no more than a symbolic gesture, and that the struggle should go on not only to compel the government to comply with the provisions of a law it enacted but also rectify the anomalies and deficiencies. At the same time, the Act also elicited criticism for downplaying learning, focussing on inputs and not outcomes, reinforcing the Inspectorate Raj, and sounding the death knell for thousands of private low-cost, low-fee-charging schools which expanded access to the poor of education of a superior to government schools.

XX

CATERPILLAR TO BUTTERFLY

Mirror, Mirror on the Wall, Am I the Fairest of All?

Till it was dwarfed by SSA, DPEP was 'the most ambitious primary education initiative in Independent India'.[1] Among the many things that DPEP attempted to do was bringing primary education centre stage, fostering competition among states, creating an enabling environment to accelerate the pace of universalization by providing financial resources, promoting a culture of outcomes, holistically addressing all aspects of universalization, focussing on quality and learning achievement, promoting the practice of decentralized planning and implementation, providing to states informational wherewithal to introduce new practices and innovate, attempting gender mainstreaming on a continental scale, and pioneering a new pattern of relationship between the recipient countries and agencies.

DPEP proclaimed again and again that it was exceptional, and prided itself on the fact that it was not an enclave but a beachhead 'to transform the entire primary education system', and the litmus test of DPEP was 'not achievement of quantitative targets or fund utilisation but [its] impact in improving systems'. Carrying forward the imagery of beachhead, a DPEP project was like the landing on a beach of Normandy; while what happened on the beach itself is of interest,

[1] Vimala Ramachandran, 'The New Segregation: Reflections on Gender and Equity in Primary Education', *Economic and Political Weekly*, XXXVII, no. 17 (27 April 2002), pp. 1600–13.

what is of greater interest is the action on the beach in relation to the campaign that followed for the liberation of France and defeat of Nazi Germany. Reinforcing the image of beachhead were other imageries relating DPEP and the larger elementary education system such as an osmotic membrane would separate the two permitting the outward diffusion of innovative practices and new thinking, while being impermeable to the negative forces of the main system. It logically follows that a proper performance evaluation of DPEP projects has to concern itself with two aspects: (*a*) evaluation of the achievements in regard to process, output, and outcome indicators of that particular project and (*b*) an evaluation of how much that project contributed to enhance the capacity of the state education systems concerned to achieve UEE as defined by NPE, 1992. The second aspect of evaluation would necessitate examination of the question whether the 'concentration of good practices within the programme was sufficiently high to diffuse rapidly and effectively through the wider system so as to bring about perceptible changes in practices and processes'. Related questions are whether the mechanisms designed were adequate to raise the 'concentration levels' (of professionalism, dynamism, and innovation) within the programme, and further to achieve the one-way diffusion envisaged by the programme.

Back in 2000 when SSA was not yet launched, K and Sajitha Bashir reviewed the progress recorded by DPEP till then in its entirety.[2] The review covered, as any normal review would, of the progress achieved in respect of enrolment, retention, and leavening the content and process of education; its distinctiveness is that it went beyond the normal reviews to answer the set of questions arising from the second aspect of evaluation. It sought to assess how well the new structures and new managerial pedagogic and participative processes DPEP introduced were functioning, the extent to which the good practices were extended to the elementary education system as a whole, and the impact of DPEP on the larger system. K and Sajitha Bashir concluded their review with the frank admission:

[2] R.V. Vaidyanatha Ayyar and Sajitha Bashir, 'District Primary Education Program (DPEP)', *Encyclopaedia on Education*, I, New Delhi: National Council of Educational Research and Training, 2001, pp. 464–76.

> DPEP has undertaken exploratory skirmishes to attack a very complex problem. Unless the processes it has initiated are carried forward, there is the danger that the dead may still seize the living. So far the philosophy of DPEP since its inception has been one of incremental action. Whether the initial successes have created the conditions for a more frontal attack and for striding forward with seven-league boots [is a moot point].

Now that 15 years had passed, it is time to judge whether the country did stride forward in seven-league boots towards the long elusive goal of UEE, and if so, what was the contribution of DPEP. In January 2001, a few months after the article was written, SSA was launched. Till June 2003 when the first two Bank-funded projects were completed, SSA and DPEP were implemented together in 18 states. Thereafter as DPEP project after DPEP project came to an end, the number of states where DPEP and SSA were implemented together began to decline till November 2008 when the last of the DPEP projects came to an end, and DPEP passed into history and SSA came to be the sole vehicle for universalizing elementary education. Consequently, the extent to which DPEP influenced the design and implementation of SSA partly answers the question whether DPEP impacted on the larger elementary education system.

In their review, K and Sajitha posed yet another question: would the programme go beyond discrete district-level projects and programme interventions at the national and state levels to an all-encompassing reform of primary education? Given that, SSA, unlike DPEP, covers the whole country and the entire elementary education, the aforesaid question has to be reframed as whether SSA is still functioning as a programme which leaves out quite a few areas of elementary education system? A seminal article written in 2004 by Shanti Jagannathan offers insightful answers for some of these questions.[3] What follows is an attempt to answer the questions taking advantage of the perspective provided by the passage of time.

[3] Shanti Jagannathan, 'Programme-based Approaches and International Collaboration: Experiences and Lessons from Education Sector', paper presented to LEPNA Forum, 'Programme-based Approaches to Diversity: Adapting to Diversity', Tokyo, 1–3 June 2004.

What We Know and What We Don't

Even with abundant archival material, it is difficult to definitively reconstruct the past; that is one of the reasons why history is an argument without an end. Strange but true, reconstruction of what DPEP did and its contribution can only be partial given the limited range of readily retrievable studies and evaluation, and further given that there is no single place which houses whole of the voluminous documentation generated such as studies and reports of the joint review missions (JRMs). In all, over the 14-year period spanning 1994–2008, there were eleven DPEP projects. The first project covered 19 districts of MP and was funded by the European Commission (1994–2002). Following the reorganization of districts and the carving out of a new state of Chhattisgarh in November 2000, the project eventually covered 17 districts of MP and nine districts of Chhattisgarh. Seven projects were funded by the Bank either by itself or as the main co-financier along with agencies such as the Netherlands government and UNICEF. These were the DPEP I Project (March 1995 to June 2003) covering 23 districts in the 6 states of Assam, Haryana, Karnataka, Kerala, Maharashtra, and Tamil Nadu; the DPEP II Project (October 1996 to June 2003) covering 92 districts in 12 states of Assam, Chhattisgarh, Gujarat, Haryana, Himachal Pradesh, Karnataka, Kerala, MP, Maharashtra, Orissa, Tamil Nadu, and UP; the DPEP III Project (March 1998 to March 2006) covering 17 education districts in the 2 states of Bihar and Jharkhand; the UP DPEP Project (April 2000 to March 2006) covering 42 districts of UP; the First Rajasthan DPEP Project (October 1999 to December 2005) covering 10 districts of Rajasthan; and the Second Rajasthan DPEP Project (May 2001 to March 2008) covering 9 districts of Rajasthan. In addition, the Bank-financed AP Economic Restructuring Project (February 1999 to March 2008) funded implementation of DPEP in 14 districts of AP. In addition to these projects funded by the EC and the Bank, DPEP was implemented in 5 districts of AP (1997–2005), 8 districts of Orissa (1997–2008), and 10 districts of West Bengal (1997–2006) with ODA funding. In all, DPEP covered 272 of India's 593 odd districts in 18 of the 20 states each of which has a population more than 50 lakhs, and over half the child population in the age group 6–11. The coverage was the most extensive in the states of UP, AP, MP, and Bihar. Together with the UP Basic education Project, DPEP covered almost all the districts of entire UP; it covered 15 of the 23 districts of AP, 34 of the 45 districts of MP (before bifurcation), and 23 of the 37 revenue districts of Bihar (before bifurcation). It covered near-about half the districts in Assam, Karnataka, Kerala, and Rajasthan. The total programme outlay of DPEP was US $2.398 billion (bn.) of which IDA contributed about 56 per cent (in absolute terms US $1.34 bn.), DFID, EC, Netherlands, and UNICEF together another 36 per cent (US $0.866 bn.), and the states together about 8 per cent (US $0.192 bn.). In rupee terms, DPEP invested over Rs 7,500 crore in elementary education, about twice that of Operation Blackboard, the largest domestically funded CSS in elementary education having a direct bearing on the improvement of elementary education. In terms of geographical coverage, magnitude of outlay, as well as scale and scope, all the previous externally funded projects such as APPEP, BEP and Lok Jumbish are minuscule in comparison. Paraphrasing a dictum of Hegel, DPEP, because of its scale and scope, was a class apart from all previous programmes relating to elementary education, whether domestically or externally funded. Unlike all previous programmes and projects, it had the critical mass required to make a noticeable dent on the primary education system.

In a nutshell, the DPEP guidelines set out what DPEP expected to achieve. First issued in April 1993, the DPEP guidelines were revised a couple of times; the revisions were marginal being limited to a few parameters such as the ceiling on the expenditure on civil construction which was raised from a quarter to a third of the outlay. The DPEP framework, the process to be followed in managing the programme, preparation of perspective and annual work plans, implementation, the system of JRMs, and most importantly, the educational outcomes expected remained unaltered all through. It is significant that of the seven DPEP projects funded by the Bank, the DPEP III and UP DPEP projects did not adopt the DPEP objectives as their objectives. DPEP III Project envisaged that 400,000 additional children in the age group 6–10 years would be enrolled from the year 2000 onwards, retention rate increased by 15 per cent; it also sought to increase learning levels without specifying the extent of increase. It had no equity-oriented goal of reducing the gender and social disparities in enrolment, retention, and learning levels. The UP DPEP Project abandoned goal setting altogether purportedly on the ground that in previous DPEP projects, setting targets had led to perverse behaviour on reporting outcomes[4]—a strange justification indeed in that none of the Bank reports including the performance assessment of the Bank's Independent Evaluation Group (IEG)[5] question the outcomes reported by DPEP I and II Projects or the UP basic education projects. It was unlikely that IEG would have taken at face value the achievements reported either by the borrower or the loan operatives of the Bank as it is an inspection panel set up in the wake of the deep turmoil within the Bank caused by the controversy over the Bank funding of the Narmada Sarovar Project, and the deep turmoil induced by the landmark Wapenhans Report which faulted the Bank's managerial culture and incentive structure which rewarded project design and lending at the expense of implementation and follow-up[6]; IEG conducts performance audit of the Bank's operations and reports directly to the Executive Board (Chapter XVI). Be that as it might be, during the implementation stage the state government used the DPEP outcome objectives as reference, and the Implementation and Completion Report (ICR) assessed the performance of the project with reference to the DPEP objectives.

It is difficult to assess what factors contributed to the success (or lack of it) of a complex programme such as DPEP with such a large outreach and variety of programme interventions, covering multiple layers of government and several institutions, and financed by multiple external agencies. Even defining *success* or *failure* is a daunting task. The question how DPEP ought to be evaluated came up within five years of the launch of DPEP when Jalan and Glinskaya attempted to evaluate the contribution of DPEP to the increase in enrolment and retention in 41 of the 42 districts where DPEP was launched during the first 5

[4] The World Bank, *Uttar Pradesh Third District Primary Education Project: Implementation and Completion Report (IDA-33070)*, 30 October 2006, p. 11.

[5] The World Bank, Independent Evaluation Group, *Project Performance Assessment Report*, Report No. 40160 IN, 30 June 2007. This report covers the two UP basic education projects and the first two DPEP projects financed by the World Bank.

[6] The World Bank, *Effective Implementation: Key to Development Impact: Report of the World Bank's Portfolio Task Force* (The Wapenhans Report). Washington, DC: World Bank, 1992.

years of implementation (1994–5 to 1998–9) . Their evaluation sought to isolate the impact of DPEP on enrolment and retention by excluding the *secular* improvement in enrolment and retention that would have happened without DPEP in 'the natural course of events'. The secular improvement between 1994 and 1999 in enrolment rates was estimated from statistically matched households in matched *control* districts not covered by DPEP, which were similar to the households in DPEP districts on a set of covariates. As there were no baseline data on enrolment in the control districts, Jalan and Glinskaya relied on secondary data such as the 1991 Census and the NSS household surveys of Rounds 50 (1993–94) and 55 (1999–2000). The first draft of the study was highly censorious and concluded that 'the (net positive) impacts are not as substantial as warranted by the massive amount of resources invested in the program or as claimed in the existing DPEP evaluation literature'. The methodology drew sharp criticism from many including Sajitha Bashir. The net positive impact estimated might have been an underestimate for two reasons. Even though implementation of DPEP began in 1994–5, 1995–6 should be reckoned as the first year of the programme as the Bank-funded DPEP I Project secured approvals only in November 1994 and the loan became effective only by end March 1995. Furthermore, programme picked up momentum only in 1998–9. Therefore, the Programme was technically four years old by 1998–9, the terminal year of the evaluation, and it was unrealistic to expect that right from the start a complex multifaceted programme such as DPEP would zoom off in all states and districts. That apart, non-DPEP districts might not provide a valid counterfactual for the reason that DPEP districts were purposively chosen for their educational backwardness as measured by female literacy rates, and the non-DPEP districts were better off educationally. Figuratively, the method adopted to assess the net impact was akin to comparing a race between a tortoise and a hare, and not to give credit for the intrinsic limitations of the tortoise even if it were ahead of the hare. In their anxiety to put forth a different point of view, Jalan and Glinskaya even misleadingly juxtaposed the total commitments of the funding agencies to all the DPEP projects with the estimated impacts in the two projects of the EC-funded project in MP and the Bank-funded DPEP I. However, as the criticism of the methodology seeped in, the criticism was toned down and became more nuanced; thus, the title of the article reporting results of evaluation 'Small Bang for Big Bucks?'

reflected the fact that the authors were no longer as cocksure of their findings as they were at the initial stage[7]; a presentation by the authors of the findings of their study concluded by posing the question, 'Was 300 million dollars (cost of DPEP-I) wasted?', and coming up with the reply, '"NO". DPEP introduced a new approach to primary school interventions in India that cannot be well assessed from secondary data'.[8] With the wisdom of hindsight, it could be said that the *DPEP effect* could have been discovered to some extent if in every DPEP state the baseline surveys of the DPEP projects covered a few control districts with levels of educational indicators as close as possible to those of the DPEP districts. The isolation of the DPEP effect is also complicated by the fact that besides DPEP many other government interventions affecting the outcome indicators were being implemented in DPEP districts, and conversely, the catalytic effects of DPEP on educational improvements went far beyond the narrow confines of participating districts. The discovery of DPEP effect in the later DPEP projects is further complicated from the fact that from 2001 (when SSA began to be implemented) till 2008 (when the last of the DPEP projects came to an end) DPEP coexisted with SSA, and in districts where DPEP as well as SSA were implemented at the same time, DPEP was a sub-set of SSA. However, given the methodological problems no one else ventured to follow the lead of Jalan and Glinskaya, refine the methodology, and attempt to isolate the DPEP effect. Consequently, all evaluations other than that of Jalan and Glinskaya attempt to compare the levels of educational outcomes *ex-ante* and *ex-post*; some supplement the comparison with data from other sources such as the NSS household surveys.

Come to think of it, to K's knowledge there is no study which covers all the eleven DPEP projects together; except for a brief section in MHRD's annual report of 2005–6, there is not even a descriptive account of what all these projects together accomplished in the matter

[7] Jyotsna Jalan and Elena Glinskaya, *Small Bang for Big Bucks: An Evaluation of a Primary School Intervention in India*, Economics Working Paper Series, Working Paper Number 9, Kolkata: Centre for Studies in Social Studies, 2003, http://www.cssscal.org/pdf/WP-2012-9.pdf.

[8] Jyotsna Jalan and Elena Glinskaya, *Improving Primary Schooling in India: An Impact Assessment of DPEP-I*, http://siteresources.worldbank.org/INTISPMA/Resources/Training-Events-and-Materials/india_primaryschool.pdf.

of outputs and educational indicators such as enrolment and reduction in dropout rates. Needless to say, even the descriptive account available is only partial as DPEP continued for two more years after the publication of that annual report. Most of the evaluations relate to the first three projects (the EC-funded Programme in MP and Chhattisgarh, and the Bank-funded DPEP I and II projects). In respect of DPEP III, UP DPEP Project, the DPEP component of the AP Economic Restructuring Project, and the Rajasthan DPEP projects, the Bank did not go beyond the customary and rather ritualistic ICRs, which, according to the Wapenhans report, tend to be written shortly after the last loan disbursement and before benefits begin to flow. Furthermore, the ICRs of these six projects are sketchy in comparison with those of the DPEP I and II projects, and one gets the impression that the loan operatives in charge of the projects were eager to close the shop once and for all without much ado.

The first three DPEP projects triggered enormous excitement and interest nationally and internationally, and the impetus given to research and studies by DPEP generated a wealth of studies. In regard to these three projects, the DPEP TSG had brought out two volumes of abstracts of studies supported by it.[9] Of these 491 abstracts, 152 pertain to evaluation studies. In addition, the background papers circulated for a research seminar in 2003 include reports of five evaluations. These include two evaluations, one by a consortium of IIMs[10] and another by Jyotsna Jha, Saxena, and Baxi on the managerial processes in DPEP.[11] A World Bank review of DPEP I and II projects[12] lists in its bibliography

[9] Research, Evaluation and Studies Unit, Technical Support Group of DPEP, EdCil., Research Abstracts in Primary Education (1994–1997), 1999; Research Abstracts in Primary Education (1997–2000), 2002.

[10] Research, Evaluation and Studies Unit, Technical Support Group of DPEP, EdCil, *External Evaluation of DPEP, Phase-I – Summary of main Findings based on the State Reports prepared by the Indian Institutes of Management, Ahmadabad, Bangalore, Kolkata and Lucknow*, 2003.

[11] Jyotsna Jha, K.B.C. Saxena, and C.V. Baxi, *Management Processes in Elementary Education and DPEP*, New Delhi: The European Commission, 2001.

[12] The World Bank, Human Development Sector, South Asia Region, *A Review of Educational Progress and Reform in the District Primary Education Program (Phases I and II)*, Report Number 1, Washington, DC: The World Bank, 2003.

as many as 224 studies, almost all of which were supported by the DPEP TSG. There are few such studies in respect of subsequent projects. EC organized a comprehensive external evaluation of its support to DPEP[13]; that was the only evaluation which evaluated the contribution to DPEP of NIEPA, NCERT, IGNOU, and other national institutions as well as of the national-level management structures such as the DPEP bureau and its Technical Support Group. True to the spirit of its support being assistance for the reform of the primary education system in India, the European Commission brought out a number of studies covering diverse aspects such as managerial processes, financing of elementary education, reaching the difficult-to-reach groups, textbooks, and teaching learning material, local area planning, and quality; these studies were not limited to MP and Chhattisgarh where EC funding was applied but a few other states covered by DPEP I and II states[14]. In spite of its deeper pockets and claims to be a 'knowledge bank' the contribution of the bank to the study of DPEP is sparse in comparison to that of DPEP TSG or EC. The studies by the bank include a review of DPEP I and II projects, IEG's evaluation of DPEP I and II projects, a case study by Subir Shukla on the pedagogic changes pioneered by DPEP[15], and two studies by Prema Clarke, one on the classroom reform in Kolar district, Karnataka[16], and another a comparative study of the MP Education Guarantee Scheme and Brazil's

[13] *Report of the Final Evaluation of EC Support to Primary Education in India*, New Delhi: European Commission, 2002.

[14] Jyotsna Jha et al., *Management Processes in Elementary Education and DPEP*; Sajitha Bashir, *Government Expenditure on Elementary Education in the Nineties*, 2000; Sajitha Bashir, *Review of the Finance Studies Conducted under DPEP*, 2000; Vimala Ramachandran, Subir Shukla, Philip Cohen, Robin Alexander, and Malcolm Mercer, 'Reflections on Equity, Quality and Local Planning in District Primary Education Programme', Occasional Papers, 2001; Rohit Dhankar and Brigid Smith, *Seeking Quality Education for All: Experiences from the District Primary Education Programme*, 2002.

[15] Subir Shukla, *Systems in Transition: A Case Study of DPEP*, World Bank, 1999.

[16] Prema Clarke, 'Culture and Classroom Reform: The Case of the District Primary Education Project, India', *Comparative Education*, 19, no. 1 (2003), pp. 25–44.

Fundescola programme[17]; it is significant that all studies except that of Shukla are by Bank staffers. The only explanation that K can think for the relative indifference to the later DPEP projects is that with the launch of SSA the focus of DOE shifted to the new programme, EC moved on to its support to SSA as its programme support to DPEP ended, DPEP lost its novelty for researchers, and the follow-up of the Wapenhans Report did not wholly uproot the loan-driven managerial culture of the Bank; furthermore, the performance audit of IEG is not universal but limited to select projects. Even in respect of the first three projects neither the DPEP TSG nor the funding agencies nor scholars thought it fit to analyse the findings of all the studies, evaluations, the reports submitted by states, and the reports of the JRMs, and come out with a comprehensive study which would have given a synoptic overview of what these three projects together achieved, what they failed to achieve, and the lessons they offer for the efforts of India and other developing countries to universalize primary education. Such a study could also have identified areas of further research and evaluation to get a more complete picture of the three projects. It is a great pity that we do not have a complete picture of all the DPEP projects as till its closure DPEP was in a state of flux and constant evolution in terms of coverage and programme interventions, and the lack of information precludes a complete picture of what DPEP accomplished and what it did not.

The DPEP strategy was heavily influenced by the lessons of earlier projects, and three such lessons gained from BEP were that the responsibility for planning and implementation should be placed squarely on the state government and that DOE officials should not descend on a state again and again and 'mother' the project development and implementation, and that the DPEP Bureau should rigorously appraise the annual work plans drawn up by states functionaries themselves with such assistance that might be available from resource organizations such as SCERT and universities. Therefore, right from the

[17] Prema Clarke, 'Education Reforming the Education Grantee Scheme in Madhya Pradesh and the Fundescola Program in Brazil', Washington, DC: The World Bank, 2003, http://documents.worldbank.org/curated/en/2003/03/2601214/education-reform-education-guarantee-scheme-madhya-pradesh-india-fundescola-program-brazil (last accessed on 29 May 2015).

beginning, assistance to the state functionaries was limited to building capacity for planning and implementation of all aspects of DPEP; it was for the states to display initiative in availing the opportunities and flexibility DPEP provided. Figuratively, the DPEP Bureau taught the states to catch fish and did not do fishing by itself; consequently, states which were keener to learn fishing and hone their new skill and catch fish fared better than the less keen states. In the first two years, the DPEP strategy exercised tight supervision in order to ensure that the culture of accountability and the new structures and processes take root. However, gradually the DPEP Bureau loosened its control, and its own supervision as well as the functioning of the JRMs did not differentiate between states which performed well and those which did not. Consequently, the responsibility of states came to be higher; it was for a state to make or break the programme, to innovate or not, and to mechanically implement the programme ignoring the organic linkages between DPEP and the larger elementary education system or to creatively avail the flexibility and resources provided by DPEP, and to mainstream the good practices tried out in DPEP and leaven the state elementary education system or not. There is some merit in the observation of the Sixteenth JRM (14 November to 2 December 2002) that 'It is difficult to comment on the progress under DPEP nationally as different states, at different stages of educational development at the time of programme initiation, have used it to varying degrees to transform primary education scenario in their states'. Therefore, 'each state had a DPEP of its own kind', and a full account of DPEP cannot be a seamless narrative but an anthology of stories—of what happened in each of the eighteen states as well as steering of the programme by DOE. Such accounts should not be limited to the project outputs and educational outcomes; they should cover aspects such as the operation of various managerial and pedagogic processes envisaged by the DPEP, managerial and pedagogic innovations, the extent to which linkages were fostered between DPEP and the main system, and mainstreaming of the good practices and innovations of DPEP. Unfortunately, to K's knowledge such detailed accounts do not exist. It is only in respect of MP many of the aspects were studied and published.

What happened in states and districts is no doubt an important aspect of DPEP; however, a full account of DPEP has to be much more than the action in states. The full account has to be an anthology of many narratives of what happened in states, and of the role played by DPEP Bureau, DPEP TSG, and national and state resource organizations such as NCERT, NIEPA, and SCERTs. It has to also record the many interplays manifested in the development and implementation of DPEP: between DPEP Bureau on the one hand and State Education Departments and state DPEP project officers on the other, DPEP Bureau and resource organizations such as NCERT, DPEP Bureau, and funding agencies, and of established structures such as SCERTs and State Education Departments on the one hand and the state and district DPEP project offices. It should also critically chronicle capacity and institution building, 'donor coordination', various aspects of pedagogic and quality improvement, and so on. Here again there are no studies; to some extent, the tension between the DPEP Bureau and the traditional structures and the politics of textbook reform were documented to some extent by a case study of the Kennedy School of Government (KSG), Harvard University.[18]

Suffice to say, dark and tangled stretches limit our knowledge of what DPEP had accomplished; however, K believes that even with the available information fairly reliable answers could be given to the questions raised above. It would be worthwhile, however, to illuminate the dark stretches through exhaustive studies which arduously cull and analyse the information scattered over several institutions such as DPEP TSG, NUEPA, and archives of agencies which were associated with DPEP, and complementing archival research with oral history would illuminate many of those stretches.

Is SSA the New Avatar of DPEP?

The answer to the above question is a resounding affirmative; except for a few mutations SSA is indeed an expanded version of DPEP covering all the districts of the country and the entire elementary stage. It embraced wholesale the DPEP strategy as well as the new structures and processes introduced by DPEP for the management of the programme and improvement of the quality of education. As *originally* designed, SSA's

[18] Husock Howard, 'Implementing Education Reform in India: The Primary School Textbook Debate and Resistance to Change in Kerala', Harvard University, Kennedy School of Government Case Study Programme, C15-00-1573.0, 2000.

approach to enhancing access and participation was the same as that of DPEP; DPEP went by the postulate of NPE, 1986, that UEE cannot be achieved in the near future by relying solely on the school system and that, therefore, schooling needed to be supplemented by an extensive alternate system that would cater to the educational needs of children outside school. The first objective of SSA envisaged that all children would be *in school or its alternative equivalents* in just two years by 2003. The other objectives of SSA comprised all children completing five years of primary schooling by 2007, and eight years of elementary schooling by 2010; all gender and social category gaps being bridged at primary stage by 2007 and at elementary education level by 2010; and universal retention being achieved by 2010. DPEP guidelines expected that all central and state programmes such as Operation Blackboard would be factored in while formulating the district plans; with the onset of the Tenth Five-Year Plan in 2002, about a year after the launch of the SSA, Operation Blackboard and NFE were subsumed in SSA. Five years later, with effect from April 2007, the Kasturba Gandhi Balika Vidyalaya scheme, a scheme for setting up residential schools at upper primary level for girls belonging predominantly to the SC, ST, OBC, and minority communities, was also subsumed in SSA. As a result, SSA came to be a sole national programme for universalizing elementary education with a couple of supporting schemes such as Teacher Education and Mid-Day Meal Scheme. And further, with the phasing out of Lok Jumbish in June 2004, Shiksha Karmi in June 2005, and the Janshala[19] in December 2005, SSA came to be the only programme that external agencies could support in the field of elementary education. Hence, the objective envisaged by DPEP of being the sole national programme for UEE that could be supported by agencies was realized.

Apart from objectives, the strategy of SSA is almost identical to that of DPEP. Thus, as with DPEP the district plan is central to SSA; so are critical appraisal of the perspective and annual plans as well as

[19] Janashala, meaning a community school, is a small-scale joint initiative of UNDP, UNICEF, UNFPA, UNESCO, and ILO. Started in 1997, UNICEF, UNDP, and UNFPA jointly committed a sum of about US$20 million for the programme; ILO and UNESCO offered technical knowhow. At its peak, it covered approximately 12.5 lakh children in over 12,500 schools spread over 125 blocks in nine states.

periodic supervision of implementation of the plans; so the simultaneous addressing of all aspects of universalization; so also is the equal emphasis on processes, community mobilization, and outcomes; so too is the implementation in a mission mode through a state-level society and core groups in the districts and blocks; and so is capacity building at all levels to plan, manage, and monitor the programme. The structures of DPEP were assimilated into SSA; these included the national-level structures such as the Mission General Council, the Project Approval Board (PAB), and the TSG. The DPEP Mission was rechristened National Mission for SSA. In fact, the national structures created by DPEP and absorbed by SSA were found to be so effective that they were adopted by the Rashtriya Madhyamik Sikhsha Abhiyan (RMSA, 2009) whose objective was to universalize secondary education and the Rashtriya Uchchatar Shikhsha Abhiyan (RUSA, National Higher Education Mission, 2013).

Apart from structures, SSA assimilated the monitoring and evaluation mechanisms put in place by DPEP. Even RMSA and even the Centrally Sponsored Scheme of Teacher Education found it expedient to go in for JRMs, and had even adopted SSA's terms of reference and template for the aide-memoire. However, to tell the truth, the JRMs are no exception to the inexorable law that, over a course of time, everything would get routinized. One cannot help feel that the report of a JRM is almost invariably a standalone document which tends to assess the progress *de novo* rather than carry forward the work of previous JRMs. The report of the action taken on a JRM is perfunctory. The JRM is swamped by so much information that it is difficult to digest the information; the field visits are too hurried and too many institutions are visited to provide anything but fleeting impressions. There is tremendous pressure to complete the remit within the brief period available by generating a standardized aide-memoire. A good practice which was introduced in recent years is to select a theme for focussed attention; however, as the representatives of agencies use the occasion, the JRM provides to pack in the aide-memoire every type of information their headquarters needs; in effect, everything is a priority which means that nothing is.

Turning to the question posed by K and Sajitha as to whether DPEP would go beyond discrete district-level projects to an all-encompassing reform of primary education, it should be said that in a strict sense, an all-encompassing reform of elementary and secondary education is not yet on cards. DPEP left out several areas such as teacher recruitment, rejuvenation of the State Education Departments and professionalization of the functionaries of those departments; so do SSA and RMSA. RUSA has a bolder vision; however, it is too early to say whether the vision would remain just a mental construct or acted upon. Invariably all critiques of DPEP are appreciative of the networking among professional institutions such as universities, IIMs, and LBSNAA, harnessing the expertise of institutions and professionals for various tasks such as studies, evaluations, appraisal, supervision, and so on, and creating new structures such as the state society; however, at the same time they are critical of the failure to make an earnest attempt to transform existing institutions. DPEP did enlist SCERTs and DIETs in its academic activities; however, there were large inter-state variations in the participation of and contribution of these institutions. SCERTs continue to be, by and large, dormant, and in many states, the functioning of DIETs suboptimal. Worse, in states such as AP 90 per cent of their time is reportedly spent on activities such as the preparation of question papers for the recruitment of teachers and evaluation of the answer papers rather on teacher training and providing support for improving the competence of teachers.[20] One only hopes that the National Teacher Mission would take up the long-delayed rejuvenation of all the resource institutions at all levels. The available evidence indicates that while good pedagogic practices introduced in DPEP districts were, to some extent, extended to districts not covered by DPEP there was little extension of management processes and styles introduced by DPEP to the broader educational system. No state seems to have adopted the principles of the annual work planning and budgeting process for other CSS and state plan schemes; it was business as usual.

As at the national level, at the state level the DPEP pattern of implementing SSA through a state society was embraced. In states where DPEP was being implemented the state DPEP societies were converted into state SSA societies, and in states where DPEP was not implemented, societies were set up for the management of SSA. It may be recalled that the management of the UP Basic Education

[20] Government of India, Department of School Education and Literacy, Minutes of the First meeting of the Joint Review Mission, 5 December 2012, http://www.teindia.nic.in/Files/jrm/Minutes_TE_JRM_1st_meeting.pdf.

Project and DPEP through a separate structure instead of the State Education Department was a very contentious issue when those projects were being developed and their financing arrangements firmed up (Chapter XIV). Looking back, the controversy surrounding the management through a society was a storm in a tea cup; neither the high expectations nor the apprehensions materialized. Except in some states such as Kerala, and thereto too for a limited period when the project was led by a director with a missionary zeal such as Suresh Kumar there were no tensions between the parallel structures of the State Education Department and the DPEP society. The fear felt in states such as MP that that nomination of non-officials as members of the state DPEP society organizations would politicize implementation did not come true as the JRM mechanism figuratively 'put the fear of God' in those who saw in DPEP yet another opportunity to extend patronage; the colonial mindset of being in awe of the foreigner was unwittingly helpful. In effect, in most states, the state society functioned as a special unit of the State Education Department for the implementation of the DPEP, and the association of non-governmental actors in the management of DPEP was generally much below expectation. The state society served mainly two purposes: it brought to bear on implementation the focussed attention required, and flow of funds from DOE to the project implementation units was smooth. Lest it should be inferred that the DPEP society was redundant and that unnecessary fuss was made over a non-issue, it should be said that departmental mode of implementing DPEP would not have as effectively served those two purposes as the society, and that, consequently, implementation would definitely have been impaired. Taking note of this fact, SSA adopted DPEP's society mode of implementation. As SSA as well as the supporting schemes covered all districts and all schools, the SSA society came to discharge developmental functions while the Director, School Education, came to discharge regulatory and administrative functions. As at the state level, at the district and local levels also SSA relied on the structures created by DPEP such as a small project implementation unit headed by a District Programme Coordinator; in most states, the project implementation unit was integrated with the District Education Office. At the sub-district level also, the SSA assimilated the Block and Cluster Resource Centres (BRCs, CRCs), and established such centres in districts not covered by DPEP. These centres did fill a conspicuous void in the training infrastructure, revive the forgotten tradition of academic supervision and guidance, and were designed to end the isolation of teachers and to serve as a close-by support mechanism 'for teachers undertaking the complex endeavour of bringing about effective change in their classroom'. RMSA had been focussing almost wholly on expansion of access and enrolment, and once it begins to focus on quality and learning outcomes, the need for creation of similar decentralized structures would be felt.

At the school level, DPEP encouraged the involvement of the local community in enhancing the effectiveness of schools. Different types of institutions were established: some states opted for village education communities, some for school management committees, some for parent teacher associations (PTAs), and some for mother teacher associations (MTAs). It is reported that 50 lakh such bodies were established; DPEP provided substantial training opportunities for these community organizations, contributing to their capacity development. Starting with campaigns to boost enrolments and school participation for first-generation learners, these bodies, over time, had expanded their role to include responsibility for civil works in school construction, monitoring teacher attendance, and planning and implementation of school improvement programmes. It is reported that their involvement led to greater attention being given to school management issues.[21] However, generalizations are precarious as there were wide variations in their role and the zeal of the functionaries across states and even among villages in a given state. SSA assimilated these structures and established them in districts not covered by DPEP; RMSA also promoted the establishment of school management committees.

Suffice it to say, but for the groundwork done by DPEP, SSA would not have taken off so smoothly. It was not only a question of SSA having in hand a tested strategy and knowledge of what might work and definitely does not; SSA was also enormously benefited by the fact that eighteen of the 20 states having more than fifty lakh population were ready to smoothly glide from DPEP to SSA, were habituated to accept

[21] Shanti Jagannathan, 'Programme-based Approaches and International Collaboration: Experiences and Lessons from Education Sector', paper presented to LEPNA Forum, 'Programme-based Approaches to Diversity: Adapting to Diversity', Tokyo, 1–3 June 2004, pp. 6–7.

the directional role of DOE, and were able to display greater initiative and creativity within the national framework. And further, it had institutional structures such as TSG to support the programme, and a well-developed mechanism for supervision, monitoring, and evaluation. In short, DPEP was the caterpillar without which the butterfly of SSA would not have come into being.

No two avatars are the same; no two human beings are genetically identical as mutations occur during conceptualization or subsequent development or both. Likewise, during its evolution from DPEP and subsequent implementation SSA acquired a few distinctive characteristics. The thrust of DPEP as well as SSA was on disadvantaged groups such as girls, Scheduled Castes (SCs), Scheduled Tribes (STs), working children, urban deprived children, and disabled children. However, in practice the first three DPEP projects gave priority to girls' participation, focused on districts that had female literacy below the state average, and did not target SC and ST children the way they targeted girls. As a result, gender disparities in enrolment, retention, and learning levels were considerably reduced across the entire programme—one of the most visible areas of success. However, the same success was not forthcoming for children from SC and ST children, particularly ST children. SSA rectified this deficiency of DPEP and focussed on the entire range of disadvantaged groups. It identified special focus districts with a high concentration of socially disadvantaged groups such as SCs, STs, and Muslims as well as districts with more than 50,000 out-of-school children. Apart from focussed attention on such districts, it also began to fix separate targets fixed for the enrolment and dropout rates of each category of disadvantaged groups and monitor the achievement of the targets.

SSA significantly departed from DPEP as well as NPE as revised in 1992 by not setting up quantitative goals for learning achievement and by regressing to the original formulation of NPE, 1986; unlike its 1992 revision, the 1986 Policy perceived a substantial improvement in the quality of education as an end in itself rather than a means to the attainment of essential levels of learning. Why this regression to the 1986 Policy formulation came about and what its consequences were would be detailed later. SSA also differed from DPEP in that the states had to bear a higher proportion of the outlay than the 15 per cent they had to bear in DPEP. Till 2006–7, the states were required to contribute 25 per cent of the outlay; thereafter the state share was increased to 35 per cent excepting the North-Eastern states which were given a special dispensation being required to contribute only 10 per cent. The Framework for Implementation of SSA (2001) was revised twice, first in 2005 and again in 2011, the later in pursuance of the enactment of the RTE Act, 2009. The most significant departure of the 2011 revision was the decision not to fund alternatives to schooling; by 2011–12 all such centres were to be either closed or converted into regular schools. All in all, the strategy followed since NPE, 1986, for achieving universal participation was given up.

Be Thou in the Driver's Seat

The imagery of DPEP as butterfly and of SSA as caterpillar is valid in another sense. DPEP had two interrelated strategies, one to universalize primary education and the other to mobilize external funding in a manner which would ensure that autonomy in managing designing, implementing, and expanding the programme is not a whit infringed. Even as DPEP was being developed and funding by different agencies such as the EC, Bank, and ODA firmed up, it was evident to K and his associates as well as the EC functionaries that DPEP was blazing a trail in accessing external funding or what in jargon is called development cooperation. Later developments in the praxis of development cooperation do indeed confirm that DPEP did blaze a trail (Chapter XIV). Before the 1990s, 'donor governments', notes Riddell in his classic study of 'foreign aid', 'have historically given little priority to the evidence of aid impact when making core decisions about how to improve the quality of the aid they provide. Now however, donors have become more reflective, giving more priority to issues of impact and trying to understand better what works and why. It led them to realize more clearly that the impact of aid depends on the context in which it is given, and on the capacity and commitment of recipients to use it well'.[22] When DPEP was being formulated, there was increasing awareness in the donor community that, in social sectors, standalone projects without a supporting policy environment and

[22] Roger C. Riddell, *Does Foreign Aid Really Work?* Oxford: Oxford University Press, 2007, p. 382.

which are not 'owned' by the recipient of aid were not efficient in terms of 'aid delivery' and attainment of the development objectives for which the aid is provided. Efficiency did not improve even when the project was sequestered from the rest of the system and even when the agency adopted a hands-on style of designing and managing the project. Agencies began to think about *new modalities of aid* [23] which would rectify the deficiencies of project mode of assistance, and in due course, lists of 'dos; and 'don'ts' made their appearance. As projects were often vitiated by the absence of a supporting policy, the list of 'dos' commended support for building the capacity of recipient countries to develop proper policies, develop strategies for implementing such policies, and further develop programmes to implement such strategies. As projects were often vitiated by lack of ownership on the part of the recipient country, the list of 'dos' commended that agencies support programmes or sector reform policies drawn up by the recipient country itself. Edward Jaycox, Vice-President, Africa Region, the World Bank gave eloquent expression to this point of view by declaring:

> There are 30 countries in economic reform in Africa where we're underwriting the economy, with hundreds of millions of dollars. We are now insisting that the governments generate their own economic reform plans. We'll help, we'll critique, we'll eventually negotiate and we'll support financially those things which seem to be reasonably making sense, but we're not going to write these plans. We're not going to say: Here you are, do this, and we'll give you money. That's out. We're not going to do this anymore, but you're going to have to find that domestic capacity.[24]

Yet another perceived deficiency of the project modality was that the project was often an enclave with few linkages with the pertinent sector; consequently, the benefits of the project were minuscule and often not sustained; like the jungle spreading and engulfing the

[23] Kenneth King, 'The External Agenda of Aid in Internal Educational Reform', *International Journal of Educational Development*, 12, no. 4 (1992), pp. 257–64.

[24] Edward Jaycox, 'African Capacity Building: Effective and Enduring Partnerships', Address to the African-American Institute Conference Reston, Virginia, May 20, 1993 'excerpts published in 'New trends in training policies', NORRAG News, NN14, July 1993, pp. 9–11.

clearance, the negative features of the larger system would overwhelm the good features introduced by the project.

Because of its underdevelopment, Africa has been the magnet which drew the bulk of aid; over the last 50 years as much as a trillion dollars—the equivalent of five Marshall Plans (1948–51) which rehabilitated war-ravaged Europe—were pumped in Africa with so little impact that aid had been described as the 'disease of which it pretends to be the cure'.[25] It was in Africa that donors had a free run, and it was Africa which presented most of the horror stories of project disasters; no wonder that it was in Africa that the new modalities were first tried out. The apotheosis of the new modalities was the Paris Declaration on Aid Effectiveness.[26] The foremost principle of the Paris Declaration is that the recipient country should 'exercise leadership in developing and implementing their national development strategies through broad consultative processes', and that conversely agencies should 'respect partner country leadership and help strengthen their capacity to exercise it'. Drawing upon the much-touted imagery of the country being in the driver's seat, the new ethics of development cooperation would require the country itself to choose the destination and route, and further to drive itself. If its driving skills are deficient, it should pick up the requisite skills; in the interim, it may allow the development partner to drive strictly in accordance with its preferences; however, it should be willing to fire the driver should the driver fail to comply with its preferences or fail to teach driving skills. Correspondingly, the new ethics would require the agencies to willingly let the country to be in the driver's seat, and, if need be, to instil in the country the necessary competence and motivation. Tokenisms such as putting the country in the driver's seat as chauffeur would not do. To say the least, the attitude of 'I know the solutions for your problems', and of 'disregarding or undermining the government capacity and systems' is no longer appropriate. The Paris Declaration also commended adoption of a programme-based approach (PBA)/sector-wide approaches (SWAp) instead of a

[25] Dambisa Moyo, *Dead Aid: Why Aid Is Not Working and How There Is Another Way for Africa*, New York: Farrar, Strauss, Giroux, 2009, p. ix.

[26] *Paris Declaration on Aid Effectiveness: Ownership, Harmonisation, Alignment, Results and Mutual Accountability*, 2 March 2005, http://www.oecd.org/dataoecd/11/41/34428351.pdf.

project approach, pooling of domestic and external resources of different agencies for implementing the national programme, adopting national systems for financial reporting and accounts, and developing joint review mechanisms.

The semantics, modalities, and good practices of PBA, SWAp, as well as of different financing patterns have been much discussed in literature[27]. PBA is defined as 'a way of engaging in development cooperation based on the principle of coordinated support for a locally owned programme of development, such as a national poverty reduction strategy, a sector programme, a thematic programme, or a programme of a specific organization'.[28] Without getting into far too many technicalities, these modalities and financing arrangements are guided by two overarching principles: first, 'one country, one strategy, one process';[29] second, the country should be the owner-driver. What these two principles state is that *ideally*

- there should be a coherent national policy which lays down the goals and objectives;
- there should be a single well-considered national strategy for achieving the policy goals and objectives;
- there should be a single well-designed national programme for implementing that strategy;
- there should be well-designed modalities of implementing that programme;
- there should be well-designed national systems of reporting, budgeting, financial Management, and procurement;

[27] OECD, *Harmonising Donor Practices for Effective Aid Delivery*, Budget Support, Sector Wide Approaches and Capacity Development in Public Financial Management, DAC Guidelines and Reference Series, Volume 2, 2006. http://www.oecd.org/dataoecd/53/7/34583142.pdf (last accessed on 29 May 2015).

[28] The definition is by the Learning Network on Programme-Based Approaches (LENPA); cited in OECD, cited above.

[29] This is one of the guiding principles of Education for All-Fast Track Initiative (EFA-FTI). Van Roemburg, Rebekka, Co-Chair of Steering Committee, EFA-FTI, *Understanding the FTI Partnership*, PowerPoint presentation, Capacity Development Workshop 'Country Leadership and Implementation for Results in the EFA FTI Partnership,' Cape Town, South Africa, 16 July 2007.

- agencies should support that programme only, and no other;
- agencies should adopt national systems of reporting, budgeting, financial management, and procurement; and
- agency coordination is not an isolated activity, but a subset of the overall coordination of the activities that together encompass the programme being supported by the agencies.

The Education for All Fast-track Initiative (EFA FTI), a global consortium of agencies and developing countries to foster accelerated progress towards the Millennium Development Goal (MDG) of UPE by 2015, commended SWAp as the model to be adopted by countries which seeks its assistance. K had an opportunity to participate in workshops organized in Africa to develop the capacity of African countries to adopt SWAp and achieve UPE. In his presentations, K elaborated on the implications of the Paris Declaration for developing countries and the agencies: how the developing countries could meet the challenges they face in exercising *leadership* in their interaction with agencies, and how appropriate the Indian experience was for them.[30] In a background study for UNESCO's EFA—Global Monitoring Report, 2009—K elaborated the themes he expounded in the African workshops.[31]

In 2000 itself, some of the agency functionaries associated with DPEP such as David Smawfield of ODA,[32] and Shanti Jagannathan and Mervi Karikorpi of EC[33] wrote about DPEP as exhibiting some of the

[30] R.V. Vaidyanatha Ayyar, *Donor Harmonization and Alignment, Organizing to Take Leadership: The Experience of India*, 2nd African Region Education Capacity Development Workshop 'Country Leadership and Implementation of Results in the EFA FTI Partnership', Tunis, Tunisia, 3–6 December 2007.

[31] R.V. Vaidyanatha Ayyar, 'Country-Agency Relationship in Development Cooperation: An Indian Experience', Background Paper prepared for the *Education for All Global Monitoring Report 2009; Overcoming Inequality: Why Governance Matters*, Paris: UNESCO, 2008.

[32] David Smawfield and Helen Poulsen, *Mainstreaming Gender through Sector Wide Approaches: India Case Study*, London: Overseas Development Institute, October 2000, http://www.odi.org.uk/sites/odi.org.uk/files/odi-assets/publications-opinion-files/2227.pdf.

[33] Shanti Jagannathan and Mervi Karikorpi, 'EC-India Development Co-operation in Primary Education: Sector-wide Approaches to Development Cooperation', Special issue on New Modalities in New Modalities for Development Co-operation, *Prospects*, XXX, no. 4 (2000), pp. 409–22.

characteristics of a SWAp, one of the new modalities of development assistance. Significantly, the developments in the praxis of development assistance were pioneered by the agencies and driven by an eagerness to improve the delivery of assistance; in contrast, the developments in DPEP were pioneered by DOE, a government department, and driven by an eagerness to access financing from multiple sources for a home-grown programme in a manner that would not detract from its autonomy in developing and implementing the programme access. In other words, the developments pioneered by DPEP were a mirror image of the developments in the *donorland*. There are few projects in the country or elsewhere in which the recipient country was so firmly in the driver's seat, a fact captured by an observation of Eimi Watanabe, UNICEF Country Representative, 'K tells each one of us, well You, you go here, and You, you go there; we all go where he wants us to go' (Chapter XIV). Shanti Jagannathan highlights the fact that outstanding and strong leadership exhibited in the beginning had a positive effect and that effect was 'in evidence even now, a decade later'.[34] DPEP as well as the financing of DPEP had almost all the characteristics of PAB outlined above except that the systems for reporting and financial management were specially developed by the DPEP Bureau for the programme. For those who had taken the trouble of even cursorily browsing this long narrative so far, it is redundant to further elaborate how DPEP was a national programme par excellence which operationalized a new national strategy for UEE in terms of a revised national education policy. Furthermore, in addition to pioneering leadership in country–agency relationships, DPEP also pioneered many of the practices such as joint review and reporting mechanisms, and country leadership a decade before the Paris Declaration. However, for all its pioneering the development and implementation of a PAB, DPEP was still a half-way house. The agencies funded DPEP separately, though, with common reporting formats and JRMs. Funds received from an agency were not pooled with those provided by other agencies but earmarked for a specific state or group of states; each state covered by DPEP was expected to comply with the procurement procedures of the agency whose funds were slotted to it. In the manner of appraisals

[34] Shanti Jagannathan, 'EC-India Development Co-operation in Primary Education', p. 5.

also, DPEP was a halfway house. DOE appraised the annual work plans of all states. While the DPEP Bureau assumed principal responsibility for appraisal of state and district plans, a World Bank Mission scrutinized the appraisal done in states where its funding was sought to be applied to satisfy itself whether the Bureau's appraisal was satisfactory; in states where EC or ODA funds were applied, appraisal was done by a joint mission of DOE nominees and the agency which sought to fund DPEP in that state. This dual mode was necessitated by the conscious decision of DOE to avail IDA credit only as specific project credit instead of sector investment credit. However, in keeping with the spirit of the programme, the JRM was a national mission. Participation of an agency in JRM was not limited to the states where its funding was applied. Thus, all in all, DPEP was still a prototype of and not a full-fledged SWAp.

In contrast to DPEP, SSA is a full-fledged PAB in that SSA does not earmark funds received from the agencies to specified states. Consequently, there were no more World Bank states, EC states, and DFID states. The World Bank, DFID, and EC appraised the project jointly and decided to pool their funds to support the programme. The agencies harmonized their procedures through a formal MOU with the central government in regard to common formats, withdrawal claims, and JRMs. The agencies also agreed to adopt the national systems for procurement, monitoring, and financial management. The agencies accepted the Manual on Financial Management and Procurement (FMP) produced by the Department of Elementary Education and Literacy (DEEL), a department which came into existence when DOE was bifurcated in 2001–2. The JRM mechanism of DPEP was modified so as to assign a greater voice for DEEL in the JRMs. Unlike the JRMs of DPEP, where DOE and the agencies supporting the programme would lead the JRMs by turns, a DEEL nominee would lead all SSA JRMs. The maximum number of members of a JRM would be 20, of which half the members would be DEEL nominees and the other half drawn from the three agencies in proportion to their financial contribution. Suffice to say, but for the groundwork done by DPEP in the matter of external financing, neither the agencies nor the DEEL would have found it so easy to opt for the modish SWAp/PBA mode. This is yet another reason why DPEP was the caterpillar without which the butterfly of SSA would not have come into being.

Coming to the process by which DPEP came to precociously anticipate and operate the Paris Declaration, exercising leadership was an article of faith which followed from an unflinching adherence to the parameters stipulated by CABE for accessing external funding, yet leadership had to be wrested and asserted again and again. In contrast to leadership, the modalities were discovered through an incremental process of search and discovery, sometimes with the cooperation of one or more of the agencies. Pioneering is not for the faint hearted. If one chooses not to travel on a trodden path, one has to pave a new path guided by one's own instincts and judgement as well as the cooperation one could elicit from fellow travellers. It is not unusual to go by wholly inappropriate past precedents and traditions. Thus, when the EC decided to assist DPEP as sector programme assistance to DPEP, a programme for reforming the primary education sub-sector, neither EC nor DOE had a clear idea how to go about. EC functionaries were right to insist that the funds provided be applied for DPEP as a whole and not to MP alone. At the same time, however, they wanted to continue the traditional project mode of assistance and be closely associated with the implementation of DPEP by way of approvals of annual work plans and positioning EC experts in the national and state management structures. Yet, given the goodwill on both sides, agreement could be reached and arrangements could be worked out which were in keeping with PAB principles and the distinctive features of DPEP (Chapter XIV). There were many hiccups in the development and Bank's approval of DPEP I Project agreement. Thus, at one point, there was resistance to fund a multi-state project instead of the traditional state-specific project. Yet with tenacious perseverance the Bank functionaries could be won over to go by the spirit of DPEP and treat Bank funding of DPEP as a sector investment loan for all practical purposes, and go in for modalities common to all the agencies funding DPEP and which are in conformity with DPEP framework and guidelines. Getting ODA to accept the DPEP framework and, by implication, the PAB principles and modalities was no easy task either. ODA did not like the stipulations of the interaction of the agency functionaries with field functionaries in AP and West Bengal being limited to the two half-yearly JRMs, and ODA's Hyderabad office should be closed down. DOE decided to avail the support only after ODA conceded DOE's requirements for participation in DPEP. The new relationship that DPEP sought to establish imposed a heavy burden of unlearning on established agencies as well as on the states, most of whom had a long experience of implementing externally funded projects in the traditional bilateral pattern of relationship between the agency and the state government. A new player like EC was at an advantage in working within the new relationship. As years rolled by and DFID began to espouse principles of development cooperation which came to be embodied in the Paris Declaration, it came to be a strong supporter of country leadership and the relation that DPEP ushered.

Getting the agencies on board is not even half the story. As the experience of India and Ethiopia indicate, the exercise of leadership by the recipient country as the Paris Declaration commends encounters two major obstacles in federal polities. The first arises from the fact that a national programme might not be flexible enough to allow local factors to inform planning and implementation. Even if, like DPEP, a programme allows flexibility it may take a long while for that fact to be recognised by the states; as the DPEP experience shows, it is possible that some states may equate flexibility with lack of a national frame and the absence of a directional role of the Federal Ministry which is responsible for operating a PAB/SWAp and interacting with the agencies funding the programme. Suffice to say, if a federal government wishes to access external resources for a national programme and pass on the resources to the states, and if it wishes to live by the Paris principles, the new relation it has to establish with agencies is a subset of the overall realignment of relations it should bring about. The new relationships fell in place only over a course of time and only after the DPEP Bureau prevailed in quite a few policy contests and power struggles which had been already narrated at length.

It would be facile to believe that the Paris Declaration had ushered a new age of idyllic relationship between developed countries and the agencies. The Paris Declaration was reaffirmed and progress in achieving the postulates of that Declaration reviewed at subsequent meetings of the High-Level Forum on Aid Effectiveness at Accra (2008) and Boesen (2011). However, for a long time to come, the Paris Declaration, like the Ten Commandments, would be more a guiding star than a destination likely to be reached by all recipient countries and agencies. SWAp/PAB modalities of assistance are not yet the predominant modes of delivery of development assistance. The country context is critical; not all countries are equally placed in their will and ability to exercise leadership 'in developing and implementing their national development strategies', and in 'taking the lead in co-ordinating aid at all levels'. Paris is redundant for counties such as China and India; it is irrelevant for many small economies and failed states. If a country's economy is no bigger than that of 'a middle-sized provincial English town', if it is chronically aid-dependent, and if it does not have a critical mass of educated manpower, what is the point in talking about country ownership and leadership, and so on? Given the colonial legacy, a high degree of aid dependence, officials of these countries are apt to be ventriloquist's dummies saying what would please donors. In K's view, the target group of Paris Declaration should be countries in the middle, which have the potential to behave in the manner Paris Declaration expects developing countries to behave. As ever there is a vast gulf between actual behaviour and what it ought to be. Riddell's study brings out that agencies differ considerably in their willingness to move away from the conventional project support to SWAp. Agencies from the Nordic countries, the Netherlands, and the United Kingdom, as well as the European Commission have been strong advocates of the new modalities, and prepared quite early to move more quickly along the spectrum away from project support, parallel, individually tracked external expenditure, and toward pooled funding by agencies in support of a government's sectoral or poverty reduction or national development programme. Some such as USAID are still 'wedded to attributable project finance', as contribution to the 'common pot' would lower their visibility.[35] In a workshop in Hanoi (2007), K heard an agency functionary contemptuously refer to the Paris Declaration as 'Paris and all that'; that expression captures the lingering resistance to new modalities and ethics of aid delivery. All in all, the Paris Declaration calls for far-reaching changes in the country–development agency relationship, akin to those brought out by the Gender Revolution, and the agencies could and *ought* to do more than the recipient countries for universal realization of the postulates of the Paris Declaration.

[35] A. Riddell, 'The New Modalities of Aid to Education: The View from within Some Recipient Countries', Background paper for *EFA Global Monitoring Report 2008*, p. 5.

The experience of SSA itself bears out the fact that, like beauty, SWAp/PAB modalities lie in the eyes of the beholder. The two most contentious issues of the negotiations for the SSA-I project were the revision of the JRM composition and leadership, and the alignment of the Bank's procurement and financial procedures with the DEEL's Manual on FMP. There was also difference between the DFID and the Bank in regard to the capacity building needed for operationalizing DEEL's FMP. DFID emphasized a developmental approach to capacity building in FMP; on the other hand, the Bank wanted to ensure adequate levels of fiduciary assurance right from the beginning of the operations.[36] The DFID's advocacy of a developmental approach to capacity building shows how far it had come from ODA's early engagement with DPEP. The alignment of the Bank's procurement procedures with the national systems removed many of the irritants that are often encountered in Bank-operated programmes. Like King Charles's Head, the very same contentious issues of SSA-I negotiations cropped up again in the SSA-II negotiations. In spite of the fact that no malfeasance was noticed in SSA-I with the use of the country systems, the Bank sought to roll back its agreement to align with DEEL's FMP; it insisted that the SSA-I financial procurement procedures should be revised so as to align with the Bank's Anti-Corruption Guidelines (2006). The problem was not so much with Bank's renewed concern for transparency; it had to do more with the new mood of control that seems to grip the Bank. It was unrealistic to insist on an explicit right to follow the Bank's funds, in each and every transaction, all the way down from the national headquarters to thousands of schools in a decentralized programme with a score of major programme components, spread over a continental nation and funded jointly by GOI, 28 states, and three agencies. The right would confer on the Bank an oversight and control role incommensurate with Bank's financial contribution which was less than 6 per cent of the programme outlay. The Bank's mood did not sit

[36] Asian Development Bank, 'How Can Programmatic Assistance Enhance Country Leadership of the Development Agenda? The Case of Sarva Shiksha Abhiyan in India', *Asian Regional Forum on Aid Effectiveness: Implementation, Monitoring and Evaluation*, 2006, http://www.adb.org/Documents/Events/2006/Aid-Effectiveness/country-papers/IND-education-swap.pdf, Asian Development Bank, 2006 (last accessed on 25 May 2015).

well with the new modalities of support delivery. The negotiations were on the verge of breaking down, and at the very last moment, the Bank withdrew from the precipice and agreed to accept the arrangements agreed to in SSA-I. Here again one faced the quintessential dilemma of balancing accountability on the one hand, and practicality and trust in improved national systems on the other. That dilemma has to be resolved by effective practical measures, and not by overzealousness which is the enemy of the good. Suffice to say, Paris or no Paris and notwithstanding the replacement of the term donor by development partner tensions are intrinsic in the relationship between agencies and recipient countries. It is in the nature of partnership that partners seek to expand the bounds of their power, and explore the limits to which they can push their partners. Every interaction is likely to be taken as an opportunity to reopen seemingly settled agreements on substantive issues and relationships.

Enhancing Access: Innovations or Smokescreens?

DPEP meticulously followed the strategy commended by NPE, 1986, for expanding access and universalizing participation. The basic premise of that strategy was that given the Indian reality, UEE could be achieved only through two systems—formal and non-formal—with provision for moving from one system to another. The school system was too rigid for millions of children who were out-of-school; it therefore needed to be supplemented by a non-formal system with flexible hours, flexible curriculum, and ungraded classrooms which enabled children out-of-school to learn at their own pace. Or to borrow the metaphor of Mao Zedong, UEE could be reached only by walking on the two legs of primary school and NFE. Given that children out-of-school are diverse, multiple strategies are needed to reach out to those whom schools fail to reach. Therefore, apart from assisting states to expand the formal school system and appoint teachers so as to bring down the teacher–pupil ratio, DPEP also encouraged states to try out a variety of alternatives to the formal school system, the most famous of which is the Education Guarantee Scheme (EGS) of MP. In addition, these alternatives contributed a significant proportion of the additional enrolment achieved in DPEP districts. In order to ensure that the efficacy of interventions under DPEP is not negated by any action of a state government, DPEP put in place strong monitoring mechanisms in place to monitor not only the implementation of the various activities financed by DPEP but also the expenditure incurred by states on elementary education and the filling of vacant teacher posts. The pressure to fill all vacancies of teachers had the unintended consequence of para-teachers coming to be a near-permanent fixture of the education system, the para-teacher being a generic term applied to any teacher who is appointed on a contractual basis at less than the regular teacher pay scale and without fixity of tenure. A para-teacher could be thus either one appointed in alternatives to schooling set up (*a*) either provide access in remote areas or to out-of-school children or (*b*) one appointed in regular schools in order to augment the number of teachers. A para-teacher was called by different names such as Shiksha Karmi, Vidya Sahayak, Shikshan Sevak, and Shiksha Mitra. The alternatives to school as well as para-teachers were among the most contentious aspects of DPEP; they triggered highly polarized debates between devout admirers and bitter critics. Till the enactment of the RTE, Act and the consequential revision of the SSA Framework in 2011, SSA followed the same strategy of DPEP to expand access and carried forward the initiatives launched under DPEP. Thus, the very first objective of SSA when it was launched was 'all children in school, Education Guarantee Centre, Alternate School, Back to School camp by 2003'. The RTE Act outlawed the dual-track strategy of NPE, 1986. However, a narration of the initiatives undertaken by DPEP and later by SSA is not of historical interest alone, as there are now strong suggestions that additional contractual teachers should be appointed in lower primary classes so that children do not leave government lower schools without learning even 3 'R's.

The strategy of centralized decentralization that DPEP pursued induced the states to seriously address the challenge of universalizing primary education by providing funding on an unprecedented scale and providing competition among states to innovate and experiment, and provided ample opportunity. The most celebrated of such innovations is the EGS started in the year 1997, which secured the Commonwealth award for the best innovation in 1998. EGS proceeds from the premise that in a state like MP with widely scattered and sparsely populated tribal settlements, lack of access was the main reason for elementary education being not universalized, that 'generations of children have wasted away waiting for primary schooling facility',[37] and that it is imperative to adopt innovative low-cost methods for providing universal access in a few years. EGS is a good example of the scope Indian polity offers to civil service to innovate and display policy and programme entrepreneurship: it was conceptualized and steered by two IAS officers, R. Gopalakrishnan, Principal Secretary to the Chief Minister, and Amita Sharma, Director, Rajiv Gandhi Shiksha Mission. It is also a very good example of the quintessential fact that the making of policy or programme is not creation *de novo*, of conjuring ideas out of thin air. It is more packaging, combination, and re-combination of 'old', pre-existing elements. EGS creatively blends three pre-existing ideas to offer a solution to the chronic problem of inadequate access: first, that only revival of the old village school can ensure compulsory primary education of masses; second, that the provision of basic services such as elementary education is best managed by local bodies; and third, that delivery of a service or benefit would be more assured if, like the Maharashtra Employment Guarantee Scheme, the government offers a guarantee. In the design of the scheme there were three overriding parameters: cost reduction, enhancing effectiveness, and ensuring that the quality is on par with that in comparable regular primary schools. Teacher cost accounted for about 90 per cent of the unit cost of a school, and hence the design focussed on reduction of teacher cost. Schools in rural areas were generally dysfunctional because teacher as well as supervising officials were 'remote'; schools in remote areas were made functional by appointing a person belonging to the village and entrusting the supervision of the school to the *panchayat*. Parity in quality was ensured by stipulating that the school hours in EGS were the same as in a regular school, laying down the same minimum eligibility qualification for the instructor as that of a regular school teacher, by adopting the curriculum and textbooks of regular schools and providing periodic in-service training similar to that of regular teachers. An EGS school was in effect a regular school except that the instructor was appointed on contract, paid a lower remuneration than a regular teacher, and belonged to the habitation in which the EGS school was set up.

[37] R. Gopalakrishnan and Amita Sharma, 'Education Guarantee Scheme in MP: Innovative Step to Universalise Elementary Education', *Economic and Political Weekly*, XXXIII, no. 39 (26 September 1998), pp. 2546–51.

While EGS has been acclaimed, it had its share of critics also. There were two strands of criticism. The first was the factual criticism which questions the claims of achievement.[38] The second was the criticism stemming from the belief that any alternative to regular schooling was inferior education. A critic bemoaned the fact that 'the government [is] not only washing its hands off providing formal quality education to the poor but declaring that rip-offs like the EGS are harbingers of a new educational dawn for the deprived and downtrodden masses in the approaching millennium'.[39] Gopalakrishnan and Amita Sharma offered a spirited defence refuting the criticisms point-by-point.[40] The critics refused to take note of the fact that arrangements for instruction were so far being provided at a staggering phase and that in faulting the scheme on the ground that the quality of education imparted was poor, they adopted an improper frame of reference. The counter-factual with which they ought to have compared was not an ideal regular school, well-endowed with physical infrastructure, teaching-learning material, and committed teachers who attended the school every day and did their very best to promote learning by their students. It ought to be the fact that at the normal pace of expansion of schools, in most habitations covered by EGS there would have been no school, and children in those settlements would not have had any learning at all. That apart, the limited evidence available indicated that there was no difference between the learning outcomes of students in EGS schools and the regular schools.[41] The actual teaching time in EGS schools was

[38] François Leclercq, 'Education Guarantee Scheme and Primary Schooling in Madhya Pradesh', *Economic and Political Weekly*, XXXVIII , no. 19 (10 May 2003), pp. 1855–69.

[39] Rahul, 'Education Guarantee Scheme in Madhya Pradesh', *Economic and Political Weekly*, XXXIV, nos 1–2 (9 January 1999), p. 64.

[40] R. Gopalakrishnan and Amita Sharma, 'Education Guarantee Scheme What Does It Claim?' *Economic and Political Weekly*, XXXIV, nos 1–2 (20 March 1999), pp. 726–8; 'Opinion or Facts? Education Guarantee Scheme in Madhya Pradesh', *Economic and Political Weekly*, XXXVIII, no. 49 (6 December 2003), pp. 5210–5.

[41] B.V. Kothari, Sherry Chand, and R. Sharma, *A Review of Primary Education Packages in Madhya Pradesh*, Ahmedabad, India: Indian Institute of Management, 2000.

significantly higher than that in formal primary schools. EGS gurujis, unlike teachers in the government schools, were not assigned additional work such as helping with the census or elections and carrying out other data collection and surveillance tasks for the government.[42] Amita Sharma elevated the fight to a conceptual plane by contrasting the epistemological approach of the critics with that of EGS.[43] She characterized the approach of the critics as *Colonial-Positivistic* and assailed the critic's perception of school as a physical entity as no more than a sum of a teacher and some materials. By its very nature, such a perception leads to exclusion. In contrast, the EGS approach is claimed to be *Rationalist-Liberal*. This approach, according to her, does not restrict reality to physical reality; it values subjectivity and tolerates differences. Consequently, the Rationalist-Liberal approach recognizes that different socio-economic situations require different institutional and pedagogic approaches, and promotes inclusion. K, however, feels that the EGS approach is better characterized as pragmatism summarized by the phrase 'whatever works, is likely true', or to use the colourful imagery of Deng Xiaoping it does not matter if a cat is black or white, as long as it catches mice.

In addition to pioneering a number of alternatives to formal schools and establishing a large number of such alternative institutions, DPEP states also went in for large-scale appointment of teachers on a contractual basis at remuneration far less than that of a regular teacher. The appointment of para-teachers was severely assailed, among others by Krishna Kumar, Manisha Priyam, and Sadhna Saxena.[44] They

[42] Vimala Ramachandran, 'A School for Every Village: The Education Guarantee Scheme', in Deepa Narayan and Elena E. Glinskaya, eds, *Ending Poverty in South Asia: Ideas that Work*, Washington, DC: The World Bank, 2007.

[43] Amita Sharma, 'Ideas of Education: Epistemic Tensions and Educational Reform', *Economic and Political Weekly*, XXXVIII, no. 32 (9 August 2003), pp. 3391–400.

[44] Krishna Kumar, Manisha Priyam, and Sadhna Saxena, 'DPEP and Primary Education in India: Looking beyond the Smokescreen', *Economic and Political Weekly*, XXXVI, no. 7 (17 February 2001), pp. 560–8; 'The Trouble with Parateachers', *Frontline*, 18, no. 22 (27 October to 9 November 2001), http://www.frontline.in/navigation/?type=static&page=archive (last accessed on 8 February 2016).

contended that the large-scale appointments of para-teachers had led to the de-institutionalization of primary education which ran counter to the DPEP's own resolve to improve the primary education system through better planning and management. They contended that justifications for appointment of para-teachers were put forth in an aggressive and euphoric manner; thus, references to politically correct features such as community involvement in the management of these schools created a smokescreen which 'discouraged people from civil society to peep behind the smokescreen and see grass roots-level realities'. So successful were the publicity and the smokescreens created that schemes such as EGS were praised for reaching the unreached, completely overlooking the abnegation of recruitment norms, the poor quality of teacher training, and the exploitative cycle in which it places primary-level teachers. They bemoaned the demonization of teachers across the board; a cliché 'Teachers don't teach' was being touted by the powers-that-be to counter any complaint about the functioning of the system of education, be it the irregular functioning of schools, poor quality of education, or the failure to universalize literacy and primary education. A corollary of this demonization was the proposition that teachers do not teach because of security of tenure and lack of accountability either to their superiors or to the community in which the school is located. A logical inference, therefore, was that educational outcomes would be better with removal of security of employment and creation of institutional mechanisms to enforce accountability to the community. In their view, however, the facts do not validate that inference. All in all, they attributed de-institutionalization of the primary education system to the promotion of the idea of para-teachers by ODA in APPEP as well as donor-driven structural adjustment programme whose objective was to increase the scope for privatization in every sphere. Handing over of primary schools to the so-called 'local communities' had enhanced the role of personal patronage, and it should be seen as an early step towards the eventual privatization of a substantial proportion of primary schools.

K's attitude to para-teachers was conditioned by his own experience in AP where because of a judgment of Supreme Court the services of thousands of para-teachers had to be regularized, with the result that thousands of persons gained a backdoor entry to regular employment, as the process for selection of these teachers was short-circuited on the ground that appointment was for a short period only. His experience left a strong impression on K so much so that as long as he was at the helm of DPEP, he rejected outright any suggestions, such that of the Education Secretary, Assam, to appoint teachers in regular schools at remuneration lower than the regular salary. K's experience was not unique, as in state after state it was only a matter of time before regular pay scales were extended to teachers appointed on lower remuneration, whatever is the manner of appointment or the terminology used to distinguish them from regular teachers. His views notwithstanding, state governments faced the real-world dilemma of expanding access and lowering teacher–pupil ratio. Their fiscal capacity did not permit the state government's appointment of the large number of teachers required if they were to be paid the normal salaries; hence, the real choice was curtailing access and putting up with unduly high teacher–pupil ratios in many classes or to lower the cost of expanding access by appointing para-teachers. The dilemma states faced was a classic ethical dilemma. To restrict access to what the state could afford was not in keeping with the constitutional obligation of free and compulsory elementary education was not ethical; at the same time, paying a lower remuneration to para-teachers violated the ethical principle of 'equal work, equal pay'.

After 1998, by when K moved out of DPEP, many states began to appoint para-teachers in large numbers in regular schools following the precedent set by states such as Himachal Pradesh and MP. Such appointments got an imprimatur from the report of the National Committee of State Education Ministers (1999). This committee considered the measures needed to accelerate UEE in a mission mode; among others, it recommended the appointment of para-teachers as a low-cost solution to meet teacher shortage, not just in remote and difficult areas but throughout the whole country. The approach to the Tenth Five-Year Plan (2002–7) endorsed the recommendation of that Committee and wanted steps to be initiated to fill up all the existing vacancies of the teachers in a time-bound manner with defined responsibility to local bodies and communities, and to remove legal impediments in the recruitment of para-teachers. So much so, para-teachers have come to be an important element of the primary education system. By 2005, over 5 lakh para-teachers of all types were in position; the number increased to over five hundred thousand.[45] A 2009 survey offered extensive information on para-teachers as well as an evaluation of their performance in comparison with regular teachers.[46] In MP and Chhattisgarh, they accounted for over half the total number of teachers; they constituted a significant proportion of teachers in AP and Rajasthan. The service conditions varied considerably from state to state. Maharashtra, Orissa, and Rajasthan were the only states where teacher training qualification is a prerequisite. About one fourth of the para-teachers in all the states were post graduates, and more than one third of the teachers are graduates. The period of appointment also varied considerably; so did remuneration. In four states, Gujarat, Maharashtra, Orissa, and Jammu & Kashmir, the services of para-teachers were regularized after a few years of satisfactory service; in effect para-teachers in these states were like untenured faculty in American universities.

While Krishna Kumar and his co-authors were right in questioning the morality of appointing para-teachers, they were wrong in claiming that para-teachers led to the 'de-institutionalization of the primary education system' and further that idea of para-teachers was promoted by ODA in APPEP as well as donor-driven structural adjustment programme whose objective was to increase the scope for privatization in every sphere. The appointment of para-teachers in regular schools began long before Jomtien Conference or structural adjustment. It was Himachal Pradesh, made famous by Jean Drèze as the land of schooling revolution,[47] which pioneered in 1984 the appointment of 'volunteer teachers'; in AP, thousands of para-teachers were appointed during 1985–7. The trend of such appointments no doubt accelerated after 1997, but to attribute that acceleration to a 'foreign hand' is a figment of imagination. ODA did not promote the idea of para-teachers in

[45] S. Pandey and Rani Raj, 'Professional Support System and Classroom Performance of Para-teachers: An Investigation', *Indian Educational Review*, 41, no. 2 (2006), pp. 35–52.

[46] Research, Evaluation and Studies Unit, Technical Support Group of SSA, EdCil, *Deployment and Competence of Para-Teachers*, Abridged Version, 2009.

[47] The Probe Team, *Public Report on Basic Education in India*, New Delhi: Oxford University Press, 1999, pp. 115–27; Jean Drèze and Amartya Sen, *India: Development and Particpation*, New Delhi: Oxford University Press, 2002, pp. 177–84.

APPEP at all. Appointment of para-teachers or reduction of budgetary expenditure on teacher salaries was not one of the 'conditionalities' of the balance of payment support extended by the World Bank or of the soft credit extended for DPEP. Contrary to what Krishna Kumar and his co-authors posit, contemporary praxis of structural adjustment does not commend privatization of elementary education. Far from it, it calls for government paying more attention to and investing more in elementary education (Chapter VII). In fact, it was UNICEF which led a spirited campaign for adjustment to have a human face by not curtailing the expenditure on basic education and primary health during the adjustment that was promoting the idea of appointment of *educational workers* by the community as a low-cost means of expanding access.

Nor is there any factual basis for their contention that large-scale appointment of para-teachers was the first step towards eventual privatization of a substantial proportion of primary schools. A more diversified educations structure of which the private sector is an important part is commended for higher education and not for elementary education. It is no doubt true that from the 1980s, a number of developed counties undertook measures to promote competition among schools and offer parents greater choice for parents though school vouchers. The most conspicuous example was United Kingdom where the New Labour governments of Tony Blair and Gordon Brown continued such measures initiated by Margaret Thatcher. The underlying idea was not to dismantle public school system but to force it to perform better by compelling public schools to compete with each other as well as with private schools. In our country these measures have not received much attention, and have so far been espoused only by writers of articles in scholarly magazine and popular magazines, that too occasionally and not as a part of orchestrated advocacy campaign. Nor have they gained currency among the policymakers in India. And as would be explained below, private unaided schools did grow substantially over the last two decades; however, the growth has nothing to do with the state retreating from its obligation to provide free and compulsory elementary education but due to the perception of parents, many of them poor, that private schools offer better education.

Krishna Kumar and his co-authors cite a DPEP study which noted that low salary, combined with the contractual character of the job, had been a major source of discontent and lack of motivation among para-teachers, and that classroom transactions are of poorer quality.[48] However, there are quite a few other studies which contend that the performance of contract teachers is on par with, if not better than, that of regular teachers. From a review of the literature, Geeta Kingdon and Vandana Sipahimalani-Rao conclude that all of the available studies on this issue so far show that the learning achievement levels among children taught by para and regular teachers were similar even though children taught by para-teachers sometimes come from poorer/more remote homes, and that the oft-heard concerns about the harm done by para-teacher schemes to children were misplaced. Those who voice these concerns conflated the issue of equity (of pay and working conditions for para and regular teachers), professional status, esteem, and security, with the issue of the efficacy or quality of education imparted by para-teachers. While concerns for equity, professional status, and security remain valid, the concerns about condemning children to poorer quality para-teachers were not borne out by the available evidence.[49] In fact, in contrast to the past, states showed a greater commitment to education. They departed from the past policy of keeping teacher posts vacant; instead, they sought to overcome inadequate fiscal capacity by filling some or all vacancies with para-teachers who cost the state exchequer less.

In K's view, the appointment of para-teachers cannot be considered to be de-institutionalization *if* three conditions are fulfilled: first, there is a credible and transparent process for appointment and review of their performance; second, para-teachers are imparted appropriate induction and in-service training; and third, the para-teachers are confirmed as regular teachers after a few years of satisfactory service. In states where para-teachers were confirmed as regular teachers after a few years of satisfactory service, the situation of para-teachers was like faculty waiting for tenure. K does not mind the concept of tenure being

[48] Research, Evaluation and Studies Unit, Technical Support Group of DPEP, EdCil, *Reaching out Further—Para-teachers in Primary Education: An Overview*, 1998; a later study is Dayaram, *Para-teachers in Primary Education; A Status Report*, 2000.

[49] Geeta Gandhi Kingdon and Vandana Sipahimalani-Rao, 'Para-teachers in India: Status and Impact', *Economic and Political Weekly*, XLV, no. 20 (20 March 2010), pp. 59–67, at p. 67.

extended to school teachers; however, he is opposed to the idea of a permanent lack of tenure. It would be utterly unfair to keep para-teachers indefinitely on contract and that too at levels of remuneration far lower than those of teachers. On a conceptual plane, K does not believe that 'managing by contract' necessarily improves delivery of education or, for that matter, the efficiency of non-commercial activities of government. While there is much that government can adopt from business management, government as an organization cannot be and should not be a clone of business. The objective, structure, process, and ethical imperatives of government are far different from that of business, and this distinctiveness should inform any adoption of business management. However, notwithstanding the general perception that RTE Act, 2009, had banned the appointment of contractual teachers[50] nothing in the Act or the Model Rules prohibits contractual appointments if the persons appointed have the minimum qualifications stipulated by the National Council of Teacher Education for appointment as a teacher. However, the appointment of contractual teachers has once again acquired salience against the backdrop of high-pitched advocacy of reinforcing teaching in lower classes by engaging locally hired contract teachers as a solution to the poor levels of basic learning.[51] It would be interesting to watch further developments.

Educational Outcomes: Enrolment, Retention, and Reduction of Disparities

Revamping the system for collection, analysis, and publication of data on elementary education is one of the most significant and permanent achievements of DPEP. India is one of the few countries in the world

[50] Ambrish Dongre, *Has RTE Made a Mistake by Eliminating Contract Teachers and Making All Teachers Regular?* http://www.accountabilityindia.in/accountabilityblog/1894-has-rte-made-mistake-eliminating-contract-teachers-and-making-all-teachers, posted on 21 December 2010 and last accessed on 29 May 2015.

[51] Karthik Muralidharan, 'Priorities for Primary Education Policy in India's Twelfth Five Year Plan', in Shekhar Shaw, Barry Bosworth, and Arvind Panagariya, eds, *India Policy Form 2012/3*, National Council of Applied Economic Research (New Delhi) and Brookings Institution (Washington, DC),Volume 9, Delhi: Sage Publications, 2013, pp. 1–46, at pp. 31–3.

where educational statistics date back to 1890. When the DPEP was conceptualized, there were quite a few statistical publications which threw much light on the state of elementary education.[52] These include DOE's annual publications *Select Educational Statistics*, and *Education in India*, NCERT's *All India Educational Survey* (conducted usually once in five years), and publications of state governments. At the national level, there was considerable uniformity in the data reporting systems; however, at the state level, the data collected and formats of data compilation and publication varied from state to state. A review of these multiple sources of data brought out that the data were not adequate for decentralized planning and implementation because of reasons such as data gaps, lack of district-specific time series data to assess the progress in enrolment, retention and school facilities, and time lags between the collection of data and publication. Furthermore, the processed data was not widely disseminated and was used more by researchers than by educational administrators as a planning and management tool. With its focus on decentralized planning, DPEP required up-to-date and reliable school- and district-level information soon after it was collected. As part of DPEP, a computerized school-based information system known as District Information System for Education (DISE) was developed by NIEPA. The first major review of the DISE software was undertaken during 1997–8. The software was later redesigned in 2001 in the light of requirements of the SSA. Initially the first 42 districts of DPEP and primary stage were covered by DISE. Over time, the coverage of DISE was extended to non-DPEP states and from primary to the entire elementary level of education. DISE could respond to complex questions such as the proportion of SC girls in enrolment in a given class in government rural schools in a given block or the number of teachers required in a given school. However, even in 2001 the extent as well as quality of use of the DISE was limited in spite of the trainings imparted, and the culture of viewing DISE as 'reporting' rather than 'information support for

[52] For a good survey of the Indian educational statistical system in the early 2000s, see Yash Aggarwal, *Revitalization of Educational Statistics: Issues and Strategies*, http://www.dise.in/Downloads/Reports&Studies/REVITALISATION%20OF%20EDUCATIONAL%20STATISTICS%20IN%20INDIA.pdf (last accessed on 29 May 2015).

monitoring and planning' was not totally displaced.[53] Over course of time the scope of DISE expanded. Apart from publishing annual analytical reports depicting the status of school facilities and detailed enrolment and dropout data by gender, social categories, and units of administration like states and districts, NIEPA also began publishing district and state report cards which helped educational administrators and the public to keep track of the progress towards UEE. DISE is the largest primary education system in the world collecting data from 14 lakh elementary schools across the length and breadth of the country. DISE now collects data on a large variety of variables including enrolment by class, age, gender and social category, teachers by class, age, and gender, contractual teachers, educational and professional qualifications of teachers, in-service training of teachers, grants for teaching learning material and school development, availability of teaching learning material and sport material, incentives to students, and number of working days and hours. It is, however, a moot point whether it is necessary to print hard copies of almost all the reports and cards when they could be accessed on line; furthermore, one is not sure of the extent to which the voluminous information and prolific publications are used for planning and implementation. Following the launch of RMSA, NIEPA developed the Secondary Education Management Information System (SEMIS), an analogue of DISE; in 2012, DISE and SEMIS were integrated to set up a Unified District Information for System for Education (U-DISE).

There is unambiguous evidence that since the mid-1990s when DPEP started, and more particularly from the year 2000 there had been an acceleration of the school participation rates; the evidence comes not only from school statistics but also from Pratham's Annual Status of Education Reports as well as from household survey data collected by the National Sample Survey Organization (NSSO) in its 42nd round (1986–87), 52nd round (1995–6), and 61st round (2004–5). Deepa Sankar's magisterial analysis of the NSSO data brings out clearly that there had been a sharp reduction in the number of children 'not-attending' schools in absolute terms as well as a proportion of the total child population. Thus, the share of children 'not attending'

[53] Jyotsna Jha, etal., *Management Processes in Elementary Education and DPEP*, pp. 54–5.

school halved from about 29 per cent of the total child population in the mid-1990s to 13 per cent in 2004–5. The gains are more remarkable in the 6–10 years age group than in the 11–13 years age group. As a share of population, children 'not attending' school came down from 47 per cent in the mid-1980s to 14 per cent in 2004–5 in rural areas, and from 23 per cent to 8 per cent in urban areas. Consequently, the gap between rural and urban areas had sharply come down from 24 per cent to 6 per cent. Similar advances were registered by girls, and socially and economically marginalized groups. Although the gender gap in participation was reduced, it still persisted, and the share of children not attending school was still largest among SCs and STs, particularly among STs, as compared to non-SC/ST communities. Most of these new enrolments (children attending school) were from the 'traditionally laggard states', a code word for educationally backward states with low levels of school participation. Thus, during the period 1999–2000 to 2004–5, among the BIMARU states, the participation rate of 6–10 age group children increased from 52.5 to 68 per cent in Bihar , 72.8 to 84.7 per cent in MP, 74.8 to 84.1 per cent in Rajasthan, and 74 to 83.4 per cent in UP. All in all, despite progress, some issues and areas of concern still remained as children who were still not participating were the hardest to reach and came from the poor and vulnerable groups; as inequities persisted, the study highlighted the need to intensify efforts towards reaching out to 'this *last horde of children*'.[54] While the gains are impressive and are indubitably due to DPEP and SSA, it is difficult to assess how much exactly did DPEP as a whole contributed in quantitative terms to the enhanced participation in elementary education because of reasons such as there being no study which covers all the DPEP projects and gives an account of what all these projects together accomplished, SSA beginning to be implemented all over the country from 2001 onwards, and the focus of SSA in its first few years being exclusively on expanding access and enrolment.

It is only in respect of the first three DPEP projects that one can have a clear idea of DPEP's s direct contribution to enhanced participation as

[54] Deepa Sankar, *What is the Progress of Elementary Education Participation in India during the Last Two Decades? An Analysis Using NSS Education Rounds*, 42112 rev. World Bank South Asia Sector for Human Development, October 2008.

they were completed before SSA picked up momentum. The achievements reported in some of the ICRs of later DPEP projects are too good to be true. Thus, the ICR of DPEP-III reported that an additional 27.5 lakh children were enrolled as compared to a target of 4 lakhs, and the ICR of the AP Project reported that an additional 20 lakhs were enrolled as compared to the target of 4 lakhs. Therefore, what all one could say with confidence is that DPEP significantly contributed to the turn around and that impressive results began to be shown from 2000 onwards as the impact of DPEP projects began to be felt and SSA vigorously began to expand access and enrolment building upon the lessons of its progenitor. A measure of the spectacular progress achieved can be gauged by the fact that in December 1993, India hosted the EFA-9 which together accounted for about two-thirds of the world's illiterate population. India was invited to host the Summit because it had the dubious distinction of being home to the world's largest adult illiterate as well as out-of-school child populations (about a sixth of the world's out-of-school population in 1990). The number of out-of-school 6–14 kids declined from 3.9 crores in 1999 to 2.5 crores in 2002; the *EFA Global Monitoring Report 2002* placed India in the group of 28 countries in 'serious risk of not achieving any of the three goals of primary net enrolment, levels of adult literacy, and gender parity in primary school gross enrolment'. A recent EFA-GMR Policy Paper places the out-of-school population in India at just 0.3 per cent the world's out-of-school population of 5.72 crore (2011).[55] A recent survey commissioned by MHRD (2014) showed that out of the estimated 20.41 crore children in the age group of 6–13 in India, an estimated 60.41 lakh (2.97 per cent) were out of school. This proportion of out-of-school children was lower than the figure of 4.28 per cent in 2009 and 6.94 per cent in 2006.[56] The drastic reduction in out-of-school children is collaborated by non-official data such as those reported in the *Annual Survey of Education Report*. The EFA-GMR Global Monitoring Report, 2015, which offers an overview of the progress towards Education for

[55] UNESCO, *Schooling for Millions of People Jeopardized by Reductions in Aid*, EFA-GMR Policy Paper 09, June 2013.

[56] Social and Rural Research Institute, *National Sample Survey of Estimation of Out-of-School Children in the Age-Group 6–13*, Draft report, September 2014, p. 7.

All during the period 2000–15, commends India for making 'marked progress in net enrolment ratio', increasing its net enrolment ratio (NER) significantly as GNP per capita improved, thereby suggesting 'a more equitable distribution of economic gains'. The report also mentions India as one of the countries which have, since 1999, achieved the Dakar Goal of achieving universal primary education with the primary adjusted net enrolment ratio (ANER) of 99 per cent and above. It also commended India for reaching gender parity for primary and lower secondary enrolment, the only country in South and West Asia to do so.[57]

We may now turn to the question of what we know from the evaluations of the first three DPEP projects. What comes out from these evaluations of these DPEP projects is that while progress had been remarkable, the quantified outcome goals were not fully achieved and that the performance of states was uneven. There was substantial growth in enrolment; however, universal enrolment was nowhere achieved and further the increase in enrolment was concentrated in a few states. The objective of reducing cohort dropout rates to less than 10 per cent was not achieved in most districts. On the whole, DPEP was more successful in reducing gender disparities than social disparities. To elaborate, MP had the distinction of VECs conducting detailed household surveys through Lok Sampark Abhiyan (LSA-People's Contact Movement) in 1996 and 2000. DPEP in MP planned for the gross enrolment ratio (GER) of 6–11-year-olds in classes I–V reaching a level of 120 per cent by 2001. Even though this target was not achieved, between 1996 and 2000, the GER increased spectacularly from 76.7 per cent to 96.5 per cent in MP and from 88 per cent to 101.5 per cent in Chhattisgarh. The performance of the states funded by the Bank was less spectacular; the enrolment in DPEP I states increased by about 6 per cent between 1996–7 and 2001–2 and by about 17 per cent in DPEP II states between 1997–8 and 2002–3. Most of the increase in DPEP II was concentrated in Gujarat, Karnataka, and UP. The main reason why DPEP II registered a higher increase in enrolment than DPEP I was the fact that DPEP I did not cover any district from the educationally

[57] United Nations Educational, Scientific and Cultural Organisation, *Education for All 2000-15: Achievement and Challenges*, EFA Global Monitoring Report, 2015, Paris: UNESCO Publishing.

backward BIMARU states which had greater scope for increasing the aggregate increase in enrolment while a third of the districts DPEP II covered were MP and UP. Furthermore, in DPEP I, everyone associated with DPEP was skimming the learning curve.

The DPEP objective of reducing cohort dropout rates to less than 10 per cent was not achieved in most districts; among the districts covered by DPEP I, only the districts of Kerala (where dropout rate was already low) realized the goal, and in DPEP II districts, only 16 per cent of districts. In 2001–2 (when the projects came to an end), among the DPEP I states other than Kerala, dropout rates were above 40 per cent in Assam, and between 20 and 40 per cent in the other four states of Haryana, Karnataka, Maharashtra, and Tamil Nadu; in DPEP II, 32 per cent of the districts had dropout rates exceeding 45 per cent and 52 per cent districts between 11 and 45 per cent. The observation of the IEG's performance audit of DPEP I and II projects that 'there was little in the way of diagnosis and rigorous measurement of dropouts, and few strategies beyond vague notions of improved quality and community support for pressing drastic reductions' is a fair comment. Equally valid is the observation of IEG that the main barrier to universalization of elementary education is not so much expansion of access as high dropout. This observation applies even now. Access is now almost universal, and the NER at the primary stage is 99.8 per cent; in other words, almost all children in the age group 6–11 are in schools. However, a large percentage of children entering primary schooling continue to drop out before entering upper primary schooling; the NER at the upper primary stage of 67.03 per cent, though higher than the 43.1 per cent in 2005–06, is far below the norms of 100 per cent, and is therefore still a matter of serious concern.[58] However, the dropout rates are still substantial, and worse the success reported is based on comparing the enrolment in the previous academic year with the enrolment in the current academic year, and there is as yet no agreed norm for defining and identifying this kind of dropout.[59] Therefore, the key to universal participation

[58] DISE: 2011–12.

[59] Ministry of Human Resource Development, Department of School Education and Literacy, *Sarva Siksha Abhiyan: Eighteenth Joint Review Mission, 17–24 June 2013, Aide Memoire*, p. 20. This Mission was led by the author, and much of the latest data cited in this article is from the data supplied to the Mission.

lies in eliminating dropout. It used to be said that children do not drop out but are pushed out because of the irrelevance of the curriculum and the teaching method which emphasized rote learning. With the popularization of a sociological view of society which views children out of school and children not adequately participating in the school as *victims* of discrimination by society, the school, and teachers, the contemporaneous discourse on inclusive education holds out that children are pushed out mainly because of the discriminatory attitudes and practices of teachers, fellow pupils, and educational administrators; that discourse lays emphasis on eliminating such discriminatory attitudes and practices, and making classrooms inclusive through measures such as gender and social justice sensitization, and preferential employment of women and persons from disadvantaged social groups as teachers.

On the whole, DPEP was more successful in reducing gender disparities than social disparities. The DPEP objective of reducing the gender disparities in primary education enrolment to less than 5 per cent was achieved in all the 12 states covered by DPEP I and II except Gujarat and UP. Between 1997–8 and 2002–3, the gender gap, as measured by the difference between the proportion of boys and girls enrolled to total enrolment, decreased from 16 per cent to 10 per cent in Gujarat and from 22 per cent to 10 per cent in UP. All in all, in 95 per cent of the districts, gender disparity in enrolment rates was reduced to less than 5 per cent; however, few districts achieved a similar reduction in social disparity. In MP and Chhattisgarh, the DPEP objective of gender and social disparities in primary education enrolment being reduced to less than 5 per cent was reportedly reached. According to data from the LSA 2000 survey, the gender equity index for enrolment was 97.3, the scheduled caste (SC) equity index 99.8, and the scheduled tribe (ST) equity index 98.2. In DPEP I and II states, additional enrolment of SC students was in line with their share in the population, but the enrolment share of ST was below that of their share in the population; in fact in all respects, the impact of DPEP on the education of STs was much below expectations.

While in the aggregate DPEP did not make much of a progress in reducing social disparities, it made spectacular progress in addressing the special needs of children with disabilities. NPE, 1986 postulated that the education of children with mild disabilities was to be common with those of other children while children with severe disabilities were to be educated in special schools with hostels. This NPE postulate was a reaffirmation of the observations in the Sarjent Committee (1944)[60] and the Kothari Commission (1966), and of the corresponding policy postulate in NPE, 1968.[61] The central government introduced a minuscule scheme for the Integrated Education of the Disabled in 1987; however, the annual outlay of that scheme by 1990 was just about Rs 2 crore for the country as a whole as compared to about Rs 125 crore for Operation Blackboard. Consequently, few state governments took no notice either of that scheme or of the NPE Policy postulate. With the clear enunciation of outcome objectives and the rigorous monitoring of progress towards attaining those objectives, DPEP put pressure on officials in the field to go into details, identify groups of children who were out of school, and ensure that they are enrolled in schools or alternative streams of education. Consequently, children with disabilities began to receive attention for the first time from officials of the State Education Departments. The fact that DPEP provided flexibility in programming and provided space for innovation enabled enterprising field functionaries to take up with a missionary spirit the education of children with disabilities. Apart from focussing on inclusion of children with mild-to-moderate disabilities, the DPEP also attempted disability-oriented pedagogic measures such as curriculum modifications, and teacher support and training. By the year 2006, in 23 districts of Rajasthan, Orissa, and West Bengal as many as 6 lakh children with disabilities were enrolled and mainstreamed.[62] Such a large-scale mainstreaming was never attempted before, and but for the resources and space provided by DPEP, the educational components of the People with Disabilities Act, 1995 might not have got such a boost. Suffice to say, it was DPEP which first struck a big blow for inclusion of the disabled in the school system. SSA carried forward the initiatives its progenitor took

[60] Ministry of Education, *Post-War Educational Development in India: Report by the Central Advisory Board on Education, January 1944*, Sixth Reprint Edition, 1964, pp. 111–20.

[61] Ministry of Education, *Education and National Development: Report of the Education Commission, 1964–66*, 1966, Volume I, pp. 221–25.

[62] The World Bank, *People with Disabilities in India: from Commitments to Outcomes*, Human Development Unit, South Asia Region, July 2009, p. 58.

to get the schools address the special needs of the children with disabilities and provide children with aids and appliances. In 2013–14, an estimated 94.64 per cent of the 27.94 lakh children identified as children with special needs were covered by one or other of the SSA interventions.[63] Full credit should go to Anupriya Chadha who, since 1997, has been leading the unit dealing with education of children with special needs in the TSG first of DPEP and later of SSA; she has been extremely pro-active in pursuing a *zero exclusion policy*. Given the importance of communication and advocacy, her unit has been publishing *Confluence*, a newsletter similar to *DPEP Calling*. Her unit has also been actively networking with other governmental organizations dealing with the disabled such as the Ministry of Social Justice and Empowerment as well as NGOs with the result that there is convergence between the activities of SSA and other programmes relating to the disabled. Of course, there are still challenges. There are still inter- and even intra-state differences in the measurement, implementation, and the understanding of what constitutes inclusive education for these children. Special efforts are also needed to ensure scholastic and co-scholastic parity of these children with other children.

The inter-state disparities in performance and the persistent high dropout rates point to possible deficiencies in the design of DPEP. DPEP proceeded from the premise that planning and implementation for UEE cannot be organized from Delhi or from any state capital, and that only through local-level planning and implementation can UEE be realized. The DPEP objectives for enrolment, retention, and reduction of disparities were uniform across the board; only the objectives for enhanced learning achievement were set in relative terms. That being so, the context-rooted process of district planning and implementation was expected to set off the disparities in the inter-district levels of educational development and administrative capability. Figuratively, in the race to the UPE, the DPEP design fixed the same winning posts for all even though the starting points varied considerably; consequently, the backward districts had a longer distance to traverse in the race. District

63 Technical Support Group of SSA, EdCIL, *Education of Children with Special Needs in Sarva Shiksha Abhiyan—RTE Act, An Overview (2013–14)*, 2014.

planning was expected to help the backward districts to overcome their handicap and reach the winning post along with others. The preparation of the medium-term perspective and annual plans, their scrutiny and appraisal at the state and national levels, the periodic review of implementation and incorporating the lessons of the review in the next annual planning cycle, action research, and feeding the research findings in the annual planning and implementation processes—all these iterative processes were expected to remove the handicap of the educationally more disadvantaged districts. What comes out clearly is that that expectation was not fulfilled in spite of enormous efforts to build capacity for planning and implementation at all levels. A rigorous managerial evaluation might have helped pinpoint whether the under-performance of several districts was due to the design deficiency or due to unrealistic uniform targets or due to inadequate performance or both. The questions that arise in a rigorous managerial evaluation are: how robust was the planning and implementation process across the districts? Were the district plans just facsimiles of templates or did they reflect the area-specific variations in the levels of developmental aid needs? How adequate were the work plans? Over the years, was there qualitative improvement in the work plans? Was learning by doing at work? Was the experience in implementation reflected in subsequent work plans? How effective was the implementation of the work plans? Can one correlate the variation in the achievement of quantitative goals by districts with variations in the quality of the district planning and implementation? Were the financial and other operational parameters mechanically applied? Is it right and proper to set uniform goals for access, enrolment, and retention for all districts? Would it have been better if districts with lower levels of educational development and more difficult environment were permitted to set realistic and credible targets rather than compelled to strive for all India goals? However, the DPEP studies and evaluations had little to say on these questions. There is not even a rigorous comparative descriptive account of the performance of different districts, much less an analytical study which correlates the disparities in performance with those in the planning and implementation process. Be that as it might be, K intuitively feels it was unrealistic to fix a uniform and absolute goal for the reduction of dropouts. Here as with other inadequacies of DPEP, K has to plead *mea culpa*.

By early January 2001 when K and Sajitha Bashir wrote the article on DPEP for NCERT's *Encyclopaedia on Education*[64] there was ample evidence that a few states such as Kerala, MP, and UP were performing better than others mainly due to two reasons: the strong commitment and executive grit displayed by the State Education Secretary or the Project Director or both, and a high proportion of districts covered by DPEP. The performance of Kerala, MP, and UP suggested that scale and a minimum threshold level were important factors in eliciting more active commitment from state governments. The scale and threshold effects appeared to be a manifestation of the law of unintended consequences. The programme was initially conceptualized to expand in an incremental manner with a limited number of districts (three to five) being funded in each state. MP was an exception in that 19 districts were included in the EC-funded DPEP Project because of the fact that it was the only one of the seven states where agencies such as EC and UNESCO had been considering funding several districts prior to DPEP. The enormous problems faced in the initial stages seemed to indicate that giving MP a special dispensation was a mistake. However, after Amita Sharma was appointed Project Director and R. Gopalakrishnan, the Secretary to the Chief Minister, began to evince keen interest in the programme and pursuit of UEE, DPEP in MP took a different turn and the problem state turned into a model state. The wide geographical coverage enabled the programme to influence primary education in the entire state. As outlined above, MP took advantage of the flexibility provided by DPEP to innovate to come up with the pace-setting EGS programme for dramatically expanding access and enrolment all over the state. DPEP in UP got a big boost once Vrinda Sarup, K's deputy in DOE and one of the pillars of the DPEP, moved to UP in January 1998 to head the Project Office. Kerala was *sui generis*; the major challenge facing DPEP was not access, enrolment, and dropout reduction but enhancement of quality, teaching-learning process, and learning outcomes. The way in which K. Suresh Kumar, the Project Director, and K. Jayakumar, the State Education introduced activity-based pedagogy in the face of opposition is the subject matter of the case on DPEP prepared by KSG, referred to earlier.

64 R.V. Vaidyanatha Ayyar and Sajitha Bashir, 'District Primary Education Program (DPEP)'.

Education Is About Learning

Never before DPEP nor later did any programme in India put the spotlight so directly on the learning outcomes of children. The focus on learning outcomes was built into the design of the programme and the states and districts forced to concentrate on quality improvement aspects in a number of ways: by specifying improvement in learning achievement as one of the three objectives of the programme, by putting direct financial ceilings on civil works and management activities and indirect ceilings on hiring of additional teachers and incentive programmes. Of course, given that a section of academics, and activists, were strongly opposed to accessing external funding for primary education, anything associated with DPEP was suspect, and the DPEP focus on learning was not exempt from that suspicion. Thus, in a 1995 article, Krishna Kumar surmised that 'our system will be asked to reveal each tiny detail of children's attainment by geographical region as such data can help in the geographical shaping of foreign investments, especially in the negotiations for investment potential of different regions'.[65] To say the least, this assertion belongs to the realm of fantasy and would not have been made if a modicum of effort were made to ascertain how funding agencies approve projects. Whatever, along with addressing all aspects of universalizing primary education, putting in practice the idea of decentralized planning and implementation, mainstreaming children with disabilities, and pioneering a SWAp-type external funding and a new paradigm of country–agency relationship, attempting a paradigm shift from a teacher to a learner-centred pedagogy through revised curricula, curricular materials, and a huge teacher training network is one of the most significant aspects of DPEP.

DPEP sought to uproot a deeply entrenched but dysfunctional system which had every feature necessary to inhibit learning: poor infrastructure, widely prevalent high teacher–pupil ratios, teacher absenteeism, low teacher motivation and competence, utterly irrelevant, ritualistic pre-service teacher training, a hardly existent in-service teacher training, dull and cognitively overloaded curriculum, chalk-and-talk method of teaching, 'completing the textbook' being

[65] Krishna Kumar, 'Learning and Money: Children as Pawns in Dependency', *Economic and Political Weekly*, XXX, no. 43 (28 October 1995), pp. 2719–20, at p. 2720.

the sole objective of teaching, a teaching methodology and evaluation system that prized rote learning, and so on. DPEP supported institution building in a big way. Even by 2000 when K and Sajitha wrote their review of DPEP, 6,300 block resource centres and 17,600 cluster resource centres were established, thereby deepening the infrastructure for academic support and guidance, ending the isolation of teachers, and putting in place a close-by institution for assisting the teachers to bring about effective changes in class room transaction. For the first time ever, large-scale, systematic, and periodic in-service training had been instituted for teachers and community leaders. In order to encourage teachers and children to develop their own teaching and learning aids, DPEP provided teachers with a small contingency grant; it also provided schools contingency grants to replace the damaged teaching learning materials such as, say, charts. Hence, DPEP went several steps beyond Operation Blackboard in facilitating schools and teachers to improve classroom transaction.

The paradigm shift DPEP envisaged encompassed five areas: curriculum, teaching–learning process, teaching–learning material, in-service training, and evaluation. The broad principles DPEP put forth were drawn from the NPE and POA as revised in 1992, the lessons inferred from Shiksha Karmi and APPEP, as well as what was taken to be forward-looking pedagogic thinking of the day. To begin with, the efforts of DPEP in the area of pedagogy were heavily influenced by MLLs. MLLs encompass three interrelated concepts. First, the levels of learning, or to use jargon *competencies*, are to be specified for each of the subjects (curricular areas) covered in a class. Thus, the Dave Committee specified the competencies to be acquired in language, mathematics, and environmental studies for classes I–V. Second, learning achievement of each student is to be measured to assess how many competencies are acquired and how well each competency is mastered so that it does not slip away. The goal was to ensure that 80 per cent of children should master 80 per cent of the identified competencies. The learning achievements of individual students could be aggregated at different levels—class, school, and administrative units—to assess how well the learning is taking place at a given level of aggregation, and to compare one unit, say, a state with another state in the matter of learning achievement. The same objective can be achieved by conducting a properly designed learning survey which covers a representative sample of schools and classes. If the same methodology for measurement and analysis is employed over time, it should be possible to gauge the trends in learner achievement at a given level of aggregation: whether they are improving or declining and so on. The third concept is the restructuring of classroom transaction and revision of textbooks so as to be *competency-based*, that is to say designed to acquire the competencies specified. It also follows that in-service training required to be reorganized so that teachers could adapt their teaching and evaluation towards attainment of the competencies. It was expected that MLL-based textbooks and teaching would lighten the curricular load, eliminate the burden of memorizing irrelevant facts, and help teachers to identify appropriate sequencing of learning, suitable transactional processes, and desirable assessment techniques which would enable a teacher to provide remedial teaching on the one hand and enrichment programmes on the other as per the needs of individual learners. All in all, they were expected to transform the teaching–learning process.

POA, 1992, spelt out in great detail the strategy to be followed for ensuring that MLLs are achieved. The main steps of the strategy were preliminary assessment of the existing levels of learning achievements; modifications of MLLs to suit local conditions, if needed be; initial and recurrent orientation of teachers to competency-based teaching; preparation of teacher training handbooks for MLL-based teaching; introducing Comprehensive and Continuous Evaluation (CCE) of students and using evaluation results for remedial action; preparation of unit tests and other evaluation materials and putting them in an item pool for using as and when required; using MLL norms as and when curriculum and textbooks are revised; and provision of competency-based teaching–learning materials. In a nutshell, to begin with, DPEP expected child-centred, activity-based learning to be introduced, and textbooks and teaching to be competency based such that the MLLs laid down by the Dave Committee were reached at the earliest. It also envisaged strengthening SCERTs, operationalizing DIETs, establishing BRCs and CRCs, putting in place a system of systematic in-service teacher training that covered all teachers periodically, developing new training modules, promoting multi-grade teaching (that is to say, a single teacher handling at the same time more than one class because of the small number of pupils in each class), and so on. DPEP TSG supported the states through academic activities such as development of prototype in-service teacher training designs and materials including those required for multi-grade teaching, development of research-based, field-tested prototype packages of textbooks, auxiliary learning materials and teacher guides based on MLL, integrated and active learning techniques for enhancing reading and mathematics skills in classes I–III, and development of training material for educational planning and management. More importantly, it followed a policy of offering the states resources as well as freedom to innovate, promoting capacity building through the personnel of NCERT, NIEPA, and DPEP TSG, and spreading the good word about good practices and innovations. And very significantly, pedagogy was one area where the DPEP Bureau issued no *diktats* as, say, with planning and management; its guiding principle was to let hundred flowers bloom so long as improvements were *sought* to be made in the five areas of curriculum, teaching–learning process, teaching–learning material, in-service training, and evaluation. It was expected that the mid-term and terminal learner achievement surveys would pass a judgement on the initiatives taken by the states.

To begin with, the states went about putting in practice most of the steps POA suggested for operationalizing MLLs. However, as states were left to go about on their own initiative without any central direction, they began drawing on whatever expertise was available for them. In quite a few states, the project directors and education secretaries began to look beyond the in-house expertise available in the SCERT. Quite a few states fell under the spell of *joyful learning* which was being promoted as a panacea by UNICEF with missionary zeal through its large network of state offices, extraordinary expertise in communication, and great strength in providing grants without asking questions. Many others began to draw upon expertise outside the government and draw inspiration from organizations outside the government and reputed for their pedagogic innovations. These trends culminated in the abandonment of MLLs which never found favour with the predominant school of educational philosophy. The joyful learning movement pushed the concept of child-centred learning to the length of not requiring children to learn anything *but* what has been made easy and interesting. It held that the best way to make learning easy and interesting is to stimulate the child through song, dance, and play. To say the least, if such extravagant extrapolation is acted upon, schools would train up 'a race of men who will be incapable of doing anything which is disagreeable to them'.[66] In terms of learning outcomes, the song and dance pedagogy was no different from the chalk-and-talk method of teaching; the customary tedium of the teacher's passive teaching is replaced by the tedium of thoughtless sequences of song, dance, and pantomime. Mercifully this movement of *ersatz* joy without learning soon faded away because the parents were put off by the *tamasha* (farce) that went on in schools which embraced the cult of joyful learning. Faded away but not dead, in July 2013 when K led a JRM for SSA he was subjected to a video presentation of the song and dance pedagogy being employed in a state to promote learning. While the fading away of the farcical joyful learning is not something to be mourned, the abandonment of MLLs is not so much for MLLs *per se* but for the fact that, like the baby being thrown with bathwater, the very idea that learning achievement is a vital element of UEE was downplayed for a while by SSA.

Even as the states were introducing competency-based textbooks, teaching, evaluation, and in-service training, MLLs fell out of favour with NCERT as well as experts associated with DPEP such as Jangira and Subir Shukla. There were three main reasons for MLL falling from favour. The first had to do with the way MLLs were promoted as a cult outside established structures such as NCERT and SCERT; the second philosophical; and the third the perception that MLLs were not properly stipulated, disseminated, and applied. Turning to the second reason, there are two schools of educationists with different pictures of human cognition. Both the schools agree that the aim of education cannot be limited to the improvement of cognitive traits; it should encompass the affective and psychomotor traits as well as higher pedagogical objectives such as thinking, creativity, problem solving, and 'learning to learn'. However, they sharply differ how the aims of education could be achieved. The first school, now dominant and anchored in the romantic tradition, believes that the aims of education are indivisible, and that the child should be treated not as an empty receptacle to be filled with information but as one engaged in making sense of the world, acting upon it, and producing knowledge. To put it in layman's language, the

[66] John Stuart Mill, *Autobiography*, New York: Columbia University Press, 1924, p. 37.

child constructs knowledge; therefore, the *constructivist* school holds that curriculum should be *interactional*, and that the child's present and potential developments should determine the kind of learning experiences the teacher must provide.[67] Whatever, from the perspective of constructivists, MLLs are the ultimate of the detested *behaviourist–connectivist* framework. They distort the educational process by limiting the scope of education to the cognitive domain; even in the cognitive domain only three of the six curricular areas were covered. The idea of chopping a subject area into discrete competencies to be mastered one by one was epistemologically unsound, and not supported by theories of learning.[68] In effect it reduced primary education to the learning of 3 'R's. Given the wide educational disparities in terms of geographical areas and social categories, nationally uniform MLLs were unrealistic. The second school considers that those who belong to the first school are deluded by the romantic idea that children somehow possess innate knowledge that can be released through play or self-paced learning or other forms of what is considered vapid ' progressive' education; consequently, they cheat poor children of learning.[69] The fund of knowledge that children acquire early in life dictates their prospects in later life. It was this belief that drove the Core Knowledge movement in the United States, a nationwide initiative to establish a curriculum based on the premise that all children should attain shared knowledge of history, fundamental political and philosophical ideas, classic literary texts, and basic scientific concepts because children from poor families are at a disadvantage as compared to better-off children whose home environment helps them to prepare better for the learning in school. That preparation determines how well the learning process takes place in the classroom. The second school also holds that a primary task of the school should be to set off the handicap of poor children from

[67] Padma M. Sarangapani, 'The Great Indian Tradition', in 'Redesigning Curriculum: A Symposium on Working a Framework for School Education', *Seminar*, Volume 493, September 2000, http://www.india-seminar.com/sem-frame2.html (last accessed on 30 May 2015).

[68] Rohit Dhankar, 'Seeking Quality Education: In the Realm of Fun and Rhetoric' in *Seeking Quality Education*, pp. 1–29, at p. 10.

[69] Andrew Delbanco, 'Dreams of Better Schools', *New York Review of Books*, 56, no. 18 (19 November 2009), http://www.nybooks.com/articles/2009/11/19/dreams-of-better-schools (last accessed on 9 February 2016).

a disadvantaged background. To that end, the school should promote cumulative learning, grade by grade, that creates the preconditions for comprehension for *all* children in the class. Therefore, chopping a subject area into discrete packages of knowledge and testing whether a package is mastered before moving to teach the next package is not the heresy that is for the first school. Another cardinal difference that divided the two schools was the attitude to testing of achievement in a few select areas such as language. For pure and unalloyed constructivists, the aims of education are indivisible, evaluation has to be continuous and comprehensive and spread over the whole range of school years, and isolated tests to ascertain what children have learnt make no sense; worse, they induce in the child fear, trauma, and anxiety.

All this philosophical discourse could have been avoided here but for the fact that competing educational philosophies impact on approaches to quality improvement as well as teaching–learning practices. Human nature is far too complex to be captured by a single framework or model; in fact, it is hubris to think so. That being so, it is necessary to view the child and approach to education from different standpoints, and to honestly accept and reconcile the multiple perceptions and approaches; in other words, act in accordance with *Anekãntavada* (the theory of many-sidedness, a key element of Jain philosophy and which has a parallel in quantum mechanics). There should be a place for imparting children 'previous knowledge' as much as there should be a place for encouraging children to make sense of the world, act upon it, and produce knowledge. To give an analogy, the famous case study method of Harvard Business School transports in a trice, as in *Star Trek*, wannabe managers to the ghastly real world and, through simulated decision making, helps them acquire and hone the instincts necessary to thrive in a competitive business environment. However, from K's own experience both as a student and a teacher, the case method has great strength as well as weakness. Moderately used, it can help students acquaint with real-world dilemmas of decision-making wherein often information is inadequate and time too short for elaborate deliberation, and help the student to cope with those dilemmas and offer a quick response to the umpteen challenges that would face them in real life. It prods the student to think more critically and cogently, and to discover by himself the fallacies in his thinking such as unquestioning beliefs and unwarranted assumptions. Yet by itself, the case method does not help the understanding of concepts; either the student has to acquire an understanding of concepts through self-study and intellectual self-reliance or better the case method is complemented with teaching of the concepts by the instructor. Or to cite other examples, in the American public school system, curricular burden is low and activity-based approach widely employed; however, the reading, writing, and mathematical skills that students acquire are generally so low that colleges have to offer remedial instruction to the new entrants. In Britain itself, the introduction of a National Curriculum and National Assessment was designed to set off the limitations of traditional approach to schooling with decentralized school-based curriculum, and the aversion to subject the students to rigorous tests. Suffice to say, by itself constructivism as well as behaviourist–connectivist framework is inadequate, and eclecticism is superior to both. Some of the MLL competencies such as 'Count 1–20 using objects and pictures', 'Identify zero as the number representing nothing or the absence of objects in a collection', and 'Arrange numbers 1–100 in ascending and descending order', are not to be derided[70] in a situation when successive ASERs bring out very low levels of learning; thus, in 2012, one in every children in class VIII could not recognize numbers 10–99 and worse, 5 per cent of children in class VIII could not even recognize numbers 1–9. As Karl Marx wrote famously in *The German Ideology*, before mankind can think and ideas can be made, man must be first fed, clothed, and sheltered. Likewise, children, particularly from disadvantaged background, must be helped to acquire *basic learning* of writing, reading, and numerical skills of a satisfactory level before they realize higher-order pedagogic goals such as critical thinking, creativity, and learning to learn. To dogmatically insist that learning should encompass all aspects and not lay emphasis on 3 'R's in the lower classes, and to condemn that any evaluation which is not is not comprehensive and does not encompass all aspects of learning—cognitive, non-cognitive, higher order—is a good example of the saying that the best is an enemy of the good. This is all the more so in a situation when children do not seem to be learning anything at all, and it is incumbent on educationists and educational administrators to keep track on what children learn through measures which might not capture all aspects of learning.

[70] Padma Sarangapani, 'The Great Indian Tradition'.

Turning to the third reason, even those educationists who were not utterly opposed to stipulation of learning achievement as an objective were critical of the way MLLs were implemented. Thus, according to Subir Shukla[71] the Dave MLLs strictly classified and rigidly sequenced and numbered the competencies, and required a child to master a competency before moving to the next one. The linear sequence in which the competency lists were drawn up became the sequence of classroom transactions as well as textbooks to such a ridiculous extent that in some states the competency-based language textbooks devoted first ten pages to listening, the next ten pages to speaking, and so on. Such linearity led to great distortions in teaching and learning. Furthermore, MLLs were erroneously treated as *the* curriculum instead of being a list of competencies providing a framework for evaluation. In their study of the implementation of MLLs, Jangira, Kaul, and Menon found fault with the Dave Committee for departing from its terms of reference by fixing competency levels for each of the classes I–V instead of classes III and V; hence, children were not allowed to learn at their own pace so that by class III and later class V they could master the competencies stipulated for class III or class V as the case may be. Furthermore, the implementation strategy was flawed. The MLLs were expected to be adapted to local situations prevailing in a district; however, in practice there was no adaptation. Teachers were not provided the skills necessary for continuous monitoring necessary to evaluate the acquisition of competencies. Priority was given to the preparation of competency-based textbooks and their revision rather than on training and classroom practice.[72]

Whatever, the decade which followed the launch of DPEP in November 1994 was a hectic period of experimentation and shifting ideas in the area of pedagogy. Hardly had the competency-based textbooks and in-service training begun when, consequent to the disenchantment with MLLs, another round of revision of textbooks and training began. The revision of textbooks in Kerala in 1997 and its introduction throughout the state had come to be a much acclaimed saga commemorated in a KSG case study. An important aspect of the revision is the active role played by practising teachers marking a

[71] Subir Shukla, *Systems in Transition*, p. 5.

[72] N.K. Jangra, Vineet Kaul, and M.B. Menon, *Implementation of MLL: An Evaluation*, NCERT, 1997.

departure from the tradition of top-down process of the revising curriculum and textbooks. Several other states undertook similar revisions guided by their own light as well as the information about revisions in other states which seeped from *DPEP Calling*, visiting experts of DPEP TSG, and the JRMs. Among the innovations which got much attention was the *Nali Kali* approach in Karnataka based on the "learning ladder" approach of the Rishi Valley schools; that approach radically changed the manner in which teachers organize teaching-learning activities. It is no doubt true that DPEP 'has achieved lift-off in respect of quality', that 'although the overall picture is extremely diverse and, in some schools the reality of teaching may still be far from the rhetoric, the culture and form of teaching in the best of them have been transformed precisely along the lines that DPEP intended', and that 'this is major achievement'.[73] However, it would be fair to say that changes were all too frequent leaving little time for consolidation, with the result that the impact on classroom practices and, consequently, on learning outcomes was less than what it could have been, and that the policy of letting the states take the initiative in regard to improving quality and learning outcomes led to more uneven spread of gains among states than would have been the case if DPEP Bureau tightly monitored quality improvement the way it did in other areas of DPEP, and prodded the underperforming states to buck up. Furthermore, even though DPEP laid great emphasis on documentation, research, and evaluation, one does not come across too many manuals to guide teachers to adopt the innovations. Consequently, there is often movement without motion as every design tends to be a new beginning without building on the lessons of past interventions. Research and evaluation were no doubt prolific till the early 2000s; however, they were largely undertaken as an independent activity, and their use to steer decision-making appears to have been relatively limited.

To make matters worse, pedagogic activities in DPEP states and later SSA could not remain immune to national developments. In 2000, NCERT revised the National Curricular Framework (NCF) after a gap of 12 years. In the run up to the revision, NCERT came up in

[73] Robin Alexander, 'In Pursuit of Quality in Elementary Education: Reflections on DPEP', in Vimala Ramachandran et al., 'Reflections on Equity', pp. 45–55, at p. 47.

1998 with a document *Primary Years: Towards Curricular Framework*; this document was rather sceptical of MLLs and held that a patently behaviourist approach of measuring learning by change in observable behaviour was not defensible, and that it was not possible to measure learning in strictly quantitative terms. Since MLLs were laid down only for three subject areas, the other important areas of learning were consciously neglected. From a historical perspective, this document is of importance in that it was responsible for the exclusion of learning achievement as an objective of SSA; the first draft of the SSA Framework (December 1999), while mentioning the NPE and POA provisions regarding MLLs, made it explicit that

> the Sarva Shiksha Abhiyan would like to situate the pedagogical interventions within the current national framework. The two volumes entitled "The Primary Years—Towards a Curriculum Framework" (NCERT) will also be used to identify most suitable processes to improve the learning environment for the child.

The Framework's guidelines for curricular reform and evaluation make no mention of MLLs at all. Rather strangely, the final version of NCF, 2000, sang paeans to constructivist concepts such as 'child as the constructor of knowledge' and the idea that the focus of education having to move away from providing mere cognitive skills (the traditional 3Rs) to fostering interpersonal and intrapersonal development far, and yet at the same time, unlike the preliminary document *Primary Years*, is not critical of MLLs. It was in fact quite appreciative of MLLs:

> The MLLs approach is based on the elements of mastery level learning, child-centred and activity-based teaching, continuous and comprehensive evaluation, diagnostic and remedial teaching, differential treatment to optimise achievement levels of all and action research. All these elements need to be practised to achieve the goal of quality elementary education for all.
>
> Emphasis has been laid on the introduction of the MLLs and the adoption of a common scheme of studies at the different stages. Simultaneously, flexibility is envisaged in the selection of strategy for curriculum transaction. This will make learning relevant to the needs and environmental contexts of the learners and allow scope for initiative and experimentation on the part of the teacher, the school and the local educational authorities. However, the scope for flexibility in the methodology and approach to curriculum transaction is not expected to

be used for introducing differential courses or similar measures which would create disparities in the standards of education in different parts of the country.[74]

Given the NCF, 2000, postulates on MLLs, one would have expected that the draft SSA Framework would have been revised to provide for operationalization of the MLLs in a manner which avoided the mistakes in the implementation of the Dave Committee. It was not; except deleting any reference to *Primary Years*, the finalized SSA Framework did not propose to act on NCF's postulates on MLLs at all. No sooner than NCF, 2000, was formulated when it was enmeshed in a bitter controversy over its views on religion and value education, and their place in school curriculum; in fact for the first time ever an NCF prepared by the NCERT was taken note by those not connected with education. The constitutionality of NCF, 2000, was challenged in the Supreme Court, among others, on the ground that in providing for study of religions, NCF was violative of the rubric of secularism which is part of the basic structure of the Constitution. This plea was not accepted by the majority of the bench; it did not see 'anything in the Education Policy or the Curriculum which is against the Constitution'.[75] Whatever, states with governments led by the Congress Party refused to accept NCF, 2000; however, in other states, efforts began to revise curriculum and textbooks based on NCF, 2000. However, before the process was completed, the NDA government lost office, and NCF was revised again as revision of NCF, 2000, and detoxification of textbooks constituted the priority agenda of Arjun Singh who succeeded Murli Manohar Joshi. The new NCF, 2005, marked the triumph of the constructivist doctrine; it strongly denounced MLLs for reinforcing 'not only the rigid adherence to year-end outcomes, but also allowed for these to be further narrowed to lessons'. The constructivist view secured a legal imprimatur in the RTE, 2009. NCF, 2005, once again triggered another round of revision of state curricula, textbooks, and in-service teacher training. Whatever might be the rationale for these frequent revisions, they disrupted the efforts to improve teaching-learning process. NPE, 1986, provided for its review after 5 years; when the Ramamurti Committee was appointed in 1990 itself to review NPE,

74 NCERT, *National Curricular Framework*, November 2000, pp. 24–5.

75 *Aruna Roy and Others v. Union of India*, 2002 7 SCC 308.

1986, NCERT was critical of the appointment, as the very setting up of the committee had an adverse effect on implementation on ongoing schemes. To quote:

> On matters like Education, there should be broad national consensus on the directions in which education has to be used as an instrument for national development and, as far as possible; it should not be subject to repeated reviews at short intervals. Such an approach may not be conducive to tangible growth and development, particularly in the field of education which requires a long gestation period, a minimum of 8 to 10 years, for programmes to be developed. The present review ... has already resulted in slackening the pace of implementation of the NPE, 1986.[76]

These observations are equally valid in respect of the curricular revisions undertaken by NCERT in the early 2000s.

The available evidence on the first two Bank-funded DPEP projects indicate that notwithstanding the strenuous efforts made to improve curriculum, teaching–learning process, teaching–learning material, in-service training, and evaluation, the impact on learning outcomes was rather limited and mixed. DPEP set three objectives for learning: first, all children should achieve an average minimum score of 40 per cent in language and arithmetic; second, the average learning levels should increase by 25 per cent over the corresponding levels of the baseline survey; and third, gender and social differences in learning levels should be reduced to less than 5 per cent. The findings of the baseline, mid-term, and terminal learner assessment surveys as well as of in-depth studies commissioned by the DPEP Bureau were commented upon in literature; there are also critiques of the testing methodology employed.[77] In a nutshell:[78]

[76] NCERT, *NCERT's Comments on 'Towards an Enlightened and Humane Society- A Perspective Paper on Education'*, October 1990, pp. 37–8.

[77] World Bank, *A Review of Educational Progress and Reform in the District PrimaryEducation Program (Phases I & II)*, South Asia Human Development Sector, September 2003; A.B.L. Srivastava, *Learning Achievement at the End of the Primary School in DPEP States*, MHRD and Azim Premji Foundation: Learning Conference 2004; Azim Premji Foundation, *Status of Learning Achievements in India: A Review of Empirical Research*, October 2004.

[78] World Bank, *A Review of Educational Progress*, p. 26.

> Most districts in the DPEP have achieved the first objective of a minimum average score of forty percent in Class I but very few have achieved this in Class III/V. For the second objective on learning achievement, 50 to 75 percent of the districts achieved the 25 percent increase in learning over the baseline levels of Class I. However, less than five percent of the districts achieved this increase in Class III/V… Both DPEP I and II have been successful in reducing gender gaps learning achievement and moderately successful in reducing social disparities in achievement …
>
> There are very few studies, however, that attempt to understand why some districts/ schools did better than others in raising leaning achievement and reducing gender and social gaps. Rampal's study [in Kerala] … is one of the few studies that undertakes classroom observation as well as administers some basic achievement tests to students in select DPEP and non-DPEP districts. The results of this study clearly demonstrated that students in Class IV in DPEP districts performed significantly better on all competencies on which they were tested relative to students in non-DPEP districts.[79]

The findings of Rampal's study, of course, cannot be generalized; the study is valuable for highlighting the challenges mainstreaming DPEP interventions. The extension of books prepared by the Kerala DPEP Society to non-DPEP districts was the *cause célèbre* narrated in the KSG case study. The fact that the learner achievement levels in non-DPEP districts were lower brings out clearly that without complementary measures such as training of teachers, introduction of innovative textbooks would result in sub-optimal learning outcomes.

The failure of SSA to fix targets for learning outcomes would have been mitigated if there were comparable data on the trends in learning outcomes which can help judge whether quality improvement led to enhance learning outcomes, and if so, to what extent. To be fair to NCERT and the designers of SSA, plans were made for NCERT conducting National Assessment Survey (NAS) as an independent project funded by SSA; the surveys were to cover classes III, V, and VIII in the three cycles, the first cycle named baseline achievement survey conducted in the period 2001–04, the second cycle named mid-term achievement survey during the period 2005–8, and the third

[79] Anita Rampal, *Curriculum Change for Quality Education: A Study of in Schools in DPEP and non-DPEP Districts of Kerala*, Trivandrum: Primary Education Development Society, 2001.

cycle during the period 2009–12. However, these surveys were standalone academic exercises, no doubt funded by SSA but having little bearing on programme interventions of SSA. The first cycle surveys were delayed and best with technical flaws. The results of the next two cycles were not comparable as they adopted different methodologies; the second cycle surveys adopted methodology based on the Classical Test Theory while the third cycle surveys adopted methodology based on the state-of-art Item Response Theory (IRT) introduced with the technical assistance of DFID. Whatever, it is really unfortunate that a quarter of a century after P.N. Dave and Snehalata Shukla of NCERT conducted National Achievement Survey and two decades after DPEP conducted baseline achievement surveys there is as yet no official time series data which bring out the trends in learning achievement the way, say, OECD's Programme for International Student Assessment (PISA) did. NCERT rightly claims that the third cycle surveys would provide baselines with reference to which the future progress in learning achievement could be compared; one hopes that these claims would come true. The SSA also encouraged the states to develop their own learning objectives as well as learner achievement methodologies, and some states had conducted learner achievement surveys. However, one is not sure of the robustness of the methodologies employed, and further, as the surveys had been standalone exercises they do not throw light on the trends in learning achievement. Nature, it is rightly said, abhors vacuum. The gap in official data was made good by Pratham through its ASERs, and what the ASERs bring about is an acute crisis of non-learning afflicting the education system in almost all states. In recent years the levels of reading and arithmetic at all levels have been declining in recent years in rural schools, and there is a pervasive 'feeling that RTE Act may have led to relaxation of classroom teaching since all examinations and assessments are scrapped and no child is to be kept back'.[80] Even the official information available confirms the existence of a crisis of non-learning. To illustrate, a presentation given by Rajasthan government to the 18th JRM of SSA (June 2013) led by K brought out that 21.76 per cent of class III children could not read Hindi, the language of the state, by the end of the school year; much

[80] *Annual Status of Education Report (Rural) 2012*, New Delhi: ASER Centre, 2013, p. 2.

worse, 4.54 per cent of class VIII children could not read Hindi. The logical question which arises is whether it is better to follow the DPEP practice of fixing quantitative targets for improvement of basic learning skills in the primary stage. As the discussion of elementary education is now conducted in the rights framework, it would be necessary to turn to the question of what the RTE Act, 2009, had to say about learner achievement.

Few human endeavours can escape the law of unintended consequences and the contingent nature of history, and the RTE Act is no exception. The primary impulse of those who campaigned first for Constitutional Amendment and later the RTE Act was the belief that the main reason why UEE was elusive was the lack of commitment to UEE by central and state governments; the logical conclusion of the belief was that an irrevocable binding legal obligation would compel the governments to do the right things necessary to ensure that UEE moves from the plane of dreams to that of reality (Chapter XIX). Seven long years intervened between the Constitutional Amendment in 2002 and the enactment of the RTE, the enabling legislation which provides the legal framework for implementing the fundamental right, created by that Constitutional Amendment, of free and compulsory education for all children in the age group 6–14. Following the enactment of RTE Act, the SSA framework was revised so as to be RTE-compliant; the changes were mainly in respect of revised physical and financial norms for appointment of teachers, provision of school facilities, provision of transport facilities, free textbooks, and uniforms to children. For the first 2–3 years after the enactment of RTE Act, the State Education Departments were preoccupied with complying with what they perceived to be the main thrust of RTE Act, to wit, the notification of the state rules under the RTE Act, making schools RTE compliant, and ensure that all out-of-school children are enrolled, this at a time when the predominant challenge was not so much access or even enrolment as the gruesome fact children were hardly learning anything. To elaborate, when the campaign for the enactment of the RTE Act began in 2002 there were as many 2.5 crore out-of-school children, and the gross enrolment ratio (GER) was about 95 per cent in the primary stage and 85 per cent in the upper primary stage. But by 2010 when the RTE Act came into force, the number of out-of-school children was reported to be only 16.84 lakhs.[81] Official data on the steep reduction in out-of-school children is also corroborated by non-official data like that of ASERs. It is quite possible that in actuality the number of out-of-school children is a little larger than the UNESCO and official estimates; furthermore, there are still a few pockets of exclusion which need to be tackled, and retention at the upper primary stage is still a challenge. However, the foremost challenge now is improvement of quality learning and achievement. Like the generals proverbially preparing for the last war, the focus of the RTE Act was on the past challenge of enhancing access and enrolment of one and all. It omits any reference to learning, and it equates good-quality education with providing teachers and facilities in accordance with the norms and standards it lays down. RTE's perception of quality and learning is an educationist version of the percolation theory of economic development. Before the late 1960s, the regnant theory of economic development commended single-minded pursuit of economic growth with the expectation that the benefit of economic growth would percolate down to the poor; if growth is taken care of, everything would be alright and no direct interventions would be necessary to reduce, if not eliminate, poverty. Likewise, according to the activists who played a major role in the crafting of the RTE Act, if the norms and standards of RTE Act are complied with, learning would take care of by itself, and learning achievement need not be monitored as it would be redundant and, worse, subject children to repeated *high-stake testing*. This approach is as unrealistic as the belief that no direct interventions need to be taken to address concerns of equity or poverty reduction. Suffice to say, the right to education that the RTE Act seeks to mandate is meaningless if it is limited to ensuring that no child of the age group 6–14 is left behind *either* at home *or* at workplace, and ensuring that every school conforms to the norms and standards stipulated by the Act and its rules. The right to elementary education makes sense only if every child *learns*, for ultimately education is about learning and everything else is an instrumental objective. It is desirable to amend the RTE Act so as to restore a correct perception of quality elementary education.

[81] UNESCO, *Schooling for Millions of People Jeopardized by Reductions in Aid*, EFA-GMR Policy Paper 09, June 2013.

All in all, learning is the final frontier of UEE and should be the predominant focus of SSA. By their very nature, improvement of quality and learning achievement are infinitely more challenging than enhancing access and enrolment. They require more intense planning, monitoring, and supervision than that required for universal access and participation. Needless to say, the annual work planning formats, *Result Monitoring Matrix*, and the reporting formats need to be modified. It is equally necessary to modify the remit of JRMs so that the Mission members expend a greater proportion of their time and energy in assessing the implementation of the pedagogic measures needed to improve learning outcomes, and to assess the extent to which learning outcomes had improved. If everything is a priority nothing is, and the usefulness of JRMs would be impaired if they do not give overriding priority to assess the trends in learning outcomes. It is easy to count the number of classrooms or toilets constructed or the number of teachers appointed or training classes conducted as they are tangible and palpable. In contrast, the extent to which training communicates the new pedagogy, the degree of absorption of those methods by teachers, and their willingness to replace their erstwhile teaching methods by the new methods are intangible are not captured by quantitative data. Therefore, much of the monitoring has to incorporate qualitative indicators which can be monitored only through rapid appraisals and quick evaluation. It is imperative to enlist a large number of individuals and organizations for appraisal and evaluation.

There are glimmers of hope. It is a happy augury that NCERT is working towards developments of learning indicators for classes I–VIII, and that following the recommendation of the 18th JRM guidelines were issued by the Department of School Education and Literacy that the 2014–15 annual work plans should give priority to improve learning outcomes. The states were requested to plan and implement three categories of interventions: defining class-wise subject-wise learning outcomes and indicators, and planning and implementing special interventions for improvement. Furthermore, an important component of SSA-III Project (July 2014–June 2017) is strengthening the monitoring of learner outcomes. The Project seeks to strengthen the capacity of NCERT to generate reliable time series data, to cover children with special needs. More importantly, it seeks to promote the use of NAS results for remedial action and improve the teacher training for measurement of learning achievement. NAS results cannot become an end in itself and is embedded in a proper frame for enhancement of quality and integrally linked with concrete measures for enhancement of quality. As demonstrated by the American *No Child Left Behind Act*, an obsessive focus on test results would be counterproductive, as it might lead to cheating scandals and imposition of such high benchmarks that half the schools fail to meet the benchmarks and are declared to be failures. SSA-III also seeks to help states and union territories to collect more disaggregated data on student outcomes at the district level for remedial action and corrective measures, that is to say do something DPEP aspired to do two decades ago. While this is welcome, it is important that disaggregated data are collected within a common national frame and the same methodology for measurement of learner achievement is adopted. This would facilitate comparison of similarly situated districts across states so that good practices developed in a district could be adapted in similar districts elsewhere in the country. All in all, learner outcomes seem to be coming back into the spotlight.

Private Schools: Do They Matter for UEE?

A cardinal postulate of education policy had been that private unaided schools do not matter for educational development. This policy eminently made sense till the early 1990s in the matter of school education as private unaided schools were relatively few, were almost wholly English medium schools affiliated to the CBSE or ICSE Council, and catered to children either of parents who because of their career could not stay in a single state for a period long enough for their children to complete school education in the local language or of aspiring parents who felt that a private English medium school offered better prospects for their children to move up in life. New genres of schools began to spring up in the late 1980s, making the schools system much more diverse than in the past. In many southern states and Maharashtra, an engineering degree came to be the target of paper chase instead of a B.A. degree, and as admission to an engineering college depended on good schooling, the demand for private education deemed to be superior to government schools began to surge. In states such as AP, well-off parents began to send their children to private residential schools which prepare students for class X and class XI examinations conducted by the state boards as private candidates as well as for entrance examinations for engineering, medicine, and other professional courses. Those with slender means began to send their children to less pricey private unaided schools whose quality of instruction was perceived to be better than government schools, as teachers were always present when the school functioned and were more accountable to parents and the management.[82] According to the *Statistics of School Education, 2011–12* (as of 30 September 2011)[83], the proportion of private unaided schools increased from 4.7 per cent of the upper primary schools in 1973–4 to 11.0 per cent in 1993–4 and to a peak of 22.3 per cent in 2006–7; therefore it had declined to 16.7 per cent in 2011–12 because of the large scale expansion of Government schools. The corresponding figures for primary schools are lower at 1.6 per cent in 1973–4, 4.1 per cent in 1993–4, 7.8 per cent in 2006–7 and 8.1 per cent in 2011–12. As of now, there are an about 3.3 lakh private schools.[84] Of these, schools affiliated to International and All India Boards, and private residential schools perhaps account for no more than 30,000. Consequently, unlike in the past schools affiliated to State Boards and charging fees considerably lower than pricey private schools now constitute the predominant majority of private unaided schools; it is they who loom large in the discourse on private versus public schools. More significant than the numbers or rapid growth of such schools is the increasing contribution they had been making to additional enrolment. Geeta Kingdon had analysed the data of NCERT's Fifth, Sixth and Seventh All India Education Surveys and her analysis brings out vividly that private unaided schools had been imparting a significant thrust to the increase in enrolment at all stages of school

[82] James Tooley, *The Beautiful Tree: A Personal Journey into How the World's Poorest People Are Educating Themselves*, Washington, DC: Cato Institute, 2009.

[83] Ministry of Human Resource Development, *Statistics of School Education, 2010–11* (as of 30 September 2011), http://mhrd.gov.in/sites/upload_files/mhrd/files/statistics/SSE_11-12Final.pdf (last accessed on 9 February 2016).

[84] Geeta Gandhi Kingdon, 'Schools without Learning', *The Hindu*, 8 February 2016.

education, and in urban areas they impart the preponderant thrust.[85] According her estimates, during the period 1993–2002, at the primary stage private unaided schools contributed about a quarter of the additional enrolment in rural areas , and about 96 per cent of the additional enrolment in urban areas. In upper primary classes (classes VI–VIII), they contributed about 23 per cent of the additional enrolment in rural areas, and seventy-two per cent of the additional enrolment in urban areas was. NCERT surveys do not include data of unrecognised schools; their enrolment according to the household data for the years 1993 and 2006 was about thrice that shown by the NCERT All India Survey date for 1993 and 2002. Hence the contribution of private unaided schools to enrolment could be higher than that indicated by NCERT surveys. The Eighth All India Education Survey (Reference date: 30 September 2009) indicates that the trends of the previous surveys gained further momentum at the primary stage. Thus during the period 2002–9, total enrolment in primary schools had increased by 0.9 per cent; however, 18.31 per cent of students studied in private unaided schools as compared to the 14.96 per cent in 2002.[86, 87] Correspondingly at the upper primary stage, during the period 2002–9, total enrolment had increased by 17.23 per cent; however, 19.97 per cent of the students studied in private unaided schools as compared to 18.33 per cent in 2002. The data of MHRD, National Sample Survey, DISE and Annual Status of Primary Education Reports corroborate the NCERT Survey data and do indicate that private unaided institutions account for an increasing proportion of total enrolment in the primary and upper primary stages. Thus according to the National Sample Survey data, in 2007–8 private unaided primary schools enrol about a fifth of the total boys enrolled

[85] Geeta G. Kingdon, 'School-Sector Effects on Student Achievement in India', in R. Chakrabarti and P. Peterson, eds, *School Choice International: Exploring Public–Private Partnerships*, Cambridge, Mass: MIT Press, 2008, pp. 111–39, at pp. 113–17. dise.in/Downloads/.../Geeta%20Gandhi%20 Kingdon.pdf (last accessed on 9 February 2016).

[86] NCERT, *Eighth All India Education Survey: Concise Report*, 2016, pp. 44–6, 48.

[87] NCERT, *Seventh All India Education Survey: Enrolment in Schools*, 2010, http://www.ncert.nic.in/programmes/education_survey/pdfs/Enrolment_in_school.pdf (last accessed on 9 February 2016).

in rural as well as urban areas; their share of girl's enrolment is only a shade lower. Private unaided schools dominate in urban areas accounting for about 59 per cent of the total primary enrolment and about 55 per cent in total upper primary enrolment.[88] All in all, private unaided schools are significant in rural areas and dominant in urban areas.

Although the jury is still out, it had been claimed that these schools draw 'their clientele from across the social spectrum'. Suffice to say that as over a third of children are now enrolled in private unaided schools, it is time to give up a cardinal postulate of education policy since Independence that private unaided schools would not matter for educational development. Before moving further, it may be said that even in respect of English medium schools, there had been greater diversification. As India got more integrated with the global economy and as there were increasingly more and more persons who could not stay in India for a period long enough for their children to complete schooling, schools affiliated to international boards began to proliferate from the late 1990s. In 2010, even CBSE had come out with *CBSE International* (*CBSE-i*), an international curriculum.

Like almost every other area of education, there are sharply divergent views on the utility and relevance of the less pricey private unaided schools affiliated to state boards. For the admirers, they are the twenty-first century equivalent of the village schools eulogized by Mahatma Gandhi in his famous Chatham House speech (1931) as constituting the beautiful tree of indigenous education. And further, the RTE Act with its elaborate norms and standards was doing precisely what the British did:

> The British administrators, when they came to India, instead of taking hold of things as they were, began to root them out. They scratched the soil and began to look at the root, and left the root like that, and the beautiful tree perished. The village schools were not good enough for the British administrator, so he came out with his program. Every school must have so much paraphernalia, building and so forth.[89]

[88] Prachi Srivastava, Claire Noronha and Shailaja Fennell, *Sarva Shiksha Abhiyan: Private Sector Research*, Study Report submitted to DFID, India, London: UK Aid, 2013, p.13.

[89] M.K. Gandhi, *Future of India*, an address given at Chatham House on 20 October 1931, London: Royal Institute of International Affairs.

The critics of private schools, however, rubbish such schools as sink schools of inequity.

These conflicting views about state and markets are reminiscent of theological disputes[90]; however, reasonable men can draw reasonable conclusions if adequate, reliable data were available. The lack of detailed data on private schools validates the saying of Bertrand Russell that the most savage controversies are about those matters for which there is no good evidence. Private unaided schools are quite heterogeneous, and the reasons for their growth are complex and vary widely. The empirical findings based on which the champions and the sceptics put forth their views are too slender to form the basis of robust conclusions which can form the basis of a national or state policy. We need to have detailed information of the different varieties of private schools, where they are located, the socio-economic profiles of students and parents, their financing modalities, fees charged, facilities they possess, and their learning outcomes; and this information needs to be collected with reasonable frequency so that it is possible to gauge the trends and assess the factors underlying the trends. As of now, *Statistics of School Education*, published by MHRD, reports details of government, local body, and private aided and unaided schools at every stage of schooling; but that publication does not report similar details of enrolment. NCERT's All India Education Survey Reports are better in that they also provide details of enrolment by management. However, beyond that they throw little light on private schools. They could but do not furnish information such as the enrolment in private schools of disadvantaged groups such as scheduled castes or details of facilities in private schools. Whenever a new survey is taken up, much is made of the attempt to focus on a new area. Thus, the Eighth Survey claims credit for focussing on degree of disability of physically challenged students; however, to K's knowledge, it did not make any attempt to offer more information on private schools any better. Private unaided schools were not covered by the DPEP learner assessment surveys; nor are they covered by National Assessment Surveys NCERT had been conducting at the behest of SSA. Nor are they covered by learner assessment surveys conducted by individual states. Needless to say, *Statistics of School*

[90] Robert Henry Nelson, *Economics* as *Religion: From Samuelson to Chicago and Beyond*, University Park, PA: University of Pennsylvania Press, 2001.

Education, All India Education Survey, and DISE should get their act together and report data on private schools on par with government schools. All types of learner assessment surveys should cover such schools. The collection of such statistics should be supplemented by periodic and nation-wide micro-studies which bring out the ground reality underlying statistical trends. It cannot be highlighted enough that evidence-based policymaking is more valuable than that based on blind belief and surmise.

Suffice to say, the basic premise of DPEP and later of SSA that only government schools and their equivalent government-funded alternatives matter for UEE did not turn out to be right. About a third of children now study in private unaided elementary schools; to say the least, to exclude them from programmes designed for improvement of quality and learner achievement makes no sense. Posing questions like as to whether the private schools be relied upon to universalize elementary education is no more than the rhetorical ploy of setting up a useful straw man who could easily be knocked down. And those who argue for handing over government schools altogether to private bodies or encourage parents to opt out of government schools by offering vouchers are oblivious of the fact that there is no country in the world without a predominant and strong government school system. Poor are poor irrespective of the type of school in which they study. As like should be treated alike, children of less pricey private schools should not be penalized by being deprived of incentives their counterparts receive in government schools. The UPA government decided to extend the mid-day meal scheme to private unaided schools in scheduled caste/scheduled tribe and minority concentration districts; poor children need to learn well. Therefore, there is no reason why their schools should not be covered by programmes for improvement of quality and learner achievement.

It Takes All the Running You Can Do to Keep in the Same Place. If You Want to Get Somewhere Else, You Must Run at least Twice As Fast As That!

The experience of DPEP as well as SSA establishes that even the best designed programmes and intentions tend to be routinized and dysfunctional, and that, therefore, they need to be continually evaluated and rejuvenated. In-service training as well as BRCs and CRCs are cases in point. The BRCs and CRCs were set up with the primary objective of providing academic support to the teachers. Over time, they had been loaded with so many functions that their utility is being impaired; figuratively, functionaries in charge of these institutions have become jacks of all trades and all-purpose journeymen.

It is well known in pedagogy that learning achievements of students in any classroom 'follow the normal probability curve', that is to say that irrespective of teaching there would always be some students whose learning achievement would be lower than that of the class average. Consequently, every teacher is required to pay special attention to such students and ensure that they also achieve average levels of learning. In other words, the teacher is expected to take note of 'individual differences' in his teaching. The desirability of teaching taking note of individual differences is all the more so when the objective is to ensure that every child acquires essential levels of learning, and a considerable number of students are first-generation learners from disadvantaged background, and children with special needs. A preponderant proportion of classrooms are much more diverse than ever in the past, diverse in terms of the home background, and diverse in terms of learning capabilities of children. Therefore, in-service training has to lay a strong emphasis on the need for teaching to address individual differences and the enormous diversity in a classroom. Design of innovative classroom practices have to be guided by four principles: 'best is the enemy of the good', 'one size cannot fit all', 'Rome is not built in day', and 'familiarity breeds contempt'. The practices should be designed not for the best only but also for the average; just as teaching is expected to take into account individual differences of learners, training has to take into account the individual differences of trainees, and should be teacher specific. Organization of training should pay greater attention to the assessment of the training needs of individual teachers. The training modules should be graded so that through successive training programmes, the less gifted and less committed teachers can progressively move up the ladder of competencies and skills. That even the best designed training module is likely to get routinized and jaded over time and needs to be periodically refurbished is vividly brought out by the evocative diary of Hemraj Bhatt, an assistant teacher in a remote village of Uttarakhand who lived for his students and whose diary published posthumously is a testament to spur the education community. Bhatt evocatively described the surcharged environment of the training sessions.

> In the initial days of DPEP and SSA, the discussions were meaningful and the participants were present for the entire duration in the training hall. Even outside the training room, there was an environment of debate and discussion. A strange glow could be seen on the faces of the participants when they came out from the training sessions, so much so that even in the bus the talk was about the issues of training, the presentations and the quality of presentations.

But after the third year, gradually the quality of training declined and 'today things have reached such a state that no one wants to even enter the training room', and 'the current scenario of the training sessions makes me weep'.[91]

On the whole, DPEP as well as SSA had not succeeded in reducing the disparities in participation and learning between children belonging to scheduled tribes and all other children, a major reason being the fact that for ST children the medium of instruction can be a formidable barrier to learning. As Hemraj Bhatt's experience as a teacher brings out, even other children might not properly and fully develop their linguistic expression, as the teachers expect that children should use the words of the standard language and make fun when they use words of the local dialect. Assam has a long tradition of using a few tribal languages as media of instruction. States such as Orissa have made commendable effort in promoting bilingual education in the lower classes whereby children begin learning the mother tongue and later switch to the language of the state; however, much more needs to be done. The sprawling tribal tract in the heart of India spans the contiguous states of Maharashtra, AP, Chhattisgarh, Orissa, and Jharkhand, and is home to several tribes. In this tract, the same tribe lives across boundaries of states. Thus, *savaras* live in Orissa, AP, as well as Chhattisgarh. It is therefore logical that these states work together and continuously share their experiences and best practices. One of the key recommendations

[91] Hemraj Bhatt, *The Diary of a School Teacher*, translated from Hindi by Sharada Jain, Bangalore: Azim Premji University, 2011, pp. 25–6, 32, http://azimpremjiuniversity.edu.in/pdf/diary-school-teacher-english.pdf. Hindi and Kannada versions can also be downloaded.

of the 18th Joint Review Mission of SSA (June 2013) was that SSA should facilitate this collaboration and critically review the efforts being made by these states to promote all aspects the education of tribal children. Even with non-tribal students, it is only of late it is being recognized that dialectical variations could come in the way of learning language, and could be 'sites of exclusion'. Often the spoken language is not only an indicator of the region to which the speaker belongs but also the speaker's position in the social hierarchy. All in all, we need to develop pedagogy of inclusion.

Your Journey Never Ends: Life Has a Way of Changing Things in Incredible Ways

India's quest for universalizing elementary education which began in 1817 has come a long way and has entered a new phase. The journey ahead is more arduous, as the experience all over the world is that improving quality and learning achievement are more complex challenges than getting children to school. That is the reason why the credo 'crisis of education' crops up again and again in many countries. To give an example, in the United States, few public institutions rival public schools in public dissatisfaction; over the last hundred years, they had time and again received unsavoury epithets such as 'public joke', 'vaudeville show', and 'destroyers of democracy'. A long journey is ahead, and it is expedient to travel light by shedding baggage of mindsets stuck in time wraps.[92]

[92] Andrew Delbanco. 1999. 'Dreams of Better Schools'. *New York Review of Books*, 56(18), 19 November 2009. http://www.nybooks.com/articles/2009/11/19/dreams-of-better-schools. Last accessed on 9 February 2016.

GLOSSARY*

Adi Sankara: One of the greatest Hindu philosophers and proponent of Advaita

Advaita: Monism: A major school of Hindu philosophy which holds that the universe and human souls are one and the same. Advaitin is one who believes in such monism.

Adult illiteracy: People aged 15 and older who cannot, with understanding, read and write a simple statement about their everyday life.

Antyodaya: A programme which targets the most deprived.

Basic education: In international parlance, particularly after the World Conference on Education for All held in March 2000, Jomtien, Thailand, basic education connotes the whole range of educational activities taking place in various settings (formal, non-formal, and informal) that aim to meet basic learning needs of children, youth, and adults. It is different from Gandhian basic education which was the dominant model for achieving universalizing elementary education from Independence till mid-1960s. The central principle of Gandhian basic education was that teaching craft should be the vehicle for imparting education. Basic education, as envisaged by the Mahatma, was a single activity of education *through* craft, and did not comprise two activities of imparting education as well as training for a craft.

* Some of the terms such as 'gross enrolment ratio' and 'net enrolment ratio' are an adaption of the definition given in the UNESCO Institute of Statistics Glossary; http://glossary.uis.unesco.org/glossary/en/home.

Batchmates: Officers who joined the civil service in the same year; similar to the American English expression, the same 'Class'. A camaraderie similar to that of the old boys' network is expected to prevail among batchmates.

BIMARU states: An acronym formed from the first letters of the names of the states Bihar, MP, Rajasthan, and UP. The word 'Bimaru' bears a resemblance to the Hindi word 'bimar', meaning sick, and connotes the backwardness of these states in terms of economic and social indicators. After the bifurcation of Bihar and MP, Jharkhand and Chhattisgarh are included in the league of BIMARU states.

Block: A block is an intermediary administrative entity between the district and the village.

Centrally sponsored schemes: Schemes drawn up and financed by the central government and implemented by state governments.

Cohort: A group of persons who jointly experience a series of events over a period of time. A school cohort is defined as a group of pupils who enter the first grade of a given cycle in the same school year.

Compulsory education: Children of a specified age group who are legally obliged to attend school; in India, that age group is 6–14.

Country Assistance Strategy: A document which outlines the World Bank's priorities and proposed lending and non-lending activities in a country for 3–5 years.

Country director: Head of a World Bank country office.

Crore: Equal to hundred lakhs or ten millions.

Directive Principle: These are guidelines and principles considered fundamental in the governance of the country which the central and state governments are obligated to keep in mind in governance. They are codified in Part IV of the Constitution of India. They are supposedly not enforceable by any court; however, through a series of activist judgments, many of them had been transformed into fundamental rights.

District: A pivotal administrative unit in India in between the state government and smaller administrative entities including villages and cities. The administrative head of a district called by different names such as district collector and deputy commissioner; he plays a key role in regulation as well as development. Officers of the IAS are appointed as the administrative head of the district.

District collector: See entry 'District'.

Dropout: A student who gives up studies before completing a given grade or stage of education, say primary or elementary.

Dropout rate: Proportion of pupils from a cohort enrolled in a given grade in a given school year, who are no longer enrolled before completing that grade or stage of education. Thus, the dropout rate at the primary stage is the proportion of pupils from a cohort enrolled in class I who are no longer enrolled when that cohort reaches class V. Dropout rates at the upper primary stage (classes VI–VIII) and elementary stage (classes I–VIII) are similarly defined.

Dvaita: Dualism; a major school of Hindu philosophy which holds that the universal and human souls are different. *Dvaitin* is one who believes in such dualism

Elementary education: Classes I–VIII constitute elementary education; of this, classes I–V comprise the primary stage, and classes VI–VII the upper primary stage. In some states, however, classes I–VIII constitute elementary education; of these, the classes 1–IV comprise the primary stage and classes V–VII the upper primary stage.

A primary school is a school with classes I–V, an upper primary school is a school with classes VI–VII, and an elementary school is a school with classes I–VIII.

In the Indian context, universal primary education (UPE) is a situation in which, among others, every child in the age group 6–11 goes to a school and completes the primary stage; universal elementary education (UEE) is the situation in which, among others, every child in the age group 6–14 goes to a school and completes the primary as well as the upper primary stage.

In international parlance, what is termed in India as 'elementary education' is termed as 'primary education', and consequently UPE in international parlance is UEE in Indian parlance.

As far as possible the international usage is used while discussing the international scene and external funding agencies; conversely, the Indian usage is used while discussing the national scene and external funding agencies.

Enrolment: Children who are enrolled in a given class or stage of education regardless of age

External funding agency: An agency based outside India which provides funding whether as grant or as loan. It is also called donor and 'development partner'. The funding can be provided either directly by a government or by a regional organization such as the European Union or a multilateral organization such as the World Bank. Where funding is provided by a government to another government, it is bilateral assistance; usually a government sets up an organization to extend assistance, for example Department for International Development (DFID) by United Kingdom.

Gross enrolment ratio (GER): Number of students enrolled in a given level of education, regardless of age, expressed as a percentage of the official school-age population corresponding to the same level of education. Thus, the GER of primary stage is the number of students in primary classes (classes I–V), regardless of age, as a percentage of children in the age group 6–11. The GERs of upper primary and elementary stages are similarly defined.

Gram panchayat: Village council; see entry 'Panchayat Raj'.

Gurudev: Literally means 'Divine Mentor', a sobriquet of the savant Rabindranath Tagore.

Human capital: The knowledge, skills, and experience of people that make them economically productive. Human capital can be increased by investing in education, health care, and job training.

Implementation Completion Report (ICR): A document which evaluates the performance of the World Bank and borrowing country in achieving the objectives of a credit extended by the World Bank; it is prepared within six months of closure of a project.

Independent Evaluation Group (IEG): Formerly the Operations Evaluation Group (OEG), IEG is an independent evaluation unit reporting to the World Bank's executive directors; it rates the development impact and performance of select projects funded by the World Bank lending operations which are completed. The results and recommendations are reported to the executive directors and fed back into the design and implementation of new policies and projects.

Indian Administrative Service: A premier administrative civil service whose members hold key and strategic positions in the union government and states

International Bank for Reconstruction and Development (IBRD): One of the five arms of the World Bank Group; it lends money to middle-income countries at near-market interest rates.

International Development Association (IDA): One of the five arms of the World BankGroup. It lends money to poorer countries at below-market interest rates with a repayment period of 35–40 years with a 10-year grace periods on repayment.

Jana Shikshan Nilayam: Continuing Education Centre.

Khap panchayat: A community council which sets the rules of conduct in one or more villages, and punishes transgression. In practice, many of them became laws unto themselves and had come to be because of the arbitrary enforcement of social taboos. Khap panchayats have come to be perceived as an embodiment of arbitrariness and the tyranny of social taboos.

Lakh: Equal to 0.1 million.

Learning objectives: Specification of learning outcomes to be achieved upon completion of an educational or learning activity. These encompass improving knowledge, skills, and competencies within any personal, civic, social, or employment-related context.

Learning outcome: Totality of information, knowledge, understanding, attitudes, values, skills, competencies, or behaviours an individual is expected to master upon successful completion of an educational programme.

Letter of Development Policy: A letter to the President of the World Bank in which the borrowing government sets out the programme of objectives, policies, and measures to be supported by the Bank's credit extended

Mahabhinishkramana: Literally means 'Great Departure'; it usually refers to the death of Buddha.

Lok Jumbish: A basic education project of Rajasthan; it literally means people's movement with a view to providing relevant basic education to all, and to generate a stimulus for human development.

Lok Sampark Abhiyan: People's Contact Movement, MP.

Ministry and department: The Government of India (GOI) is organized as ministries; each ministry is in charge of a minister who can be a Cabinet Minister or a Minister of State with independent charge. Often large ministries have several departments. Thus, as of now the Ministry of Human Resource Development (MHRD) comprises two departments: the Department of School Education and Literacy and the Department of Higher Education. A secretary to GOI is the administrative head of each department.

State governments are organized as departments; it is in charge of a minister. A secretary to the state government is the administrative head of a department. Each department has executive arms called directorates or commissionerates. The head of a directorate or commissionerate is called a head of the department.

Multigrade teaching: A single teacher simultaneously teaching many grade levels (for example, classes I–V) in a single class.

National assessment: Assessment of learning outcomes which aims to describe the achievement of a given target population and provide feedback on a limited number of outcome measures that are considered important by policy makers, politicians, and the broader educational community. It is generally administered to a sample of individuals and also collects background information that are important to link analysis to policy questions at the national, sub-national, and local levels.

Naxalite: A member of any of the Communist guerrilla groups in India.

Net enrolment ratio (NER): Total number of students belonging to a specified age group who are enrolled in a given stage of education expressed as a percentage of the total population in that age group. Thus, the net enrolment ratio of primary stage is the enrolment in classes I–V of children of the age group 6–11 as a percentage of the total population in that age group; net enrolment ratios for upper primary stage and elementary stage are similarly calculated for the age groups 11–14 and 6–14, respectively. For assessing the extent to which the policy objective of universal enrolment is achieved, the net enrolment ratio is a more accurate measure than the gross enrolment ratio (GER); to illustrate at the primary stage, GER includes in the numerator children who are enrolled and below 6 years as well as those above 11 years while the denominator is the population of children in the age group 6–11. Consequently, the GER might exceed 100 per cent, while NER can never exceed 100 per cent.

ODA: This acronym is used in this book in two senses:

- Overseas Development Agency of United Kingdom; in 1997, it was transformed into the Department for International Development (DFID).
- Development Assistance, or aid as is popularly called by OECD-DAC, offered by 23 countries and the European Union that are members of the Development Assistance Committee (DAC),

an organ of the Organisation for Economic Cooperation and Development (OECD). These countries are Australia, Austria, Belgium, Britain, Canada, Denmark, Finland, France, Germany, Greece, Ireland, Italy, Japan, Luxemburg, Netherlands, New Zealand, Norway, Portugal, Spain, Sweden, Switzerland, South Korea, and the United States.

Out-of-school children: Children in the officially specified age group who are not enrolled in the relevant stage of education or the next stage of education. To illustrate, at the primary stage, out-of-school children are children in the age group 6–11 who are not enrolled at the primary stage or upper primary stage; the upper primary stage is included because children may join class I earlier than the official age of 6 years and might complete the primary stage before they compete 11 years.

Overage children: Students who are older than the official school-age range for the educational programme they are enrolled in. Thus, the official age group for primary stage is 6–11 years, and consequently overaged children at the primary stage are children who are enrolled and whose age is above 11 years.

Panchasheela: Literally five principles of conduct.

Panchayat Raj: Local self-government in rural areas; usually it is three tiered with a *zilla parishad* (district council), *panchayat samithi* (Block Council), and *gram panchayat* (village council). A block is an intermediary administrative entity between the district and the village. The Panchayat Raj bodies were vested with a constitutional status by the 73rd amendment to the Constitution.

Primary education: See Elementary Education.

Province: During British rule, states were called provinces.

Rishi: Sage.

Sā Vidyā Yā Vimuktaye: Knowledge is that which liberates.

Shiksha: Education

Shiksha Karmi: Literally 'education' workers. This term is used in this book in two senses. The first connotation is a programme in Rajasthan to provide education for children in remote villages where teacher absenteeism is rampant, by engaging local youth as instructor. The second connotation is a teacher appointed on contractual basis; other names for such teachers are para-teachers, Vidya Sahayak, Shikshan Sevak, and Shiksha Mitra.

Tambrahm: the mildly derisive expression for Tamil Brahmins used by North Indian yuppies, and sportingly adopted by Tambrahm yuppies themselves.

The Mahatma: Literally means a 'Great Soul'; in this book, M.K. Gandhi is referred to as the Mahatma.

Underage children: Students who are younger than the official school-age range for the educational programme they are enrolled in. Thus, the official age group for the primary stage is 6–11 years, and consequently overaged children at the primary stage are children who are enrolled and whose age is less than 6 years.

Union territory: An administrative entity in whose administration the Union has a greater role than in the administration of states.

Vernacular: Language or dialect spoken in a region.

Vishishtadvaita: Qualified monism; a major school of Hindu philosophy whose position is in-between the *Advaita* and *Dvaita*.

Women's Development Programme: A precursor of MS, which was started in Rajasthan in 1984.

Zilla Parishad: District Council; see the term 'Panchayat Raj'.

Zilla Saksharatha Samithi: District Literacy Council.

SELECT BIBLIOGRAPHY

Books, Monographs, Reports, and Speeches

Allison, Graham T. 1971. *Essence of Decision: Explaining the Cuban Missile Crisis*. Boston, MA: Little, Brown & Company. (The second edition was published in 1999 by Longman, New York, and it was co-authored with Philip D. Zelikow).

Aggarwal,Yash. *Revitalization of Educational Statistics: Issues and Strategies*. http://www.dise.in/Downloads/Reports&Studies/REVITALISATION%20OF%20EDUCATIONAL%20STATISTICS%20IN%20INDIA.pdf. Last Accessed on 29 May 2015.

ASER Centre. *Annual Stats of Education Reports*.

Austin, Granville. 1966. *The Indian Constitution: The Cornerstone of a Nation*. Oxford: Clarendon Press.

Ayyar, Vaidyanatha R.V. 2009. *Public Policymaking in India*. New Delhi: Pearson Longman.

Azim Premji Foundation. *Status of Learning Achievements in India: A Review of Empirical Research*, October 2004.

Basu, Moushumi. 'World Bank's Lending to Social Sectors in India'. Jawaharlal Nehru University thesis, 2003.

Bashir, Sajitha. 2000. *Government Expenditure on Elementary Education in the Nineties*.

———. 2000. *Review of the Finance Studies Conducted under DPEP*.

Berkman, Steve. 2008. *The World Bank and the Gods of Lending*. Sterling VA: Kumarian Press.

Berlin, Isaiah. 1953. *The Hedgehog and the Fox: An Essay on Tolstoy's View of History*. London: Widenfeld & Nicolson.

Bhaskar Rao, Digumarthi. 2007. *Success of a Primary Education Project*. Delhi: A.P.H. Publisher Corporation.

Bhattacharya, Sabyasachi, ed. 1997. *The Mahatma and the Poet: Letters and Debates between Gandhi and Tagore, 1915–1941*. New Delhi: National Book Trust, 1997.

Bhoothalingam, S. 1993. *Reflections on an Era: Memoirs of a Civil Servant*. New Delhi: Affiliated East-West Press Private Limited.

Black, Maggie. 1986. *The Children and the Nations: The Story of UNICEF*. New York: UNICEF.

———. 1996. *Children First: The Story of UNICEF, Past and Present*. Oxford: Oxford University Press.

Bordia, Anil. 1990. *Working Together for a New Education*. Opening Speech at the NIEPA Seminar on Education for All: UP, 6–9 November 1990, National Institute of Educational Planning and Administration, New Delhi.

Callaghan, James. 1976. *Toward a National Debate*. Speech at Ruskin College, Oxford, October 18.

Cardozo, Benjamin N. 1928. *The Paradoxes of Legal Science*. New York: Columbia University Press.

Caves, Richard E. 1982. *Multinational Enterprise and Economic Analysis*. Cambridge: Cambridge University Press.

Chakrabarti, R. and P. Peterson, eds. 2008. *School Choice International: Exploring Public-Private Partnerships*. Cambridge, MA: MIT Press.

Chandler, Alfred Dupont Jr. 1962. *Strategy and Structure: Chapters in the History of the American Industrial Enterprise*. Cambridge, MA: MIT Press.

Chinapah, Vinayagum. 1997. *Handbook on Monitoring Learning Achievement: Towards Capacity Building*. Paris: UNESCO.

Citizens for Democracy. 1978. *Education for Our People: A Policy Frame for the Development of Education (1978–1984)*. New Delhi: Allied Publishers.

Clark, Charles E. 2001. *Uprooting Otherness: The Literacy Campaign in NEP-era Russia*. Cranbury, NJ: Associated University Presses.

Clayton, Pamela. *Literacy in Kerala: Report of Research Undertaken November 2005–October 2006*. University of Glasgow, Scotland, November 2006. http://www.scribd.com/doc/17375060/Literacy-in-Kerala.Last accessed on 22 May 2015.

Colclough, Christopher with Keith M. Lewin. 1993. *Educating All the Children: Strategies for Primary Schooling in the South*. Cambridge: Cambridge University Press.

Colclough, Christopher and Anuradha De. 2010. 'The Impact of Aid on Education Policy in India'. RECOUP Working Paper No. 27, University of Cambridge, London: DFID.

Compulsory Education and Child Labour. 1994 RGIC Proceedings. No. 4, New Delhi: Rajiv Gandhi Institute for Contemporary Studies.

Constitution Assembly Debates, available on websites such as **indian**kanoon.org/doc/ and parliamentof**india**.nic.in/ls/debates/.

Coombs, Philip H. 1967. *The World Educational Crisis: A Systems Analysis*. 1967. New York: Oxford.

———. 1985. *The World Crisis in Education: The View from the Eighties*. New York: Oxford.

Coombs, Philip H., Roy Prosser, and Manzoor Ahmed. 1973. *New Paths to Learning for Rural Education and Youth*. New York: International Council for Educational Development, 1973.

Cornia, Giovanni Andrea, Richard Jolly, and Frances Stewart, eds. 1987. *Adjustment with a Human Face: Protecting the Vulnerable and Promoting Growth: A Study by UNICEF*, two volumes. Oxford: Clarendon Press.

Dar, R.K., ed. 1999. *Governance and the IAS*. New Delhi: Tata McGraw-Hill Company.

Das, Maitreyi. 1992. 'The Women's Development Program in Rajasthan: A Case Study in Group Formation for Women's Development', Working Papers, Women in Development, World Bank, WPS 913.

Dhankar, Rohit and Brigid Smith. 2002. *Seeking Quality Education for All: Experiences from the District Primary Education Programme*.

1990. *Final Report of the World Conference on Education for All: Meeting Basic Learning Needs*. New York: Inter-Agency Commission, WCEFA (UNDP, UNESCO, UNICEF, World Bank).

Drèze, Jean and Amartya Sen. 2002. *India: Development and Participation*. New Delhi: Oxford University Press.

Durant, Will. 1926. *The Story of Philosophers: The Lives and Opinions of Great Philosophers*. New York: Simon and Schuster.

Dyer, Caroline., 1996. 'The Improvement of Primary School Quality in India: Successes and Failures of Operation Blackboard', Edinburgh Papers In South Asian Studies Number 4, Centre for South Asia Studies, University of Edinburgh.

Evans, David. 1981. *The Planning of Non-formal Education*. Paris: International Institute of Educational Planning.

Evans, Eric. 2004. *Thatcher and Thatcherism*, 2nd edition. London: Routledge.

European Union, New Delhi Office.

Frankel, Francine R. 1978. *India's Political Economy, 1947–1977: The Gradual Revolution*. Princeton: Princeton University Press.

Fraser, Alastair. 2006. *Aid-Recipient Sovereignty in Historical Perspective, Global Economic Governance Programme*. Managing Aid Dependency Project, Department of Politics and International Relations, University College, Oxford University.

Gadgil, D.R. and V.M. Dandekar. 1995. *Primary Education in Satara District: Reports of Two Investigations*. Pune: Gokhale Institute of Economics and Politics.

Gandhi, M.K. *Future of India*. An Address given at Chatham House on 20 October 1931, London: Royal Institute of International Affairs.

Garrett, R.M., ed. 1984. *Education and Development*. London: Croor Helm.

Ghosh, Avik. 2006. *Communication Technology and Human Developments: Recent Experiences in the Social Sector*. New Delhi: Sage.

Govinda, R. and N.V. Varghese. 1993. *Quality of Primary Schooling in India: A Case Study of Madhya Pradesh*. Paris: International Institute of Educational Planning.

Guhan, S. 1995. *The World Bank's Lending in South Asia*. Washington, DC: The Brookings Institution.

Haddad,Wadi D. (with the assistance of Terri Demsky). 1994. *The Dynamics of Education Policymaking: Case Studies of Burkina Faso, Jordan, Peru and Thailand*. Washington, DC: The World Bank.

Haig, Alexander. 1984. *Caveat: Realism, Reagan and Foreign Policy*. New York: Macmillan.

Heath, John. 2006. *An Evaluation of DFID's India Programme 2000–2005*. Evaluation report EV 670. London: Department for International Development.

Heilbroner, Robert. 1993. *The Great Ascent*. New York: Harper and Row, Inc.

Hennessy, Peter. 1993. *Never Again: Britain 1945–51*. London: Jonathan Cape Ltd.

International Institute of Educational Planning. 1967. *Educational Development in Africa*, Volume III: Integration and Administration Paris.

Kirk, Jason A. 2011. *India and the World Bank: The Politics of Aid and Influence*. New York: Anthem Press.

Jenkins, Simon. 2006. *Thatcher & Sons: A Revolution in Three Acts*. London: Penguin.

Jha, Jyotsna, K.B.C. Saxena, and C.V. Baxi. 2001. *Management Processes in Elementary Education: A Study of Existing Practices in Selected States in India*.

Jolly, Richard, ed. 2001. *Jim Grant: UNICEF Visionary*. Florence: UNICEF Innocenti Research Centre.

Jones, W. Phillip. 1988. *International Policies for Third World Education: UNESCO, Literacy and Development*, London: Routledge.

———. 1992. *World Bank Financing of Education: Lending, Learning and Development*, 1st edition. London: Routledge.

———. 2007. *World Bank Financing of Education: Lending, Learning and Development*, 2nd edition. New York: Routledge.

Jones, P.W. with David Coleman. 2005. *The United Nations and Education: Multilateralism, Development, and Globalisation*. New York: Routledge.

Kafka, Franz. 1999. *The Complete Novels: The Trial, America, The Castle*. London: Vintage.

Kapur, Devesh. 2010. *Diaspora, Development and Democracy: The Domestic Impact of International Migration from India*. Princeton, NJ: Princeton University Press.

Kapur, Devesh. 1997. John, Prior Lewis, and Richard Charles Webb, eds. 1997. *The World Bank: Its First Half Century*, two volumes. Washington, DC: Brookings Institution Press.

Karlekar, M., ed. 2000. *Reading the World: Understanding the Literacy Campaigns in India*. Bombay: Asia South Pacific Bureau of Adult Education.

Kenez, Peter. 1985. *The Birth of the Propaganda State: Soviet Methods of Mass Mobilization, 1917–1929*. New York: Cambridge University Press.

Killick, Tony with Ramani Gunatilaka, and Ana Marr. 1998. *Aid and the Political Economy of Policy Change*. Routledge/ODI: London.

King, Kenneth. 1991. *Aid and in the Developing World: The Role of Donor Agencies in Education Analysis*. Harlow, Essex: Longman.

King, Kenneth and Lene Buchert. 1999. *Changing International Aid to Education: Global Patterns and National Contexts*. Paris: UNESCO.

Kingdon, John W. 1995. *Agenda, Alternatives and Policies*, 2nd edition. New York: Longman.

Klitgaard, Robert. 1990. *Tropical Gangsters*. New York: Basic Books.

Kothari, B.V., Sherry Chand, and R. Sharma. *A Review of Primary Education Packages in Madhya Pradesh*. Ahmedabad, India: Indian Institute of Management, 2000.

Lax, David A. and James K Sebenius. 1986. *The Manager as Negotiator: Bargaining for Cooperation and Competitive Gain*. New York: The Free Press.

Le Grand, Julian. 2003. *Motivation, Agency and Public Policy: Of Knights and Knaves, Pawns and Queens*. Oxford: Oxford University Press.

Little, Angela, Wim Hoppers, and Roy Gardner. 1994. *Beyond Jomtien: Implementing Primary Education for All*. London: Macmillan.

Lockheed, Marlaine, Adriaan M. Verspoor, and Associates. 1991. *Improving Primary Education in Developing Countries*. New York: Oxford University Press.

Laubach, F.C. 1940. *India shall be Literate*, Nagpur: National Church Council; Reprinted in 2015 by Andesite Press.

Lyons, Raymond and Raymond Poignant, eds. 1967. *Educational Development in Africa*. IIEP African Studies Series, three volumes. Paris: International Institute of Educational Planning.

Mahbub ul Haq. 1976. *The Poverty Curtain: Choices for the Third World*. New York: Columbia University Press.

Mathur, Anurag. 2000. *Scenes from an Executive Life*. New Delhi: Penguin.

Majumdar, R.C. 1961. *Three Phases of India's Struggle for Freedom*. Bombay: Bharatiya Vidya Bhavan.

Medel-Ationuevo, Carolyn. 1996. *Women Reading the World: Policies and Practices of Literacy in Asia*, Hamburg: UNESCO Institute for Education.

Mehta, Pratap Bhanu. 2003. *The Burden of Democracy*. New Delhi: Penguin India.

Mid-day Meal in Primary Schools, http://www.righttofoodindia.org/data/wsfmdm.pdf. Last accessed on 28 May 2015.

Mill, John Stuart. 1924. *Autobiography*. New York: Columbia University Press.

Morsy, Zaghloul, ed. 1995. *Thinkers in Education*, four volumes. Paris: UNESCO Publishing.

Mosley, Paul, Jane Harrigan, and John Toye. 1995. *Aid and Power: The World Bank and Policy-Based Lending*, 2nd edition, two volumes. London: Routledge.

Moyo, Dambisa. 2009. *Dead Aid: Why Aid Is Not Working and How There Is Another Way for Africa*. New York: Farrar, Strauss, Giroux.

Mukherji, Rahul, ed. 2007. *India's Economic Transition: The Politics of Reform*. New Delhi: Oxford University Press.

Myrdal, Gunnar. 1968. *Asian Drama: An Inquiry into the Poverty of Nations*, three volumes. New York: Pantheon.

Naik, J.P. 1965. *Educational Planning in India*. New Delhi: Allied Publishers.

———. 1969. *Educational Planning in a District*. New Delhi: Asian Institute for Educational Planning and Administration.

———. 1975. *Equality, Quality and Quantity: The Elusive Triangle in Indian Education*. New Delhi: Allied Publishers.

———. 1975. *Elementary Education in India: A Promise to Keep*. Delhi: Allied Publishers.

———. 1975. *Policy and Performance in Indian Education 1947–74*. Dr. K.G. Saiydain Lectures, 1974. New Delhi: Allied Publishers.

———. 1997. *The Education Commission and After*, 2nd edition, New Delhi: A.B.H. Publishing Corporation.

Naik, J.P. and Syed Nurullah. *A Student's History of Education in India (1800–1973)*, 6th edition. Delhi: Macmillan, 1974.

Nair, Kusum. 1961. *Blossoms in the Dust, The Human Factor in Indian Development*. New York: Praeger.

Narasimha Rao, P.V. 2000. *The Insider*. New Delhi: Penguin Press.

National Planning Committee. 1948. *General Education and Technical Education and Development Research*. Reports on the Sub-committees Series. Bombay: Vora and Co., 1948

Nelson, Robert Henry. 2001. *Economics* as *Religion: From Samuelson to Chicago and Beyond*. University Park, PA: University of Pennsylvania Press.

Neustadt, Richard E. 1960. *Presidential Power: The Politics of Leadership*. New York: Wiley, 1960.

Neustadt, Richard E. and Ernest R.May. 1986. *Thinking in Time: The Uses of History in Decision-making*. New York: The Free Press.

O'Neill, Onara. *A Question of Trust*.BBC Radio, 2002, http://www.bbc.co.uk/radio4/reith2002/lectures.shtml. Last accessed on 26 May 2015.

Oakeshott, Michael. 1991. *Rationalism in Politics and Other Essays*. Indianapolis: Liberty Press.

OECD. *Budget Support, Sector Wide Approaches and Capacity Development in Public Financial Management, DAC Guidelines and Reference Series, Harmonising Donor Practices for Effective Aid Delivery*. Paris. http://www.oecd.org/dataoecd/53/7/34583142.pdf, 2005. Last Accessed on 29 May 2015.

Padmanathan, C.B. and Jandhyala B.G. Tilak. 1986. *External Financing of Education*. New Delhi: National Institute of Educational Planning, 1986.

Paris Declaration on Aid Effectiveness: Ownership, Harmonisation, Alignment, Results and MutualAccountability, 2 March 2005. http://www.oecd.org/dataoecd/11/41/34428351.pdf. Last Accessed on 29 May 2015.

Raiffa, Howard. 1982. *The Art and Science of Negotiation*. Cambridge, MA: The Belknap Press of Harvard University Press.

Rajput, J.S., ed. 2001. *Encyclopaedia on Education*, two volumes. New Delhi: National Council of Educational Research and Training.

Ramachandran, Vimala, Subir Shukla, Philip Cohen, Robin Alexander, and Malcolm Mercer. 2001. 'Reflections on Equity, Quality and Local Planning in District Primary Education Programme'. Occasional Papers.

Rampal, Anita. 2001. *Curriculum Change for Quality Education: A Study of in Schools in DPEP and non-DPEP Districts of Kerala*. Trivandrum: Primary Education Development Society.

Rao, Mamta. 2002. *Public Interest Litigation*. Lucknow: Eastern Book Company.

Riddell, Roger C. 2007. *Does Foreign Aid Really Work?* Oxford: Oxford University Press.

Rustomji, Nari. 1971. *Frontiers: Sikkim, Bhutan, and India's Northeastern Borderlands*. New Delhi: Oxford University Press.

Saldanha, Denzil. 2010. *Civil Society Processes and the State: The Bharat Gyan Vigyan Samiti and the Literacy Campaigns*. Jaipur: Rawat Publications.

Samoff, Joel, ed. 1994. *Coping with Crisis: Austerity, Adjustment and Human Resources*. London: Cassel.

Schelling, Thomas C. 1960. *The Strategy of Conflict*. Cambridge, MA: Harvard University Press.

Sebenius, James K. 2006. *3-D Negotiation: Powerful Tools to Change the Game in Your Most Important Deal*. Boston: Harvard Business School Press.

Sen, Amartya. 2014. *Beyond Liberalization: Social Opportunity and Human Capability*. The First D.T. Lakdawala Memorial Lecture, 29 June 1994. New Delhi: Institute of Social Sciences.

Shaw, Shekhar, Barry Bosworth, and Arvind Panagariya. 2013. *India Policy Form 2012/3*, National Council of Applied Economic Research (New Delhi) and Brookings Institution (Washington, DC), Volume 9. Delhi: Sage Publications.

Sharma, Aradhana. 2008. *Logic of Empowerment in Neoliberal India*. Minneapolis: University of Minnesota Press.

Shirer, William. 1969. *The Collapse of the Third Republic: An Inquiry in the Fall of France in 1940*. Simon & Schuster, 1969,

Shukla, Subir, Philip Cohen, Robin Alexander, and Malcolm Mercer. 2001.

2002. *Report of the Final Evaluation of EC Support to Primary Education in India*.

Sivadas, S. 1991. *How Ernakulum Became the First Literate District of India*. No. 195, UNESCO-UNICEF-WFP Cooperative Programme.

Smawfield, David and Helen Poulsen. 2000. *Mainstreaming Gender through Sector Wide Appraches: India Case Study*. London: Overseas Development Institute.

Sorensen, Theodore. 1963. *Decision-Making in the White House: The Olive Branch and the Arrow*. New York: Columbia University Press.

Srivastava, A.B.L. 2004. *Learning Achievement at the End of the Primary School in DPEP States*. Ministry of Human Resource Development and Azim Premji Foundation Learning Conference.

Tamm, Gordon, Jörgen Person, and Uno Winblad. *Lok Jumbish: Appraisal of Programme Documents*. A Note to SIDA, May 1991.

Tandon, Prakash. 1981. *Return to Punjab*. Berkeley: University of California Press.

The Probe Team. 1999. *Public Report on Basic Education in India*. New Delhi: Oxford University Press.

Tooley, James. 2009. *The Beautiful Tree: A Personal Journey into How the World's Poorest People Are Educating Themselves*. Washington DC: Cato Institute.

UNESCO. 1988. Report of The External Auditor, Executive Board Document 155 EX/27 Addendum; Report by the DG on the Progress Made in the Implementation of the Recommendation of the External Auditor, Executive Board Document 156 EX/31.

———. 2013. *Schooling for Millions of People Jeopardized by Reductions in Aid*, EFA-GMR Policy Paper 09.

———. 2015. *Education for All 2000–15: Achievement and Challenges, EFA Global Monitoring report, 2015*. Paris: UNESCO Publishing.

Valderrama, Fernando. 1995. *A History of UNESCO*. Paris: UNESCO Publishing.

Vernon, Raymond. 1971. *Sovereignty at Bay: The Multinational Spread of American Enterprises*. New York: Basic Books.

Weiner, Myron. 1991. *The Child and the State in India*, Princeton, NJ: Princeton University Press.

Weiner, Norbert. 1994. *Invention: The Care and Feeding of Ideas*. Cambridge, MA: The MIT Press.

Wheeler Bennett, John W. 1962. *John Anderson: Viscount Waverley*. New York: St. Martin's Press Inc.

Whitehead, Clive. 2003. *Colonial Educators: The British Indian and Colonial Educational Services, 1858–1983*. London: I.B. Tauris.

Whyte, William H. 1956. *The Organization Man*. New York: Simon and Schuster.

Woodruff, Philip. 1971. *Men Who Ruled India*, two volumes. London: Jonathan Cape.

Woolf, Virginia. 2008. 'Mr Bennett and Mrs Brown'. In: *Virginia Woolf: Selected Essays*, Oxford World Classics. Oxford: Oxford University Press.

World Bank. 1992. *Effective Implementation: Key to Development Impact: Report of the World Bank's Portfolio Task Force*.

———. 1995. *India: Social Safety Net Sector Adjustment Program: Completion Report*.

———. 1997. *Primary Education in India*.

———. Clarke, Prema. 2003. *Education Reform in the Education Grantee Scheme in Madhya Pradesh and the Fundescola Program in Brazil*. http://documents.worldbank.org/curated/en/2003/03/2601214/education-reform-education-guarantee-scheme-madhya-pradesh-india-fundescola-program-brazil. Last accessed on 29 May 2015.

World Bank—District Primary Education Projects

Shukla, Subir. 1999. Systems in Transition: A Case Study of DPEP.

2003. *A Review of Educational Progress and Reform in the District Primary Education Program (Phases I and II)*, Report Number 1, Human Development Sector, South Asia Region.

2006. *Uttar Pradesh Third District Primary Education Project*[1]*: Implementation and Completion Report (IDA-33070)*, Report No:ICR-000164, 30 October 2006.

———. 2007. *Project Performance Assessment Report*. Independent Evaluation Group, Report No.: 40160 IN, 30 June 2007.[2]

———. 2007. Narayan, Deepa and Elena E. Glinskaya, eds. 2007. *Ending Poverty in South Asia: Ideas That Work*, Washington, DC: The World Bank.

———. 2008. Sankar, Deepa. *What Is the Progress of Elementary Education Participation in India during the Last Two Decades? An Analysis Using NSS Education Rounds*, 42112 rev. South Asia Sector for Human Development.

[1] Some of the World Bank documents erroneously include UP basic education projects among DPEP projects.

[2] This report covers the two UP basic education projects and the first two DPEP projects financed by the World Bank.

World Education Forum, Education for All Assessment. *Funding Agency Contributions to Education for All*. Thematic Studies, Dakar, Senegal, 26–28 April 2000.

———. 2000. *Final Report*, Paris: UNESCO.

Journal Articles

Acharya, Poromesh. 1994. 'Universal Elementary Education: Receding Goal'. *Economic and Political Weekly*, 29(1–2):27–30.

Adiseshiah, Malcolm. 1977. 'Literacy's Functionality and the Fight for Social Justice'. *Convergences*, 8(24):23.

Asian Development Bank. 2006. 'How Can Programmatic Assistance Enhance Country Leadership of the Development Agenda? The Case of Sarva Shiksha Abhiyan in India', *Asian Regional Forum on Aid Effectiveness: Implementation, Monitoring and Evaluation*. http://www.adb.org/Documents/Events/2006/Aid-Effectiveness/country-papers/IND-education-swap.pdf.AsianDevelopmentBank. Last accessed on 29 May 2015.

Ayyar, Vaidyanatha R.V. 1995. 'Placing DPEP and NLM in Perspective'. *DPEP Calling*, January 1995.

———. 1995. 'Let Not the Dead Seize The Living: The DPEP Saga'. *DPEP Calling*, December 1995.

———. 2007. 'Donor Harmonization and Alignment—Organizing to Take Leadership: The Experience of India'. 2nd Africa Region Education Capacity Development Workshop 'Country Leadership and Implementation for Results in the EFA FTI Partnership' Tunis, Tunisia, 3–6 December 2007. http://www.fasttrackinitiative.org/library/moduleIIIcoordination.pdf. Last accessed on 25 May 2015.

———. 2008. 'Country–Agency Relationship: The Indian Experience'. Background paper prepared for the *Education for All Global Monitoring Report 2009*, UNESCO, 2009/ED/EFA/MRT/PI/02, 2008.

Banerjee, Sumanta.1993. 'Revisiting the National Literacy Mission'. *Economic and Political Weekly*, 28(25): 1274–8.

Barnes, Julian. 2012. 'Daddy's Girl'. *New York Review of Books*, 3, http://www.nybooks.com/issues/2012/feb/23/. Last accessed on 22 May 2015.

Basu, Moushumi. 2006. 'Negotiating Aid: World Bank and Primary Education in India'. *Contemporary Education Dialogue*, 3(2): 133–54.

Bhattacharya, Sabyasachi. 2014. 'Professor Bipan Chandra (1928–2014)'. *Economic and Political Weekly*, 39(41): 26–9.

Bhola, H.S. 1988. 'A Policy Analysis of Adult Literacy Education in India: Across the Two National Policy Reviews of 1968 and 1986'. *Perspectives in Education*, 4:213–28.

Brock-Utne, Birgit. 2003. 'Formulating Higher Education Policies in Africa- the Pressure from External Forces and the Neoliberal Agenda'. *Journal of Higher Education in Africa*, 1(1):24–56. http://www.netreed.uio.no/articles/high.ed_BBU.pdf. Last Accessed on 24 May 2015.

Chayes, Abraham. 1976. 'The Role of Judges in Public Law Litigation'. *Harvard Law Review*, 89(7): 1281–316.

Clarke, Prema. 2003. 'Culture and Classroom Reform: The Case of the District Primary Education Project, India'. *Comparitive Education*, 19(1):25–44.

Delbanco, Andrew. 1999. 'Dreams of Better Schools'. *New York Review of Books*, 56(18), 19 November 2009. http://www.nybooks.com/articles/2009/11/19/dreams-of-better-schools. Last accessed on 9 February 2016.

Dongre, Ambrish. 2010. 'Has RTE Made a Mistake by Eliminating Contract Teachers and Making All Teachers Regular?' http://www.accountabilityindia.in/accountabilityblog/1894-has-rte-made-mistake-eliminating-contract-teachers-and-making-all-teachers. Posted on 21 December 2010 and last accessed on 29 May 2015.

Fernandez Aloysius P. 2006. 'History and Spread of the Self-Help Affinity Group Movement in India', Occasional Papers, Knowledge for Development Effectiveness, Rome: International Fund for Agricultural Development.

Gandhi, M.K. 1939. 'Discussion with Teacher Trainees'. *Harijan*, 18 February 1939; Reprinted in Government of India, *The Collected Works of Mahatma Gandhi*, Volume 68, Publications Division, pp. 372–73.

Gopalakrishnan, R and Amita Sharma. 1998. 'Education Guarantee Scheme in Madhya Pradesh: Innovative Step to Universalise Elementary Education'. *Economic and Political Weekly*, 33(39):2546–51.

———. 1999. 'Education Guarantee Scheme What Does It Claim?' *Economic and Political Weekly*, 20 March 1999, 34(12):726–8.

———. 2003. 'Opinion or Facts? Education Guarantee Scheme in Madhya Pradesh'. *Economic and Political Weekly*, 38(49):5210–5.

Husock, Howard. 2000. 'Implementing Education Reform in India: The Primary School Textbook Debate and Resistance to Change in Kerala'. Harvard University, Kennedy School of Government Case Study Programme, C15-00-1573.0

Ingram, Helen. 1977. 'Policy Implementation through Bargaining: The Case of Federal Grants-in-Aid'. *Public Policy*, 25(4):499–526.

Jagannathan, Shanti. 2004. 'Programme-based Approaches and International Collaboration: Experiences and Lessons from Education Sector'. Paper presented to LEPNA Forum , 'Programme-based Approaches to Diversity: Adapting to Diversity', Tokyo, 1–3 June 2004.

Jagannathan, Shanti and Mervi Karikorp. 2000. 'EC-India Development Co-operation in Primary Education: Sector-wide Approaches to

Development Cooperation'. *Prospects*, Special issue on New Modalities in New Modalities for Development Co-operation, 30(4):409–22.

Jalan, Jyotsna and Elena Glinskaya. 2003. 'Small Bang for Big Bucks: An Evaluation of a Primary School Intervention in India'. Economics Working Paper Series, Working Paper Number 9, Kolkata: Centre for Studies in Social Studies, 2003. http://www.cssscal.org/pdf/WP-2012-9.pdf. Last accessed on 29 May 2015.

———. 2003. 'Improving Primary Schooling in India: An Impact Assessment of DPEP-I'. http://siteresources.worldbank.org/INTISPMA/Resources/Training-Events-and-Materials/india_primaryschool.pdf. Last accessed on 29 May 2015.

Jaycox, Edward. 1993. 'African Capacity Building: Effective and Enduring Partnerships'. Address to the African-American Institute Conference Reston, Virginia, 20 May 1993. Excerpts published in 'New trends in training policies', NORRAG News, NN14, July 1993, pp. 9–11.

Jones, W. Phillip. 1998. 'Globalisation and Internationalisation: Democratic Prospects for World Education'. *Comparative Education*, 34(2):143–55.

Kamat, A.R. 1982. 'The Pilgrim's Progress'. *Bulletin of the Indian Institute of Education*, J.P. Naik Special issue, 3:104–18.

Kameswari, Jandhyala. 2003. 'Empowering Education: The Mahila Samakhya Experience', Background Article for the EFA Global Monitoring report 2003/4, 2004/ED/EFA/MRT/PI/29, Paris: UNESCO.

———. 2012. 'Ruminations on Evaluation in the Mahila Samakhya Programme'. *Indian Journal of Gender Studies*, 19(2): 211–31.

Khatkhate, Deena. 1995. 'Always a Borrower Be'. *Economic and Political Weekly*, 30(52): 3361–2.

Khera, Reetika. 2013. 'Mid-day Meals; looking Ahead'. *Economic and Political Weekly*, 48(32): 12–14.

King, Kenneth. 1992. 'The External Agenda of Aid in Internal Educational Reform'. *International Journal of Educational Development*, 12(4): 257–64.

Kingdon, Geeta Gandhi and Vandana Sipahimalani-Rao. 2010. Para-teachers in India: Status and Impact. *Economic and Political Weekly*, 45(20): 59–67.

'Kissinger Returns'. *Harvard Magazine*, March–April 2012.

Kumar, Krishna. 1994. 'Myopic Education: Foreign Aid to No Purpose', *Times of India*, April 30, 1994.

———. 1995. 'Learning and Money: Children as Pawns in Dependency'. *Economic and Political Weekly*, 33(43):2719–20.

———. 2004. 'Quality of Education at the Beginning of the Twenty First Century: Lessons from India'. Background Paper for *EFA Global Monitoring Report 2005*.

———. 2011. 'Teaching and the Neo-liberal State'. *Economic and Political Weekly*, 46(21):37–40.

Kumar, Krishna, Manisha Priyam, and Sadhna Saxena. 2001. 'Looking beyond the Smokescreen: DPEP and Primary Education in India'. *Economic and Political* Weekly, 36(7):560–8.

———. 'The Trouble with Para-teachers'. *Frontline*, 18(27 October to 9 November 2001). http://www.frontline.in/navigation/?type=static&page=archive. Last accessed on 8 February 2016.

Leclercq, François. 2003. 'Education Guarantee Scheme and Primary Schooling in Madhya Pradesh', *Economic and Political Weekly*', 38(19):1855–69.

Lindblom, Charles. 1959. 'The Science of 'Muddling Through'. *Public Administration Review*, 19 (2):79–88.

———. 1979. 'Still Muddling, Not Yet Through'. *Public Administration Review* 39(6): 517–26.

Mathew, A. 2005. 'Literacy: Real Options for Policy and Practice in India', Background paper prepared for the *Education for All Global Monitoring Report 2006*.

Mitra, Ashok. 1983. 'How Is India Doing? An Exchange'. *New York Review of Books*, Volume 30, 3 March 1983. http://www.nybooks.com/articles/archives/1983/mar/03/how-is-india-doing-an-exchange/. Last accessed on 22 May 2015.

Mukherjee, Mridula and Aditya Mukherjee. 2014. 'Tribute: Remembering Bipan Chandra', *Mainstream*, 52(37), 6 September. http://www.mainstreamweekly.net/article5172.html. Last accessed on 4 June 2015.

Pandey, S and Rani Raj. 2006. 'Professional Support System and Classroom Performance of Para-teachers: An Investigation'. *Indian Educational Review*, 41(2): 35–52.

Paris Declaration on Aid Effectiveness: Ownership, Harmonisation, Alignment, Results and Mutual Accountability, 2 March 2005. http://www.oecd.org/dataoecd/11/41/34428351.pdf. Last accessed on 29 May 2015.

Porter, Roy. 1994. 'A Seven-Bob Surgeon: "Pope" Huxley and the New Priesthood of Science'. *Times Literary Supplement*, 18 November.

Psacharopoulos, G. 2006. 'World Bank Policy on Education: A Personal Account'. *International Journal of Educational Development*, 26:329–38.

Putnam, Robert. 1988. 'Diplomacy and Domestic Politics: The Logic of Two-Level Games'. *International Organization*, 42(3):427–60.

Rahul. 1999. 'Education Guarantee Scheme in Madhya Pradesh'. *Economic and Political Weekly*, 34(1–2):64.

Raju, Jagmohan Singh. 2013. 'Saakshar Bharat Mission'. UNESCO Effective Literacy Website. http://www.unesco.org/uil/litbase/?menu=9&programme=132. Last accessed on 25 May 2015.

Ramachandran, Vimala. 1999. 'Adult Education: A Tale of Empowerment Denied'. *Economic and Political Weekly*, 34(24): 870–80.

———. 2002. 'The New Segregation: Reflections on Gender and Equity in Primary Education'. *Economic and Political Weekly*, 37(17):1600–13.

Rath, Nilakantha. 2002. 'D.R. Gadgil on Planning at the District Level'. *Economic and Political Weekly*, 37:2219–22.

Rebekka , Van Roemburg. 2007. PowerPointPresentation, Capacity Development Workshop 'Country Leadership and Implementation for Results in the EFA FTI Partnership', Cape Town, South Africa, 16 July 2007.

Riddell, A. 2007. 'The New Modalities of Aid to Education: The View from within Some Recipient Countries'. Background paper for *EFA Global Monitoring Report 2008*.

Rao, Govinda M. 1992 'Some Proposals for State-level Budgetary Reforms'. *Economic and Political Weekly*, 27(5): 211–21.

———. 1993. 'Subsidies in Higher Education'. *Economic and Political Weekly*, 27(28):891–2.

Rath, Nilakantha. 2002. 'D.R. Gadgil on Planning at the District Level'. *Economic and Political Weekly*, 37(23):2219–22.

Sadgopal, Anil. 2008. 'Common School System and the Future of India'. Posted by *Parisar* (a forum of progressive students) on March 24, 2008, http://parisar.wordpress.com/2008/03/24/common-school-system-and-the-future-of-india/. Last accessed on 24 May 2015.

———. 2003. 'Education for Too Few'. *Frontline*, 20(24).

Sharma, Amita. 2003. 'Ideas of Education: Epistemic Tensions and Educational Reform'. *Economic and Political Weekly*, 38(32): 3391–3400.

Sarangapani, Padma M. 2000. 'The Great Indian Tradition.Redesigning Curriculum: A Symposium on Working a Framework for School Education'. *Seminar*,Volume 493, September 2000. http://www.india-seminar.com/semframe2.html. Last Accessed on 30 May 2015.

Sen, Amartya. 1982. 'How Is India Doing?' *New York Review of Books*, Volume 29, 16 December 1982. http://www.nybooks.com/articles/archives/1982/dec/16/how-is-india-doing/. Last accessed on 22 May 2015.

Thapar, Romila. 2009. 'The History Debate and School Textbooks in India'. A Personal Memoir. *History Workshop Journal*, 67(1):87–98.

Tilak, Jandhyala. B.G. 1993. 'Financing Higher Education in India: Principles, Practice and Policy Issues'. *Higher Education*, 26:43–67.

———. 2004. 'Fees, Autonomy and Equity'. *Economic and Political Weekly*, 39(9):870–3.

———. 2004. 'Education in the UPA Government Common Minimum Programme'. *Economic and Political Weekly*, 39(43):4717–21.

Tilak, Jandhyala. B.G. and N.G.Varghese. 1991. 'Financing Hither Education'. *Higher Education*, 21:83–101.

UNESCO. 1986. 'UNESCO in Asia and the Pacific: 40 Years on'. *Bulletin of the UNESCO Office for Education in Asia and the Pacific*, Number 27, November.

UNICEF, 1997.'Interview with Aklilu Habte'. *Education News*, 6(3):19–23.

Vaidyanathan , R. 2008. 'Developing Healthy Contempt Is a Must'. *Daily News and Analysis*, 1 July. http://www.dnaindia.com/report.asp?newsid=1174759. Last accessed on 22 May 2015.

Varghese, N.V. 1995. 'Decentralisation of Educational Planning in India: The Case of the District Primary Education Programme'. *International Journal of Educational Development*, 16:355–65.

Verspoor, Adrian. 'Lending for Learning: Twenty Years of Support to Basic Education'. World Bank Working Papers on Education and Employment, WPS 686, May 1991.

Magazine and Newspaper Articles

'Literacy by Compulsion in Durg'. *HindutanTimes*, 20 April 1992.

'Schnorr Enough'. *Economic Times*, 15 November 1992

'Back to UNESCO: Renewing Old Ties'. *Newsweek*, 14 June 1993.

'The Tuesday Interview: Dr Eimi Watanabe'. *Economic Times*, 27 July 1993.

'The Tiger Came for Breakfast'. 1993. *The Vigil*, Volume X.

'Controversy over Revised Guidelines'. *The Statesman*, 31 March, 1994.

Mazumdar, Tapas. 'Financing Higher Education: Beyond 'Public vs Private'. *The Observer of Business and Politics*, 26 March 1996.

Alagh ,Y.K. 'Financing Higher Education: State Must Bear the Major Brunt'. *The Observer of Business and Politics*, 27 March 1996.

Nair, C. Gouridasan. '"Mahila Samakhya" Caught in a Spat'. *The Hindu*, 1 July 2002.

Sadgopal, Anil. 'Education for Too few'. *Frontline*, Volume 20, Number 24, 2 December 2003.

'Survey of India and China'. *The Economist*, 5 March 2005.

Indian Express, 31 July 2009.

'Parliament Is Supreme: CJI'. *Times of India*, 26 August 2012.

Menon, Sreelatha. 'Mid-day Meal Monitoring Is Defunct'. *Business Standard*, July 2013.

Kingdon, Geeta Gandhi. 'Schools without Learning'. *The Hindu*, 8 February 2016.

Official Documents

I. Government of India

Government of India

1913. *Government Resolution on Education Policy*.

1927–32. *Quinquennial Report of the Progress of Education in India*.

Ministry of Education

1944. *Post-War Educational Development in India* [Sarjent Committee Report].
1960. *Central Advisory Board on Education (1935–1960): Silver Jubilee Souvenir.*
1966. *Education and National Development: Report of the Education Commission, 1964–66*, 4 Volumes[Kothari Commission Report].

Ministry of Education and Social Welfare

1972. *Report of the Secondary Education Commission (October, 1952 to June, 1953)*, 2nd Reprint Edition[Mudaliar Commission Report].
1979. *The National Education Policy, 1947–1978*, July.

Ministry of Finance, Department of Economic Affairs

1993. *Economic Reforms: Two Years After and the Task Ahead.*

Ministry of Human Resource Development, Department of Education

Select Education Statistics (Annual Series)
1985. *Challenge of Education.*
1986. *National Policy on Education, 1986.*
1986. *Programme of Action, 1986.*
1990. *Bihar Education Project* (along with Government of Bihar).
1990 *Lok Jumbish: People's Movement for Education for All: Rajasthan* (along with Government of Rajasthan).
1990. Committee for Review of National Policy on Education, 1986, *Towards an Enlightened and Humane Society: A Perspective Paper on Education* [Ramamurti Committee Report].
1992. *National Policy on Education, 1986 with Modifications Undertaken in 1992.*
1992. *Programme of Action.*
1994. *Evaluation of Literacy Campaign in India: Report of Expert Group.*
1995. *Report of the Committee on Mid-Day Meals.*
1997. *We can Change Our World: The Mahila Samakhya Experience.*
1997. *50 Years of Education.* http://www.teindia.nic.in/mhrd/50yrsedu/home.htm. Last accessed on 1 June 2015.

Ministry of Human Resource Development, Department of Education—Research, Evaluation and Studies Unit, Technical Support Group of DPEP (DPEP TSG), Ed Cil

1995. *Budgetary Resources for Education, 1951–52 to 1993–94*.

1995. Ayyar, Vaidyanatha, R.V. 1995. Let not the Dead Seize the Living. *DPEP Calling*, December.

1996. *Evaluation of Managerial Structures and Processes under DPEP—A Synthesis Study*.

1998. *Reaching out Further—Para-teachers in Primary Education: An Overview*.

1999. *Research Abstracts in Primary Education (1994–1997)*.

2000. Dayaram, *Para-teachers in Primary Education: A Status Report*.

2002. *Research Abstracts in Primary Education (1997–2000)*.

2003. *External Evaluation of DPEP, Phase-I*. Summary of Main Findings Based on the State Reports Prepared by the Indian Institutes of Management, Ahmadabad, Bangalore, Kolkata, and Lucknow.

Ministry of Human Resource Development, Department of School Education and Literacy

2003. *Education for All: National Plan of Action INDIA*.

2012. Minutes of the First meeting of the Joint Review Mission, 5 December 2012, http://www.teindia.nic.in/Files/jrm/Minutes_TE_JRM_1st_meeting.pdf. Last accessed on 29 May 2015.

2013. *Fourth Joint Review Mission of Mahila Samakhya (12 to 21 March 2013)*.

2013. *Sarva Siksha Abhiyan: Eighteenth Joint Review Mission*, 17–24 June 2013, Aide Memoire.

2014. *Statistics of School Education (As on 30 September 2011)*.

Ministry of Human Resource Development, Department of School Education and Literacy—Research, Evaluation and Studies Unit, Technical Support Group of Sarva Shiksha Abhiyan, EdCIL

2009. *Deployment and Competence of Para-Teachers*, Abridged Version.

2014. *Education of Children with Special Needs in Sarva Shiksha Abhiyan—RTE Act: An Overview (2013–14)*.

Ministry of Human Resource Development, Department of Higher Education

2005. *Report of the CABE Committee on Financing of Higher and Technical Education.*

National Council of Educational Research and Planning

1990. *NCERT's Comments on 'Towards an Enlightened and Humane Society- A Perspective Paper on Education.*
1997. Janghira, N.K. Vineet Kaul, and M.B. Menon, *Implementation of MLL: An Evaluation.*
1998. *Primary Years: Towards Curricular Framework.*
2000. *National Curricular Framework.*
2005. *National Curricular Framework.*
2007. *National Focus Paper on Work in Education,* Position Paper, 3.7.

National Institute of Educational Planning and Administration (Now Known as National University of Educational Planning and Administration)

1990. *Education for All by 2000: An Indian Perspective.*
2000. *University Finances in India.*
2006. *Implementation of Operation Blackboard Scheme in Primary Schools in India,* National Evaluation of Operation Blackboard.
2013. *Elementary Education in India: Analytical Report, 2012–13.*

Planning Commission

1969. *Guidelines for District Planning.*
1978. *Report of the Working Group Report on Block Level Planning.*
2003. *Successful Government Innovations and Best Practices: Experience from Indian States.*
2006. *Towards Faster and More Inclusive Growth: An Approach to the Eleventh Five Year Plan.*

University Grants Commission

1993. *Report of Justice Dr. K. Punnayya Committee: 1992–93.*

University Grants Commission and Association of Indian Universities

1992. Report on National Colloquium on Right to Education as a Fundamental Right. *Journal of Higher Education*, 18: 1–139.

II. Government of West Bengal

1992. *Report of the Education Commission.*

Case Law

Aruna Roy and Others v. Union of India, 2002 7 SCC 308.

Bandhua Mukti Morcha v. Union of India and Others, AIR 1984 SC 802.

Mohini Jain, Miss v. State of Karnataka & Others, AIR SC 1858.

People's Union for Civil Liberties v. Union of India and Others, Civil Writ Petition 196 of 2001.

S.R. Bommai v. Union of India, AIR 1994 SC 1918.

Unnikrishnan, J.P. & Others v State of Andhra Pradesh & Others, AIR 1993 SC 2178.

INDEX

ABOUT THE AUTHOR

R. V. Vaidyanatha Ayyar is an independent researcher. He was a member of the Indian Administrative Service (1966–2003) and Visiting Professor, Centre for Public Policy, Indian Institute of Management, Bangalore (2003–9). He was Secretary to the Government of India (1997–2003), and has extensive experience of dealing with a variety of international organizations and of negotiating with a number of countries including China, Pakistan, and Russia. Among others, he had been the Chief Coordinator of the Education for All Summit of Nine High-Population Countries, New Delhi (1993), a member of the World Bank External Advisory Panel on Education as well as the UNESCO High Level Committee on Statistics, and Chairman of the Drafting Committee of the WIPO Diplomatic Conference on Internet Treaties (1996). He is the author of the book *Public Policymaking in India* (2009). The author may be contacted at vaidyarv@gmail.com.